Anonymus

Financial Relation between Great Britain and Ireland

Interim Report of 28th March 1895

Anonymus

Financial Relation between Great Britain and Ireland
Interim Report of 28th March 1895

ISBN/EAN: 9783742832641

Manufactured in Europe, USA, Canada, Australia, Japa

Cover: Foto ©knipser5 / pixelio.de

Manufactured and distributed by brebook publishing software
(www.brebook.com)

Anonymus

Financial Relation between Great Britain and Ireland

ROYAL COMMISSION ON THE FINANCIAL RELATIONS BETWEEN GREAT BRITAIN AND IRELAND.

SECOND VOLUME

OF

MINUTES OF EVIDENCE,

Comprising that taken between the 29th March and the 15th November 1895,

BEFORE

HER MAJESTY'S COMMISSIONERS

APPOINTED TO INQUIRE INTO THE

FINANCIAL RELATIONS BETWEEN GREAT BRITAIN AND IRELAND,

WITH

APPENDICES,

BEING A FURTHER SUPPLEMENT TO THEIR

INTERIM REPORT OF 28TH MARCH 1895.

Presented to both Houses of Parliament by Command of Her Majesty.

LONDON:
PRINTED FOR HER MAJESTY'S STATIONERY OFFICE,
BY EYRE AND SPOTTISWOODE,
PRINTERS TO THE QUEEN'S MOST EXCELLENT MAJESTY.

And to be purchased, either directly or through any Bookseller, from
EYRE AND SPOTTISWOODE, EAST HARDING STREET, FLEET STREET, E.C., and
32, ABINGDON STREET, WESTMINSTER, S.W.; or
JOHN MENZIES & Co., 12, HANOVER STREET, EDINBURGH, and
90, WEST NILE STREET, GLASGOW; or
HODGES, FIGGIS, & Co., LIMITED, 104, GRAFTON STREET, DUBLIN.

1895.

[C.—7720.-II.] *Price 2s. 1d.*

TABLE OF CONTENTS.

Terms of Reference to the Financial Relations Commission.

To inquire into the Financial Relations between Great Britain and Ireland, and their relative taxable capacity, and to report :—

1. Upon what principles of comparison, and by the application of what specific standards, the relative capacity of Great Britain and Ireland to bear taxation may be most equitably determined.

2. What, so far as can be ascertained, is the true proportion, under the principles and specific standards so determined, between the taxable capacity of Great Britain and Ireland.

3. The history of the financial relations between Great Britain and Ireland at and after the Legislative Union, the charge for Irish purposes on the Imperial Exchequer during that period, and the amount of Irish taxation remaining available for contribution to Imperial expenditure; also the Imperial expenditure to which it is considered equitable that Ireland should contribute.

WITNESSES EXAMINED SINCE 29TH MARCH.

Name.	Description.
18. Giffen, Sir Robert, K.C.B., LL.D., [illegible] days	Controller-General of the Commercial, Labour, and Statistical Department at the Board of Trade
19. Lough, Thomas, M.P., [illegible] and [illegible] days	Member of Parliament for West Islington
20. Hamilton, Sir Edward W., K.C.B., [illegible] days.	Assistant Secretary to the Treasury . . .

INDEX TO EVIDENCE

INDEX TO APPENDICES.

MINUTES OF EVIDENCE

TAKEN BEFORE THE

ROYAL COMMISSION

ON THE

FINANCIAL RELATIONS BETWEEN GREAT BRITAIN AND IRELAND.

EIGHTEENTH DAY.

Friday, 29th March 1895.

At Committee Room B, House of Lords.

PRESENT:

THE RIGHT HON. HUGH C. E. CHILDERS, *Chairman*.

LORD FARRER.	BERTRAM W. CURRIE, Esq.
LORD WELBY.	J. E. REDMOND, Esq., M.P.
Sir DAVID BARBOUR, K.C.S.I.	THOMAS SEXTON, Esq., M.P.
The Hon. EDWARD BLAKE, M.P.	GUSTAV W. WOLFF, Esq., M.P.

Mr. B. H. HOLLAND, *Secretary*.

Mr. ROBERT GIFFEN, C.B., LL.D., called and examined.

7609. (*Chairman.*) What is your official position?—I am Controller-General of the Commercial, Labour, and Statistical Department at the Board of Trade.

7610. What, in that capacity, have you specially done, to what has your attention more especially been called?—In that capacity, and previously as Assistant Secretary to the Board of Trade, holding much the same office, and having much the same duties, I have had to give special attention to trade questions, and lately to wages and other labour statistics.

7611. Have you done so with respect to other countries than our own?—My attention has always been given to the statistics of other countries as well as our own, and I may say I have a general acquaintance with the statistics of a great many countries. That is part of my official duty.

7612. You propose, I think, to put in, in the first instance, two tables. Will you describe them to the Commission?—I propose to put in two tables, both relating to the wages paid in Ireland in different employments as compared with wages in the United Kingdom. The first of these tables is a comparison of statistics which were published some years ago in which an attempt was made not merely to give rates of wages, but also the average earnings of great masses of labour, deduced from the rates compared with the numbers of people at different rates. It seemed to be a very important matter in order to bring out a true average, that you should not only look at particular rates but that you should inquire how many people were paid at the different rates, and then deduce the true average, having regard to that fact. Most of these tables were published some years ago, and from the average results contained in them, the first table, which I now submit to the Commission, has been compiled.

7613. What is the general result, statistically, of the first table?—Before I state the general result, I should like to explain that the second table is merely a comparison of rates, and for the most part of rates supplied to us by trade unions. The figures are taken from a volume which is about to be published by the Board of Trade, and it will be observed it is a comparison of rates mainly, and not only that, but a comparison of urban rates, and it seems to me that putting the two tables together they throw a great deal of light upon the facts as to what wages are in Ireland and in the United Kingdom as a whole.

7614. (*Lord Farrer.*) You do not I see, in the heading to these papers, give the dates. Do they refer to the present time?—They refer, practically, to the present time or a period a few years ago, but I may say that in matters of wages when you look at the broad statistical results, you may take it that wages are not things that fluctuate as a rule, very much from year to year. So that, substantially, the rates that are given, although some of them go back to 1886—those in the first table are mainly derived from data obtained in 1886—yet it may be considered that they apply fairly well to the present time. And we know from other sources of information that there

Mr. Robert Giffen, C.B.

[illegible]

Wage [illegible].

has been no great change in rates since the date at which the first tables commence. The matter has been looked at now very steadily by the Department for several years, and information has been published from time to time, and more information will be published, as to changes in rates; but looking at things on a very considerable scale from inquiries we made in 1892, we were satisfied that although in some cases, particularly in mining, there was a very considerable advance in wages between 1886 and 1892, yet in railways and other things we found that looking at averages, for various reasons, there was no considerable change between 1886 and 1892, although there was some improvement. That is the general state of facts as to wages.

7615. Referring now to our special question, what is the general effect of Table 1 in a comparison between Ireland and Great Britain?—Table 1 appears to me to show that the average wages in Ireland, when you compare great masses of labour, range from 10 and 15 per cent. up to very nearly 50 per cent. lower than for similar masses of labour in Great Britain. That is about the general effect of that table, so far as I can judge.

7616. Then, as to Table 2, what do you say?—I think one may say the general effect of Table 2 is, when you look at artisan rates, you cannot say there is so very much difference in artisan rates in Ireland and in Great Britain; although I think the general effect is that artisan rates are a little less in Ireland than they are in Great Britain, yet you will find a good many instances the other way. The suggestion arises that as, when you compare artisan rates in Ireland with artisan rates in Great Britain, you are comparing a very small class indeed in Ireland with an enormous class in Great Britain, but you must recognise when you come to wages of that kind, there is not so much difference in Ireland from Great Britain as perhaps you would have expected, looking to the general inferiority of wages in Ireland. The explanation, no doubt, is that artisan labour is very mobile, and that in employments of that kind you could not have wages much higher in places so near, for instance, as Belfast and the Clyde, without labour going from one place to the other. Again, all these are subject to the remark that although when you compare artisan rates in Irish towns with towns in Great Britain of a similar size, you have always to remember that Great Britain includes the metropolis, in which, as you will see from some of the figures, wages as a rule are much higher, not only than they are in Ireland, but than they are in the rest of Great Britain itself. But the metropolis is a part of Great Britain—and you have to take that into account. Substantially the average wages of artisans, if you could take account of the masses, would be much higher in Great Britain than they are in Ireland, if you include the metropolis. Then added to this there is the point, as these second tables show, as regards unskilled labour in Ireland—the lower classes of labour—that the difference between Ireland and Great Britain is much greater than it is in the case of artisan wages, and that so far the inference is in correspondence with the indications in the first table.

7617. (*Mr. Sexton.*) What the Commission is particularly endeavouring to fix is the relative taxable capacity of Ireland and Great Britain, and I notice that the average in your Table 1, in the second column is a United Kingdom average, it would be still higher if it were a Great Britain average, would it not?—I took these figures because it so happens the comparison was made in that form in the tables when they were published originally, and I have simply collected, from tables already published, the comparison which I had already made. But the point would be this, that not much difference is made in comparing Ireland with the United Kingdom, and in comparing Ireland with Great Britain, excepting in one or two cases, because the proportion of Ireland is so small that whether you compare Ireland with the United Kingdom or with Great Britain the figure is much the same. The proportion of Ireland would appear smaller if you compared it with Great Britain only, but there would not be a great difference. In the case of agriculture, it is necessary to take account of that because the number of people connected with agriculture in Ireland approaches so closely to the number of people connected with agriculture in Great Britain that if you make a comparison between Ireland and the United Kingdom you get to far an unfair [illegible], because Ireland, in that case, is so big as to bring down the average, but it would not be so much so, I think, in the other cases, because the proportion of Ireland is so small.

7618. Agriculture is an extremely important in regard to Ireland, is it not?—Yes, and you will observe that in regard to agriculture, I have stated the proportion for Great Britain as well as for the United Kingdom on that account.

7619. (*Chairman.*) Then you point out that, allowing for the different distribution of people employed at high and low rates, the preponderance in Ireland of wages at the low rates compared also with the numbers at the low rates for Great Britain, these differences in the wages rates between Ireland and Great Britain suggest that the average remuneration of the wage earner, man for man, is probably only half or little better, than the average remuneration of the wage earner in Great Britain. Will you develope that suggestion?—I think, perhaps, that will come afterwards, but I am calling attention to the point at the outset in order to enforce the importance of it—that whatever the facts as to comparing individual rates may be, yet when you compare the great masses, and take account of the different masses in each country at the different rates the result will be that the average income of the wage-earner in Ireland is about a half, or little more than a half, of the average income of the wage-earner in the United Kingdom. That will be developed later, but that is the general impression of the tables as they are put before you now, when you read into them that you have to take into account the different masses of labour at the different rates.

7620. What is your next table?—The next table which I put in is an extended statistical comparison between Ireland and the United Kingdom on a great many points which would appear likely to assist the Commission in the general inquiries they are making as to the resources of Ireland and Great Britain. I have observed that you have had one or two tables put in by different witnesses. I think Sir Edward Hamilton gave you one, and some of the other witnesses have given you tables of a similar character to these, but much shorter, and I think it would be of interest that you should have an extended comparison with a good many of these data before you. That I put in as Table 3.

7621 How do you arrive at the estimate in Table 3, in the absence of custom duties as between Great Britain and Ireland; you estimate the imports and exports. How do you arrive at that?—To a certain extent there is an account of the foreign trade of Ireland directly. As far as that goes you have absolute figures. Then you have an account of the quantities of cattle, sheep, horses, and pigs exported from Ireland, and if you apply current prices to them you get an amount of what these exports are. With regards to the imports into Ireland, you can take account, for instance, of such commodities as tea, and so forth, which are subject to duty, because if you know what the quantity paying duty and going to Ireland is, you will know that one year with another there must be an import of the same quantity into Ireland. Then a good many years ago, I think as far back as 1874, there was an account published of the quantities of imports into Ireland of grain stuffs and things of that sort, which, to a certain extent, may still be useful at the present time. I did not think it would be desirable to put the detailed estimate in, because, of course, in a comparison of this kind there is a certain amount of conjecture; but I may say, as far as exports are concerned, the chief articles in the table

Sir Robert Giffen, K.C.B. — [illegible] — *Imports and exports.*

before me are exports of cattle, horses, sheep, and pigs. You put a value upon them, and then you get the result. Then I have a catalogue made of the quantity of bacon and hams—of things exported in that way, with a statement of how it is arrived at. Then butter is dealt with in a similar way. Of course there is a certain element of conjecture in it, but you know these must be items of export trade from Ireland—you know these are the things which must be exported. Then, with regard to the linen trade, the gentleman who has prepared this table for me has made a good many calculations as to what the exports from Ireland would be in that trade, where we have the statements of the exports from the United Kingdom, we know a great deal of the work in Ireland is done for foreign countries. Then, similarly, you can make a calculation as to the value of Irish spirits exported, the value of beer exported, and the value of fish. Of course there is a great deal of conjecture in it, but in the absence of any customs returns, one would like to see how the thing would work out in a rough manner, and that is how it has been done. Then coming back to the imports, you have no less than 8,000,000*l.* sterling directly imported into Ireland in the foreign trade. That is something with which you start in making up an account. Then you happen to know, for instance, as regards coal—the quantity of coal imported into Ireland, because there is a special return which shows that; you make a calculation of the value of that coal at the usual export price of English coal, and you get a figure which may be roughly about the value of the imports of coal into Ireland. Then coffee, currants, foreign spirits, tea, tobacco, sugar, wine, and so on, are all treated in much the same way, and reasons are given for arriving at the particular figure. I think if anyone takes an interest in these matters they can see for themselves it is possible to make up an account in the way that I have described which would approximate to the truth very roughly, and, perhaps, give you a better figure than none at all, if you wish to think about these matters. That is all I would put forward with regard to the figures in this table as to imports and exports.

7622. So that the total figures in supplement B to table 3, on page 6, where you give exports of 27,674,000*l.*, and imports of 22,000,000*l.*, may be taken to be approximately correct, may they not?—Yes. I may say it is not done by myself, it is done by a gentleman in my office, whom I got to look into it, but it is following similar lines to what I followed when I wrote upon the subject of the resources of Ireland and Great Britain, in the "Nineteenth Century," in March 1886, and it is a kind of calculation that statisticians often make in the absence of anything better. You try to make up an account of how much the exports and imports would be.

7623. (*Mr. Sexton.*) Do you intend to put in a memorandum as to the process by which you arrive at these results?—I think I can, if the Commission wish it. I have it here, and will simply hand it in; always subject to the observation that so much conjecture enters into these things that it must be taken as a very rough approximation; and that is all it can pretend to be.

7624. (*Chairman.*) What you have told us in detail you can put into a very short statement, can you not, not tying yourself to the exact accuracy of any of the figures?—Yes. I think it might be just as well to put in the statement itself, as I have received it, and the Commission will apply their own judgment and discretion to it, as to whether it is made up in a fair way or not, and arrive at an idea of what the result would probably be if we had all the figures. I may say that I have compared it with some of our colonies, for instance, and I think if you compare these imports and exports with the imports and exports of Canada, that the Irish figures are about equal to the Canadian figures; but if you compare them with the imports and exports of the Australasian Colonies, where the population is about 4,000,000, the Irish figures are considerably below the figures of the Australasian Colonies.

7625. The rough difference between exports and imports into Ireland may be stated to be about five and a half millions?—It would appear so in that account; but that is one of those conclusions which I should say, ought not to be drawn from a rough account of this kind, unless you can confirm it in some other way, because there is so much conjecture entering into almost all the figures that the margin may be much more out than the total of each side of the account itself. The margin may err much more readily than the total upon each side of the account.

Economic drain from Ireland.

7626. But taking it roughly, would that difference of 5,500,000*l.* measure what has been called the economic drain from Ireland?—I do not know that it would. At one time in this country we were also exporting much more than we were importing. I should say about 30 years ago, we were exporting on balance more than we were importing; but the interpretation was, we were investing in foreign countries, and it was no indication of an economic drain from this country at all. You must hesitate before you apply conclusions of that kind to figures of that description.

7627. You would not admit the wisdom of stating the economic drain at 5,500,000*l.*?—I do not think the figure would justify you in saying that. I give you the figure exactly as I got it, but, considering the way in which it is obtained, and considering the difficulty of interpreting what the exact meaning of a balance of imports over exports, or exports over imports, may be, you would not be justified in speaking of it certainly as indicating that there is an economic drain of that amount.

7628. (*Sir David Barbour.*) That difficulty, of interpreting the exports and imports, exists in the case of all countries, even though you have accurate statements of exports and imports, does it not?—That would be so.

7629. There are transactions of the nature of borrowing and lending which do not appear in the statistics of imports and exports?—Yes. I should think there is a certain amount of saving in Ireland which goes into foreign investments; I do not know how much, but possibly to some extent it is so.

7630. (*Chairman.*) That has always been put forward, has it not, as almost the first item in correcting that calculation to which attention must be drawn?—That is one of the things; but as this subject of the economic drain from Ireland has been mentioned, I should say that I had the curiosity some years ago to inquire in the city whether there was any indication of a perpetual adverse exchange in Ireland, which would be one sign of an economic drain, at least of an economic drain eventually of a serious kind, and the information which I got was that on the whole the exchange was even between Ireland and Great Britain. That is all I can say. I see nothing in the figures themselves, or in any figures with which I am acquainted, to indicate that there is a drain of any very great amount.

7631. No more than the steady and very small drain on between the metropolis and the country?—There is a kind of drain always going on to the metropolis from all parts of the country, but that results in a very moderate pressure, indeed, upon the remittances from the provinces to London.

7632. (*Mr. Sexton.*) Does any other reason, except foreign investments, occur to you at present for counselling hesitation in drawing any inference from the relation between exports and imports as to the economic drain?—I think there is a good deal of evidence that Irish investments are held very largely in Ireland itself. For instance, Irish railways are held very much in Ireland itself, and I am not aware that in the City there is any very great market for Irish securities outside what there is in Ireland itself.

7633. (*Lord Farrer.*) The tendency has been, has it not, rather to transfer investments from London to

Sir Robert Giffen, K.C.B. — *Remittances from Ireland.*

Ireland, for instance, in banks?—I cannot say how far that has been so of late years.

7634. (*Lord Welby.*) Have you ever heard that that is so with regard to Guinness's?—I have heard that a very large transfer of that stock has been passed from England to Ireland?—I could not say about that; I have not had so much acquaintance with the City of late years as I once had, but I do know that Ireland is considered to be a strong country to come against, and a country which has securities and investments, and to which the people interested in the securities on the Stock Exchange go when they wish to get them placed. That I do know, and that has been going on for many years. But if you look at the number of securities, the income of which can be sent from Ireland to this country, or sent abroad anywhere, I do not think you will find that the income of those securities would represent any very large amount in comparison to the total income from the securities in Ireland.

7635. (*Chairman.*) Take, for instance, the leading Irish railways; there are not above three at least of them, practically, quoted on the Stock Exchange in London, are there?—They are not much quoted on the Stock Exchange in London.

7636. One or two of the very best may be, but, as a rule, the Irish securities which are not railway securities are very little dealt with in London, are they?—I never heard them much talked of at all in the City when I was acquainted with it.

7637. (*Lord Farrer.*) Are you acquainted with any case in which the meetings of Irish banks were formerly held in London only, and are now held in Ireland?—No, I could not say anything about that. If there was any large economic drain from Ireland, it would be probably by the owners of landed property or of houses—the class who receive a large amount—but that is not a very large sum so far as one can judge altogether. A very large part of Schedule A, in Ireland, appears to be held by a few people, judging by the income-tax returns; and, as to Schedule B, only a very small part of it really pays income tax at all, so that you are chiefly limited to schedule A, I would consider. Probably there are no remittances abroad in connexion with Schedule D at all, as the people who are carrying on trade and manufactures must for the most part live where the trade or manufacture is carried on, so that it would only apply, I should consider, to a part of Schedule A, if there are any remittances abroad, and that would be on the part of people who receive rents and who do not live in Ireland. How much that would be I have no means of estimating.

7638. (*Lord Welby.*) *Primâ facie* if you have reason to think that the exchange between England and Ireland is even, that is a reason for thinking there is no very great drain, is it not?—No large drain one way or the other. Of course some things enter into that calculation of exchange again. For instance, you have a considerable number of officers connected with the army in Ireland who, no doubt, spend a much larger amount in Ireland even than the pay that they receive; and any remittances made to them on that account would be a set-off, as far as exchange is concerned, against any economic drain from Ireland of another kind. Whether it would be important enough to enter into the matter very much I do not know, but any rental interest in Ireland would affect the Exchange to some extent, in the same manner.

7639. (*Sir David Barbour.*) Do you think that over a long series of years the exchange affords any indication as to whether there is or is not an economic drain?—I think, if there was an economic drain, that it would tell upon the exchange in a series of years.

Relative population.

7640. (*Chairman.*) I will now pass to other considerations. In the first place, what would you suggest to take as the test of the resources of the two countries?—In comparing the resources of any two countries, I think as a statesman would look at the subject, the first thing to take into account always, would be the population. That is the starting point of your investigation to a very large extent.

7641. What is the ruling figure as to the relative population?—As to population, I should like to repeat for convenience here (there is no doubt you have the figures before you in many other ways) that in 1894 the population of the United Kingdom was 38·8 millions, and the population of Ireland only 4·6 millions, and that gives the proportion of Ireland to the total of 11·9 per cent.

7642. All but 12 per cent.?—All but 12 per cent., and, of course, I shall have occasion to mention the point later on, but probably, in a year or two, owing to the increase of population in Great Britain that is always going on, and the slight decrease of population in Ireland that seems always to be going on, that figure will very likely become a smaller one—the proportion will be less than almost 12 per cent., it may become 11 per cent., and, perhaps, less; that is the probability of the next few years.

7643. Then passing from the actual proportion of population to the details upon which it is built, what would you say?—I should like to call the attention of the Commission to certain facts as to population which seem to bear upon the general economic condition of Ireland and the United Kingdom generally when we compare them. The first figure of that kind which I have thought would be of value to the Commission is the figure of what is known as the excess of births over deaths. There is sometimes an impression that a high birth-rate is a sign of prosperity, and a high death-rate a sign of adversity, but that is not quite so when we look at it in detail, because we often find that a high birth-rate and a high death-rate go together. The reason is the great amount of infant mortality, and you always find that when you have a high birth-rate, as a rule, you have a high death-rate. The advantage of taking the excess of births over deaths is that you know whether the general conditions appear to be favourable to the increase of population or not, and I may say that amongst statisticians who have worked out the subject, the best indication of general wholesome conditions of living in the community is furnished by the existence of a considerable excess of births over deaths along with a moderate birth-rate, and a low death-rate. The supposition is that in a community of that kind marriages are deferred, owing to the saving habits of the people, and although the birth-rate is low, yet there is much less infant mortality—the children who are born live, and so you have an excess of births over deaths which is of a very satisfactory kind. When we take the comparison on that head between Ireland and the other countries of the United Kingdom, we find according to the latest statistical abstract (I think it was 1893), the births in Ireland were 105,000, the deaths 83,000, and the excess of births over deaths 22,000, giving a proportion per thousand of the population of that excess of births over deaths, of 5 per thousand. In England in the same year the births were 914,000, the deaths 570,000, the excess of births over deaths 344,000, and the proportion of the excess of births over deaths per thousand of population comes out at 11·4, or more than double the corresponding excess in Ireland. Similarly for Scotland the births in the same year were 127,000, the deaths 80,000, and the excess of births over deaths 47,000, giving the proportion per thousand of the population of the excess of births over deaths of 11·5 just about the same as the proportion for England, and in both cases much more than double the excess of births over deaths in Ireland. I should say that the reason of it is, so far as one can judge, not any excessive mortality in Ireland, because the deaths, you will observe, in Ireland are very little more than the deaths in Scotland with a somewhat larger population, but it is a deficiency of births, and that seems connected with another characteristic of Ireland's population which I shall put before you presently—that the population in Ireland appears on the whole to be an older population than that of either England or Scotland.

7644. Then, on the whole, do you give us the range, or do you not give it as the case, the inferiority of the general condition of the population?—I think it indicates a certain inferiority in the general condition of the population, that you have such a small excess of births over deaths in Ireland; that it is not so progressive or advanced a community as the communities of England and Scotland. I think that is a fair inference, so that if you have a proportion of close upon 12 per cent. of the population in Ireland as compared with the United Kingdom, you may almost assume that the resources of Ireland as compared with the resources of the United Kingdom are less than 12 per cent. That is a fair inference from the figures as to population so far as we have gone.

7645. (*Mr. Sexton.*) The salient fact appears to be that the population of Ireland is older?—I am going to give figures on that head presently.

7646. (*Chairman.*) Putting it in general words, what is the broad conclusion you would draw from these figures?—What I have stated—that the presumption from the evident inferiority of the general condition of the population, man for man, is that the resources of Ireland must be much less than in the proportion of one to eight. That is what I have stated, the population is close upon one eighth, but the resources are not probably so much as one eighth, if you take into consideration the conditions of inferiority that are apparent even when you look at the population statistics.

7647. Do you also wish to call attention to the different composition of the population?—Yes, I put in two tables, Tables 4 and 5, which bear on the composition of the population in Ireland, and in England and Scotland respectively, and I have drawn it out in this way to show the numbers and proportion of people under 20, between 20 and 40 (which I consider the prime of life), 40 to 50, and then 50 and upwards. I do not think I need read the numbers in Table 4, but I thought it useful to give the actual figures, so that the Commission could look at them.

7648. Any conclusions which you draw from these you will, perhaps, state to the Commission?—The conclusion is that in Ireland no less than 15·6 per cent. of the male population are upwards of 50, but in Scotland and England the percentages are 13·6 and 13·7 respectively. The percentage in Ireland between 20 and 40 (that is of the male population) is 29·6 per cent., and in Scotland and England 29·9 and 29·0 respectively. The percentages of female population are much the same as the percentages of the male population. The conclusion is, therefore, that Ireland has fewer people in proportion, in the prime of life, and more above 50, than Great Britain has.

7649. That is fortified, is it not, by the statistics of emigration?—Yes. I have now to call attention to the statistics of emigration. I put in Table 6, which is extracted, I may say, from the annual report on emigration and immigration which is presented to Parliament. The general effect of this table appears to me to be this. In 1893 there were 116,000 passengers outward of English adult persons to places out of Europe, and 16,000 children, the children being thus about 11 per cent. of the total—and while there were 19,000 adult Scotch persons with 4,000 children, the children being about 18 per cent. of the total—the corresponding records for Ireland show an emigration of 46,000 adults, and 4,000 children, the latter being thus about 8 per cent. only of the total. That is to say that emigration from Ireland is in proportion, not so much an emigration of families as the English and Scotch emigration is, but an emigration of adult persons, so far as one can tell, much more largely than the emigration from England and Scotland is. Before passing from this table I may notice there is another point in it to which attention may be called, that is that while there is an excess of males over females of a considerable amount in the emigration of English and Scotch persons, in Ireland there is more of an equality between the sexes, and in the year 1893, there is actually an excess of females over males in the emigration from Ireland.

7650. (*Mr. Sexton.*) What do you infer from that?—That corresponds with the fact which we have had as to the small excess of births over deaths, and it also corresponds with the smaller proportion in Ireland of people between 20 and 40 than there is in either England or Scotland, whereas in Ireland there is a much larger proportion above 50 than there is in either England or Scotland. All the facts that I have given you as to the excess of births over deaths, as to the the actual composition of the population, and as to emigration which I have now given you, are in correspondence, and point to the same fact of the actual population in Ireland being weaker, man for man, counting everybody, than the actual population of either England or Scotland.

7651. (*Chairman.*) Having brought together these preliminary figures, what do you infer from them with regard to the main point of our inquiry?—That they indicate the probability of the resources of Ireland being less per head than those of Great Britain which I propose now to enquire into directly. It seems to me, if you compare the resources of the two countries, the main point, if you can ascertain it, so far, is a comparison of the aggregate of individual incomes in the two countries. There are two elements always to be considered, property and income, but on the whole income is the proper thing to compare, because people with the same amount of property may have different incomes, and of course the man with a good income from a small property is really in as good a position, to a large extent, as the man who has the same income from a large property. It is not quite the same thing, but it counts in that direction. I may give as an instance of a community which has a large income in proportion to its property, the case of the United States; and other new countries. These are countries which borrow in order to carry on their business, and the result is that the communities there have a large income in proportion to their property, whereas in an old country like England, the community with a large amount of accumulated property, does not seem to have an income in proportion to the property of quite the same amount, yet the community that has the income can make use of it in all sorts of ways, and the income is an actual resource at the time just the same as if they derived it from property. There is another illustration which one may give, and that is often given as a defence of the English artisan in comparison with foreign artisans for not accumulating property. The argument is that the artisan here by spending his income upon developing his own strength and comfort, makes himself a better instrument of production, so that he has a larger income, although he has not the accumulated property of a foreign artisan.

7652. We will deal, then, with the income first?—I think it important, therefore, that we should consider the question of income mainly, when we deal with the resources of two different countries. There is this other point to be considered; that is it is quite possible that in two countries the aggregate of income which you may get from statistics would not bear the same proportion to the real income in the two countries. That is to say, there is a real income, and an income expressed in money. In one country you might have certain services rendered to the whole community which were not the subject of exchange, and so, not being the subject of exchange, they could not be reckoned as income, but in another country the same services becoming the subject of exchange would be reckoned as income. An illustration of this is given by the well known facts as to wives and other members of households. The wives and other members receive no income, there is no exchange of incomes; but when the household is disorganised sometimes a housekeeper has to be employed, and then there is no exchange of income although the housekeeper is really performing the services which the wife would do in another household. In applying this consideration, however, to countries like Ireland and Great Britain, we may assume that the account would be affected alike in both by any considerations of that kind. We have no reason to believe that the exchanges are less in proportion to the total real income in the one country than in the other, and, therefore, there is a good reason for using the method of ascertaining the money income in both cases respectively, if you can do so.

Assessment to income tax.

7653. There are most important reservations which ought to be borne in mind, but will you now go to the general question, or have you any other remarks to make?—That is all I have to say generally about it, because, statistically, all we can do is to count up the aggregate of individual incomes as they are actually exchanged, without going behind into the question of what the real force of the two communities would be, if we are to get at the whole facts. When we come to the subject, practically we find that a portion of the incomes of Great Britain and Ireland is dealt with for the purposes of taxation by the Income Tax Commissioners, and it is a great convenience when we come to study such a question as the present, that you find a large portion of the incomes of the respective countries is dealt with continuously for the purpose of taxation, and therefore you can get something in the one country which you can compare with the other country. If there were reason to believe that income tax incomes bore the same proportion to the total in the two countries compared, and that the returns were accurate to a fraction, hardly any other inquiry would be necessary than an inquiry into the income tax. I propose now to state the figures as to the income tax as they appear to me. The basis of the income tax is the gross assessment of the whole of the incomes from certain kinds of property, lands, and houses, and the assessment of the incomes from other sources above the limit of 150*l.* (now 160*l.*), the object being to tax the incomes above the limit with certain deductions. From the income-tax statistics, therefore, we get first, a gross assessment which includes all incomes above 150*l.* per annum from all sources, and in addition the whole of the incomes from certain property, land, houses, &c., whether they are above or below that limit. Second, a net assessment which includes incomes above 150*l.*, with a deduction from incomes between 150*l.* and 400*l.*; and third, the *yield* of the tax which for the present purpose, of course, is much the same thing as the net assessment in another form. For our purpose the last two comparisons appear the best, because the thing to be compared in the two cases is the aggregate of individual incomes above a certain standard, whereas the gross assessments deal with the whole of certain kinds of property which may exist in a different proportion in the two countries from what property or income generally does. In the net assessment you compare two things exactly on the same basis; in the gross assessment you include some kinds of property which may be in different proportions in the two countries, and therefore it is not a good test of the whole. However, it is important to see how all the figures compare.

7654. You take the gross first, I presume?—I will take the figures for the gross first, for the year 1893-94. You find that out of a total income of 718·3 millions in the United Kingdom assessed to income tax, Ireland has 38·2 millions, or 5·4 per cent., England has 609·4 millions, or 84·4 per cent., and Scotland has 69·6 millions, or 9·7 per cent., thus showing that Ireland has rather more than a twentieth part of the income-tax income of the United Kingdom, and if the income-tax income is fairly representative, has rather more than a twentieth part of the resources. But, as I have said, the gross assessment is not quite so satisfactory as the net assessment, to which I will now advert. When we look at the net assessment, we find that you have a total of 597·1 millions in the United Kingdom, of which Ireland has 27·3 millions, or 4·6 per cent. of the total; England has 510·2 millions, or 85·5 per cent. of the total; Scotland has 59 millions, or 9·9 per cent. of the total. So that Ireland, while appearing as rather more than a twentieth part of the United Kingdom where gross assessments are taken, that is, assessments which include, besides all incomes above 150*l.*, the whole of certain kinds of incomes, now appears when net assessments are taken, that is, incomes of above 150*l.* only, with certain deductions, as only about one twenty-second of the United Kingdom.

7655. And that calculation you prefer to the calculation of gross assessments, do you?—I think it is more useful and more perfect as a test than the gross assessment, for the reason that I have given. Now I pass to the yield of the tax. I take the Return No. 334, Session 1893, in which the actual yield of the tax is given. In that return a complication is introduced by making a certain small part of the yield, 171,000*l.*, appear as contributed from Imperial sources, and not distributed between England, Scotland, and Ireland respectively, but for convenience sake the amount will be here credited to England only, as it is not a matter of very great importance. When we look at the comparison of the yield, the figures which we get are these. The *yield* in 1892-93 was 13,159,600*l.*, of which the amount contributed by *Ireland* was 652,000*l.* or 5·1 per cent.; England, 11,671,000*l.*, or 88·9 per cent.; Scotland, 1,216,000*l.*, or 9 per cent. The results I consider, are substantially the same as those shown by the net assessment above given. The slight differences may be due to minor corrections, or some small changes, which perhaps for the purpose you are now concerned with, it is not necessary to take account of, because I do not think that in any case it will be possible to get at more than an approximation to the actual facts, and the differences between the net yield of the tax and the net assessment seem to me to be almost immaterial. You get much the same figure whichever you take.

7656. (*Mr. Sexton.*) It seems to bring the proportion of Ireland down from one twenty-second to one twenty-fourth?—I do not think, when you come to taxation, when you come to state a proportion, that you will be able to make much distinction between a twenty-second and a twenty-fourth—they are practically much the same thing.

7657. (*Chairman.*) You take the twenty-second, do you? I take the twenty-second as being rather more convenient, and I think it is possible that some small differences in payment may arise to account for the smaller net yield. Then, of course, there is the 171,000*l.* which I have credited to England only, and which the revenue authorities think ought to be distributed in a way which they do not know between the three countries.

7658. (*Chairman.*) Apart from this smaller adjustment, our attention has been called to one or two other questions in connexion with income-tax figures as a test of relative taxable capacity. It has been contended by some of the witnesses who appeared before us, that Ireland is less highly or strictly valued and assessed to income tax than England, and by others that it is more strictly assessed. Have you anything to say on that point?—I considered that question a good many years ago, and the conclusion to which I came then, was that, on the whole, I thought that Ireland was more strictly valued. I derived that impression in part from the Committee of 1864, which investigated the subject a good deal. But I think also that it arises in this way, that in England, especially as regards foreign incomes, it is very difficult, I believe, to get at the true facts at all, and I should say that it is almost quite certain that there is a considerable part of the foreign income of the British people, which is never brought home and accounted for to the income-tax authorities—in fact it is a large element in the matter.

7659 (*Lord Farrer.*) That is as regards foreign securities. I think the Chairman's question rather pointed to the valuation of land?—The question was quite general to me whether the one country was over-valued or not, and the question being put in that general way, and it being very important to look at it in that general way, I gave the most general answer. In addition to that, I think we have had various statements in Budget speeches and other documents. I recollect one very strong statement by Mr Gladstone in one of his budget speeches, in reference to the strange difference in assessments under Schedule D., which was found when the income-tax authorities compared the returns which had been made to them with the claims which the same people made when the property happened to be taken by railways or for some other purposes. Really the cases were very striking indeed, and it is obvious that in a very wealthy country like England, and especially in a metropolis like London, that the assessing authorities, as regards Schedule D. have very little means indeed of getting at the true facts, and there are many people in businesses who hardly know themselves what their profits are, except after a long series of years. Practically what is done very often, I believe, is that the surveyor takes a shot at a man and keeps on raising the assessment until the man begins to feel that the pressure is becoming rather too severe, and objects. I have heard of cases of that kind.

7080. (*Lord Welby.*) May I ask if you have heard of cases—I do not want to generalise too much—in which people have kept on paying on an income much above that which they really earned, because they did not like it to be known that they were losing?—There are not many such cases, I think, not so many as on the other side. I have heard a good deal more on the other side, but I have no doubt it would be so, to some extent.

7081. (*Mr Sexton.*) That would be just as likely in Ireland as in England, would it not?—I do not know that it would be quite so in Ireland, because being a smaller place, everybody is much more under observation. What I think is this, that in the metropolis, the income-tax authorities have special difficulties in their assessment under Schedule D., of which the illustration given by Mr. Gladstone, no doubt, a good many years ago, was a very striking one. I think there are very important matters with regard to the assessments of income tax generally. With regard more particularly to Schedule A. and Schedule B., I could not say how the facts may be at the present time. I should think it very likely that the practice in England has become more strict as the years have gone on, but I do know in past times, the valuation for the income tax from many parts of England, was far below what the real value of the property was. I am speaking now of Schedule A., and I am speaking, to some extent, on official authority, because some years ago I was the instrument of obtaining a return, which was never published, from the Inland Revenue authorities comparing the agricultural rental of England in the period before 1812 with the present time, and I was warned at that time by the Inland Revenue authorities that this must be subject to the observation that about 1812, the assessment to the income tax could not be taken to a fair assessment of the rental—that probably the rental was considerably more. They believed the thing had been more strictly taken account of since, but then it had been gradual, and I am not at all sure, from what I have heard, that it has been done at all completely throughout England. In many parishes and many places the necessity has hardly arisen for making the valuation complete so far as local purposes are concerned, and local people have so much to do with the valuation, that the valuation has really not been made so complete as it might be.

7082. (*Chairman.*) There is one other point which has been raised in this comparison, and that is this: It has been pressed upon us very strongly that a large portion of the income derived from land in Ireland is withdrawn into England by absentee landlords, or by mortgagees, and it has been urged upon us that this should be deducted from the gross assessment under Schedule A. in Ireland, and added to the gross assessment under Schedule A. in England; what do you say as to that point?—I think that is covered a little by what was said at the beginning of my evidence about the exchange between England and Ireland. I should doubt if there is very much to be made upon that head, because if you go into a strict account in that way you would also have to invert means to find out in some way or the other what the share of Ireland is in the investments in foreign securities which really come to London, and are all dealt with in the English assessments. You would have great difficulty if you went into matters of that kind, I consider. There is also a sense in which the absentee rents are as taxable as any other rents in Ireland, that they are a resource of Ireland, as far as taxation is concerned, although they are remitted and spent elsewhere. I think that is a fair consideration—that real property is necessarily a resource of the country which has it; it is always there, and cannot go away, and it is a resource for the purposes of taxation.

7083. (*Lord Farrer.*) What should you say if it is mortgaged; supposing Irish real property is mortgaged up to the hilt to mortgagees living in England, and receiving in that way the income of the property?—The rates and taxes in the country itself would always come before mortgage interest. It would not cease to be a resource to the country which has the property.

7084. But the surplus, after paying the rates and taxes, would go to England instead of to Ireland, would it not?—That would, no doubt, be so. I am only pointing out, just now, that practically, so far as purposes of taxation are concerned, because of that land is available for taxation in the country which has to resort to absentees and others, it remains completely available for the purposes of taxation.

7085. (*Mr. Sexton.*) But after the question of taxation comes the question of income. It is quite true real property cannot be carried out of the country. Yet if the person owning the real property, whilst he does contribute, no doubt, his share to the local rates, takes away the income, and spends it in another country, does not that affect the taxable capacity of the original country, although the real property remains there?—I do not think so, as far as real property is concerned, for the reason I have given, that it cannot affect the taxable capacity in that way. It is a thing you might take into account if you are going to be extremely equitable in dealing with your taxation. I may say it is a point which has frequently occurred to me when I look at the extent of our own investments in foreign countries, and it is a thing which statesmen will have to consider. If you were going to be at issue with the United States, for instance, a large part of the income which now, in a state of peace, we consider to be a resource of the people of the United Kingdom, would disappear, and would, as a matter of fact, be a resource of the people of the United States, because they have the thing in their own hands—the property and the income. It is a matter to be considered. What would happen in time of war would be that everything would be available to the country which has got it.

7086. But even though they have the real property, whilst you have the income, is it not part of your taxable capacity. It is only when the income disappears from your hands that your taxable capacity disappears?—I am stating all the facts; it is for the Commission to judge, because it is quite obvious that, so far as real property is concerned, the country which has it has a power of taxing whoever may be the owners of the income, and wherever they may be.

7087. (*Lord Farrer.*) And will get its tax before the foreigner gets his income?—Yes.

7088. (*Sir David Barbour.*) A country in such a position would not exempt a man from the income tax simply because he lived abroad?—We see that now in the United States, where they are imposing an income tax which a great many people in this country will have to pay. It happens in a good many countries, you have the income tax in Italy and India. The people in India have to pay it, and then the same

Sir Robert Giffen, C.B.

28 May 1894.

Taxable capacity as affected by absentee-ism.

Sir Robert Giffen, C.B.

20 Mar. 1895.

Taxable capacity [illegible] affected by [illegible].

income, when it is remitted to this country, has to pay a further income tax here—that is a well-known thing which besets us in dealing with taxation.

7669. (*Mr. Sexton.*) When you take the yield of income tax as a measure of taxable capacity as between two countries, do you not assume that the income from which the tax is paid is expended in the country and credited with the tax?—I do not think so—not very much. It would be an important matter if it was a serious amount, if, for instance, there was any reason to believe that Ireland had to remit 10,000,000*l.* or 15,000,000*l.* sterling annually, or some sum of that kind, but I do not think it can be a question of more than two or three millions at the outside one way or the other, and then it does not become a question of so much practical importance.

7670. (*Chairman.*) As a statistician you would discard, however much as a politician you might give it weight, any such argument?—I do not think it is very material for any purposes of these figures that we have been dealing with, because we can only get an approximation at best, and any difference that would be made by taking that into account would be comparatively small and would not turn the balance much one way or the other—that is the impression which I have.

7671. (*Sir David Barbour.*) There is this difficulty also, is there not, that if you take the money paid as interest on mortgages from Ireland, and if you take also the absentee rental, you take two sums which are to some extent identical, that is to say, a portion of the absentee rental goes or may go to pay the mortgage interest?—I could hardly go into that, because I do not think the amount can be very much one way or the other.

7672. But it is a difficulty, is it not, in attempting to make an exact calculation?—It would be a difficulty, and I think that you could not go into such minute calculations with any satisfactory prospect at all, that it is not a case for minute calculations of that kind.

7673. (*Lord Farrer.*) In illustration of what you said before, supposing that Ireland had her own Government, and was to impose her own income tax, these revenues drawn out of Ireland, and going into England, would undoubtedly be taxable in Ireland and be subjects which she could tax?—Real property is always taxable in a way no other property is.

7674. And other property, investments in railways or banks which are held by foreigners—supposing Ireland had the power of imposing her own income tax, would be, or might be, subject to her taxation, and form part of her taxable capacity?—Subject always to this, that you cannot tax property generally except real property (anything like circulating capital), without running the risk of driving it away from the country.

Income tax [illegible] Ireland [illegible].

7675. (*Chairman.*) I will now go back from that digression. The last express point dealt with in your evidence was the proportion of one-twenty-second, with which you credited Ireland. We went to two very important points from that, and I will now go back to your evidence at section 29, in which you give reasons why the inference drawn cannot be disproved. Will you enlarge upon that?—The point is this, that if you have such a proportion as one twenty-second established by a considerable part of the income of the respective countries, you may assume that that proportion is likely enough to hold good, or nearly so, as regards the total income. That is the *primâ facie* assumption which you would be entitled to make. I may give a short explanation. Suppose the income tax income to be about a half, if you have any reason to suppose it is about a half, or some such proportion of the respective incomes of the two countries you are comparing, then the other half would either be in the same proportion in the two countries, or in a slightly different proportion, or in a very different proportion. If you, for instance, thought that the other income (not the income tax income) would be in the proportion, say, of one-eighteenth in one country instead of one-twenty-second, then that would only affect the final result in this way, that you would have to take the mean between one-eighteenth and one-twenty-second, and your general figure for the whole would only be affected by the alteration from one-twenty-second to one-twentieth. That is a very important consideration, to keep in mind when you come to investigate the question of what the other income of the two countries respectively is. You have got a large lump of income very well ascertained, establishing a definite proportion, and when you have to consider it, that if you are to change that proportion materially, the proportion of the other income must be very different from what that of the income tax income is. You must show, as regards Ireland and Great Britain, that the other income is in a greater proportion than one twenty-second—that it amounts to one-fifteenth or one-tenth, or some such higher proportion—before you can alter the impression which this figure of income tax gives.

7676. It depends upon the volume, of course?—It means a great difference in the other income to make a great change in the proportion which you have once established by means of this large mass of income tax income. I think we shall find that there is no reason to believe that the proportion of the other income is widely different; but what I am calling attention to now is that it would have to be widely different before, for practical purposes, you could say that the proportion of the income tax income is not to hold generally.

7677. On this point you would now like, would you not, to call attention to the matter we have dealt with before—the wages question?—On this head I think now the returns as to wages, which I put in at the beginning of my examination, will come to be of use, especially the first table, which I think most important. In the first table it seems to me that in most of the trades included in the returns there given, where Ireland is at all represented, there is hardly an exception to the rule of the average Irish wages being lower than the average of the United Kingdom, and in the case of the larger trades, as a rule, considerably lower. Linen, for instance, appears an exception, the Irish wages come near to the level of those of Great Britain. The linen trade, however, is a trade not carried on in the whole of Great Britain, but in Scotland only, where wages run lower than in England, that is a thing which we ascertained from our former wages returns. The trades, likewise, where Ireland is not represented, are, as a rule, the better paid trades of the order to which they belong, that is, the cotton trade among textiles, and various of the mining trades. For instance, you will find that whereas in the United Kingdom the average wages in the cotton trade are 35*l.* per head (that is for men, women, and children), and in the woollen trade 34*l.* per head; in the woollen trade, where Ireland is represented, the average Irish wages are 21*l.* per head. But in the cotton trade where the average is a little higher than it is in the woollen trade, Ireland is not represented in our returns at all, and as a matter of fact, I think there is hardly any cotton manufacture in Ireland—at least there are very few people in the census put down as engaged in the cotton manufacture. That is, taking a group of trades together, you find Ireland is not represented in the better trades of the group, and that its average, say, for instance, of 20*l.* to 23*l.* in the linen trade, although it compares with about 23*l.* in the linen trade for the United Kingdom, has to compare with 33*l.* and 35*l.* per head in the cotton trade, which is really the important trade so far as the amount of labour are concerned.

7678. (*Mr. Blake.*) It only compares favourably with the worst paid trades, does it not?—It only compares favourably with the worst paid trades, and that is an element which you have to consider.

7679. (*Mr. Currie.*) Have you the figures in the ship-building trade?—I do not think the figures are worked out in that way, but I think it is quite obvious,

Sir Robert Giffen, K.C.B.

from the second table I have put in, that the ship-building wages in Belfast run on a level with the ship-building wages on the Clyde, there is no doubt about that, but then the other point comes in, that there is a comparatively small ship-building industry in Ireland; it is not such a great mass of labour as it is in Great Britain.

7680. (*Chairman.*) Will you develop any further points on No. 1?—I do not know that I can, but I should like to call special attention to the figures as to railways, and the amounts which you get there are 48*l.* 4*s.* for Ireland, and 61*l.* 10*s.* for the United Kingdom. That is for the year 1891. With regard to these figures, I should say that they are practical averages of the whole mass of railway labour in Ireland and in the United Kingdom respectively. They are built up from actual ascertained payments in the whole trade. There you have the difference—something intermediate between the great difference that there is in the unskilled trades, and the slight difference that there is in the highly skilled and artizan trades.

7681. In the railway wages, to which you have called my attention, you give two figures for 1886 and 1891?—Yes; that shows improvement between 1886 and 1891.

7682. An improvement in both cases, and nearly in the same proportion?—Yes, not a great improvement. It is a very curious study to compare the railway wages in detail. You find that there is a considerable advance of rates, but when you come to multiply the rates by the number of people employed, you find that there must have been a great infusion into the railway service of people at the lower rates, because when you work out the average you do not get so great an advance between 1886 and 1891 as you would have expected from the advance of rates themselves.

7683. (*Mr. Sexton.*) In both countries?—In both countries.

7684. (*Chairman.*) To what do you attribute that?—To the taking on of new hands. Porters and that class of labour have been extending more in railway service, I imagine, than the highly skilled operatives.

7685. The management of railways has been compelled to employ cheaper labour?—I do not think cheaper labour, but it has been compelled to employ a larger mass of the inferior unskilled labour on railways for certain purposes. That is the sort of idea which we have.

7686. (*Mr. Sexton.*) Would it be due to an extension of lines with—or a corresponding extension of the number of upper officers?—I do not like to theorise about it. I observe the fact in detail, and that seems to be the fact which has arisen, that along with a considerable increase of rates you have had a greater infusion of people at lower wages than was the case six or seven years before, and that would be the natural effect of greatly increasing the staff in a short period, you would take on the people at the lower rates and by-and-by they would improve.

7687. (*Chairman.*) Taking the whole of Appendix I., may it be said that skilled labour remuneration in Ireland and in England compare pretty nearly. Is the percentage of difference between the different classes of skilled labour in the United Kingdom and Ireland pretty uniform, or are there any great divergences?—I do not think we have got sufficient data to go into that altogether. The rates in the second table are very largely the rates of the building trade and one or two other trades.

7688. I was referring only to Table 1. I will put my question in another way. Is the difference in the average of the United Kingdom and the average of Ireland pretty uniform throughout in the skilled trades?—I do not think you can say it is uniform, because there are skilled trades, where you find that in some of them the Irish proportion comes comparatively near to the English. You find, for instance, in the police that the Irish figure is 66*l.* and the English 71*l.* per head.

7689. That is hardly a trade, is it?—It is an industry of a kind, and I suppose the police pay taxes like other people.

7690. But in the regular skilled trade employments, practically, is not the percentage between Ireland and the United Kingdom pretty nearly the same?—I do not think you can say that. You find, for instance, in the textiles, that the Irish may be taken at about 21*l.*, and in the best and most numerous of the textiles of Great Britain it is 34*l.* or 35*l.*, and that is a difference of nearly 50 per cent. But if you look at the building trades, you will find that in Ireland it comes out at 52*l.* 12*s.* in 1891, and 62*l.* 6*d.*, in Great Britain, at the same time; that is a much less difference than that which you have in the textile trades.

7691. (*Lord Farrer.*) And that includes London, does it not?—That includes London.

7692. (*Chairman.*) Before we pass from the skilled trades to the agricultural wages, have you any further remark to make?—No, except this, that if you look at the unskilled rates in the second table you will find this. Take, for instance, bricklayers' labourers and masons' labourers, you will find that while there is a fairly close correspondence in the two artizan rates, and that in Ireland the wages for the bricklayer and mason are not so much below those of the bricklayer and mason of Great Britain (except in London, I think), yet the rate for the bricklayers' labourer in Belfast, from which place we have returns, comes out to about 16*s.* a week, as compared with much higher rates, as a rule, in Great Britain. That is another indication that in the unskilled rates Ireland falls behind Great Britain much more than it does as to skilled rates.

7693. But when you rise to the skilled rates of which the proportion is comparatively small in Ireland, then the difference is not so great, is it?—That is so.

7694. Do you lay that down as a general principle?—That is the general effect of the comparison of wages.

7695. (*Mr. Blake.*) Because they are so easily mobilised?—I think so. And I should suppose the difference of rates as regards unskilled labour expresses some difference of quality arising in some way or other.

Agricultural wages.

7696. (*Chairman.*) However, by far the largest class after all is the agricultural labourer, is it not?—Yes, that is the largest class of all.

7697. As to that, the Commission would be glad if you would develop your view?—I do not know that I can develop it very much except to say that these figures at the end of the first table are based on a comparison of rates in different parts of Great Britain and Ireland, with an allowance, as much as possible, for the difference of numbers at each rate. This is the summary of a great deal of work, and I do not think it differs from other investigations into agricultural labour which have been made, such for instance, as Mr. Little's, which you have had before you. I do not know whether reference has been made to it or not, but he has written very extensively about it.

7698. (*Mr. Sexton.*) Does your computation with regard to agricultural labourers take any note of the degree of continuity of employment?—Not so much as I should have liked; and I may say, as far as this average rate of 13*s.* 6*d.* for Great Britain is concerned, I should be disposed, after hearing the evidence which has been given before the Royal Commission on Agriculture, to raise it a little so far as the net earnings of the agricultural labourers are concerned, and that it should be more nearly 15*s.* a week on the average, than 13*s.* 6*d.* That was the general effect, I think, of the evidence which we have had, and that the statement as regards English agricultural labour in general, rather understates the position than anything else.

7699. And, of course, the comparison would be further materially affected for our present purposes, if it were found that the employment of agricultural labourers is tolerably regular and continuous in

Mr. Robert Giffen, C.B.

29 Nov. 1895.

Agricultural wages.

England, and to intermittent and precarious in Ireland? —That would be so.

7700. (*Chairman.*) When you gave us 9s. 6d. as the average for Ireland, and 13s. 6d. as the average for Great Britain, you do not take into consideration the continuous employment, do you?—I think to some extent it would be taken into consideration in this way—that in Ireland, there is a great difference between winter and summer in the rates for labour, so far as I can observe, and so far as that is concerned that would be taken into account in these rates.

7701. (*Mr. Blake.*) What would be taken into account is a change in the rates of wages, but not a time of non-employment?—We do not take much account of the effect of the harvest in the two countries respectively, which I think very likely pulls up the English average more than the Irish.

7702. (*Mr. Sexton.*) Have you not already taken into account the change of rate in wages at winter and summer and computed the wages?—Yes, I think it would be noted here.

7703. (*Chairman.*) But not the non-employment? —No.

7704. So that 13s. 6d. to 9s. 6d. puts the comparison as to Irish wages a little too favourably, does it?—If there is a great deal in the question of regularity of employment; I should like to see it discussed, locality by locality.

7705. (*Lord Farrer.*) There is less continuity of labour in Ireland than in England, is there?—Apparently, from all I have heard, there is, but whether that would be true of all districts of Ireland I am not sure. I see in some parts of Ireland there are yearly hirings, then of course, you have continuous employment. Perhaps the better class of labourers may be more continuously employed than the inferior class, and there may be other things to consider, which only shows the importance, I think, if we are to have a continuation of such inquiries in the future, that these matters should be studied locally very much more than has been the case hitherto, and that really to make up a statement of the aggregate income of two communities, it would almost be essential that a great many people should be set to work, and you should, as it were, have a statement, county by county, written with local knowledge so as to bring out the whole facts. That would be the only means of getting a completely satisfactory account of the whole matter.

7706. Stating it very roughly then, you would say that agricultural wages in Ireland compared with agricultural wages in Great Britain are two to three? —Something like that.

7707. (*Mr. Sexton.*) I think your more recent researches, since 1892–93, lead you to say that the figure of 13s. 6d. might be 14s.?—Yes. I think two to three comes near it.

7708. (*Lord Welby.*) We were told in evidence that there were a very large number of labourers, in different parts of the country, who were boarded and had their food given them; I suppose, if that is the case, that would be one of the difficulties to which you have alluded?—One of the difficulties in dealing with wages' statistics is the money value you put upon board sometimes—what it ought to be, 5s., or 6s., or 7s., or 8s., or 9s. a week.

7709. (*Sir David Barbour.*) In many parts of Ireland the labourers live with the farmer and board with him, do they not?—Yes, that is so, but there you have difficulties of this kind. Sometimes they have partial board, they get one or two meals per day, and are not lodged, and what money value you have to put upon that is a question which would hardly be got otherwise than by locally building up your information.

7710. (*Mr. Sexton.*) How far does the system of payment partly in money and partly in kind prevail in England?—Not very much in England; in Scotland a good deal. In Scotland, agricultural wages all round come up to 18s. and 19s. a week, but then there are very few of them in Scotland. Whereas, in Ireland, you have about 600,000 males above the age of 20 connected with agriculture, in Scotland you have only only about 150,000; that is the difference between the two.

7711. Does your gross computation endeavour to take note of the value of payment in kind and turn it into money?—Yes, that would be so.

Adjourned for a short time.

7712. (*Chairman.*) Before luncheon we were discussing the figures of 13s. 6d. and 9s. 6d., the proportion of wages in Great Britain and Ireland. You would even still further qualify those figures, would you not, by the preponderance in Ireland of the wages at the lower rate?—That is the point I should like to go into now. I think the point to bring out is, that whilst we can establish such a difference between rates for labour in Ireland and Great Britain, we do not complete the investigation without taking into account the different numbers at the different rates, and I may say that the relative numbers at different rates of wages are important in all such comparisons, and I am not making it for the first time for the purpose of this discussion. To show how important it is theoretically, I should like to quote to you from a paper which I read nearly four years ago at a meeting of the Australasian Association for the Advancement of Science, and which has been reprinted in the Journal of the British Economic Association. I was looking at the question of comparisons of wages in different countries or between different periods in the same country, and I was led to see then how important the question of the relative numbers of people at different rates was in any proper investigation on the subject. The passage which I read was to the following effect: "It is quite conceivable that in one of "two countries the earnings, and still more the "nominal wages, may be higher than in the other in "every single employment which can be enumerated "and compared, and yet the average earnings of the "average wage-earning man may be higher in the "latter country than in the former, the reason being "the different distribution of the people according to "earnings. This can be shown very clearly in a "theoretical comparison. Take first a community of "1,000 wage-earners, with the people distributed "according to earnings in the following classes, A, "B, C, D, and E, as follows:—The first community, Class A, earnings per annum, 30l.; numbers, 500; total, 15,000l. Class B, earnings per "annum, 60l.; numbers, 200; total, 12,000l. "Class C, earnings per annum, 70l.; numbers, 100; "total, 7,000l. Class D, earnings per annum, 80l.; "numbers, 100; total, 8,000l. Class E, earnings per "annum, 90l.; numbers, 100; total, 9,000l. This "gives you a total number of 1,000 people whose "aggregate wages in the year amount to 51,000l., and "whose average per head is, accordingly, 51l. Compare "these with another community of equal numbers in "which there are also five grades, each remunerated at a "lower rate than the corresponding grade of the first "community, but in which the average of the whole "is higher because of the different distribution of the "people among the grades. Second community:— "Class A, earnings, 40l. per annum; numbers, 100; "total 4,000l. Class B, earnings, 50l. per annum; "numbers, 100; total, 5,000l. Class C, earnings, "60l. per annum; numbers, 100; total, 6,000l. "Class D, earnings, 70l. per annum; numbers, 200; "total, 14,000l. Class E, earnings, 80l. per annum; "numbers, 500; total, 40,000l. There is now a total "number of 1,000, the same as in the first community, but the aggregate earnings are 69,000l., and "the average per head is 69l. In a comparison of "rates of wages merely according to the nature of "the employment, the wages in the first community "would obviously appear higher than in the second, "and this would be strictly true in a sense, but the "inference would be untrue that the average earnings "of the wage-earning classes of the first community, "striking a true average, would be higher."

7713. *How would you apply that to Ireland?*—I would apply that to Ireland in this way, that there we have a case where nearly all rates are lower in Ireland than in Great Britain, but there is also a disproportionate number at the lower rates for Ireland as compared with the number at the lower rates for Great Britain. The case for Ireland, therefore, is the very opposite of the theoretical case I have quoted, because it is a case where the one community that has the low rate is also the community where the great number of people are at the lowest rates; the case which I gave you was that the community with the lowest rates happened to have a greater proportionate number of its people in the higher paid classes, and therefore the average came out better than another community which had higher rates. But here, in the case of Ireland, you have both the lower rates for Ireland and the greater numbers of people at the lower rates for Ireland compared with the numbers at the lower rates for Great Britain. The result is that while in the United Kingdom, omitting agriculture, according to the evidence I gave before the Labour Commission, the average wage per man is about 60*l.* per head, about 15 per cent. of the wage earning class being above the average, about 60 per cent. about the average, and about 25 per cent. under the average—in Ireland, as far as I can judge, the average could not be put at more than about 35*l.* per head, made up in something like this way—60 per cent. at 25*l.* only, 1,500*l.*; 30 per cent. at 40*l.* only, 1,200*l.*; 10 per cent. above 60*l.* (at, say, 60*l.*), 600*l.*; that gives you a total of 3,300*l.* for the 100 people, or an average of rather more than 33*l.* per head. That is a sort of general view as to how the wages in Ireland would run, including, however, in the wage earning community peasant farmers who are pretty much in the same social condition, and you treat them for that purpose as belonging to the wage-earning community.

7714. (*Lord Welby.*) For that purpose do you take peasant farmers below a certain valuation?—Peasant farmers practically below a certain valuation are really wages earners. You will find constantly in the references to the wages rates in Ireland, the labourer is spoken of as being better off than the peasant farmer who is living on his own holding. You find that frequently in the statements as to the rural condition in Ireland.

7715. Would you put any line below which you would take the peasant farmers?—I am going to give you some statements shortly about the numbers of agricultural holdings in Ireland, but the point seems to be this, that the greater number of the agricultural holdings in Ireland is absolutely under 15*l.* valuation. I may say that I have some difficulty about the numbers, because in one return which I find in the census, the number of holdings is given at 486,000, and in the agricultural statistics of Ireland for a later year the number of occupiers is given at 520,000, and you find that practically you have before you the same table, but in the one table—the table in the census—the holdings under one acre (speaking of agricultural holdings) are stated at 14,000 in number, and in the agricultural statistics they are stated at 58,000 in number. I have been looking the last two or three days to see if I could find any explanation of the apparent discrepancy, but I can make nothing of it at present. I am merely stating that because in the one case, of course, you would have a larger number under 15*l.* than you would have in the other case, but practically there is no doubt about the fact that the bulk of the agricultural holdings in Ireland are under 15*l.* annual valuation. As far as I can judge, taking the figure of 486,000, which you get in the agricultural statistics, you have absolutely 232,000, or half the number under 15 acres; you have another 130,000 between 15 and 30 acres, and my impression is that up to 30 acres, you have practically the valuation of 15*l.* or something like it. According to that you have very nearly 400,000 occupiers under 15*l.* valuation, and under 30 acres.

7716. (*Mr. Blake.*) Was I right in understanding you to say, with reference to the 60*l.* which you mentioned for England, that you excluded agricultural labourers?—Yes, but whether you include them or not, it would not make much difference.

7717. (*Mr. Sexton.*) You did exclude them on both sides, did you not?—No, not in Ireland. I merely stated to you the figures that I gave to the Labour Commission. I think it very important when I give you a figure which I have given before for a different purpose it should be so stated, and that I have not been giving you a figure I have been making up for the Commission, but am giving you a figure which I have had in existence for general purposes some time. I should like also to add that the 60*l.* was not for England only, but for the United Kingdom.

7718. (*Mr. Blake.*) Do you think with regard to the relative numbers engaged in agriculture and other industrial employments in England, and to the relative wages, it would make no serious difference in the average rate over the whole?—I think not, because the statement which I gave did not include the building trades on the other side at that time. I had not got that out, and various other trades where wages are comparatively high.

7719. (*Chairman.*) Going back to your previous answer and the difference between the averages, will you tell the Commission what you arrive at as to the comparative wages rate for each?—Taking it at 33*l.* a head, and taking 60*l.* for the United Kingdom, the result is that the incomes of the wages-earning classes in Ireland, man for man, are little more than half of those of the United Kingdom, and as the population is only between an eighth and a ninth, that would make the Irish share of such incomes, about one-seventeenth only of a similar income in the United Kingdom. Then allowing that the proportion of people in the prime of life in the two countries is the same (whereas in fact the proportion is lower in Ireland), that would not bring up the proportion of the total income very much, as the working-class income I think is only about three-eighths of the total income. The point is, that you have one-twenty-second for the income tax income, and if you take the wage-earning income at about one-seventeenth, that being only three-eighths of the total, you would still get a proportion of about one-twentieth for the total income. You do not bring up the proportion of the total income of Ireland to the total of the United Kingdom very much, even by allowing that they have a larger proportion of the wages earning income than they have of the income tax income. That is the sort of general information I wish to put before you. My own opinion is that if you allow for this fact, that the numbers in Ireland have got to be reduced by the consideration that they have a smaller proportion of people in the prime of life, that you do not get such a large aggregate as you do in Great Britain, given the same number of the general population—therefore the effect would be not to change the income tax proportion of one-twenty-second very much.

7720. (*Mr. Sexton.*) Were you about to draw any general inference from your statement that four-fifths of the Irish holdings are valued under 15*l.* a year?—I think that will come a little later on. When I propose to compare the agricultural production of Ireland with reference to the total resources of the country, my point is going to be that two-thirds of the Irish people depend upon agriculture. That being the case, you find if two-thirds of the Irish people give you so much income, and the balance is to be made up in any other way, it must be made up out of the wages the others earn, and I think in that way you will find you cannot get at much more than one-twenty-second for the whole of Ireland as compared with the United Kingdom.

7721. (*Chairman.*) Then there remains the incomes under the 150*l.* limit?—In addition to the income above the income tax limit, and to the income of the wage-earning classes, you have a certain amount of income intermediate between those two, which Mr. Dudley Baxter used to speak of as the income of the lower middle class. He arrived at a sum at that time—about 25 or 30 years ago—of about 13,000,000*l.* as the income intermediate between the income tax income and the wage-earning income in Ireland. My recollection is he figures were about 13,000,000*l.* for Ireland; the corresponding figure for Scotland was about 7,000,000*l.*, and for England about 60,000,000*l.* My impression is that the figure for Ireland, even then, was altogether too much, because I think he had somewhere about 330,000 people as the recipients of that middle-class income, and, looking at the population statistics of Ireland at the present time, I do not see where these 330,000 are to come from. That was the sort of general notion that I had. As regards England and Scotland, in dealing with this question, we have something to go by. We find that in Schedule A., for instance, and Schedule B., about 57,000,000*l.* of income, which is assessed in the gross, is exempted afterwards in the net assessment to income tax, for various reasons, including about 44,000,000*l.*, because the income of the people is under the 150*l.* limit. Still, you know what the income is from the gross assessment, and then you find when you come to the net assessment that there is a difference of the amount stated. But when you come to look at this difference for Ireland, you find that, apart from Schedule B., it is very small indeed, and you have also this to consider, that a great deal of the income which is exempt in Ireland under Schedule B., is probably not middle class income, but really, peasant income.

7722. (*Mr. Sexton.*) Already in the wage-earning class?—Yes. Although you may conclude, as regards England and Scotland, it is middle-class income, probably you cannot draw the same conclusion as regards Ireland, because you know, as regards Schedule B., there is about 7,000,000*l.* which is exempted, part of which is probably peasant-class income. For these and other reasons it seems to me that Dudley Baxter's estimate of 13,000,000*l.* was too high, and I should be inclined to put it, at the outside, at not more than 10,000,000*l.*, at the present time. The figure is a little uncertain in many ways, but looking at where the numbers are to come from, who are to be the recipients of the income, and the small amount which is exempted in connexion with Schedule A., and the probability that a large amount of what was exempted under Schedule B is not middle class income at all, but peasant income, I doubt very much if you could get to a sum of even 10,000,000*l.* as the intermediate income in Ireland. Then, as the figure for the United Kingdom altogether comes up to between 180,000,000*l.* to 200,000,000*l.*, if I am right in the idea of the amount of 10,000,000*l.* for Ireland, that would not vary the total amount shown by the income tax to any extent worth considering.

7723. (*Chairman.*) Summing up the whole case as to England, how would you put it to the Commission?—To bring the matter to a focus, it would be desirable to make an estimate of the aggregate income of Ireland and of the United Kingdom in much the same form as Dudley Baxter did in 1868, but this I have not ventured to do in the absence of complete official statistics at present, for a detailed account. I may say that to make up such an account officially, and from official statistics, and doing it in an official manner, would involve the labour of many months and years of a very considerable department indeed; to do it in a way which you could submit to, and discuss before, a Commission of this kind. But without making up such an account, what I should like to point out is that the conclusion is not dependent on any such estimate, but on the direct comparison of the income tax already made, and on the comparison of rates of wages in different employments, as qualified by the preponderance of the lower paid employments in Ireland. I should like, as a rough way of giving an idea of the subject, to state that according to former experience, it appears a tolerably safe rule to double the gross assessment to income tax in order to arrive at the aggregate income of the country, which would give about 76,000,000*l.* for Ireland, of which 27,000,000*l.* would be above income tax level, 10,000,000*l.* intermediate between income tax and wages, and the remainder of close upon 40,000,000*l.* working class income. These figures compare with the usual estimate of nearly 1,500,000,000*l.* for the United Kingdom, which I gave to the Labour Commission, and which shows a proportion of just about one-twentieth. I may say that I consider the figure of about 1,500,000,000*l.* for the United Kingdom rather under the mark, and I would like to refer the Commission to a paper which has just been read before the Statistical Society by Mr. Bowley, in which he states a figure of, I think, over 1,600,000,000*l.* for the United Kingdom. That is, perhaps, an over-estimate. I am rather inclined to think that it is so; but it is the latest statement made by an independent investigator to which I can refer you.

7724. If 1,600,000,000*l.* were the figure for the United Kingdom, how would that be divided for the three countries?—I do not recollect exactly how Mr. Bowley does it. I am rather referring the Commission to a document upon which they may form their own conclusions to some extent. I wish to give them all the information I can, so that they may form their own conclusions.

7725. Has the paper just been read?—It has just been read before the Statistical Society. I think you will be able to get copies of it by applying to the Statistical Society.

7726. Passing from that there are, I think, other facts as to the relative resources of Ireland and Great Britain which you would like to refer to?—Yes. The next set of facts which I should like to discuss are the figures of the probate and succession duties, which we used to call the legacy and succession duties, because these are duties levied on property passing at death. If you had reason to believe that the property passing at death in one country bears the same proportion to the total property as it does in another country, then you would have some means of comparing the property in the two countries. I have seen the figures of legacy and succession duty in Ireland and Great Britain, respectively, employed, even by so great an authority as Mr. Gladstone, in this way. All you had got to do seemed to be to take the amount of property passing at death in the two countries, and then you had an absolute comparison. But before giving you the figures, I should like to point out that this is not an absolute comparison by any means; that you do not know, as a matter of fact, given any two countries, that the amount of property in them passing at death bears the same proportion to the total property, and there are one or two reasons why it is unlikely that they should bear the same proportion. You might have death-rates varying in the two countries, and even if you had the same death-rates for the population generally, you could not know, *à priori*, that the death-rate of the people who had property was the same in the two countries. That is a totally different question from the general death-rate—the death-rate of the people who have property might not be the same. Then some difficulty arises in the comparison, when you find that the property passing at death, which appears in the returns, is not the whole property, but really the life interest of the successor in the property, and that introduces a totally new element into the comparison, because when you introduce this element of the life interest of the successor, you will find that in a country where the property sells for a small number of years' purchase of the income, the life interest of the successor may very nearly approach to the total value of the property; but in another country, where the property sells for a larger number of years' purchase of the income, the life interest of the successor may be a very small part of the total value of the property. This seems to me to apply very much to the succession duty as between Ireland and Great Britain. In Ireland, the number of years' purchase for which land passed some years ago, when I was looking into these matters, appeared

I do not think the figures really give a different impression from those which the income tax figures give. | Mr. Robert Giffen, C.B. — 18 Nov. 1895. — Agricultural produce of Ireland.

7731. Your next point is to inquire whether there is anything in the circumstances of the main industry in Ireland, agriculture, to throw doubt on the comparison of income generally which has been made?—Yes, that is the next point to which I wish to refer. Ireland being mainly an agricultural country, if there are any means of taking note of what the net production of agriculture really is, then you find that you have a statement of the resources of two thirds of the people of Ireland, and if the remaining third produces in proportion to the two thirds, then you have one figure, but if the amount has to be increased very much above, then the remaining third must produce a great deal more per head than the two thirds do, and it is very important to ascertain what is the production of the two thirds, and then make a separate inquiry as to what the one third is likely to do.

7732. (*Mr. Blake.*) That is the dominating factor, the agricultural produce?—It seems to me that is one of the main points to which attention ought to be directed.

7733. (*Chairman.*) I propose not to interrupt, but to give you an opportunity of stating the matter in your own words, as you have prepared it so very carefully?—I have given a statement which has been before the Commission of the idea which I have of the net income of the agricultural population of Ireland, and the round figure which I state is 40,000,000*l.* sterling. That seems to me the net income which all the people connected with agricultural labour in Ireland, labourers, farmers, and everybody connected with it, can have to divide amongst themselves.

7734. (*Mr. Sexton.*) Net?—Net. I may say that, although the statement I have given in the Appendix is somewhat different in form from that Dr. Grimshaw gave you, it is not really so different in substance. What he did was to make a statement as from the farmers' point of view; he showed you the gross income on the one side and deducted what the farmer had to pay for rent and labour as well as for other things; and I think he arrived at about 27,000,000*l.* as the probable return to the farming classes in Ireland. Then there would be about 10,000,000*l.* to the landowning classes, and then he added about 9,000,000*l.* for the labour.

7735. It was 46,000,000*l.* altogether, was it not?—That was the figure at which he arrived. The figure I have arrived at is 40,000,000*l.*, but in a somewhat different manner, because I wished to get at the case in a little more direct way for all classes. I found, when I came to analyse it, the chief differences between his statement and mine was in two things, the first being the value which he puts on the dairy produce, which is about 3,000,000*l.* more than the value I have been able to put upon it. You will see when you refer to the statement I have given that my authority in respect of the dairy produce is practically Mr. Rew, the Secretary, I think, of the Chamber of Agriculture in England, who read a paper at the Statistical Society about two years ago as to dairy produce in which he gives an estimate of the number of gallons of milk produced, and so on. I have followed him as to the quantity of milk produced in Ireland, and put a value upon it of about 5*d.* per gallon, which seems to me, taking all things, to be about the fair average value the milk would be. You will see in what way Dr. Grimshaw arrives at the larger figure. The other difference is in regard to the value of hay, which must be the value of hay which is used for non-agricultural purposes, and I think Dr. Grimshaw puts at a figure, to the best of my recollection now, of about 2,500,000*l.* sterling, which seems to me in excess of what the actual figure ought to be. If you consider the number of non-agricultural horses in Ireland, which cannot be so large as to consume such a quantity of hay; and if you also take into account the computations which have been made by the farming people in England as to the total value of hay consumed for non-agricultural purposes in the United Kingdom, viz., about 16,000,000*l.* sterling altogether. I do not think you can say that even one-fifth of that is consumed for non-agricultural purposes in Ireland. These are matters for the judgment of the Commission, and it seems to me of use to point out that there are the substantial differences between the estimate which Dr. Grimshaw laid before you, and the estimate I have now given. I think on the whole my estimate is probably a little nearer the mark, but I do not wish to put forward any of these things as more than suggestions for the consideration of the Commission, and for you to apply your judgment to, with all your knowledge of Ireland, which other witnesses might give you.

7736. (*Mr. Sexton.*) Your figure of 40,000,000*l.* stands precisely on the same basis as his figure of 40,000,000*l.*, that is, it includes the farmers' profit, together with rent and labour?—That is so.

7737. (*Mr. Blake.*) There is a difference of about 3,000,000*l.* in milk, and 3,000,000*l.* in hay, is there not?—That is nearly what it comes to, and of course that would bring it to a point for you to investigate and see how that difference arises, and see how you would be inclined to say which estimate is right.

7738. (*Mr. Sexton.*) We have already had it from Mr. Murrough O'Brien that, instead of the 14,000,000*l.* for milk, he would put about 8,000,000*l.* You say, 11,000,000*l.*?—Yes, I think the great thing is to submit full data on these matters for discussion. It seems to me always, the agricultural people could help in this matter much more than they do, because agriculture is much more suitable for an estimate of the total production than almost any other industry, because the turnover is practically only once a year, or thereabouts, and you have more means of ascertaining what the production is, as it is pretty much the same year after year.

7739. (*Chairman.*) And the 40,000,000*l.*, we may take it, may we not, is your deliberate opinion?—It is my deliberate opinion.

7740. After considering it for some time?—I have been considering it for some years, and I have made the best use of the computations which I could get in different directions.

7741. (*Mr. Sexton.*) Would you attribute to any particular point of time the calculation of the prices in relation to the 40,000,000*l.*?—The time I have taken is about the present time.

7742. (*Chairman.*) What other point do you wish to deal with in connexion with agriculture?—The point would be this, assuming this figure of 40,000,000*l.*, the question is how much is to be added to it by looking at the other kinds of production in Ireland, and the first question which we have to discuss is really whether in point of fact the statement is true, which I have made to you, that two-thirds of the Irish people are dependent on agriculture. I think you have had some statements made to you which somewhat dispute that, and I should like to give you some figures which would help you to a judgment upon the point. For this purpose, I have taken note of the occupations of Irish people according to the Irish census of 1891, and I have made a statement here in three columns. In the first column I take the figure, which is given in the Irish census, of all persons of specified occupations; in the second column, I give you the figure of specified occupations of males only; and in the third column, I give you the figure of specified occupations of males above 20. The result of the three columns is not the same. If you take the first column, this is what you get: All persons of specified occupation, 2,110,000. That divides itself into, first of all, professional class, 211,000; second, domestic class, 250,000; third, commercial class, 83,000; fourth, agricultural class, 937,000; fifth, industrial class, 630,000. Then, upon that, you would say that the agricultural class is less than half the total number of people of specified occupations. I think that figure was put before the Commission. But if you look at the second column, dealing with males only, you find the number of people of specified occupations is now 1,504,000. Then you have the professional class, 138,000; domestic class, 34,000; commercial class, 71,000; agricultural class, 845,000; industrial class, 404,000. You would see upon that that the agricultural class is more than one-half of the population, conveying quite a different impression from the first set of figures. Then you take the third set of figures, and now the males above 20 of specified occupations are 1,213,000; the professional class, 83,000, the domestic class, 27,000; the commercial class, 65,000; agricultural class, 701,000; industrial class, 333,000. Here the agricultural class now becomes seven-twelfths of the total, and I think, before it is legitimate to use the first column to show that only half the people of Ireland are dependent on agriculture, you ought to inquire into the bearing of the other two columns on the subject. I have looked into the matter a little, and what I find is that the impression given by the last column of all, which really is the distribution of the bread-winners of the community, is not an untrue one, and you find that the numbers in the professional class in the other two columns, and in the domestic class, are in fact unduly swollen in various ways, especially the professional class, which includes a great many people who may be of specified occupations but who are not engaged in occupations which bring in an income. You have there, you have students between 15 and 20, male and female, at colleges and universities, and people of that kind, and the only thing you practically can do is to take the third column of all, which gives you the distribution of the bread-winners. But this is subject to the observation that the 701,000 of the agricultural class is itself understated in this figure, according to notes on the figures in the census returns themselves. It is stated in the Census of Ireland (General Report, note, page 110,) that the industrial class includes persons called general labourers, the majority of whom may be assumed to be agricultural labourers, although not having returned themselves as such. The total number of these "general labourers" is 111,000, and of these the number of the age of 20 and upwards is 96,000. If we transfer three-fourths of these to the agricultural class we should increase that class to 773,000, and the proportion of this number to the above total of 1,213,000 is nearly 64 per cent.

7743–4. (*Mr. Sexton.*) Practically two-thirds?—Yes, practically two-thirds. I have not been satisfied with that, I have thought it would be interesting to look a little further, and I find that in the General Report of the Census, which I have been quoting, there are two tables, Tables 59 and 60, at pages 310 and 311 of the General Report of the Census. These tables profess to show the proportion of the population of Ireland living on agricultural holdings, with the numbers living on each description of agricultural holdings, and the proportion of the population of Ireland not living on agricultural holdings at all. I think it may be convenient that I should state that according to this table the numbers of the people in Ireland in 1891 living upon agricultural holdings altogether was 2,978,170, or close upon three millions. That is the actual statement in the Census itself.

7745. There, again, you have two-thirds?—Yes. Furthermore, of these 1,631,000 were living upon holdings under 15*l.* valuation, 1,347,000 were living upon holdings above the 15*l.* valuation. Then in Table 60 the percentages of the whole of Ireland and of each province of Ireland are stated in respect of the numbers living upon agricultural holdings, and those not so living; and it seems to me it would be of great interest you should see not only what are the proportions for the whole of Ireland, but the corresponding proportion for the different provinces of Ireland. Taking the whole of Ireland, you find that 34·7 per cent. of the population are living upon agricultural holdings under 15*l.* valuation; 28·4 per cent. are living upon agricultural holdings above 15*l.* valuation; and 36·9 per cent. are not living upon agricultural holdings at all; all which seems to me to confirm the plea that two-thirds of the Irish people are dependent upon agriculture, and that is their occupation. When you go further and go to the different provinces of Ireland themselves, what you find is in Leinster 19·7 per cent. are on agricultural holdings of under 15*l*, 28·1 per cent. are upon holdings above 15*l* valuation, and more than half the people, 52·2 per cent., are not upon agricultural holdings at all. In Munster 29·3 per cent. are upon holdings under the 15*l* valuation; on holdings above 15*l* valuation, 35·8, not on agricultural holdings, 34·9 per cent. In Ulster on holdings under 15*l*. valuation, 33·5 per cent.; on holdings above 15*l* valuation, 28·8 per cent.; and not on agricultural holdings, 37·7 per cent. In Connaught on holdings under 15*l* valuation, 70·6 per cent.; on holdings above 15*l*. valuation, 16·3 per cent.; and not on agricultural holdings, 13·1 per cent. I think that gives us some idea as to where the pressure of population is, as well as helps us to understand the dependence of the people on the industry of agriculture.

7746. And I think the foot-note which you read from the General Report of the Census Commissioners, as to the extent to which people called industrial are really agricultural, suggests that beyond those living on agricultural holdings in Ireland there are a large number of labourers living in towns and villages who depend on agriculture?—I think probably the transference of the majority of general labourers which I made will cover the thing very nearly, but the two things are quite in correspondence. The figures I gave you as to the distribution of the bread-winners and the figures we have now got as to the distribution of the population do seem to me to be quite in correspondence.

7747. It is the first time I have heard these later figures given in an inquiry of this kind, and they certainly confirm fully what you have already said?—I should like to read an extract from the General Report on the Census of Ireland of 1891 which deals with this very point—it is not an obscure point at all. The passage is from page 16 of the General Report of the Census, and it is:—"As stated in the General Report "of the Census Commissioners of 1881, page 18, these "large proportions of smaller holdings in Connaught, "and in some portions of Ulster point to the insufficient means "of subsistence for such small agriculturists. These "deficiencies are, however, to some extent compensated "for in the case of Mayo, and other Connaught counties, by the earnings of the agricultural labourers who "annually visit Great Britain, as shown by the returns "of migratory labourers published annually by the "Registrar-General. In the case of Armagh and other "Ulster counties in the north-east of Ireland the "deficiency is made up by the earnings of hand-loom "weavers in those parts where this industry is still "carried on. Again, the small agriculturists along "the coast of the west and north-west supplement "their earnings from farming operations by fishing, "and the manufacture of kelp. The former occupation has been always carried on under great difficulties and the kelp trade has of late years become "unremunerative." Then the report goes on to say:—"The distribution of the population on the agricultural holdings also points to an excessive struggle "for existence in some of the remote agricultural "districts of Ireland. Thus the proportion of the "total population living on agricultural holdings not "exceeding 15*l* in rateable value is for Ireland 34·7 "per cent., for the province of Leinster 19·7, Munster "29·3, Ulster 33·5, and Connaught 70·6. In the "county of Leitrim the percentage is 79·2, in Mayo "74·6, and in Donegal 64. The proportion of the "population living on agricultural holdings over 15*l*. "in rateable value, is for Ireland 26·4 per cent., for "the province of Leinster 28·1, Munster 35·8, Ulster "28·8, and Connaught 16·3. Of the population in "Ireland on census night 1891, 38·9 per cent. did "not reside on agricultural holdings; in Leinster the "percentage was 52·2, in Munster 34·9, in Ulster "37·7, and in Connaught 13·1." I gave that quotation from the report to show that I am not simply taking a table, I am taking a thing that was discussed in the report, and that that was the statement which the report made as to the distribution of agricultural population in Ireland.

7748. You have still, I think, to adjust these figures by the transfer which you made from the industrial class?—No, I think not. I think these latter figures as to the population resident on agricultural holdings are definite figures by themselves, and would not be dependent on the other figure. It may still be the case that there are labourers in Ireland who are not resident upon agricultural holdings, and these would have to be added to the population dependent on agriculture.

7749. The transfer you have made from the persons classed as industrial is chiefly a transfer of persons who live in towns and villages, but who live by agricultural labour, is it not?—But still that transfer did not bring up the proportion to more than two-thirds. That seems to be near enough in a broad way for practical purposes.

7750. (*Chairman.*) You propose to make one qualification with reference to the males under 20, and female labour generally?—Yes, with reference to my first calculation as to the distribution of males above 20, and the apparent proportion of about 64 per cent. being engaged in agriculture, the qualification suggested to me is that the labour of males under 20, and of female labour generally, may be more largely employed in non-agricultural than in agricultural industries. Of course the inference from that would be that, although the distribution of males above 20 is what we have stated, yet the population of Ireland may not be quite in the same proportion, provided female labour generally, and male labour under 20, is more largely employed in non-agricultural than it is in agricultural industries. But, while that may be the case to some extent, I doubt, looking at the total number of males under 20, and of females engaged in occupations altogether, whether any calculation of that sort would affect us to a material extent, and I think the figures which I have given as to the people resident upon agricultural holdings would rather tend to show that that is not a very material point.

7751. What conclusion, taking these facts as established, do you draw?—If, then, 64 per cent. of the Irish people only produce a value of, say, 40,000,000*l*. per annum, the remaining 36 per cent., if their labour were no more productive per head, would produce in round figures about 22,000,000*l*., total 62,000,000*l*., which is a mere matter of arithmetical computation.

7752. But is the remaining industry of Ireland more or less productive?—That leaves us the question whether the remaining industry of Ireland is more or less productive or not, and on this I should like to say that wages are no doubt higher in some other industries at least than in agriculture. That we have seen from these figures as to artisans, with which we have been dealing. But, per contra, the value produced in agriculture includes the large element of rent, not merely the rent which goes to the landlord, but also the beneficial rent, if any, enjoyed by tenants, though a great part of this rent is likewise not ordinary profits, but what is called economic rent. I should doubt if there is any justification then for concluding that Irish income as a whole is much more per head than what is shown per head as the result of its agriculture to those engaged in it. I think you must allow something more per head for people not engaged in agriculture, because there we include the professional and other people, as well as the wage-earning classes; but I doubt whether it would be a very large sum, for the reasons I have given, and at any rate it is a matter for investigation how much it ought to be. It seems to me that the onus is now upon people who would maintain that Irish resources are brought up by a consideration of the non-agricultural resources, to show in what way they are much superior per head to those resources from agriculture. Before passing from this point I

Sir Robert Giffen, K.C.B.

19 Nov. 1895.

Position of non-agricultural population.

should like to refer to the table before you in which I compare the agricultural population of England, Ireland, and Scotland. I think it would be rather interesting we should see how different the figures are in England and Scotland to what they are in Ireland. That is Table 8. I again deal with the males above 20, the bread-winners of the population in this distribution. You find there that for England the males above 20 with specified occupations were 7,088,000, and of those enumerated as belonging to the agricultural class there are 894,000, or just about 200,000 more than the numbers in Ireland, if we rectify that 701,000 by adding the "general labourers." In Scotland the males above 20 with occupations specified, are 951,000 and of these the males above 20 enumerated as belonging to the agricultural class are 181,000; so that practically against rather less than 800,000 belonging to the agricultural class in Ireland, that is, males above 20, you have 1,145,000 in Great Britain, or just 50 per cent. more than in Ireland; although with so much larger an agriculture you have not so very much larger an agricultural population.

7753. (*Mr Sexton.*) The figure seems to be one out of seven in England and Scotland, and about two out of three in Ireland?—Yes, that is how it works out, and of course the wealth of England and Scotland is so large because you have such an enormous population outside of agriculture altogether.

7754. That is about six times as many in proportion?—Yes, that is so. The non-agricultural population of Great Britain must be many times that of Ireland.

Aggregate estimated incomes of Great Britain and Ireland.

7755. (*Chairman.*) Going back to the comparison of the proportion of Irish income and capital to that of the United Kingdom, do you make that, as you have said before, $\frac{1}{20}$th?—If you will take the income of the United Kingdom as about 1,400,000,000*l.* and you find that you must put the aggregate income of Ireland on the basis of this statement with reference to agriculture at somewhere between 60,000,000*l.* and 70,000,000*l.*, you get a very small proportion, indeed.

7756. You have already assumed that the population of Ireland is less than the value man for man as for the people of Great Britain, so that their resources must be less than half the proportion, that is less, than $\frac{1}{11}$th per cent.?—That is my general idea.

7757. That tallies, you think, pretty fairly with the calculation of England?—It seems to me the figures are generally very much in correspondence, that there is nothing to suggest a difference from the income tax proportion which I take as the primary calculation.

Consumption of articles.

7758. Then going back to Table 1, you wish to repeat your former proposition, I think?—No, I should rather say Table 3, comparing that table in which I make a comparison between Ireland and the United Kingdom on a great many points. I do not know whether the members of the Commission have looked at the table or not, but perhaps there may be some questions to put to me upon it. There are a large number of different points involved in the table, and I should like first of all to refer to the one I have put in the forefront, and that is the consumption of coal. Whereas in the United Kingdom the home consumption exclusive of export is over 135,000,000 tons, the proportion consumed in Ireland is 3·3 million tons, or only 2·4 per cent of the total, and if we allow that coal is the great instrumental article of production then of course Ireland bears a very small proportion indeed.

7759. (*Mr. Sexton.*) That bears on the question of manufacturing industry?—No doubt.

7760. (*Chairman.*) The imports and exports you have discussed already have you not?—What seems to me important is that there is nothing really to suggest that that proportion we have arrived at from income tax is an unfair one. No doubt some of the proportions are rather higher, for instance, the capital of new joint stock companies paid up in cash in 1893 Ireland's proportion comes out as 7·5 per cent for that one year, but if you look at the much more stable figure as to the "number of joint stock companies doing business 1883 to 1894" you find the proportion is down to 4·2 per cent. So that if you really look at the figures carefully there is nothing to lead you to suggest anything different to what you have got.

7761. What conclusion do you draw from the figure as to savings banks?—I think the figures as to savings banks seem to show a certain amount of saving in Ireland but then we have of course always to remember that savings banks figures are not conclusive by any means, that is may be a question of convenience and custom merely whether saving takes one form or another; and even if the proportion for Ireland shows up more than it has done, it would not induce me to change my conclusion; but the proportion is not much higher; it comes to about 6 per cent. or $\frac{1}{16}$th.

7762. Do you draw any conclusion with regard to the proportion of letters delivered in each country?—Not much; it is interesting to watch. If all indications corresponded with those of the letters then you would have some reason for throwing up the proportion but merely because one or two things seem to throw up the proportion it does not alter your general conclusion when you have such facts before you as the relative consumption of coal and things of that kind.

7763. Then, what do you say as the number of passengers carried?—I think there Ireland comes out rather low, but she comes out in a rather larger proportion, if you will observe, as regards tramways; but that again is not sufficient to alter the general impression, because tramways are not such a very important matter compared with the other great things of the two countries.

7764. Is there any other point on Appendix III. which you wish to state?—There is nothing which I wish to bring before the Commission. It is more for the Commission to put any question to me.

7765. The comparisons of the amount contributed by Ireland to Customs and Excise revenue I think we have threshed out already?—I do not think we have quite. I have something more to say upon that point. As regards Customs and Excise revenue the proportion of Ireland comes out to rather over 11 per cent., and if you could suppose that the contributions of people to Customs and Excise were absolutely in proportion to their resources then that would be a proportion rather inconsistent with what we have had before us. I should like to say, however, that there is nothing singular in certain taxes discriminating against one of two communities, though nominally at the same rate, that it is a thing with which we are quite familiar in discussions upon trade and discussions upon finance, and this proportion of 11 per cent. does not even suggest to me that the resources of Ireland may be in the proportion of 11 per cent. to those of the United Kingdom. I may say that we are acquainted with similar difficulties in the application of the most favoured nation clause in commercial treaties. A country might give us most favoured nation treatment nominally, and yet by adjusting its tariff to the articles which it imports from other countries, excepting the special articles it imports from us, it might subject our trade to higher duties than it subjects the trades of other countries; and this matter is one which is frequently before us practically in the Commercial Department of the Board of Trade, in dealing with tariffs, and it is one of the points to which we have to give our minds. It is quite conceivable that a country like France, for instance, might have an average duty of 20 per cent. upon its imports from all countries, and you might find that the average duty upon goods imported from England alone was not 20, but 30, and even 40 per cent. It is quite possible so to adjust the tariff that that would be the effect, and similarly it is quite possible for a Government so to adjust its taxes that it would take, say, 10 per cent. of the taxable income of one community and take 20 per cent. of the taxable income of another community, and the taxes would be both the same. That is quite a feasible thing theoretically.

Sir Robert Giffen, C.B. 25 Nov. 1895. Taxable capacity.

7766. (*Mr. Blake.*) We have had an example of it in practice in Canada, on the importations from England of late years, where it was decidedly higher from England than on the whole of the importations from the States?—I can quite conceive that. That is a point which we have constantly before us.

7767. (*Chairman.*) Summing up all these considerations, and having come to the conclusion as to the relative means of the two countries, will you express it in your own words?—Taking a round figure, I should say the proportion of Irish resources would be one-twentieth, probably rather less. I have a notion it is rather less, but I put it at a round figure.

7768. It might be the twenty-second which you produce in the income tax returns, but you think it cannot be more than a twentieth?—I think it cannot possibly be more than a twentieth.

7769. Then you wish to add to that a remark in respect to the rapid growth of Great Britain, do you not, both in wealth and population?—I think that is rather important. I have mentioned it already with reference to population. I said, although the proportion of Irish population was 11·9 per cent. last year, it will probably be very different two or three years hence, and one must enforce that when you look at this question of resources.

7770. As to wealth, is the wealth of the United Kingdom increasing more rapidly than that of Ireland?—I think the wealth of the United Kingdom is increasing more rapidly than the population. I have seen no signs of the wealth of Ireland increasing more rapidly per head than that of Great Britain. It has increased a little, I think, by the diminution of the population, especially the agricultural population, from time to time, the resources remaining the same, but apart from that I see no great increase of Irish wealth to resemble the enormous increase of wealth constantly going on in England.

7771. That being the case both as to population and as to the well-being of the different parts of the United Kingdom, do you think it should be subject to revision?—I think so, but I think the more practical point would be if you have a figure of one-twentieth at a given time, as practical people, if you are going to do business upon it for the next 10 or 15 years or so, you should assume a proportion, not of one-twentieth, but of one twenty-fifth, even at starting, because you know the thing is constantly changing in a certain direction. Then, in addition to that, you ought to provide for a periodical revision.

7772. You would begin by a more favourable [illegible] than the present facts would require as to Ireland, and you would provide for still further adjustments in future, having regard to the movement both as to population and as to wealth being less favourable to Ireland than to England?—That is my idea. Of course, as regards periodical revisions, if they were enforced over a long period it might happen that there would have to be revisions in the opposite sense. The practical thing would be to look forward to the proportion of Ireland rather diminishing than increasing in the immediate future, and I should propose to provide for that by adopting a proportion more favourable to Ireland than the actual arithmetical proportion which the figures at the present time show.

7773. Then, dealing with the question of taxable capacity, you say that there is a strong body of economic opinion that it may be taken as in strict proportion to income; what have you to say further about that?—This is rather a curious theoretical technical point, I think, to which we are coming now. Suppose you establish the income of two different nations that you are going to tax alike, the question arises whether you are going to take the actual proportions of income or not, and it seems to me that this is a matter which can be looked at from two points of view, and the one which was a very common one with the Chancellor of the Exchequer at a former time, was that the question was always one as to which the remark might be made *cujus* [illegible]. The object of a Chancellor of the Exchequer was to get as much as he could possibly get from every community under him, and really the question of taxable resources became a question to some extent of the squeezability of the two communities, and you might take more than you ought from a rich community or a poor community, or vice versa. It all depended, not so much on actual cash resources, purely considered, but, as I say, upon the squeezability of the two communities. But when you are not trying from communities the absolute and adequate sum of them can contribute, and something far below that amount, then the question of equity, I think, comes in, at any rate it is a fair question for discussion. And when we come to discuss it, I think we must admit at the beginning that there is a very large body of economic opinion, especially in France I may say, to the effect that you ought not to take any account whatever of the relative poverty or the reverse—that taxation ought to be adjusted absolutely to the actual incomes of different peoples and different communities. That is not an opinion which I accept at all, but I think it is fair to mention to the Commission that it is an opinion which is pretty extensively and pretty authoritatively held.

7774. (*Lord Farrer.*) I do not quite understand what the proposition is. Is it that the tax is to be proportionate to the income?—Yes, absolutely. That was the French idea.

7775. That you take a penny out of ninepence, and twopence out of a shilling?—Yes, but the whole idea of progressive taxation is regarded as wrong, and, I may say, is one which is apt to put the French economist into a fury, it is like holding a red rag to a bull; they think it lets in socialism and other evils. The opinion relates to the same class and amount of income in the same country, and I do not think it has ever been discussed with reference to a comparison of two countries; that is quite a novel point.

7776. So that if a man has only 10*l.* a year to live upon, you take the same proportion from his income as if he had hundreds or thousands of pounds?—That is the French idea.

7777. (*Mr. Sexton.*) As between two citizens of the same country?—Yes. Then the great exponent of the opposite idea, is Mr. Mill, and I think it may be convenient I should give the passage in which he discusses the question. It is Book 5, chapter ii., section 3, in which he goes at length into the question, and shows that simply it is not the same thing to take 2*l.* from a man who has 40*l.* a year, as to take 4*l.* from a man who has 80*l.*, or 10*l.* from a man who has 200*l.*, that the sacrifice imposed on the taxpayer, is greater upon the man from whom you take 2*l.* out of 40*l.*, than it is on the man from whom you take 10*l.* out of 200*l.*, although the proportion is the same. It seems to me that the argument as stated by Mr. Mill is quite conclusive, and appeals to our common sense in the matter, and that the sacrifice is not so great in proportion from the larger income as it is from the smaller, and that when we come to deal with the matter equitably, that is a thing which ought to be allowed for. In what way exactly, it is difficult to say, because the matter has not been so frequently discussed from that point of view.

7778. (*Chairman.*) How do you apply that to the case before us, as to the comparative taxability of Great Britain and Ireland?—If you deduct a minimum sum, so much per head from each community, as a sort of minimum sum, though you would not wish to take anything from a man who had no more than that, then the taxable income would be the whole income in each country, above that sum. That was the sort of general idea. If you apply that to Ireland, and take a maximum sum, say, of 10*l.* per head, you would get, upon the basis of an Irish income of 76,000,000*l.*, a taxable surplus, I think, now of about 72,000,000*l.*, and in Great Britain your taxable surplus would come to over 600,000,000*l.* But these, of course, these are very rough computations indeed, and are only meant to be illustrative of what the effect of applying this principle would be. I do not think you mean, say, from the point of view of superannuability that you could possibly ever take as much as 100,000,000l. out of the taxpayers of Great Britain. That is from the point of view of superannuability.

7779. (*Mr. Blake.*) And considering who is to assess those taxes?—Considering who is to assess those taxes; but the suggestion is that something ought to be allowed under this head when you come to go into the matter as a practical one. When I considered the subject first of all, I suggested to apply the minimum to each individual member of the community, and then say that all above that was taxable income; but when you come to look into it, it is not quite so, because you may have a great many members of the community, as I think you have in Ireland, who are far below the minimum—below the figure at which you would be disposed to go in levying taxation, and therefore if you are to arrive at the taxable income, you should only deduct—not the 12l., or whatever sum you may fix upon—but the actual income which these people receive per head, which may be 6l. or 7l., or some smaller sum, and then deduct the minimum only from those in the community who have more than your minimum—that is the 12l. But a rectification of that kind is not important, because the whole figures are too wide to be practically discussed. I am only giving them to illustrate what the effect would be.

7780. (*Chairman.*) But, speaking broadly, you would say that a poorer community has a smaller taxable surplus in proportion to its gross income in comparison with the richer community?—I think that is evident, and if you apply it to the case of Ireland and the United Kingdom, the point would be this, that if you are going upon actual income, and considering Ireland's portion to be one twenty-fifth, you might reduce it still further, say to a thirtieth, or something like that, to make some allowance for the fact that its taxable resources upon the same income are less in proportion than those of Great Britain. Some rough mode of calculation of that kind is all you can do.

7781. Was your attention ever called to Mr. Pitt's answer, if I may use the expression, on this subject in the discussion of 1785 as to the commercial relations between Great Britain and Ireland?—I do not recollect.

7782. I will read it to you, and ask you what you say to it. Mr. Pitt said he must most earnestly caution the House not to suffer themselves to be carried away by the idea that a poor country, merely because she enjoyed some comparative exemption from taxes, was therefore able to cope with a rich and powerful country. The fact he was ready to contend was by no means so. On the contrary the smallest burden on a poor country was to be considered when compared with those of a rich one by no means in proportion to their several abilities, for if one country exceeded another in wealth, population, and established commerce in a proportion of two to one, he was nearly convinced that that country would be able to bear ten times the burden that the other would be equal to. That is an exaggeration, I suppose, in your view?—I think that is a powerful statement, and in the main, I should say, quite a true one.

7783. But the proportion of 10 to 1 is a little exaggerated, is it not?—You could not with advantage get such taxation in proportion out of a country whose people had only on an average 5l. per head, as you can out of a people who had an average of 10l. per head.

7784. (*Mr. Sexton.*) The figures you have quoted point to just the same conclusion?—I think that is quite obvious, and I think the Commission would do well to look at the passage from Mill because it is very well argued in that passage.

7785. You apply Mr. Mill's principle as to the minimum of subsistence per head before arriving at the taxable property, and you have stated figures to carry that out?—I have stated the figures already very roughly. I do not think I need go over them.

7786. Yes, as 22 is to 300?—Yes.

7787. (*Chairman.*) Those figures you would adhere to, would you?—I merely give them as illustrations. They are quite arithmetical, they are not more than that if you apply that rule in a strict arithmetical way, but I do not suggest and never suggested such a rule could be applied in a strict arithmetical way.

7788. (*Mr. Blake.*) That is to say if you were to assume that this was all taxable?—Yes.

7789. But of course if you do not, in the case of either country, approach anything near to your ultimate limit, your last observation would not have so much force, would it?—No, and I do not think you can lay down that you are absolutely able to calculate taxable resources in that way, and say that you will tax each country equally.

7790. (*Mr. Sexton.*) The difficulty of levying the whole taxable income would be as great in Ireland as in Great Britain, would it not?—I should say it is quite impossible. I only say that in some countries the levy of taxation comes up to 25 or 30 per cent. of the total income. There have been such things in the way of taxation, and in this country at the beginning of the century I am not sure but what the levy exceeded 30 per cent. of the total income.

7791. During the French war?—During the French war.

7792. It was a 10 per cent. income tax at one time?—Yes. It was considered about one-third of the income of the nation went through the pockets of the Government.

7793. But the point that you could not levy 300,000,000l. in England does not apply against the principle, because there would be an equal impossibility of levying 22,000,000l. in Ireland?—I do not think it could be done.

7794. (*Chairman.*) Have you anything to say on this subject with reference to the accumulated wealth in Great Britain and Ireland?—I think not, except that I have not put before the Commission any calculation of the accumulated wealth, because I doubt if figures of that kind are of any special value to the Commission, after you have the figures of the income-tax, as they are only the figures of the income tax in another form—they would raise great difficulties, and many questions for which a discussion of this kind, I think, would be unsuitable. You want something more exact and definite than it is sometimes necessary to introduce into calculations of that kind which I have made. All I can say is that there is nothing in any calculations of that kind which I have made which would alter the impression which has been made upon my mind by the income-tax figures alone.

7795. (*Mr. Sexton.*) That is as a test for income simply?—Yes.

7796. (*Chairman.*) There is one important point before us upon which you have not touched. It has been argued that before estimating what Ireland's contribution to Imperial services should be, account should be taken of what money is spent from the exchequer upon services internal to Ireland, such as the civil and judicial services, police, and so forth, and the question to be considered is not whether the whole Irish Revenue but whether the balance remaining after these payments, is or is not in proportion to Ireland's relative taxable capacity; what do you say to that?—I have thought of that subject a little, partly in reference to discussions before the Commission, and partly in reference to returns which have been issued by the Treasury, and some discussions which I think have taken place in Parliament. The opinion which I have formed is that on the whole it is not possible to make the distinction between the different objects of Imperial expenditure which is made in some of these returns and discussions, that in fact all the expenditure by an Imperial government is to be considered expenditure for Imperial purposes, and although part of it may be spent locally you cannot consider it in any way expenditure for the special benefit of that locality. It is expenditure for the general objects of the Imperial government. That is the general idea which I have forward and I should like to illustrate that with relation to military expenditure which is allowed to be an Imperial expense. But if you look into it you will find that one of the primary objects of military expenditure, one of the primary objects of an army, is to maintain order inside a given community; that the ultimate guarantee of civil order in every community is not the policeman, but the soldier. If, therefore, you consider the police a local object—for the benefit of the locality where the police are stationed—you are just as much obliged to consider the military expenditure locally as expended for the locality where the military are stationed as used. But then if you do not consider the military expenditure to be for the local benefit of the locality where the soldiers happen to be, then you must also consider that the police expenditure is on the same footing, because both the police and the soldiers are engaged in guaranteeing the general order of society. They are fulfilling exactly the same functions and doing the same duty and services. Then, if you take an expenditure like the expenditure on education, I think you will find that the expenditure on education is not absolutely for the local benefit of the community which receives the money to be spent upon the education, but it is considered highly desirable in the interests of the whole community that education should be up to a certain mark and standard, and the government would endeavour to promote that education quite apart from the feelings or wishes of the local community, and might engage in expenditure quite irrespective of their wishes and their needs. For these reasons practically I cannot see any difference in the objects of the Imperial expenditure by the Imperial government, they are all Imperial from beginning to end, and you cannot consider that any part of them is for the local benefit of a particular part of the country.

7797. (*Mr. Sexton.*) I gather from what you say and the very clear discourse you have just addressed to us, that the amount of expenditure from the Imperial revenue in any particular country could not be justly pleaded as a reason for the taxation of that country beyond what might be its resources?—I do not see that it enters into the question in any sort or degree.

7798. (*Lord Farrer.*) This rather gives one a different impression from the impression your article in the "Nineteenth Century" gave me, because there you took into consideration, did you not, the very large expenditure on Ireland?—I think, if I recollect that article—it is rather hard to be examined on an article you wrote eight years ago—but if I recollect rightly, there were two points of view in that article, and the one point of view from which I wrote was I think according to the opinion of some people to discuss the question whether England got any benefit out of Ireland, or not. Looking at it from that point of view I think the conclusion to which one came was that on the whole the English Government was not benefited by having Ireland to draw upon, because, in fact, according to the system which was practised in England, you had to spend more in Ireland than what you received. But I think I went on in the same article to point out that there was matter for dissatisfaction on both sides, because from the Irish point of view they could not take account of it in that way; they could only look at it that they were contributing more than they ought to do.

7799. I do not want in the least to argue it or cross-examine you now, but I want to get at your view. Do you think now, we ought to consider the question of the taxation of Ireland independently and apart from the expenditure on Ireland?—I think so, absolutely.

7800. And that we have nothing to do with the expenditure of Ireland?—Nothing to do with it.

7801. Then you dissent entirely from all the views which are put forward by the Treasury, and the propositions contained in Sir Edward Hamilton's memorandum?—Entirely.

7802. Do you say that you go so far that you would relieve Ireland to whatever extent may be necessary according to your views of her taxable capacity, and at the same time that you would do nothing whatever to reduce the expenditure of Ireland?—That opens up a very wide subject indeed.

7803. (*Mr. Sexton.*) I think you said nothing very decisive appeared to you to suggest that the earning of the non-agricultural part of the community in Ireland differs from the earning of the agricultural body?—I think I said it ought to be put at rather more, but I did not say very definitely that it would be very much more if you allowed for the element of rent.

7804. You gave us 40,000,000*l.* for the agricultural community, and 23,000,000*l.* for the other. I presume that leads it would be 63,000,000*l.* total income?—That was a mere arithmetical computation, giving the same to the third as I gave to the two-thirds, but if you give them more, you must give them something between the 63,000,000*l.* and the 76,000,000*l.* which I mentioned at an earlier part as the valuation which I arrived at by doubling the gross assessment to income tax which gives one a rough idea of how a thing of that kind would turn out.

7805. But in order to give a taxable income to Ireland of 27,000,000*l.*, after deducting the non-taxable subsistence you have to take the higher figure and not the 63,000,000*l.*?—The 63,000,000*l.* is too small.

7806. But in order to yield the 28,000,000*l.* you have to take the 76,000,000*l.*, have you not?—Yes, that is so.

The witness withdrew.

NINETEENTH DAY.

Thursday, 2nd May 1895.

At Committee Room B, House of Lords.

PRESENT:

THE RIGHT HON. HUGH C. E. CHILDERS, *Chairman*.

LORD FARRER.	BERTRAM W. CURRIE, Esq.
LORD WELBY.	CHARLES E. MARTIN, Esq.
The Right Hon. THE O'CONOR DON.	J. E. REDMOND, Esq., M.P.
Sir THOMAS SUTHERLAND, K.C.M.G., M.P.	THOMAS SEXTON, Esq., M.P.
The Hon. EDWARD BLAKE, M.P.	HENRY F. SLATTERY, Esq.

Mr. R. H. HOLLAND, *Secretary*.

Mr. ROBERT GIFFEN, C.B., LL.D., recalled and further examined.

Mr. Robert Giffen, C.B.
2 May 1895.
Agricultural produce of Ireland.

7807. (*Chairman.*) Before your cross-examination I think you wish to supplement your evidence in chief on one or two points?—That is so.

7808. In the first place with respect to your estimate of the net produce of Irish agriculture, will you say what you wish to put before the Commission?—I wish to make an additional statement with reference to the average price obtained for milk in Ireland. The figure which I gave was 5*d.* per gallon, and I applied that figure to the estimate of the quantity of milk produced, based upon Mr. Rew's calculations. I have since come into possession of facts as to the price actually realised for milk by the Irish co-operative creameries which seem to me to throw light on the subject. The average price paid by the creameries to the farmers in the last few years has varied between 3·55*d.* and 4·25*d.* per gallon, and it is stated that in addition the farmers receive back 80 gallons of separated or skim milk for every 100 gallons they send in, which separated or skim milk is estimated to be worth 1¼*d.* or 1½*d.* a gallon, that is about a penny to a penny farthing on the gallon of milk sent to the creameries. Adding this to the price paid by the creameries, the figure comes out at 4½*d.* to 5*d.* per gallon. The creameries exist mostly, it appears, in comparatively rich pastoral districts of Ireland, so that the price is probably higher than that received by a large number of farmers in Ireland, though, of course, some who are in the neighbourhood of large towns, like Belfast or Dublin, may receive more. It seems to me there, that the figure obtained from the actual returns of the co-operative creameries on a large scale supports the figure of 5*d.* per gallon which I put before you. I should like at any rate to mention the facts to assist your judgment in the matter.

7809. Then also with respect to oats, I think you wish to make a correction, do you not?—I should like to state that in addition to the differences between Dr. Grimshaw's estimate and mine regarding the produce of agriculture, there is a difference of about 1,000,000*l.* for oats, which is due in part to a difference in price. I may also mention that in giving my evidence I overstated by an oversight the difference between us about hay, making it 6,000,000*l.* sterling, but the correct figure of 2,500,000*l.* has been put in the proof, the total difference between us remains much what I said, and is accounted for under the three heads of dairy produce, hay consumed for non-agricultural purposes, and oats.

7810. (*Mr. Sexton.*) The difference remaining 6,000,000*l.*?—About that, three or thereabouts.

7811. (*Chairman.*) You also wish to make a remark as to the point raised by Lord Farrer, I believe?—Yes. I have looked further into the point raised by Lord Farrer as to my article in the "Nineteenth Century" in March 1886 being different from what I now say respecting the treatment of expenditure for Irish purposes as a set-off to the contribution of Ireland to the general taxation of the United Kingdom. Having looked at the article again, instead of speaking from recollection merely, I wish now to say that, so far as I can judge, there is nothing in the article bearing out Lord Farrer's view that that article recognised the propriety of deducting the amount expended from the Imperial Exchequer in Ireland, or for so-called Irish purposes, as a set-off to the contribution of Ireland to the Imperial Exchequer. I merely discussed, as a matter of hard fact, whether Ireland had been of economic value to Great Britain or the reverse. In this way I took account of what we spent in connection with Ireland, which but for any connection with it we should not have had to spend, and I said that this was a set-off to Ireland's contribution to the Exchequer from the point of view of Ireland's economic value to us, that is to say, to the people of Great Britain; but I did not suggest at all that in a question of what the taxation ought to be, this set-off could be considered. In fact, I said a good deal to the opposite effect. Having further considered the matter also, I may say that I know of no economic authority of any sort or kind for the proposition, that in considering the question of the equality of taxation throughout a community, a distinction may be made between so-called Imperial objects, and objects special to some geographical division of the community or some special group of taxpayers, so that in considering the question of equality of taxation so far as that geographical division or special group is concerned, the amount which they receive back for expenditure for special objects is to be deducted from the total contribution so as to show their contribution for so-called Imperial objects. It seems to me there is no authority for such a view. Having also considered the matter, I must repeat my observation that I do not think any such distinction can be drawn between Imperial and other objects. All the objects of a central government are, in my view, Imperial. The welfare of the community as a whole is always in view, or it ought always to be in view, whatever the particular expenditure. I should like to add, with reference to that definition, viz., that all the expenditure out of an Imperial Exchequer is to be considered to be for Imperial objects, that that definition

tion is actually given in Mr. Goschen's Report on Local Taxation in 1870, and that the distinction there made is between local and Imperial expenditure; the local expenditure being what is raised and spent by the local authorities. That is the distinction which is made. Everything which is spent by the Imperial Government is set down as Imperial expenditure, and this distinction which is now made between so-called Imperial objects and other objects is entirely ignored, and I think was never heard of until the recent returns made by the Treasury. I mentioned on the last occasion also one or two difficulties in making a distinction between Imperial and local objects, which seemed to me insuperable, but the list of such difficulties could be increased indefinitely. I may say that this goes even so far as what are so-called local objects now. Take even such things as poor relief and road making. These are objects of local expenditure where revenue and expenditure are both local; but the primary object of localising expenditure is not always that the expenditure is of special local benefit, but because local management out of local revenue is the only way of guaranteeing the whole community against excessive waste. As far as local benefit goes, good roads, for instance, are a military requirement of the first urgency, and the State must make them or see that they are made, in fulfilment of its first duty of keeping civil order. I wish further now to make a remark upon the reference to the Commission. The reference to the Commission appears to assume the opposite theory, that a distinction can be made between special objects and Imperial objects, the expenditure on the former to be deducted from the gross revenue before showing the amount available for Imperial objects. You are asked to inquire into "the charge for Irish purposes on the Imperial Exchequer, and the amount of Irish taxation remaining "available for contribution to the Imperial expenditure," and also "the Imperial expenditure to which "it is considered equitable that Ireland should "contribute." I was not aware, or had forgotten when the question was put to me, that the reference to the Commission had been of this nature; but if it is open to you to take the view that there are no Irish purposes corresponding to the definition in the reference, and that all expenditure out of the Imperial exchequer is to be considered Imperial, then I should press most strongly the absence of economic authority for the distinction which is attempted and its inconsistency with any view of the functions of an incorporating union of two or more countries which implies the abolition of all such distinctions and the interest of every part of the united community, in the expenditure from Imperial funds, from the point of view of the welfare of the community as a whole.

7812. These answers you wish incorporated with your answers the other day, do you not, in your examination in chief?—I think I should like to express them so as to give my view a little more fully, because they arise in part from what Lord Farrer put to me.

7813. Then we may consider your examination in chief concluded by those answers given now, and you can be cross-examined upon them later on each member wishes to take up the questions?—That is so.

7814. (*Lord Farrer.*) I want, first of all, to ask you one or two questions, in order that I may understand more distinctly some small points in your evidence. I want to understand exactly what you meant when, in answer to the Chairman, you spoke of an economic drain. Did you mean what we have called elsewhere a balance of liquidation, or did you mean something that was drawn from Ireland for which Ireland received no benefit in return?—I meant something that Ireland had to pay in respect of its being in the position of a debtor State—that that causes a flow of things from Ireland to some other place.

7815. Simply that without reference to the question of what the origin of that debt had been. The debt may have been one, for instance, of a beneficial mortgage employed in increasing the revenues of Ireland?—Yes, that is quite so.

Sir Robert Giffen, C.B.

4 May 1895.

Economic drain on Ireland.

7816. But you would still call the interest paid upon that mortgage an economic drain, would you?—Undoubtedly.

7817. So that you would not confine it to such a case as the following. Supposing that rent is paid to an Irish landowner living out of Ireland, from the expenditure of which Ireland receives no benefit, you would not confine the words "economic drain" to a case of that kind?—I should think not. I would extend it to every case of a payment from Ireland for which there is no immediate return. Of course it is quite true that it is to the interest of a community to pay its debts, but it is also quite true that a man who has a debt to pay is so much less rich than a man with similar means who has no debt to pay.

7818. Would you call, for instance, the 10,000,000*l.* which is paid annually by India to England an economic drain?—Undoubtedly.

7819. Although India may have received and may be receiving full benefit for it?—And also although it may be to the advantage of India to maintain credit and to keep on making the payments.

7820. The mere fact of there being a [illegible] payable is what you call an economic drain, is it not?—I think so; that is the sense in which I used the words.

Assessment to income tax.

7821. Then I want to understand exactly your reason for preferring the net assessment to the income tax to the gross assessment as a test of the capacity of Ireland; I did not fully understand you as to that?—The gross assessment happens to include the total annual income from certain kinds of property, which kinds of property, or some of them, happen to be the principal kinds of property in Ireland, and are not the principal kinds of property in Great Britain, whereas the net assessment is the assessment of all incomes above a certain amount, therefore the net assessments in both countries is exactly on the same footing.

7822. Of course it may happen, may it not, that the net income assessed for the payment of the income tax is not an exact measure of the income of the country, because the incomes below the limit may be larger in one country than in the other?—That is so; that is quite possible.

7823. You go on to deal with that point afterwards?—Yes, I go on to deal with that point afterwards, but as far as they go the two things are on the same footing if you take all incomes above a certain amount in two countries, but if, as you do in the gross assessments of income tax, you deal with the total value of some kinds of property only, then you vary the proportion between the two countries, if those kinds of property you deal with in that manner are the chief kinds of property in one country and not the chief kinds of property in another country. That is the case with lands in Ireland which are assessed under Schedules A. and B., which are the chief property in Ireland, and are not the chief property in Great Britain.

7824. (*Mr. Sexton.*) What do you say is the chief property in Great Britain?—Railways, houses, shipping property, mines, and many other kinds of property which you see from the assessments of income tax.

7825. (*Lord Farrer.*) I think after all the result you get from the net assessment of the Income Tax agrees very nearly, or almost entirely, with Sir Edward Hamilton's figure, does it not?—As far as the figures go, they are the same figures.

7826. On question [illegible], I should like to ask you this question. You stated, and I entirely understand the answer, that where the income, such as rent, is spent out of the country, it does not affect the original taxable income of the country, because the tax is taken before the rent is paid to the landowner, who lives out of the country?—That is so.

7827. But at the same time, the fact that a man may spend say 10,000*l.* a year in London instead of spending it in Ireland, affects the general prosperity and taxable property of the country, does it not? Suppose that the whole of the rent of Ireland was spent in England instead of being spent in Ireland, that would affect the prosperity and the taxable resources of Ireland, would it not?—The aggregate resources of Ireland, you might consider, would be so much more.

7828. So much more if it were spent in Ireland than if it was spent in England?—If it were received by a person living in Ireland. He might not spend it in Ireland although living in Ireland.

7829. Supposing he were living in Ireland and spending it in Ireland, there would be so many more persons employed there, so much more produce bought, and in one way or the other the country would be the richer for it, would it not?—I am not quite sure how that would be, because the effect of his spending it in Ireland might be to divert employment to some extent, and it would be extremely difficult to follow it up. If it was to be spent in Ireland, and there was to be no diversion of other money that would be spent out of Ireland in consequence of that sum being spent in Ireland, then it would be an addition, but it is quite impossible to say beforehand what the effect of keeping a particular 10,000*l.* in Ireland would be until you know whether another 10,000*l.* would not go out somewhere else.

7830. Taking the case of a landlord with 10,000*l.* a year, if he lives in Ireland we will suppose that he spends it in labour on his estate. Then suppose that instead of living in Ireland he lives in London, or lives on the Riviera, and he spends it in personal luxuries, and employs a number of persons, surely in that case would not Ireland be worse off than if that money was spent in Ireland?—I think that is somewhat difficult to follow out completely, because it might be the case that the retention of that particular sum of money in Ireland might raise wages in certain employments in Ireland, so that it would no longer be profitable to carry on certain industries, and the money might be sent out of the country by somebody else. There is always a balance in these matters, and the difficulty is even to account in theory for all the effects of omitting a particular factor.

7831. But you would say, would you not, if one country pays to another a very large sum by way of tribute (taking, for instance, the Spanish tribute from the West Indies), the West Indies would be the worse off for paying that tribute, and Spain the better off?—In the aggregate, so far as the general resources of the country are concerned, but not as regards particular individuals in the countries. I do not admit at all that sending money to elsewhere, as it is called, impoverishes any particular individual in the country from which the money is sent. It may or may not diminish the aggregate resources of that country.

7832. Take, for instance, all the money which is spent by Irishmen in London, and suppose that instead of their living in London they lived in Dublin, and employed Dublin shopkeepers, would not that be to the benefit of Dublin as compared with London?—Precisely, but then you would probably have so many more people to receive the benefit. It does not follow that any large number of individuals in Ireland would be much better off, and any large number of individuals in Great Britain so much worse off. In that case, probably, there would be some transfer of population.

7833. (*Mr. Sexton.*) Suppose a landlord living in Ireland spent 10,000*l.* in Ireland last year, and this year transfers his residence with his income and expenditure to London, and ceases to employ labourers on his estate in Ireland, are not those labourers directly impoverished?—That is the effect of a change. No doubt every change has certain effects, but I am speaking of the thing in a state of equilibrium, and when a change has taken place.

7834. Some time after it had happened?—Some time after it had happened. There are always two views, the dynamic view and the static view. It might happen that after a very little time the labourers in that case would go away elsewhere.

7835. (*Mr. Currie.*) Does not the expenditure of a capital in a country benefit the country?—Undoubtedly, it adds to the aggregate resources of that country, but it may or may not add to the individual wealth of particular people in that country.

7836. But you would say, would you not, that a country where capital is largely expended is in advance of a country where it is not so?—Provided the population of the country where the capital is largely expended is not growing even faster.

7837. Supposing you go through a country, either England or Ireland, and you see a pauperised landlord who spends nothing by the side of a rich landlord who spends much, would you not say that the tenants of the rich landlord are better off than those of the poor landlord?—To some extent, but I do not think it is quite so material on a broad scale as it appears to be, because labour and capital have the power of transferring themselves from one place to another.

7838. (*Lord Farrer.*) Can labour transfer itself so easily as capital?—I think so now.

7839. (*Mr Sexton.*) Does it not appear that the presence in a country of a resident landlord class, employing a proportion of their incomes in labour on their estates, must have a powerful and healthy influence on the labour market in that country, and the development of the population, such as marriage, and many things?—To a certain extent it may be so, and yet you may find that some of the most prosperous places in the world are places where the income or rent is remitted to a landlord living elsewhere.

7840. Do you not consider that what you have defined with great precision in your evidence in chief as the general inferiority of condition in the population of Ireland, one of the evidences of which is the emigration of the vigorous and young—is due, to a great extent, to the impoverishment of the labour market by the absence of a large proportion of the landlords in other countries which employ labour?—I think if you look at the case of a country which also remits a great deal of its income to a distant country, Australia for instance, you will find that the remittance of a very large amount to absentees is coincident with the very highest state of prosperity in the country.

7841. Yes, if the labour of the country is already fully employed, but supposing there is spare labour and that that unemployed labour is increased in volume by the withdrawal of the income of the landlords from the country and the contraction of the labour market, is not that a distinct evil?—At the time when the change takes place it is a distinct evil, but as a permanent arrangement I do not think that it matters very much to individuals, and I give the case of Australasia as a case in point. There the remittance of a very large sum to a distant country is quite consistent with the very highest state of prosperity in the country itself. The United States is another case of the same kind.

7842. But even after a time the labour market being more contracted than it would have been if the natural income of the country had been spent there, does not that lower the population, and lower therefore the general prosperity of the country?—I should not like to go so far, because you would require to take into account so many other things, and you could not assume that on a change occurring by which money is remitted to certain classes from a particular country that other changes may not come to balance these things.

7843. (*Lord Farrer.*) You have taken the case of Australia and the United States. In those cases the remittances to this country are due to the fact that this country has advanced large sums to those countries which have been profitably employed in making railways and otherwise, and in sending those remittances to this country they are paying interest on their debts, are they not?—I was putting rather a different case, a case in which there has been no *quid pro quo* in the first instance, but where the landowner lives out of Ireland, and without having anything remitted to him than England, spends his rent out of Ireland?—I do not think I can carry it any further than I have done. It is a question which has been discussed at great length in economic books, and I do not think that putting questions and answers in this way would help the matter very much, because it takes a great deal of time to think out what the effect of the existence of a particular factor would be, and to follow out all the consequences.

7844. (*Mr. Currie.*) Do you not think that recent experience, both in Australia and the United States, shows this, that unless those remittances which are made to this country in respect of those obligations are practically returned back in the form of new advances, all those countries would be materially impoverished?—That they are beginning to feel the pinch when they are asked to pay their debts, there may be something in that effect.

7845. (*Lord Farrer.*) On questions 7718 and 7719, in dealing with the comparison of the wages in the two countries, you say you omit agricultural wages?—I do not omit them in the final comparison.

7846. You omit them in that comparison, and you afterwards add them in order to get at your final results, do you not?—I cannot explain question 7713 without reading it all over again, but I think my general view was quite clear and the figures have all been completely stated.

7847. Are you quite satisfied with those figures although the agricultural wages, etc., as you say, excluded there?—I do not say they are excluded there, because I am not acquainted with the answer until I have had time to read it over again.

7848. Perhaps when you read it over you will look at the point. I only wanted to understand distinctly what you meant. Read it through to yourself?—I do not think it would be much use reading a question of that kind in the midst of a great many questions after having put all the figures before you.

7849. In question 7713, the figures you refer to are not contained in any table you put in, are they. You gave them in your answer, which is probably sufficient?—The figures, as stated here, were read from a table which was printed in my proof, and which you have had before you there, but they are not in the tables in the appendix. They are taken from the same figures, and I think you may depend upon them being absolutely accurate.

7850. You have given a table with a great deal of most useful information as to a comparison of the resources of Ireland at different periods. Do you happen to have looked at Tables 11 to 27, which were put in by Sir Edward Hamilton?—I looked at them, not very minutely, because I did not lay myself out to criticise Sir Edward Hamilton in any way. But that table which I put in I may say is one which I have had in the office some years. I merely added to it a few things before coming here.

7851. In some respects it differs from Sir Edward Hamilton's not in actual results, but in the mode in which it presents different things. Have you looked at Sir Edward Hamilton's tables sufficiently to be able to criticise upon them?—I have no criticisms to offer; I have looked at them generally, but I do not propose to offer any criticism upon them myself.

7852. Where you give the figures on the same basis, so far as I can make out there is no difference between you?—I should say that is very likely, but I give figures on a good many points which he does not deal with, I think.

7853. You do. Then I come to a rather more important point upon which I want to get your opinion, and for that purpose I will refer to Sir Edward Hamilton's tables, because the figures are put together there, though, perhaps, we might not all agree with them entirely. It is with respect to the receipts of Customs and Excise, Table 7. We know according to your view and according to the other comparisons which have been made, that whilst the whole revenue received from Ireland is comparatively small, and the revenue derived from direct taxation comparatively very small indeed, yet that in the shape of customs, Ireland pays 12·11 per cent. of the whole, and in the case of excise 10·24 per cent. Then with respect to tea in Table 23, Sir E. Hamilton shows that in Great Britain the expenditure upon tea is 10s. 1d. per head, whilst in Ireland it is 11s. 10d. per head. Then in Table 24, he shows that the expenditure on tobacco in Great Britain is 12s. 7d. per head, and in Ireland 14s. 7d. per head. Probably that last figure would be a little reduced by subsequent corrections, but substantially it remains. Then with regard to spirits, the consumption in Great Britain is 1*l.* 8s. per head, in Ireland 1*l.* 4s. 6d. per head. Of beer, 2*l.* 13s. per head in Great Britain, 1*l.* 7s. 2d. in Ireland, and the total of beer and spirits in Great Britain, 1*l.* 9s. per head, and in Ireland, 2*l.* 11s. 8d. per head—the total on all the items on tobacco and spirituous liquors, according to Table 23, brings the expenditure in Great Britain, 5*l.* 4s. 6d. per head, and in Ireland, 4*l.* 0s. 1d. per head. Now, an argument has been founded upon that—I do not say by the Treasury—and no doubt will be founded upon that elsewhere that these are luxuries, that they show that the Irishmen spend upon luxuries very nearly, and in some cases even more, than the Englishman, and that taxation being a matter of a charge upon an individual, the Irishman has only to consume less of these luxuries in order to bring down his taxation to an equivalent with that of the Englishman. I am not pressing that as my argument at all, it is not my argument, but it has been put, and I want to know what is your view upon it?—I do not see that it is an argument at all. It does not alter the fact that the Irishman pays more in taxation in proportion to his resources, actually. It may be quite possible for him to diminish his taxation by voluntarily abstaining from certain things, but it does not alter the fact that he does pay the taxation.

7854. It does not, but you see the strength of the argument lies in this, in the allegation that these are luxuries, which it is easy for him to do without?—But I do not see how it bears upon the problem at all; the problem is whether you pay in proportion to your resources or do not, and, as a matter of fact, you do pay more than in proportion to your resources, whether you do it by expending it in so-called luxuries, or in paying taxes which you cannot evade at all, is only material to this extent, that if the tax is to some extent quasi voluntary, it is not so severe as taxation which you could not evade at all, but it does not alter the fact in the slightest degree as to the proportion of the contribution.

7855. I think that somewhere or other you have taken as a basis for argument what may be considered as the minimum what a man ought to have in order to live a decent life, and then you have taken the surplus above that as the real margin upon which taxation can be imposed?—That is a suggestion as to arriving at a better understanding of the taxable capacity of different places and their resources.

7856. But supposing it is stated that such and such a man spends so much upon bread, meat, clothes, and house, and that he also spends so much on tobacco, and that the quantity he spends on tobacco is out of all proportion to what he spends on food and clothing, then the argument is that whatever his condition may be there is a superfluity which he can cut off, and that it is that superfluity which is taxed. I want to see what your view about that is?—That would involve a discussion into which I am not prepared to enter, as to what is a luxury and what is a necessary.

7857. We are getting into the point now?—I am not prepared to say that the expenditure in Ireland upon tea, for instance, is an expenditure upon a luxury; I am not prepared to say that the expenditure to a very large extent upon spirits is an expenditure upon a luxury. We speak of these in a rough and general way as luxuries; as a matter of fact, if we were studying physiological questions more carefully, it might be found that many of these things which are called luxuries are perhaps to some extent more

Mr. Robert Giffen, C.B.

9 May 1895.

[illegible]

8 May 1895.

necessary than things which are spoken of as luxuries. That is not a question into which I am prepared to enter at all.

7858. But it is a question which is very difficult to avoid here, because the argument is quite sure to be pressed. The argument is that the evidence shown by the expenditure upon those articles that there is a superfluity which may be taxed, and that is an argument which has to be met?—If I could see any statement of physiological and other reasons for calling an article like tea, for instance, a luxury, I should be prepared to go into the subject, but I have never seen any statement of the reasons for making certain definite articles in that sense luxuries.

7859. Then I will put it to you in this way. Do you not think it probable that a very poor person, almost in consequence of his poverty, is disposed to spend a larger proportion of whatever he has to spend upon stimulants than a man who is better off?—Perhaps he is involuntarily the best judge of what is the most advantageous mode of spending his small means, and that method may be one which does not commend itself to people who are looking upon him from above. For my part, I never criticise in a matter of that kind. I should never dream of criticising.

7860. But the criticism is made and has to be answered?—I do not think it has to be answered until the people state their reasons for making their criticism. They only say these things are superfluous, but as far as I have seen they never give you any evidence why they are.

7861. Then do you think very probably they are not superfluous?—I think that is a thing to be considered. We, who are outside, cannot go into the accounts of every small budget in Ireland or anywhere else, and the people who are outside are not in a position to offer their criticism, and to say that this expenditure is an expenditure upon superfluities and luxuries. It may be the most necessary expenditure of all to a person in a given position.

7862. I will read you a passage from a work of a countryman of your own, and ask you whether you agree with it. It is the answer that Maggie Mucklebackit makes in reply to the Antiquary, when he expressed the hope that the distilleries would not work again. She answers thus:—"Ay ay, its easy for your honour and the like of you gentlefolks, to say sae, that hae stouth and routh and fire and fending and meat and claith and sit dry and canny by the fireside—but an ye wanted fire and meat and dry claise and were deeing o' cauld, and had a sair heart whilk is warst ava', wi' just tippence in your pouch, wadna ye be glad to buy a dram wi't to be eilding and claise and a supper and heart's ease into the bargain till the morn's morning." Do you think there is good sense in that?—That is a passage with which I am very familiar, and which I think expresses a good deal of good sense.

Death-rate in Ireland.

7863. (*Sir Thomas Sutherland.*) Apropos of what Lord Farrer said just now, I should like to ask whether the mortality in Ireland is greater than the mortality in Great Britain?—Not so, I think, but that is a question I am not prepared to go into, because it is most important in questions of comparative rates of mortality to look at the rates in detail, and not take the general death-rate, and I have not looked at the rates in detail between Ireland and Great Britain.

7863a. I suppose it would not surprise you a great deal, would it, if the last statistical abstract shows that the mortality in Ireland is quite as small as the mortality in Scotland?—But then you cannot compare general death-rates. A difference may arise from a difference in the composition of the population. As I explained, I think, on the last occasion, you have a high death-rate very often where there is a high birth-rate, and the two are connected.

7864. You see the object of my question with reference to Lord Farrer's classical quotation. I wanted to ascertain whether the habits of the people tended to bring them to a premature end?—For that purpose I could not go into the question without examining rates in detail. The general death-rate is no use for such a purpose as you are putting the question now.

7865. (*Mr Sexton.*) Even though their food may be more meagre and their lodging worse than in England, still the death rate would be affected in their favour in Ireland by the circumstance that the bulk of them lead an outdoor life, would it not?—I suppose it would be so, but I cannot go into the question, not having dealt with it in detail, and having some acquaintance with these matters statistically, I must press the importance of looking into this matter in detail when you come to compare the question of death-rate in the two countries.

7866. (*Lord Farrer.*) I think, generally speaking, that your evidence was to this effect, that the population is diminishing proportionately, and that not only is it small compared to what it has been and diminishing but it is also a weaker population for the purpose of earning wages or profit. Then you take as the same point on which you rely to regards the capacity of Ireland to pay the income tax, and you make out according to that, the resources of Ireland are somewhere in the proportion of $\frac{1}{15}$th or $\frac{1}{16}$th compared with those of England?—As compared with those of the United Kingdom as a whole.

7867. Then you say that any information we can get from the probate and succession duties rather confirms this; that the figures you give with regard to agricultural produce also confirm it, and the figures you gave with respect to wages, and you say further, that the resources of Ireland are gradually growing less and less in proportion to those of the United Kingdom?—Yes.

7868. In considering all that, do you think it is safe to take $\frac{1}{15}$th as a starting point of the two countries?—That is the suggestion I made.

7869. With a provision for revision from time to time?—Yes.

7870. Then you go on with a very interesting argument to show that there are reasons why taxation should not be in arithmetic proportion but should be rather favourable to the poorer country, and you would take as a starting point $\frac{1}{20}$th?—That is the suggestion I made. Of course that is rather a question for a jury than for one individual.

7871. I mean that is the conclusion you have come to, is it?—That is so.

7872. I want to ask you whether the endeavour has not been since the amalgamation of the English and Irish Exchequers, to make taxation identical in the two countries?—I think some steps towards that were taken between 1850 and 1860.

7873. But surely steps were taken before that time; one Chancellor of the Exchequer after another of all parties have attempted to do that. You have had the income tax applied to Ireland and you have had the customs and excise duties gradually altered until they have become the same in the two countries, is not that so?—That is not a complete account of all the steps which have been taken; I think some of the steps which have been taken have been the remission of taxes in Great Britain which were not payable in Ireland at all, such as the house duty.

7874. Quite so, but that has all tended to make taxation identical in the two countries, has it not?—To make the rates of taxes identical.

7875. And with very few exceptions the taxation is identical now; there are a few taxes which Ireland does not pay, but otherwise taxation is identical, is it not?—The rates of taxation are identical.

7876. The customs tax, the excise tax, the income tax, are the same, subject to the qualifications of valuation, are they not?—The rates are the same.

7877. Do you think that it is a right principle to make taxation identical, and if not, why not?—If you can arrive at the final object of your taxation, that is to say, to levy an equal sum in proportion to the resources upon every member of the community by that method, then it would be a right method, but

Mr. Robert Giffen, C.B.

3 May 1895.

Points of taxation.

if not, clearly it does not attain the object of equal taxation.

7878. Then how do you answer Mr. Lowe's view, that taxation is a taxation of individuals, and not of nations, and consequently that each Irishman is only charged just as each Englishman or Scotchman is charged?—That is not so, because if you tax an Irishman upon the things that he consumes and do not tax Englishmen and Scotchmen upon the things that they consume, the taxation is not equal.

7879. Then may not the same argument—to use Mr. Lowe's argument—be applied to the crofter of Scotland or to the peasant labourer of Dorsetshire or Wiltshire; the taxation does not fall in the same way upon them as it does upon the richer, well-to-do citizen, does it?—I have not gone into that question. It is quite possible that you may have to consider many questions of taxation, if you look at them from the point of view of equality and look at them from additional points of view, points of view which have hitherto been rather neglected; you may find you may have to introduce a good many amendments into your scheme of taxation—it is quite possible.

7880. I want to know how you would justify dealing with Ireland on a different basis than that with which you deal with England and Scotland?—I do not propose to deal with it on a different basis.

7881. You propose to make the taxation different between the two, do you not?—I do not make any proposal at all, I only state the fact.

7882. But why do you take Ireland as a separate unit? Why do you not take Wiltshire or Dorsetshire as compared with Lancashire or Middlesex?—because it so happened when I took up the subject, that point was of interest to the public.

7883. (*Mr. Sexton.*) You have probably noticed that the reference to the Commission treats the two countries as two units?—Quite so. Speaking with reference to Lord Farrer's question as to why I took up one subject and not another, I took up a subject that happened to be of interest to the public at a certain time and of interest to myself. I have not taken up the others because they have not interested me.

7884. (*Lord Farrer.*) But we are here not for the purpose of making a report in the air for the Statistical Society, but for the purpose of getting at some practical conclusions. I am not saying there is not a perfect reason, but I want to know on what ground Ireland is to be taken as a separate unit rather than Wiltshire or Dorsetshire or the Isle of Skye?—I do not say that Wiltshire or Dorsetshire or the Isle of Skye should not be taken as separate units; I have never said anything to the contrary.

7885. Then what you are saying has nothing to do with what has got practically to be done, has it?—I do not know what has got practically to be done.

7886. But we are here for a practical purpose, in order, if possible, to make a report upon which it might be possible to frame legislation?—I do not go into that. I merely speak with reference to what I have studied.

7887. But what is the use of a statement that Ireland is overtaxed unless upon that you were to build some remedy for preventing her being overtaxed?—I find knowledge is always useful, whether you can apply a remedy or not.

7888. Then you are only giving this to us as a matter of knowledge, not as a matter of practice, are you?—I think you can take it as the result of a good deal of practice; but what practice may or may not follow on the statements I have put before you is not a point which I have considered. I am not prepared to make recommendations that seem to carry the thing a stage farther.

7889. Then your evidence really has no reference to the practical question, has it?—I think it has reference to the practical question so far as exact knowledge is useful on any practical question.

7890. (*Chairman.*) May I interrupt by asking you whether your evidence is evidence with regard to the reference to the Commission?—Yes, on the two points, undoubtedly.

7891. And you have not felt it your duty to go outside that?—I have not gone outside that; and, looking at the matter as a private investigator, I find that you have materials for dealing with the subject of Ireland which you have not for dealing with the subject of Dorsetshire or the Isle of Skye.

7892. (*Sir Thomas Sutherland.*) The point of your evidence in chief really was that some 2,000,000*l*. or 3,000,000*l*. of taxation ought to be removed from the shoulders of Ireland, but now I understand you to say you do not quite see how it is to be done?—I do not think I gave any evidence as to the taxation of Ireland at all. My evidence was confined exclusively to the relative resources of the two countries. In March 1886 I made some remarks on the taxation, but any evidence which I have submitted to this Commission relates exclusively to the resources of the two countries, and I purposely abstained from the other subject because, as a matter of fact, all the figures are new since I wrote upon the subject in 1886, and it would have taken me too much time and involved too much labour to go into the figures anew, and I have not gone into them since 1886.

7893. (*Lord Farrer.*) You see the reference to the Commission goes a good deal further. You see the question is, "Upon what principle of comparison, "and by the application of what specific standards, "the relative capacity of Great Britain and Ireland "to bear taxation may be most equitably determined." Now, there is no use in saying the resources of Ireland are so and so, unless you can say how you are to apply that specific standard to the taxation of Ireland?—I think I have given the answer to that question.

7894. According to your view, looking at the figures, it would appear that Ireland is overtaxed by about 4,000,000*l*. But surely there is no use our reporting that unless we can say how that is to be dealt with, is there?—Of course I should not like to go into the question of what the reference to the Commission is upon that point, but, speaking statistically chiefly, I confine myself to the question of the relative resources. The practical question of how the Chancellor of the Exchequer is to apply his knowledge involves questions of finance, and of great detail, and of prolonged study, I should think. At the present moment I am certainly not prepared with a scheme by which the thing could be adjusted equally, and I did not consider that any part of my business.

7895. Then your evidence is simply to the point that Ireland is overtaxed to that extent, is it not?—No, I have not even given any evidence upon that subject. I have simply given evidence as to the resources which you may apply yourself to the consideration of the taxation. I have given no evidence about the taxation.

7896. But your evidence is that her capacity for bearing taxation is $\frac{1}{20}$th of that of England, and you say we ought to take $\frac{1}{20}$th as the starting point?—I suggested that.

7897. That has no meaning, has it, unless it is to be the starting point of something?—If it is thought desirable, I think I should be quite prepared to go into the question of practical application, if the Government would sanction the use of my official time for that purpose, but because I give evidence upon one subject, I do not think that is a reason why, as a matter of course, I should be asked questions on a totally different subject.

Expenditure on Irish services.

7898. You have already given evidence to the effect that you do not think the expenditure upon Ireland ought to be taken into consideration at all. Surely that is dealing with a practical question, is it not?—I do not think so. That is a question of general principle in dealing with it which arises out of certain returns

Mr. Robert Giffen, C.B.

1 May 1895.

[illegible]

bearing upon a certain part of the reference to the Commission. In answer to the chairman I gave my view as to something upon that question of principle.

7899. And you give your views upon that that we are not to take into consideration the expenditure upon Ireland at all?—That was the suggestion.

7900. That is directly contrary to the terms of the reference, is it not, because it tells us to do that?—I pointed out the difficulty I was met with after the chairman put his question, and I cannot suggest at all how that question should be dealt with by the Commission.

7901. I have been led into these questions by your article of a few years ago, and I confess that article led me to the same view which the Treasury have taken now, that, whilst Ireland was very much overtaxed, there is a very large expenditure upon Ireland which is excessive as compared with similar expenditure in England and Scotland?—All I can say is that is quite a novel view to take up in dealing with the question of equity of taxation, and that was not the point of view from which I approached the subject in my article in the "Nineteenth Century."

7902. Your article, if I remember rightly, was on the relative economic value of Ireland to England; and you considered first how much Ireland does contribute, and then you considered further how much does Ireland receive, and I thought it a very fair and reasonable view to take of the matter?—I think it was not so much what Ireland received, it was how much we had to spend in connection with Ireland which we would not have to spend if Ireland were not part of the United Kingdom. I did not say that Ireland received it or received any quid pro quo in respect of that expenditure; in fact I suggested that Ireland did not receive a quid pro quo, although we had to spend the money. I suggested Ireland did not benefit by it. That was the general tenour of the article.

7903. (*Mr. Sexton.*) It really was what the title suggests. The title was "The Economic Value of Ireland to Great Britain," and the point to which you applied yourself was the point of how much it cost?—Yes; a pure arithmetical question so far, and not at all with reference to the question of equity. May I point out to Lord Farrer, that in dealing with the question, I dealt very largely with the military expenditure in Ireland, and I think very properly?

7904. (*Lord Farrer.*) You dealt first with the military expenditure?—Yes, very largely.

7905. Then you dealt with the civil service expenditure?—Yes.

7906. Then you dealt with the local expenditure. What you said was this:—

"Turning to the other side of the account, what we find is that the Imperial Government has, first, to garrison Ireland to a degree unnecessary in Great Britain; and, second, to pay disproportionately for the local government of Ireland. If the home troops were to be stationed in Ireland in proportion to the population, the troops in Ireland would be about 19,000 only; if in proportion to revenue, about 6,000 only. Actually Ireland has at least 31,000 troops, sometimes more,* an excess on the first basis of 12,000 troops, and on the second basis of nearly 25,000. At 150*l.* per man, which is the cost of the British standing army, we thus spend in Ireland on the first basis 1,800,000*l.* which we might save, and on the second nearly 3,000,000*l.* Next the Imperial Government spends a certain amount of money on the internal administration of different parts of the United Kingdom, the Civil Service expenditure. Altogether it spends in this way the sums shown in the following table (the particulars being extracted from the last finance and revenue accounts):—

"STATEMENT of CHARGES on IMPERIAL REVENUE for LOCAL ADMINISTRATION in GREAT BRITAIN and IRELAND compared. From the Finance and Revenue Accounts 1884–85.

(In thousands of pounds, 000's omitted.)

	Total.	Great Britain.	Ireland.
	£	£	£
Pensions for judicial services, pp. 42–43	[illegible]	[illegible]	[illegible]
Salaries and allowances, pp. 43–45	[illegible]*	[illegible]	[illegible]
Courts of justice salaries, pp. 48–73.	[illegible]	[illegible]	[illegible]
Civil Service, Class I.—Public works and buildings† (last great classed)	[illegible]	[illegible]	[illegible]
Civil Service, Class II.—(Civil departments)	[illegible]	[illegible]	[illegible]
Civil Service, Class III.—(Law and justice).	[illegible]	[illegible]	[illegible]
Civil Service, Class IV.—(Education).	[illegible]	[illegible]	[illegible]
Civil Service, Class VI.—(Non-effective).	[illegible]	[illegible]	[illegible]
Total	17,4[illegible]	[illegible]	[illegible]

"In addition there have been numerous grants of loans to Ireland in the last 40 years which have never been repaid. It is easy to see that, on any hypothesis, the Imperial Government spends on Ireland more than its proper share whether measured by its resources, its population, or its actual contributions to Imperial revenue. Out of a sum of 17,400,000*l.* spent out of Imperial revenue for the internal administration of Great Britain and Ireland, it absorbs very nearly a fourth. The following compares what Ireland would be entitled to on three different hypotheses, with what it actually receives out of the sum of 17,400,000*l.*:—

	The portion.	Sum due to Ireland from Imperial Revenue.	Sum actually Received by Ireland.	Excess of Actual Receipts.
Proportion to resources	[illegible]	[illegible]	[illegible]	[illegible]
Proportion to population	[illegible]	[illegible]	[illegible]	[illegible]
Proportion to contributions	[illegible]	[illegible]	[illegible]	[illegible]

"In any case Ireland gets more than is due to it, assuming in the last two cases that a contribution according to population or on the present scale is just. In these two ways, then, partly through excessive military expenditure, and partly through excessive civil expenditure, Great Britain spends upon Ireland a disproportionate sum. Taking the resources as a measure, the account would balance as follows:—

	£	£
"Over spent for British troops in Ireland	[illegible]	
" " local administration	[illegible]	
		[illegible]
"Deficient excess of receipts from Ireland as proportioned to its resources		[illegible]
"Deficit		[illegible]

"The English Government is thus a loser by Ireland to the extent of about 2,750,000*l.* per annum, although it receives from Ireland over 3,000,000*l.* more revenue than Ireland, on any fair computation, ought to pay. If Ireland only paid a fair contribution for Imperial purposes we should be out of pocket by the 3,000,000*l.* more, or nearly 6,000,000*l.* Actually, it is beyond question, we lose as a Government nearly 3,000,000*l.*, while taxing Ireland over 3,000,000*l.* more than it ought to be taxed."—That

* In 1884 the numbers were [illegible], out of a total of [illegible] at home.

* Including salary of Lord Lieutenant and Queen's Colleges. I have only included salaries and allowances special to Great Britain and Ireland.

† Ireland gets the benefit of part of the sum.

even quite clear from the point of view of our purchase, but has nothing to do with the question of the equity of the taxation itself.

7907. It has a good deal to do, has it not, with the question of remedying the over-taxation?—I am not quite sure how far you can usefully go into it.

7908. (*Mr. Sexton.*) In fact, you declare here to me to-day the exceedingness of the taxation, and at the same time the exceedingness of the expenditure?—It seems to me the two things are quite consistent.

7909. (*Lord Farrer.*) Then, if you tell me you do not want to go into this question at all, I will not ask you any more questions, but so far as I understand Ireland at present pays about 1/13th of the whole of the Imperial revenue. You may take that from me as correct?—I must take it from you because I have not gone into those figures.

7910. You may take it from me that it is 6·29 per cent., or about 1/16th; you would make it 1/20th, or about 1,000,000*l.* less than it is at present, I understand. If you do not like to answer me you need not answer me, but I want to know how this 1,000,000*l.* is to be obtained?—Surely that is a question for the Chancellor of the Exchequer from time to time. That is a thing which would require weeks and weeks of study. How can it be possibly answered offhand by a question put at this table?

7911. You have pointed out in your article one mode of spending less upon Ireland?—I do not think I have pointed that out.

7912. That follows distinctly, does it not, from your figures?—I think not.

7913. Of course any statement of that sort must be followed by some attempt at a remedy; would you justify the charging of this 4,000,000*l.* on England and Scotland with all their poor inhabitants?—It is quite possible you might save the greater part of the 4,000,000*l.* that nobody would spend it, and I think upon that it would be quite proper to suggest that upon these Treasury statements it is quite obvious that considerable savings might be made. I was looking over the statements this morning before I came to the Commission, and I find an item like this—the Registrar-General's office in England is put down at 40,000*l.*; in Scotland at 6,000*l.*; and in Ireland at 16,000*l.*, showing quite a disproportionate sum spent in Ireland for doing apparently the same work. These are the figures for 1892-93. I give that as a small item.*

7914. If you go to the judicial services and others, I suppose you find the same thing, do you not?—Yes, you find the same thing, so that it is quite possible the solution might be that a large part of that 4,000,000*l.* might be saved to everybody.

7915. Provided proper arrangements were made. I think, taking Sir Edward Hamilton's figures, the expenditure upon local services in Ireland comes to about 1/4th of the whole expenditure on local services in Great Britain?—What does he mean by local services in that connexion?

7916. What the Treasury put as local services?—That is one of the inconsistencies of the Treasury returns. Local services have hitherto been spoken of as the expenditure of local authorities out of local revenue. Now you introduce a distinction between Imperial and local objects out of the Imperial expenditure, which is entirely novel and very confusing to me.

7917. I think that is exactly what you did yourself in your article, is it not?—I think not.

7918. That is the way in which I read your article, certainly?—I spoke of the expenditure for civil government, and I spoke of military government.

7919. "Next the Imperial Government spends a "certain amount of money on the internal administration of different parts of the United Kingdom." Then you give a comparison of what is spent in Great Britain and Ireland and that is what the Treasury have done?—But I do not suggest it is not Imperial expenditure. The Treasury suggest the one thing is for an Imperial object, and the other is not.

7920. But that is a question of words, is it not? The question is whether they are not analogous expenditures in the different parts of the United Kingdom?—I carefully avoided the phrase "local expenditure."

7921. You avoid the phrase, but you do not avoid the fact?—I think the phrase here is rather material, because if I use a descriptive term for a certain service, still speaking of it as Imperial service, that is a very different thing from the phraseology in which it is spoken of as not an Imperial service. Only one kind of service is spoken of as Imperial, and the other as local.

7922. Then the whole of your evidence has proceeded upon the principle of distinguishing between Ireland and Great Britain for the purposes of taxation, has it not, as our Commission does?—I do not know what you mean exactly by "proceeded upon the principle."

7923. Ireland is one unit and the rest of the United Kingdom is another unit?—That is so for the purpose of this discussion.

7924. Then how can you definitely distinguish between Ireland and Great Britain for the purpose of taxation, and not also distinguish between them for the purpose of expenditure?—You can make distinctions between them for the purpose of expenditure if you like so as to ascertain what you spend and things of that kind, but I do not see that that has any bearing at all upon the question of the equality of taxation which treats the taxed community as a whole.

7925. (*The O'Conor Don.*) You do not see any connexion between the expenditure and taxation of the two countries as separate items, do you?—I view the expenditure as an expenditure for the benefit of the whole united community. It may be spent in this place or in that, but it is an expenditure for the benefit of the whole united community.

7926. As I had not the benefit of hearing your examination in chief, I have very few questions to ask you. I would ask you one question with regard to the point which was raised at the beginning of your examination to-day as to the so-called luxuries indulged in by the Irish people. Take the item of tea. Is it not the fact that tea is very largely used in Ireland, because the class of people in Ireland who use it so largely are not able from their poverty to purchase meat, cheese, and bread which are largely used by the same class in England?—I think there is a good deal of evidence that tea is consumed in that way, but I am not prepared to go into the question in detail.

7927. You do not know the general mode of living of the labourers in Ireland—that they very seldom get meat?—I do not know especially about it, but from what I know of agricultural districts generally, and similar districts in Scotland, where I have lived, and what I have read about Ireland, I should say that tea is a substitute for more solid food to some extent.

7928. And food upon which there are no taxes?—That would be so now.

7929. So that that would not be a proof, would it, that the Irish were better off in consequence of their using these taxable commodities?—I think not. I do not see any evidence in the use of certain kinds of taxable commodities to prove the well-being of a population without considering many other elements.

7930. With regard to the answer you gave to question 7713, you allude in that answer to the apparent discrepancy between two returns of the

* Note by Witness.—With reference to the observation, Dr. Grimshaw, the Registrar-General of Ireland, has forwarded me, in connexion with a statement to the effect that the Office of which he is the Chief has a much larger sphere of work than the separate offices in either England or Scotland. The Irish office, in addition to the ordinary work of a registry office, collects agricultural, emigration, and other statistics, a duty which is in Great Britain discharged by other departments. Dr. Grimshaw also states that the average cost of his office is 13,000*l.* per annum, and that the year mentioned by the witness, in which the estimate rose to 16,000*l.*, was exceptional.

Mr. Robert Giffen, C.B.

4 May 1895.

Agricultural holdings.

number of agricultural holdings in Ireland, and what I want to ask you in connexion with that is do you take those returns of the number of agricultural holdings as indicating the number of occupiers in Ireland?—I think one of the returns is described as the number of occupiers, and the other as the number of holdings. I think I am careful to mention the nature of the return which I quote from.

7931. But are you not aware that the number of holdings in Ireland is very largely in excess of the number of occupiers of land in Ireland?—I believe so, but the return from which I quoted I think was the number of occupiers, not the number of holdings.

7932. If you are reported correctly the number of occupiers is the larger number in your answer?—I mentioned that. I cannot speak for the tables, because they are not mine, and I called attention to the apparent discrepancy.

7933. (*Mr. Sexton.*) It is a discrepancy between what are called the agricultural statistics and the Census?—Yes.

7934. (*The O'Conor Don.*) As a matter of fact, all your tables here are based on the assumption, are they not, that those holdings in Ireland represent an equal number of occupiers?—I think the return from which I quoted is given in the agricultural statistics as the number of occupiers. I was very careful to take a return of the number of occupiers, and not the number of holdings.

7935. Has there been any return either in the Census or in the agricultural statistics showing the actual number of the occupiers of land in Ireland?—I think that is discussed in the Census—that very point that you speak of—whether the conclusion is absolutely right or not, I can say nothing about, as I can only speak from what is in the books, but certainly the point is discussed, and they deliberately give it as the number of occupiers—not the number of holdings.

7936. I believe there is some mistake there. From my experience of Ireland, the number of occupiers is very very much smaller than the number of holdings, and that any argument derivable from the number of holdings under a certain figure (15*l.* as you put it here) will be misleading?—The difference between the two tables, I may say, arises entirely upon holdings of the lowest valuation of all. How it arises exactly I cannot explain to you.

7937. But you have arrived at a certain conclusion that there are a certain number of holdings occupied by occupiers under 15*l.* valuation, upon the assumption that every one of those holdings is held by a distinct and separate occupier?—I think, so far as the figure I quoted is concerned, you will find that it is the number of occupiers, and I think if you were to refer to a figure I gave in a later answer as to the number of people living upon different kinds of holdings in Ireland you would see that the matter has received a considerable amount of attention in the statistics.

7938. Do you not think it would make an important difference?—Not in what I have said. There may be discrepancies to explain, but I do not think the figures I have given will mislead you at all.

7939. (*Mr. Sexton.*) You went beyond the actual occupiers, did you not?—Yes; I gave the number of people actually living on the different descriptions of holdings.

7940. (*The O'Conor Don.*) When you go into the consideration of the number of people living in the different descriptions of holdings you consider the whole family—men, women, and children—do you not?—Yes, that would be so; but still it gives you the number of people actually living on the holdings, and that is a comparatively definite thing which you get from the Census statistics.

7941. But that will not give you any means of arriving at the number of separate holdings held by separate individuals, under a certain figure of valuation, will it?—But the Agricultural Statistics do profess to give you that figure, and that was the table which I quoted.

7942. But you say the Agricultural Statistics are based on the number of holdings, quite irrespective of the occupiers?—No; they give the number of occupiers; they have taken some trouble about the matter.

7943. (*Mr. Sexton.*) I think the object at which you were aiming was this: You desired to show the Commission what proportion of the population of Ireland is economically dependent upon agricultural income?—That was the thing at which I wished to arrive.

7944. And no matter what might be the number of agricultural occupiers, that is, tenants, the moment you were able to show the actual number of persons living on holdings, your demonstration was practically complete?—That seemed to me to add materially to the demonstration. That was my object. But in any case I do not think it is of much value to put questions across the table upon a point of this kind, because it is quite possible for you to look at the Census tables themselves, and the tables in the Agricultural Statistics, and see what they profess to do, and the people who bring out these statistics are the people who are responsible for telling you whether a particular table refers to the number of holdings or the number of occupiers. They can tell you all about it.

7945. (*The O'Conor Don.*) But I think I may state from my own knowledge that the figures in the Agricultural Statistics do not give you the number of occupiers, and that they have never taken an enumeration of the number of distinct occupiers?—All I can speak of, then, is that the table I quoted, which professes to give the number of occupiers, compares with a certain table in the Census professing to give the number of occupiers. The two tables are identical, except as to the valuation at the lowest limit of all, and I presume therefore that that table does mean the number of occupiers.

7946. Which table?—The one I referred to in Question 7718.

7947. You refer to two figures there, one being 486,000 and the other 539,000?—The 486,000 is the figure in the Census and the 539,000 is the figure in the Agricultural Statistics, and they are given in both as the number of occupiers, with a description showing the importance of treating the number of occupiers as a distinct question from the number of holdings; and when you come to compare the two you find the difference between the 486,000 and the 539,000 is in the number of occupiers at the lowest valuation of all. In other respects the two tables are identical, but they profess to give the number of occupiers with quite a distinct understanding that it is a different problem from the number of holdings. However, it is quite a simple matter, on which you could get evidence from the authorities who brought out the Census and the authorities who brought out the Agricultural Statistics.

7947*a*. The Agricultural Statistics, as I understand them, are ascertained by taking the number of separate rating in the General Valuation Office in Dublin?—I am not prepared to go into the question, except to state that they do profess to give the number of occupiers, and not merely the number of holdings.

7948. I will not press that any further. There was a difference of 6,000,000*l.* between your calculation of the agricultural income of Ireland and the paper presented by Dr. Grimshaw in Dublin, not as emanating from himself, but as drawn up by a gentleman in his office some years ago. Supposing that 6,000,000*l.* additional income stated in Dr. Grimshaw's paper were added to the income of Ireland, would it make any substantial difference in your totals in the comparison with England?—Not a great deal.

7949. In fact it would be unimportant, would it?—I do not say it would be unimportant, but it would not make a great deal of difference.

7950. (*Sir Thomas Sutherland.*) I was very much struck with your statistics with regard to the population in Ireland, and especially with the fact, which I was not aware of before, that the population of

Ireland is older in point of age than that of the United Kingdom?—Yes.

7951. And that the births in Ireland are numerically in a lower ratio than in the United Kingdom?—Yes.

7952. I suppose one may assume from that that the numbers of children in families in Ireland are less numerous than they are in the United Kingdom?—I would not like to say that; it is, to some extent, like the population of France. You happen to have an unusually large number of old people, but it does not follow that the actual families of young people are different in size from what they are in Great Britain.

7953. You do not know either way which it is, whether the families are smaller or not?—No, there are no sufficient data in that respect.

7954. From the average population being older, and the number of births being fewer, families would in all probability be less than in England and Scotland, I suppose?—No, it would not be quite safe to say that. The births are fewer in proportion to the total population, but it does not follow that the births are fewer in proportion to the people at marriageable age.

7955. But assuming that my interpretation upon that point may possibly be correct, and it may be that the families are smaller proportionately, is it possible to account by that fact for the other fact that the consumption of luxuries is so much greater than we would suppose it ought to be, or would be, from the facts which you put forward in reference to the income of the people?—That would be so to some extent. If you have a smaller number of children in Ireland in proportion to the total population, and a larger number of grown up people, then the consumption of certain things per head would probably be more in Ireland than it would be if there was a larger number of children in proportion to the population.

7956. I suppose there is no question that the fewer children a man has the more tobacco he can afford to smoke?—And not only that, but if there is a large number of children and you divide the consumption of tobacco per head of the community, you water the consumption of the tobacco as it were, and you have a smaller consumption per head. Whether the individual consumes more tobacco or not is a different question.

7957. (*Lord Farrer.*) Do not the statistics show the proportion of the different ages in the two countries?—I gave some statistics on that head.

7958. And whether there are more children in proportion in Ireland, or fewer?—Yes. If you look at Table 3, which I put in, you will find that in England and Wales the proportion of the population under 20 years of age is 45·3 per cent., in Scotland 45·[illegible] per cent., and in Ireland it is 45·5 per cent., showing a smaller proportion of children, that is for males only, under 20, and there are similar figures for the female population.

7959. (*Sir Thomas Sutherland.*) Passing from that point to another point, I should like to know, in a word, how you can possibly prove over taxation in the case of indirect taxation?—I do not see any difficulty in the matter. If you can establish what the income of a man is, and how much he pays in indirect taxation upon articles which he consumes, then you can easily arrive at the result I should think. It is a mere question of arithmetic as it seems to me. You first of all establish what a man can pay, and then you establish what he does pay. Then you have an answer to your question.

7960. But no one can possibly prove that that which a man consumes is more than he can afford to consume, can he, unless you prove at the same time that the mortality in the population is greater than the average mortality of a population of a similar kind?—But surely you can say if a man can afford to pay 2*d.* in taxation and that is his fair proportion, and you find that he pays 3*d.*, that is a thing you can establish—you can establish an average.

7961. You know very well, of course, that in India, or even in China, the cost of living of the people per head would appear inherently small even in comparison with Ireland, but you know very well that the people there can still afford their little luxuries in the way of opium for instance, and you know that quite recently the Royal Commission demonstrated that the use of that luxury has not been attended with any danger to life or any cause of mortality. That is a case in which the use of a luxury vis-à-vis the income or means of living would appear to be totally out of place, yet we know that it actually occurs, is not that so?—I do not see what the question is that you wish to put to me upon that statement which you have made. *Sir Robert Giffen, C.B.* *1 May [illegible]* *Policy of taxation.*

7962. The question I put to you before was, how is it possible to prove a man can be overtaxed by indirect taxation. That was my first question. And I say, is it not an illustration of that point that in India, where the incomes of the population are infinitesimally small, which is a matter of popular knowledge, the population can afford to consume such luxuries as opium?—I do not see that that throws much light upon the question at all.

7963. Then I will pass to another point which Lord Farrer raised. Inasmuch as the net result of your figures and your argument is that Ireland is overtaxed to the extent of 4,000,000*l.*, and in reply to Lord Farrer's question as to how that taxation could be adjusted, you said you were hardly in a position to say. Speaking broadly and fairly on that matter, can you imagine that any suggestion can be made with regard to that re-adjustment of taxation, except one which would involve a reduction in the duty on whisky, and an increase in the duty on beer. Can you imagine any other. I have tried to and I cannot?—I think I could if I was taking time to go into the question, but I should not dream of answering such a question on the spur of the moment.

Adjourned for a short time.

7964. (*Mr. Sexton.*) You were asked by the right honourable gentleman near me some questions as to the discrepancy disclosed by the agricultural statistics and the Irish census with regard to the number of agricultural occupiers and holdings. That point no doubt is one which could be better elucidated, could it not, by the Registrar-General, who is himself one of the Census Commissioners?—I think so. The difference troubled me a little, and I made the best I could of the figures with all the knowledge I had, and I did not think it was material for the purpose for which I was using them. *Agricultural holdings.*

7965. At that point in your evidence you were endeavouring to ascertain, were you not, what proportion of the people of Ireland are directly dependent upon agriculture?—Yes, that was the point.

7966. Apart from what the fact may be as to the discrepancy, you had other figures showing the number of persons actually resident on agricultural holdings in Ireland?—Yes, figures also derived from the Census, and not only figures, but a statement in the Census that the point had been considered and discussed.

7967. These figures, which stand apart from the particular discrepancy, coupled with the correction, suggested by a note in the Census as to the extent to which those who are called general labourers depend upon agricultural industry, enabled you to arrive, did it not, at the conclusion that 64 per cent. of the people of Ireland depend on the agricultural industry for subsistence?—I have no doubt about the practical conclusion.

7968. Then I may pass over that, because it stands independently of the question raised by the O'Conor Don. You were asked by Sir Thomas Sutherland how can you prove over taxation in the case of indirect taxation. The question suggested that where taxation is indirect proof that it is excessive is impossible. Does the question of the excessiveness of taxation depend in any degree upon the mode of *Policy of taxation.*

difficult questions as to the incidence of taxation which arise, and that many people think they pay taxes upon whom the taxes in reality do not fall, and that that is a very important point as between individuals in the same community.

7971. But the question for us is, as I take it, not how the tax is paid, but how much is paid?—That seems to me the question, and almost an arithmetical one.

7972. Sir Thomas Sutherland suggested that if the taxes in Ireland were excessive it would follow that there should be more than the average mortality, but do you see any connexion between the two things. Does it follow that there is no proof that a man is over-taxed unless he dies?—I think that that perhaps arose from some misunderstanding of expressions on Sir Thomas Sutherland's part, now that I think over the question as he put it. Of course there may be an excessive taxation in this respect, that the Government takes so much from the taxpayer as to diminish his resources so materially as to affect the length of his life, but you may have taxation which is excessive in comparison with that of another community which raises totally different questions, and in that case the taxation may be excessive without having that effect on the length of life of the community which a really excessive taxation in proportion to the means of the community would have. It was the use of the word "excessive" in two totally different meanings.

7973. Taxation may be so excessive as to shorten the length of life conceivably, but on the other hand, taxation may be greatly excessive without shortening life, and as between two communities may inflict injustice and even hardship upon one without affecting the death-rate?—I would hardly like to use the words "greatly excessive." I should say, excessive as between the two communities, and a certain amount of injustice.

7974. I rather failed to follow—I do not know whether you intended—the suggestion of Sir Thomas Sutherland, that as people in India with very small incomes are able to pay the opium tax they cannot be excessively taxed?—I do not know anything about the circumstances of the people of India, and of course the answer might be that the people of India are not excessively taxed in proportion to the benefits which they receive from the Government, and the necessity they have for having that Government with them, but that hardly applies to the case with which we are dealing, of a comparison between the two countries and the taxation upon them in proportion to their means.

7975. At any rate the mere fact of the payment of a tax by a population upon what may be considered a luxury, does not of itself in any way establish, does it, that their subsistence may not be trenched upon by the tax?—That would be so. It may be possible that the subsistence of the people of India is trenched upon by the taxation although that taxation is very small, and although it may be also true that they are better off with the taxation and the English Government to boot than they would be without both.

Expenditure on Irish services. 7976. I regard you as a scientific witness brought here to assist the Commission to determine so far as we can between Great Britain and Ireland what I supply good government to the whole community concerned in it, and you do not consider minutely how much is spent in one spot and how much in another, it is all spent for the benefit of the community.

7977. Do you hold firmly by the principle that in equity the taxation of the people of the two countries should be in proportion to their resources, and that the expenditure in either country or in both is a question of Imperial justice and policy which cannot be pleaded as a set-off against the excessive taxation in either country?—That is the general view I have. I can conceive, theoretically, exceptions, but that is generally the broad view which it seems to me must be taken of the expenditure by any Government that it expends out of its income for the benefit of the whole community which is governs equally.

7978. And that there is no more reason for pleading the cost of the constabulary or any other item of charge in Ireland to justify the taxation there, than there would be in pleading the use of soldiery in Manchester or in Skye?—I think the cases are exactly upon the same footing. It might happen that in some particular part of the country, such as one of the mining districts, you might require, as was the case a year ago, soldiers to keep order in a certain emergency which had occurred, but that would not be a set off to any plea which the people of that locality might have been putting forward that they were unjustly taxed; it is only a part of the ordinary expenses of Government to which they were entitled as the whole community were entitled, and that is all you can say about it. It happens that a Government has to spend more in one locality than in another, according to what the exigencies of the situation may be, and there is no set off between the two things.

7979. It is not because the people of Ireland wish it, or because they have accepted it as a set off, that a special expenditure has been made there, but because an Imperial policy dictated it, is it not?—That seems to me to be the general view to take of it. There seems to have been some general idea, on the part of those who were spending the Government money, that they were giving some special advantage to Ireland by that expenditure; but still the paramount motive always was the benefit of the whole community of the United Kingdom, and ought to have been, that being the general object for which the Government existed.

7980. I take it then, Dr. Giffen, that on an inquiry appointed to ascertain the true relative capacity of the two countries, the introduction of the question of expenditure on either of them is rather irrelevant, and tends to confuse the issue?—I think the use of the phrase in reference to your Commission about expenditure for Irish objects, is somewhat an unhappy phrase, and that it will not conduce to a serviceable inquiry on your part, because the objects of the Imperial expenditure are necessarily Imperial all the way through, and not English, Scotch, or Irish.

7981. You have pointed out already, and I think it important that emphasis should be thrown upon it, that until recently expenditure from the Imperial purse, no matter where made, was considered and called Imperial expenditure?—I mentioned that and

I mentioned Mr. Goschen's Report on Local Taxation in 1870 in which you will find that that phrase is constantly used, and that the distinction there is between Imperial and local, Imperial being expenditure out of the Imperial Exchequer, and local, the local expenditure by local authorities out of local revenues.

7282. In fact, I think you suggest also that the phrase "local expenditure from the Imperial purse," or "expenditure for Irish purposes from the Imperial purse," only began after the proposed legislation of 1886, and after the Treasury began the series of papers called the "Financial Relations Papers" in which they endeavoured to adjust revenue?—I was not aware of it before that.

7283. Therefore you have made it quite clear that in your opinion the question of just taxation is not only separate from any question of expenditure, but cannot be properly identified with it?—I think that is so, and I think if you were going into detail as to the expenditure set forth in these papers of the Treasury, you would find that almost upon every item you could raise questions as to whether the Treasury distribution between Imperial and English, Scotch, and Irish, is correct or not; upon almost every item, so far as I can judge, questions could be raised, and there would be no end to them.

7284. And principle dictates that this question of taxation should be considered alone, does it not?—That is my opinion.

7285. So much has been said about your very remarkable article in 1886 which was, I think, the standard authority upon this discussion until you came to give evidence here, that I should like to ascertain from you exactly what you meant by it?—I do not know that I would care to go into that; I rather deprecate going back.

7286. I think you will find I will go no further than you desire. I think you proposed in the inquiry as to the economic value of Ireland to England, to examine it in the spirit of an auditor examining a ledger account?—Yes.

7287. You found two things—you found that the taxation of Ireland was excessive, but nevertheless that the United Kingdom lost by Ireland?—I think that was the general effect of the article.

7288. By reason first of a civil expenditure in Ireland from the Imperial purse in excess of the proportion created by the resources of Ireland?—That was so.

7289. And, secondly, by a military expenditure in Ireland in excess of the proportion created by those resources?—That was so.

7290. And you concluded, did you not, that under certain circumstances a much smaller revenue might be sufficient for the administration of Ireland, and yet at the same time that the United Kingdom might not lose?—I think that is quite conceivable theoretically, and there are many things in practice to suggest it, but I would rather not express an opinion now upon points of that kind, as that article was a very special one, written under special circumstances, and entering perhaps more into politics than I care to do without full consideration and without the knowledge of the Government at the time.

7291. I have no desire whatever to approach any question of politics with you, and your answer is sufficient that it is conceivable, because it is often argued that no readjustment of the burdens of Ireland could take place without Imperial loss. You, I think, made it clear that there might be a readjustment for a relief to Ireland and at the same time a relief to the United Kingdom?—I think that is quite possible.

7292. Our main function is to report to Her Majesty what is the true proportion of relative capacity between Great Britain and Ireland. I understand that you conceive—and if you do I entirely agree with you—that that proportion being reported the function of applying that report is one not of principle, but of policy, detail, and convenience into which you do not enter?—It would be opening up, I consider, a very large and very wide subject as to how the adjustment is to be made.

Mr. Robert Giffen, C.B.

8 May 1895.

Suggestions on Irish taxation.

7293. At the same time, under conditions which you have outlined, you do not shrink, do you, yourself from the function of making suggestions should it be thought desirable?—If the Government chooses to enter into that inquiry; but I should require to consider a great many matters which I have considered very little.

Economic drain from Ireland.

7294. I for one greatly desiring your presence here and expressing you to give evidence on questions of principle, never expected you to draft Acts of Parliament. I now pass on to the question of the economic drain from Ireland. I think you have defined an economic drain to be a paying out of money from a country without any immediate return?—I think that that is the most convenient definition, and what I think people had in their minds, that a country is in the position of an indebted country, and that therefore there is a drain from it, and when you speak of an indebted country, you mean moneys to go out in various ways; not exactly in payment of past debts, but to the owners of property in the country who may happen to be absent, and to other people abroad who may have claims upon it.

Imports and exports.

7295.* The more detailed return of the export and import trade of Ireland which you have given us seems to show that the export trade being 24,000,000*l*. a year and the import 17,000,000*l*., the one exceeds the other by 7,000,000*l*. a year?—But I think I stated at the time that this is a case in which the figure of imports and the figure of exports may each of them be approximately true and no great margin of error perhaps not more than five or ten per cent. or something of that kind, but the margin must be subject to a much greater amount of error. If you were to correct the imports for instance, by adding to them by 1,000,000*l*. or so and correct the exports by diminishing them 1,000,000*l*. or so, you would diminish that margin very seriously indeed. The figures are not quite good enough for carrying a margin, I consider.

7296. Undoubtedly if you were to take 1,000,000*l*. off the exports and correct the imports in the opposite direction by adding 1,000,000*l*. to them, you would take 2,000,000*l*. off the margin?—Yes. It is a well known case in mathematics, I believe, that some figures, which are approximately good for the general circumstances of what you are doing, for a margin may lead you into very wide error indeed.

7297. In this case, in order to affect the amount of the margin, you have to make the somewhat violent assumption, have you not, that the figures are to be corrected in opposite directions?—Still, that may be as likely to happen as to correct them in the other direction. I am afraid that involves difficult arithmetical considerations which I would be hardly prepared to discuss.

7298. I would venture to suggest a doubt whether from year to year the exports would necessarily be diminished by correction and the imports increased. However, the figures, subject to what you say, appear to suggest a considerable margin against Ireland, do they not?—I think you may say that. At any time I have tried to put figures together on that head and make up an account of imports and exports in that way it always would come out much the same; the facts seem to lie rather that way than the other way.

* *Note by Sir R. Giffen.*—The detailed return referred to here and in subsequent questions and answers, is a [illegible] [illegible] dealing with the principal articles of Irish import and export trade only. It does not contain any estimate as to [illegible] of certain [illegible], and is thus [illegible] incomplete. The complete estimate which I placed before the Commission [illegible] allowance for these "[illegible]" articles (see Supplement B. to Table III., page 174), and on comparing the figures given in that table, it will be seen that the difference between the estimated total values of the imports and exports of Ireland is about five millions only instead of seven millions as would appear from this and the following questions. (See also Qs. [illegible], &c.)

Sir Robert Giffen, C.B.

1 May 1895.

Imports and exports.

7999. I understand that ordinarily speaking an excess of imports over exports is considered one of the tests of a prosperous condition?—I think by some of the economic authorities it would be, but I could not say that that is the general opinion among the mass of mankind. That is my own opinion. I should rather look for an excess of imports in a satisfactory state of things, than for an excess of exports.

8000. For instance, taking past times in regard to British trade, you said that at a certain time when the exports greatly exceeded the imports, that British people were at the same time investing largely in foreign securities?—I believe that was the case. That was the beginning of our large interests in foreign countries.

8001. You felt how important it was to explain the excessive exports by that consideration?—No, I think I gave the answer in reply to a question which seemed to imply that an excess of exports necessarily signified that the country having an excess was an indebted country. I meant merely to show that there were cases where the excess of exports might have a different meaning.

8002. And that in this case the apparent excess of exports was explained by a profitable use of a portion of their value elsewhere than in England?—That was so.

8003. You suggested, I think, rather in a tone of speculation, that some material portion of the value of the exports of Ireland may be represented by the foreign investments of Ireland?—That may be possible.

8004. But is it a mere speculation. Have you any evidence either from the investments themselves or from the condition of any class in Ireland, that they have a large surplus to apply in that way?—I speak from a general knowledge of Irish people being interested in foreign securities, a knowledge which I gained when I had more acquaintance with the city than I have now, and I have no doubt that to a certain extent certain portions of the community in Ireland are interested in foreign investments—how much I could not say exactly—but that the numerous [illegible] a considerable number of individuals I can say positively.

8005. But neither absolutely nor generally could you offer any evidence as to the extent of it?—I can offer no evidence as to the extent of it.

8006. Is it a reasonable suggestion that when you find the exports put at 24,000,000*l.* the imports would be larger than 17,000,000*l.* in a country like Ireland, deriving so much of the necessaries of life, such as food, clothing, and articles of manufacture from abroad, unless a substantial portion of the capital of 24,000,000*l.* represented by the exports, were in some way diverted from profitable use by the people in Ireland. Would it be right to say that the tendency in Ireland would be, unless some circumstances intervened to bar, to spend more upon imports than 17,000,000*l.*, the exports being 24,000,000*l.*?—I do not know that I could give any distinct answer to that question. That would involve so many considerations. I should think it would be very desirable, considering the general condition of Irish people, that they should have resources larger than they are, in which case I believe their imports would be still greater. That would also mean that their exports would have to be increased.

Economic deduction.

8007. I was rather suggesting that the standard of life in Ireland being as it is, rather low, and depending so much as it does upon the use of imported articles, that the gap of 7,000,000*l.*, or so between the exports and the imports suggests that a large portion of the capital of the country is in some way withdrawn from its use in elevating the standard of life?—I do not feel that you can depend upon that difference of 7,000,000*l.* so completely as to draw inferences of that kind, when you consider that possibly part of the difference may be the export of certain sums for investment in foreign countries by those particular parts or portions of the community of Ireland who have moneys to invest.

8008. I rather gather, both from your article in 1886 and from your evidence now, that what you call the capital of Ireland is locally held, which is not quite the same question?—It is not quite the same question; it is for the most part locally held, but when you come to narrow margins there is a great want of sufficient data to form any exact opinion about it.

8009. But if you find the various forms of capital in Ireland mostly held by Irishmen, it goes some way to suggest that they invest at home rather than abroad, does it not?—That is always the case with almost every country, the largest portion of investments are at home, and not abroad.

8010. In your article of 1886, you summarise the capital of Ireland at 470,000,000*l.*, and attribute that 400,000,000*l.* to local investment, as I think you did almost wholly?—For the most part I have no doubt that would be so.

8011. Under the several heads of value of land and houses, tenant's capital, railways, furniture of houses, and other capital, the 64,000,000*l.* which you said included the banking capital does not appear to leave room for any larger amount of capital invested in foreign securities, does it?—I think I rather gave the go by to that question at that time, and I did not profess to go into it very exactly. I made a hasty calculation, I think in my book, upon the Growth of Capital, but it may well be that there is a certain amount of capital in Ireland invested in foreign securities, yet not large enough to vary that figure of 400,000,000*l.*, or rather more, to a very large extent.

8012. But if it were found that no very large amount was invested by Irishmen in foreign securities, coupling that finding with the actual relation between the imports and the exports, would it suggest to you that any large amount of the income earned from year to year in Ireland goes out of it by way of absentee drain?—I do not think that the amount which can go by way of absentee drain exceeds more than a very few millions, putting all the evidence together and forming the best judgment that I can, and being also guided by the fact that as far as I could ascertain the exchange between Ireland and this country, as I told you, appears to be about even.

8013. Have you read the evidence of Mr. Murrough O'Brien?—I have read it generally—not very carefully.

8014. Are you aware that he handed in a paper in which, under the several heads of absentee rents, interest on mortgage and various other specified payments, he calculates that a sum of about 6,000,000*l.* is yearly paid out of Ireland?—I would not like to go into that matter in detail except in communication with some gentleman in Ireland who knew local circumstances better than I can do, but that seems to me rather a large sum. I do not express a final opinion upon it, but that seems to me rather a large sum.

8015. I am not anxious at all to press you upon that as I consider your true character that of a scientific expert, but it is notorious is it not, that a large number of Irish landlords never see Ireland, and that a large proportion of mortgages are held in this country. I submit to you that whatever may be the exchange, the exchange cannot get rid of the obvious fact?—That must be worked out by people who have knowledge of local circumstances, and I should not like to express an opinion upon Mr. Murrough O'Brien's evidence which I have not gone into carefully, and which I have not had the means of checking in details; that is rather a matter upon which you must form your judgment.

8016. There was a Parliamentary paper issued some 20 years ago showing that a couple of millions of rent is expended out of Ireland. Is approximate equality of exchange from year to year compatible with the payment of, say 2,000,000*l.* or 3,000,000*l.* of rent, and a million of mortgage interest out of Irish funds to persons resident in England?—I should look for it rather depressing the exchange a little, and as Ireland bills upon London would be at a slight premium in consequence of that.

8017. But if the fact convinces you that the landlords do live in England, would you present the state of the exchange as final evidence to the contrary?—You must look into all the circumstances because it might happen at the time those questions were asked, some particular expenditure was going on in Ireland. The Government expenditure that goes on tends to reduce the exchange again, and there are a good many things to be considered in the matter, but 5,000,000l. seems to me a very large sum indeed; if you consider that Schedule A. in Ireland amounts to about 13,000,000l. altogether, and that is the principal source of investment income in Ireland, 5,000,000l. seems a very large sum indeed to be sent away.

8018. The 5,000,000l. was not altogether from Schedule A., it was under various heads. No doubt the principal heads were referable to Schedule A.?—Yes, I should have thought so.

8019. Dealing as you do with hundreds of millions in Great Britain, even a scientific man is apt, is he not, to minimise the importance of 3,000,000l. or 4,000,000l. a year to Ireland. It is very unimportant to you, but it would be very important to Ireland, would it not?—No doubt that would be the effect, and it comes to be a question of what would come to be a small margin. I should expect if I were studying the question minutely, to have a great deal of information from people acquainted with local circumstances, not only of Ireland generally, but of particular parts, and fill it up to detail, taking a survey considering how the property is really occupied, who were the absentees, and how much land they had got. I need not say that one meets with Irish landlords in England who make a general complaint that they received no rents from Ireland at all.

8020. What you have said about the expenditure of the government in Ireland reducing the exchange, and what you said formerly about the private incomes of officers in Ireland and money expended by tourists, all seems to me to suggest that the exchange itself is not offered by you as real evidence?—Not as complete evidence, it is only as an indication.

8021. But do you suggest that whilst the removal of the income of an absentee from Ireland to Great Britain is felt for the moment, its effect disappears. What seems to me is this, that at the moment of the transfer of the income of a person who becomes an absentee, there is a local dislocation in consequence, but when that process goes on from year to year and extends from individuals to classes, and to absentees over the country as a whole, the country does no doubt adjust itself to the change, but does it not do so by a contraction of the labour market, and by the disappearance of that part of the population which can no longer find employment?—That would be the general effect as far as you can trace out that particular cause; but I think what I pointed out was that if that cause did not exist you might have some other drain arising; it did not necessarily follow if you stopped that, that nothing else would happen.

8022. I have noted in your answers from time to time the natural desire of a scientific man to give a complete view of anything he touches, but I should wish for my part, to disentangle one matter and have it noted, even if we can go no further. I would suggest to you that even if the landowners (taking the two countries) of one country or a large proportion of them, passed out of their own country and live in the other that the subtraction of their incomes from their own country does debilitate the body politic there, does lessen the fund for employment and purchases, and necessarily sets the country on a downward grade?—I do not know that I would go as far as that: that would raise the question as to when absenteeism from a particular country began, and if it be the case that absenteeism is not new, that it has existed for generations, I do not know how far you could speak of it as having had any general effect at all, because the country must have long before been reduced to that condition.

8023. If 3,000,000l. a year of the rents raised upon Irish soil are spent in England, would not that in a sense produce an injury to Ireland and a benefit to England?—I do not know that you could say an injury to Ireland and a benefit to England in that broad way, except in the aggregate that it makes England so much stronger and Ireland so much weaker, but it would not necessarily imply that the people of Ireland individually suffered by it and the people of England individually gained very much by it. I am making a distinction between the aggregate resources of one nation compared with another and the particular welfare of the individuals.

8024. Absenteeism began long ago, no doubt, but it has continued incessantly, and has continued to develop; and what presses upon me is the consideration that when a body of income disappears and continues to disappear from that country, and the income natural to that country goes into another, the employment of labour is diminished in one country and extended in the other; that the poorer country has emigration to look to simply, and the richer country keeps the people at home?—That is to say, that the aggregate of one country is less, and the aggregate of the other more?

8025. Yes.—That applies to all cases of absenteeism, but I made a distinction between that and the individual welfare of the people of the respective countries.

8026. I should like to submit to you a concrete case, the case of the city of Dublin, which was at one time not very remote, the residence of a great number of Irish peers and other landlords. Owing to familiar causes they have left, and live now in England, and the result has been that the prosperous industries in the city of Dublin have disappeared; the dwellings and mansions of the peers and landlords are tenement-houses of the most squalid class; the market for employment almost nothing; and the effects there are unmistakable; they have turned the city of Dublin from a prosperous city to one that is struggling under a great load of poverty?—That is so; the aggregate of Dublin is so much less than it was at a certain other time or than it would be if those people were to continue to live in Dublin. I may mention, as you have referred to Dublin, that I have heard of Turin in Italy exhibiting somewhat the same kind of phenomenon, not perhaps to the same extent. Since that place ceased to be the capital of a considerable part of Italy, and a new capital has been founded in Florence, and then in Rome, Turin has suffered in consequence; but that is a different thing from saying that the people of Italy as a whole, including the people of Piedmont, are not better off than they were. I make the distinction between the two cases, that you might have one locality diminished in its aggregate, but yet the welfare of the whole community, including even the people of that locality, might be improved.

8027. You have given very striking evidence about the relative ages of the population, the relative excess of births over deaths, and the character of emigration, both as between males and females and as between adults and children. Does it not occur to you that this chronic and continual absenteeism, by lessening the means for the employment of labour, has promoted the spirit of emigration and has brought about what you have called that inferiority of condition which you describe as one of the causes of a lower taxable capacity?—I should rather be inclined to say that many of these evils, and this absenteeism itself, are due to the more general causes which divert population from agricultural places to other places and to large towns.

8028. You have been very careful in all that you have written and said, I think, to deal with the assessments under Schedule A., as indicating only the capacity of the persons dealt with in those assessments, and not the general capacity of the country?—Yes.

8029. That is one thing, but frequently in these discussions and in the House of Commons we find

Sir Robert Giffen, C.B.

8 May 1895.

Basis of taxable capacity.

the assessments under Schedule A. cited as proof of the relative taxable capacity of the two communities as a whole?—That would not be fair at all, because you could not use Schedule A. in that manner unless you had reason to believe that the proportion of property dealt with in Schedule A. to the whole property and income of the two communities was the same in both.

8030. And where an effort is made to apply Schedule A. in that larger use which I have mentioned, then the subtraction from one country of a large part of the income covered under Schedule A. would become a matter of some importance, would it not?—That would be so, undoubtedly.

8031. In your evidence upon the relative taxable capacity you suggest the two gross heads of capital and income, and you prefer income as a test, as I understand?—Yes.

8032. You prefer income as a test, do you not, because capital itself is not a test of income?—Yes.

Relative capital of Great Britain and Ireland.

8033. A country with a relatively small capital may have, may it not, a relatively large income, and the converse may be the case?—Yes.

8034. In your article in 1886 you put the capital of Great Britain at 9,600,000,000l., and Ireland 400,000,000l., or 1 to 24?—I should say that both figures were rather too low.

8035. How do you modify them now?—I think you will find later figures in my book on the Growth of Capital. I cannot carry them in my head, but both were somewhat increased, though the proportion was about the same when I came to take a year or two later, with all the advantage of the income tax figures, to make a calculation in the way I had done before.

8036. But you would not say, would you, that the proportion of 1 to 24, which you stated in 1886, has greatly varied since?—I think not. I do not think there is sufficient evidence to say it has greatly varied since, but then I have not looked minutely into any income tax figures for that purpose later than 1887 or 1888 I think. I have not looked into the figures recently for that purpose.

8037. The capital of Ireland, I take it, can always be more minutely ascertained than that of Great Britain, can it not?—I think it can be. It is more easy for one man to look into the facts with regard to a country like Ireland with less than five millions of people than it is to look into the facts with regard to the United Kingdom with close upon 40 millions; the last problem is much bigger than the first.

8038. The wealth of Ireland is substantially within her shores, but the wealth of England being diffused, it is more difficult to estimate, is it not?—There are other difficulties; the manufacturing and mercantile business of England is a business to which it is very difficult to affix a capital sum; you cannot get at the figures of capital very well.

Assessment to income tax.

8039. When you come to income, I think you suggested three different lines of inquiry. You suggested generally that if you double the gross assessment to income tax, you acquired an idea as to the amount of the gross income, did you not?—That seemed to be the rough deduction from what Dudley Baxter did nearly 30 years ago, and so far as I can judge it works out fairly well, but it is not a thing conclusive, it is only to help one to investigate and form ideas as one goes along, it is not conclusive and definite of course.

8040. Then you proceeded more closely to take the net assessment under all the schedules?—Yes.

8041. Which you consider more reliable, do you not?—That gave a proportion of 1 in 22?—Yes.

8042. Then the yield gave a proportion of 1 to 24; why do you prefer the net assessment to the yield?—Because I think there are some questions respecting the yield which I was not quite able to follow—questions of detail, and the Treasury in their statement made certain adjustments which they thought brought out the yield as between England, Scotland, and Ireland more accurately. I did not follow up those questions of detail in any way, because I did not think they were very material for any purpose.

8043. You have no doubt, I think, that Ireland is more strictly valued than England in the income tax?—Generally speaking.

8044. For obvious reasons in a small poor country, where property is easily ascertained, the valuation is likely to be more full, is it not, than in a country where fortunes and incomes exist in multitudes?—That was one of the general reasons which I gave, and also that there are special difficulties in a metropolis like London in making your assessments, because no man knows what his neighbour does.

8045. What you have stated as to the difficulty of valuing industrial profits, and also as to the diffusion of British property throughout the world, would apply not only to the capital, but also to the valuations for income tax, would it not?—That would be so.

8046. And suggests that a great deal of British property escapes assessment?—I am not quite sure but what some of it, according to the strict reading of the Income Tax Acts, ought to escape assessment. I believe there is a question as to whether profits made abroad, which are not brought home to this country, are liable to be assessed at all.

8047. But it is British wealth?—Yes, but it is not liable to be assessed until the profit is brought home; that is a point of law of some difficulty, and I do not know how far the decisions have fixed it.

8048. Whatever may be the relative fulness of the valuation of Ireland and Great Britain under the separate schedules, taking the proportion of 1 to 22 afforded by the net assessment, you then pass on to consider whether that proportion could be modified by the receipts of the wage-earning class, do you not?—Yes.

8049. And you found, did you not, after a very exhaustive inquisition, dependent upon many details, that the wage-earner in Ireland, man for man, earns about half what is earned by the wage-earner in Great Britain?—That is what I thought would be the case.

8050. That, taking the population at between one-eighth or one-ninth of the United Kingdom, as it now stands, would give a proportion of one-eighteenth, would it not?—Something like that, so far as that part of the matter is concerned.

8051. But that proportion of 1 to 18 has to be considered by the light of a more precarious employment for the great masses of people in Ireland, and also by what you have brought out in your evidence, the inferiority of power and condition of the population, the greater number of the aged?—Yes, and that you have a larger proportion of people above the age at which earnings are earned in Ireland than what you have in Great Britain.

8052. You conclude, do you, that the proportion afforded by the income tax is certainly not to be modified by the proportion existing between the wage-earning classes?—I think not, or not sensibly modified. I think I pointed out, if you took one-eighteenth for one-half of the income and one twenty-second for the other half of the income, and put them together and took the average, you would get one-twentieth, which was not a figure very widely different from one twenty-second, so that you do not sensibly modify the figures by even allowing that the income of the working classes of Ireland is one-eighteenth.

8053. Having pursued these two modes of inquiry first by doubling the assessment and then by comparing the proportions afforded by the wages, you passed on, did you not, to a still closer inquiry by ascertaining the actual earnings of the whole actual agricultural population, and comparing that with the remainder?—I entered upon that as a separate inquiry to see how it would work out. Of course there are great advantages in these matters in absolutely independent lines of inquiry.

8054. You ascertained the actual number of people dependent on agriculture, did you not?—Yes, according to the Census.

8055. And you ascertained the income from agriculture by very elaborate inquiries, and you found, as I understand, that very year the landlords' rent, the labourers' wages, and the farmers' profits all three added together make 40,000,000*l.*?—That was about the figure at which I arrived.

8056. Sixty-four per cent. of the people, making 40,000,000*l.*, you conclude that the remaining 36 per cent. might make about the same?—I think the remaining 36 per cent. perhaps make rather more. I think that was the conclusion I came to.

8057. More altogether?—More per head.

8058. But weight has to be thrown, has it not, upon the consideration that the 40,000,000*l.* which you allot to the 64 per cent., includes 10,000,000*l.* of rent, includes the whole income of the landlords?—I think I stated that at the time I gave evidence.

8059. That seems to suggest, does it not, that an equal measure of income would certainly be ample for the 36 per cent. left because you distribute over the 36 per cent. left, the proportionate income of the tenants and the landlords taken together?—Are you speaking of the income per head now?

8060. No, on the aggregate?—I do not think I suggested that the aggregate of the remaining 36 per cent. would be equal to the aggregate of the 64 per cent.

8061. Did you not?—No, I did not suggest that.

8062. It would be important now if you were to state what your investigations lead you to suggest?—I said if you took it arithmetically and allowed as much per head to the remaining 36 per cent. as you do to the 64 per cent., you would come at a figure of rather more than 60,000,000*l.*, to 62,000,000*l.* That would be the arithmetical comparison, but I suggested that probably the income of the remaining 36 per cent. was rather more than 22,000,000*l.* That is how I put it. I gave you how the exact comparison would be. If you took it that the industry of the remaining part of the people of Ireland was as productive as the 64 per cent., you would get a figure of 22,000,000*l.*, but, for various reasons, I think you must take it as somewhat more, but what precise figure I have no means of stating exactly.

8063. Can you suggest any reason for supposing that the 36 per cent. have an income of more than 22,000,000*l.*, seeing that the 64 per cent. includes the landlord's rent?—The 36 per cent. would include the professional classes in Ireland for instance.

8064. But the 64 per cent. excludes professional classes who receive by far the larger share of the gross income of the country?—Not quite. Because the 64 per cent. may also include professional people as well as landlords, but in their character as landlords and as dependent upon agriculture, the 40,000,000*l.* includes everything; if you have to consider that they are rendering services and receiving income in some other capacity, then they are not included. They should rather go with the 36 per cent.

8065. The amount that individual members of that class would receive in any other capacity would apparently be but a small proportion of the amount of 10,000,000*l.* as received as rent?—But still it would add to what the 36 per cent. receive. Then the 36 per cent. would include the creameries in Ireland and the profits upon brewing, ship-building, and industries of that kind.

8066. Certainly, those would pass to the things, would they not, to supply the wages?—I do not propose to submit any figures but I did make some calculations in my own mind as to the general product of other industries in Ireland, and I think that you must increase that 22,000,000*l.* to some extent.

8067. Do you make any suggestion?—I do not like to suggest any definite figures more than what I have suggested in connection with the Income Tax—the doubling of the Income Tax figures.

8068. (*Chairman.*) In the last question in which you referred to these figures, you based it as between 60,000,000*l.* and 76,000,000*l.*, do you not?—That was so.

Mr. Robert Giffen, C.B.

1 May 1896.

8069. You leave it open to that extent, do you?—Yes, on that line of inquiry I do not like to be more definite than the actual data which you have.

8070. (*Mr. Sexton.*) If that were done, the effect of it would be, would it not, to attribute to the 36 per cent. an income in the aggregate of nearly double that obtained by the 64 per cent., although the 64 per cent. includes the whole rental of the country as well as the farmers?—That is my impression; that it is more in proportion per head from the non-agricultural districts of Ireland than it is from the agricultural.

8071. If we assume for the purpose of making a computation that the income of the non-agricultural classes is the same on the whole as that of the agricultural classes, that would make the gross income 63,000,000, would it not?—That is so.

Consumption of dutiable articles as a test of taxable capacity.

8072. Sir Edward Hamilton in a memorandum in which he professes not to offer any opinion, but to submit facts, hazarded this statement. "But 'the "taxable income' (to quote Mr. Giffen) is the income "remaining after 'allowance for the maintenance "'necessary to maintain a population upon a given "'standard of living'; and that minimum may vary "greatly. It is quite conceivable that an Irishman "with a weekly wage of only 10s. or 12s. may have a "larger margin to spend as he pleases than an "Englishman or Scotchman with a weekly wage of "18s. The Irishman may be able to house himself "more cheaply. He may have less to spend on his "fuel. His food may be cheaper. His clothing may "cost him less. Therefore the amount of a man's "income is not necessarily a test of his capacity to "bear taxation. Perhaps a better test of the amount "which the taxpayer can afford to pay for being "governed, protected, and educated, is the residue of "income remaining after bare necessaries of life have "been met, and probably the best and readiest means "of gauging that residue is to be found in the amount "which he spends on luxuries. Now it so happens "that the only dutiable articles of consumption are "luxuries of the masses, unless tea be excepted from "that category, and as the amount of duty paid on "such articles is approximately ascertainable, it is "possible to make an estimate of the amount which "the people of Great Britain and Ireland respectively "consume, and the amount which they respectively "spend in buying it. I submit the estimate with "much diffidence." Then he appends tables which exhibit the conclusion not yet in any measure affected, that per head of the population in England 4*l.* 1*s.* 6*d.* is spent on the duty and cost of excisable articles, and in Ireland 4*l.* 0*s.* 1*d.* Do you observe that after having stated that the true test is the residue remaining after the necessaries of life have been met, Sir Edward Hamilton instead of estimating the cost of necessaries, and deducting that from the income in order to find the margin, begins at the other end, and taking the articles which are usually the subject of taxation, he finds what is spent upon them, and he suggests that what is spent upon them is in itself a justification of the tax. How does that course of reasoning appear to you?—That would rather involve me in a criticism of Sir Edward Hamilton, and it seems to me inconsistent with a good deal I have said, and to which I would still adhere; but if the question is put to me so directly, I think I should say that there is no reason to believe that a man with 10s. a week in Ireland could by any possibility have a surplus approaching that of a man with 18s. a week in England, that there is nothing on which he can expend his income, as far as we know, cheaper in Ireland than in Great Britain. The food, the clothing, the articles of import, such as sugar, tea, and things of that kind are just as cheap in this country as they are in Ireland—sometimes cheaper—and possibly if the poorer people of Ireland pay less for house rent, for instance, and consequently have a larger surplus than they otherwise

Mr. Robert Giffen, C.B. 13 May 1895. Consumption of "luxuries" as a test of taxable capacity.

would have, the reason would be that they have not the same accommodation, they are not getting the same article, and I think we might consider that they are not even expending what it is necessary they should expend in order to live in a proper manner. That is what I should say with reference to that suggestion, that it is possible for people in Ireland with that large difference of income from people in England, to have an equal surplus. I do not think that is at all possible, and I do not think it is possible given an expenditure upon the same things, and equal accommodation that you can do any better with 16s. a week in Ireland than what you can do in Great Britain generally. I do not view the mere fact that people in Ireland spend more upon tea, tobacco, beer, and spirits, much more than you would think in comparison with people in England, shows anything as to the taxable capacity whatsoever.

8073. If a legislator having before him the fact of the prevalence of certain habits of consumption amongst the people of food and drink, chooses to lay taxes on the use of that food and drink, and those taxes took a heavier part of the income or the margin of income of one country than the other, can the circumstance that a certain sum is expended on those articles be pleaded in justification. In other words can the fact of the tax be used to justify itself?—I do not think in that way. Of course you must study all the evidence you can get as to the resources of the two particular communities you are comparing, and that particular fact may be evidence so far as it goes, but it may be overridden by other evidence, and I think in the case of Ireland and Great Britain the other evidence is so overwhelmingly strong that you can have no doubt about the relative resources.

8074. If the Imperial Government avails itself of the existence of certain habits of consumption to levy a revenue is it reasonable to say to people, having so availed itself, "change those habits and you will not pay any longer"?—I think that is quite unreasonable. That is what was said about the time of the Committee of 1865, and I recollect some will remarking upon it as a most curious thing to say, because whenever it came to be a subject of real debate between the people of two communities, the community which was paying more than its proportion to the revenue would have so strong a case that the other side would not be arguable.

8075. And if the people did change their habits and cease to consume the articles, is there anything to assume so that the same revenue would not be raised by some other mode?—I think that would be so, and one can almost conceive if you were to tax potatoes instead of whisky and tobacco, probably the relative revenue obtained from Ireland would be still greater than it is.

8076. As to the use of the term "luxuries," does it not appear that in a country where the conditions of housing, clothing, and food are such as to maintain physical vigour and comfort, that an article may be a luxury which in a poorer country where cold, hunger, and other privations are suffered, the same article may be a necessary?—I do not agree with the distinction which is often drawn between luxuries and necessaries at all, and I do not think it is an economic distinction; it is a sort of sumptuary distinction, and what the exact value of it in a scientific sense may be it is very difficult to tell, but there is no doubt that as regards a great many articles which are generally spoken of as luxuries, it may also be quite true that a great deal of the consumption of those articles is not the consumption of luxuries but the consumption of necessaries by those people who consume them, although in popular speech they may still be spoken of as luxuries.

8077. In fact by the use of them they become necessaries, do they not?—I think as regards tea, and a certain portion of the consumption of tobacco, beer, and spirits, they may be spoken of as almost necessary articles of consumption in a country with the climate of these islands.

8078. Regarding the country as we are instructed to regard it not only from an equitable but "from the most equitable point of view." Is it to you conceivable that in a country where the average income of the working man is 10s. or 12s. a week, there can be a larger margin, and that there must not be a smaller margin than in a country where the wages are 18s.?—I think that seems self-evident, and if the members of the Commission would look at some of the budgets of working-class expenditure which have been published at different times (we have published some at the Board of Trade), they will find that as the income diminishes the proportion spent upon articles of food increases, and vice versa. If you have an income of 40l. a year, say, perhaps 60 per cent. will be spent on articles of food; if you have an income of 80l., perhaps less than 50 per cent.; if you have an income of 100l., perhaps 40 per cent. only on articles of food, and so on. As the income increases, the proportion spent upon articles of food diminishes—that is what you actually find in practice.

8079. The important inference seems to be, does it not, that if you take two countries, one with a large average individual income and the other with a smaller average individual income, and apply what is loosely called taxes, but what may be more precisely called identical taxes on the same articles of consumption, the so-called tax will reach more in one country than in the other?—I think that is quite evident. With reference to articles of luxury, I should like to say this. You will find in Adam Smith, for instance, that meat is spoken of as a luxury, and not as an article of necessary food at all.

8080. Meat is distinctly a luxury in Ireland, there are many people in Ireland who only eat meat two or three times a year, while they smoke tobacco every day?—Yes, so many questions might arise the moment you tried to apply this sumptuary distinction to economic and financial discussions.

8081. In the endeavour to ascertain what is the taxable margin of the incomes of the people of the two countries, do you think it is an appropriate way instead of determining what subsistence costs, and leaving a margin in, to take it at the other end, and by ascertaining the amount paid for what may be termed luxuries, call that a margin?—I do not think that is satisfactory.

The witness withdrew.

TWENTIETH DAY.

Friday, 3rd May 1895.

At Committee Room B, House of Lords.

PRESENT:

THE RIGHT HON. HUGH C. E. CHILDERS, *Chairman.*

LORD FARRER.	CHARLES E. MARTIN, Esq.
LORD WELBY.	J. E. REDMOND, Esq., M.P.
The Right Hon. THE O'CONOR DON.	THOMAS SEXTON, Esq., M.P.
The Hon. EDWARD BLAKE, M.P.	HENRY F. SLATTERY, Esq.

Mr. R. H. HOLLAND, *Secretary.*

Mr. ROBERT GIFFEN, C.B., LL.D., recalled and further examined.

[illegible] (*Mr. Sexton.*) At what amount do you estimate the current annual income of Great Britain?—I cannot put any exact figure upon it, but I should think not less at the present moment than 1,350,000,000*l*.—out of the United Kingdom, I should rather say.

[illegible] In order to ascertain the income of Great Britain we have to deduct from that, what?—What I would assign to Ireland, but that does not make much difference one way or the other.

[illegible] But if we do deduct it, you would deduct how much?—70,000,000*l*. to 75,000,000*l*.

[illegible] Then the income of Great Britain at present you estimate at between 1,250,000,000*l*. and 1,300,000,000*l*.?—That would be so, but I think I ought to say as these matters there is some difficulty, because after an interval of two or three years you always get a different figure.

[illegible] But I think you will agree with me, that in order to afford a basis for discussion and recommendation, it is much better to have a figure, even though it may be qualified by arguments, than to have no figure?—No doubt it would be better to put it in that way.

[illegible] You valued the income of Great Britain in 1886 at 1,200,000,000*l*.?—I think I put that as a [illegible] which was good enough for me to take—I did not put it as an exact figure, but as a minimum sum which was good enough for the purposes for which I was discussing the subject.

[illegible] Your memory is quite correct. You said, "I "have a strong feeling that in those figures, which "were based very much on what Mr. Dudley Baxter "and Mr. Leone Levi had done, I gave too little to "Great Britain if not too much to Ireland?"—I think it is very important to draw attention to that point, that to use figures which were good enough for that discussion is not quite the same thing as a considered figure which you have arrived at after a statistical investigation, and it is not to be treated in the same manner.

[illegible] But the comparison of the two figures of 1,200,000,000*l*. ten years ago and over 1,400,000,000*l*. now would suggest a marvellous rate of progress, would it not. It would suggest that the increment to the annual income of Great Britain in ten years has been equal to two or three times the whole annual income of Ireland?—I should not be surprised at that result. The addition to the population of Great Britain in ten years is close upon 3,000,000, and that bears a very large proportion to the total population of Ireland, and if you allow even for a moderate increase per head in the income of the people of Great Britain you soon get out a figure of increase in ten years which exceeds the total figure of Ireland at a given time.

[illegible] We know that in about every 15 years Great Britain adds to its population a number now about equal to the whole population of Ireland?—That is so.

[illegible] These considerations remind one of a very striking saying of yours, that is Ireland may come to be, in relation to Great Britain, a larger Isle of Man?—That was the sort of idea I had of the drift of events—that if you have Ireland going on as other agricultural districts are doing, not increasing in population, and Great Britain increasing as it has been, that would be the final effect before many generations are over unless something happens to reverse the movement.

[illegible] The population of Ireland is on a declining scale, and the agricultural income of Ireland, which is at any rate the main bulk of her taxation, whatever may be said, is diminishing, and has depreciated seriously in recent years?—I think in recent years it has suffered to some extent as expressed in money by the general fall in prices, and that that has been a disadvantage to the Irish people as to other agricultural communities.

[illegible] We have your evidence fortified by the facts as to the course of prices by the evidence of the Irish Registrar-General, and by the proceedings on the Irish Land Commission as to [illegible]?—I know those proceedings and the efforts that were made to obtain a continuous record of prices, and there is no doubt there has been a fall of prices in recent years which must have affected Ireland as an agricultural community disadvantageously.

[illegible] Have these facts suggested to you that in the efforts to strike a proportion for a permanent scheme of taxation it would be necessary to have a regard to the wonderful progressive condition of Great Britain, and to the stationary, if not retrogressive, state of Ireland?—That was the meaning of my suggestion.

[illegible] As to the income of Ireland between the figures which you have been considering, the figure of 76,000,000*l*., founded upon a rather arbitrary assumption that the gross income may be double the agricultural income, and the figure of 62,000,000*l*. founded on the idea that the income of the non-agricultural body is the same as the agricultural body, I would wish to submit two or three considerations to you. In the first place, if we were to prefer the figure of 76,000,000*l*., we have to consider, have we not, that although the rent of the landlord, the labourers' pay, and the farmers' profits are all included in the 40,000,000*l*., and the agricultural body have two-thirds of the whole, the one remaining third earn nearly as much as the two-thirds?—I think that is quite possible, but that you would have to assume.

[illegible] Although I should suggest the inclusion of the sum of 10,000,000*l*. in the 62,000,000*l*. would amply cover the professional and mercantile incomes on the other side, and would make it just to assume that the non-agricultural earnings were no greater than the agricultural on the whole?—My impression is that the figure of 62,000,000*l*. would be too low. If, as it is quite easy for anyone to do, you take the figures of the census and the numbers of people in different occupations, and apply very roughly the average income which you derive from those different figures of wages I have given you, I think you would find that the figure of 62,000,000*l*. would come out rather too low.

[illegible] At present I find it hard to realise that the non-agricultural third earn nearly double as much as the agricultural two-thirds, although that two-thirds includes the rent?—I have put all the figures before you for the purpose of enabling you to form a judgment, but I think if you would take the trouble to make a rough calculation in the way I suggest, you would find you would come at a figure of more than 62,000,000*l*.

[illegible] I am explaining the difficulties I find in my own mind with the view of getting light from you. In 1886, you thought the valuation of 76,000,000*l*. rather high, did you not? You said "I put down the

Mr. Robert Giffen, C.B.

6 May 1895.

whole income of Great Britain at about 1,300,000,000*l*. and that of Ireland at just over 70,000,000*l*. But I have a strong feeling that in those figures, which were based very much on what Mr. Dudley Baxter and Mr. Leone Levi had done, I gave too little to Great Britain, if not too much to Ireland?—I think I have looked into matters a little more fully since that time. That was one figure out of a great many in a very short article which took a great deal of trouble, and since that time I think very likely to some extent there has been an improvement in Irish wages of a non-agricultural kind, and that there have been other changes. At any rate, I had not looked into the matter so fully in 1886, as I have since done.

6099. Anyone living in Ireland and studying her affairs from day to day would be surprised to hear that if 70,000,000*l*. was too high or high enough in 1886, there should be a higher income now, the income raised by much lower rents at all, even, considering the great fall in agricultural value, which is the main bulk of the income?—I think, on the other hand, you will find that in industrial business in Ireland as in other parts, there has been some improvement in wages, and I think probably in some respects a greater improvement in Ireland than in Great Britain, because they have been coming up to the level of Great Britain more and more in regard to artisan and industrial pursuits.

6100. I rather gathered from your evidence as to wages, that wages do not fluctuate; that you regard them as a non-fluctuating quantity, and that estimates of wages taken 10 years ago would be good enough for the present time?—I do not think I quite said that. In the United Kingdom generally that might be so, but it might be the case that in a special part of the United Kingdom like Ireland, the process of coming up to the general level might have been going on.

6101. Your calculation of average income quoted by Sir Edward Hamilton gives 14*l*. as the average income all over Ireland. If you multiply that on the present population, it will give a figure very nearly approaching the 63,000,000*l*., will it not, and if to some extent the resources of Ireland remain the same although the population diminishes, then you ought to increase the figure per head.

6102. Certainly, but on the other hand, do you not see the figures of the Registrar-General, and the proceedings of the Land Commission suggest that agricultural values which amounted to 40,000,000*l*. a year have shrunk by about one-third during the last few years?—But there has perhaps been a special decrease of agricultural income owing to that circumstance and yet an increase of the other income in Ireland which has not been affected in the same way by the fall of prices.

6103. But is it not a difficult assumption in regard to a country dependent so much upon agricultural prosperity, that if the income of the farmer diminishes materially, the other wages of the country can have much increased?—I think not, for this reason, that a considerable part of the other income of the country is derived from an export trade and that it is comparatively independent of the conditions of the agricultural industry. For instance, the ship-building in Belfast is a kind of export trade, the linen manufacture trade is an export trade, brewing and distilling trade is an export trade, and they are not so much dependent—at any rate they are not dependent exclusively by any means—upon the home trade, that is to say upon the agriculture of the rest of the country.

6104. Quite true, but the ship-building is confined to one town, the linen trade to two or three, and the distilling and the brewing to two or three, the numbers employed in those trades are so infinitesimally minute compared to the total mass of the labouring and agricultural population that I hesitate to attribute to that cause any material importance on the whole average?—Still their numbers make up a considerable part of the numbers of people employed in Ireland outside of agriculture.

6105. Out of a million and a half of Irish people sustained outside of agriculture, I suppose there will be certainly 300,000 or 400,000 male adults, and I should not think that above one-tenth of that number would be employed in these particular industries?—I think more than that, and with regard to the linen manufacture, for instance, you have very considerable numbers, no doubt, of women and children employed.

6106. In Belfast?—And the neighbourhood.

6107. I will not press that further. I would like to remind you now of the method you pursued in 1886 in estimating the total income of Ireland. You took the agricultural income, but you deducted from it the rent before finding the average income of each individual of the agricultural community. Then you applied the average income of the agricultural person, namely 16*l*., leaving out the rent to the remainder of the population, assuming that half the remainder of the population earned the same as the agricultural body, and the other half 50 per cent. more?—I really have forgotten the method which I employed then so as to arrive at those approximate figures.

6108. That method appears to have been carefully considered as the whole article was [illegible] as carefully considered a document as I have ever read. If we apply that method now, taking the agricultural income at 50,000,000*l*. and deducting the rent of 10,000,000*l*. dividing into the balance of 30,000,000*l*. the 2,000,000 of people engaged in agriculture you find an average of 15*l*. You then assume that of the remaining population of one million and a half, half of them, namely 750,000 earn an average income of 10*l*. each, or say, 7,500,000*l*.; that the other 750,000 earn an average income of 15*l*. each, or say, 11,250,000*l*. Adding the two together you have a non-agricultural income of about 19,000,000*l*. which added to the 30,000,000*l*. of agricultural income and the 10,000,000*l*. of rent, makes together a total of 59,000,000*l*. or 60,000,000*l*., as the gross income of Ireland so that this amount approximates closely to the lower of the two estimates, namely 63,000,000*l*., and indicates that such estimate is not likely to be under the mark?—I have no doubt I did the best I could in 1886, but I have really quite forgotten at this moment the method I employed. I think if I were doing the same now, I should find that in consequence of those figures as to wages which have been obtained altogether since that date, I should proceed by a somewhat different method, and apply those figures of wages to the figures of the census which I recommend you to follow, and other members of the Commission to follow. I think you would then find that you would arrive at a somewhat larger sum than 63,000,000*l*. for the total income of Ireland.

6109. The same difficulty I feel is that in the case of a country more purely agricultural perhaps than any other in Europe, that the incomes of more than one-third of the people not employed in agriculture are supposed to be nearly relatively double those of the parts so engaged?—No doubt there are many difficulties in the matter. I will give you an illustration of how the thing works out in detail. You will find that the constabulary, for instance, have an income of 1,400,000*l*. or something like that, and if you apply that to the numbers you find you get a figure much above any sort of average for Ireland. There are one or two other employments of that kind, and you find they do have some effect on the whole figure of the total income of Ireland, when you take those things into account.

6110. I would consider that of great weight if the rent were not included, but I consider the rent of 10,000,000*l*. to be so large a factor as to overbear any other consideration?—No doubt these are very fair considerations, and you must weigh them with the other evidence when you come to put it together, but I think I should recommend you to give your mind to it a little and look at the figures of occupations in the census and the rates of wages which I have given. I think you will then find that there is probably some reason for believing that the income per head outside of agriculture is more than the income inside of agriculture.

6111. (*Chairman.*) Parenthetically, as to what you have said about the constabulary, do you count the constabulary as married men with their families, or do you take them simply?—I was simply comparing them with reference to the average income of people in Ireland.

6112. But the average income is of people married and not married, and children, all round, is it not?—Yes. I was simply mentioning it as a case of people employed in Ireland who get much larger incomes than people would get employed in agriculture.

6113. (*Mr. Sexton.*) There are 13,000 police, their pay is 900,000*l*., giving an average of 70*l*.?—I think you [illegible] will find there has been some increase in the pay of recent years.

8114. I am giving the present pay [illegible]—I am comparing it with the estimates made in 1868. That was one of the elements as to the increase in incomes, and although the numbers are small, yet when you find there is [illegible] as to one class of people, and when you find that similar things have been occurring with reference to other classes, that helps to pull up the total.

8115. So then. I quite realise that the non-agricultural income may be larger than the agricultural income, but I find it hard to realise that it may be double, especially as that involves the assumption that the valuation which you thought rather too high in 1868 is much exceeded now, and the average income which you calculated a few years ago points to the lower and not to the higher sum. However, we shall apply ourselves as well as we can, to that matter. You have said, having regard to the data which you have submitted, that no scheme of permanent taxation could be founded on the assumption that the gross income of Ireland stands in a higher proportion to that of Great Britain than 1 to 20?—I think so.

8116. Having found the income, we have to find the taxable income, and you lay down the measure and equity of the matter in these terms in your article of 1886, page [illegible], "The taxable income of Ireland must "bear a still smaller proportion to the taxable income "of Great Britain than does its gross income or "capital to the gross income or capital of Great "Britain. The taxable income is the income remain"ing after allowance for the maintenance necessary to "maintain a population upon a given standard of "living. In this sense, giving the people of Great "Britain an average of 15*l.* per head as the minimum, "they have a taxable income of about 800,000,000*l.* "sterling annually." That is to say, from the gross income of 1,300,000,000*l.* you deduct 15*l.* per head upon 35,000,000?—Yes.

8117. "On the same scale, 5,000,000 of people in "Ireland would absorb 60,000,000*l.* out of say "75,000,000*l.* gross income, leaving a taxable income "of 15,000,000*l.* sterling only." Then on the next page you sum up the matter in this way: "To put the "matter shortly, and in the roundest figures—there "can, of course, be no exact figures of income and "capital—Ireland in population has sunk from one"third to less than one-seventh, in gross income, from "two-seventeenths to less than one-seventeenth in "capital, from a proportion that was material to about "one-twenty-fourth only; in taxable resources, from "a proportion that was also material, being perhaps "about one-tenth" (I think you are speaking of the "period of the union) "to a proportion that is almost "inappreciable, the proportion of only 1 to 50." Then later on you say that "nearly the whole taxable income "of the Irish people is, in fact, absorbed by the State. "The taxable income being about 15,000,000*l.* only, "the Imperial Government, as we have seen takes "nearly 7,000,000*l.*, and the local taxes are over "3,000,000*l.* more, or about 10,000,000*l.* in all. So "large a proportion of taxation to taxable income "would be a serious fact for any country, and there "can be little accumulation in Ireland under such "conditions." Would you apply that method to the figures we now have, say about 1,400,000,000*l.* for Great Britain, and what figure would you prefer for Ireland?—Suppose you take 75,000,000*l.*

8118. The population of Great Britain is about 34,000,000, which at 15*l.* each would still be 510,000,000*l.*, leaving the taxable income of Great Britain 1,000,000,000*l.* The gross income of Ireland is suggested by you at 75,000,000*l.*, the population is 4,500,000, which at 15*l.* is 55,000,000*l.*, giving a taxable income of 20,000,000*l.* The taxable income of Great Britain being 1,000,000,000*l.*, and the taxable income of Ireland being 20,000,000*l.*, it would appear that the proportion of one to 50 which you stated in 1886, holds good at present?—I think that those are something like the figures which I gave to the Commission in my evidence in chief, but I think I pointed out that that was not strictly correct, that that calculation was somewhat rough in that respect, that you ought not to deduct the minimum from each person per head in the community, but that you ought to deduct the total income of the people who are below the minimum, and then you should only deduct the minimum from the people who have something above that, and that that would give you somewhat different figures, if you were going into it accurately, that would be the proper method to apply, and unfortunately we have no means of applying that method very well. I think there would be the figures to some extent.

8119. Of course we are proceeding in this and in other branches of the data in the main in large measure of the kind upon doctrines of average and general assumptions?—No doubt, but when you come to business when you have to go into things much more strictly than what one does in opening up a subject for the first time, and suggesting matters really for the consideration of other people, and that is a very obvious qualification to make, that although it was good enough roughly and for practical purposes to deduct the minimum from every person in the country and to multiply it by the number of persons, yet perhaps it is not quite good enough when you come to business, because there are so many people who are under the minimum altogether, and clearly the correct method, if you can apply it, is to deduct the total income of all the tax-payers who are below the minimum, and then deduct the minimum only from those who have an income above that limit.

8120. (*Chairman.*) But making that correction what result would there be—would it be more favourable to Ireland or less favourable?—I think that it would be less favourable to some extent in that way, that Ireland probably has a much larger number of people absolutely below the minimum. Say for instance if the average below the minimum is only 7*l.* per head, or something of that kind instead of 15*l.*, you multiply the number of people below the minimum by that sum, and then you have a smaller sum to deduct than if you applied to all those people the proportion of 15*l.*

8121. To a certain extent that applies to England too does it not?—That applies to England too, and as I said when one is dealing with the subject quite generally, and opening it up for the first time, that is a point which you would perhaps not give much attention to, but when you come to business it may be a thing which you ought to give some attention to, and see if it would affect you. I think it would affect the comparison a little.

8122. (*Mr. Sexton.*) Of course it is obvious, for instance, in the case of the English agricultural labourer you have given his wages as ranging from 15*s.* to 20*s.* a week, but even a labourer who earns the maximum of 20*s.*, if he has a wife and three small children, and his earnings are not supplemented through having an income of 52*l.* a year would be under the minimum, would he not?—Yes, but clearly, if you deduct from the aggregate income of a community in one case, say for Ireland, for a large number of people 10*l.* per head or something of that kind, and you deduct from the aggregate income of England a sum of 15*l.* per head, the result is a little different from what it would be if you were deducting the same sum in each case.

8123. If the proportions of persons below and above the minimum in the two countries varied greatly, that is, if the number of those be much below the minimum in Ireland, that would affect the computation, would it not?—That is the general idea I have expressed and that is a consideration of some importance which ought to be kept in mind. I was very much surprised indeed that that article of mine remained so long and that no comment was ever made by anybody who looked at the subject. It became quite clear to my mind when I was preparing to give evidence before this Commission that that was a point which really ought to receive some attention.

8124. I can assure you your article has been subject to continual attention and thought since it was written. From your evidence as to the cost of living in Ireland and from the fact that the Irishman pays as much as the Englishman for the main necessaries of life, and [illegible], I assume you would give no countenance to any idea that a different minimum should be fixed in England to that in Ireland?—I think not—not for a purpose of this kind, because from the point of view of the community of the United Kingdom as a whole, the idea is that all should come up to the same level and that the minimum for the purposes of taxation would be fixed at the same amount.

8125. If you fix a lower minimum for Ireland, that would be taking advantage of the greater poverty of Ireland in order to exact a larger measure of taxation?

—It would be stereotyping the lower standard of living, which I think it is undesirable to stereotype.

8126. It would be doing what I have said, and also what you say, would it not, it would be dictating by law that the standard of life should continue to be lower in Ireland than in Great Britain?—It would be something in that direction, which I should consider to be very undesirable.

8127. (*Lord Welby.*) You said, in speaking of the supposed under assessment of Great Britain, you thought there was a considerable part of the foreign income of the British people which is not brought home and accounted for. Do you know of any estimate of the amount of British investment in foreign securities?—I do not know of any that have been made except by myself, and that was some years ago. I cannot say that I recollect the figures at this moment, because I have not been looking into them lately.

8128. I have a recollection that it was 100,000,000*l.*, but I am not quite sure that I am right?—I do not think I ever put any such figure as that into a statistical form. I may have said at different times that I think the figure would be that, but I think at any time I made a statistical observation, I arrived at no more than 60,000,000*l.*

8129. I understand that the Inland Revenue have made an estimate of their own on the subject, and they think 60,000,000*l.* to 70,000,000*l.* is about the mark?—I do not think there are materials beyond a point for forming a very good estimate. When I made that estimate, and arrived, I think, at somewhere about 60,000,000*l.*, I had a great many figures before me as to Stock Exchange securities, and the probable amount held in this country of such securities as compared with what were held in foreign countries, and I made a very elaborate list indeed, or rather, had it made for me. I arrived at some estimate of what the income would be of a visible kind that would come to this country in connexion with foreign securities. But the uncertain element, to my mind, as a single investigator, has always been the amount of income received by British subjects abroad in connexion with mercantile and financial firms who probably account for it in Schedule D somewhere, and yet I am satisfied do not account for all the profits which they make abroad.

8130. That is to say, you draw a distinction between the profits made in trade and investments in that case?—Not altogether, because there are profits from investments to a very large extent as well.

8131. But would these be returned under Schedule D?—I think some of them would be. Then you have a considerable number of British people living in foreign countries who are still British subjects, and who eventually come and reside in this country, but who have their capital abroad, and I do not think that at any time the Inland Revenue authorities would be able, even if they tried, to get hold of all the income of that kind.

8132. But you would apply a certain force to the estimate made by the Department that is always handling the income figures, would you not?—I should form an opinion upon it if I had a full explanation of what is done, but I should attach no great value to a mere statement, that it should be estimated so and so without seeing what the process is which they have gone on the matter. The process is really all important, because it is quite possible that otherwise you might be speaking of different things, unless the process happened to be fully explained.

8133. I quite agree with you on that point, and I only wanted to call your attention to the fact that that figure is the Inland Revenue estimate, quite agreeing with you that the value of that estimate must be judged by the manner in which it is computed?—I can form no opinion upon it until I see what the process is.

8134. You speak of a considerable part of these investments as not accounted for. May I ask whether your impression is founded upon any actual facts coming to your knowledge upon that point?—Undoubtedly. I have been consulted by different people in the city at different times, as to the returns which they were making to the income tax.

8135. Does that lead you to consider that a considerable amount does remain to be accounted for?—That is so, that to some extent these people were engaged in investments and undertakings in foreign countries, the profits of which were very fluctuating and very difficult to estimate; and it seems to me that where a large amount of profit happened to be made, it is a thing which those who received it would probably say nothing about. It would be quite impossible for the Inland Revenue to follow it up. I am not clear in my own mind as to how the law stands in respect of profits made abroad and which are not brought home. On one occasion I was consulted by a gentleman who had been paying income tax on 10,000*l.* a year made abroad; he had no sort of idea whether that was the true figure or not, and then I understood it was ascertained that not having brought the money home he was not liable to return it at all. How that may be exactly I do not know, but the whole case is this, that the incomes and profits are of such a kind that the Inland Revenue authorities would have the utmost difficulty in getting hold of them.

8136. I may say that the Inland Revenue, while agreeing with you that a certain amount of such investments escape them, do not think a very large proportion escapes?—I cannot speak about that until I see how they have formed that impression.

8137. Here again I am only anxious to bring before you the conclusion to which I think more importance ought to be attached than you attach to it, viz., it is a conclusion that which a skilled department has arrived on these things?—I think in this case that there is some knowledge to be gained from long experience and acquaintance with the City, which probably that Department would not have.

8138. Quite so, but at the same time the question is always before them, and I remember one or two instances of investigations made by them which certainly left upon my mind the impression that they were not otherwise than skilled and acute in following up any indication or clue which came across them of such investments existing and not being accounted for?—I think it might be of some interest to the Commission to give a concrete illustration of what I mean by the difficulty of estimating profits made abroad. I believe that contractors undertaking large works abroad like a foreign railway—a large firm like Brassey's, for instance—would make a calculation that the speculation would not be carried over for a period of something like ten years. They would go into the business and they would make advances, and they would not be able to show their accounts for a period of something like ten years. At the end of the ten years I do not suppose large firms having made large capital profits, would sit down and calculate exactly what the profits had been; probably the money would remain abroad and not be brought home, and if they were not liable until it be brought home, there it would remain. I do not say the firms are intending to defraud the revenue in any way—that is not the point—but really there is a certain difficulty in knowing what the profits are, because the business has to extend over such a long period; sometimes, again, it may be quicker than they expect.

8139. I think possibly we are a little bit going on different lines. When I am speaking of what the Inland Revenue have done and do, my attention is confined to what I call simply *bonâ fide* investments. Your evidence rather turns on what I should call Schedule D, does it not?—That may be so, and I think I mentioned when I began that it was that part of the business as to which I had most doubt. Probably, as regards the investments, I think one might attach some value to the calculations of the Inland Revenue authorities, because a great deal of it is visible, and you can follow it up, but this uncertain element which exists no doubt, above and beyond all that, and which is very important, I think it would be very difficult for them to get hold of.

8140. I am glad to hear you give that answer, because what I was anxious to do was, as far as possible, to bring the line of your thought into connexion with that of the Inland Revenue, so as to ascertain where the separation between you was, and I expected that while I have been putting to you the view of the Inland Revenue, as confined to those investments, your attention was turned to the more difficult subjects of profits in trade?—That shows the importance in expressing opinions on things of that kind—that the whole process should be before one, and not merely the final figure. But if you could tell me now what the exact state of the law is as to profits being brought home before they are assessed to the Income Tax, perhaps I could form a better opinion as to whether much escapes or not. I believe the mere

Sir Robert Giffen, C.B. 8 May 1895. [illegible]

fact that the law is somewhat unsettled shows that there is a real difficulty in the matter.

8141. (*Chairman.*) That would depend on the result of an appeal in a case that is now before the House, would it not, a very important case on that very question?—I believe that is so, and that there are great differences with regard to the law on the matter.

8142. (*Lord Welby.*) I think anyone who has had any experience of the appeals made to the Treasury, would know first of all that there are great difficulties on the law point, that the most skilled administrators would speak with the greatest doubt as to what the state of the law actually is. That leads me to what you mentioned just now, a point which I was going to put to you. It seemed to me that that point is of so great importance that I would ask you whether you can suggest any method by which better information on that matter could be obtained. I rather gather from what you say, that the difficulties are so great, that it is only by rumour and occasional information that the returns [illegible] to you?—I think there is a little difficulty on the part of any man engaged in undertakings, the turn-over of which is extended over a long period, in knowing the profits himself, that is a difficulty which is very [illegible] and which, perhaps, could never be got over. But besides that, I am extremely doubtful whether, as a matter of principle and for the purposes of taxation, the Government ought to endeavour to tax the income of people made abroad until it is brought home. Although it may be a resource of the people and add to the wealth of the country, it ought to [illegible] as a matter of taxation not to attempt to tax it until it is brought within the jurisdiction. As to your being able to tax it, I have extreme doubt whether it can be done at all.

8143. Do you think that, so far as investments in foreign countries are concerned, you have made allowance for that kind of [illegible] which the law does not [illegible]?—I certainly allowed for that, because it was necessary for me to allow for that, whether the income escaped [illegible] because of the Inland Revenue authorities not following it up or because the law did not enable them to follow it up, was a point of no consequence for my purpose.

8144. (*Lord Farrer.*) I gather if you think the money made abroad is not brought home, it cannot be said to add to the taxable resources of this country?—Not in the same way as other income does, although it may add to the wealth of the people of this country and to its [illegible] ability to tax themselves when great emergencies [illegible] as a thing one ought to take account of.

8145. (*Lord Welby.*) Without expressing any strong opinion upon that point, I confess I hear the view you are giving now expressed [illegible] for the first time, but if the taxation is to be equally apportioned, ought not a man who invests his capital abroad and lives here, to pay income tax upon that income just as much as the man who invests at home?—Theoretically that would be so.

8146. Do you question the advisability of following the man very strictly on account of the inherent difficulty of the case, or on any other ground?—Mainly on account of the inherent difficulty of the case.

8147. The reason I put that question to you is this. As an economist you would not encourage the Inland Revenue to pass over such cases and thereby give a premium to people to set up abroad in order to escape?—It depends upon what the law is which the Inland Revenue authorities have to enforce.

8148. But at all events you made no suggestion, could you, any method from your great experience and the inquiries you have made on these subjects, by which more definite information on that point could be obtained by the department itself?—I think one of the difficulties of an income tax [illegible] such as we have is that, if you are to apply it to incomes under Schedule D with great stringency, it means declarations of a very [illegible] kind, and I do not think that the endeavour to enforce the declarations of incomes, however strictly, in doubtful cases, meets with such success that it ought to be encouraged. That is my feeling about it.

8149. If I may put it in another form, you are referring to what is a very old cause of the Revenue Departments, namely, that people become more honest as the rate goes down?—I believe so. At any rate with regard to these matters made abroad it is difficult to [illegible] where people can hardly tell what the profits are, there is [illegible] endeavouring to enforce them to strict declarations by a process of that kind, and, therefore, I do not see how you can get at that income very well at all.

8150. I will not press the matter, but of course one would like to point out that it is a mere shifting of the burden, and that what one man who is able to pay does not pay, is put on someone else's shoulders?—No doubt that is the difficulty, and it is a difficulty with regard to the Income Tax Acts, where it applies to incomes of people who have to make declarations of profits where those profits are somewhat difficult to ascertain.

8151. I observe that you derived the impression that there was under-assessment from the proceedings of the Committee which sat in 1869?—I think I was speaking of the Irish Committee of 1865. I am afraid it was a slip if I said 1869; I was thinking of the Irish Committee of 1865.

8152. You would admit, would you not, that the Inland Revenue, with the great increase of its experience since that time, has become much more strict and close in its methods of assessment than it was 30 years ago?—I believe that would be so just at the present time, and the thing has become more strict from time to time.

8153. In my experience there has been one continual course of approach nearer and nearer to strict assessment, and the attention of the department has been very much devoted to that point. Therefore I would ask you whether, though at that time the evidence as given before the Committee might fully justify you in the opinion you formed, you would somewhat qualify that if applied to the present assessment?—I think I would put it exactly as I put it in my evidence in chief, in which I allowed for the continual improvement you are speaking of now.

8154. You gave us a ground for thinking that property in Great Britain is under-assessed, a statement of Mr. Gladstone's many years ago in which various compensations had been claimed; that was the case of Cannon Street, was it not?—It was either Cannon Street or Holborn. I forget which it was, but the discrepancies were tremendous.

8155. The celebrated case we remember is that of 1864, Cannon Street, in which the compensation claimed was 85,000*l*., the jury awarded 17,000*l*., and the income returned was 9,500*l*.?—Yes, something like that; the discrepancies were tremendous.

8156. Those are the figures; that is a very striking case. I would venture to call your attention to the fact that when that took place the Income Tax Act was only eight or nine years old, and though I do not think for a moment that the income tax returns now would coincide with the claim for damage which might be put forward, might we not assume that probably the Inland Revenue Commissioners, with their long experience, would have assessed some of those gentlemen at higher rates than they accepted at that date?—I think with the greatest goodwill in the matter that the real difficulty of the Inland Revenue in dealing with people of that kind is that they have no adequate knowledge in order to check the returns made to them, or in order to make their assessment in the absence of returns.

8157. I do not like to press upon you anything [illegible] opinion, but it is a subject which has often interested me. Of course, when at the Treasury, I got no direct information, but only information from the Inland Revenue officials, and from them I learned that they were collecting, and are collecting a larger amount of information about the means of people?—I have no doubt that the thing is much better conducted than it was, and yet that a great deal escapes them.

8158. I do not mean to suggest to you that the point on which you based your view that there was a good deal of under-assessment, has been entirely removed. I only mean that every year does make the assessment stricter and closer to facts. I might also perhaps call your attention to another fact very much of the same kind. Do you remember when the [illegible] of the Probate Court were compensated?—I do not recollect that.

8159. That was a case very much of the same kind, which amounted almost to a scandal did it not?—With reference to the difficulties, I think I may mention that some years ago the Inland Revenue Department made a kind of raid upon distinguished artists. They found they were having pictures at the Academy, and some authority at the Inland Revenue Department put down the prices that these premises were supposed to fetch, and checked the returns of income which the actuaries had been making by this information; but I do not think the result was quite satisfactory so far as the money derivable to the Exchequer was concerned, because they were met by the sellers in different ways. The actuaries had to explain to them, that although such prices were paid upon the sale they were not always sold, and things of that kind, and then it might happen that some years afterwards the premises were sold and the Inland Revenue Department were not informed.

8159. There was a little friction, I believe, between the Inland Revenue and the Royal Academy, was there not?—I am afraid so.

8160. Did you happen to read the evidence which was given before us by Mr Howe of the Inland Revenue?—I think I glanced over it, but it did not seem to me to bear upon any points which I was making myself so far as my recollection goes.

8161. Why I would call your attention to that evidence was, that he was an official of the Inland Revenue, who had been employed in the income tax collection in England and also in Ireland, and therefore he had a singular experience and facility for forming a correct comparison of the two kinds of assessments in the two countries. His evidence was that the assessment in Ireland was not stricter than it is in England, which is a point which has been brought before us?—That might be as regards the detail of assessments under particular schedules so far as the surveyors could follow it, but it would not affect very much the kind of observation which I have been making, which is of a much more general kind.

8162. I do not quite follow where the difference would be. Given the official and allowing him to be a fairly intelligent man, if he tells you that the system of assessment in Ireland is as strict as it is in England, would you accept that?—But if Ireland has not the kinds of income which are the subject of under-assessment, I do not see how that would apply very much.

8163. I understand you draw a difference in this, that in England there is a considerable amount of income, which escapes, and that that is very much smaller in Ireland, therefore there is much less field for under-assessment?—Yes, and also Ireland is a smaller place altogether, where people are more under the observation of their neighbours, and that you have no place in Ireland like the metropolis where people have little knowledge of their neighbours, and where undoubtedly there is a great difficulty in getting profits.

8164. But on the other hand, the method of assessment is somewhat different in Ireland and England, and I would put it to you whether the method of assessment in England is not such as would lead to greater strictness than that in Ireland. For instance, in Ireland, there is only one person to make the assessment, namely, the government surveyor, whereas in England there is in every parish an assessor and in every district local commissioners of taxes, men resident in the district, and who have therefore very good ways of ascertaining what the means of the people are?—Of course there are details as to particular assessments under Schedule A or Schedule B or whatever they are, into which it would be impossible for me to enter, but so far as my own knowledge goes I should say the part of the United Kingdom which is most strictly assessed is neither England nor Ireland, but Scotland, where you really have a scientific system thoroughly and logically applied.

8165. But still, taking Schedule D, I would put to you that if there is in one case a local assessor and local Revenue commissioners and in the other case only the government surveyor, you have in the first case a number of people at work, many of them with special knowledge in one place, and therefore more likely to arrive at correct information than if you have the government surveyor alone, who naturally is not a local man, that is to say, a man who is employed only in the district?—I could not form an opinion upon that point because I am not acquainted with the details as to the methods.

8166. It is rather an important point, is it not, because we are all endeavouring to form a judgment upon this question. Is it not rather an important point in judging the question whether Ireland is severely taxed or not, to consider what the methods of the assessing of taxation are?—I think it would affect very little, as I have said before, the kind of observation I had been making, and to which I attach the greatest importance.

8167. I will read you one question and answer on Mr. Howe's evidence, 7510. "As you have touched upon "Schedule D, do you think the self-made assessments "under Schedule D in a country like England, where "the volume and number of assessable returns is so "great, can have been so searching an assessment as in "Ireland?—(A) My opinion is that it is more searching. "Taking the area, speaking roughly, Ireland is half "the area of England, there are [illegible] surveyors in "Ireland and [illegible] in England with the result that in "England each man has a much smaller area to "supervise, and the considerations I have mentioned, "namely, the existence in England of a number of "bodies of local men, each of whom have special "knowledge (speaking from what has come under my "own personal knowledge) lead me to the conclusion "that the assessments in England are certainly made "in a more stringent manner than in Ireland." Of course that is the opinion of an officer who is acquainted in some detail with the methods actually employed, and yet as he gives the reasons I do not think they are quite satisfactory, and would not overcome the presumption from the fact that in Ireland it is much easier to know than in England, and I do not think the officer deals specially at all with the metropolis as what he speaks of. There are no income tax authorities in the metropolis who are so well acquainted as one would suppose, with the incomes of different classes of people. I speak in this matter from observation as a member of the community, and what people tell you as to their income tax and matters of that kind—what I have seen myself, and I should doubt very much indeed if there is that close acquaintance which would enable them to assess their incomes properly.

8168. My information rather differs from yours?—I may tell you, privately, until I entered the Board of Trade, I never made a return for income tax at all, and other people did the same, the thing was as loose as possible.

8169. At the same time has not Ireland one government officer who is still a skilled officer, whereas in England there are these district authorities with larger knowledge of the people around them, who make the assessment in the first instance, and whose assessment is therefore as likely to be more effective than the assessment of the one government officer in Ireland, with the result that it is likely to be rather more strict with regard to England than with regard to Ireland?—I should think not, from the general fact that in Ireland knowledge is so much more easily obtained without weighing the other considerations which have been mentioned.

8170. (Mr Sexton.) May I ask, Sir Giffen, whether where local bodies make assessments, their interest is to make assessments equal as between individual and individual, but they have no interest in making a high assessment for Imperial purposes, rather the other way?—I do not like to go into details of that kind, because I am not acquainted with the local machinery in that way, except in Scotland, where they really have a good machinery for doing the business properly.

8171. (Lord Welby.) You have submitted a number of important figures to the Commission to aid them in framing a judgment, but you have taken care to guard yourself by stating that they are approximate, and by warning us not to draw inferences too hastily from them?—Not to draw inferences too hastily, but not to press approximate figures into use as if they were final and absolute figures. An approximation should always be dealt with as an approximation, as being made from certain imperfect materials, the best that can be got, and the proper plan in which to use them, I always think, is to compare one approximation with another derived in different ways, and form a judgment on it as a jury would do.

8172. What I mean, is this, for instance, these approximate figures show an excess of imports of 3,000,000 or 4,000,000. We at once got into a conversation as to whether that represented an absentee drain, and I think you warned us against taking these approximate figures as a fact, and then considering how that fact is to be dealt with in the way of adjusting the balance?—Yes, I took the opportunity yesterday, in reply to Mr Sexton, of explaining a good deal more as to the dangers of using that margin as if it were an absolute figure.

Sir Robert Giffen, K.C.B.

4 May 1894.

8173. For instance, I take it that in your figures of exports you mentioned as exported half the butter, half the poultry, half the eggs, a quarter of the [illegible], in the absence of any statistics collected by competent officers as to exports, that must be a conjecture, must it not?—But altogether a conjecture. The gentleman at my office who did it took some trouble to get some kind of data for each figure, and I think it is explained in the return itself what the calculation is, although he does not always explain how the suggestion was made to him. I think you will find that any corrections that could be made upon items of that kind would not be likely to alter the total very much, and it was the total for my purpose which I wished to arrive at.

8174. Your conjecture is what I may call a very plausible one upon that point. You know that there is a considerable export of butter, and if it is a large one, you come to the conclusion that it represents a very considerable proportion of all the butter made?—You also know what the limit of butter may be.

8175. You do not know what the consumption at home is, do you; that is where the conjecture comes in. You know that a considerable amount is exported, and a considerable amount is consumed at home, but, drawing the line between them, it might be a third, might it not?—But the export of butter cannot possibly be more than the amount of butter made; you have an absolute limit in that respect.

8176. Quite so, but you say half that is export?—Then the limit of error would be between that half and the totals, assuming that half is really exported, of which we practically can have no doubt.

8177. You say you know the whole amount made. That also is a certain extent is conjecture, is it not, because there is a considerable amount of difference as to what the produce of cows is, and so on?—When you have such a paper as that of Mr. Rew as to the produce of dairies, I think you may say that you have some knowledge on the subject.

8178. I have read his article, and it is the very article which led me to make that remark, because my recollection of it was that he pointed out that very different estimates were given of the butter-producing power of a dairy?—No doubt there are different estimates, but I think a paper like Mr. Rew's forms a starting point, because he compares, and gives returns, and goes into the subject much better perhaps than has been done before.

8179. I have no wish to question what your experience has led you to think are the probable results, but I desire to bring home to the Commission an illustration of the [illegible] which you expressed to the Commission not to press the actual figures further than they ought to go?—You must not use approximations as though they were absolute figures for all the purposes for which absolute figures can be used.

8180. (*Chairman.*) I was a member of the Royal Commission which inquired into the Irish butter trade, and my recollection is that the amount of butter brought to market could be determined to a nicety, and that that was really the only figure which was absolutely ascertainable?—Just so.

Drain from Ireland.

8181. (*Lord Welby.*) From your experience, can you suggest any method by which we could learn whether there is any, and what drain, from Ireland to England such as has been suggested?—Not completely, I think. You must be content with not knowing a good deal upon these matters. What the exact figure which Ireland pays over its borders, in consequence of its being an unbalanced country, may be, I do not think it would be possible to ascertain with any exactness.

8182. Do you not think, for instance, that if you could get the real judgment of the Irish bankers, that they would be able to tell you, not closely or accurately, but approximately, what the adjustment between Ireland and England is over an average year?—I think not. I may say, for instance, with reference to information obtained from Irish banks and the Post Office, we used at the Board of Trade to obtain information, and I think we obtain the information still, although we do not publish it, as to the remittances by people in America to their friends in Ireland, and you would quite see that there was a serious difficulty on the part of the banks in really giving you the information, because they could not always tell what the precise history of a cheque had been, or what it was for; that would apply to almost all the money which is remitted from Ireland, as it were.

Sir Robert Giffen, K.C.B.

4 May 1894.

Balance of trade as to Ireland.

8183. What I am thinking of is this: one knows that in the adjustment of trade questions, how very dangerous it is to rely upon that adjustment as being confined to the two countries concerned, that adjustments are constantly made through third countries. It struck me, however, that probably between England and Ireland such would not be the case, and I was going to put the question to you. Do you think from your experience that the relations between England and Ireland are adjusted more simply, because Ireland has not very great communications abroad independent of England, through which such adjustments could be made, has she?—I think Ireland has communications abroad, directly with the United States and to some extent with European countries, in consequence of [illegible] living in those European countries, which would give rise, more or less, to direct relations abroad, which would have to be taken account of.

8184. Would you put weight upon the statements of bankers here whom you might choose as likely to know. Suppose they were to say to you, "We do not "think there is any adjustment of any very large "amount between England and Ireland; that is to "say, the remittances one year practically balanced "the remittances another, and therefore there is no "large balance of adjustment," would you lay stress upon that?—I would attach some value to it as an element in the consideration of the question, but then that equal balance might arise from the fact that money is sent to Ireland to pay there of the expenses of the army there, and to provide individuals who are living there in connection with the army, and so on, and you might have a good deal to take into account.

8185. I am not putting this forward as an argument against there being large sums remitted to absentees, but I am merely putting it for this purpose, that so far as actual money remittances go for whatever purposes, the money sent into Ireland pretty nearly balances the money sent out of Ireland, and I am led to this train of thought by a remark which you made to me some years ago that you did not think there was a very large balance of adjustment?—I think that is so, I think that is a kind of fact that would be well worth considering.

8186. I rather gathered from one of our colleagues who was sitting near me and who is a banker, that he was inclined to agree with you?—I took some trouble about the matter at the time. I thought it was of some interest to see whether Ireland showed the condition of a permanently indebted country in that form.

8187. And no information that you came across then satisfied you that it was, did it?—No information that I got at that time seemed to show that there was a very large amount remitted in consequence of an indebtedness, but it is quite possible there may be a few millions, and yet all the facts may be what I was led to understand they were.

8188. Repeating my first question do you know any way in which you could recommend the Commission to endeavour to obtain information upon that point which it would be worth having?—Whether it could be obtained locally or not, I am not quite sure. If you ask a banker, and people who have the locality said, "A B and C D are living abroad, and remit money to "them," then you would arrive at a figure probably.

8189. Looking to the fact that the banks in Ireland are fewer than the banks in England, do you not think it probable that between them and the post office you would be able to ascertain whether on the balance large sums were remitted every year one way or the other?—I think you could get at some information if you selected your bankers and took some trouble about it, but cheques do not tell their own history on the face of them.

8190. They do not, but still when the banks come to adjust they would know which way the balance would be by these clearings, would they not?—They must know, for instance in a given year, whether they placed more money with their agents in London than they did the year before. Points of that kind must be known to them.

8191. And that would tell one, would it not, unless there were adjustments made through relations with the United States, what the balance of adjustment was roughly ?—You see, there is so much difficulty in the matter, however, owing to the operations of trade, that it would be excessively difficult to follow.

5192. In discussing the population returns for the three countries, you refer to the conditions, do you not, that the difference between Ireland and Great Britain is that there is a deficiency of births in Ireland. You have before mentioned, as a consequence of circumstances, that a moderate birth-rate was the best subject of a wholesome condition of living?—I do not think I used a moderate birth-rate alone, I think I suggested a moderate birth-rate, and a moderate death-rate, with as large an excess of births over deaths as was compatible with those conditions.

5193. You took the figures as against Ireland, and I was looking at the question of moderate birth-rate in order to ask you whether you do not consider that the birth-rate in Ireland satisfied that condition; it seemed to me from the figure you quoted, it was a moderate and not a very high birth-rate?—It is not a high birth-rate. I do not think a moderate birth-rate by itself means very much, it must be accompanied by the other conditions,—a large excess of births over deaths.

5194. The reason why I ask the question is that it rather points, does it not, to the habits of the people with regard to deferred marriages?—I do not think that would be a sufficient reason, because to some extent it is obviously due to the fact that you have a large proportion of old people in Ireland, that makes both your death and birth-rate lower, or your birth-rate at any rate, because you have a larger number of people who are not likely to have children.

5195. The birth-rate being moderate, do you think it at all points to what are called prudent marriages?—I have heard that among some classes in Ireland that would be so, but how far it goes in degree I have no means of telling.

5196. (*Chairman.*) On the average there are more imprudent marriages in England than in Ireland, are there not?—I believe that is the case, but I could not speak as to that exactly, not having gone into the figures lately.

5197. (*Mr. Sexton.*) But the figures you presented to the Commission show that the marriage-rate in Ireland is lower than in any other part of the United Kingdom, do they not?—I do not think I gave you the marriage rate myself, it was given by one of the other witnesses; but the marriage rate may well be lower in Ireland than in Great Britain, and yet there may be as much marrying among people of the marriageable ages, because there is not so much among the people of non-marriageable ages.

5198. (*Lord Welby.*) It may be that that moderate rate may point to what may be called prudent marriages, may it not?—I am led to believe it is so to some extent among the better classes of the farming population of Ireland, but I cannot speak of the degree to which it exists.

5199. When you estimate the wages of agricultural labourers in Ireland at 10s. a week, do you make allowance for the extra earnings, such as for harvesting in England?—Not especially for extra earnings made in England, because that is perhaps not such a large figure now; it applies to one or two parts of Ireland only.

5200. Still it is a point which should be borne in mind, is it not, if you are taking the agricultural population of Ireland as a whole?—No doubt, but I do not think it would affect the matter very materially, taking the whole mass of people in Ireland.

5201. Taking the people who have mixed occupations, say partly agricultural and partly fishing (although I do not lay stress on the latter, because it is not very great), in great parts of England the agricultural labourer has no assistance of that kind, so that we ought to take that into consideration in judging the earnings of the agricultural population of Ireland and England respectively, ought we not?—That would be so, but then unfortunately we know the extent of the produce of the fishing industry in Ireland, and it is so small that it does not affect the question very much.

5202. Do I not gather from you that in the North the agricultural population assist themselves to a considerable extent by small manufacturing industries in their homes?—If you compare the factory returns with the census statistics of occupations you will find that there are a great many more people employed in the textile industries of Ireland than are accounted for in the factory returns, and that seems to show that women and children, and possibly, to some extent, male adults are employed in these textile industries outside of factories.

5203. And that would tend rather to bring up—perhaps not to a very great extent—the earnings of the agricultural classes, would it not?—I do not think so very much. I think you will find that as far as adults are concerned no one engaged in agriculture could also be engaged in any of these textile industries.

5204. But the wives or boys?—Possibly the wives and children may be employed to some extent, but then you get at that by counting them amongst the products of the other industries of Ireland.

5205. In fact, then, the only thing which is really omitted is the small occupations of fishing, and a somewhat considerable sum earned by people who do these other things?—I do not think it would be a very large amount altogether.

5206. In speaking of death duties as a test of wealth, you say that property which passes at death under succession is not the whole property, but the life interest of the successor, and you draw the conclusion that the life interest may approximate very nearly to the capital value of the estate in a country where property is sold for a small number of years' purchase. I did not quite follow the bearing of that argument. Can you explain it to me a little more fully?—The point was that in a country where property sold for a small number of years' purchase the amount returned for the purpose of duty would correspond more closely to the amount of property actually passing at death than in a country where similar property sold for a larger number of years' purchase of the income, and the effect of that was by comparison with Great Britain to throw up the property of Ireland and to diminish the property of England relatively, if you took the succession duties as the test.

5207. But as each successor, the successor pays, or I think paid (because under the Finance Act of last Session there is an alteration in that point) a percentage on his rent capitalised on the number of years the life is worth, and in both cases it is capitalised equally, is it not?—As far as that one goes, but I am using the figures as a test of the relative property in the two countries. Say in one country the property is purchasable at 15 years' purchase, and in the other country at 30 years' purchase, and that the life interest in both is on the average 10 years' purchase, clearly in the country where the property sells at 15 years' purchase the proportion of that life interest would be two-thirds of the total value, and in the country where it sells for 30 years' purchase it would only sell for one-third of the total value. Therefore in the one case the figure which you get is two-thirds of the total value of property passing at death, and in the other case it is only one-third of the total value passing at death, so that if you are going to compare the two as tests of the property in the two countries respectively, you must take that into account.

5208. My difficulty about it is this. I notice in the statistical returns presented by the Board of Trade that cultivated and stock land in Ireland produces per acre rather more than in England. I will take the cereal crops, oats, and taking roughly an average of five years, I find that the average produce is [illegible] bushels per acre in Ireland and about 40 bushels in Great Britain. I will take, in the same way, hay, which produces at two tons an acre in Ireland to one and a half in England. I am only giving those figures roughly. If that is so, the produce of land in Ireland is greater than in Great Britain, and its taxable power, therefore, larger. As the death duties must be paid eventually out of the produce of land, if the landlord's interest is measured by the number of years at which he can sell, and is less in Ireland than in England, the interest of the tenant must be larger, must it not?—I do not know that that follows at all, but in any case it comes to the question again that the produce of agriculture in Ireland is much inferior to the produce of agriculture in Great Britain. I do not know what special figures you have, but you have only got to look at the results in general and I think you will find that the produce of agriculture in Ireland, although there are nearly as many people employed as there are in Great Britain, is very much less indeed.

8209. I am quoting from your Board of Trade returns?—But those are only returns as to one or two particular crops. They do not bear upon the general produce of agriculture in Ireland at all.

8210. I beg your pardon, as far as what I call cultivated land, excluding stock land, in Ireland is concerned, the oats and hay take up by far the largest amount?—But then they are not so important crops in England and Scotland perhaps as they are in Ireland relatively. The chief crop to be taken account of in a complete comparison would be permanent pasture, and I am bound to say that, having looked into the matter a little, the produce of agriculture in Great Britain is evidently much greater any way you take it than the produce of agriculture in Ireland very, very much greater.

8211. I am put upon that train of thought by an article of yours on the progress of the working classes, and perhaps you will let me read you an extract from it. "The rise in the remuneration of labour in Ireland in the last 50 years is one of the facts which has been conspicuously brought before the public of late. In no other way is it possible to account for the stationariness of rents in Ireland for a long period, notwithstanding the great rise in the prices of cattle and dairy produce which Ireland produces, and which it has been contended would have justified a rise in rents. The farmer and the labourer together have, in fact, had all the benefit of the rise in agricultural prices"?—I do not quite see the bearing of Lord Welby's question, it is quite possible all you have read to me in that passage is true, but what I have said elsewhere is true; there is no inconsistency.

8212. I rather gathered that you were basing your comparison on the fact that in Ireland Death Duties approach much more nearly to the capital value of the land than they do in England, thereby giving the idea that land in Ireland is worth much less than land in England. When I turn to the only official documents to which I can go, namely, the returns made by the Board of Trade in the Statistical Abstract, I find that the produce of land in Ireland is as large, and as I read the figures, larger than in England. Therefore, as far the value of the land is at least equal. If the taxable value of the land as ascertained by the Death Duties is reduced so much less in Ireland than in England, then the difference must, upon the train of thought suggested to me by that extract from your article, be in the hands of the farmer?—If I may make the remark, my comparison was not about land specially, but between property liable to Succession Duty and property liable to Probate Duty. What I pointed out was evidence to show that as regards Succession duty, whatever the property may be which is subject to it in Ireland, you get a much closer approximation to the total value of that property passing on death than you do in England. As regards all other property, you get hold of it in the Probate Duty, where the mode of levying is exactly the same in both countries.

8213. (*Lord Farrer.*) Are not you making a confusion between the total value of the landlord's interest in the property and the total value of the property?—No, I am taking the total value of the property liable to succession duty in one case and liable to succession duty in the other.

8214. What is the reason why the landlord's interest in the property is worth a smaller number of years' rental in Ireland than in England?—That may be a totally different question. I do not believe it is that it is because the tenant has an interest, but I think we should confine ourselves to the subject, because that is not material to the question of the comparison which I put before you. You have two heads of property, one is liable to succession duty and the other is liable to probate duty. I point out that as far as succession duty is concerned, the mode of valuing the property passing at death gives you in one country a closer approximation to the real value of the property than it does in the other. Therefore, so far as that property is concerned, in comparing Ireland with Great Britain you must assume that you have got a larger figure relatively than you have in Great Britain. As regards all other property, including the tenant's interest, whatever it is, you have got the probate duty figures.

8215. Do you assume that the landlord's interest is the whole interest in the land?—I do not. I merely took the succession duty—the property liable to succession duty, whatever it is, because the two things cover all the property—the one is the succession duty and the other is the probate duty, the probate duty is on the same basis in both; the succession duty, by the nature of it, is not on the same basis in both—that is all.

8216. (*Lord Welby.*) It must be charged on the land?—I have nothing to do with that—for the purpose of this comparison that is quite immaterial.

8217. I cannot follow you really?—But it is quite simple, you take the two figures to compare the total property in the two countries; one figure as regards certain property—the probate duty is on the same basis in both; the other figure, the succession duty, is not on the same basis, because in the one country the mode of assessment gives you a figure which approximates much more nearly to the actual value of the property passing than it does in the other.

8218. Then I say that that land pays less under the head of death duties, to the State, than the land in England?—Because it is worth less.

8219. Is it?—Whatever the reason may be, so far as it is liable to succession duty it is worth less.

8220. (*Mr. Sexton.*) It cannot be attributed to the interest in the tenant, because the disparity in the prices of land in Ireland and England existed before the tenant was allowed to have any legal interest?—I think there is some misunderstanding on Lord Welby's part as to the effect of the comparison.

8221. (*The O'Conor Don.*) You are using the comparison, are you not, simply as a test?—I am not comparing the value of land in England and Ireland; I am merely comparing the value of property subject to succession duty, which includes a great deal which is not land.

8222. I am merely taking the official figures?—But I am dealing with the whole property in Ireland, part of it is covered by probate duty and part by succession duty. The probate duty in Ireland and Great Britain is on absolutely the same basis; the succession duty is not; but the whole property in both countries is covered.

8223. (*Lord Farrer.*) What you say is, that in Ireland the interest of the landlord in the property approaches much more nearly to the valuation of the succession duty than it does in England?—No, I say the life interest of the successor to real property in Ireland subject to succession duty approaches more nearly the total value of the property belonging to the successor than it does in England.

8224. The total value of the property belonging to the successor?—Yes.

8225. Because the number of years' purchase in Ireland is less than in England?—That is so.

8226. But that does not exclude the whole property, does it, that excludes the successor's interest in the property?—The assessment for the succession duty is of the interest of the successor, and in Ireland the interest of the successor, in consequence of the mode of assessment, approximates more closely to the total value of the property passing to the successor than it does in Great Britain.

8227. Taking him to be a tenant in fee, it approaches more nearly to the value of his interest, but why is that?—I do not quite follow the question which you are putting now.

8228. Is it not because someone else, the tenant, has a larger share of the whole interest in the property?—Not at all. I am merely dealing with the ownership of the property, and to the extent that it is owned.

8229. But it is the property you have to consider, not the ownership, is it not?—It is the property liable to succession duty which we are dealing with, if there is any other property it is dealt with in the probate duty.

8230. (*Mr. Sexton.*) Any interest of the tenant is in the probate, is it?—Yes, you get both the probate and the succession duty, covering the whole property; the probate duty in both countries is on the same basis; the succession duty, in effect, is not on the same basis, because it gives you a figure more closely approximating to the total value of the property in Ireland than it does in Great Britain.

8231. (*Mr. Blake.*) As I understand, the tenant's interest comes in under the probate duty, does it not?—It would.

8232. And the landlord's under the succession duty?—Yes.

F 2

Sir Robert Giffen, K.C.B.

1 May 1896.

Death duties.

8832 So that when you put both the duties together, you have the whole interest in the property?—That is the view I take, and then, I say, that by the mode of assessing the succession duty, you get a figure which approximates more closely to the total value of that property in Ireland than the corresponding figures in Great Britain, and I do not see that any of the matters raised by Lord Welby have any relation to the point at all.

8833 (Mr Sexton.) You have shown that it is nearly about double in Ireland to what it is in England, have you not?—I do not think I went into that in detail. I gave merely a hypothetical illustration.

8834 (Lord Welby.) I rather demur to your way of putting it, in which you speak of making a comparison of the death duties, as not a fair test of comparison?—I like always to understand the nature of an objection, and I do not understand Lord Welby's objection at all; I do not understand it in the least degree.

8835 In the same way I am unable to understand Dr. Giffen's argument.

Material progress of Ireland.

8836 Do you think, on the whole, Ireland is advancing in prosperity?—If you take long periods for comparison the people in Ireland are generally better off than they were 50 years ago.

8837 Taking the death duties, I observe, in 1838, the property passing under probate was in round figures 4,500,000*l*., and now it is 8,460,000*l*., is it not?—Just so.

8838 Does not that show very material progress, especially when we recollect that that large increase is shared amongst a reduced population?—I have no doubt there has been large progress in Ireland during that time; everybody acquainted with Ireland says the same thing, and the figures no doubt say so.

8839 Shall we be agreed that consumption of articles is one of the best tests of the material wellbeing of a people?—Yes, the consumption of all articles put together.

8840 And that there has been a very considerable increase now, taking a lengthened period, of articles of consumption?—I have no doubt that would be so; there would be some difficulty in establishing what the figures were at the beginning, I should think.

8841 I am basing myself again on a statement of yours as to the progress of working classes, because I have another extract of yours with which I so much agree that I shall read it to you. You give a table, and you say, "This wonderful table speaks for itself. Rice, tea, sugar, tobacco, spirits, wine, malt, all, coffee only excepted, tell a clear tale. The increase in tea and sugar (153 lbs. to 436 lbs.) appear specially significant, the consumption being now four times in round figures what it was 40 years ago. There could be no better evidence of diffused material well-being among the masses. The articles are not such that the increased consumption of the rich would have made much difference. It is the consumption, emphatically, of the poor man which is here in question"?—Of course, I am speaking of the United Kingdom there. What I said was, there would be a difficulty in establishing figures for Ireland specially.

8842 I say you take tea, which is very nearly at the same rate of consumption as in England. We should be so far agreed, should we not (because, I think, the tendency of evidence has rather deserved to limit, that Ireland has shared in the increase of material well-being of the United Kingdom?—I have never said anything to the contrary. Ireland has shared, to some extent, in the general advance.

8843 I did not mean to say that you had said anything to the contrary; I wanted to see whether we were agreed upon that point?—There is no doubt that Ireland has made a great advance.

8844 (Chairman.) I should like to ask you one or two questions upon a point which has been brought before us in the evidence of the late Mr Chalmers Smith. Mr Chalmers Smith, I am sorry to hear, died soon after he gave his evidence, and very material evidence it was. At the Board of Trade you know a good deal about railway matters, I believe?—Yes.

Railways in Ireland; suggested reductions.

8845 I am not going to ask you any detailed questions, but if you have read Mr Chalmers Smith's evidence by any chance, you will know that he proposes and argues, as one of the best means of meeting what he considered the excessive burden of Ireland as compared with Great Britain, not purchasing the railways, as has been proposed several times, but an arrangement whereby out of Government resources there might be made a great reduction in rates and fares. You at the Board of Trade will know the bearings of that question. Speaking generally, have you anything to say to us upon that evidence?—If I saw Mr. Chalmers Smith's evidence I could answer you. I do not recollect what he said specially upon that head, but there is no doubt that a reduction of rates and fares would be of great benefit to Ireland, and would be a particular form of benefit that would be as good as, and perhaps better than, many of the other forms of remission of taxation—that it would help the trade of Ireland, and be of benefit.

Sir Robert Giffen, K.C.B.

1 May 1896.

[illegible]

8846 My other question is this. From your Board of Trade experience, do you think there would be any practical difficulty in ensuring such a great reduction of rates and fares, which the companies ought to be compensated for in some shape or other from public resources?—That would be a question more for the Treasury than the Board of Trade, I should think, but it would be quite easy to arrange in some way that the railway companies should get some benefit.

8847 And that the passenger rate and fares should be greatly reduced at the cost of the Executive Government. I do not ask you for any details as to the financial operations which would be necessary, but as a matter of business with which in connection with railways you are so familiar at the Board of Trade, do you see any practical difficulty in carrying out Mr Chalmers Smith's proposal?—Nothing, except the practical difficulty of the State making advances to particular joint-stock companies, which is always a serious difficulty, and involves many important questions.

8848 It would be more than advances, it would be payments practically, which would have to be secured in some way?—I think the time has almost passed now, but there were schemes suggested some years ago, if I recollect rightly, by which the State was to assume the liabilities of the railway companies, borrow the money at a less rate of interest itself, and use the difference in some such way as you have mentioned now. There is no doubt, in some form or other, the thing could be done.

8849 I have carefully avoided asking you anything upon that point, because it has been the subject of such very close consideration and report, both by commissions and committees, if I remember rightly. What I wanted to get your opinion upon was the practicability of doing something short of the purchase of the railways by the State, and of dispossessing companies, I should hope, as conditions of efficiency for the compulsory reduction of rates and fares?—I think something could be done, but I should be much more in favour of the purchase out and out of the railways, and their administration by the State, in a country like Ireland.

8850 So I should think many would be, but the operation would be a very difficult one, and one which practically has met with great objection from former inquiries, has it not?—I remember taking a great interest in the subject at the time of some of those inquiries, and I think it was a misfortune, on the whole, that the decision finally come to was adverse to the purchase of railways in Ireland.

8851 (Mr Sexton.) If it were once done, it would be rather, would it not, to much less difficulty afterwards than the administration of a system of advances or payments to joint stock companies?—Perhaps that would be so. I think, on the whole, the administration of the railways by the State in Ireland would give you more benefits than any other mode of treating the railways.

Canal [illegible]

8852 (Chairman.) There is one other question which I am specially address to you, because I know you have taken great interest in it. There have been schemes, have there not, for tunnels across the narrow passage between Ireland and Scotland?—Yes.

8853 Do you consider that these schemes, so far as you know of them at the Board of Trade, have an element of practicability in them?—Speaking for myself, I should think that they have an element of practicability, and it would be eminently to the interests of the communication of Great Britain and Ireland that they should be taken up by the State, and pushed forward irrespective of any question of profit or loss upon the undertaking, the political advantages are very great, and although you might not be able to been beforehand to capitalists that a profit would be likely to arise, yet the State might have great confidence that, directly or indirectly, the result would be beneficial to it. I think I should say that my attention was very much attracted to the subject at the time of the discussions about the proposed tunnel between England and France—the Channel tunnel, and I gave evidence before the Joint Committee on that subject as to the commercial advantages which the making of that tunnel would have. It seems to me that, although the commercial advantages might not be so great in some respects between Great Britain and Ireland, yet looking at the immense trade between the two countries, and the possibilities of developing mutual traffic, and extending the residence in Ireland of people living in Great Britain, the effect of making a tunnel between Great Britain and Ireland would really be enormous in its commercial advantages, apart from all the political advantages that we might expect to follow.

9314. Do you happen to have read the Reports of the engineers which have been made on the subject?—As to the practicability?

9315. Yes?—My attention has not been given so much to that part of the matter, because it seems to me that is a question much more for engineers, but I have no doubt that in some form or other engineering skill would be equal to the making of a tunnel between Great Britain and Ireland.

9316. But assuming that it was not impracticable, and that the burden of making such a tunnel did not fall entirely, if at all, upon Ireland, do you conceive that a great benefit would be gained by the Irish people, if communication with the mainland of Great Britain were given to Ireland?—I think the benefits would be very great indeed, that it would lead to a kind of close intercommunication between Ireland and Great Britain, that is prevented, to some extent, by the sea passage, which is not so pleasant to every person as the tunnel would be.

9317. And for commercial purposes, what do you say?—For commercial purposes the facility of transferring goods without breaking bulk would be very great indeed, and I think it would lead to a much greater portion of the passenger traffic between this country and America coming through Ireland than what takes place now by way of Queenstown, which would be a very important matter.

The witness withdrew.

Sir R. Giffen's evidence is continued at Question 11,[illegible] (Twenty-Seventh Day).

TWENTY-FIRST DAY.

Thursday, 23rd May 1895.

At Committee Room B, House of Lords.

PRESENT:

THE RIGHT HON. HUGH C. E. CHILDERS, *Chairman.*

LORD FARRER.	THE HON. EDWARD BLAKE, M.P.
LORD WELBY.	THOMAS SEXTON, ESQ., M.P.
The Right Hon. THE O'CONOR DON.	GERALD W. WOLFF, ESQ., M.P.
Sir DAVID BARBOUR, K.C.S.I.	HENRY F. SLATTERY, ESQ.

Mr. B. H. HOLLAND, *Secretary.*

Mr. THOMAS LOUGH, M.P., called and examined.

Mr. T. Lough, M.P. — 23 May 1895. — Taxation of Ireland in 1794 and 1894 compared.

9318. (*Chairman.*) You are a member of Parliament, are you not?—Yes.

9319. Will you tell us what your connexion with Ireland is?—I am an Ulster man, and I spent the first half of my life in Ireland. Since then I have lived in London, but I have paid a great deal of attention to Ireland. I go over two or three times every year, and have spent my time always when there, during the last 25 years, in the south of Ulster, in the rural districts. I have given a great deal of thought to the questions of the political economy, so to speak, of those parts of Ireland.

9320. Your evidence would therefore chiefly be as to rural Ireland?—Yes; in fact, strictly speaking, it would be confined to rural Ireland. The counties I know best are Cavan, Monaghan and Fermanagh, three counties in the south of Ulster.

9321. You wish to draw attention, I understand from your paper, to the taxation of Ireland to-day compared with what it was 100 years ago, and to indicate whether there is anything in the condition of the country to justify the great changes which have taken place as to taxation?—Yes, that was the first point I wanted to draw attention to. I have taken the year 1794 to compare with 1894, because 1794 seems to me to have been the last normal year we had in Ireland before the union.

9322. (*Lord Welby.*) That is before the French war broke out?—Practically before the French war broke out, and before the union with England.

9323. (*Lord Farrer.*) Was that before the expenses of the revolution?—Yes. I wanted to avoid the expenses of the revolution, and any abnormal expenses. I have prepared the following table:—

Year.	Population.	Taxes.	Per Head.	Income.	Annual Income per Head.	Tax per £ of Income.
		£		£	£	
1794	[illegible]	[illegible]	[illegible]	[illegible]	[illegible]	[illegible]
1894	[illegible]	[illegible]	[illegible]	[illegible]	[illegible]	[illegible]

I find that the population then, according to the tables which have been submitted to the Commission, was just a little under what it is now. The figures are mentioned in my heads of evidence, 4,[illegible]; now it is about 4,600,000, so that the population was about the same in 1894 as in 1794. Then coming to the taxes, I include a rough amount, 500,000*l.*, for local taxation. I take that because I find that the local taxation amounted in 1834 to 700,000*l.*; therefore I think 500,000*l.* is an outside figure to assume that the local taxes may have come to in 1794. I include those because I want to bring before the Commission what the peasants have to furnish altogether, and local taxation is just as onerous upon them as Imperial taxation. I include them also because the people have very incomplete control over local taxation. In one sense local taxation is as much fixed by Parliament as Im-

Mr. T. Lough, M.P. 22 May 1895.

Taxation of Ireland in 1791 and 1894 compared.

parial taxation—the machinery under which local taxation are levied, such as the Poor Law, is fixed here in Westminster; therefore I think Parliament is nearly as much responsible for the local taxation as it is for the imperial taxation, therefore I include both at both periods. The amount in 1791 was a little under 2,000,000l., and the amount in 1894, 11 millions and a quarter. That is an average per head of the population in 1791 of 8s. 9d., and in 1894 of about 49s. That seems to me to be an extraordinary increase in the amount, and I do not think it ought to take place in a country unless two conditions exist there, one is that the country is growing richer, so that it can afford to pay the heavier amount of taxation, and the other that the country wanted the institutions for which the taxation was levied.

8264. (*Lord Farrer.*) Are these figures taken from Sir Edward Hamilton's memorandum?—Yes, they are.

8265. (*Lord Welby.*) Not the capital?—No; I have not mentioned the capital yet. If you will allow me I will deal with that presently.

8266. (*Chairman.*) You are dealing now with the taxes local and imperial together?—Yes, and I have taken them from Sir Edward Hamilton's table, which he furnished as the best table he can give of the amount paid by Ireland.

8267. (*Lord Farrer.*) I only want to know for this reason. You are taking the figures as given by Sir Edward Hamilton, you are not criticising them?—Not in the least; I do not want to criticise any figures. I will accept them.

Increase [illegible] of Ireland [illegible]

8268. (*Mr. Sexton.*) You have taken what the Treasury calls the true revenue, have you not?—The true revenue, not the amount which may be collected in Ireland, but the true revenue. As I was saying, in a country where such a great increase in taxation takes place, it seems to me there ought to be some proof that the country was getting richer, so that it could afford it, and that the institutions for which the taxation is granted are required. It seems to me that neither of these two things existed in Ireland. I do not think the country has got richer. I think it is poorer, and I do not think the institutions on which the taxation is spent are required to any considerable extent in Ireland, if at all. The first reason that I suggest for this taxation having gone on is that the question has not been looked at, especially during the last half century, from an Irish standpoint, but that it has been looked at from a British standpoint. We in Great Britain have been engaged in our own concerns, which are engrossing and interesting, and the country has been taxed quite irrespective of what Ireland can pay or what Ireland might require. Then I want to make another suggestion about a reason with regard to Belfast. Belfast is perhaps about the most advanced place in Ireland. It is looked at as the one success in Ireland, and of course we are all proud of Belfast, but it seems to me that it throws no light on the problem as to the 32 rural counties of Ireland. Belfast is a manufacturing city that happens to be situate in the north of Ireland, and the extent to which its progress is confined to itself is illustrated by the fact that the two counties in which Belfast is situated have diminished, including Belfast, in population during the last 50 years. In 1841 the population of the two counties, including the city, was 782,221. In 1891, notwithstanding the growth of the city, the population had fallen to 694,251. It seems to me also that early in the century the Irish problem was much better understood in Great Britain, because Ireland then was much like Great Britain, no change had taken place, and there was a great deal of information obtained as to the conditions of rural Ireland of a kind that does not interest the people of Great Britain now. I want just to mention as authority for the statement I am making that there were surveys, as they are called, made of each agricultural county. I have brought one of my own county, Cavan, for the year 1802. Then there was an inquiry made into every parish in Ireland by Mr. Mason, and there were [illegible] on these [illegible], particularly Wakefield's in 1811. In these we get a description of Ireland which seems to me to be unanswerable, and which shows that there was a great deal of prosperity in the rural districts then such as does not exist now.

8269. Speaking broadly, do you say that Ireland was self-supporting early in the century?—Yes. If the Commission will allow me, I want to read two very short paragraphs as a description of the rural parts in 1802, and I may say that I have looked through all these books, and I give the two sentences I am going to trouble the Commission with, as types perfectly average of the County Cavan and most of the rural districts. "The farms range from 5 to 50 acres, very "few of them exceed 50 acres, but on all these "farms are one or more cottiers who are bound to "work, not in the fields, but at the loom for a regular "day's hire, according to agreement." "The farmer, or "the employer, who is more commonly called the manufacturer, lives well and has a good profit from the "industry of his cottiers. A pig, a small lot of flax, "and a calf pay his rent, for these people hold their land "on very easy terms; a manufacturer who is able to "work four looms in his own house and employ his "cottiers, soon acquires a comfortable independence." That, I think, is a fair description of a farmer at that time.

8270. (*Lord Farrer.*) Was that in the neighbourhood of Belfast?—No; it was far away from Belfast, in the County Cavan—this is the statistical survey of my own County. I want to read one other sentence as to the domestic economy. "The men are principally employed "in husbandry, though some few manufacture linen. "The women and children spin both yarn and wool. "Their markets are distant and discouraging; labour "may average 7d. per day through the year, but they "have everything cheap, provisions in abundance, and "turf quite convenient, and only for the cost of cutting. "Clothing is mostly furnished at home, so that their "expenditure is trifling if their incomes are small. In "fact they rely on themselves chiefly for their necessaries, and are in a great degree independent and "confined to their own counties. Few are without "a cow, and the greater proportion have two or three "cows."

8271. (*Lord Welby.*) Are you reading from Wakefield?—No, that is one of these county surveys. This is a book published by the Royal Dublin Society by Sir Charles Coote, Baronet, a description of the County Cavan, which afterwards, as I show, is one of the poorest counties in Ireland to-day, and I read those sentences as a fair type of what it was then.

8272. (*Chairman.*) Comparing the state of Ireland then with its state now, what would you say?—It seems to me that for about 20 years after 1791, there was fair progress made in Ireland till Waterloo, but from Waterloo to the time of the famine, progress was slower, elements of prosperity were not entirely destroyed but after the time of the famine the agricultural classes have suffered severely. For the last half century rural Ireland seems to have been a failure, and it is a strange coincidence that in the time of greatest prosperity the taxes were very light, and in the time of greatest distress they have become very heavy.

8273. (*Lord Farrer.*) Were they very heavy during the French war, prior to the amalgamation of the Exchequers?—The revenue went up considerably during the first 15 years of the century, but there was great progress in Ireland during those 15 years, most remarkable progress. I shall illustrate that a little more as I go on.

8274. (*Lord Welby.*) You said, first of all, that taxes went up, and I think you corrected yourself and said the revenue. Do you mean to draw a distinction between the two? Did you mean by altering the words to imply that taxes had not gone up?—No, the taxes did go up. I used both words in the same sense.

8275. (*Mr. Sexton.*) I suppose you are aware that, comparing what you call the normal year of 1791 with the years immediately before Waterloo, that the taxation of Ireland trebled?—Yes, I remember that it went up very considerably.

8276. (*Sir David Barbour.*) And nevertheless the prosperity continued?—The prosperity continued very much up to Waterloo. I think that is undoubted, notwithstanding the increase of taxation. Without going into great detail, I think that the prosperity of European agriculture then was great owing to there being no competition from abroad. Now every competition has arisen, and there is very little increase of production, or improvement in the method of agriculture. So I think that a survey of agriculture tends to show that the wealth is not so great now as it was in the beginning of the century. Then I turn to manufactures, and, speaking broadly, it seems to me that all these industries have been extinguished, and there is only the manufacture of linen, stout and whisky.

and perhaps a little shipbuilding worth mentioning now.

8277. (*Lord Farrer.*) When you speak of the manufactures, are you referring to the domestic manufactures you spoke of just now?—I am referring to them also—all sorts of manufactures. In 1794, everything the people used was made in Ireland—hardware, plate, cutlery, clothes, boots, hats, agricultural implements, furniture; but now all are imported. All the food of the people and the cattle was produced at home, and after feeding the population, much flour, grain, and meal was exported. Now, all flour is imported, and the oil cake and feeding stuffs are imported, and Indian meal and American bacon brought in to replace Irish meal and bacon, which is either not produced or else exported, and which would be much better food for the people. The corn mills, which were once great sources of wealth, are now silent in every part of Ireland. There are 17 in Clonmel alone, on the Suir; but in the County Cavan there is a splendid mill at every village which has been closed during the last quarter of a century.

8278. What evidence have you that hardware, plate, and cutlery were made in Ireland?—I can give you detailed evidence on all those points.

8279. You have looked into that, have you?—Yes; there was a great manufacture carried on in Dublin and in other parts. If you wish for any details upon that point I can give you them. The another sort of loss point, as compared with then, is the great increase of absenteeism. That, of course, commenced when the Parliament was removed. There was large expenditure before the union in Dublin every season. I have heard that put at very high figures, and the country mansions were all maintained on an extravagant scale. That absenteeism has gone on increasing all through the century, and the last 25 years seems to me to have cleared every person out of my district who could possibly go; that is since the disestablishment of the Church, which gave the final blow with regard to people who could get away remaining any longer in Ireland.

8280. (*Mr Sexton.*) Why?—There is not the attraction to people who are connected with the Church on the Society in our three counties, and it is a very noticeable feature which exists pretty well all over Ireland. I could mention houses within a circuit of two or three miles which have been closed. The tithes in the district used to amount to something like 1,800*l.* or 2,000*l.* a year, and they were enjoyed by a few resident and spent locally up to 1869. Now the tithes are levied, but are taken into a central fund and wasted to a great extent. That has increased absenteeism.

8281. Why did the local landlords go away? They could not escape the tithe by going away too, because the clergyman was no longer a State functionary?—No. There was no society or attraction. I was not going into the question of why. I was only speaking of my own knowledge that they have gone away, and that therefore there is a great decrease in local expenditure and employment.

8282. (*Sir David Barbour.*) And the rents have fallen—is that one of the reasons?—Rents have fallen somewhat.

8283. (*Lord Welby.*) You do not mean that merely the clergy have gone away, but that the well-to-do people who supported the church have gone away because the clergy are no longer established?—Yes. Well-to-do people of all kinds have gone away. I think it is generally assumed that absenteeism took place, say, at the beginning of the century or half a century ago. So far as my experience goes I can point to many cases around me where it seems to have developed very much in the last 20 or 25 years in Ireland. Then the last point upon that I wanted to put was that the population in country places was a good deal larger in 1794 than in 1894. There were only 70,000 people in Belfast then. Now there are 300,000 people there. Dublin has increased greatly, and therefore I think the country population must have been 4,000,000 in 1794, and it is placed now at about 3,400,000. So that that is a proof also that there was more employment for people in the country then than now. I want to read one other extract from the book I have already referred to, of 1802, illustrating how the towns have gone down. That is as to a village near my own home, but I could quote a hundred; it seems to me to be more or less true of every country town in Ireland, especially in the south, the west, and the centre. This is a description of Killeshandra at the end of last century: "The population is yet very considerable, and the linen "manufacture more engaged in, and much encouraged "by the market at Killeshandra, where coarse linens "are purchased every week to the average value of "1,200*l.* The appearance of this town is engaging, "being neat and clean, and industry and its rewards "are very conspicuous, everything appears comfortable, a good market house and a brick hotel." Now it is one of the most squalid places you would find in Christendom, there is no trade of any kind. There have been some of those houses which have been described as second-class houses built in Killeshandra, but they are fearful structures, and the whole town is in a terrible state, and, generally speaking, in the counties I am referring to, the towns have decayed and are in a decaying condition at present. You will see ruins of houses in main streets and very few windows in prosperity.

8284. (*Sir David Barbour.*) Do you say that that prosperity was due to domestic manufacture?—I was really only troubling with the fact that it existed then, and does not exist now. I think we may conclude that the domestic manufacture helped it very much.

8285. But you do not think a reduction of taxation would bring back that domestic manufacture, do you?—Certainly, that is my argument. I think it is the chief thing to restore it.

8286. (*Chairman.*) Speaking generally, how would you compare the state of things in this respect between 1794 and 1894?—That the wealth of Ireland was greater in 1794 than in 1894, but that the taxation has increased greatly notwithstanding the increasing poverty. That is the conclusion I arrived at on the facts I have stated. I have left out one point, the point of the capital of the country. A member of the Commission referred to it a moment ago. I have been giving the facts that have struck myself as to that comparison, but it is a remarkable thing that in Mr Giffen's book, which I suppose is the best authority we have about the wealth of these countries at the beginning of the century, and, in fact, at various periods, we find a calculation made by Colquhoun in 1812, who devoted a great deal of attention to the subject, which places the capital of Ireland at 351,000,000*l.* I think that, probably, was a hundred millions higher than it would have been in 1794. But it has not been suggested to the Commission that it is now more than 347,000,000*l.*, and I believe Mr. Giffen puts it at an extreme figure of 400,000,000*l.*, so that this calculation made by quite independent authorities in England lends colour to my general argument, which is, that Ireland is poorer to-day than it was 100 years ago.

8287. And more heavily taxed?—And six times as heavily taxed.

8288. (*Mr Sexton.*) The capital is probably from 100,000,000*l.* to 150,000,000*l.* sterling less than it was at the beginning of the century?—Yes, and those are not my figures.

8289. (*Lord Welby.*) Do you happen to know whether Mr Colquhoun gives any data?—Yes, he does, elaborate data; it is here, and I have brought the book.

8290. Is it criticised by Mr Giffen?—Yes, it is criticised by Mr Giffen, and highly spoken of. Mr Giffen says as regards England he is roughly right.

8291. (*Mr Sexton.*) As regards Ireland, does Mr Giffen, in regard to the year 1812, see any cause for dissenting from those figures?—He sees no cause for dissent, and that is an extraordinary support, you may say, to my own conclusions obtained by a study of the localities.

8292. (*Chairman.*) Passing from Ireland to Great Britain for a moment, what was the comparative state of things during that 100 years?—Turning to Great Britain I have taken the year 1800, because I have been able to get accurate figures for 1800—they are the figures which have been submitted to the Commission—and 1894. First as to population; the population of Great Britain was 10,500,000 in 1800; in 1894 it was 34,000,000. The revenue (again including local taxation) amounted in 1800 to 36,000,000*l.* I have taken the local taxes for the year 1803, but I think that is nearly accurate. In 1894 it was 117,000,000*l.* The taxation per head in Great Britain itself was 70*s.*, and in 1894 it was 69*s.* Going on with the rest of my table, which is quoted from the same authority as I have already mentioned, the capital was

		£	£ s. d.			£
Great Britain, [illegible]	[illegible]	[illegible]	[illegible]	[illegible]	[illegible]	[illegible]
„ [illegible]	[illegible]	[illegible]	[illegible]	[illegible]	[illegible]	[illegible]

We thus see that in all respects the greatest contrast exists between Ireland and Great Britain. In Ireland the taxation is six times greater; in Great Britain it is [illegible] times greater. In Ireland the population has not increased. In England it is [illegible] times greater. In Ireland the wealth has not increased, in Great Britain it is eight times greater. In Ireland the increase of taxation per head is [illegible] per cent. In Great Britain it has declined—there is no increase.

[illegible] (*Chairman.*) That is comparing the [illegible] years of Ireland with the 95 years of Great Britain?—Yes.

[illegible] Then going into the figures Sir Edward Hamilton has given us, how would you sum those up?—Sir Edward Hamilton has given us a contrast between [illegible] and [illegible], which is really almost as startling as the contrast we got for the period I have already given. According to Sir Edward Hamilton, the indirect taxes in Great Britain fell from [illegible] to [illegible], but in Ireland they rose from [illegible] to [illegible] per head in the two periods mentioned. The direct taxes fell in Great Britain from [illegible] to [illegible], and they rose in Ireland from [illegible] to [illegible] per head.

[illegible] (*Mr. [illegible]*) You have given the figure of [illegible] for Great Britain, but it appears to be [illegible] from the return. Have you the return before you?—I have not.

[illegible] Look at it and see if it corrects your figure. Compare the indirect taxes for Great Britain—what are they in the return?—The indirect taxes are given in the return as [illegible].

[illegible] Now look at your paper?—I have [illegible], that must be a misprint.

[illegible] Then it is [illegible], as compared with [illegible]?—Yes; rather a serious difference. Let me quote it from the return. They fell from [illegible] to [illegible]. The printer has misplaced the figures. In Ireland they rose from [illegible] to [illegible]—that is the indirect taxes. The total revenue in Great Britain fell from [illegible] to [illegible], but in Ireland the total revenue rose from [illegible] to [illegible]. I think the same remark applies to these two periods, namely, that that country was richer in [illegible] than in [illegible].

[illegible] Of course it is important to remember that these figures which you have taken for [illegible], and also for [illegible], are the figures which the Treasury after adjustment declare to be the true revenue?—That is so.

[illegible] (*Chairman.*) How do you sum up the comparison of these figures?—I think they give a fair picture of the great progress which has taken place in Great Britain, and which is still proceeding, and which may be summarised by saying that the increase in local and imperial taxation there by no means equals the growth of the people in population or in wealth, so that the relative burdens of the people have diminished and the general standard of efficiency is greatly raised. That is how I sum it up as regards Great Britain.

[illegible] Will you indicate what, in your opinion, is the reason why Irish taxation has so much increased?—Yes, I desire to go into one or two points upon that in a little detail. It seems to me that the first reason is that the subject has been looked at, owing to the enormous interest of the British [illegible], exclusively from the British standpoint, and I will give two examples. The first example is the year [illegible], when the duty was taken off corn. It will be remembered that the agitation arose in English manufacturing centres and that it benefited them, I suppose, will be admitted, without raising any debateable point, more than it could benefit purely agricultural districts. The whole discussion of the subject was from the standpoint of the crowded centres of population in England.

[illegible] (*Lord Farrer.*) That was so with regard to the general agitation, but with regard to the immediate occasion and cause of Sir Robert Peel's action, it was the failure of the potato crop, was it not?—I cannot tell. I believe he attributed it to that, but the actual effect did not help the poor people who were starving. The effect was quite different. Little advantage came to the starving Irish, for prices rose in 1847 and did not fall materially till [illegible] and [illegible], and they rose again during the Crimean War. The disastrous effect on Ireland arose gradually, but grew permanent and terrible in the destruction of her great market for grain through the opening of the ports to foreign wheat, flour, and meal. Before [illegible] it is difficult to obtain reliable figures. Since that time the tables furnished by Dr. Grimshaw show how the home trade fell off. The export trade was extinguished altogether.

[illegible] But that would be in favour of those who consumed corn in Ireland, would it not?—Exactly, but that is not what you said a moment ago. You suggested that it was to give the people cheap bread who were starving, and of course if you are to give people cheap bread to preserve them from dying from starvation you must give it them quickly.

[illegible] (*Lord Welby.*) If I recollect rightly, the argument was this, the restrictions on the import of corn at the time the Irish were starving under the famine, were so great that it was necessary at all events to suspend the corn law at once in order to make it possible that the people should live, and I think Sir Robert Peel's argument was, that looking at the state at which the question had arrived in England, it would be impossible, once the Corn Law was suspended, to put it on again. I think that was the line of argument?—My only point is that the argument is probably good enough from the British standpoint, but supposing Sir Robert Peel's object was what you have said, to relieve the Irish, it did not relieve them, because nothing would relieve them, only low prices, and the low prices did not come until the people were dead.

[illegible] (*Sir David Barbour.*) Might not prices have risen still more if the Corn Laws had not been abolished?—I could not answer that.

[illegible] (*Lord Welby.*) That is another way of looking at it. The people would have starved in far greater numbers than unhappily they did?—Quite so.

[illegible] (*Lord Farrer.*) Your general argument is this, is it not, that the repeal of the Corn Laws, however beneficial it may have been to the people of Great Britain, was not equally beneficial to the people of Ireland?—Quite so, and Ireland was not looked at separately to see whether when it was necessary to carry out that policy some adjustment might not have been made in other directions which would have made it fit Ireland better than it has.

[illegible] And although there may have been an immediate necessity for introducing fresh food into Ireland, yet considering that Ireland was an agricultural country, the repeal of the Corn Laws was not so beneficial to Ireland in the long run as it was to England?—In the way it has been carried out it was not. No attempt was made to adjust it to Ireland.

[illegible] (*Sir David Barbour.*) Do I understand you to argue that the Corn Laws ought not to have been repealed as regards Ireland at that time?—No. I do not go that length.

[illegible]	Wheat	Barley, &c.	Oats	Potatoes	[illegible] Crops	Total Crops
	£	£	£	£	£	£
[illegible], 18[illegible]	[illegible]	[illegible]	11,[illegible]	[illegible]	1[illegible]	[illegible]
[illegible], 18[illegible]	[illegible]	1[illegible]	[illegible]	[illegible]	[illegible]	[illegible]

[illegible]. (*Lord Farrer.*) Where are these figures taken from?—They are Dr. Grimshaw's figures, I think they are [illegible] accepted. There are no export figures given, but I believe it is undoubted there was a large export trade from Ireland before the Corn Laws were repealed. After the people had lived on their crops and produce they had a good deal over for export, and now they have to import most of the food on which they live.

[illegible]. I suppose they lived largely on potatoes, and exported their corn?—I think they had more than potatoes; they lived on grain and meal, I think, as well as potatoes. [illegible] used to be nearly as big then as now, but the sheep were eaten at home; now many are exported to England.

[illegible]. (*Mr. Sexton.*) I see these figures of yours are taken [illegible] from Table C of Dr. Grimshaw's return on page [illegible] of the appendix to the Blue Book, and represent the average of the [illegible] produce?—That is so. I think the produce would have been greater if it could have been taken earlier, and Dr. Grimshaw suggests that. I do not think it is easy to realise how much hardship has been produced [illegible] by the direct conversion of the country from a grain-producing to a cattle-growing country. By cattle each acre of land can only produce [illegible] or [illegible] a year. With any grain crops, even at low prices, the produce will be [illegible] or seven times as much.

[illegible]. (*Lord Farrer.*) That has been the case in England, very largely too, has it not?—Quite so. I do not dispute that. Much of what I say would apply to rural England, but they have been able to live by other means in England. They are unable to live [illegible] no other means in Ireland, which makes the difference great. In any part of Ireland it is necessary, if land is to be kept in good order, that a large proportion should be broken up from time to time. This has been neglected in the last century and the result has been a great deterioration in the quality of the land.

[illegible]. (*Chairman.*) Can you mention another critical time when the interests of Ireland were inadequately considered?—Yes, I think in the year 1853, after Sir Robert Peel was dead, we had perhaps a worse example. I think that was the great period when the capacity for considering Ireland disappeared altogether from the English Parliament. In 1853, when the taxation was equalised all over the Kingdom by Mr. Gladstone, the net results of the changes were that during ten years the taxes were increased by [illegible]. (I have taken these facts from the tables) and the payment of [illegible] rose from [illegible] per head in 18[illegible] to [illegible] 7*d.* in 18[illegible]. The [illegible] was gradually raised from [illegible] the gallon to 10*s.* 6*d.*, and the income tax was imposed on Ireland for the first time. The facts are very well described in Sir E. Hamilton's memorandum. The [illegible] of one or two members of Parliament were brushed aside, the main argument being that the wiping out of a bad debt (that was the debt which had been incurred during the famine period) and the adoption of a policy of granting loans would compensate for the amount of [illegible] heavy taxation. That was a reversal of Sir Robert Peel's policy with regard to Ireland, and it appears that Mr. Gladstone would not have done it, only he thought that the [illegible] at any rate would be temporary. This has not proved to be so.

[illegible]. You then proceed to discuss the change in the Whisky duty. Will you state roughly why you think it more oppressive in Ireland than in England?—It was assumed then, and I think it has been accepted ever since, that the severe taxation of whisky is an aid and [illegible] in Ireland as it is in Great Britain. I do not think that such is the case. The manufacture of whisky is a great Irish industry which could not but be unfavourably affected by quadrupling the tax. Probably the most obvious effects were to extinguish local distilleries and to encourage illicit manufacture. In England spirits are not consumed to any great extent, the national drink is beer, which has all along been favoured in the matter of taxation. The habits of the people in the country districts of Ireland favour the consumption of whisky rather than other stimulants.

[illegible]. (*Mr. Sexton.*) And the climate, I suppose?—Yes, and the climate. The lives of the people, the way in which they have to go to fairs and spend their time away from home, and the inadequate means of obtaining refreshments at the places to which they go, all favour the consumption of the stimulant.

[illegible]. The climate is much more humid, is it not, than that of Great Britain?—Yes, as is [illegible] there [illegible] and [illegible] at times.

[illegible]. (*Lord Farrer.*) What is your view of the nature of the injury inflicted on the Irish by the taxation—that they do not get their whisky so cheap?—That is it.

[illegible]. Is it that they want more whisky and that but for the tax they would have more whisky, or is it that but for the tax money would have been saved upon whisky and would have been spent upon other things?—Yes, both seem to me to be the same. Money would have been saved on whisky which they would have been able to spend on clothes.

[illegible]. Whisky is a sort of necessity, is it?—Yes, whisky is a sort of necessity at times [illegible]. I have devoted a good deal of attention to the point. I have had a coffee house opened for 10 years in one of the little towns. That is a well-furnished coffee house on the London model; it is as well patronised as any one of the [illegible] public houses in the town.

[illegible]. (*Mr. Sexton.*) What town?—Ovens, but there are no coffee houses in the other towns where the people congregate; there is no money or enterprise to supply them with more suitable refreshments than whisky; that is the reason, I think, that they require whisky in a way that the English do not require it, and you could not have hit them a more deadly blow than by taxing it.

[illegible]. (*Sir David Barbour.*) You say the increased taxation did not [illegible] sobriety. Do you mean to say the people drink as much as before?—I think they do, per head of the [illegible] population.

[illegible]. Assuming they do drink as much, how is the manufacture destroyed or interfered with?—By the depopulation of the country reducing the number of purchasers, and by the heavy rates and expenses connected with collection, as well as the heavy duty itself.

Mr. T. Lough, M.P. [illegible]

local distilleries have been extinguished. On the point of sobriety, the only way of encouraging sobriety is to develop the well-being of the people. To starve them and stint them as they have been, in my opinion, by these heavy taxes, is the best way to encourage drunkenness and other vices.

6332. (Mr. Sexton.) Of course, where the Legislature levies a constant habit, like the drinking of spirit in Ireland or beer in Great Britain, then they take a tax off the part of the income devoted to the purchase of that article. If the tax were lowered, then the same quantity of the article could be purchased at less expense, and the balance of the tax would remain part of the income of the purchaser?—That is my point.

6333. (Chairman.) Have you looked at it from the point of view that the reduction of the tax increases the tendency to consume, or that the increase of the tax reduces the tendency to consume?—I think the reduction of the tax would develop the well-being of the people, and if that were done they would not resort any more to excess, drunkenness or vices of any kind.

6334. (Lord Farrer.) What that really comes to is, is it not, that a certain amount of whiskey is a necessity for the Irishman, that he must get that, that if he has to pay so much more for it he will pay so much more for it in the shape of taxation, but that if you take off the tax and it becomes cheaper, then the money will very probably go in clothes or food or something that will improve the life of himself, his wife, and his family?—I accept that statement fully with that slight qualification that you have described the state of things now and in the past. But, I think, if there were good coffee houses, such as I have kept in our place, that they might be gradually got to take more civilised substitutes for the coarse bad raw whiskey that they drink. But as things are, I accept your description.

6335. (Sir David Barbour.) I suppose you are aware that experience shows that an increase of prosperity amongst the working classes in England, is immediately followed by an increase in revenue from spirits, beer, and so forth?—I believe that is true, but I do not think that it is relevant to this point, because the working classes in this country are in a far higher state of prosperity than we could get the people in Ireland to for a long time.

6336. (Lord Farrer.) If that were so, ought not the conclusion to be that the more prosperous and the more civilised workmen would be less inclined to excess in spirits, and would apply a larger portion of his income to the other necessaries of life?—It would, if other conditions favoured a development in that line. Now the other conditions are good in Ireland—they have fresh air and that sort of thing. In England, they live in slums, and although they are prosperous there are many temptations.

6337. (Lord Welby.) There has been a habit of speaking as if the whole of the population of England was highly prosperous. You say a number of them live in slums. Have you ever considered what the proportion of the English population is which is not so well to do. Do you know that a very large proportion of the population of England live in extreme poverty and in a worse condition than the people of Ireland?—Yes. I represent one of those constituencies, and I have studied the question all my life.

6338. Then must not we draw some distinction, and do not we fall into error when we lay down that everybody in England is prosperous and everybody in Ireland is poor?—Quite so. Still I think you may look at the question broadly, because the nation is prosperous in England and in Ireland very poor.

6339. With the experience we have of our population in big towns, can we speak of the population of England in a sweeping manner as prosperous, and taking Ireland in the same way, say they are poor?—I think so, and if you will allow me I will come to that point presently, for I make a contrast between the average income of the Irishman engaged in agriculture with the Englishman in a large town.

6340. (Mr. Sexton.) Of course in Great Britain, as in Ireland and every other country, there is a certain portion of the population—in fact, human society is not conceivable, scarcely, without a certain proportion of the population being either destitute or on the verge of destitution, but I suppose you would say there is at least as large a proportion in Ireland as in Great Britain destitute or on the verge of destitution, and that, on the other hand, the bulk of the Irish community is composed of people who are always very poor as compared with the bulk of the community of Great Britain who are often in actual distress?—Yes, there is a far larger section of the people submerged—to use the English word—in Ireland than in England.

6341. (Chairman.) I believe you wish to give other instances of the inability of England to deal with Irish affairs?—I think in almost every instance of taxation since 1853, and I might take notoriously the one in 1894, there is an utter forgetfulness in Parliament of the Irish situation. In 1894 we had the demand to increase the taxes. It arose in London and other great cities where the value of a strong navy is fully realised, but the full proportions of taxes were put on Irishmen as well as a matter of course. There was no separate discussion in Parliament of the possibility of the poor people in Ireland paying those taxes. India is separately discussed. India generally gets one or two days in Parliament for the discussion of her financial position, and there is a very pressing plea made on the ground of the poverty of the Indians. It seems to me that the poverty of the Irish as a nation is far greater than that of the Indians, because the Indians are increasing more rapidly in population than the people of Great Britain, etc., whereas the people in Ireland are being starved out. So I think the feature I mentioned about 1853 has continued down to this moment, and there is never any separate consideration of Ireland as regards taxation.

6342. (Sir David Barbour.) Do you think there is more consideration given to Indian affairs than to those of Ireland?—No. I am speaking of taxation. It is assumed that what suits this country will suit Ireland, which I think is the most false assumption which could possibly be made.

6343. (Chairman.) You wish to indicate another reason for the excessive of taxation, do you not?—Yes, I think there is very little attention paid to local opinion from Ireland. The valuations in Ireland are fixed, and the incidence of taxation to some extent settled by officials appointed from the Treasury, who do not look sympathetically at the local claims, and I think, whether we succeeded the local claims or not, it would be of great advantage to have it stated. These officials consider it their chief business to defend every detail of the system which they have to enforce.

6344. (Lord Farrer.) Are you speaking there of rates or of valuation?—A little of both. The valuation affects the amount the people have to pay—settles the amount.

6345. (Mr. Sexton.) The Valuation Act was passed in 1852, was it not?—Yes.

6346. The income tax was imposed in 1853?—Yes.

6347. And the valuation proceeded up to 1865?—Yes.

6348. (Lord Welby.) The law was passed in 1852. It was not passed with a view to income tax, which was not then dreamt of?—Quite so, but it was passed with regard to other incidents.

6349. But you are speaking of the Treasury, and that brings it into line with Imperial taxation, which was not in contemplation at the time?—Quite so. In England valuations are done to a large extent by local authorities, by people of the localities and paid by the localities. Sometimes there is an agreement—there is particularly now, I believe, in London—or some attempt is being made, to agree between officials who are appointed to act with the local authorities, but in Ireland all was done by a purely central official. Sir Richard Griffith went through Ireland and made his valuation, and he did it fairly, from his standpoint.

6350. He was sent by the Lord Lieutenant purely for Irish purposes; the Treasury had nothing to do with it?—Exactly, but in Cavan they ought to have had a Cavan authority, instead of Sir Richard Griffith, who came down and said Cavan is worth so much, and he did not know much about it.

6351. (Mr. Sexton.) Did not Sir Richard Griffith know that the valuation he made would measure the income tax to be paid by Ireland?—Yes.

6352. (Chairman.) Do you think historically that that was the case?—Yes, I certainly think so, because the valuation was going on after the income tax was imposed.

8353. (*Lord Welby.*) But the regulations under which Sir Richard acted were laid down before the income tax was thought of?—Yes.

8354. I quite acknowledge the valuation was going on after the income tax was imposed, but the law under which the valuation was carried out was passed before the income tax was ever thought of, and the regulations under which Sir Richard acted were drawn up before the income tax was thought of?—Yes, I think it is true up to [illegible].

8355. (*Lord Farrer.*) I think your words perhaps [illegible] what you do not mean. You would not wish to encourage what we have had complaint of in the London County Council—a sympathetic valuation of the rich houses in Marylebone or St. George's—it is a question of exactness, is it not?—It is.

8356. It is a question of which is the more exact and just valuation—not of local sympathy at all?—I think what I said was that the clients of the locality ought to be listened to sympathetically. You may have to decide against it, but there is no harm in having a little sympathy.

8357. (*Mr Sexton.*) The point I urge is that as those Imperial officers knew very well that their valuation would measure the amount to be paid for Imperial tax to the Imperial Exchequer, they would be certain to make a high rather than a low valuation?—Perhaps so.

8358. (*Lord Welby.*) And on the other hand I venture to say that the [illegible] had no connexion whatever with the Treasury, and I can hardly agree that they would have that extreme affection for the Treasury and for the Exchequer as to make them vary their valuation with that view?—Just so.

8359. (*Chairman.*) Can you state the actual increase in Imperial taxation contributed by Ireland from money collected there?—Yes. I submit a table which shows that the Imperial taxation in 1820 was 15s. 3d., and that it decreased to 13s. 2d. in 1840, now it has increased to 1l. 13s. 4d. per head.

TABLE showing the AVERAGE INCREASE per head of the population in the IMPERIAL TAXATION contributed by IRELAND from 1820 to 1894.

Years.	Population.	Taxes.	Per Head.
	£	£	£ s. d.
1820	[illegible]	[illegible]	0 15 3
1830	[illegible]	[illegible]	0 11 9
1840	[illegible]	[illegible]	0 13 9
1850	[illegible]	[illegible]	0 14 9
1860	[illegible]	[illegible]	1 6 7
1870	[illegible]	[illegible]	1 7 5
1880	[illegible]	[illegible]	1 8 2
1890	[illegible]	[illegible]	1 10 3
1894	[illegible]	[illegible]	1 13 4

8360. (*Lord Farrer.*) Is this the true revenue according to Sir Edward Hamilton?—Yes.

8361. (*Chairman.*) Passing to local taxation, you make a similar comparison, do you not?—In local taxation the year we first get is 1826. The amount per head was then 2s. 6d., and it has steadily increased until 1891, when it stands at 13s. 9d. It is increasing now almost every year.

TABLE showing the INCREASE of LOCAL TAXATION per head of the population in IRELAND from 1826 to 1891.

Years.	Amount.	Population.	Per Head.
	£		s. d.
1826	[illegible]	[illegible]	2 6
1841	[illegible]	[illegible]	3 6
1851	[illegible]	[illegible]	7 1
1861	[illegible]	[illegible]	4 6
1871	[illegible]	[illegible]	10 4
1881	[illegible]	[illegible]	10 1
[illegible]	[illegible]	[illegible]	14 10
[illegible]	[illegible]	[illegible]	15 6
1891	[illegible]	[illegible]	13 9

8362. (*Sir David Barbour.*) I suppose as the taxation has increased the people get more for that taxation?—I think not. The people have disappeared, and there seems to be no way of causing institutions to disappear—they stay on.

8363. It is wastefully expended, you think?—It is wastefully expended.

8364. (*Chairman.*) I understand that you wish to suggest some cause for this increase—perhaps you will enlarge upon that?—I am now speaking of local taxation, and I suggest one or two reasons why local taxation has increased so disastrously, as I think. There has been a policy proceeding all through the century of stripping the localities of their public property, and the little sources of revenue that they possessed. It has gone on right on as if the object of Parliament, or whoever the authorities were, was to destroy the public property in Ireland. The first example I quote is in connexion with Municipalities. It will be remembered that instead of passing the Municipal Franchise Acts quickly in 1834, as the British Acts were passed, the Irish Acts were delayed from 1833 to 1841.

8365. There was a difference between the two Houses?—Yes.

8366. (*Mr Sexton.*) A refusal of the House of Lords to pass the Commons' Bills?—Yes, by the time they were passed the property had nearly all disappeared.

8367. (*Lord Farrer.*) Was much parted with between the time of the passing of the Municipal Reform Act in England and the passing of the Irish Act?—I think that a million's worth at least of local property must have disappeared.

8368. (*Lord Welby.*) Who got the money for it?—It disappeared in various ways. I was going to explain the Cavan case.

8369. (*Mr. Sexton.*) Do you mean a million of income?—No; I mean property worth a million. I think that was the object of the delay, to put it plainly—to make away with the property, and as soon as the property was made away with, they let the Act pass, because it conferred nothing on the Irish people but the right to tax themselves.

8370. (*Chairman.*) You would not say it was the parliamentary object, would you?—No. Parliament always meant well.

8371. (*Lord Welby.*) But the Acts were simply delayed, not by any local action, but by the refusal of the House of Lords to pass them?—Quite so.

8372. And the House of Lords were not actuated by any desire to see this property disappear, were they?—They might have sympathy with the Irish landlords who desired delay and who were interested in the disappearance of the property.

8373. (*Mr Sexton.*) At any rate the delay of the House of Lords gave local oligarchy free play during that time with regard to the conversion of property?—That is exactly my point. I wanted to show an example of that, again keeping to my own county, Cavan. I have brought here the old Cavan charter to show how Ireland was treated about 300 years ago when these things were better understood. This charter was given by James I. and then confirmed by James II., and it makes the people of Cavan a corporation for ever, and allows them to build a common hall to be called by the name of the town hall of Cavan, which I believe did get into existence, but even it has disappeared. Then it gives them all the land within a mile of the town—these are the town parks; all those town parks have disappeared, and they are the most highly rented part of Ireland now.

8374. (*Chairman.*) Have they disappeared really?—Yes, they have gone into private hands. They are the most highly rented parts. I believe the "town park" means a park that belonged to the town originally.

8375. (*Mr Sexton.*) To the municipality?—To the municipality, and my argument is that these parks if they had been preserved would have enabled a good many of the town expenses to be paid. We have such towns in England. At Aldeburgh in Suffolk, they have still common lands. The result is they have no rates in the town.

8376. (*Chairman.*) As much as the sea has left?—The sea has left a good deal. I know of a place in Ireland, Belturbet, where a part of the town park remains. They have no rate there. A couple of hundred acres of the land still remains to them. Carrickfergus

Mr. T. Lough, M.P.

10 May 1895.

Loss of local property generally.

I believe, has a little of its town parks left, but such cases are quite exceptional. In Cavan all the lands have been taken away and the market also. The dues of the market were to be the property of the town for ever. I remember when the market was worth 800*l.* a year, but it belonged to the lord of the manor, and even now only 100*l.* a year, or something like that, is contributed by the people who hold the market to the town, and I believe that is all perfectly illegal. But without going into that, my first point is that the alienation of this property has greatly increased local rates.

8577. (*The O'Conor Don.*) In this particular case of Cavan, was the property taken away during those six years which you speak of?—It is hard to put your finger on the time when the property was taken away, and I suggest, as Mr Sexton put it, that the delay of the six years gave facilities for its removal, from which Ireland has suffered a good deal since.

8578. But can you say whether it was taken away before or after those six years?—I cannot quite.

8579. You see it does not support your contention unless you show that it was taken away during those six years?—Certainly, because my contention is simply that the public property as regards these municipalities has disappeared to a large extent in Ireland, and I hold that whoever had charge of Ireland, is responsible for it.

8580. (*Lord Welby.*) Do you mean taken away by the Government?—Not taken directly by the Government, but the Government did not protect it as they ought to have done.

8581. (*Sir David Barbour.*) Were there no local authorities whose duty it was to look after this property, or was it the local authorities who took it themselves?—I think it was the local authorities; I think they got a little of the plunder themselves.

8582. (*Mr. Sexton.*) The old unreformed bodies were of a mere rings, they were not public bodies as we understand them at the present day. They were not representative bodies, were they?—No, they were not representative bodies.

8583. (*The O'Conor Don.*) What is the date of these charters?—This charter was granted in 1613 by James I. and confirmed by James II. in 1688, I believe.

8584. Then that was probably taken away during the existence of the Irish Parliament?—Oh, no. Well, I could not say. Perhaps some of the property was, but I think a good deal of it continued down to the beginning of the century.

8585. You have not made any inquiry, have you, to know when it was taken away?—I have made inquiry, but it is hard to get at absolute proof, which I can state to the Commission. There are old inhabitants who tell me that they remember fields belonging to the town which are now enclosed and have disappeared. There was no attempt made to protect them.

8586. (*Mr. Sexton.*) Do you happen to have heard that in Dublin, for instance, under the old unreformed Corporation, before 1840, that what was at one time a very wealthy city property has almost wholly passed away, and that what is now one of the most populous and fashionable suburbs of Dublin was transferred for a peppercorn rent, or rather the land on which the buildings stand?—I have not gone into any detail as to that, but I am ready to believe it from what I know of my own county. Then the second point I wanted to suggest was, that even in country parishes, bog lands, [illegible] in commons and rivers which the public enjoyed, have gradually been taken possession of for private purposes, and examples are given in the report of the late Land Acts Commission, of how inefficiently Parliament protects the interest of the people in Ireland, and when you take away fields or any means of subsistence from the people, you throw them on the rates, and that tends to account for the great increase of local rates.

8587. (*Sir David Barbour.*) Are there any commons in Ireland?—I think there were a good many. In Mr. Shaw Lefevre's book he defines there were commons, but I think the town parks might be treated as commons, and I have also noticed places that looked like village greens.

Effect of Church Act, 1869, on local funds.

8588. They do not exist now, I suppose?—No, nothing exists now which required protection. Now I come to the great alienation which we can put our finger on, that is the Church Act of 1869. Now as to that, from time immemorial the tithes had been spent locally, and belonged to the parishes. The tithes in my own diocese were worth £9,000 a year. The Act was passed, and those tithes although collected in the locality ever since, are not spent in the locality, and the claim of the locality upon them is not at all acknowledged. I think that has been perhaps the most crushing thing with regard to Ireland during the last half century, for the tithes were worth 400,000 a year, and the localities have not succeeded in preserving their claim to a single penny of money. But now when the same principle is going to be applied in Great Britain (we have the Welsh Bill before the House), the claim of the localities is acknowledged there, and we are going to discuss at least the point of the parishes retaining the benefit. Then in the Scotch Bill it is promised that the tithes shall be given to the localities if the Church is disestablished, but in Ireland no guarantee was taken in the same way.

Mr. T. Lough, M.P.

10 May 1895.

[illegible]

8589. (*Chairman.*) Do you attach great importance to the clergyman of a particular locality having the endowment?—No. I am against the parson having the endowment, although I am in favour of disendowing the Church, I am against the disestablishment of the locality.

8590. (*Mr Sexton.*) Against disendowing it?—Yes. I am in favour of disendowing the Church but not the locality. I want all the local property kept in the locality.

8591. (*Chairman.*) I am speaking now of the change in Ireland. Formerly the greater part of the tithe went to the parson, did it not?—It did.

8592. And now since disestablishment it has gone to a central fund?—Yes.

8593. Do you think its not going to the parson is a grievance there in the locality in which the parson lives?—I must put that at a little greater length. When it was first given to the parson, my opinion is that the Church was a very different institution to what it is now. Centuries ago the Church practically took the place of the Poor Law, furnished the hospitals, and a good deal of the hospitality of the locality. That state of things passed away.

8594. (*Mr. Sexton.*) There was education also was there not?—Yes, the Church gave whatever education there was. That state of things passed away, but the public money, namely the tithe, which was used for those purposes, was now retained by the parson. I thought that an abuse, I think so still, and I think it should be taken from the parson, but that care should be taken to keep it in the locality, that care is being taken in Great Britain, in Wales, and in Scotland, but no such care was taken in Ireland. A terrible blow was thus given to the localities at that time, and we can put our finger on that, and give you the whole history of it. These are the three points which seem to me to have caused a great increase of local taxation in the first instance.

[illegible]

8595. Have you any other cause for an increase to which you wish to call attention?—Yes. I think that the new local taxing authorities have been constituted in such a way in Ireland that the public control over them is practically inoperative and that great encouragement is given to extravagant administration. I think the grand jurors, although they are bodies that try to do their duty, owing to their extraordinary constitution, can hardly resist favouring works that may be expensive to the rates but useful to members. There is no electorate for this taxing body and there is not even a tenure of office which would make them responsible, therefore I think that the grand jury cannot, according to our modern notions, be recognised as a good taxing authority.

8596. They sit twice a year for a few days and you have a new body each year?—Yes, and even the same body I think does not always sit the second time. It may be a different body. A body comes up, their names are hardly recognised, they are not represented, they go into a room and to a certain extent they fix the rates. Of course the rates have been before the presentment sessions.

8597. (*The O'Conor Don.*) Can they fix anything that has not been before the presentment sessions?—I do not know that. I know most of the rates come before the presentment sessions.

8598. (*Lord Welby.*) Do you think if the system of grand juries is reformed or another body is elected by the people it would be more economical?—I think so, I have faith in the principle of election. Although I will admit at first they might be a little extravagant, I think gradually people would see where the shoe pinched. The second authority I wish to mention is the Board of Guardians; they are very differently constituted in Ireland to what they are in Great Britain. I think that the whole system is extravagant and unsuitable. In County Cavan we have still five unions which were formed when the population was 243,000. Now the population has diminished to something a little over 100,000, but the five unions are kept up still, and each one, I think, is a seat of maladministration and extravagance. I believe in the Cavan workhouse there are only two Protestant children and a school teacher gets [illegible] a year for looking after those children because there were a number of Protestant children there years ago.

8399. Is it the case that half the guardians are elected?—Yes.

8400. By what sort of constituency?—By a system of plural voting, a very bad constituency from our English standpoint.

8401. Who nominates the other half?—The lord lieutenant nominates them; he makes them magistrates and then they are *ex officio* guardians.

8402. (*The O'Conor Don.*) They are not nominated, they are *ex officio* guardians being magistrates?—Yes, they are magistrates and up to the number they want, the magistrates of the county are *ex officio* guardians.

8403. (*Lord Welby.*) Do you know whether any report has ever been made from the county of Cavan on the subject of reducing those five unions?—I do not think so, and I am aware that there has been a party under which nothing could have been amalgamated, but I think it is quite hopeless to expect that those little bodies enjoying their brief spell of authority will themselves suggest their own extinction.

8404. But there is the great public outside them quite able to express their opinion, have they ever done so?—I am one of them; I am expressing my opinion. I do not think they have. I have always advocated that.

8405. [illegible] in some public manner, and pressure brought to bear on the Government. I hear it constantly stated, and we have heard evidence about extravagant expenditure, but I have not been able to trace any action on the part of the public in Ireland themselves to get some extravagant local expenditure stopped?—I am afraid the public are a bit demoralised in Ireland. They have been so long subjected to a bad system that they want assistance in getting on to better lines. I think, at the same time, they will welcome a more economical system; they feel it to be very oppressive, although they do not know how to cure it.

8406. (*Mr. Sexton.*) The public in Ireland, for instance, see that we, as their representatives in the House of Commons, press these matters forward in the House, get the Bills read a second time, and then that the Government find they have no time to go through with them?—Quite so.

8407. (*Lord Farrer.*) In England, as to the quarter sessions and board of guardians, there has never been a complaint of extravagance. Of course, we know that people desire to make the whole constitution more democratic, but the complaint certainly has not been that they were extravagant. Now, I understand you think these old-fashioned bodies in Ireland have been extravagant?—I quite agree with your statement that in Great Britain they are not extravagant, but the reason is that there is so much wealth in England as compared with Ireland. I do not think that they would be extravagant in Ireland if the country were richer. If we had the wealth it would not matter, but we have not, and it is and, therefore, to see anything wasted.

8408. (*Lord Welby.*) If that is the case, would not you rather expect to have from the suffering constituencies a rather lively expression of opinion. It seems to me that the Irish people who suffer have, in the main, been rather passive about the matters they have not expressed themselves as I should have expected on the subject of a reform in expenditure?—You are throwing on these poor peasants the responsibility of saying what ought to be done, as it seems to me, and I do not think you can fairly expect them to generalise on a great matter like that.

8409. (*Lord Farrer.*) But do the rates fall upon them?—Half the rates fall upon them.

8410. (*Lord Welby.*) But I should expect them to express themselves through perhaps they cannot point out the best method of reform. Do they not complain?—They would as soon complain of the rain as of the poor law; they think the poor law is just as permanent as the rain or the frost.

8411. (*Mr. Sexton.*) I think you have conceded, have you not, to the suggestion I made that the efforts of the Irish members in Parliament for twenty years to remedy things of this kind have been abortive?—Yes.

8412. And that people have expressed themselves with great force and energy, as to the establishment of a separate legislature in Ireland which could deal with these and other questions in Ireland and until that legislature is established they never will be dealt with properly?—I must say they are very chary of going into any details in Ireland. They do not express an opinion upon any detail. The third point that I suggest which has tended to increase the local rates is the limited municipal franchise that has been granted in the towns. There are not nearly as many voters for the affairs of the municipalities in these little towns all over Ireland as there are for Parliamentary elections, therefore that limited franchise has checked the development of public spirit and has favoured a little group controlling the affairs of the town and I think has tended towards jobbery, local tyranny, neglect and waste.

8413. (*Chairman.*) Have you any other reason to suggest why the payment of these local and Imperial taxes has been found so oppressive?—Yes. I think this point, which is quite uncontroversial, is perhaps the most important of all, namely, that the taxes have to be paid out of a produce which has gradually depreciated in value as the century has proceeded. From 1793 to 1815 wheat averaged about [illegible] per quarter therefore [illegible] of taxation could be paid with one quarter of wheat. Last year the price of wheat was [illegible] per quarter therefore it would now require three quarters of wheat to pay the same amount of taxation. To grow the three quarters would require three times as much land, and labour, and wages have doubled in price. It may be said that wheat is not at present grown so much in Ireland, but it is used largely and I think Ireland is poorer and not richer because it is not grown. Oats which is the chief Irish grain crop has not depreciated so much, still it is cheaper than it was. Barley has and rye have fallen as much as wheat. This year owing to the [illegible] from Australia butter has fallen greatly. I hear that in the markets in Ulster a week or two ago butter was sold at [illegible] a lb and that it was very hard to get [illegible], for a pretty fair quality. Of course it is not the best butter. I know it is difficult to sell because I have a little creamery there and the people are pressing milk at [illegible] a gallon on us because they do not know how to get rid of their butter. That is a desperate blow to Ireland this year. I believe there are 2,000 tons of Australian butter at present in cold store in London which will keep down the price of butter all through the season that is a new development.

8414. (*Sir David Barbour.*) Has not the agricultural condition of Ireland improved somewhat during the last year or two?—I do not think so, we have had a famine, and we are giving the people free seed. We had a good harvest in Ireland last year. I drove myself about 150 miles through some of the most beautiful country during the harvest but those very parts were sunk in famine three months afterwards.

8415. (*Chairman.*) How has this great fall in value affected rent?—I was going to sum up the fall in values that it takes twice the amount of produce now to pay every million of taxation which it did 100 years ago. It is a curious thing that Mr. Wakefield, whom I have already quoted, makes a very careful estimate in his book of what the rent of Ireland was in 1811. He after going through every parish and county, makes the total rental 17,[illegible], an average of [illegible] per acre for 13 millions and three-quarter acres.

8416. (*Mr. Sexton.*) That was a rent on the war prices?—Yes, on the war prices. This, I think, illustrates what has been suggested that up to 1815 there was great progress made in Ireland—the war prices were producing plenty all over the country, and the rent got up there to this enormous large figure. The rent has been reduced to [illegible] millions or [illegible] millions, but the taxes instead of going down with the rent have been doubled and trebled, so that the fall in rent supports my argument, that that decrease of produce and decrease in prosperity of the district should have led to

Mr. T. Lough, M.P.

[illegible] May 1895.

Administration by local authorities in Ireland.

Limited franchise in towns.

Agriculture in Ireland. Depreciation of values.

a decrease of taxation, rather than to the great increase that has taken place.

8417. (*Sir David Barbour.*) Unless the taxation was unduly low in former times. I do not say that was the case, but it is a possible and conceivable state of things, is it not?—But, even if it were unduly low and the people got poorer, the increasing poverty of the people would not be a reason for raising the taxes.

8418. (*Mr Sexton.*) It has been found that the taxation of Ireland between the Union and Waterloo did increase relatively more rapidly than the taxation of England, has it not?—Yes, I think so, far more. I think Ireland for the first 19 years of the century was really making better progress than Great Britain, and there was a curious suggestion made in the year 1816, that Ireland should have more than her 100 members of Parliament, because she had become to be so much more important a country than England during the 16 years, owing to the war prices.

8419. (*Sir David Barbour.*) You would not suggest another war in order to bring about that state of things, would you?—No.

8420. (*Chairman.*) In proportion to population she would have been entitled to a still larger number of members, would she not?—She would at that time. The claim was based on the increase of wealth and the increase of population.

8421. (*Mr. Sexton.*) Of course, any benefit from a war, so long as it depends on prices, is always subject to the reaction when the war ceases?—Quite so.

8422. (*Chairman.*) Has the farmer received any compensation for this great fall?—No, that is a point I want to put to the Commission. There is no compensation at all for this depreciation in the amount of produce. In his purchases, the farmer may get his cloth cheaper or he may get other things he has to buy cheaper, because other products may have gone down as well as his, but the taxes have to be paid in gold, and it seems to me there is no amelioration in the situation so far as taxes are concerned.

8423. Will you kindly sum up what you have been saying on this important point?—I cannot quite sum it up without also reminding the Commission that the rent which has to be paid on the agricultural lands is admittedly too high. I think that may be accepted without discussion. The present state of the land courts in Ireland and the unanimous opinion lately expressed in Parliament, of the need of further reductions, may be taken as placing this beyond controversy. If we assume that agricultural rents all over the island are now three millions more than they should be, the situation may be summed up by saying that the farmers of the country have to provide each year four millions more of Imperial taxation, one million more of local taxation, and three millions more of rent than is just or necessary, and these eight millions have to be provided from produce which has been depreciated to half its former value, so that Ireland is called upon to furnish each year a tribute not less onerous than an addition of 16 millions per annum would have been to the sum paid 100 years ago.

8424. (*Lord Farrer.*) Does not part of that increase of taxation fall upon rent?—Yes, a small part of it falls upon rent.

8425. Then to whatever extent that is the case it is not the farmer but the landowner who is injured is it not?—Yes, I think that is so to a very slight extent. I deal with that later on.

8426. (*Mr Sexton.*) To what extent?—About half a million a year.

8427. Has Parliament done its duty, do you think, in the matter?—I wish to say that I think our Irish Members of Parliament have been a good deal to blame all through the century because they do not press this taxation question more. I have already stated that in the House of Commons the question of Indian taxation is being pressed but we do not hear this question of Irish taxation discussed. It seems to me if it were, it would be more intelligible to the English than the land question, because all revolutions of the Anglo-Saxon peoples have arisen out of questions of taxation and I do not know of any more grave than these Irish exactions. Landlords are as much interested as tenants and the Catholics as Protestants and the North of Ireland as the South. I think that is one reason why Ulster is not so much interested in public affairs as the representatives of the South think it ought to be, because the people in Ulster think enough is not being made of this point of taxation, they feel the burden of taxation very keenly up there and if they were satisfied that the National movement included a reduction of taxation and would lead to it I believe they would be more sympathetic with it.

8428. (*Mr. Sexton.*) You are aware, are you not, that in the last ten years an Imperial Government lost office because of this finance question, and you are also aware of the representations of Irish members which led to the appointment of this Commission (and I am glad to see something is being done now) but I am speaking of the last 40 or 50 years. It seems to me terrible that the Irish case was not put more clearly before.

Adjourned for a short time.

8429. (*Chairman.*) You now desire, I believe, to indicate some of the results which have been produced in Ireland by over-taxation?—Yes, mainly by over-taxation, I think over-taxation is the first cause. The first result is that the population has been decimated. While the corn laws gave unnatural protection to agriculture a prosperous [illegible] of the people [illegible] possible who had increased until then in numbers in proportion to the growth in Great Britain notwithstanding the taxes. But when the corn laws were repealed, two millions died or disappeared in five years, and since 1851, it seems to me that the suffering caused by the disappearance of the people has been greater, because it has been more prolonged. I have the figures of population here, 8,175,1[illegible] in 1841, 6,5[illegible] in 1851, 5,798,[illegible] in 1861, 5,412,[illegible] in 1871, 5,174,[illegible] in 1881, and [illegible] in 1891. Really I think the continued decrease is more startling than the incidence of the famine.

8430. (*Lord Welby.*) Do you put those two on the same footing? I can understand your being struck by the continued decrease, and the cause of it from 1851, but surely you do not put down to over-taxation the decrease which took place during the time of the famine? There was a special cause to which we must ascribe that decrease, must we not, the absolute failure of the potato crop?—I do not want to go into what took place at the time of the famine any more fully than I have done in my evidence. I simply state here that within five years of the occurrence two millions of people disappeared; it is the later time I want to speak of.

8431. But then you give it as one of the results of over-taxation. I can understand it being an argument for the prolonged decrease in population, from 1851, but surely we must admit that there are other causes except increase of taxation, must we not?—That is so. It is since 1851 particularly that I wish to refer to.

8432. (*Lord Farrer.*) I think you said that Ireland was very prosperous during the first two decades of the century when taxation had increased very much, so that there must have been other circumstances than those of increase of taxation to account for the decrease of the population in Ireland?—The population did not decrease until 1846, it steadily increased up to 1845.

8433. But still you said that in the earlier part of the century, in spite of increased taxation, Ireland was very prosperous?—It was during the first 15 years.

8434. So that you would not look to over-taxation as the only cause, would you?—I want to begin at 1851. I do not go further back than that. Besides, the over-taxation only commenced in its most grievous form in 1853, therefore I only speak of the last 40 years.

8435. It did increase very largely, did it not, during the time of the war?—It increased during the time of the war, but it decreased from 1820 to 1850.

8436. Taxation decreased, did it?—Yes, and as to local taxation, there was scarcely any increase from 1820 until 1842.

8437. (*Chairman.*) Going back to the question of emigration, you say that you do not consider that the emigration from Ireland was normal, such as it was from Scotland or Wales; will you enlarge upon that?—The emigration of the last 10 years seems to me the most extraordinary fact that we can find in the history of any country. I generally hear it spoken of in England as a healthy sign, that the people undertake it willingly for their own improve-

[illegible] or [illegible]. I do not think it has been a normal emigration of that kind. The country would have furnished such a number of emigrants as Scotland furnished, or as Great Britain or Wales furnished in proportion to its population. There I would have called normal emigration, but the vast emigration which decreased the population in increasing proportion after 1851 seems to me not normal, but that the majority were driven away by the impossibility of obtaining a livelihood, substantially driven out, and not from a desire to improve their condition. I think that the scenes, the grief exhibited at railway stations, which everybody has heard of, illustrate that point. There have been the most piteous and agonising scenes that any country's history has afforded, showing that it was not a hopeful departure of a young fellow, or of a normal mass of the population to improve their condition, but that really the people were being torn violently from the place they would like to stay in. I think Scotland ought to furnish a larger proportion of emigrants than Ireland, because the people are a little better off there, and better educated. Therefore, if we regard the person who emigrates as one taking an intelligent view of the world, and who wants to go to a place where there are better opportunities, there ought to be more of that class of person in Scotland than in Ireland.

8438. Do you think you could lay down any general [illegible] as to what induces people to emigrate?—I [illegible], perhaps, a little too freely, but speaking from experience of the families and individuals I have known, I have seen them make every struggle to remain in Ireland, and go away most reluctantly.

8439. Even when they have had friends on the other side of the water who have urged them to go there?—That would be a case which would perhaps come within the description of normal emigration, but the cases I have seen—cases which have produced a profound impression on my mind—have been cases of farmers who have had a fair capital, house and land in Ireland, and who have made a hard struggle for years, and have then been finally driven out and obliged to go.

8440. (Lord Farrer.) You have told us that it largely due to the fall in agricultural prices, and the depression in profits of agriculture?—Quite so.

8441. You would not attribute that to over-taxation, would you?—The increase of taxation was an infliction which could easily have been prevented.

8442. But it is one thing, is it not, to take a cause which you can prevent, like taxation, and another to take a cause which you cannot prevent, perhaps, like a fall in prices?—I think the Government should have taken account of the fall of prices, and the difficulties the people had to contend with, and should have said, "We will demand no augmented contributions from these people owing to these circumstances." Instead of that being so, as the fall of prices took place the people were charged with more and more taxes.

8443. You do not mean that the fall in prices was due to over-taxation, but that when the fall in prices took place, then taxation ought to have been less instead of more?—That is my point.

8444. (Mr. [illegible].) The capacity to bear taxation diminished?—That is exactly my point, and at that time the taxation was increased.

8445. (Mr. Sexton.) And to meet double taxation required four times as much produce as in the early part of the century?—Exactly.

8446. The taxation being doubled, and the produce being able to pay only half as much taxes, you require four times as much produce as you did in the beginning of the century?—Yes, out of every little farm they had to get four times as much to pay the demand.

8447. (Lord Welby.) In talking of this taxation, we might, ought we not, to make a certain distinction?—The taxation on a great number of articles in the greatest consumption has fallen immensely on the one hand, while on the other hand on one article of consumption, as far as the poorer classes are concerned, spirits, it has been largely increased; but while we admit that, let us not lose from sight that the tea duty has been reduced something like 300 per cent. and the sugar duty—a most important article of consumption amongst the poor classes—entirely swept away?—My answer to that is that the total amount [illegible] from these people has increased all the time.

8448. Must we do not fall into an error. Supposing the taxation on every article are reduced all the way round, and supposing that led to a great increase of consumption, the people are paying less upon a pound of tea and upon a pound of sugar, but in consequence of some reason or other they are consuming a good deal more; we must take into consideration, must we not, and only the amount derived from taxation, but what that taxation is. Take such a case as this. I suppose my greatest boon has been conferred than the abolition of sugar duties?—It has been a great boon.

8449. And we must take that into consideration, must we not, though at the same time we admit fully that the duty on spirits has been very largely increased. I freely admit that the contribution to the exchequer has been increased?—Yes.

8450. But on most articles of absolute prime necessity, the taxation has been very much decreased, and, in some places, abolished, has it not?—Yes, I hardly know how to take account of your point, because I have merely looked at what you have made each person pay.

8451. I am explaining that. I only want to couple with it the qualification that we must not count from sight, when talking of over-taxation, the large amount which has been remitted on most important articles?—Quite so.

8452. As you put it, without contesting the rather limited view you take of it, I want at the same time to say then that must be coupled with the consideration of what the rates of duty paid are. Would you admit that?—I do not quite admit it; I cannot quite see it. It does not appear to me to affect the matter, because if you tax the thing a person wants most the only point you need take account of is how much has the man to pay.

8453. Taking tea and sugar, if you look at the remission of taxation, which has taken place with regard to these two articles of consumption, the boon has been enormous, and against that you have only to put, as far as the lower classes are concerned (putting aside local taxation), the spirit duty, which has been largely increased?—But you forget one which is more oppressive than either—the tobacco duty.

8454. That has not been altered. That is the only duty in which there has been no alteration. It is quite open to you to say it is over-taxed, but there has been no change in it?—They consume a much larger quantity of tea.

8455. But you pay less to the Exchequer on tea and that must be taken into consideration?—I think where you are wrong is, you assume there is a great variety of foods. Now, there is not a great variety; it is very limited. Probably the variety of food has diminished rather than increased, and you take the two or three things which the people want, and which, therefore, in most instances are essential to them, and you charge a very heavy tax on them. Then with regard to your point about the reduction of the tea duty——

8456. But we have not increased the taxation on a great number of articles. I will grant you spirits, but after spirits we have increased the taxation upon nothing, and upon the prime and necessary articles of life we have enormously decreased the taxation. Both these points ought to be fairly brought in, at all events, as a corollary to your statement about the over-taxation of Ireland, ought they not?—I have no objection.

8457. (Mr. Sexton.) Of course, the remissions of taxation on articles of consumption have benefited Great Britain as much as they have benefited Ireland?—Certainly, more.

8458. Do you consider that may be left out of account, then?—Yes.

8459. Then the taxes which are still imposed have resulted in an increased levy per head on the inhabitants of Ireland as compared with that of Great Britain?—Yes.

8460. And the inhabitant of Ireland at the present day, taking all the articles of consumption together, pays double as much as he did at a former date, because he requires four times as much agricultural produce to pay the tax as he did at the former date?—That is my point; that is the way I like to put it.

8461. ([illegible].) Going back, now, for a moment, to the subject of emigration, what is the present condition of emigration from Ireland?—If you look

Mr. T. Lough, M.P.

[illegible]

of the emigration returns, you will find emigration has gone up wherever the distress has been most severe. That seems to me to associate emigration with the suffering of the people in the most direct way.

8462. (*Lord Farrer.*) Is that so or has emigration, on the whole, generally gone up when things have been prosperous in the United States, and when the attractions on that side have been greatest?—That, I think, is the result of Mr. Giffen's very valuable tables, is it not?—I think if you look at the returns, you will find they do not at all confirm that view. You will find in 1880 and 1881—1880 being the largest year we had in Ireland—and in 1886 and 1887, an increase of emigration exactly contemporary with the severe distress in Ireland.

8463. I will only ask you if you have looked at the papers which have been published from time to time by the Board of Trade, containing a careful analysis of emigration, and referring it to its apparent causes?—I have not.

8464. I think it would be well worth your while to do so, because by a very large induction Mr. Giffen has come to the conclusion that, on the whole, emigration depends more upon the attractions in America than upon what happens in this country?—I will look at them.

8465. (*Mr. Sexton.*) Have you noticed that the Irish Registrar-General reduces the matter to an axiom, he says when the potato crop is a bad crop, the next year the stock of pigs decreases, because they are mainly fed on the surplus of the potato crop, and when the potato crop is a failure, in the next year the emigration reaches the maximum?—Yes, those are my views. I am not, to tell the truth, very much inclined to accept the somewhat [illegible] calculations which are made on these Irish subjects on this side. I look at them simply as we see them in Ireland.

8466. (*Lord Farrer.*) It is a thing I could not possibly enter upon now, because it is a careful induction from a great many figures which require a very careful study?—Just so. Then it seems to me that the present decrease of emigration will probably be temporary, according to my past experience, because we had some suffering in 1890, and have passed measures for giving relief for famine and providing seed for the people.

8467. (*Chairman.*) Do you think that emigration is coming to an end?—No, I do not see any reason for the reduction of the emigration of last year, which was the lowest we have had for years; it fell to 35,000.

8468. Do you know whether it is still diminishing?—We cannot tell anything about 1895 yet, but I think we must not assume too hastily on the figures of 1894 that any permanent decrease in the rate is taking place.

8469. I believe you wish to put in some very interesting papers as to three counties?—Yes. Those three Ulster counties are the counties I know best. They are supposed to be prosperous counties, and they are very quiet counties; they always have had a good character, excepting the English standpoint. There there has been the most terrible decline, as I think the Commission will see if they examine the figures. I will hand in the table, which is as follows:—

Counties.	1841.	1851.	1861.	1871.	1881.	1891.	Per Cent. Decrease of 1881–1891 over 1871–1881.	Per Cent. of Decrease since 1841.
Cavan	243,158	174,064	153,906	140,735	129,476	111,917	13·56	[illegible]
Fermanagh	156,481	116,047	105,768	92,794	84,879	74,170	[illegible]	[illegible]
Monaghan	200,442	141,823	126,482	114,969	102,748	86,206	16·1	[illegible]
Total of three Counties	600,081	—	—	—	—	272,293	14·20	[illegible]
Total of Ireland	8,175,124	—	—	—	—	4,706,162	9·08	[illegible]

I will take Monaghan first. It is a splendid county, has good land, and is well cultivated, yet Monaghan showed the largest percentage of decrease in Ireland between 1881 and 1891, so that you need not go to the West of Ireland where the Englishman generally looks for examples of misery. I think the misery is much worse in the so-called prosperous parts of Ireland.

8470. (*Lord Farrer.*) Comparatively mostly?—Yes, and I take Monaghan as my first example. In Monaghan the population had fallen from 200,000 in 1841 to 102,000, or to half, in 1891, far more than the proportion of the whole country.

8471. (*Mr. Sexton.*) Much more than half, because the population of the other counties increased up to 1841?—Yes. In the next decade it falls to 86,000. It falls 16·1 per cent., while the average decrease over Ireland in that decade was 9·08 per cent. I think that shows that in this excellent county you had more acute suffering, and there is more acute suffering at present, perhaps, than in the parts of Ireland you generally look to for examples of distress. Now in Fermanagh, another splendid county, the figures are almost the same, and I will not repeat them. Then in the County Cavan there were 243,000 in 1841, they had fallen to 129,000 in 1881, and to 111,000 in 1891, showing a reduction of 13·56 per cent., so that the average of decrease in these three prosperous counties is 14·20 per cent., while the average over the whole of Ireland is only 9·08 per cent. That is in the 10 years between 1881 and 1891. This is the best part of Ireland, so that whether I am suggesting the real disease or the real cure or not, there is some disease existing, and more acute disease, not for the bad and distressed parts of Ireland, but for the parts which are making a desperate struggle to keep their heads above water, and are not able to do it.

8472. (*Sir David Barbour.*) These being the best parts of Ireland, how does it happen that there is more distress there in the 10 years than in the poorer parts?—Distress does not exactly convey the evil, if I am right. I do not think there is distress, in the sense in which we use that word, but there there is no hideous pauper population unable to live under the conditions the Government enforces.

8473. But the conditions are the same there as regards taxation, as they are in the western parts of Ireland, are they not?—It may be so. I have not taken out the figures of particular counties in the west; I have only compared them with the whole of Ireland; but they live in a more wretched state in the west.

8474. (*Lord Farrer.*) Are not the facts you state also consistent with the hypothesis that it may have been the attractions of a superior life in America that may have led persons who were rather better off to emigrate, while those same attractions would not have had the same force with regard to persons who were worse off?—I think a consideration of these three counties will show you that that line of argument will hardly do, because the attractions of America have been diminished during the last 10 years. That is the general tendency of the statistics.

8475. It goes up and down. You know the attractions of America are diminished or increased according to the state of business and occupation there. For the last two or three years, no doubt, they have gone down, but they increased before that time?—I think, generally, America has not presented the attractions from 1881 to 1891 that it presented at earlier periods, such as 1841 to 1851, and yet in that period when there is no great attraction in America, we find these people, who are intelligent people, pouring out of Ireland.

5476. (*Mr. Sexton.*) Did America attract any material part of the population of Ireland until the Famine and the repeal of the Corn Laws began their joint operation in 1846?—I do not think so; I think it is the circumstances in Ireland which have driven the people out.

5477. (*Chairman.*) Not since the early part of last century; there was a considerable emigration then, was there not?—Yes, but it was a normal emigration, the population still increased.

5478. (*Mr. Sexton.*) And absolutely immaterial in comparison with the numbers since 1846?—Yes; I do not object to a healthy emigration.

5479. (*Chairman.*) It was a normal emigration?—Yes.

5480. And had been for a long time?—It was a normal emigration until 1846, and after 1851 (leaving out those five years to avoid controversial matter), it has been abnormal and unhealthy, I think, owing to the circumstances in Ireland.

5481. (*Lord Welby.*) Do you think the condition of the people in Monaghan has gone down since the Famine?—Yes.

5482. Taking the county of Monaghan and taking the classification of houses into first, second, third, and fourth class, I find in 1841 that of the fourth class, which are the most miserable mud huts or houses with one window, there were 31 per cent., while in 1891 there were only 3 per cent. That does not seem to me to be going along with the idea of the great increase in misery. I will give you another figure. When we come to the first class houses, where there was 1 per cent. in 1841, there was 3 per cent. in 1891, and when we come to the second class of house, which is a very good class of house, there were only 10 per cent. in 1841 and over 30 per cent. in 1891. That represents an advance in well-being, does it not?—There are no Irish figures [illegible], which I think are so curious and so untrue as those figures about the first and second class houses. I think they give no true picture of the state of things in Ireland at all.

5483. Will you say why, because the description of a house is a thing which we can bring down to certain form. For instance, when you take the fourth class, the mud cabins, a house without windows, that is intelligible and you get at an actual fact. If they were 31 per cent. of the whole number of houses in 1841 and only 3 per cent. in 1891, that is as true a fact as you can have, is it not?—The mud house, so called, of 1841 was not such an uncomfortable and unsanitary place as you imagine it to have been. The building of mud houses has become a lost art in Ireland, but these mud houses used to be a sort of concrete structure, and were not so uncomfortable dwellings as you imagine. But, I think, the most ghastly dwelling in which a man can live will be found in Ireland now amongst these new slated houses. I will read a sentence again that, from the book I quoted from just now, the "Survey of Cavan": "To what purpose then is the "face of a country to be changed, to gay and chequered "scenes, if the peasant on whom its stability depends, "is gradually emaciated, not by luxury, but by keen "poverty and too often by savage oppression? What "does it avail, if the proud lord of extensive domains "shall raise neat slated cottages on the verge of the "[illegible] road, if he does not take care to ameliorate the "condition of the peasant, who cannot warm the walls "of his ill-fated habitation, whose misery but ill "agrees with the outer view?" I think that is very pertinent to this point of the first and second class houses. I do not believe in the statistics at all. I think there was a great deal more comfort in many of these mud houses than there is now in many of the slated houses.

5484. Then I must again appeal to you with the definition of what houses are: "The fourth class includes "all single room houses constructed of mud or perishable material; the second class consists of a good "house having five to [illegible] rooms and windows." With a definition of so clear between these two, is it possible to argue from a [illegible] or any other point of view, that you could compare a hut of mud with a single room with a house having five to seven rooms and windows. It is not possible to put the two together, is it? The bigger house with the more rooms and more air must be a proof of an improvement, is not it so?—I will leave it. I can only express my own opinion. I think the old notion of a house with one great big living room in it, common in England as in Ireland, would be a good deal more wholesome than these residences with small rooms, and as for sanitation, these houses have no sanitation at all in Ireland either.

Mr. T. Lough, M.P. [illegible]

[illegible]

5485. There is another point I wish to call attention to, taking Monaghan, namely, the return of cattle. Among that large population of 200,000, there were 87,000 cattle, and in 1891 there were 87,000 head of cattle among the smaller population. Nearly all the other figures are in the same proportion. Does not that show that the 86,000 people who had 87,000 head of cattle must be rather better off than the 200,000 people who had only 87,000 head of cattle?—That is not a necessary inference. The greatest proof of degradation of an agricultural country is to see it turned into a great cattle ranche, and village declining. The whole country was tilled in 1841, the people ate their own wheat, their own meal and none of this wretched Indian meal; they ate their own bacon and not American bacon. They had not room for cattle then. I think you may take it that an increase of cattle means a decrease of agricultural prosperity.

[illegible]

5486. (*Mr. Sexton.*) Do you think that the substitution of stone for clay in the walls of houses of the peasantry, and the slate for straw in the roof, at all diminishes the significance of the fact that half the population has been swept away in 50 years, and does it indicate an improvement in the condition of those who remain if we see that the income on which they have to live is heavily diminished?—I do not think so. I do not think any of the facts mentioned by Lord Welby take anything off the weight of the figures I have submitted.

5487. (*Lord Welby.*) But if you have a population of 86,000 people with cattle increasing to that extent, it must mean, must it not, a state of things which is hardly represented by greatly increased poverty?—I visited Monaghan at Christmas and spent two or three days in the agricultural parts. On the farm on which I stopped there was a good house, such as would have been occupied by a middle class gentleman, and a school and a forge in ruins. That was a farm of about 120 acres, and the one remaining house was the one in which we were, a very good house. I could not help thinking that 40 or 50 years ago when there was work for the forge and children in the school, that place was in a better condition than it is now. The gentleman who was entertaining me took me across to see his brother, about three miles away. I found his brother, a young unmarried man, camped out as you would expect to find a settler in Australia, but in a house which within my recollection has belonged to one of the gentlemen of the county, with stabling for a dozen horses, with beautiful grounds, and a magnificent lake, a farm of about 150 acres of land, and here this young fellow was living by himself camped out, as it were, in a desolate mansion, and finding it hard to make a living for himself in a place where dozens of happy beings had lived half a generation ago, so that with these pathetic pictures before my mind and knowledge of actual facts I am not inclined to accept these statistics.

5488. (*Lord Farrer.*) Do you think with your knowledge, taking man for man, woman for woman, and child for child, that they are worse off than they were 40 or 50 years ago?—Relatively I think they are. We can never answer that question directly, but I think the whole population in 1845, let me say, as compared with the other populations of countries in Europe, were on a far higher grade than the whole population is in [illegible] as compared with the population of surrounding countries.

5489. (*Mr. Sexton.*) You have shown already that the value of the agricultural produce has shrunk enormously since 1846. Have you noted the fact given in evidence by [illegible] that the value of stock upon which Lord Welby relies has fallen considerably since [illegible], when it was [illegible] and is now only [illegible]? Can you from these data as to the enormous fall in the agricultural produce and the heavy fall in the value of stock, deduce any such inference that there is anything in the figures as to stock to make up for the loss of agricultural produce?—I cannot. I disbelieve in the stock argument entirely; stock gives no employment to the labouring classes; it is the most easily carried on occupation.

Mr. T. Lough, M.P.

22 May 1895.

8490. And moreover, the value of it has fallen?—The value of it has fallen.

Report of Devon Commission.

8491. (*Sir David Barbour.*) Have you seen the Report of the Devon Commission?—I do not like to say I have with sufficient accuracy to answer a question on it.

8492. It gives a very unfavourable report of the condition of the people of Ireland just before 1845?—That was a bad time.

8493. (*Lord Welby.*) That was in the year of prosperity which preceded the famine. If I remember rightly 1843, 1844, and 1845 were distinctly prosperous years?—I have avoided saying much about 1845, it is 1895 which interests me.

8494. But the Report of the Devon Commission came out in 1845?—I know that.

8495. (*Sir David Barbour.*) Does not the Devon Commission give a picture, not of the temporary condition of the people for a year or two, but of what may be called their permanent condition about that time?—I am willing to agree to that if you like, but if you look at these tables I am supplying, they refer to this year.

8496. The only thing I wish to bring out is that there was great distress in Ireland in former years, nothing more than that?—I think there was, I am prepared to admit that.

Decline of trade in some [illegible]

8497. (*Chairman.*) Have you made any comparison in your mind between the emigration from Ireland and the migration to England from the more populous districts?—I have made a comparison about it, but if you will allow me I want to point attention to another figure with regard to the three counties with which I have been dealing. The total decrease over the 50 years in these three counties is 54·63, whereas the decrease in the whole of Ireland is only 32·44 per cent. So from that I argue that the pressure, to whatever cause it is due, must have been hard on these counties. I have known a very few prosperous tradesmen. I know many tradesmen in Monaghan, but I do not know any who are making satisfactory progress. There is no new trade arising to replace the old trades, and I remember myself manufactures of leather, tobacco, hats, candles, nails, boots, furniture, soap, rope, tiles, meal, flour, and bread. I remember all these created in the counties but they are all extinguished and nothing has arisen to replace them.

8498. (*Lord Farrer.*) Is not that what has been going on throughout England, and, indeed, throughout the world generally, that small local manufactures have diminished, and that the manufacture has been transferred to large factories?—Very often when that has taken place some other satisfactory has been developed in its place, but I do not want to go into that. I want to say that where that diminution of wealth takes place, then the taxation ought to be reduced.

8499. I suppose you would say there has not been the compensation in Ireland by the establishment of large factories which there has been in England?—No, no compensation at all.

8500. That is your point?—That is my point, and the other point is that the taxation has been increased.

8501. Because we have all of us known how cottage industries, of looms, for instance, in Yorkshire, which I knew somewhat in my youth, have all disappeared?—Yes.

8502. And the work is done in large factories instead?—Yes.

8503. Shoes that were formerly made throughout all the villages are now made at particular seats of manufacture?—You would think if there was any possibility of doing anything in Ireland that something might have been done with leather, considering the number of hides there are in the country, yet that has been swept away, as everything else has been.

8504. (*Mr. Sexton.*) The transfer of trade in England being merely from one part of England to another it has increased the taxable capacity of England?—Yes.

8505. On the contrary, it has gone from Ireland, and so decreased the taxable capacity of Ireland?—That is true, and I want to avoid a discussion of whether a change to manufacturing centres is inevitable or not; because my point is that where the trade of a country has been cleared out, as in Ireland, the taxation should be reduced.

8506. (*Lord Farrer.*) My point was with reference to your statement as to what results over-taxation in Ireland produced in Ireland. I want to point out to you that what has been happening in Ireland is what has been happening elsewhere, and although that may have been a reason for not continuing taxation so heavily, and not increasing taxation, yet that the actual causes of the want of occupation are different, that they are commercial and not financial?—I accept that, to a large extent, but I think that heavy taxation prevents industries growing up in Ireland, which would have grown up if the circumstances had been favourable.

Mr. T. Lough, M.P.

22 May 1895.

Belfast industries [illegible]

8507. (*Chairman.*) Have you any remark to make upon the similarity or dissimilarity between the migration from one part of Great Britain to another and the emigration from Ireland?—Yes. The statement is often made that we have had a similar movement in England. In my opinion there is no parallel between the movement of the people clearing out of Ireland, and the movement which has taken place in England into towns. When I look at the decline in the population of Ireland, I always take a large district like Ulster or Munster, or any one of the four divisions, or draw a line across and take the district north of Dublin, or south of Dublin; and in any of these districts you will find the population has diminished in the proportion stated, but in England, although you hear of migration into towns from agricultural districts, you can take no group of three counties altogether where there is not a great increase of population during this period.

8508. You can take the eastern counties as an exception, can you not?—The eastern counties have increased in population, if you draw a line from the Wash down to the Thames, a broad line, the size of Ulster.

8509. (*Lord Farrer.*) You mean if you include the towns?—Certainly, I do that in both cases.

8510. (*Mr. Sexton.*) The towns are a part of the county for the present purpose, are they?—Yes.

8511. (*Sir David Barbour.*) Why are not these manufactures established in Ireland?—Because they would be crushed out by heavy taxation.

8512. But the system of taxation is the same in England as in Ireland, is it not?—I do not know that it is so heavy, and at any rate you would want to give the Irish greater relief if you want to get them planted out there.

8513. (*Mr. Sexton.*) Is the scale levied on the same income?—Certainly not.

8514. (*Lord Farrer.*) Taxation has not prevented the growth of the Belfast industries, has it?—No, it has not, and that has proved that where it is possible to put up an industry, it can be done in Ireland, but in the country districts they require more encouragement.

8515. But does not that show that you must go to some other causes than taxation. If taxation is the same in Belfast as in the other parts of Ireland, why should industries have grown up in Belfast and not in other parts of Ireland?—Of course in Belfast very few industries have grown up. The only one that has grown up has been the shipbuilding in addition to the linen industry, which existed in Ireland all along. Belfast has gathered the linen industry into itself.

8516. I am only addressing myself to the question of whether it is over-taxation which has prevented these industries from growing up in Ireland?—Just so.

8517. (*Sir David Barbour.*) Are there not a great many small industries in Belfast?—I do not think there is any industry of great extent excepting the linen and shipbuilding. In a large city like that there will be some small industries, there is whiskey, tobacco, and ginger ale, for instance.

8518. (*Lord Welby.*) Tobacco is a large industry, is it not?—Yes, it is a large one; but I think the prosperity of Belfast does depend on two great industries, linen and shipbuilding. Shipbuilding was obviously an industry on which the taxation did not press very heavily. The shipbuilders took a bit of waste shore at Belfast, at first and so got on gradually.

8519. (*Mr. Sexton.*) And the wages were lower?—Yes, at lower wages and lower rents.

8520. (*Lord Farrer.*) How would taxation touch such an industry as shoemaking, for instance?—If any machinery were brought into Ireland, or any mill erected, immediately those rates which you have heard described would be put upon it.

8521. (*Lord Welby.*) Still there would be rates, I take it, in Belfast on the shipbuilding yards, would there not?—Quite so.

Mr. T. Lough, M.P.

[illegible]. (*Sir David Barbour.*) I think you said that the [illegible] industry is [illegible] on account of the lower rates of wages in Belfast?—Yes.

[illegible]. Is that really the case? I have heard that the workmen employed in Belfast will not take less than the rate of wages prevailing on the Clyde?—I have nothing on my notes about the comparative wages in Belfast and on the Clyde; I only answered a [illegible] case from memory to a remark made by a member of the Commission.

[illegible]. (*Chairman.*) Do you ascribe any evil to over-taxation, besides the diminution of population?—Yes. I come to another evil in a moment, but I should like to say first that I think with regard to the comparison with England that you must not only do what you do in England, where the people can go into the towns and live, but you must do more; you must enable the people to live so cheaply in Ireland that they will be able to live on the land. That is the point I wanted to draw out of the comparison with England. It is not enough to make a system the same as in England where people who cannot live by agriculture can go into a town 20 or 30 miles away; there is no need to go further in England. But in Ireland, where the effect of the present system is to turn the country into a desert, I think some change should be made sufficient to enable people even in those bad times to live on the land. The next evil that I trace is the increase of pauperism. Between 1864 and 1894 there has been a great increase in pauperism in Ireland. This is a point on which some unsatisfactory returns are presented. I wish I had time to deal with the returns which Lord Welby brought forward, as I have dealt here with the returns of pauperism, because I think we might get a clearer explanation of it. The Local Government Board in Ireland publish averages taken on a certain day for the last 30 or 40 years. These averages may be less, and pauperism greatly increased. Therefore I got the figures of pauperism from the Irish Office, and they show a most startling increase during 30 years. The total number of indoor paupers in Ireland in 1864 was [illegible], with a population of [illegible], giving a proportion of [illegible] per 1,000 of the population. Now, in 1894, the indoor paupers were [illegible] with a population fallen to [illegible], or a proportion of [illegible] per 1,000. I had better put the table in. It is as follows:—

TABLE showing the total Number of Persons receiving Out-door and Indoor Relief in Ireland, and their Percentage to the total Population in 1864, and in every fifth Year since then until 1894.

Year.	Total Number of Indoor Paupers.	Total Number of Out-door Paupers.	Total Paupers.	Population.	Proportion to each 1,000 of Population.
[illegible]	[illegible]	[illegible]	[illegible]	[illegible]	[illegible]
[illegible]	[illegible]	[illegible]	[illegible]	[illegible]	[illegible]
[illegible]	[illegible]	[illegible]	[illegible]	[illegible]	[illegible]
[illegible]	[illegible]	[illegible]	[illegible]	[illegible]	[illegible]
[illegible]	[illegible]	[illegible]	[illegible]	[illegible]	[illegible]
[illegible]	[illegible]	[illegible]	[illegible]	[illegible]	[illegible]
[illegible]	[illegible]	[illegible]	[illegible]	[illegible]	[illegible]

[illegible]. (*Mr. Blake.*) Do not these figures include the ins-and-outs paupers?—Yes, they do, but that does not affect my argument.

[illegible]. (*Lord Farrer.*) How are these figures made out; are they the number of individual persons who have received relief?—I think I had better say yes to that question, but one person may be included twice.

[illegible]. So that if John Smith has been in the workhouse once in January, once in February, once in March, and so on throughout the year, he will count as twelve?—If he has been in for a short time every month, but if he has been in continuously, which I think would be the case of a man appearing every month, he only counts as one. If a man goes into the workhouse for a fortnight in January, and for a fortnight in May, he will count as two.

[illegible]. Then this is not the number of persons in the workhouse, but the number of persons who have gone into workhouses?—That is so.

[illegible]. Is that a fair test?—I think it is the fairest test.

[illegible]. (*Lord Welby.*) You know that the Local Government Board takes an opposite view, do you not?—I think the Local Government Board view in Ireland is an unfair view.

[illegible]. And here?—I have the English figures below, and will quote them. My reason for thinking that theirs is a perfectly [illegible] view is that, if the conditions of affairs is such that John Smith can rub through the year by going into the workhouse once, then I say the conditions are better than if John Smith has to go in three times.

[illegible]. (*Lord Farrer.*) But supposing his visit has been the whole year?—Then he only counts one.

[illegible]. Is that a good condition of things?—I am not saying that that is a good condition of things; my other answer is that I am taking the same returns for each year.

[illegible]. (*Chairman.*) It is a comparison of statistics?—Yes.

[illegible]. Not a justification of them?—No, they are the same statistics in 1864 as in 1894.

[illegible]. (*Lord Farrer.*) But is "The total number of in-"door paupers" a correct heading to your return?—I think so.

[illegible]. Should it not be the total number of persons who have been inside the workhouse?—That would do.

[illegible]. (*Lord Welby.*) Then again the rate per mille stated in this form gives the idea that so many out of each thousand have been relieved, which, inasmuch as many of them have been relieved two or three times, is hardly a fair statement, is it?—But I point out that that applies to any one of the years, therefore, my comparison is quite right.

[illegible]. (*Sir David Barbour.*) Why do you not take the correct statistics for comparison?—I do take them, these are the correct statistics.

[illegible]. Hardly; for instance, if a man went into a workhouse for half a month in each month, he would under your system of statistics count as 12 men, but if he were so badly off as to remain in for the whole year he would only count as one pauper?—That is so.

[illegible]. But surely if he can support himself half the year, it would indicate a better state of things than if he could not support himself at all, taking an extreme case?—I think it is a pity to look at it in that way, because, if you do, you will make any statistics false; probably there will be an equal proportion of these people in each of the years.

[illegible]. (*Mr. Sexton.*) Do you compare these figures with corresponding figures of Great Britain?—I do.

[illegible]. And these are prepared exactly there of the same kind, are they?—Exactly.

[illegible]. What I understand as pressing on your mind is that the frequent return of the same person to the workhouse every year is an indication of poverty?—Considerably. I think it is just the same as if 12 people came.

[illegible]. It shows also rather the severity of the struggle for subsistence, does it not?—I think so.

[illegible]. (*The O'Conor Don.*) How do you substitute the out-door paupers on that system?—That return is given by the Local Government Board. All these figures are taken from the Local Government Board figures.

[illegible]. (*Chairman.*) You have no alternative but to accept those figures, have you?—None. I will produce the annual return to-morrow if I am here.

[illegible]. (*Mr. Blake.*) I think you stated that you got these figures through the Chief Secretary for Ireland, did you not?—Certainly, and the figures for 1864 for [illegible] paupers are [illegible] out of a population of [illegible], while in 1894 they are [illegible] out of a population of [illegible]. Now I compare these with the English figures exactly the same. We see in Ireland that the proportion is nearly doubled; it has gone from [illegible] per 1,000 to [illegible] per 1,000, and in the same period in England the figures fell from [illegible] per 1,000 to [illegible] per 1,000.

[illegible]. (*Lord Farrer.*) The statistics being taken on the same basis?—Exactly.

[illegible]. (*Lord Welby.*) You do not happen to have the figures with regard to England to which you refer, do you?—I do not, but I will bring the returns. There are

Mr. [illegible] Lough, M.P. — [illegible] May 1895. — Agriculture in Ireland. [illegible]

five submissions to it. I quoted two, and will give the others.

8530. (*Chairman.*) On this point you wish to call attention to a calculation of the average subsistence of the farming classes in Ireland, I believe?—Yes. I will finish my point on pauperism by saying that whereas in Great Britain in the 20 years pauperism has halved; in Ireland in the 20 years it has doubled. I think that it will really make the point quite clear about the increase of pauperism, if we look at the average subsistence of the people at the land, and remember the intense poverty which they have got to endure. According to the tables of Dr Grimshaw, the population which has to subsist upon the land is roundly 3½ millions. The total produce of the land each year is 38,000,000. If this were divided equally amongst 3½ millions, it would give each person [illegible] a week to live upon. The agricultural rent amounts to [illegible] millions. This is received by a few individuals, not exceeding at the most 50,000. It therefore takes one-fourth from the total amount of money without any appreciable diminution of the numbers. We must, therefore, reduce for rent, the [illegible] to [illegible] per head per week.

8531. (*Sir David Barbour.*) When is that figure of 3½ millions Dr Grimshaw gives, does it not include the inhabitants of the small villages, the small shopkeepers, blacksmiths, and shoemakers, and so on?—It does.

8532. But they all earn something, which should be added to the produce of the land, should it not?—It is all included. I think all such would be included in the 38,000,000, which the land produces.

8533. But then there is a large proportionate income earned, is there not, by the shopkeepers, and people of that sort?—There is no industry apart from the land, and they have all to live out of the profit made from the land.

8534. Supposing a person has to [illegible] a week to live upon and he pays [illegible], or whatever it may be, for a pair of boots, that is income to the shoemaker, is it not? He pays away a portion of his income in exchange for a pair of boots, so that there is a larger total income than merely 38 millions?—I do not think there is much.

8535. There may not be much, but there is some, is there not?—I have tried to state it quite accurately. I think the 38 millions is a great deal too large.

8536. But there is that item, large or small, which is not taken into your account?—I wish to say that I did look at it, and as I saw in these agricultural villages no industry but agriculture I thought I was quite safe in assuming that there was nothing except that which was made out of the land.

8537. (*Chairman.*) Does your figure of 50,000 include families?—I think it might be taken to include the families of those who receive the rent. I meant it so. I took 10,000 landlords and five to a family, which made 50,000.

8538. (*Mr. Sexton.*) Do you accept the suggestion that the wealth of the country as a basis of taxation is to be increased every time an income changes hands in the country?—I do not; that is where I differ.

8539. Is it not a question of the creation of wealth?—That is it.

8540. And you have in Ireland only the produce of some two or three industries?—Yes.

8541. And you cannot add to the income produced by those?—You cannot. You will find that the figures are sufficiently startling. I do not want to have any conflict about the figures, because I will give you [illegible] if you like.

8542. (*Sir David Barbour.*) But there is that item which is not in your calculation, is there not?—I cannot quite accept it, but I recognise your point. The share of local and Imperial taxes which fall upon the agricultural section of the community cannot be less than 7½ millions. We must, therefore, deduct for taxes another 10d. per week, leaving the actual subsistence of the people no more than 2s 6d. per head per week, on the average. That makes for the family of five 12s 6d per week. The minimum wage allowed to the lowest class of worker by the London County Council is 24s per week. When we remember that the 12s 6d per week, which is all that the family of the Irishman engaged in agriculture enjoys, is an average, and that everything

in excess of this which the richer tenants secure has to be deducted from the share remaining for the poor, it is clear that there is a vast population, probably two or two and a half millions, eking out a most miserable subsistence. How great then is the responsibility of encouraging the payment by such a community out of its depreciated agricultural produce of 7½ millions in gold each year for rent and taxes. I have brought out these figures to illustrate the point, that the whole community, numbered at 3½ millions, roughly, engaged in agriculture in Ireland, have an extremely narrow subsistence, and therefore any help—a pound or two or three pounds a head or whatever we can give to them—will have a great deal to do with the increase or decrease of pauperism.

8543. (*Chairman.*) Do you know anything else in the question of taxation?—I will take famines next. I do not think we can lose sight of the famines which have become regular incidents in Ireland, and which we in Parliament take, as a matter of course. There is no surprise at present whenever a famine occurs in Ireland. We had one this year after the beautiful harvest of last year. Leaving out the great famines of 1846 and 1847, we had serious outbreaks in the years 1879, 1880, 1886, 1891, and 1894. They are always marked by the same features of discontent and increased emigration and pauperism, and are always allowed to pass without any serious inquiry into their cause.

8544. Do you wish especially to call our attention to the fact that these famines are not due to the failure of the potato crop?—Yes. It is always assumed that it is due to the failure of the potato crop, and I want to go into that. Take the present famine we are dealing with, for example, and it is a very fair illustration. We had an excellent harvest in Ireland last year, except as regards potatoes, and they were 33 per cent. short all over the country. I want to show that this applied really all over the country, so I have taken out from the Irish agricultural statistics the report of every county in Ireland, and I find that there is not a single county in which the potatoes were not short, and in some of the counties which are not scheduled for distress, the crop was more short than in the parts which have been scheduled. For instance, I think Cavan was one of the worst counties, and it got practically no relief; the crop yielded only about half a good crop, it was almost a total failure. With regard to the 12 counties of Leinster I will read you the results:—Carlow: Deficient in quantity, and quality bad. Dublin: Below the average of other years. Kildare: Bad crop, decidedly below the average. Kilkenny: Extremely damaged, only half crop in some districts. King's County: Very bad, scarcely up to half average yield. Longford: Yield inferior, quality bad. Louth: Light crop. Meath: General bad yield, some districts half rotten. Queen's County: Poor crop in all districts. West Meath: Below average in quantity, size, and quality. Wexford: Crop small, general poor quality. Wicklow: A marked failure. Then for Munster the results are:—Clare: Barley half a good crop. Cork: Good crop in one or two districts, but poor in others. Kerry: Inferior quality and quantity. Limerick: Much below average. Tipperary: Deficient crop, poor quality. Waterford: Light crop. Then for Ulster the observations are:—Antrim: Fair in most districts, others partial failure. Armagh: Bad light crop generally. Cavan: Yield only about half good crop; almost total failure. Donegal: Only 33 per cent. in quantity, quality poor. Down: Poor crop. Fermanagh: Low average yield. Monaghan: Yield small. Tyrone: General [illegible] crop, some districts total failure. Londonderry: Fair in one district, in others more or less failure. Then for Connaught:—Galway: Under average in all districts. Leitrim: Total failure some districts; bad generally. Mayo: Only half or one-third average crop. Roscommon: Not more than half a crop. Sligo: Below average generally; only half in some districts.

8545. (*Chairman.*) Are these all relating to 1894?—Yes. The short yield of potatoes was spread absolutely all over Ireland, and there hardly appears to be one district better off than the other. The best is Cork. It says, "Good crop in one or two districts, but poor in the other districts," and that is the best report in the whole of Ireland, so that the shortness of the crop was spread all over the island. Now there was an excess in the hay crop (which is even more valuable than the potato), and also in corn. Seeing the whole value of the potato crop is only 7,000,000, and 33 per cent. = 2,300,000, it is sufficient for our purpose if we amount that 2,000,000*l.* was the total loss incurred by the short crop of potatoes.

8166. (*Mr. Blake.*) After allowing for the excess in hay and corn?—Yes.

8167. (*Chairman.*) Hay was very large?—Yes, hay was a good crop.

8168. (*Mr. Sexton.*) Do you say a full potato crop would be 7,500,000*l.*?—Yes.

8169. Then if that fell 25 per cent., there was a loss of 2,500,000*l.* irrespective of the increase in hay and seed corn?—Yes.

8170. (*Lord Welby.*) Do you find the hay crop more valuable?—Yes, it is really more valuable. You get no price for it, but it feeds the cattle, and therefore I allow for it and I say the loss was only 2,000,000*l.* That is not an unreasonable fluctuation in an agricultural country. I think no agriculture can be carried on in any country where there is no room for such a fluctuation as that. It is 5 per cent. of the total agricultural produce. The total agricultural produce is 40,000,000*l.*, and 2,000,000*l.* is 5 per cent. Broadly, I say that it is not an unreasonable fluctuation. We had in England, I think, a much greater loss by the depreciation of prices in wheat and barley last year, and yet no famine. Very well, in Ireland we have a famine attributed to that fluctuation, but the very same year that we lost that 2,000,000*l.* we had to pay 10,[illegible] of rent, and 7,500,000*l.* of taxes. It is contended that the sole cause of the calamity was the failure of the potato, the loss on which only is 2,000,000*l.*, and we take no account of the 17,[illegible] rent and taxes in [illegible] the causes.

8171. (*Mr. Sexton.*) The rent and taxes go on every year, but the 2,000,000*l.* loss arose in this year?—The 2,000,000*l.* loss arose in this year. I will admit it might be an important cause, but my argument is that the taxes and the rent should be such as to enable the people to sustain such a fluctuation as this without being forced into famine, and it is so in any other country except Ireland.

8172. (*Sir David Barbour.*) But are you not applying to particular districts, arguments drawn from the average of the whole country, that is to say, the loss on the potato crop may have been much more heavy in one part of the country than in another, and in that person there may have been no gain from hay or oats?—It was to avoid that question that I read so much from this [illegible]. The loss is spread equally over every county.

8173. (*The O'Conor Don.*) But is it not the fact on that point that in certain parts of Ireland the people are much more dependent on the potato crop than in others?—I do not think so. I think the people who have suffered most in the present famine—and it is well to speak of the present one, because it is a type of them all—owing to the failure of the potato crop, are not the people who eat the potato, but the people who [illegible] upon the potato, the farmers who are a little above the lowest class. All the potatoes had run out by the [illegible] in January, and owing to that means of making money being withdrawn the distress has become very serious.

8174. Do you think there really was a famine in Ireland last year, it is a rather large word to use, is it not?—You have the symptoms which in any other country would be taken as a proof, and in the [illegible] Act which we have passed through the House of Commons we are giving relief to every union in Ireland, we are giving at the public expense, so far as the loan goes, free of interest, their seed, recognising the fact that they have eaten the seed, which is the last symptom of distress in an agricultural country.

8175. Is it the fact that every union in Ireland has taken advantage of that?—I think we may assume they will, they have before.

8176. You are giving them the money without interest, but the money will have to be repaid, will it not?—It is a loan without interest, and we give them years to repay it, and we forgive them easily if they do not repay it.

8177. Do you think they will accept that where they do not really want it?—But they want it everywhere.

8178. Can you say as a fact that they are accepting it everywhere?—So far as I know.

8179. (*Mr. Sexton.*) I think your main point is that the burden of rent and taxes in Ireland being equal to nearly half the value of the agricultural produce, that a fluctuation which any other country could withstand though relatively slight in Ireland causes distress and sometimes famine?—That is my point. The rent and taxes are 55 per cent. of the total produce. The loss by failure of crop is only 5 per cent., and that seems to me a not unreasonable fluctuation. The Irish harvests on the whole are steady, and I say it is more reasonable to suppose that the distress is owing to the 45 than to the 5 per cent.

8180. (*Lord Farrer.*) Are you right in putting rent and taxes together as an aggregate burden on the resources of Ireland? Surely the rent is a part of the resources of Ireland, and the taxes follow upon rent to a certain extent?—I think so in the Irish case, where so much of the rent is absentee rent.

8181. If you can get at it?—We know it is 4,000,000*l.* or 5,000,000*l.*

8182. But to take the rent of the country and treat it as an addition to the taxes of the country seems to be a curious way of arguing?—I think it is true, absolutely true in Ireland. In my county of Cavan we have hardly any resident landlords at all.

8183. (*Lord Welby.*) But surely partly the taxation comes out of that very land, does it not?—Yes, about [illegible]

8184. But you take them together?—No, I have allowed for that. I have only assumed 7,500,000*l.*, whereas the total taxation of the country is 11,[illegible]

8185. (*Mr. Sexton.*) About half the rent goes out, does it not?—I think so.

8186. Does not four-fifths of the taxation of the country come out of the articles of consumption, particularly from this very class we are discussing?—Yes.

8187. (*Lord Welby.*) On what do you base the statement that there are six millions of absentee rent?—I would rather say five millions.

8188. (*Mr. Sexton.*) Absentee rents and mortgage interest together?—Yes.

8189. (*Lord Farrer.*) But the five millions of rent which goes to absentees out of Ireland pays income tax, does it not?—Yes, it pays income tax.

8190. And that same rent on death pays succession duty?—Yes. So far we allow those taxes to the good.

8191. I mean it is part of the resources of Ireland for the purposes of bearing taxation?—Yes, up to the extent they pay.

8192. (*Mr. Sexton.*) But the yield of the income tax is so trivial in comparison with the whole amount that it hardly affects the argument, does it?—Very little, it is only [illegible]

8193. Half a million out of seven millions is so trivial that it does not affect the main drift of your argument?—No, it does not, and I tried to allow for that in putting only seven and a half millions, for I want to include both local and Imperial burdens, and I think I have allowed for income tax and all that the classes that live on the land do not pay.

8194. (*Chairman.*) Passing from famine and these other subjects, what other evils do you attribute to the burdens of taxation?—I think the increase of lunacy in Ireland, which is a most startling fact, must be traced to the severe burdens which prevent the people making a living. We find that the number in 1851 was 3,674 of registered lunatics, or one to 1,[illegible], in 1861 it had increased to 7,0[illegible], or one to 8[illegible], in 1871 to 9,7[illegible], or one to 5[illegible], in 1881 to 9,7[illegible], or one to [illegible], and in 1891 they had increased to 14,945, or one to 315. I have the table here, which I will hand in:—

—	1851.	1861.	1871.	1881.	1891.
Lunatics	[illegible]	[illegible]	[illegible]	[illegible]	[illegible]
	1 to [illegible]	1 to [illegible]	1 to [illegible]	1 to [illegible]	1 to [illegible]

8195. Are these lunatics in public charge, or are they lunatics whether in public charge or not?—They are lunatics in public charge in all the institutions of the country.

8196. Is not the proportion of lunatics who have been found out, if I may say so, very much greater of late years than formerly?—Yes, but I think we may take it we have a very fair comparison between 1871 and 1891, and there is a most startling increase between these periods, a far larger increase than in any previous years. I think we only assume we had captured all the lunatics by 1881.

[illegible]7. (*Lord Farrer.*) Do you remember what Swift said in the last century:—

> "He left the little that he had
> To build a house for fools and mad,
> To prove by one satiric touch,
> No nation wanted it so much."

So that there was a complaint of lunacy in those times too. In Swift's time there was great complaint of the misery of the people, was there not?—Yes.

[illegible]8. The complaint of the Irish people is no new thing, is it?—No.

[illegible]9. (*Mr. Sexton.*) You have shown the extraordinary increase of lunacy between 1851 and 1891 to coincide with the extraordinary increase of emigration of the same years, have you not?—Yes.

[illegible]0. (*Sir David Barbour.*) Was there any great increase of taxation between 1851 and 1891?—Oh dear, yes.

[illegible]1. Do you think that has anything to do with the increase of lunacy in that period?—Yes.

[illegible]2. (*Lord Welby.*) Not an increase of taxation, was there?—Yes. In 1850 the amount demanded from each person was 11s. 6d., and in 1894 1l. 12s. 6d. per head for imperial taxation alone. The increase in local taxation was 5s. 7d. per head.

[illegible]3. (*Sir David Barbour.*) But were the duties on articles of common consumption raised during that period?—I only look at it from the aspect of what you ask each person to pay.

[illegible]4. There was an enormous increase in the lunatics between 1851 and 1891, and you put down high taxation as one of the causes. I ask you, do you think the increase of lunacy was due to an increase in rates of taxation?—There is an increase in the amount we demand per head, and nothing would seem to me more likely to cause an increase in lunacy than pressing for these impossible sums while the whole prosperity of the country was sinking.

[illegible]5. But there was no rate of duty raised, was there, the spirit duty was not raised, was it?—It may have been raised a little.

[illegible]6. (*Lord Farrer.*) Supposing that I pay 6d. in the £ income tax in this year, and I have to pay a 100l. a year, and supposing the rate remains the same, and next year I have to pay twice that amount because my income has increased, you would not on that account say there has been an increased burden of taxation put upon me, would you?—No.

[illegible]7. (*Mr. Sexton.*) Of course you would admit that where it is a question of income tax, the man with an increased income suffers nothing by paying the tax, but where it is a question of decreased income of the [illegible] classes of the kingdom there it is an increasing burden?—Quite so. In regard to this increase of lunacy, there has been a suggestion made that it was owing to tea drinking. That seems to me one of the most foolish suggestions we have ever heard about the Irish question. It seems to me it can be traced to no other cause except the struggle for existence, and the difficulty people have in making ends meet.

[illegible]8. (*Chairman.*) Have you any other social effect to attribute to over-taxation?—Yes, the decrease of marriages and births. I think that the connection will be readily acknowledged between want and reluctance to marry. The proportion per cent. of the population of 17 years and upwards married is as follows:—

—	[illegible]	[illegible]	[illegible]
Ireland	[illegible]	[illegible]	[illegible]

So that we see a steady reduction in the number of people who are married.

[illegible]9. (*Mr. Sexton.*) Together with greatly increased emigration at the same time?—Yes, then the annual average of persons married to 1,000 living, is lower in Ireland than in any other European country now. It is 90, and I may say it has been steadily decreasing during the 20 years. This is a very remarkable figure as to the Irish, who are supposed to be a fertile people. The figure is 90 in Ireland; Sweden, 151; Belgium, 118; Switzerland, 107; France, 1[illegible]; Italy, 1[illegible]; Prussia, 167; England, 1[illegible]; Scotland, 1[illegible]. All these figures of European countries compare with 90 in Ireland. Then the figures as to births are just the same, the births in Ireland have fallen now to [illegible]; in Sweden they are 2[illegible]; England, 2[illegible]; [illegible], [illegible].

[illegible]0. (*Chairman.*) How do you connect these figures with over-taxation?—I say that over-taxation produces want, and that these are the fruits you may expect to see when a country is reduced to a state of semi-destitution.

[illegible]1. (*Sir David Barbour.*) But is not the decrease, to which you have alluded, brought about by the emigration of young people?—That again is caused by the same thing. The whole figures with regard to the country, I think are unexampled, and this is one of the most serious. I trace all these evils simply to the excess imposed annually on the nation in the shape of financial burdens, and we may answer the question as to what results the over-taxation taken in connection with the over-renting has produced in Ireland by saying it has decimated the population, ruined the agricultural districts, led to a vast increase in pauperism, [illegible] a most intelligent, gay, and healthy community to produce the largest proportion of lunatics, and changed the most [illegible] people in the world into the most sterile.

[illegible]2. You ascribe, do you, all these evils to over-taxation?—In connection with over-renting.

[illegible]3. But from some other parts of your evidence I gather you would be prepared to say that Ireland suffering from economic causes has had that suffering aggravated by over-taxation and over-renting. Is that your view, or do you say that the evils are not due to economic causes but have been produced by taxation and over-renting?—I will take your view.

[illegible]4. I ask is it your view?—I will accept it that the suffering which the country has had to bear in any case has been greatly aggravated.

[illegible]5. (*Mr. Sexton.*) Except that the economic difficulty in Ireland, which has been aggravated by over-renting and over-taxation, was itself, if not produced at least stimulated by Imperial policy in the repeal of the Corn Laws for the interests of Great Britain?—Yes, I think it was stimulated; I will adopt that word. I am not against the abolition of the duty on corn.

[illegible]6. I am not discussing that in principle at all, but do not you conceive that an economic condition which compelled the change from agriculture, which you consider suitable to Ireland, to the rearing of cattle, was stimulated at least by the repeal of the Corn Laws, a measure itself stimulated by the necessities of Great Britain?—I do, certainly—it was largely stimulated; I quite agree there was need for a violent change, it was forced on, the country could not help it, and it is that violent change which has wrought such terrible evil.

[illegible]7. And it was the manifest interest of Great Britain, was it not, which dictated that change?—Exactly. I will put it further, the necessities of her great manufacturing communities forced the change along, and that change ruined agricultural Ireland.

[illegible]8. (*Chairman.*) But as you qualified it before it was not the only cause which led to the repeal of the Corn Laws, but Irish distress itself led to the repeal of the Corn Laws?—No.

[illegible]9. I thought I understood you to say so?—No, I only want the distress as saying that Sir Robert Peel gave that as one of his reasons.

[illegible]0. (*Lord Farrer.*) The great cause—the larger cause—had been at work for years, but that was the immediate moving cause?—I am always sceptical about immediate moving causes.

[illegible]1. (*Mr. Sexton.*) Whatever may have been stated by Sir Robert Peel did the measure operate to mitigate or increase Irish distress?—It tended to increase it, and I think we must go to the opinion of Mr. Cobden

TWENTY-SECOND DAY.

Friday, 24th May 1895.

At Committee Room B, House of Lords.

PRESENT:

THE RIGHT HON. THE O'CONOR DON, *Chairman*.

Lord Farrer.
Sir David Barbour, K.C.S.I.
The Hon. Edward Blake, M.P.
Bertram W. Currie, Esq.

Charles E. Martin, Esq.
Thomas Sexton, Esq., M.P.
Gustav Wolff, Esq., M.P.
Henry F. Slattery, Esq.

Mr. B. H. Holland, *Secretary*.

Sir Edward W. Hamilton, K.C.B., recalled.

Sir E. W. Hamilton, K.C.B.

24 May 1895.

6624. (*Chairman.*) You have given the Commission a most valuable and interesting statement of the Financial Relations between Great Britain and Ireland, both before and after the legislative Union, and before I deal with any particular figures I should wish to ask you whether it does not appear from your statement that prior to the year 1782 (the year of independence) taxation in Ireland was altogether dissimilar from that of Great Britain?—I think that is so, certainly.

6625. Was not the contribution of Ireland towards Imperial expenditure in that period, previous to 1782, rather of an indirect character?—It was. I think it may be said to have consisted entirely of a certain number of soldiers who were placed at the disposal of the Imperial Government.

6626. Did it not amount to what you call in your paper, the constitutional right of the Crown to a contribution to the military establishment?—Yes; it was fixed in a more definite form by an Act of Parliament in 1769.

6627. And there was no special grant at that time made towards the navy or any other Imperial expenditure?—No.

6628. Of course, Ireland at that time did not contribute to the British debt in any way, did it?—No.

6629. In the year 1782 and during the continuance of the Irish Parliament, I suppose all grants towards Imperial expenditure were absolutely at the discretion of that Parliament?—I should hold that to be the case.

6630. And there was no constitutional right to interfere with that discretion?—No, I think not.

6631. Of course it follows from that, that taxation during that period was absolutely dissimilar in the two countries?—Yes, under the control of the Irish Parliament.

6632. Then coming to the later period when the Act of Union was passed, and up to the time of the amalgamation of the Exchequers, Ireland contributed in certain proportions, did she not, to the general expenditure of the Empire?—After the Union yes, in the proportion of 1 to 7½.

6633. During that period the taxation was dissimilar?—Yes, it was dissimilar.

6634. Was it not also one of the conditions of the Act of Union that even after the amalgamation of the Exchequers, and after a general indiscriminate taxation was applied, there should be exemptions or abatements to Ireland according as her circumstances required?—That was in the Act of Union no doubt.

Act of Union.

6635. Therefore was it not clear that it was intended even after the amalgamation of the Exchequers, that Ireland should be treated as a separate unit or entity for taxation?—I do not know that I should go so far as to say that it was a separate entity for taxation, because I think if you have indiscriminate taxation you can hardly say there can be a separate entity for taxation, but I think there is no doubt the terms of the Union did contemplate that the matter should be reviewed from time to time, and that any special circumstances should be taken into account as had been done in the case of Scotland.

6636. Up to the present date is it not the fact that there are differences between the taxation of the two countries?—There are several taxes to which Ireland is not subject.

6637. Does it not follow from all that that from the time of Ireland's connection with England up to the present date Ireland has never been treated in the same way as if she were merely a county of England?—That is so, I think, certainly.

Distinctive fiscal position of Ireland.

6638. And, I suppose, you will admit that it is possible to have separate and distinct taxation for the two separate islands?—I think it would be attended with an enormous amount of inconvenience.

6639. But there is nothing impossible in the suggestion, is there?—I think it would be impossible short of having, so to speak, a customs barrier.

6640. I am not speaking now of having differential customs duties, but is it not possible to have a different system of taxation in the two countries irrespective of customs duties?—As far as indirect taxation is concerned, I think you would be bound to have a customs barrier. Of course if you wholly exempt the country from a direct tax, that is quite another matter.

6641. What I mean is this. It has been said, and said in Parliament, very much before the Committee on which I served in 1864, that countries were not taxed, but individuals were taxed, and what I want to ask you is this: whether it is not really the fact that a country (meaning by "country" the individuals that live in a certain island, we will say) can be taxed differently from individuals who live in another part of a country under the same government?—I do not quite understand what you mean by the word "can"—when you say can be taxed, of course you can, from a practical point of view, do so if you treat them as two separate countries, and, as I say, raise up customs barriers, but I do not see how you can treat them otherwise separately from a fiscal point of view.

8642. You could, for instance, treat them as Ireland was treated up to the year 1853 as being free from the income tax?—My remarks had reference to indirect taxation.

8643. I was speaking of taxation generally?—Yes, just in the same way as Ireland now is not subject to the inhabited house duty, that being a direct tax.

8644. Do not the terms of reference to this very Commission justify the assumption that we have to inquire into the relative capacities of Ireland and Great Britain as distinct countries?—Yes. I think the terms of the reference certainly contemplate that.

8645. Coming to the financial arrangements made under the Union, each country, as we know, had to contribute to the general expenditure in a certain proportion, 15 to 2, and each country was to be liable for its separate debt, but outside that, was there any separate charge upon either country?—No, I think not.

8646. At the bottom of page 31 and the beginning of page 32 of your paper you allude to a slight departure from that. There is a small sum put down there for separate charges?—It is the time between 1801 and 1817 you are alluding to.

8647. Yes, there are some trifling charges there besides the expenses of the separate debt which are charged separately, are there not?—Yes, that is the case.

8648. Would it not appear from that return that nearly the whole of those charges were in the first two years after the Union and that they probably had some connection with obligations incurred before the Union?—Yes, I should think that is certainly the case, that they had reference to some of the charges that had been incurred by Ireland herself prior to the Union.

8649. But under the Act of Union was there any provision which would have made expenditure on account of the government of Ireland anything else than Imperial expenditure?—No, I think not, but, of course, the separate charge for debt.

8650. Whether right or wrong all expenditure then voted by Parliament was to be regarded as Imperial, excepting the charges for the separate debt?—Yes, the pre-Union debt.

8651. I would ask you then, did not the Act of Union, following from what I have said, really affirm these three principles: first, that Ireland was to be regarded for financial purposes as a separate country?—Yes.

8652. And even with the amalgamation of the Exchequers she was to be entitled to special exemptions according as circumstances might require?—That is so.

8653. Secondly, that she was to contribute to the Imperial expenditure, that which was supposed to represent her taxable capacity in certain proportions which were settled by Act of Parliament?—Yes.

8654. And thirdly, that this Imperial expenditure included all expenditure voted by Parliament, no matter to what part of the United Kingdom it became necessary, excepting the expenditure for the separate debts?—Yes, except that I think the Act of Union must be held to have contemplated the possibility that Ireland might incur a debt charge separate from that of Great Britain.

8655. These proportions of 2 to 15 you have told us were adopted on the supposition that they represented the taxable capacity of the two countries. Might I ask you, who have given so very much attention to the subject, is it your opinion that that proportion was a just one, and really represented the taxable capacity of the two countries?—I think it is very difficult so many years after to express a definite opinion upon it. I think it was the best calculation that was able to be made at the time, and I think it is very possible that had there not been the enormous charge in connexion with war and the disturbed state of Ireland herself, that might have turned out to be a fairly equitable arrangement. I think, in consequence of the enormous war expenditure which was incurred, the arrangement turned out certainly to the disadvantage of Ireland; in fact, I will go so far as to say that the charge was a very burdensome one for Ireland.

8656. You believe, then, it was in excess as things turned out, do you?—Yes, as things turned out.

8657. (*Sir David Barbour.*) If the two countries were to contribute in proportion to their taxable capacity that would involve the assumption that taxation would be levied equally heavily in both countries, putting aside the charge of debt? That is to say, if the two countries are to contribute in proportion to their taxable capacity, you must assume that taxation is equally heavy in both countries?—Would that follow, because a tax might produce a great deal more relatively in one country than in another? It might be more productive in one than the other.

8658. But would not the general assumption be that you must take an equal amount?—Certainly.

8659. In proportion to the wealth?—Yes, but not necessarily by the same taxes.

8660. An amount of revenue in proportion to wealth or capacity?—An equal amount of revenue.

8661. And to do that you would have to put on taxes roughly of equal burden in the two countries, would you not?—I do not think it would follow of equal burden. They might be much more burdensome in one country than in another.

8662. In point of fact taxes were not put on in Ireland to the same extent as in Great Britain?—No, not to the same extent.

8663. (*Chairman.*) Have you a copy of your evidence before you?—Yes.

8664. I find, that in answer to Question [illegible], on the very point asked you by Mr. Sexton, you say, "I have come to the conclusion, speaking entirely for myself, that Ireland was taxed as heavily as probably she could reasonably be expected to be taxed without leading to the result which may come from over-taxation, that is to say, a diminished revenue." Do you adhere to the opinion therein expressed that during that period Ireland, although she had not exactly similar taxes as England, was taxed to the full extent of her ability?—I should like to qualify that in one respect. I was thinking at the time of the general mass of the people. One, of course, must remember that it might have been possible to have got something out of Ireland in the way of income tax without it relatively being a greater oppression than it was in Great Britain at the time, but speaking of the masses of the people, I think the conclusion I came to was that she had been subject to as high duties as could be reasonably expected.

8665. And consequently the point put by Sir David Barbour would not apply, that Ireland's failing to pay her proportion was due to her being too lightly taxed?—Except as regards the income tax, yes.

8666. Who was responsible for this taxation of Ireland at that period?—I think the Executive Government of the United Kingdom.

8667. And the Imperial Parliament?—And the Imperial Parliament.

8668. And if Ireland was not taxed up to the full amount of her abilities the Imperial Parliament was to blame?—Certainly, the blame would fall upon Parliament.

8669. Assuming that Ireland was, as you have stated, taxed as heavily as she could bear without the result of producing a diminished revenue, is it not evident that the proportion placed upon her by the Act of Union as circumstances turned out was excessive?—Yes, as circumstances turned out.

8670. Owing to the enormous war expenditure?—Yes, owing to the enormous war expenditure.

8671. One of the results arising from that has been this, has it not, that the Irish debt was raised up to the same proportion as the English debt, or a little more?—I do not quite understand what you mean by the same proportion.

8672. Before the Union the Irish debt was in a much lower proportion to the English than as 15 to 2, was it not?—Yes, that is so.

8673. And by the failure of Ireland to contribute this 15 to 2 in revenue, her debt was more largely increased than the debt of Great Britain?—Yes, that is so.

8674. And consequently Ireland has lost the advantage which she possessed at the union of having a proportionately smaller debt?—Yes.

6675. So that if it be true that the proportion of [illegible] to [illegible] was excessive, through that circumstance Ireland has been deprived of an advantage which she enjoyed at the time of Union?—Yes.

6676. Because, as it appears from your paper, although she did not make up her proportion in revenue, she did make it up in some shape or form by raising the debt?—Yes, the greater part of it.

6677. With the exception of a small proportion, a couple of millions, or something like that?—Yes.

6678. Is it not also a fact that this large war expenditure, and in fact, the very existence of those wars in one way served Great Britain in improving her trade, and making her the carrying nation of the world?—I doubt if that was so in the first years after the Union, but later on I think that would be the case.

6679. But do you not think during those commercial wars, that one effect arising out of it was to improve very much the trade of Great Britain? Do you not think the wealth of Great Britain largely increased during that time in spite of the large taxation?—You will see, on page 17 of the edition of the Memorandum which I have before me, I give the relative value of imports and exports from Great Britain and Ireland in 1815 as compared with 1801. It will be observed that the increase was relatively greater than it was in Ireland, but not so much as might have been expected. It rose from [illegible] to [illegible] millions, roughly speaking.

6680. What was the proportionate increase?—I put it out from [illegible] to 1 to [illegible] to 1.

6681. You do not think that the relative increase was at very much more in Great Britain than in Ireland during that period?—I do not think it comes out in a very marked manner.

6682. With regard to the increase in the debt, I gather from your former evidence you consider it doubtful whether the form in which the debt was incurred was justifiable, or contemplated by the Act of Union?—I thought it was doubtful whether it was contemplated in so many words by the Act of Union, but at the same time, I think it was the only practicable way in which the terms of the Union could be carried out. That, I think, may be inferred to be the conclusion to which the Committees which sat between 1807 and 1815 came.

6683. (*Sir David Barbour.*) Do you not consider, having regard to the terms of the Union—that is to say, assuming that the terms of the Union were equitable—that the mode of working it was equitable?—I think so, there was no other way. There is a passage in one of the reports of the Committee of 1815, from which they evidently thought it would have been manifestly unfair to work it in any other way.

6684. Do you think it was equitable, having regard to the terms of the Union?—Yes, in the sense that I think there was no other way of working it.

6685. And that there was no injustice done?—As it turned out, of course, the debt charge pressed very heavily upon Ireland.

6686. But that would have come, upon it now, in any case?—Yes.

6687. Assuming the equity of the terms of the Union, then, the mode of working it was equitable, was it not?—Yes.

6688. (*Mr Blake.*) And assuming the terms of the Union inequitable, it does not aggravate any injustice there was?—Quite so.

6689. (*Chairman.*) Was not the Irish debt raised upon the credit of Ireland as distinct from the credit of the United Kingdom?—The greater part was raised in Great Britain, and Ireland got the benefit of the market of Great Britain, but the credit, I suppose, in the first instance was that of Ireland.

6690. And in consequence of that had not she to pay a larger amount for the raising of the debt?—Her credit, I presume, did not stand equal to that of Great Britain.

6691. You state, in answer to Question 1530, "What
"I meant was, that the debt raised separately for
"Ireland primarily rested on the credit of the Irish
"revenue"?—Yes.

6692. "I presume the Imperial credit was behind it,
"but at the same time the fact that Ireland had been in
"a perpetual deficit in those years must have made
"her borrow on much more onerous terms than she
"would had she been able to make ends meet." Now, if the debt had been raised as a joint debt, and not in the form of a separate debt upon Ireland, I presume it could have been raised on more reasonable terms?—I presume so; but it is difficult to speak with any certainty at this distance of time about the loan arrangements.

6693. And could it not, under the terms of the Act of Union, have been raised as a joint debt, and subsequently apportioned between the two countries?—I do not know. I should not like to express an opinion upon that after this long lapse of time.

6694. You expressed the opinion a moment ago, in answer to Sir David Barbour, that there was no other way of meeting the difficulty, except in the form which was adopted?—Certainly, so far as the apportionment of the charge is concerned, that is the only way in which it could be met as regards the apportionment of the charge. Now, I think, you are speaking to me as regards raising the loan?

6695. Yes. You see the charge that was placed upon Ireland depends, to a certain extent, upon the rate at which the loans were raised?—Yes, no doubt.

6696. And if the system which was adopted in borrowing was one which, the security not being so good, being only Irish instead of Imperial security, caused the loans to be raised under more disadvantageous terms, does it not follow that a higher charge was placed upon Ireland than if the debt had been raised directly upon Imperial security?—That, no doubt, would be the case, but to what extent I have formed no opinion.

6697. I want to go back to the question whether the Act of Union did not contemplate raising a joint debt, and subsequently apportioning that debt between the two countries. If you would look at Question 1527 and your answer to me you will see there Article 6 is quoted?—Yes.

6698. Article 6 provides "If at any time in raising
"their respective contributions hereby fixed for each
"country, the Parliament of the United Kingdom shall
"judge it fit to raise a greater proportion of such respec-
"tive contributions in one country within the year than
"in the other" (that is the point I want to draw your attention to), "or to set apart a greater proportion of
"sinking fund for the liquidation of the whole or any
"part of the loan raised on account of the one country
"than of that raised on account of the other country,
"then such part of the said loan for the liquidation of
"which different provisions shall have been made for the
"respective countries, shall be kept distinct, and shall
"be borne by each separately." Does not that contemplate making a separate provision in the way of sinking fund for debt in one country rather than in the other, but leaving the debt raised upon the Imperial security?—I think it is open to that interpretation.

6699. That is another mode in which the deficiency of revenue in Ireland might have been met, is it not?—Yes; to a certain extent.

6700. And if that mode had been adopted instead of the one which was adopted of raising those loans primarily upon Irish security, as you have said before, the loss to Ireland would not have been so great?—No, not so great.

6701. I do not think you have told us, but could you tell the Commission what was the loss to Ireland between the capital sum created in debt, and the actual receipts in cash?—I do not think I have any statement on that point, but no doubt I could furnish the Commission with the information.

6702. (*Mr. Sexton.*) It is in the returns of the Committee of 1815, is it not?—But I should like to have that figure analysed again. The debt charge has been gone into a great deal lately, and perhaps the result would not work out exactly the same.

6703. (*Chairman.*) It was stated before us on the Committee of 1815?—I will endeavour to furnish some figures.

6704. There was a considerable sum at all events, was there not, between the capital debt created and the amount of cash received?—Yes, and it was the same in Great Britain—there was an enormous difference.

6705. You have quoted a number of statements made by very distinguished Irishmen to the effect that after the Union, Ireland was treated not merely with justice, but even with partiality. I suppose there is nothing

Sir E. W. Hamilton, K.C.B.

30 May 1895.

inconsistent in that statement with the test of the proportion of contribution placed upon Ireland being excessive?—I was only quoting what the view of Irishmen at the time was.

8706. But that did not show that they considered that the proportion placed upon Ireland was one which would show partiality towards her?—No.

Presumed hardness of taxation to Ireland relatively to Great Britain.

8707. Assuming that Ireland is to be treated as a distinct country, or entity, for financial purposes, and assuming also, that she ought only to be taxed in proportion to her taxable capacity, is it, or is it not, your opinion, that she is now paying in taxation a greater proportion out of her wealth or income than Great Britain is paying?—I should like to be allowed to make one general remark with your leave. Of course, in expressing any opinion here, it must be understood I do not commit the Treasury in any way. I only speak for myself individually. I am authorised to appear here as a member of the Treasury to furnish you with any information that I can; but I am not in a position to commit the Treasury by anything I say.

8708. Quite so?—The honourable member now refers, I suppose, to the present state of things?

8709. Yes?—I think it is difficult to give a direct aye or no to that query, but I think there is no question that, relatively to her resources, as regards indirect taxation—but only indirect taxation, owing to the particular habits and tastes of the Irishman—Ireland is paying more than Great Britain is.

8710. With regard of course to direct taxation that is paid in proportion to the income?—I think that is so; assuming that Ireland's income is about one twentieth of that of Great Britain.

8711. In support of that view which I am very glad to have obtained from you, you have given a number of very interesting tables in your paper, among them being a table showing the various standards of comparison of wealth. In those standards of comparison first of all the Probate and Succession duty shows that Ireland's capacity is 5·6 per cent.; income tax 5·5 per cent.; assessed capital 4·5 per cent.; railway receipts 8·9 per cent.; savings banks' deposits 8·7 per cent.; money orders, 5·5 per cent.; postal orders, letters and telegrams 5·7 per cent. These all show, if they are to be taken as guide, that Ireland is paying a larger proportion than her taxable capacity would justify?—As regards indirect taxation, yes.

8712. Of course when you say as regards indirect taxation, we presume that direct taxation is paid in proportion, and therefore we may set that aside. Ireland is not paying more upon the direct taxation than England is, is she?—No.

8713. Therefore, as far as direct taxation is concerned the two countries may be said to be paying on the same basis?—There are certain taxes from which Ireland is exempt, the inhabited house duty, the land tax, and establishment licences. She is entirely exempt from those taxes.

8714. But with the exception of those?—As regards the other main branches of direct taxes, Ireland stands on the same footing as Great Britain.

8715. Taking the whole taxation of each country and the total amount that is contributed out of each country, and contrasting that with the tests of either the wealth or the income of the respective countries, is it not clear that as a whole Ireland pays a larger proportion out of that income than Great Britain does in taxes?—Relatively to her population and relatively to her presumed taxable capacity, yes.

Test of taxable capacity.

8716. I want to deal for a moment with the qualification which you put in your paper to these statements. You qualify your statement by saying that a man's income is not necessarily a test of his ability to taxation, and you say that Ireland's capacity to bear taxation may be greater in proportion to its income than the capacity of Great Britain, inasmuch as the Irish income may go further in meeting the requirements of the owners, because Irishmen, as a body, may have certain advantages; and you refer to those advantages. The Irishman may be able to house himself more cheaply, spend less on his food, his food may be cheaper, and his clothing may cost him less; therefore the amount of a man's income is not necessarily a test of his capacity to bear taxation. You say these things may be the case; have you any reason to believe that they are the case?—No. I was taking the test of income, and I thought it was a very obvious thing to say: "Yes, but that is not "a fair test to take, because a given income in one "country may go further than the same income in "another country." I only made the remark so as to qualify myself, or rather, so to speak, to forestall an argument that might naturally be used.

8717. You do not urge these things as facts, do you? —No, not in the least. It was simply that I thought it was an obvious retort to make upon anybody who was contrasting income as a taxable test.

8718. I presume you do not mean, when you suggest that the Irishman may house himself more cheaply, for instance, that he can have a similar house at a cheaper rate in Ireland than in England?—I am afraid I am not sufficiently well acquainted with the country to say that; I was only speaking on general grounds.

8719. I want to find out whether you meant that the Irish possibly might not have the same wants as the English, or that that those wants could be supplied more cheaply?—I meant on general grounds that it was quite conceivable a man might be able in one country to provide himself better with the necessaries of life than a man in another country on the same means.

8720. On similar means and similar necessaries of life?—Yes.

8721. I want to ascertain whether you meant if the Irishman, for instance, lived on a lower class of diet, or lived in a lower class house he would have more?—No, I was only speaking generally.

8722. What was in your mind was that such things should be both similar, that the mode of living should be similar and the ability to pay should be similar?—Yes, but the Commission will understand that I was only speaking in the broadest possible sense, I was not drawing any conclusions.

8723. (*Mr. Sexton.*) You indicated it as a possible argument?—Yes, as a possible argument which might be brought up against such a test as that of income.

8724. (*Chairman.*) You also suggested as a possible argument that the amount the taxpayer actually spends in taxation on what you call luxuries may be a better test of his ability than any of those other tests that have been quoted?—Yes, that was my personal opinion; I thought it a better test or rather a less misleading one.

8725. Which would you think the most frequent and expensive dinner, beef or bacon with bread, or dry bread and tea?—I suppose beef or bacon with bread.

8726. And the English labourer, as you know, partakes of that much more largely than the Irish?—There are a greater number of people, no doubt, in Great Britain, who are able to indulge in those luxuries, but at the same time I suppose there are quite as many poor people in Great Britain who are unable to indulge in those luxuries as there are in Ireland.

8727. But if the Irishman, out of his poverty is unable to indulge in the luxuries which pay no taxes, such as beef, bacon, and bread, and is obliged to have resort to tea and dry bread, how can that be taken as a proof of the taxable capacity of the Irishman more than the Englishman?—I should have hardly thought that tea was a substitute for beef or bacon; I do not quite see the analogy.

8728. As a matter of fact it is so. In a great many parts of Ireland with which I am acquainted, that is the dinner, breakfast, and everything of the working classes?—But tea can hardly be considered to be food.

8729. Tea and bread?—Tea is hardly a nutritive article, is it?

8730. No, but it helps to get down the bread. Is it not also a notorious fact, going a little further, that even the use of alcoholic drinks often arises from poverty?—Yes, I believe that is the case.

8731. Therefore, how can you regard it as a proof of the capacity to pay taxes?—I will not go so far as to say that tea and alcoholic drinks are luxuries, but they are expensive items, at any rate, in which the Irishman indulges, and I should have thought that the consumption of such articles was a fair test—I will call it a complementary test—of the taxable capacity of a country, and one that occurred to me, on the whole, as being least misleading. I will not say more than that.

8732. I should like now to go to the expenditure question. Will you turn to page 39 of your Memorandum. You see there you have a table showing the expenditure incurred on local services in Great Britain and Ireland respectively?—Yes.

6733. Can you tell me when this distinction between local services and Imperial services was first drawn?—In the way in which it has been drawn in these accounts?

6734. Yes?—It must be said, I think, to owe its origin to the return of returns drawn by Mr. Goschen in 1890 for the Committee which was never appointed.

6735. But up to that date the distinction was never heard of, I suppose?—I don't it always existed; I do not think any returns had been made upon that basis. But we always considered that Imperial and local expenditure ought to be distinguished.

6736. The distinction hitherto that one has always heard of is between Imperial and local expenditure was the expenditure voted by the Imperial Parliament, and the expenditure incurred by local bodies?—But I do not think that is really the true distinction to draw.

6737. Why not?—For instance, under recent financial arrangements a part of the expenditure which was met out of rates is now met out of revenue which is collected by Imperial officers, and handed over to the local authorities. It is manifest that that expenditure is quite as much local as expenditure out of rates.

6738. That is a grant in aid of those local rates?—Yes, but still it is an expenditure met out of Imperial revenue.

6739. But excepting that which is of course Imperial revenue, why should the preservation of order, or the collection of the revenue, or any of those other purposes, be considered local? Is it not as much for the benefit of the Empire that order should be preserved in one part of the country as in another?—Yes; but surely a part of that expenditure is incurred solely and entirely for Ireland. Let me illustrate my meaning by an extreme case. Suppose Ireland, owing to some terrible catastrophe of nature, disappeared tomorrow, there is no doubt we should get rid of a great many charges; we should not have to educate the Irishmen, we should not have to keep up a large police force in Ireland, we should be rid of many other administrative charges, but we should not get off one sixpence of the National Debt charge, and we should probably have to keep up the same army and navy. That is the distinction which I draw in my own mind between Imperial and local expenditure. It is a distinction which has been drawn for a great many years. I remember when Mr. Gladstone first introduced his Bill of 1886, he drew exactly the same distinction between Imperial and local expenditure as Mr. Goschen did in 1890.

6740. Then according to that definition you would think, would you, that the expenditure chargeable on Great Britain is that expenditure only which would have to be incurred if Ireland met with such a catastrophe as you suggest?—Yes.

6741. Accepting that definition, supposing Ireland was swallowed up in the Atlantic by some extraordinary convulsion, would England have to spend any shilling less on the navy and army than she now does?—No, I think not, and therefore I regard it as Imperial expenditure. It is possible the army might be somewhat reduced, but I do not suppose any material reduction would be tolerated by the authorities in Pall Mall.

6742. But the army and navy are essential for England alone, are they not? If Ireland were not there England would have to pay exactly the same amount?—I have no doubt that the War Office authorities would make out that it would be absolutely essential for us to have as big an army as ever.

6743. Upon the principle you have just laid down then why should Ireland contribute anything towards that Imperial expenditure?—Why should it be regarded as expenditure on the part of Ireland if it be absolutely essential for Great Britain?—Because surely Ireland gets the benefit equally with Great Britain—I will not say equally—but, at any rate, to a certain extent, she shares the benefit which we gain by keeping up our credit in the way of paying our debt, and in maintaining the Empire by our army and our navy.

6744. But do you think that expenditure would be required supposing Ireland were an independent country, do you think she would require that expenditure on the army and navy?—She would surely require an army.

6745. Do you think she would?—I am not aware of any country in Europe or any civilised country that has not got an army.

6746. Supposing Ireland started perfectly independently tomorrow, do you think she would require an army?—I should have thought so most certainly. I cannot conceive the existence of any country without an army of some kind.

6747. Do you not think Great Britain would rather make it a condition that she should have no army?—You are talking now of her as an independent country?

6748. Yes?—No, I cannot conceive that. I should have thought that Ireland under such restrictions would not be an independent country. An independent country surely would have the right of fixing her own army, and determining for herself whether she would require an army. I should imagine it would be impossible for a country to exist without an army.

6749. Has Canada an army?—She has a certain number of troops.

6750. Only militia, not a standing army?—Not a standing army, but she has troops.

6751. Has she a navy?—No.

6752. Have the Colonies of England standing armies or navies?—They have troops certainly, in Australia they have very considerable troops.

6753. Only for local purposes?—Yes, for local purposes.

6754. Let us confine ourselves to the navy. Why should Ireland contribute at all to the navy upon the definition you have now given of Imperial and local services?—Because I think that Ireland benefits by the defence of the Empire through the navy just as much as the rest of the inhabitants of the United Kingdom do.

6755. Does she benefit a bit more than the Colonies?—Yes, I think so, by her close proximity to Great Britain.

6756. But in what way does that give her a greater benefit than the Colonies. Would not England, for her own sake, quite irrespective of the interests of Ireland, take care that nobody attacked Ireland. Would it not be absolutely essential for England to do so?—That may be the case, but then surely Ireland must have to care her own protection. If she is a separate country she would be bound to take steps to protect herself.

6757. Are the Colonies separate countries?—No, they are not separate countries.

6758. They do not pay anything towards the navy of Great Britain, do they?—Australia contributes towards the navy of Great Britain.

6759. Take Canada, does she?—I do not think so.

6760. If you lay down that definition which you laid down a moment ago as to Imperial charges, I ask you on what grounds Ireland should contribute more than Canada?—I laid down that definition as an extreme definition. I was trying to illustrate my meaning, as one often does, by taking an extreme illustration, but the distinction drawn between Imperial and local expenditure, I say, has been one which has been drawn on the highest authority. I can quote two very high financial authorities, who for the last 25 years have drawn that distinction, one, Mr. Gladstone, and the other, Mr. Goschen. I think Mr. Giffen said there was no authority for it, but with all due deference to Mr. Giffen, I think Mr. Goschen was a very great authority indeed, and he drew a distinction, and, in fact, Parliament accepted the distinction. I will not say Parliament, because this is not a parliamentary reference, but the distinction is clearly contemplated in the terms of reference to this Commission itself.

6761. (Mr. Sexton.) The origin of the distinction, I think, is rather clear, because Mr. Gladstone's Bill, and the political proceedings then consequent on the Bill, have always contemplated such a change as would establish in Ireland a government to be provided for out of an Irish Exchequer, and also the expenditure required within that country, and a contribution to Imperial expenses as well?—Certainly.

6762. (Mr. Blake.) I understand you to suggest the origin of it to be Mr. Gladstone's proposals in 1886?—Yes.

8763. I was dealing with the future by the light of the past considering that all the local expenditure would be in the future under the new scheme?—In discussing a question of this kind, I can quite understand anybody not wishing to regard Ireland as a separate fiscal entity, but if you once begin to regard her as such I think you must look to much at one side of the account as at the other side of the account.

8764. (*Mr. Sexton.*) You are obliged to ask yourself the question after the Government of Ireland have maintained the machinery of government in that country what can they afford to pay towards the Empire?—No doubt.

8765. And in that way a distinction necessarily arises?—Yes.

8766. (*Chairman.*) Why should not the collection of the revenue of Ireland be regarded as an Imperial service?—I think it is an open question whether collection of revenue in Great Britain and Ireland should be regarded as an Imperial service or not.

8767. I see you have put it down as a local service?—I think I am right in saying that in the last Home Rule Bill it was treated as an Imperial service.

8768. (*Mr. Sexton.*) What was?—The collection of the customs revenue in both countries was treated as an Imperial service in the Bill of 1893 as introduced, and in the Bill as passed by the House of Commons that of both Customs and Inland Revenue was so treated.

8769. (*Chairman.*) Your tables show that a very considerable portion of the revenue nominally paid in Ireland is really contributed by Great Britain; that is so, is it not?—Yes.

8770. And surely it is not fair to set down the collection of that as a local charge in Ireland, is it?—I quite admit it is open to argument that you ought to make a deduction from the collection charge; I admit that, and I remember that point distinctly coming up in connexion with the financial proposals of 1893.

8771. If the collection of the revenue is an open point, which ought to be perhaps regarded as an Imperial matter, rather than a local one, do you not think that the protection of the revenue ought also to come under the same category?—I do not understand what is meant by the protection of revenue.

Expenditure on Irish constabulary.

8772. I will explain: One of the largest items I find under Irish expenditure is that upon the constabulary?—Yes.

8773. Is it not one of the duties of the constabulary to protect the revenue, especially in regard to illicit distillation?—Yes, that is so.

8774. Was it not one of the reasons why Irish spirits so long escaped high duty that it was feared from previous experience that a high duty on that article would lead to a very great amount of illicit distillation in Ireland?—Yes, I think that was the case.

8775. And when Mr. Gladstone increased the spirit duties, he at the same time transferred the looking after illicit distillation to the constabulary, did he not?—Yes.

8776. And one result of that has been that illicit distillation has almost disappeared, has it not?—Yes.

8777. Then does it not follow from that that this charge for the constabulary must be regarded, to a certain extent, as an Imperial charge, and not one relating merely to Ireland?—It never has been disputed, I think, that part of the police charge in Ireland may be considered as an Imperial charge; in fact, I remember that in the original "financial relations" return that was presented to Parliament prepared by Mr. Goschen, or at least under his superintendence, he did draw distinction by taking out the constabulary charge, and treating it as an Imperial charge; in fact, he treated the whole of it as an Imperial charge.

8778. The whole of the constabulary charge?—Yes, I think so.

8779. (*Mr. Sexton.*) I do not know what the object of that was, but the effect of it was, I think, to show that Ireland made rather a larger contribution out of her revenue to Imperial expenses than Great Britain, was it not?—That would be so, no doubt.

8780. (*Chairman.*) The object of these late returns now appears to be the opposite, namely, to show that the Irish do not contribute sufficiently largely to Imperial expenditure?—These returns have not been drawn with that view, certainly; they have only been drawn to show the facts as near as they can be shown. Of course, every return based upon any estimate is open to be taken exception to and criticised.

8781. But you see the effect of transferring this very large charge for constabulary from one side of the account to the other, would make an enormous difference, would it not?—I should not transfer the whole, certainly; I do not think it can be possibly said that you should transfer the whole. You would have to transfer the whole of the police charge in Great Britain as well, which would not be so big. Similarly you would have to transfer the whole of the collection charge for Great Britain, and make it an Imperial service.

8782. (*Mr. Sexton.*) Would you say, that if 600,000*l.* represented the cost of a police force for Ireland upon the model of Great Britain, the difference between 600,000*l.* and 1,500,000*l.* might be claimed as Imperial?—I think that would be more reasonable. I think I have worked it out that if the police force in Ireland cost the same as in Great Britain per head of population, it would be between 600,000*l.* and 700,000*l.*

8783. (*Chairman.*) Does it not appear from these returns, looking at them just as they stand without much examination, that the cost of these local services in Ireland are very much higher than in Great Britain?—They are higher, no doubt, relatively, owing to a very great extent, to the constabulary charge, and, as the Commission know, the legal charges in Ireland are very high, relatively, to what they are in Great Britain.

8784. But it does not follow from that, does it, that they are in reality excessive in themselves? You say they are, compared with Great Britain, apparently excessive, but it does not follow from that they are in reality so, does it?—No; I am not prepared to say that the constabulary are paid too highly. I believe the legal charges might be reduced, but I will not say that of the constabulary.

8785. Is the fact that these charges are, apparently, compared with Great Britain high, any justification whatever for the existence of higher taxation in Ireland? Is the fact that there is larger expenditure on local services any justification for excessive taxation upon Ireland, as compared to her resources?—I think it is a consideration to be taken into account. If Ireland is being regarded as a separate fiscal entity you must examine both sides of the account, and if her expenditure is very large, a larger amount of revenue has to be raised from her.

8786. That expenditure is under the control of Parliament, is it not?—Yes, that I admit, of course.

8787. And that expenditure, I suppose, ought to be regulated according to the actual requirements of the case?—Yes.

8788. Quite irrespective of taxation?—Yes, from an Imperial point of view, but at the present moment I understood you were rather approaching the consideration of Ireland, as if she were a separate country.

8789. No. I am regarding her now as part of the United Kingdom with this difference, that she is to be regarded for financial purposes as a distinct unit?—Then as a distinct unit, I think you are bound to look at both sides of the account.

8790. If you regard her as a distinct unit, you think that if a certain expenditure is required in Ireland, Ireland alone should pay for it, do you?—I would not say Ireland alone, but I think it is a consideration in regard to the amount of revenue to be raised from Ireland.

8791. Do you think that would justify a higher taxation being placed upon Ireland in consequence of the larger proportionate expenditure?—I think the larger proportionate expenditure is a consideration that ought to be taken into account; I will not go farther than that.

8792. But you do not say it is a justification for the other if the other exists?—I will not say a justification, but it is a consideration which ought to be taken into account.

8793. (*Mr. Sexton.*) Allow me to draw attention to an observation of Lord Castlereagh in a speech in introducing the matter. He said "If the proportion of "the expense shall be rightly fixed and ascertained upon "just principles, for every part of the Empire, it is "immaterial to Great Britain where the expenditure "takes place. If the internal circumstances of Ireland "call for a larger proportion of that my to be [illegible] "is the island, the expense will be greatest here. If the "southern coast of England requires to be strengthened, "the expenditure will be directed to that quarter; but "are Scotland and other parts of the Empire, which "equally contribute, but do not require any expensive "protection, to [illegible] or jealousy that their state "of security requires a less portion of troops, and a less "proportion of expense than the more exposed or con-"tested part of the two islands." That passage appears to contain the principle already expressed, that while it is proper to consider the proportion in which taxation ought to be raised, when once the Imperial purse is filled the Imperial authority cannot consider the expenditure in any particular part of the United Kingdom as a reason for special taxation there or as a special justification?—I did not go so far as to say that the amount of local expenditure was a justification for special taxation, but I said I thought the amount of such expenditure was a consideration which ought to be taken into account if you regard one part of the United Kingdom as a separate fiscal unit.

8994. (*Sir David Barbour.*) Was not Lord Castlereagh at that time arguing in favour of indiscriminate taxation, the same system of taxation throughout both countries?—I think he had that ultimately in view but not when he made that speech.

8995. (*Mr. Sexton.*) He was arguing the contrary?—But he had in view eventually, I presume, the fiscal Union as well as the legislative Union.

8996. Certainly, and that passage, as I submit to you, means this: that whilst you may consider the resources in raising taxation, once it is raised, you need not consider the scale of expenditure in any particular part of the kingdom as justifying any special levy there, but that every part of the kingdom may claim upon the common purse in proportion to its needs judging from an Imperial point of view?—I do not think I should go as far as Lord Castlereagh in that direction. If you regard Ireland as a separate entity for the purposes of taxation, you are, I think, bound to look at the other side of the account to see what the expenditure, which is necessarily, or perhaps unnecessarily, incurred in that country, is.

8997. If there are two Governments and two Exchequers, and the Irish Government is contributing besides its own expenditure to the Imperial expenses, then the question arises; but if there is a common Government, using a common purse, what I submit to you is that Imperial policy would require that the expenditure in each part should be measured by its needs?—But then it might be argued, surely, that Imperial policy would equally require that taxes should be uniformly raised throughout the United Kingdom.

8998. I started with the principle that the taxation should be justly framed according to the resources?—I venture to think you have the choice of alternatives. If you treat Ireland as a separate entity and frame taxation according to her resources, I think you must compute the expenditure as well as the amount derived from taxation in that country. If you are content to treat Ireland as part of the United Kingdom without drawing such distinction, then the whole of the expenditure of Great Britain and Ireland may be regarded as amounts of Imperial expenditure met out of a common purse.

8999. Taking it as it stands; taking it as a United Kingdom, do you think that the amount of expenditure in any one part of the United Kingdom, in Scotland, or in Yorkshire, or in Ireland, can be pleaded as a reason for justifying taxation which might otherwise be admitted to be excessive?—I did not say "justifying." All I said was that I thought it was a consideration that ought to be taken into account if you look at Ireland, from your point of view, as a separate fiscal entity.

9000. (*Chairman.*) Ireland was regarded as a separate fiscal entity under the terms of the Union?—Yes.

9001. And no such point as you now allude to was taken into consideration then?—No, I admit that.

9002. So that your opinion differs from the text of the Act of Union in that respect?—Yes; because, since the Union, separation of fiscal entities has disappeared.

9003. The principle we have before us, laid down as a precedent, is, that with regard to expenditure as explained by Lord Castlereagh, expenditure ought to be Imperial although for taxation purposes Ireland and Great Britain were to be regarded as separate entities?—Yes, that was his statement at the time of the Union.

9004. (*Mr. Sexton.*) He went so far as to say that it was immaterial to Great Britain where the expenditure took place?—Yes, that appears to have been his opinion. Sir R. E. Welby, K.C.B. — [illegible] May [illegible].

9005. (*Sir David Barbour.*) But that is always subject to this, that Lord Castlereagh looked forward to the time when there would be the same system of taxation in both countries?—I think he had that ultimately in view. Relation between expenditure and taxation in Ireland.

9006. But he said so, did he not?—He said it ultimately, but at the moment he was making his speech he was not proposing indiscriminate taxation.

9007. The proportionate contribution was to be only temporary?—Yes.

9008. (*Mr. Sexton.*) What he said was, "If the proportions of expense shall be rightly fixed and ascertained upon just principles," whether by proportionate or indiscriminate taxation?—Yes.

9009. (*Chairman.*) If expenditure on local services in Ireland is greater in proportion than in Great Britain, you do not at all wish to imply that that local expenditure in Ireland is excessive in itself, do you?—I do not go so far as to say that the local expenditure in Ireland might not admit of reduction; on the contrary, I think it might be reduced with advantage. I do regard it in some respects as excessive. Expenditure in Ireland.

9010. Do you regard it as excessive simply from the fact that it is greater in proportion than in Great Britain?—No.

9011. You think the question whether it is excessive or not must be ascertained by examination into each particular item of expenditure?—Certainly.

9012. And it might be greater in proportion in Ireland than in Great Britain and still not be excessive?—That is quite conceivable owing to the different circumstances of the two countries.

9013. I suppose if the expenditure is greater in Ireland than in Great Britain, as you have said before, it is under the control of Parliament?—That is so.

9014. And it comes before Parliament through the ministers and before the ministers through the [illegible] of Government departments?—Yes.

9015. And, therefore, it is really the heads of Government departments who are responsible primarily for that expenditure?—That is so.

9016. I find that even as to your own department—the Treasury—the expenditure is larger in Ireland than in Great Britain in proportion?—Yes, that is quite conceivable.

9017. Do you believe that the charge for the Treasury is excessive?—No; but the administration of a small country may be proportionately much more costly than the administration of a big country.

9018. And that would to a certain extent, justify a greater proportion for Ireland *primâ facie*, would it not?—In certain respects no doubt it would.

9019. Have you, in making these calculations of the expenditure on local services in Ireland, taken into account the local payments that were made in aid of them? Are not there considerable sums paid in aid of these local services under miscellaneous receipts in both countries?—I do not quite follow the question.

9020. To put it in another way, the local services both in Great Britain and Ireland are composed of services for which payments are made to a certain extent, are they not?—Yes.

9021. For instance, for these judicial services there are payments made in the shape of fees. Then, again, as to the constabulary, there is a certain amount of payment made for it and so on. What I want to ask you is, in taking into account the expenditure for local services in the two countries, have you taken into account the miscellaneous receipts on the other side?—Yes, under the head of miscellaneous revenue.

9022. I want to ask you a question in connexion with that, because I find that these returns have altered considerably in form since they were first presented to Parliament. The first return, I think, was presented by Mr. Jackson, and is No. 329 of Session 1891. You will find, if you look at page 14, under the head of Miscellaneous Revenue in Ireland, a number of entries, for instance, you will find, "Constabulary, [illegible]," do you see that item?—Yes.

9023. Then "Valuation office, 10,[illegible]"—I will take one or two as an example. Let us take the last one—

Mr. J. W. [illegible] K.C.B. — [illegible] — Expenditure in Ireland.

"Valuation Office, Ireland, 10,257." that is on the receipt side of the account. Now will you look at the expenditure side of the account at the bottom of page 60, where you will see an entry there of 23,130?—Yes.

6824. There you have, you see, a set off to one charge by a payment to the other of nearly a half?—That is so.

6825. If you will turn to the last return, which purports to be the same (No. 314, of Session 1894 (Mr. Sexton's return), you will not find any entry there of a receipt under the head of "Valuation Office"?—No, that is owing to a change in the system by which the receipts have been appropriated in aid of expenditure. In the last 12 years, as I daresay may be remembered by those who are members of the House of Commons here, the system of appropriating these extra receipts has been introduced. Instead of paying them into the Exchequer they have been appropriated in aid of the actual expenditure itself, and the consequence is that you may see in the latest returns a smaller expenditure on the one side and a smaller sum paid into the Exchequer on the other side; but, of course, the net result is the same.

6826. That is the explanation, is it?—Yes.

6827. You have deducted on both sides?—Yes, it has been gradually introduced into all the civil expenditure of this country. All the extra receipts which are cognate to a particular service have so far as possible been appropriated now in aid of the expenditure, and the vote of Parliament now is taken net, so to speak.

6828. (*Mr. Sexton.*) I think you went some way in regard to the change, then went back again, and finally adopted the change more fully, did you not?—No, it has been gradually adopted.

6829. Was not there a movement at one time back to the old system?—No, not during the last 15 years or so.

6830. (*Chairman.*) What I want to point out in connexion with this is, taking the first return, where the receipts and expenditure are both entered, does it not appear from that return that Ireland contributed even in a larger proportion to meet these local services than Great Britain did?—I have not got the proportion here, but that may be the case.

6831. It is entered in the Return at page 15, you will see. The proportion of Ireland is 30 per cent.?—Of course the larger the unappropriated receipt was the larger would be the revenue with which Ireland was credited.

6832. But it shows these local services were charged for and paid for in Ireland in a greater proportion than they were in Great Britain, does it not?—That may be so.

6833. (*Mr. Sexton.*) What effect had that change upon the miscellaneous revenue?—It diminished it, of course, considerably.

6834. The miscellaneous revenue which is called Imperial?—It would not affect the Imperial revenue.

6835. How is it the Imperial miscellaneous revenue has so very much diminished in recent years. It used to be about three millions a year at one time, now it has come down to one million?—You will see in 1889 and 1890, for instance, there was one item alone of 800,000*l.* for the Mint, that was an extraordinary year, in which we got out a very large amount of silver. That was a very special receipt.

6836. Is that part of the miscellaneous revenue?—Yes, that is part of the miscellaneous revenue; that is on page 14 of Mr. Jackson's return. You will see a sum of 800,000*l.* there; that would be now about 160,000*l.*

6837. It has run down from two millions and a quarter in the first of the series to one million?—I do not see the two millions and a quarter.

6838. Look at page 4 of the first return?—Yes, it is now down to a million and a half according to the latest return.

6839. According to the return of 1893–4 it is one million?—No, it is 1,500,000*l.* in the latest return.

6840. (*Chairman.*) How do you account for that?—There are various details; I do not know that I could explain them at this moment.

6841. Is it a mere change of account?—To some extent, and a change of term also, as well as account. For instance, as I said, there was that enormous receipt in one year from the Mint, 800,000*l.*

6842. (*Mr. Blake.*) In the 2,250,000*l.*?—Yes, in the 2,250,000*l.* year.

6843. That is, of course, altogether an exceptional year?—Yes.

6844. (*Mr. Sexton.*) Has the change affected at all the apportionment of revenue between the three countries in the financial relation returns?—No, I do not think it can be said to have affected it, certainly not perceptibly.

Mr. J. W. [illegible] K.C.B. — [illegible] — Loans to Ireland.

6845. (*Chairman.*) Turning to another point, I see you state at the very end of your paper "Any record of "the financial treatment of Ireland by the Imperial "Government would be imperfect if no account was "taken of the amount of public money which has been "placed at the disposal of that country on loan, and "still more so the amount of loans the repayment of "which has not been exacted." Then you go on to show that 46,510,000*l.* was advanced to Ireland, and that no less than 10,780,000*l.* of that, or about one-fifth of the amount, had been remitted or written off. I should like to ask you a few questions in connexion with that. In instituting these comparisons of the respective amounts remitted between the two countries, is it not of importance that we should examine whether the loans remitted were of a similar character?—Undoubtedly so, and this statement includes the very exceptional loan made to Ireland in the famine time, which Parliament afterwards considered as a grant.

6846. (*Mr. Sexton.*) I rather think it would fall within Lord Castlereagh's idea of Imperial expenditure, would it not?—Perhaps so.

6847. If you have the United Kingdom, and a famine arises in one part of it, would you consider the raising of loans and the remission of them as grants, as any argument in favour of excessive taxation there?—No, but if you take up one part of the United Kingdom separately from the other, these special grants out of the Exchequer to that part may be taken into account.

6848. We are treating the whole as one kingdom?—No; surely you are looking at Ireland now as if she were a separate country.

6849. We are considering what would be her just proportion, and assuming she pays her just proportion to the Imperial purse, is such an expenditure as an expenditure upon a local famine to be regarded as a reason for exceeding the just proportion?—No, I do not say so.

6850. (*Chairman.*) I should like to see whether a good many of these are loans at all. I suppose you will admit that in every loan transaction there must be two parties, the lender and the borrower?—Certainly.

6851. And I suppose further, that in all ordinary loan transactions the borrower is a free agent?—Yes.

6852. He borrows because he wishes to borrow?—Yes.

6853. And further, that concurrently with applying the money advanced to the purposes for which it is advanced, that he should have the spending of the money and the dealing with the loan?—Yes.

6854. Taking first of all this large item of 4,[illegible] which you have returned here as remitted for employment of the labouring poor, I would ask you who was the borrower there; to whom was the money lent?—It was lent to Ireland, so to speak at the moment, and it was no sooner lent, than it was treated as a grant.

6855. I want, in the first instance, to know who actually borrowed the money. To whom was the money lent by the Treasury?—I think it was partly to landlords and partly to local authorities.

6856. If it be the fact that it was lent to the Board of Works, a Government Department, and if it be the fact that the Board of Works had the expenditure of it, can it be said that, that was a loan to local authorities in Ireland?—No, I think it was such an exceptional transaction that it could hardly be considered a local loan, and in fact when the whole question of loans was considered in 1887 by Mr. Goschen he specially excepted it from remitted loans altogether, and regarded it as a grant.

6857. But you see you have brought it into these 10,000,000*l.* again?—Yes, because it has always figured so, we cannot now strike it out of the Parliamentary returns.

6858. Is it fair to bring into a return of this sort, which on the face of it would show that Ireland has been a defaulter to the extent, we will say, of one-fifth of the money lent to her, a loan which you now say was struck off as not being really a proper loan at all?—It was not done with any intention to imply that Ireland was a defaulter; it was merely to state the fact that there had been a large grant made to Ireland in addition to the expenditure incurred at the time.

8659. We are not dealing here with grants, because if we were we would have to bring in grants also for public purposes in England. We are dealing now solely with loans, and there is a comparison made in your paper between the amount of loans advanced to Ireland and the amount of loans advanced to Great Britain, and on the other hand the amount of loans written off or remitted on the one side and the other. In that return you first large item is an loan which you now admit ought not to be included in the category of loans at all?—I think it may properly be regarded as a grant, but it has always been in the loan account, because the money was ostensibly a loan in the first instance. I ought perhaps to have put a footnote calling special attention to the item.

8660. (Mr Sexton.) Also there ought to be a footnote saying that one half of the 10,000,000*l.* was remitted in consideration of the imposition of the income tax?—Yes.

8661. Which was to be a temporary tax, but has been now made permanent, and has been levied for 40 years at a rate of half a million or so, 20,000,000*l.* say?—That is so. But the statement about loans was itself rather in the nature of a footnote to previous statements about taxation and expenditure.

8662. (Chairman.) Mr Sexton has rather forestalled what I was coming to. I wish to examine not merely into this 4,294,947*l.*, but the other items that were included also in what are called the consolidated annuities. First with regard to the 4,294,947*l.* Is it not the fact that Parliament the year after it made these advances to the Board of Works, decided that a moiety of it should be considered as a grant in consequence of the great famine that existed in Ireland?—Yes.

8663. And the balance of the amount was confirmed, was it not, as a charge upon the land in the different counties up to the year 1853?—Yes. I think it is the same thing as what were called the "consolidated annuities" which meant the famine loan.

8664. The consolidated annuities you will find included a number of other items besides the famine loan. There is a little confusion about this that I want to clear up. The amount that was remitted under what was called the famine loan, was 4,294,947*l.* A moiety of the expenditure under that loan up to the year 1849 was remitted by Parliament directly, the year after the grant was made, was it not?—Yes. I think that is so, but I have not the facts accurately in my mind.

8665. Then the balance, which amounted to something over 2,000,000*l.*, remained as a charge upon the counties?—Yes.

8666. There was also a charge upon the counties, if you look at your return, page 13, of 797,870*l.*, which is entered as "Temporary Relief, Consolidated Annuities, and Distressed Poor Law Unions"?—Yes.

8667. Now, if you will turn back to the advances made under another Department, by the Public Works Loan Commissioners, you will find "Union workhouses 1,270,[illegible]"?—Yes.

8668. These were all consolidated into what was called the consolidated annuities, were they not?—Yes. That was so, I believe.

8669. And these consolidated annuities continued to be paid up to the year 1853, did they not?—Yes.

8670. The annual payment upon these consolidated annuities amounted to how much?—I think about [illegible] a year.

8671. Are you not aware that during the whole of that period the Irish members were continually protesting against these charges being placed on the land on the ground that the money had been spent by a public Department, and according to their view Ireland had not received adequate value for it?—Yes, I believe that to be the case.

8672. In 1853 was not that the form in which they were remitted? The charge being [illegible] a year, Mr. Gladstone imposed in lieu of it a charge of [illegible] in the shape of additional income tax?—Yes.

8673. Which he represented would be a gain to Ireland, inasmuch as it was to last only for seven years, whereas the charge of 240,000*l.* was to continue spread over from 10 to 40 years?—Yes, I believe that to be the case.

8674. Looking at it from that point of view, can it be truly said that those different items which I have enumerated were ever remitted?—They were remitted in the sense of their being written off the loan account by Act of Parliament.

8675. As a matter of account they were remitted, but as a matter of charge to the country, after what you have now admitted to have taken place, can it be truly said that Ireland got a remission of those sums, inasmuch as a charge was placed upon her very considerably higher, which has continued more than the 40 years?—I think it may be considered as an Imperial grant.

8676. Was not the year 1853 a year of surplus?—Yes. It was.

8677. Do you suppose for a moment that Mr. Gladstone would have imposed this enormously heavy increased burden upon Ireland at a year of surplus if it were not that he had in view this apparent remission to grant to Ireland?—I am afraid I cannot say what was in his mind at the time.

8678. As I want to go through these 10,000,000*l.*, I would thank you to take down those items which I say should be struck out. Will you take down first of all the 4,294,947*l.*; then Union workhouses, 1,270,[illegible]*l.*, Relief works, 137,[illegible]*l.*, and Temporary Relief, 797,870*l.* Have you taken those down?—Yes.

8679. Now I want to proceed to another item, leaving that for the present. If you look at page 13 you will see River Drainage and Navigation, 1,[illegible]*l.*?—Yes.

8680. I would again ask you, do you know to whom that loan was made—who was the borrower?—I am afraid I am not sufficiently well acquainted with it to tell you.

8681. Will you take it from me that the borrower there again was the Board of Works, and that the river drainage and navigation was carried out by the Board of Works—a Government department. Do you think that can be considered as a loan to the people of Ireland?—Not, I think, in the sense of an ordinary local loan.

8682. Do you know why that loan was remitted? Was it not remitted because these navigation works and drainage works which were carried out were, to a very great extent, found to be useless, and that neither the counties nor the owners of the land received any benefit from them?—I believe that to have been the case.

8683. I will read to you the preamble of the Act under which they were remitted. "Whereas in many "instances the estimates of the expense of such works "have been exceeded, and many of them are still "unfinished, and in certain cases the assents required "to authorise the charge on the lands to be improved "have not been obtained"; then the Act was passed remitting them?—Yes.

8684. Was not this remission then a remission because the money had not been properly spent, that the proper assents had not been got for the expenditure, and because no real benefit arose from the expenditure?—Yes, I presume so.

8685. Then can you say that that is properly speaking, a loan which can be compared with these loans made in Great Britain for local purposes?—No. I do not think it does stand on all fours with them.

8686. (Lord Farrer.) There might be some loans, might there not, made in Great Britain which stand on the same footing, the loan for Wick Harbour, for instance?—No doubt if we look into it we shall find some bad loans made in Great Britain.

8687. (Mr. Sexton.) Has part of it been remitted?—Part of it has been.

8688. (Chairman.) Now will you look at page 6 of that return? There is a figure there of 900,000*l.* called Tithe Relief?—Yes.

8689. Then you will find under the head of "Relief of Clergy," 33,[illegible]?—Yes.

8690. Then "Board of First Fruits," [illegible]?—Yes.

8691. Then "Tithe Composition," 237,[illegible]?—Yes.

8692. Have you got those figures down?—Yes.

8693. Is it not the fact that all these loans were loans made to the clergy of the Established Church or to the charities of the Established Church, the First Fruits for

* Sic.

Sir E. W. Hamilton, K.C.B.

16 May 1894.

Public loans for Irish purposes.

the repair of the churches, and the rest to the clergy in consideration of the impossibility of collecting the tithes and the first fruits?—I believe that to have been the case owing to the disturbed state of the country.

6894. The loan was originally made to the clergy secured upon the tithes and other rates which then existed, was it not?—That I believe to be the case.

6895. And Parliament, a few years subsequently, deciding that those tithes and those rates should be abolished, and were unjust, had to give up the money that they had lent to the clergy, had they not?—Yes.

6896. Now can that be considered as a loan for local purposes in Ireland?—No. I think it stands on a different footing to an ordinary loan for local purposes.

6897. It was an attempt, was it not, to enforce an alien church on an unwilling people?—I suppose that may be said to be the case.

6898. And Parliament deciding that was wrong, it having advanced money to these clergymen in the meanwhile, who were its agents throughout, had to forgive the loan to the clergy, it having taken away the security from the clergy for which the money was lent?—That is so.

6899. I should like you to add that to the figures already already given you?—Yes, the additions come to 9,000,000*l.*

6900. (*Lord Farrer.*) Can you tell me what was the motive in making these loans—was it free will on the part of the Treasury?—I think it was in order to cope with severe social evil at the moment in Ireland.

6901. Under pressure from Irish members?—I should imagine it may have been under the pressure of Irish members, but I think the executive governments of the day have themselves made proposals to Parliament.

6902. Has it was for the purpose of meeting some want in Ireland?—No doubt.

6903. It was not a simple dole given out of the kind heart of the Treasury to the Irish people, was it?—No, it was to cope with very special circumstances.

6904. (*Chairman.*) Are you referring to the tithe loans?—I am referring to the whole of them.

6905. But they are all of a different character, these last loans relating to the church simply arose from the impotence of the Government to collect the tithe charge, did they not?—Quite so.

6906. And they considered that the clergy who were starving owing to not receiving their dues, ought to have some compensation for their abolition?—Yes.

6907. And when they altered the law and did away with the tithes, and in place of the tithes established a rentcharge, this money really was granted to the clergy, was it not, as compensation for the loss of the salaries which they had previously held by law?—Yes, I believe that to be the case.

6908. (*Lord Farrer.*) Still, it was for the purpose of remedying what was felt to be a grievance in consequence of the state of the law in Ireland, was it not?—Yes.

6909. (*Mr. Sexton.*) The Irish people never asked the Government to lend money to the clergy of the Established Church upon the security of tithes which they wanted to see abolished?—That may be so.

6910. (*Chairman.*) The next item I would draw attention to is not a very large one, but I do not see why it should be included here, and that is an advance to Dunleary Harbour. Is not that the harbour of Kingstown?—Yes. This is part of the cost of that harbour.

6911. Was not this sum advanced first on dues—what are called passing dues?—I am afraid I do not know the details.

6912. You may take it that is so. Was not that tax then really a tax upon shipping and therefore more a tax on England than on Ireland?—It seems to me to be so. I am not acquainted with the history of the loan I am afraid.

6913. If there was a tax upon passing ships, ships that passed Dunleary Harbour, that tax was hardly made for the benefit of Dunleary Harbour, was it?—I am afraid I do not know; I have forgotten the history of Dunleary Harbour.

6914. The tax on passing ships being abolished it was lent to Dunleary Harbour, was it not?—Just so.

6915. I should like to know how much money has been spent on Holyhead Harbour on the other side of the Channel?—I do not know what the sum was.

6916. Do you think, if this comparatively small sum of 140,000*l.* advanced to Kingstown is to be put down as a loan which Ireland has not repaid, that we should not consider how much has been spent on the opposite harbour on the Welsh side of the coast?—Yes.

6917. On the face of it unless explained, would not the table relating to these loans lead any one reading it to the impression that out of the loans that have been made to Ireland, one-fifth has not been repaid whereas, out of the loans made to England, only about a million has not been repaid?—I am afraid that is due to my having put it in that particular form. There was no intention on my part to have that inference drawn from it; I merely wanted to point out that an expenditure had been incurred of very large amount in Ireland, and likewise there had been an expenditure in Great Britain of a smaller amount which ought to be taken into account in considering the financial relations of the two countries.

6918. (*Lord Farrer.*) The expenditure on Holyhead Harbour has had something to do with Ireland, has it not?—I presume so, very considerably. The harbour would be of comparatively little importance if it were not for Ireland.

6919. (*Mr. Sexton.*) This return, occurring as it does in the sequence of the argument, and pointing to an estimate of the relative proportions of taxable capacity, appears to convey this sort of hint, does it not: "Possibly you do pay too much in Ireland, but look at all we have remitted?"—It was not intended to convey that hint.

6920. (*Mr. Morton.*) Is not Holyhead Harbour looked upon as the principal harbour of refuge on the west coast of England?—I am afraid I do not know.

6921. (*Chairman.*) The next item I would draw your attention to, is one which is called Suitors' Fund, Court of Exchequer, 172,000*l.*?—Yes.

6922. Was that money remitted at all?—I am afraid I am not acquainted with the details of that loan.

6923. Here is the Act of Parliament in which it states that it was not. I will read from the Schedule to the Act of Parliament. "This money was issued for the "purpose of compensating officers of the Court of "Exchequer, whose emoluments were diminished by "the first mentioned Act, and were repayable out of "Suitors' fund. A small sum only was to be paid "direct, but under the 31st and 32nd Victoria, Chapter "91, the stock standing to the credit of the fee fund "of the Court of Chancery, and the Court of Exchequer "was sold, and the proceeds of the same, together with "the cash standing to the account amounting to "172,000*l.*, were paid into the Exchequer, consequently "the debt may be considered to have been virtually "paid although not actually cancelled." That is from the Schedule to the Act of Parliament which goes through the operation of formally cancelling it?—Yes.

6924. Surely that sum should not have been included here as "amount of debt remitted to Ireland," should it?—No. I think it perhaps would have been better if it had not been included, but it has always been treated as a loan.

6925. The last amount I come to is a very small sum, but it shows, I think, how many of these loans were remitted, though nominally remitted—it is a small sum of 13,917*l.* to Maynooth College. Was not that remitted under the Church Act?—I am afraid I do not know the history of that.

6926. It states in the note here that it was so?—Yes, it does.

6927. Perhaps you are not aware that under that same Church Act, a sum of over 300,000*l.* was calculated to be due to the professors and others of Maynooth in consequence of vested interests arising out of the previous parliamentary grant?—I am afraid I am not sufficiently acquainted with the Act to say that.

6928. You may take it from me that was so, and that Parliament decided at that time that this was a sum due to those persons for their vested interests, and that sum of over 300,000*l.*, which was due by the Imperial Parliament, was taken out of the church fund, which was disestablished at the same time?—Yes.

Sir E. W. Hamilton, K.C.B.

16 May 1894.

Public loans for Irish purposes.

8029. Do you think if the Imperial credit was extended to Maynooth to the extent of over 300,000*l*., that it was a very great gift to forgive a building debt of 11,000*l*.?—No, but my opinion is worth nothing, because I do not know the circumstances of the case.

8030. But assuming that to be the case, it would appear to be so, would it not?—Certainly.

8031. Then this transaction instead of being a remission to Ireland of 11,000*l*., was, in reality, a remission of the Imperial obligations of over 300,000*l*. was it not?—Apparently so.

8032. Then all these items added together, come as you admitted a moment ago, to nine millions?—About 9,300,000*l*.

8033. Therefore before we compare these ten millions of Irish remissions, with the remissions made to England, we have to reduce that ten millions down to about one million?—No, I do not see that you can reduce it. It is a remission with the exception of perhaps one item, and I do not know how it came into the loan account, that is the Thames Fund, Court of Exchequer. But as I have said there were no remissions passed against Ireland. The statement was made in order merely to point out that in addition to the expenditure which had been incurred in Ireland over that long period there had been an expenditure connected with loan transactions in Ireland of 10,730,000*l*., and in Great Britain of one million odd.

8034. But as you admitted to me, before we can draw this comparison, we should see that the loans were on all fours—that they were of the same character, and I have endeavoured in my examination to show that these loans, at least, are not of the same character as ordinary loans to local authorities?—I admit that, and I also admit that I might have qualified that statement more than I did.

8035. (*Mr. Sexton.*) Taking it in this connexion, it seems to ignore the Imperial idea, and to treat the government of Ireland as a financial speculation, does it not?—I do not quite follow the question.

8036. It seems to ignore the Imperial idea which I have quoted from Lord Castlereagh, does it not?—I think the whole of these returns ignore the idea of Lord Castlereagh.

8037. Certainly it does, so far as they represent that the rate of expenditure in Ireland is to be considered as properly influencing the amount of taxation to be raised there?—I do not think the two things go together.

8038. You do not think they suggest it, do you?—No, I do not think the one necessarily follows the other.

8039. But when you invite us to take into consideration, not only what has been spent in Ireland upon administration there, but what has been lent or remitted, does not the whole calculation seem to assume the character of a financial speculation, and as if one should judge the propriety of the taxes raised in Ireland by the amount expended or lent?—No, that was not the idea, the idea was that you should examine both sides of the account, that is, not only the income side of the account, but the expenditure side of the account in order to approach the consideration of this question, it was necessary to treat Ireland as a fiscal entity by itself, and, therefore, I venture to think that it is only proper that both sides of the account should be examined.

8040. The term "account," which you have used so often, seems rather to suggest a commercial than an Imperial spirit, does it not?—No, I do not mean to imply that. If you examine the state of a country, surely the thing you examine is the state of her revenue and her expenditure, and you want to see whether she is solvent; whether she is paying her way, or whether her expenditure ought to be reduced or her taxes raised in order to cover that expenditure. You object to my using the word "account"?

8041. I do not object. I want to know how you use it?—I used the word because it covers both sides. I think you must consider both the expenditure of a country and the revenue of a country. The whole object here is to find out whether Ireland is overtaxed, as I understand; and if you examine one side of the account I think you must examine the other side of the account as well, otherwise you cannot get at the true position which that country occupies.

8042. What perplexes me is, how you can suppose that expenditure, whatever it may be, ought materially to affect the result of an inquiry into the just taxation in proportion to resources?—If you once begin to inquire into the taxable resources of one part of the kingdom, I think it necessarily follows you must inquire and see what the other side of the account is.

8043. I should suppose that an Imperial statesman or financier would simply consider how much revenue was required for the expenses of an Empire without relation to the special locale how much money is required for carrying out Imperial policy, and would raise that in proportion to the resources of each part of the country?—If you regard Ireland as part of the fiscal system of the United Kingdom you need not then inquire so much about the expenditure incurred in that particular country; it may all be regarded as Imperial.

8044. Our present inquiry does regard it as part of the fiscal system?—Yes, but the terms of reference imply that you are to examine how far Ireland, if she were a separate country, would stand by herself, otherwise you cannot see whether she is taxed in proportion to Great Britain or not for Imperial purposes.

8045. It may possibly include that, but it may also contemplate the continuance of the present relations?—But you must consider her as a separate entity, I understand.

8046. As a separate entity so far as concerns her resources?—Yes.

8047. (*Lord Farrer.*) Do you think you can separate Ireland for the purpose of seeing what she ought to pay without also separating her for the purpose of seeing what she gets?—No, I think it is very difficult to do that. If you once begin to treat Ireland as a separate entity, you must then look at her in the same way all round.

8048. If you treat her not as a separate entity then one identical system of taxation suits Ireland just as much as it suits Wiltshire or the Highlands of Scotland?—I think so.

8049. But if you treat her as a separate entity for the purpose of asking what she ought to pay, you ought also to treat her as a separate entity for the purpose of seeing what she costs?—I think it is very difficult not to do so.

8050. (*Chairman.*) With regard to these particular loans, you have stated in your paper "The State has "advanced to the poorer, the smaller country, 38,000,000*l*. "for local purposes, and no less than 10,000,000*l*. or more "than one fifth of the amount advanced has been "written off and treated as a free grant." What I have endeavoured to point out to you in my examination is that these 10,000,000*l*. were not advanced for local purposes at all; that the greater proportion consists of items that ought not to come under the head of loans, and, therefore, any point that is contained in the sentence I have read, has no force?—No. I think there is very little in the point. I did not intend to attach much importance to it. I put it at the end of my memorandum, and I should have preferred to have qualified it a little more.

8051. Can you tell me what is the meaning of remitting loans by Treasury letter, has the Treasury power to do that?—In old days it assumed the power, but it does not do so now. We have to go to Parliament. It was done in old days by a Treasury warrant. It was an assumption on the part of the executive of the day. I do not know, really, under what authority, but it was done away with about the year 1875 or 1876 if I recollect rightly, by an Act of Parliament which said that no loan was to be remitted hereafter without the authority of Parliament.

8052. Because I see a very large amount of the remaining balance of one million is remitted by Treasury letter?—Yes; that was done by the executive government of the day which took upon itself to do so.

8053. (*Mr. Currie.*) I suppose when recovery was hopeless?—Not necessarily so, but when for practical, or other reasons, it was considered well not to press the claim.

8054. (*Chairman.*) I see 220,000*l*. is remitted by Treasury letter with regard to the constabulary, that is about one-fourth of the balance remaining out of that ten millions. It may have been possible, may it not, that that money was remitted at the time that the charge for constabulary was placed upon the Imperial funds?—I am afraid I am not now well acquainted with the history of these loans. I did know something about them at one time, but I have forgotten the details.

6955. You see we have no means of knowing this, because we do not know the grounds upon which the Treasury letter was issued. In case that was remitted in the way I said, it would not be a remission of a loan at all, except technically, would it? Originally, I believe, the constabulary were charged locally, and the charge was subsequently placed on the Imperial funds, and that sum of [illegible] came to be necessarily [illegible] balance [illegible] from one account into the other, and remitted on that change being made?—It may be so. I am afraid I am not acquainted with the history of the loan.

6956. (*Mr. Sexton.*) Was it not by way of a set-off to the injury caused to Ireland by reason of the repeal of the Corn Laws?—Throwing the whole cost of the constabulary on the Imperial funds certainly was a sort of set-off against the repeal of the Corn Laws.

6957. (*Lord Farrer.*) I suppose in treating these as loans which have been remitted for the general purposes of your argument, it does not very much signify whether they are treated as loans remitted or as grants to Ireland?—No. I meant really that they were grants to Ireland.

6958. There may be the further question whether the system of making a loan under pressure and then remitting it, is not a worse system than the system of direct grant?—I regard it as a much worse system.

6959. And there may be the further question whether all these loans were made under proper arrangements, and whether they were made in such a way as to be an advantage to Ireland?—No doubt.

6960. That is a totally different question, is it not?—Yes, and of course the circumstances were extremely exceptional at the time when the Government was late to face with a great national catastrophe in Ireland, and they had to do the best they could to try and cope with it.

Adjourned for a short time.

6961. (*Chairman.*) We have been dealing up to the present with the question of loans remitted, and I should like to ask just before passing from the subject a few questions upon the loans that have been repaid, or that are in the course of repayment. I find by the Local Loan's Fund Paper that 25,871,650*l.* have been been repaid, with interest, the interest amounting to over 9,[illegible]*l.* I should like to ask you has not the rate of interest on these loans varied very much?—Yes.

6962. And does it not very very much upon the loans that are outstanding?—Yes, it varies from 3½ to 5 per cent. There are very few at 5 per cent. now, but there are a few.

6963. Is it not the fact that 5 per cent. is charged in some cases where the security is of the very best description?—I am afraid I cannot answer that without further details of loans.

6964. The rate of interest on these loans made by the State, is not regulated, is it, as loans made by banks usually are, according to the security?—Yes, to a very great extent they are. The lending bodies, no doubt, consider that the security offered by local authorities is better than the security which an individual can offer. Take an undertaking like a harbour. In that case the risk is much greater than it would be in the case of a loan secured on the rates for (we will say) sanitary purposes.

6965. Take, for example, the loans that were made in Ireland to grand juries of counties for the building of bridges, could there be a better security than that, that is to say, the first charge on the rates of the county?—No, I think that is a good security.

6966. Is not the rate 5 per cent.?—It was so formerly, but that rate would not apply to new loans, I think the new loans would be at 4 per cent.

6967. When has the change been made, because we were informed by Sir Richard Sankey in Dublin, that the rate was 5 per cent.?—He is much more likely to be right than I am, but I am under the impression there was an amendment made about five years ago, and what they called the rate of interest under their general powers was reduced from 5 per cent. to 4 per cent. I know there a great many cases in which the rate of interest on Irish loans has recently been reduced from 5 per cent. to 4 per cent., but I am not aware whether this is the case as regards that particular class of loans on county roads and bridges.

6968. Do you see any reason why this dissimilarity in the rate of interest should exist in loans advanced on equally good security?—Not on equally good security.

6969. Do you think the rate ought to depend, as in commercial transactions, on the value of the security?—I think so to some extent.

6970. (*Lord Farrer.*) You do reduce the rate on the existing loans, do you?—Yes, the rate has been reduced in many instances—in a good many of the railway loans, for instance.

6971. On application of the debtor?—Yes, and taking all considerations into account, of course.

6972. (*Chairman.*) A paper has been handed in by the Board of Works in Dublin, showing that the annual average interest realised in the year is 3*l.* 7*s.* 10*d.* per cent. on the capital outstanding?—Yes.

6973. And the average rate chargeable on the advances out of the Local Loans Fund was 3*l.* 11*s.* 2*d.*?—The averaged rate charged?

6974. Yes, and the average rate realised 3*l.* 7*s.* 10*d.* In making this average, I find that they include all loans free of interest, do you think it is fair to put in a loan that is given free of interest in making up the average rate?—I think it must be a very limited amount of loan in Ireland now, which is made free of interest nominally, but I have not the paper before me to which you are referring now, prepared by the Board of Works; but from a calculation I worked out not long ago, I found that on the total amount outstanding in Ireland at the present moment, 13,750,000*l.*, the amount of interest received in the last completed year, 1892–3, was 407,000*l.*, and that really only represented about 3 per cent.

6975. (*Mr. Sexton.*) But what about the arrears that may be paid hereafter. The almost receipts of any year do not indicate the receipts of the Treasury for interest, do they?—I do not know. Arrears are a very doubtful quantity.

6976. You collect them, do you not?—In the course of time. I have no doubt that 407,000*l.* included some arrears.

6977. As The O'Conor Don has shown you, 3*l.* 7*s.* 10*d.* was really raised?—I have not that return before me, the other figure is one I happened to have before me at the moment.

6978. (*Chairman.*) Taking it at 3*l.* 7*s.* 10*d.*, is not that a very high rate of interest, considering the present value of the money market?—It may appear to be so, but perhaps the Commission will remember that in 1887 a measure was passed in Parliament by which the Local Loans Fund was established, which became a self-supporting fund, and the money lent was represented by stock at 3 per cent. interest, which is irredeemable till 1912. Therefore, to start with, we are bound to pay 3 per cent. on that stock.

6979. Was there a particular stock formed?—Yes. It is called "Local Loans Stock." It is a 3 per cent. Government Stock, which is irredeemable till 1912.

6980. What does it amount to?—41,000,000*l.* Then, in addition to having to pay 3 per cent. interest upon local loans stock, we have also to pay a good many other expenses; there is the expense of managing the Local Loans Stock, the expense of administering the loans incurred by the various lending departments which, of course, is a very considerable sum. I think these expenses amount to nearly 60,000*l.*

6981. Before you pass from the administrative expenses, does that include any of the expenditure on the Irish Board of Works?—Part of it. The Public Works Loan Commissioners, of course, are a lending department pure and simple, you take their administrative expenses; then you take so much of the Irish Board of Works as represents the loan business of that department, and there would also be a certain amount of expense incurred by the Irish Land Commission on account of loans. If you add the whole of these administrative expenses together, they came in the year 1892–3 to 57,000*l.*

6982. Do you include that expenditure in the account of general expenditure of these different departments?—Yes, and in order to make out an income and expenditure account for the Local Loans Fund, we have to take these administrative expenses into account; they are repaid by the Local Loans Fund to the Exchequer.

6983. But you include, as I understand you, the amount of expenditure on administering these loans in the general expenditure account of the country?—That is so.

8984. And you do not give us credit for the extra interest which you charge on account of that expenditure, do you?—I do not follow you.

8985. Your argument is that you cannot lend at a lower rate of interest than you are lending?—Yes.

8986. Inasmuch as the expenditure upon the administration of these loans has to be looked at as an item that has to be repaid by these loans?—Yes.

8987. If that expenditure is an item that has to be repaid by these loans, surely it should not be entered in the expenditure account as an amount to be repaid out of the taxes of the country, should it?—The administrative expenses are incurred in the first instance out of voted money, and then an equivalent sum is recovered from the Local Loans Fund, the money so recovered is paid into the Exchequer as miscellaneous revenue, and so much of it as relates to Irish loans is credited to those returns to Ireland.

8988. (*Mr. Sexton.*) What is the Ratification Annuity?—In 1887 when Mr. Goschen established this Local Loans Fund, the idea was that it should be made self-supporting and it was decided at the time and Parliament accepted the proposal, that there should be set upon the fund an annuity of 130,000*l.* a year, which was about the amount we thought at that time the Loans Fund could afford as a set off against some of the bad debts which the State had incurred in making the loans in past times, but when that calculation was made, we specially excluded all the loans connected with the Irish famine.

8989. Then 130,000*l.* a year, which you take out of the income of this fund, may be applied to recouping the State for the loss of some loans previously made or uncollectable?—Yes.

8990. In Ireland?—It would be in Ireland and Great Britain.

8991. Do you in dealing with the Local Loans Fund treat Great Britain and Ireland strictly as one unit, or do you differentiate in the accounts of the fund between Ireland and Great Britain?—We do not differentiate.

8992. So that if a loss were incurred on loans in Great Britain, the contributions of Ireland might be drawn upon to make good that loss?—No, because if a loss connected with a loan is incurred subsequently to 1887, a vote has to be taken by Parliament. If, for instance, on a railway loan in Ireland there is a bad debt of 30,000*l.*, we have to go to Parliament to replace that sum, and carry it to the credit of the Local Loans Fund. It need not be done in one year. We have power to borrow it on a short term, but Parliament has to make good now every expense that is lost since 1887.

8993. Then what was the use of the ratification annuity?—That was in respect of bad debts incurred prior to 1887.

8994. (*Chairman.*) Would it apply to all these loans we have been talking of to-day?—No. In the calculation which was made at the time, upon which the annuity of 130,000*l.* was arrived at, all these loans relating to the famine were looked upon as grants, not loans, and were excluded from the calculation.

8995. Would all these other accounts, as to the church and so on, be included?—I am afraid I have not the exact calculation at hand, but I could give information which would show what were included and what were excluded. It was only a rough and ready way of reckoning what the State had lost, and the annuity of 130,000*l.* was, I think, calculated to replace the amount lost in about 100 years.

8996. (*Mr. Sexton.*) Then the operation of this 130,000*l.* may give back to the State the capital of some loans which you have set down as being lost, may it not?—That might be so.

8997. (*Lord Farrer.*) And that is spread over the whole of the Local Loans Fund; you do not separate between Ireland and the rest of the United Kingdom, do you?—No.

8998. (*Mr. Sexton.*) I do not yet quite understand it. In case Parliament now by direct vote makes good any loss incurred by the fund since 1887, what do you do with the surplus income of the fund?—I am sorry to say there has been practically no surplus income; we had a surplus income this year of 7,000*l.*, but that is the first time we have had one; since the fund has been established, it has hardly been able to pay its way.

8999. Then you have found by experience that the fund is just able to maintain itself without incurring a loss, and that, therefore, Parliament in case of a bad debt, must make good the loss by a vote?—Yes.

9000. (*Sir David Barbour.*) Does that loan maintain itself after paying the annuity?—Yes.

9001. (*Chairman.*) We were informed by Mr. Murrough O'Brien in Dublin, that the loans from the Board of Works and other bodies in Ireland were made out of deposits in the Post Office and Savings Banks; is that so?—They are, to a certain extent, indirectly. Prior to 1887, there was a considerable amount of money taken from the savings banks direct and lent by the Government to the local authorities; but when the Local Loans Fund was established, there was a stock set up, and as part of the savings banks money was invested in that stock—and the National Debt Commissioners hold on account of savings banks a considerable amount of this stock—indirectly you may say that the savings banks money is being lent out in Ireland. In the first instance it is lent on the security of the loans fund; but the guarantee of the Consolidated Fund is behind the Local Loans Fund.

9002. What is the rate of interest payable to depositors?—The rate of interest payable to depositors is 2*l.* 10*s.*

9003. And you lend it out at 3*l.* 10*s.*, do you not?—Yes, but the net result is that we are barely able to pay our way.

9004. How is that accounted for?—The administrative expenses are very heavy, and the bulk of the savings banks money has to be invested in consols, which are not at the present moment paying more than 2*l.* 12*s.*

9005. That makes the Local Loans Fund bear the loss on all those investments?—No, hardly so.

9006. You charge the people to whom you lend the money a high rate of interest in consequence of your not being able to invest your money well, I am speaking now of the Savings Banks deposits. You pay depositors 2*l.* 10*s.* Would it not pay you to lend that money out at 3*l.*?—I should say that, while the rate payable to depositors in the Post Office Savings Banks is 2*l.* 10*s.*, the rate which has to be paid to the trustees of other savings banks is 3*l.* 15*s.*

9007. The post office has a much larger proportion, has it not?—Yes.

9008. Would it not pay you better to lend that money at a lower rate of interest than investing in consols?—But we can only now under the law advance money for local purposes out of the Local Loans Fund, which has to pay 3 per cent. on its stock, and that stock is not now to be bought under 110.

9009. (*Lord Farrer.*) Are you limited as to investment?—Yes, to government securities. There is a power also to invest in Metropolitan stock, but it has never been exercised.

9010. (*Chairman.*) May I take it as your evidence that you could not make advances for local purposes at a lower rate of interest than you are now charging without being at a loss?—Yes, unless the Act of 1887 were amended.

9011. Assuming that the Act might be amended could you do so?—Of course if you relieved the local loans account of a charge to the extent of 130,000*l.*, that would make a difference.

9012. (*Mr. Sexton.*) But if you make the fund responsible for these and not for past transactions, what would be the result?—You would have a margin of 130,000*l.*

9013. Of the total amount due from Ireland more than half I see has been advanced under the Land Acts?—Yes.

9014. The rate there is 4 per cent. for interest and sinking fund?—It is 3½ per cent. for interest.

9015. Then the half of the money which has been lent under the Land Acts is at 3½ and on the other loans there is an average interest of 3*l.* 11*s.*?—Yes.

9016. Therefore there would be a difference of nearly ¼ per cent. paid by borrowers under the Land Acts as compared with other borrowers?—Yes, there is no doubt that borrowers under the Land Acts are accorded more favourable terms.

9017. (*Chairman.*) I see here there is an item of 1,300,000*l.* lent at 4 per cent. Do you know to what body that was advanced?—Under what heading is it?

9018. There is no heading except "rate of interest"?—I have some figures here as to railways which are at 4 per cent., fishery piers also are at 4 per cent.

9019. I see "Public Health and Waterworks"; that would be a large item, would it not?—Yes, but part of that is lent at 3½ per cent., I think. The rate of interest on some of these loans rather depends on the currency of the loans. We give a more favourable rate of interest for loans which have a shorter currency than for loans which have a longer currency. There is a sinking fund on almost all these loans except those under the Land Act, which of course is fixed.

9020. Can you say with regard to these loans in the past, that the Government have not made money on them at the rate at which they have lent?—I do not think we have ever made any money out of it. We have incurred heavy losses.

9021. I am not talking of setting the loss against the gain; but assuming that the loss is a loss which is to be accounted for as it is here in these tables of remissions, have they not made a gain upon the loans which were not remitted?—Of course, an account has only been kept separately since 1887 when the Local Loans Fund was established, and since that time, allowing for the 130,000*l.* charge, there has been, I think in some years a slight deficit. In 1893–94 there was a surplus of 6,000*l.*

9022. (*Mr. Sexton.*) In the case of the Purchase Act of 1891, you may remember that 4 per cent. was the annuity, as under the previous Act?—Yes.

9023. That ¼ per cent. was returnable for Irish use to the counties?—That was so, but that was a separate stock issued.

9024. I am speaking of the general policy of the loan. Under Mr. Balfour's system the State takes 2¾ per cent. as interest?—That is all.

9025. Whilst the general interest payable under the Board of Works is 3*l.* 11*s.*?—Yes.

9026. That makes a difference of nearly 1 per cent., does it not?—Yes, a considerable difference.

[illegible margin note]

9027. (*Sir David Barbour.*) You said, in answer to The O'Conor Don, that the Irish debt actually raised in the Union was raised on less favourable terms than if it had been raised as a joint debt. Did you say that simply as a matter of inference, or as meaning it to be a matter of fact?—I can only state it as a matter of inference.

9028. Perhaps you will ascertain whether, in fact, it was raised on worse terms?—I think that if it was raised simply on Irish credit, it must have been raised on worse terms; but I will see if I can make out some calculation throwing light on this point.

[illegible margin note]

9029. You say in your Memorandum that before 1782 the Sovereign had a constitutional right to dispose of the Irish revenue?—Yes.

9030. Do you mean that the Sovereign had the right to place any charge he thought fit on the Irish revenue?—That raises rather a difficult and technical point, and with the leave of the Chairman I should like to read a short note on that point (which perhaps I ought to have put in the Memorandum). It explains the matter more fully in detail. It is this: "Irish expenditure was regulated by the civil and "military establishments, settled by warrants under "the Royal Sign Manual at the beginning of each "reign. These establishments could be varied, and "could only be varied by special Royal Warrants. "Additional payments in form and required the authority of a King's letter. Irish revenue consisted of "the hereditary revenues of the Crown, and additional "duties granted by aid thereof. The surplus of "revenue over expenditure, thus determined, was at "the absolute disposal of the Crown. At one time the "surplus was annually remitted to the King. Then "the revenue, charged with the expenditure, was "farmed out, and the King received the surplus in the "form of a stipulated payment by the farmer. Later, "the surpluses accumulated in the Irish Treasury, and "were applied from time to time in reduction of debt "or otherwise at the King's discretion. The King "could not impose taxes, and to meet a deficiency he "had to ask the Irish Parliament to vote the necessary "supplies. About 1750 the Parliament tried to control "the disposal of the surplus, but failed. They then "set to work to destroy the surplus by appropriating "their additional grants to special purposes. The "hereditary revenue being, by this time insufficient to "meet expenditure, the King was driven to cede to "Parliament a certain share in the settlement of the "military establishment, which resulted in the passing "of the Act of 1769" (to which I refer in my Memorandum), "fixing that establishment. But the Crown "retained sole control of the civil establishments up "to 1793. The Irish Civil List Act of 1793 (33 George "III., Chapter 34), formed all the unappropriated "revenues into a consolidated fund, to which were to "be carried during the King's lifetime the hereditary "duties of the Crown, and on which the cost of the "civil establishment was thenceforth charged." I think that really answers the question put, but it is rather a technical point.

[illegible margin note]

9031. There were certain aids granted; that is, aids granted by the Irish Parliament?—Yes.

9032. What was the power of the British Parliament as regards the Irish revenue and expenditure before 1782?—The British Parliament, of course, claimed the power to make laws binding Ireland, but the power I do not think was ever exercised as regards finance.

9033. But they claimed the power, did they?—I think they did; I mean prior, of course, to 1782.

9034. And after 1782 I believe the British Parliament no longer possessed any authority over the Irish Parliament, or over the Irish revenue and expenditure?—I think that is so. [illegible margin note]

9035. Did the Sovereign retain after 1782 any right to dispose of the Irish surplus revenue?—I think the right was retained even after 1782, but I do not know of any case in which the right was exercised.

9036. I think after 1782 the state of affairs was this: Ireland paid the costs of the civil and military establishments required in Ireland?—Yes.

9037. And kept up 15,000 troops, of which 3,000 might be used for service outside Ireland?—That was the case down to 1792, when the military establishment was increased to 20,000 plus the militia.

9038. I am talking of the time immediately after 1782?—That was the case for the next 11 years.

9039. That maintenance of troops, I understand, was at the discretion of the Irish Parliament. The Irish Parliament could have reduced the number of troops, and could have increased them?—I think so. There was a proposal made by Mr. Flood in 1783, to which I refer in my Memorandum.

9040. Then I believe after 1782 Ireland was "in case "of war or any extraordinary emergency" (using the language of Mr. Pitt) "called upon and expected to "contribute, as in reason and justice she ought, to "such further exertions as the situation of affairs and "the general interests of the Empire may require." That is what may be called a moral obligation?—I think so, and I think it was recognised on the part of Ireland. The Commission will remember that I quoted one instance in my Memorandum of a vote for the navy being taken in 1782, and an increased number over the 15,000 troops for service abroad.

9041. So that in fact the amount of assistance that Ireland would give to the Empire was at the discretion of the Irish Parliament?—Yes.

9042. And there rested on the Irish Parliament a similar obligation to support the interests of the Empire as rested on the English Parliament?—Yes, and there is no doubt that towards the end of the century Ireland made very considerable contributions.

9043. I believe that in the years immediately succeeding 1782 the Irish revenue was adequate to meet the Irish expenditure of those days?—Yes. I think that is shown by Table I. in part I of my Memorandum. It will be seen that the revenue very nearly covered the expenditure in each year.

9044. And before the Union the taxation in Ireland was light?—Yes, I think so, certainly much lower.

9045. Before the Union Ireland did not contribute much to Imperial expenditure, did she?—No, very little really.

9046. Outside Ireland?—Nothing outside Ireland, with the exception, I think, of the 3,000 troops that were placed at the disposal of the Empire, and that contingent of troops may, I think, be said to have cost about 100,000*l.* a year; that is all that she really contributed.

9047. Before the Union Ireland was not on the same footing commercially as Great Britain—there were certain commercial disabilities or restrictions, were there not?—Yes.

9048. Do you know what they were?—The export of certain articles was prohibited altogether, such as woollen manufactured goods and raw wool. Then there were a great many import duties in England which were practically prohibitive, particularly on certain kinds of linen I think; and the trade with the Colonies was wholly prohibited.

9049. So that on the whole Ireland was under serious commercial disabilities?—Very great, no doubt.

9050. It is the case that when the war with France broke out in 1793, the Irish Parliament granted further supplies than it had been giving, and the Irish expenditure increased in consequence?—No doubt, but of course the further assistance was in regard to expenditure incurred in Ireland, because the Imperial expenditure in Ireland, was very heavy.

9051. And it had always been understood that Ireland would share the Irish expenditure?—Yes, certainly.

9052. And I think the Irish expenditure increased still more when the Irish Rebellion broke out in 1798?—Yes, that is so.

9053. You have attempted—you only call it an attempt—to draw a distinction between the amount of expenditure due to the war and the amount of expenditure due to the Rebellion, but I think you admit that your calculation is largely hypothetical?—Yes, I should like it to be regarded as hypothetical only.

9054. Because it is a fact, is it not, that the disaffected portion of the Irish population looked to assistance from France, and the French Government entertained the project of invasion in the hope that there would be a rising in Ireland?—Yes, I think that is so.

9055. And the Irish Parliament had to keep up forces in Ireland to meet enemies of both kinds, and it is very difficult to say how much of the expenditure on those forces was due to fear of invasion and how much to fear of internal disturbance?—Just so.

9056. Is it not the case that the Irish expenditure in the years immediately preceding the Union was very high?—That is so.

9057. I find that it was [illegible] in 1799, with a deficit of [illegible]; [illegible] in 1800, with a deficit of [illegible], and in the broken period of a year just before the Union, [illegible], with a deficit of [illegible]?—Those are the figures.

9058. And I believe it is the fact that the Irish debt increased more rapidly in the years immediately preceding the Union, than it did in the years immediately following the Union?—Yes, that is so.

9059. I find that in the four years preceding the Union the increase was slightly more than [illegible] sterling, and in the four years following the Union, only [illegible] sterling?—That is so, as shown by the tables at the end of Part I.

9060. I think you said in your Memorandum at page [illegible], that during the years of heavy expenditure preceding the Union, the amounts spent in maintaining Irish regiments abroad or in manning the fleet were very insignificant, and that practically the whole of the increase of expenditure was incurred in Ireland, and for the purpose of defending Ireland against foreign and domestic enemies?—I think that is clearly established by the accounts which I have very carefully examined. There was no trace of any expenditure incurred outside Ireland which was paid by Ireland.

9061. Have you compared the expenditure in the years immediately succeeding the Union with the actual expenditure in the years immediately preceding the Union?—I think it will be seen from my Memorandum that in the three years preceding the Union the total expenditure came to [illegible], and in the three years subsequent to the Union it was [illegible], about. It was about [illegible] larger in the first three years succeeding the Union than in the last three years preceding the Union.

9062. In those years succeeding the Union were not certain arrear charges paid off?—I understand by arrear charges, you mean charges incurred by Ireland prior to the Union?

9063. Yes?—There were such charges.

9064. And in the first year Ireland paid about [illegible] more than she was bound to pay under the system of contribution, and afterwards got credit for it?—That is so. That appears from the account which I gave in my Memorandum, [illegible].

9065. Am I right in holding that the whole intention of the Government (and I suppose by "Government," we must say the British Government here) at the time of the Union was to ultimately amalgamate the two Exchequers, all expenditure being defrayed out of the proceeds of equal taxes indiscriminately imposed on the same articles?—I think that may be said to have been the ultimate intention of the authors of the Treaty of the Union.

9066. And that arrangement was intended to be subject to such abatements and exemptions in the case of Ireland as circumstances might from time to time appear to demand?—Yes, that is so.

9067. In the matter of abatements and exemptions, Ireland was to be put on the same footing as Scotland?—Yes, according to the terms of the Treaty of Union.

9068. And I think that this intention to amalgamate the revenues and expenditure of the two countries, and impose indiscriminate taxation was avowed both by Mr. Pitt and by Lord Castlereagh?—Yes, that is so, I think.

9069. I want to read to you what Mr. Pitt said on the 21st April 1800, on this matter, at page [illegible] of your Memorandum. "The object of the financial arrangements was to effect the gradual abolition of all distinction in finance and revenue between the two countries, and to accelerate the time when both countries shall have but one fund and pay one uniform proportion of taxes throughout each"?—Yes; that is so.

9070. Was it not also intended that the Union should put an end to the commercial disadvantages under which Ireland laboured?—That was certainly the intention of Pitt immediately afterwards.

9071. Were not those disadvantages removed by the Union?—Yes.

9072. As part of the Union?—Yes.

9073. So that the avowed object of the Union was that, a common Exchequer, and the same system of finance and revenue?—I have no doubt that was the ultimate object of the Union.

9074. And uniformity in taxation, subject to certain abatements, of course, in the case of Ireland?—On the ground that that was thought to be the fairest system.

9075. And absolute commercial equality?—Yes, certainly.

9076. I wish to ask you a few questions about what Lord Castlereagh said in the Irish House of Commons on the 5th January 1800, when he was making his principal explanations on the message from the Lord Lieutenant, recommending a legislative Union. You will find his remarks at page [illegible] of your Memorandum. Lord Castlereagh said, "It were to be wished that there was not an insurmountable bar to a common system and a common Treasury, and that we could become like counties of the same kingdom subject to the same system of finance. Were our entire expenditure common, (which would happen if neither kingdom had any separate debts or if those debts were in proportion to their ability,) by no system whatever could they be made to contribute so strictly according to their means as by being subject to the same taxes equally bearing on the same objects of taxation in both countries." That was what he said on that occasion, was it not?—Yes.

9077. And that shows that he held (rightly or wrongly) that the best means of making the two countries contribute according to their means was to impose the same taxes on both?—I think so, under the same system of taxation.

9078. Did not Lord Castlereagh also say, on that occasion, that the first principle of incorporation was "that there should be no retrospect in regard to expenditure. Ireland is to have no concern with the past debt of Great Britain"?—Yes, that is so.

9079. And he held on that ground that a common system of finance was, for the time, impossible, the debt of Great Britain being much greater in proportion than that of Ireland?—Yes.

[illegible]
[illegible]

Act of Union.

Sir E. W. Hamilton, K.C.B.

30 May 1895.

9080. He therefore proposed, I understand, that the debt of each country should be a separate charge of that country, and that as regards other expenditure their contribution should be proportionate?—Yes.

9081. Did he not also say, in regard to the question of contribution, that it was necessary to ascertain "the "best criterion that can be found of the relative means "of the two countries in order to fix the relative "proportion of their contributions"?—Yes.

9082. And he then said that the best criterion would be the produce of an income tax levied on the same description of income in both countries, and equally well levied in both?—Yes.

9083. But as that criterion was not available he sought for the next best, and believed that he had found it in what he calls the "joint result of commerce and consumption"?—Yes, that is so.

9084. He took the ratio which the aggregate export and import trade of Ireland bore to that of Great Britain, and also the ratio in which certain dutiable articles were consumed in the two islands, and from a combination of these two ratios he deduced the proportion of 1 to 7½ as that in which the two countries should contribute to joint expenditure?—Yes.

9085. I believe the accuracy of the figures he used has been attacked?—Yes, that is so, and I refer to that fact later on in my Memorandum.

9086. But whether they were correct or not, it is obvious that the means of a country, so far as regards its capacity to bear taxation, are not, necessarily, proportionate to its foreign trade?—That would be so.

9087. And in the same way the relative consumption of certain articles is not, necessarily, a correct test of the means of two countries?—No. I do not think either of them are absolute tests, but both foreign trade and the consumption of principal articles of food would, at any rate, be contributory tests of the means of the two countries.

9088. But being only what you might call approximately accurate, or contributory tests it follows, does it not, follow that you cannot say positively that Lord Castlereagh had deduced a correct proportion?—Not certainly not. I think he took the best test at his disposal. I cannot say more than that.

9089. And even if the proportion of 1 to 7½ had been a correct proportion, it would have been necessary to tax both countries to what we may call the same extent in proportion to its capacity, in order to raise the due proportion of revenue to meet the contributions?—That is to say, to extract from Ireland the same proportionate amount of revenue, or rather an amount of revenue from Ireland in proportion to the amount which she had to contribute.

Taxation of Ireland after the Union.

9090. Making that assumption it would be necessary to exact the same proportion, we will say, of her total income or resources as you did in England?—Yes, but it would not follow that it would be the same taxes—they might be heavier or lighter.

9091. But, in point of fact, the taxation was considerably lighter in Ireland than in Great Britain, after the Union—there was no income tax, was there?—There was not.

9092. There was a 10 per cent. income tax at the time in Great Britain, was there not?—Yes, in Great Britain.

9093. And the taxation in Ireland continued to be lighter than in Great Britain for a great many years. For instance, there was the lighter spirit duty?—No doubt it did.

9094. (*Chairman.*) Is it quite correct to say the "taxation" of Ireland; ought it not to be "the rate"?—Yes. I mean the rate, but there are also the exemptions.

Act of Union.

9095. (*Sir David Barbour.*) I will read you another remark that Lord Castlereagh made at the same time in reference to the arrangement for the accumulation of any Irish surplus in time of peace. This is what he said: "Great Britain has at length established the "great principle of raising a great part of the supplies "within the year; this island is not at present in a "situation to adopt a similar system, the consequence "of which is that the debt of Great Britain will here-"after increase in a much less degree and be more "rapidly liquidated, while the debt of Ireland will be "increasing with greater rapidity." He also said, "It may happen that if war should continue and Ireland "fund her supplies, whilst England raises a great part "of hers within the year, and mortgages her income "tax to their rapid reduction in time of peace, that the "proportion of the debt of Ireland may rise and her "scale of taxation increase accordingly." I wish to ask you whether it is not clear from what I have read that Lord Castlereagh contemplated that either one or other of two things would happen after the Union—either there would be peace, and the debt of Great Britain would be more rapidly reduced than that of Ireland, or there would be war, and the debt of Ireland would grow more rapidly than that of Great Britain?—I think those are the two alternatives that he had in his mind.

9096. And in either case would not the result be the same, to bring the two debts (sooner or later) to the proportion of 1 to 7½, and pave the way for that complete union of the revenue and expenditure of the two countries and for that system of indiscriminate taxation which it was the avowed object of the Union to establish?—I think so.

9097. Whichever result followed it must be the same?—It must bring the two debts together, according to what Lord Castlereagh said.

9098. I wish to read from the seventh of Mr. Pitt's resolutions which passed the House of Commons with reference to this point; it is at page 6 of Mr. Holland's Memorandum. "The mode of jointly defraying such "expenses shall be regulated according to such rules "and principles as shall be in like manner agreed upon "previous to the Union, for the purpose of establishing "gradually a uniform system of taxation throughout "every part of the United Kingdom"?—Yes, that is so. I have not got the words before me, but I know the passage.

9099. And as I said before, the concluding words of this resolution show what the intention of the government was at that time?—Ultimately, yes.

9100. It has been said that the charge imposed upon Ireland, after the Union was too high. Is it not desirable to compare the charge imposed on Ireland under the proportionate system with the charge Ireland would have had to bear if there had been no Union?—Since I wrote my Memorandum, I have looked a good deal more into the accounts of Ireland between 1801 and 1817, and I find, what is, perhaps, rather a striking fact, although much must not be drawn from it. It is this,—that with the exception so far as I can see of the 16,750,000*l.*, which was practically remitted from Ireland to Great Britain, in order to make good the quota, the large expenditure paid by Ireland was in respect of expenditure wholly incurred inside the country. Therefore, of course, it might be inferred that, Union or no Union, Ireland would, with the exception of that 17,000,000*l.* have had to bear this enormous expenditure, for there is no trace, as far as I can see, of any expenditure incurred outside Ireland, excepting those sums that were remitted from Ireland to Great Britain.

9101. So that the very heavy expenditure which Ireland incurred after the Union was almost entirely or chiefly incurred in Ireland itself?—Yes, that is so, at least, according to the best information I have been able to obtain.

9102. From which I suppose one might infer, not with absolute certainty, that she would have had to bear that charge if there had been no Union, because she always bore the charges in Ireland?—That is the inference to be drawn, no doubt.

9103. I quote what Lord Clare said in the Irish House of Commons, as it throws some light on the state of things to which I have referred. This was said with reference to the proposals made for the Union. "We "have not three years of redemption from bankruptcy, "or intolerable taxation . . . . If England were at "peace at this hour with all the powers of Europe you "would be compelled to maintain a war establishment "for defence against your own people." Does not this remark show that it was possible or probable that if there had been no Union, the Irish expenditure would have been very high in the beginning of the present century?—I think so, inasmuch as prior to the Union, Ireland had to bear all the charges incurred in Ireland.

9104. And were those charges heavy?—No doubt they were very heavy.

9105. I think we have seen that the avowed object of the Union was to bring about a state of things under

Sir E. W. Hamilton, K.C.B.

30 May 1895.

Sir E. W. Hamilton, K.C.B.

[illegible]

which there would be a common system of revenue and finance and indiscriminate taxation?—I think so.

9106. And I think we have seen that it was held that such a state of things would exist as soon as the debt of Ireland bore a certain proportion to the debt of England?—Yes.

9107. If Ireland were charged too highly at the time of the Union, the only result would be to bring about the proportion of the two debts more rapidly than would otherwise have been the case, would it not?—I think that would have been so, because the greater Ireland's liability was the more she would have had to borrow in order to meet it.

9108. And, consequently, if she were more highly charged the result would be to hasten the time for complete amalgamation and indiscriminate taxation?—That would be so.

9109. And if that indiscriminate taxation were a higher taxation, to hasten the time would undoubtedly be a loss to Ireland, would it not?—Yes.

9110. So that the question of the fairness of Ireland's contribution after the Union really resolved itself, did it not, into a question of time, namely, the time for complete amalgamation of revenue and expenditure, and equal and uniform taxation?—That would have been the case, I think, on the assumption that Ireland would have had to borrow to meet her liability.

9111. If there had been peace, as Lord Castlereagh said, the English debt, according to his argument, would have been reduced more rapidly?—No doubt that was the other alternative.

9112. (*Lord Farrer.*) Do you not think that was the alternative that Mr. Pitt had in view, that he was sanguine of the war being over, and that England's charges would be reduced?—I think there was no question about it. Mr. Pitt's own idea was that the war would not last, and I do not think anybody could have foreseen that it was going to last 15 more years.

9113. (*Sir David Barbour.*) In point of fact, though the Exchequers were amalgamated in 1817, taxation was not really made uniform in the two countries till 1853, was it?—That is so.

9114. It is not absolutely uniform at the present day, is it?—No; because Ireland is exempted from the inhabited house duty, the land tax, and establishment licences.

9115. Consequently Ireland enjoyed certain advantages in the matter of taxation up to 1853, and the system of equal taxation, which it was the avowed object of the Union to bring about, did not come into complete operation for more than 50 years after the Union?—That is so.

9116. I am now going back a little. The proportion of contribution to be paid by each country was to be settled by what Lord Castlereagh called the "joint "result of commerce and consumption"?—Yes, those were his words.

9117. And he had previously said that the best system would be to make both countries subject to the same taxes, had he not?—Yes.

9118. Making them contribute in proportion to their ability?—Yes.

9119. Was it this system of uniform taxes equally bearing on the same subjects of taxation that the Union was intended ultimately to secure?—I think so.

9120. But pending the introduction of this common system there was to be a system of proportionate contribution?—Yes, a proportionate contribution of 2 to 15.

9121. Lord Castlereagh said he would have preferred to settle the proportionate rate of contribution by a consideration of the produce of an income tax, if there had been an income tax in both countries?—Yes.

9122. And failing the criterion of an income tax he took "the joint result of commerce and consumption"?—That is so.

9123. Is it not the case that under the Act of Union the proportion of 2 to 15 was only to be maintained in the first instance for 20 years, and that provision was made for its revision from time to time?—That is so under the second paragraph of the seventh article of the Treaty of Union.

9124. And certain rules are laid down in the Act of Union regarding the data to be used from time to time in revising the proportion of contribution?—That is so.

9125. And these rules were to be followed, were they not, so long as the system of proportionate contribution was in force?—Yes.

Act of Union.

9126. Have you found anywhere in the papers connected with the Union a single passage which indicates that it was intended after a common system of revenue and finance had been introduced, and the same taxes indiscriminately applied to both countries, that their contributions to joint expenditure should be regulated by a consideration of the respective trade of the two countries, or of the respective consumption of certain articles, or of the proceeds of an income tax?—I do not think there is anything on record.

9127. Are not these the words of the Act of Union, that there are to be "equal taxes imposed on the same "articles in each country subject only to such particu- "lar exemptions or abatements in Ireland and in that "part of Great Britain called Scotland, as circum- "stances may appear to demand"?—Yes, those are the words of the seventh paragraph of the seventh article.

9128. So that there is nothing in the Act of Union which binds the present Parliament to consider the question of particular exemptions and abatements with reference to the proceeds of an income tax, or with reference to any criterion specified at the time of the Union, is there?—No.

9129. In fact, in determining now and at any future time, whether any and what abatements and exemptions should be granted to Ireland or Scotland, the hands of Parliament are absolutely unfettered by anything said at the time of the Union?—Except the qualification at the end of the same paragraph which said, "as circumstances might appear from time to time to demand." There was that qualification.

Taxation of Ireland after the Union.

9130. You say at page 9 of your Memorandum that it was doubtful whether the taxation of the country—that is, of Ireland, after the Union, had not been carried to the point beyond which further impositions would have ceased to be productive?—Yes.

9131. I understand that statement to be based rather on opinions expressed by others than upon any facts you have come across?—I expressed it to a certain extent, no doubt, on the authority of others. McCulloch, for instance, was a man who dealt with the question, and I regard him as a considerable economic authority. I have looked at his book more carefully since I wrote that, and he mentions this as a very striking instance of the impotency of taxation, when carried beyond a certain extent, to produce revenue. I confess I cannot quite identify his figures. He makes out that between the years 1807 and 1816 taxes were imposed in Ireland which ought to have produced something approaching to 3,500,000l. Then he compared the receipts of 1807 and those of 1817, and the increase of revenue according to his figures, was practically nil. I confess that does not quite agree with the figures in the tables that I have placed before the Commission, and I cannot identify his figures, but I do not think there is much doubt that the taxes did not produce anything like what they were expected to produce. They were expected to produce, according to the statement of the Chancellor of the Exchequer of that day, about 3,500,000l. altogether, and, I think, that the outside sum they produced was a million or a million and a half.

9132. I believe the income tax was not in force in Ireland at that time. That at any rate could have been imposed, and would have produced something?—No doubt it would. Mr. Pitt himself, at the end of the last century made up his mind to impose it and made an estimate of what it would be likely to produce. He put it down at 1,000,000l. Of course, the income tax at that time was yielding an enormous sum in Great Britain at the high rate of 2s. in the £, and if you take a moderate estimate of 1 per cent. which is about what it produces in Ireland now, as compared with Great Britain, the imposition of the income tax in Ireland would at the close of the war have brought in about 600,000l. or 700,000l.

9133. In connexion with this matter I should like to read you a passage from the Report of the Select Committee which reported in 1815. That Committee prepared a statement showing the increase or diminution of the gross and net permanent revenue at the end of every three years from 1791 to 5th January 1815, and they said: "On this statement it is satisfactory to "observe that the net payments into the Exchequer

Sir E. W. Hamilton, K.C.B. — [illegible] — Taxation in Ireland after the Union.

"for the year ending 5th January 1815 exceed those for the year ending on the same day, 1819, by 1,300,000*l.*, and that the increase has been uniformly progressive since 1811." Further on they say:—"And although your Committee cannot pretend to form any correct opinion as to what may be the actual produce of the existing taxes of Ireland in future years, subject as that must be to the influence of various causes connected with the general state of the Empire, yet they are strongly induced to hope for a continued increase, founding their opinion on what has actually happened in recent times, on a full consideration of the growing prosperity of Ireland, and on a belief that improvements are yearly taking place in the financial collections and arrangements of that country." Are not these remarks opposed to the conclusion that the last straw in the way of taxation had been laid on Ireland, and that further taxation would be unproductive?—No doubt the revenue did increase in Ireland, as will be seen by reference to some of the tables I have handed in; in fact, between 1807 and 1816 the revenue rose from 4,300,000*l.* to 6,100,000*l.*, and to that extent I thought Mr. McCulloch's figures were hardly borne out; but of course it is very difficult to form an opinion at this distance of time, as to what the state of facts was; but it was held generally at that time, putting aside the income tax which would never have affected the bulk of the population, that Ireland was taxed as heavily as she could bear.

9134. But are not these remarks that I have read rather opposed to the conclusion that Ireland was taxed as heavily as she could be?—They may be slightly opposed to it, I admit, but I think, if one reads the thing, that that is the general conclusion to be found, but that does not apply to the income tax, as I say. It is then that, in the absence of that tax, it cannot be said that the last straw was laid on Ireland.

9135. The resources of Ireland had undoubtedly been very much increased?—Yes, very materially.

9136. And when you have increased very much the taxation of a country, even though it is able to bear more, there are great practical objections to increasing it still further at the time, are there not?—Certainly, because you may very likely prevent the tax from being further productive.

9137. At any rate, great opposition would be raised to it?—Certainly.

9138. But it does not follow, does it, at that moment that absolutely the last straw in the way of taxation has been laid on the country?—No, not the last straw.

9139. (*Chairman.*) In consequence of the last statement which you have made, do you alter the opinion you gave on the first day that you were examined when you said "I have come to the conclusion, speaking entirely for myself, that Ireland was taxed as heavily as she could reasonably be expected to be taxed"?—No, I think not, because, as I have said, I was talking of the mass of the people, to whom, of course, income tax would not have applied.

9140. But with the exception of income tax, do you still adhere to that opinion?—Yes, I adhere to that opinion myself.

The witness withdrew.

TWENTY-THIRD DAY.

Thursday, 13th June 1895.

At Committee Room B, House of Lords.

PRESENT:

LORD FARRER, Chairman.

The Right Hon. The O'Conor Don.	Bertram W. Currie, Esq.
Sir Thomas Sutherland, K.C.M.G., M.P.	J. E. Redmond, Esq., M.P.
Sir David Barbour, K.C.S.I.	Thomas Sexton, Esq., M.P.
The Hon. Edward Blake, M.P.	Henry F. Slattery, Esq.

Mr. R. H. Holland, *Secretary.*

Sir Edward Hamilton, K.C.B., re-called and further examined.

Sir E. W. Hamilton, K.C.B. — 13 June 1895. — [illegible]

9141. (*Sir Thomas Sutherland.*) You have been asked a good many questions with regard to the historical part of our reference, but I understand from your paper that you consider the settlement made at the time of the Union, financially speaking, was intended to be a perfectly fair settlement?—I think that was clearly the intention of the framers of the Treaty of Union. There is no doubt that the intention was that it should be a fair and equitable arrangement between the two countries.

9142. But of course the result was altogether upset by the unforeseen long war that ensued?—Yes, and the colossal expenditure which that war involved.

9143. In consequence of that war I think you stated that the taxation of Great Britain was increased enormously, to the extent of 30,000,000*l.* or 35,000,000*l.* a year?—That I think may be said to be the case. It was, in fact, almost doubled.

9144. And that the debt of Great Britain was increased also to the extent of something like 360,000,000*l.* in round figures?—Yes, that is so.

9145. While the taxation in Ireland was increased by about 2,000,000*l.*, and the debt in Ireland ran up from 30,000,000*l.* to 110,000,000*l.*, or thereabouts?—Yes.

9146. Of course, the resources we know was very much greater in the case of Ireland than in the case of Great Britain, and if that state of things had been prolonged, it seems clear, does it not, that the conclusion which one draws from your memorandum is, that it would have been quite impossible for Ireland to continue borrowing?—I think, I shall be able to bring that out rather more clearly when I explain about the debt.

9147. If you please. That is the conclusion I draw from reading your memorandum, namely, that if the state of things had been prolonged it would have been practically impossible, looking at it from a business point of view, for Ireland to continue to borrow?—I will not say she would have exhausted her credit, but I think the burden would have been intolerable to her.

9148. At all events, in the judgment of Parliament in 1817 the state of things made the Union of the exchequers inevitable?—That is so.

9149. And whatever Ireland had to do with the debt of the United Kingdom, all that she would have to do would be to contribute her quota of taxation which she would reasonably bear, towards the general expenditure [illegible], was it not?—Yes.

[illegible]

9150. Now, I understand from your figures that the estimated contribution of Ireland to the general revenue of the United Kingdom is something like 7,[illegible] as round figures?—That is taking the latest year, I think. The total revenue of Ireland, according to 1893-94, may be said to have been 7,[illegible]

9151. Of that amount I gather that about 1,[illegible] is derived from direct taxation?—That is so.

9152. And about 6,[illegible] from indirect taxation?—Yes.

9153. And about [illegible] is received from the Post Office and from miscellaneous sources?—Yes, in round figures.

9154. I understand from your point of view there is no question whatever as to the 1,[illegible] of direct taxation being levied with as much fairness as the same taxes are levied in Great Britain?—I think it represents about the relative amount which is paid by Great Britain in proportion to what is supposed to be the capacity of the country.

9155. What I mean is the 1,[illegible] is levied really upon the same principles, or at all events, with no harshness towards Ireland as compared with the mode in which it is levied in Great Britain?—That is certainly so.

9156. And I think it results in this, does it not, that the direct taxation in Ireland is at the rate of 6s. [illegible] per head, while the direct taxation in Great Britain is at the rate of [illegible]?—For 1893-94 the exact figure worked out as under the head of direct taxes 6s. [illegible] a head in Ireland and [illegible] in Great Britain.

9157. It has been attempted to be shown in the [illegible] by my right honourable friend, and of course in many other ways, that Ireland cannot afford to pay the indirect taxation which she pays, that is so, is it not?—Yes, I think so.

9158. As a matter of fact one of the questions which I think my right honourable friend asked you was whether you were not aware of the fact that Ireland used so much [illegible] in order to enable her to consume so much dry bread instead of bacon and bread which the labourer gets in England?—Yes.

9159. And similarly that the consumption of whiskey was partly to be accounted for by the poverty of Ireland; I think that was the nature of the questions of my right honourable friend?—I believe so.

9160. I do not think the O'Conor Don pushed it quite so far as tobacco, but I think he was going a little in that direction and he generally suggested that the consumption of these duty paying or excisable commodities was really due to the poverty of the country?—That was so, I think.

9161. If that sort of argument were to hold good with a Chancellor of the Exchequer, I presume there are districts and masses of population in Great Britain, to say nothing of Scotland and the east end of London, which would be able to put in a similar plea?—Yes, I am afraid that is one of the great difficulties which underlies that problem.

9162. For the sake of argument, granting the relative poverty of Ireland, is there in your knowledge any proof that her population is suffering from poverty and from the habit of using whiskey and tea instead of bacon to such an extent as to affect the physical health of the country?—I am afraid I am no judge of that.

9163. Are you aware that in the year 1891 the death rate in Great Britain was 19 per 1,000, and that in Ireland it was only at the rate of 18 per 1,000?—I think I saw that in one of the tables presented to the Commission.

9164. If the health of Ireland were affected by the habits of the people, do you think that the lowering of the duty on spirits would be likely to lessen the consumption of whiskey and increase the consumption of bacon?—I do not think so; the general result of lowering the duty on a commodity is that there is a larger consumption of that commodity.

9165. If there is any argument as to the lowering of duty on spirits, Scotland would have as fair a case to present as Ireland I suppose?—Yes, that would be so.

9166. I think we may assume that your opinion is that all the customs and excise duties in the United Kingdom must be levied at the same rate throughout?—I think there is no question about that; and if there were any attempt made in the direction of differentiation, the first people to complain about it would probably be those who live in Ireland themselves. I do not know whether it is generally known to the Commission—but it is the fact—that, when the equalisation of spirit duties was undertaken in 1858, what appears to have been one of the considerations taken into account by the Chancellor of the Exchequer of the day was the pressure put upon him by the spirit distillers in Ireland to remove the inconveniences resulting from differential duties.

9167. Assuming that that must be so, of course a generous legislature might exempt Ireland from, say, income tax, or death duties?—Certainly, but that would not relieve (what may be called) the masses, because the consuming classes would not be affected by such taxation.

9168. It would act as a bounty to the manufacturers, would it not? My friend Mr. Webb is not here, but I intended to use him as an illustration. If he or any other [illegible] were exempt from income tax he would have a decided pull over his [illegible] there, whom I represent, in another part of the kingdom, would he not?—No doubt.

9169. Really, as a question of practical politics you would hardly consider it desirable, would you, that the direct taxes should be varied so as to make them more favourable in one part of the United Kingdom than another, especially as Ireland already enjoys a certain amount of exemption in that respect?—I should certainly not expect that line to be taken.

9170. Do you consider from your investigation of the matter that there is any proof whatever that Ireland cannot afford to pay the contribution to the revenue which it now makes?—I think it is very difficult for me to express a definite opinion upon that point, but the greater part of what she contributes to the revenue is from indirect taxation, therefore to some extent voluntary.

9171. (Mr. Sexton.) The question for us is not whether she can afford to pay, but whether she can afford to pay what she pays as well as Great Britain can afford to pay what she pays, is it not?—I think so.

9172. (Sir Thomas Sutherland.) If, for the sake of argument, we were to admit that Ireland is overtaxed, how could the indirect taxation be mitigated except by lowering the duty on tobacco and spirits, because I suppose everyone will agree that the duty on tea is low enough, if we are to have any duty at all?—I think so.

9173. And by increasing the beer duty. That, of course, I presume, would be one way of diminishing the amount of revenue collected in Ireland and Scotland, and of raising a greater revenue in England, unless, of course, the higher taxation on beer was to injure the revenue from beer?—Yes, I think that would be so. It is a remarkable fact that the consumption of beer in Ireland has considerably increased of late years. I have a figure here before me which may interest the Commission. In 1879-80 there were 5½ million gallons of spirits consumed, and in 1893-94 there were only 4,730,000 gallons consumed. Therefore there was a decrease of over 700,000 gallons. If you take beer, on the other hand, you will find that in 1879-80 there were 1,300,000 barrels consumed, and in 1893-94 no less than 1,[illegible] barrels consumed. Therefore there is an increase of 415,000 barrels, and one would infer from that that the taste of the Irishman is undergoing at any rate some change.

9174. (Mr. Blake.) There was an increase in beer of about one half, was there?—There is a decrease of 13 per cent. on spirits and an increase of 40 per cent. upon beer.

9175. (Mr. Sexton.) Can you put this into money. Is the reduced amount paid for spirits much greater than the increased amount paid for beer?—I am afraid I have not that calculation by me, but I have no doubt I can furnish it.

9176. (Chairman.) Have you compared that with the figures relating to Great Britain or Scotland?—No, I have not.

9177. (Mr. Sexton.) The duty on a barrel of beer is, how much?—6s. 3d.

9178. (Mr. Currie.) And the duty on spirits is 10s. 6d., is it not?—Yes.

9179. (Mr. Sexton.) Then it would appear that the decrease in duty on whiskey would be 400,000l., about, and the increased duty on beer about 800,000l.?—Yes.

9180. So that the decrease is double the amount of the increase?—Yes, I think about that.

9181. (Mr. Blake.) Perhaps you could get out the figures of the total amount of the duties?—Yes, I will endeavour to do so.

9182. (Sir Thomas Sutherland.) I understand the real point of your observation to be that it is possibly owing to the increase in the consumption of beer, and that of the

Sir E. W. Hamilton, K.C.B. — [illegible] 1895. — Relief of [illegible] Irish [illegible].

beer duty were increased, and the spirit duty diminished, the revenue derived from Ireland might still remain as large as it is now?—Yes, if it is not due to some temporary change.

9183. In the interests of Ireland it might not be going in the direction of alleviation?—Not necessarily so.

9184. But it would be going in the direction of alleviation so far as Scotland is concerned, where I fancy the national beverage is still whiskey, and the consumption of beer has not largely increased?—I fancy so, but I have not looked at the figures as to Scotland.

9185. Assuming, for the sake of argument, Ireland pays too much in taxation, I suppose the position could be altered by making a large grant of, say, a couple of millions or so out of the taxation of the United Kingdom for local purposes. I see some such suggestion of the kind is made in the current number of the "National Review." Of course if that were done, a couple of millions or so would have to be taken out of the pockets of the people of Great Britain towards which the poor down-trodden people of Scotland contribute in order to elevate Ireland?—I am afraid there would be no other means of meeting the grant.

Constitution [illegible] Imperial [illegible].

9186. There is only one other question I want to ask, and that is, supposing we had in Ireland the equivalent of Grattan's Parliament (and as that is rather a political question you need not answer it unless you like) do you think it is possible that the representatives of that parliament would be satisfied to rest under any enforced contribution, and that they would not claim to make their own bargains, as Grattan's Parliament did? Supposing that the present representatives of Ireland, in the House of Commons, for whom I have the greatest respect, agreed to pay a fixed contribution to the revenue of the country, do you suppose that their successors in this supposed parliament would be content to make any contribution of the kind?—I think that is perhaps a question somewhat beyond what I ought to answer.

9187. You were asked a question, I think, at the beginning of your evidence, whether the Cape contributed towards the Imperial expenditure?—Yes.

9188. It does not, does it?—No.

9189. We should like her to contribute very much, should we not?—Certainly.

9190. Do you know, on the other hand, that such colonies as the Straits Settlements, and Hong Kong, and Ceylon, are made to contribute by the Treasury and the War Office pretty smartly?—I do not know that I ought to adopt the words "pretty smartly," but there is no doubt they do contribute.

9191. Supposing Ireland were to have a representative and an executive authority like the Cape, do you not draw a little analogy as to what the position might be in that case so far as the Exchequer of the Imperial Parliament is concerned?—I do not think the two cases are on all fours.

9192. In the time of Grattan's Parliament they offered, I think very fairly, to contribute towards the Imperial Government, always provided that they did it as a matter of bargain as between one independent body and another independent body; that was so was it not?—Yes, I think that may be said to be the case.

9193. (*Chairman.*) Can you tell the Commission whether the Isle of Man contributes anything towards Imperial expenditure?—I think there is some small payment of about 10,000*l.* a year made, but as regards the Channel Islands there is no contribution at all.

9194. (*The O'Conor Don.*) You have been asked questions from which one might deduce the conclusion that I had on the last occasion asked you questions on the assumption that Ireland was over taxed beyond her ability. Did I ask you any question whatever that would lead to that conclusion? I referred, did I not, to her relative ability, not to her absolute ability?—I think it was "relative ability" which you put to me.

9195. Were not all my questions directed to the relative ability of the two countries to bear taxation?—I think so.

9196. Therefore it does not follow, does it, from any of my questions, that I assume that Ireland was absolutely overtaxed beyond her present ability?—I inferred, from what you said, that you were dealing with relative ability, and not actual ability.

9197. Therefore, the conclusions drawn from my examination by my friend are not exactly correct, are they?—I think perhaps the questions went rather beyond the terms of the reference to the Commission, which have reference to the relative ability of the two countries.

9198. I understand that since you were here on the former occasion, you have looked into the question of the loans before and after the Union, and the rates at which they were raised. Perhaps you will now give us the information which you were then unable to give with regard to that?—I think when I gave evidence on the last occasion, in answer to questions put by the right hon. gentleman, I led the Commission to believe that the credit of the loans raised in respect of Ireland between 1801 and 1817, rested, in the first instance, on the credit of the Irish Exchequer only, and presumably—I was speaking then under reserve—on the British Exchequer behind it. I am afraid I was not accurate in my facts, and having examined the question more carefully, with the leave of the Commission I hope I may be able to explain the position of affairs better than I could then. I have two documents to put in which I hope will interest the Commission. I will first of all explain what they are and I will then make one or two comments upon them. I first of all propose to put in a statement which shows "the amount received in cash as "compared with the amount of debt created on account "of Ireland both before the Union and after the Union, "until the Exchequers were amalgamated."

9199. (*Mr. Sexton.*) For each year?—For each year.

9200. (*The O'Conor Don.*) Both before and after the Union?—Yes. Then I propose to put in a second statement which shows the rate per cent. for interest incurred on each of the loans given in No. 1 as were raised solely by Stock and Bills on account of Ireland (1) in Ireland, and (2) in Great Britain. That shows I think in the fairest possible manner the rates at which the money was raised at the time. I cannot apply that system strictly to all the loans, because some of the loans were raised partly by annuities, and it is impossible to capitalise them; but I think the bulk of the loans was raised by stock or bills, and if one calculates at a rate from those loans, one may take that such rate represented the credit on which Ireland or Great Britain could borrow. It is a fair inference to draw that the rate which applies to the greater part would apply to the whole. Before the Union, Irish loans, whether raised in Ireland or in Great Britain, rested solely on the credit of the Irish Exchequer, and I make out that during that time the average rate at which she was able to raise money was in Ireland itself about 6½ per cent., while when she came to the British market, it was at about 5 per cent. She only came to the British market just at the end of that period. That, I think, explains the position of affairs as regards the loans raised by Ireland prior to the Union. After the Union the bulk of the loans was not raised in Ireland, but in Great Britain. In fact, out of the total amount of stock created, about 91,000,000*l.* was raised in Great Britain, and about 19,500,000*l.* was raised in Ireland.

9201. (*Mr. Sexton.*) Between 1801 and 1817?—Yes.

9202. (*The O'Conor Don.*) For Irish services?—Yes, for Irish services. When a loan was raised in Ireland itself, the dividends on the stock so issued were charged on the Consolidated Fund of Ireland alone, and there was no other guarantee; though I presume that, if Ireland had got into difficulties so great that she could not pay her interest, the Imperial Parliament who passed the Act would have been bound to come to her rescue. With regard to loans raised in Great Britain on Irish account, it is quite clear that so far as the lender was concerned the security was the credit of the Consolidated Fund of Great Britain and not Ireland. With the leave of the Commission I will take an instance—namely the loan that was raised in 1826 under the Imperial Act of 1808, Geo. III. Cap. 33. I need not explain the terms on which that loan was raised, but the dividends on the whole of the 30,000,000*l.* were charged on the Consolidated Fund of Great Britain, and out of the 30,000,000*l.* 2,000,000*l.* were assigned to Ireland, and in respect of that 2,000,000*l.* assigned to Ireland it was directed by the Act of Parliament that an amount equivalent to the dividends on the portion remitted to Ireland should be periodically paid out of the Irish Exchequer to Great Britain. Therefore, I think it is clear that as regards the bulk of the debt created between 1801 and 1817 the credit rested solely upon the British Exchequer. Here is a remarkable fact (though I think it admits of explanation) that really the loans which were raised in Great Britain for Ireland were raised on rather less favourable terms than the loans raised in Ireland on account of Ireland. I presume that must be due to the abundance of the sums raised in Great Britain by Government loans during that period—in fact Ireland may have had more loanable capital left in the country than Great Britain.

9203. (*Mr. Currie.*) Might not it also have depended on the price of the public funds at the time?—I am only comparing now the rate of interest paid upon the cash received.

9204. (*Mr. Blake.*) Do the loans made in Ireland run over the period to which you have referred?—I think they may be said to run with tolerable uniformity over the whole period. For instance, in 1803 there was raised in Ireland a loan of 1,500,000*l*.

9205. At what price?—I am afraid I have not the terms of that loan at hand. But I have an example here before me of a loan actually raised in Ireland, and that was in 1808, when an Act was passed authorising the raising of 2,000,000*l*. to be paid into the Bank of Ireland, and the terms were these: every contributor of 100*l*. was to receive at his option 139*l*. of 3½ per cent. Stock, or an Irish Treasury Debenture of [illegible] bearing 5½ per cent.

9206. (*The O'Conor Don.*) What would that rate of interest be?—I think it came here worked out at about 4*l*. 15*s*. I am not quite certain, but about that time there was a loan raised in Ireland at that rate.*

9207. What would the rate be at the same time on loans raised in England?—At that time the rate in Great Britain was slightly lower,—about 4*l*. 9*s*., but over the whole period between 1801 and 1817 the average rate on which loans were raised on Irish account in Ireland was about 4*l*. 16*s*., and the average rate at which loans were raised on Irish account in Great Britain was very nearly 5*l*.

9208. (*Chairman.*) I suppose it does not follow because they were raised in Ireland that they were raised from Irishmen?—No, not necessarily so.

9209. Or, vice versa, that because they were raised in Great Britain they were raised from Englishmen?—No, I do not think that follows. With the leave of the Commission I will hand these papers in. (*The papers were handed in, vide Appendix.*)

9210. (*Mr. Sexton.*) Have you answered the question whether the borrowing on Irish account in Ireland extended over the whole period of 16 years?—Yes, off and on.

9211. (*Mr. Blake.*) I mean relatively with the proportion of the English borrowings?—This Return shows the exact scale of things.

9212. (*Mr. Sexton.*) What was the reason there was a small amount of money raised in England for the Irish not by way of part of a large loan but by way of separate loans; there was about 4,000,000*l*. raised in the period by separate loans, and not as part of greater loans, of which a part was remitted to Ireland. Can you tell us anything about that?—I am afraid I have not the particulars here. I ought, perhaps, to point out that Ireland, whether she raised loans in Great Britain or in Ireland during the period between 1801 and 1817, raised them on more favourable terms under the Imperial Acts of Parliament, than she did before the Union. The average rate at which she raised loans on her own credit in Ireland between 1801 and 1817 was at about 4¾ per cent., but prior to the Union it was 6¼ per cent.

9213. (*The O'Conor Don.*) Prior to the Union, at what rate did Great Britain raise loans?—I am afraid I have not my figure before me, but it certainly was not anything like that. For instance, take the first loan which was raised in Great Britain on Irish account subsequent to the Union, the rate was about 5½ per cent.

9214. (*Mr. Blake.*) Was not there a general tendency to an increase of the rate when these enormous borrowings were taking place?—No doubt.

9215. (*Mr. Sexton.*) I am rather at a loss to understand how you infer that the Union had a beneficial effect upon the credit of Ireland, seeing that the loans raised for the account of Ireland, in Ireland, after the Union, appear to have been raised upon more advantageous terms than the loans raised for account of Ireland in Great Britain after the Union?—I think that was due to the enormous amounts raised up in Great Britain.

9216. How, then, did the Union benefit the credit of Ireland?—I think that if Ireland could only borrow prior to the Union at an average rate of 6*l*. 10*s*., and subsequently to the Union at about 4*l*. 15*s*., it must have been due in the main to the fact that Ireland had the Imperial credit behind it, or rather that the loan was under the aegis, so to speak, of the Imperial Parliament.

9217. Have you observed that taking the relative charge for the debt of Ireland and for the debt of Great Britain at the time of the Union, and comparing them with the relative charge of each at the time of the consolidation of the exchequers, the charge of Ireland increased relatively more than the charge of Great Britain in that time?—Yes, I believe that is so.

Sir E. W. Hamilton, K.C.B.

11 June 1895.

Borrowings of Irish debt 1801–1817; rate of interest on them.

9218. That does not look as if the Union had benefited her credit, does it?—I am afraid I cannot reconcile that fact with the figures which I have before me here.

9219. (*Chairman.*) What you have been saying is not at all inconsistent with what Mr. Sexton puts. It only goes, does it not, to the question of how the loans were raised, and whether the English credit came to the assistance of the Irish credit in raising those loans?—Yes. What I pointed out was that according to the figures before me Ireland was apparently borrowing on more onerous terms prior to the Union than subsequently to the Union.

9220. That does not touch the question of whether she was compelled to borrow more after the Union, does it?—No, it does not.

9221. (*The O'Conor Don.*) Where did you ascertain the facts with regard to these loans?—I have got them out from our old records with the help of the National Debt Office, and from old Parliamentary Returns. I hope that, when these papers are put in, it will be tolerably clear to you how the calculations are worked out.

9222. Speaking merely from recollection, your figures do not seem to me to correspond with what we were given to understand in 1865 before the Committee which sat in that year?—I do not think they had these figures before them.

9223. But they had some figures before them?—Yes, but I do not think the calculations have ever been worked out in this way before.

9224. (*Mr. Sexton.*) Is this a correct account of the way in which money was raised on account of Ireland? First it was raised in Ireland to the extent of 14,000,000*l*.?—About 15½ millions.

9225. I think that 10,000,000*l*. of yours includes 4,000,000*l*. raised by separate loans?—When I said 94,000,000*l*. in Great Britain and 15,500,000*l*. in Ireland, I was speaking of the stock created, and not of the actual cash raised; because of course there is a very great difference between the two. The cash raised by loans in Ireland amounted to about 16,750,000*l*.

9226. In Great Britain for the account of Ireland by loans separate from the British loans, and solely dedicated to Ireland, there was raised 4,000,000*l*.?—I am not acquainted with any particular loan of 4,000,000*l*.

9227. And then the whole balance of 60,000,000*l*., or 70,000,000*l*. was raised from year to year under the authority of Acts of the Imperial Parliament raising one loan for the whole service, and remitting a part of it to Ireland?—That is so.

9228. The part remitted to Ireland being raised on identical terms with regard to annuities and sinking fund, and so on, as with regard to Great Britain?—Yes.

9229. (*The O'Conor Don.*) Is that all you wish to say upon that point?—Yes.

9230. Is there any other point arising out of my examination the other day on which you wish to say anything?—No, I think that is the main point.

9231. (*Mr. Sexton.*) Could you furnish the Commission with particulars of the debt created and redeemed on account of Great Britain, and on the account of Ireland in each year from the Union to the consolidation of the Exchequers?—I think that information is practically given in the great report of the National Debt Office presented to Parliament about three years ago. The full particulars are given in that Parliamentary paper—I do not happen to have it with me.

9232. The papers you have given in so show at the end of each year the amount of debt outstanding—the result of the two factors?—Yes.

9233. It does not show the amount of debt created in the year, or the amount redeemed in the year?—No, the Governments of Great Britain and Ireland were borrowing with one hand and paying off with the other.

9234. As that is the resultant factor, you have no doubt in your hands the material necessary to inform the Commission how much amount of debt was created on account of Great Britain, and how much on account of Ireland, and how much redeemed on account of Ireland in each year?—That is fully given, I think, in the Parliamentary Returns year by year, and I will put in the paper. I will have the tables extended and separated for the Commission.

* The actual rate at which the loan of 1808 was raised in Ireland was [illegible]

Sir E. W. Hamilton, K.C.B. 18 June 1895.

9235. Could you exhibit that simple matter from summarily the debt contracted on account of Great Britain, and on account of Ireland from 1801 to 1817?—Yes, I think a reproduction of two or three pages from the Returns would give it.

9236. (*The O'Conor Don.*) With regard to the miscellaneous revenue and the expenditure on what you call "local services" in the two countries, upon the last occasion you explained that the form in which the miscellaneous revenue was recorded, has been altered of late years?—Yes, that is so.

9237. And I think you gave the Commission to understand that the alteration could not affect the relative proportion of revenue contributed by Great Britain and Ireland?—Yes, that is the case.

9238. Does it not appear from these returns that a larger proportion of the revenue raised in Ireland is spent on these local services than is spent in Great Britain out of what is raised in Great Britain?—I am afraid I do not quite follow the honourable member.

9239. In part of these financial returns it is shown that there is a larger proportionate expenditure upon what you call local services in Ireland than in Great Britain. Is it not the fact, without going into details, that the expenditure upon local services in Ireland is greater than the expenditure upon those services in England, proportionately?—Undoubtedly so. What we call local expenditure, no doubt, is relatively greater in Ireland than in Great Britain.

9240. That being so, does it not follow as a necessary consequence that if you change the form of account, and instead of giving Ireland the credit of the whole of the miscellaneous receipts, you set off the receipts against the local services, and only deal with the balance, it must affect the relative contribution of Ireland to the whole contribution of the United Kingdom?—No, I do not see that, I am afraid. The system of what we call "appropriating revenue" or "extra receipts" in aid of expenditure is this. Supposing under the old system there was an expenditure of 100,000*l.* and 10,000*l.* extra receipts belonging to the same service, the present system would be that the expenditure would be voted net; therefore, so far as Ireland is concerned, surely it is the same thing if, instead of having spent upon her 100,000*l.*, and being credited with 10,000*l.*, she is debited with 90,000*l.* for local expenditure.

9241. Not when you come to tot up the whole?—Yes, I think it would be exactly the same.

9242. Supposing the whole of the expenditure on local services in Ireland was met by devoting a certain proportion of the revenue received in Ireland directly to the payment of this and that, then, striking the balance in the way you do in the changed accounts, and only transferring the balance over and above to the credit of Ireland's contribution to the general revenue, would it not follow that you would altogether alter the proportion of that contribution to the general revenue from what it now is?—I am afraid I cannot see that.

9243. There was a time, was there not, when you charged on the one side the gross charge, and showed on the other side the whole of the miscellaneous receipts?—Yes.

9244. If these miscellaneous receipts come from Ireland in a larger proportion than the ratio of the ordinary revenue, then by assigning those receipts to the expenditure, and only showing the balance as Ireland's contribution, do you not depreciate the contribution of Ireland to the whole revenue?—I am afraid I do not follow that.

9245. Let us say that the proportion of ordinary revenue between Ireland and Great Britain is 1 and 12; let us say that the contribution of Ireland to miscellaneous receipts in proportion to Great Britain is 1 to 6—taking merely arbitrary figures. Supposing 6,000,000*l.* and 1,000,000*l.*, it is manifest if you allow that 1,000,000*l.* to remain in the Irish receipts, the Irish receipts taken altogether will show a larger proportion to the British receipts than if you take that 1,000,000*l.* first off the Irish expenditure, and only show the balance, because the effect of that will be to reduce the expenditure, and also to reduce the receipts more in Ireland than in Great Britain, the miscellaneous receipts being higher there than on the average?—I am very sorry; but I am afraid I cannot follow you.

9246. Can you follow my idea?—No, I cannot follow your idea. It is quite impossible that the system which has been adopted—which is a pure matter of account—can upset the calculation in any sort of way.

9247. It cannot upset the relative proportion?—No, it cannot upset the relative proportion.

9248. (*Mr. Sexton.*) Do you not take a certain amount of the Irish revenue?—Yes, but you reduce the expenditure pro tanto.

9249. We are not considering the expenditure now at all. Will you kindly answer from your mind all question of expenditure?—But the whole of these returns are built upon the principle of showing the local expenditure and the balance of revenue after that expenditure is met. I understood that you were asking whether it affected the contribution of Ireland to Imperial expenditure.

9250. (*The O'Conor Don.*) I am afraid you mistook my question, which was not with regard to Imperial expenditure, but with regard to Ireland's contribution to the gross revenue?—If you are talking about the gross revenue it would be so, but you are for ways at cross purposes. I thought you meant it would upset the proportion of contribution to Imperial expenditure.

9251. (*Mr. Sexton.*) Your mind is firmly fixed upon a certain proportion between expenditure and revenue, but we desire to regard it as revenue only?—If you regard it as revenue only, I admit that would be so; but it is not business.

9252. It is revenue?—Yes, it is revenue, but the amount would be small.

9253. (*The O'Conor Don.*) But the change would affect the gross amount of revenue, would it not?—Yes, the gross amount of revenue raised or derived from Ireland.

9254. And the proportion of the gross amount between the two countries?—I do not think it would upset the proportionate amounts of the two countries.

9255. (*Mr. Sexton.*) Necessarily one thing follows the other, does it not?—I do not think so, because you would apply the same system to Great Britain. I think they would come out relatively very nearly the same.

9256. Unless the miscellaneous revenue of Great Britain and Ireland bore the same proportion to each other that the general revenue did, would it not be obvious that the alteration would alter the proportion?—Certainly, but I think you would find it would work out just the same as it is now. However, the amount in question is very unimportant.

9257. (*The O'Conor Don.*) You say, do you, the reason why it does not affect it is first, because the amount is small, and secondly, because the amount of miscellaneous revenue in the two countries is practically in the same proportion?—Yes, that is the case.

9258. One question with regard to the Local Loans Fund. You told us that it barely pays its expenses?—Yes, that is so.

9259. And that it is burdened with an annuity of 130,000*l.* for paying off old bad debts?—Yes.

9260. I suppose so far as the annuity for paying that annuity goes, that that tends to raise the rate at which the loans can now be made?—Undoubtedly it does.

9261. So that it practically comes to this, that the present borrowers of the money have to pay a higher rate of interest in order to recoup the State for loans that were written off or remitted long ago?—That is so, no doubt.

9262. Upon what principle, may I ask, is a charge made upon the present borrowers more than on anyone else to recoup the State for old loans that have been written off?—The right honourable gentleman is aware that it is an arrangement made only eight years ago by the late Chancellor of the Exchequer, Mr. Goschen, and he thought it was only fair that some reparation should be made to the State in respect of loans that had been lost.

9263. But why should that particular form of reparation, namely, making the present borrowers recoup the State for losses which for some good reason ought to be blotted out, be adopted?—It may be put it in that way, but evidently if a bad debt occurs now, say in respect of a Scotch harbour, the taxpayer has to make it good.

9264. (*Chairman.*) Might not you put the question in another way. Why, on the other side, should the general taxpayer pay for loans which have been lost rather than the class of persons who are interested in loans?—No doubt the loss would more properly have been made good by those people who were themselves the borrowers.

9265. It is a question of who shall bear the loss?—Yes, and ultimately the State has to bear the loss.

9266. (*Mr. Sexton.*) At present the State bears it?—Yes.

9267. (*The O'Conor Don.*) Can you give us a list of the remitted loans for which the 130,000*l.* a year is raised as an annuity?—There was a rough calculation made but the general idea was that to set up as large an amount as the Local Loans Fund might reasonably be expected to bear, the amount that was set up (viz., [illegible]) being a small amount as compared with the sum of loans which had turned out to be bad and were lost.

9268. (Mr Carew.) When it is alleged that the borrower pays an excessive rate, is it not a fact that the market rate?—That depends, of course, on who the borrower is. If the borrower is a local authority which can offer the security of rates, then the rate at which it could obtain a loan from the Government ought not to be so good a rate as it could borrow at [illegible].

9269. In fact, they only come to you when they cannot borrow outside, do they?—Very often so.

9270. (Chairman.) At any rate they are not bound to come to you, are they?—No.

9271. If they can get better terms outside, they are at liberty to do so?—Yes.

9272. (Mr Sexton.) In the case of the City of Dublin, you would not allow them to go to anybody but you. They could not promote a Bill to move [illegible] three years ago. As soon as you gave them power to issue Parliamentary Stock they paid off every penny they owed to you, did they not?—We should be only too happy to see facilities given to Bills which encourage borrowing in the open market in lieu of from the Government.

9273. I have no doubt whatever if public authorities in Ireland were allowed to use their own credit without restriction, they would get money at a less rate than they are getting you at present?—I am sure we should be only too delighted to encourage that. Please do not be under the supposition that we wish to be lenders in Ireland. It is not a profitable business for the State.

9274. But 3¼ per cent. is higher than the market value of money is it not?—There was a case that came before me only the other day from some local authority in Ireland, and we said, "So far as we are concerned, you "shall have every facility to enable you to borrow in the "open market."

9275. (The O'Conor Don.) Is it not the fact, whether the State wishes to make these loans or not, that it is making a profit on them to pay off these old debts?—Yes, if you call that a profit.

9276. Debts that have been wiped out of your accounts altogether?—No doubt, I admit that.

9277. You are making a profit now to enable you to recoup the State for having wiped out those former debts?—It admits of being put in that way, no doubt. (If one is the Right Honourable gentleman is aware that it is a statutory enactment, and it was an arrangement made only a very few years ago by Parliament—indeed less than eight years ago.

9278. Sir David Barbour asked you the other day, whether, in making the financial arrangements for the Union, Lord Castlereagh did not contemplate the ultimate amalgamation of the Exchequers, and indiscriminate taxation of Great Britain and Ireland, and I understand you to agree to that?—I think that was certainly the ultimate intention of Lord Castlereagh.

9279. And that this result might be brought about either by a reduction of the British debt, or an increase of the Irish debt, and that in either case the result might be the same?—That is so.

9280. But would the result be the same if it were brought about in either way, or had the result to be different according to the way in which it was brought about, if the result were brought about by a diminution of the English debt, would not that lead to a diminution in taxation subsequently to the amalgamation?—Yes, I presume it would.

9281. I think it is rather an important point of view to see the form in which that amalgamation was brought about. If the amalgamation had been brought about by the diminution or by the absolute extinction of the two debts, Ireland then would never have had to pay any proportion of the interest upon the pre-Union British debt, is not that so?—I think I should prefer to reserve my opinion on that point until I have had time to consider it more fully.

9282. It is quite clear, is it not, if the debts were extinguished and an amalgamation took place after the extinction, upon the principle that the two countries were on an equality, it would be upon an equality on which neither country would have to pay anything towards the cost of previous debts?—Yes, and the same with Ireland if Ireland had not [illegible].

9283. So the result is not the same if brought about in different ways, as Sir David Barbour seemed to imply?—I do not see the point quite clearly.

9284. (Chairman.) It is the same, is it not, so far as regards identity of taxation, but not the same so far as regards the amount of taxation?—I think that is the way to put it.

9285. (The O'Conor Don.) Am I correct in saying that the amalgamation might have been brought about in three different ways, first by a reduction of the British debt down to the same standard as the Irish?—Yes.

9286. Secondly, by an increase in the Irish debt arising out of the fact that Ireland was not taxed in the same proportion to her resources as Great Britain was?—Yes.

9287. And thirdly, by the increase of the Irish debt owing to the great burdens being placed upon Ireland by the terms of the Union?—Yes; that would be so.

9288. I understood you to say that as circumstances turned out, after the great war expenditure, the last mode by which the Irish debt might be increased was the one which really came into force—that is to say, that the proportion placed on Ireland of 2 to 15 turned out to be too much?—Yes, I think that was the case.

9289. And then the Irish debt was increased up to the full proportion of the English debt in consequence of having that excessive proportion placed upon her?—Yes; what proved to be an excessive proportion.

9290. That being the result, was that an alternative to which any honest statesman could have looked forward in 1800?—I do not think any statesman could have foreseen that we were going to be at war for 15 years, involving that gigantic expenditure.

9291. Do you think Mr. Pitt or Lord Castlereagh could have looked forward to what actually did happen; that is to say, that the proportion of 2 to 15 would turn out to be excessive?—It is very conjectural to offer any opinion upon that.

9292. Would it not be really the greatest slur to place upon a statesman, that he looked forward to that?—I think it would, it was of course not possible for a man like Lord Castlereagh to see what was going to take place during the next 15 years.

9293. As I understand, Sir David Barbour asked you whether what happened was not what Lord Castlereagh and Mr. Pitt looked forward to as likely to happen?—What I meant to imply was that both Mr. Pitt and Lord Castlereagh looked forward to an ultimate amalgamation of the Exchequers.

9294. But did they look forward to that as likely to arise from a diminution of the British debt?—That I cannot say.

9295. How could it arise in any other way if the proportion placed upon Ireland was a just proportion, and if Ireland was compelled to pay that just proportion, and able to raise it by taxation?—I am afraid I do not follow the point.

9296. How could the debts be equalised if the proportion placed upon Ireland by the Act of Union was a just proportion, and if the Imperial Parliament compelled Ireland every year to pay her just proportion?—I do not see the drift of the question.

9297. There would be no necessity for borrowing a greater proportion in Ireland if she paid her proportion of taxation?—I admit that.

9298. Then either that proportion was unfair, and Ireland was unable to pay it, or the Imperial Parliament, it being just and fair and Ireland being able to pay it, did not ask her to pay it, is not that so?—I think that might be so.

9299. Then how could any statesman in 1800 have looked forward to amalgamation except upon the principle of the English debt being reduced, if he assumed that the proportion of taxation payable by Ireland was a just one?—But I think there are certain passages in Lord Castlereagh's statements and in Mr. Pitt's from which it may be inferred that they did contemplate the possibility of amalgamation if it so happened that the Irish debt increased so as to bring it up to the same level proportionately as that of Great Britain.

9300. Was not the raising of the revenue by Ireland after the Union, whether by taxation or by debt, absolutely at the disposal of the Imperial Parliament?—That is so certainly.

9301. In which Ireland was in the minority?—Yes.

L 4

9302. If the proportions placed upon Ireland by the Act of Union were a just one, and if, instead of raising it by taxation, it was raised by loans, was not that the fault of the Imperial Parliament?—The Imperial Parliament no doubt would be responsible for it.

9303. And it would be the effect of their action?—Certainly.

9304. And could statesmen in 1800 have honestly looked forward to the fact that the Imperial Parliament, in order to bring about an proportion of debt or equalise the debts, would not raise by taxation what ought fairly to be raised?—No, I think not.

9305. Therefore, does it not follow as a necessary consequence that any statesman looking forward to equalisation by the raising of the Irish debt, must have assumed that that proportion was too high or that the Imperial Parliament would not do its duty in raising it?—I do not know that that necessarily follows.

9306. What other alternative could happen? If the proportion of 2 to 15 was a just proportion, and Ireland was able to pay it, and she did pay it, the Irish debt would not be raised in higher proportion than the English, would it?—No.

9307. On the other hand it being a just proportion, and the Irish revenue being raised by loans instead of by taxation, does it not follow that the Imperial Parliament did not do its duty?—I think it is difficult to hazard an opinion upon these points at this distance of time.

9308. The reason I ask you is this. It seems to me Sir David Barbour's questions reflected most strongly on the political character of Mr. Pitt and Lord Castlereagh?—I did not infer that. I thought the point Sir David Barbour wished to bring out was whether it was a fair inference to draw from the speeches of Lord Castlereagh and Mr. Pitt, that they did contemplate, sooner or later, identity of taxation and amalgamation of the Exchequers. That was the broad inference I drew from his questions, and I did not intend to say more in my answers.

9309. (Mr. Sexton.) You remember that very statement that Ireland in the time of peace would save half a million, and in time of war would save a million?—Yes, but it is impossible to follow those calculations.

9310. But admitting those statements, does it not follow that if those assurances were made good, that Ireland would have been able to raise her quota by taxation?—Yes, but I think the whole of these calculations were completely upset by the vast expenditure which had to be incurred.

9311. (The O'Conor Don.) I admit that these calculations were upset, and that they were not justified by events, but I rather gathered from your admission to Sir David Barbour that you thought their calculations included what actually did happen?—No, I did not mean that.

9312. Is there anything to show that Mr. Pitt or Lord Castlereagh ever contemplated that the Irish debt would be raised in the manner in which it was through the proportion turning out to be excessive?—My recollection is that there was a passage or two in one of the speeches of either Lord Castlereagh or Mr. Pitt which bore that out.

9313. That the proportion was excessive?—No, but that the debt which would have to be raised in Ireland might be relatively greater than the debt which Great Britain might have to raise.

9314. (Mr. Currie.) Are you generally doing a great injustice to a man when you increase the burden of his debt without increasing the remuneration?—No.

9315. I fail to see the hardship?—Quite so, but I do not gather that that was quite the point put to me by the right honourable gentleman.

9316. (Chairman.) The O'Conor Don's questions rather point to this, do they not, whether Mr. Pitt and Lord Castlereagh would have made the arrangement they did at the Union if they had foreseen the facts that actually occurred?—I think it is very possible they would not.

9317. It is extremely difficult, of course, to say exactly what they did think, or what they did not think, is it not?—Yes; it is purely conjectural.

9318. Might it not have been the case they thought the great probability was that the war would come to an end, that the English debt and burdens would be reduced, and that of Ireland reduced with it?—Yes.

9319. But that they also might have had in their minds, the opposite might take place, and if it did take place, then it might be necessary to amalgamate the Exchequers in the way it has been done. That alternative probably was not entirely absent from their minds?—Quite so.

9320. When you see what the arguments of some of the opponents to the Union were, it is possible that that second alternative may have been in their minds too?—Yes, I think that is a fair way of putting it.

9321. (The O'Conor Don.) Did not Lord Castlereagh contemplate, even when amalgamation of the Exchequers took place, and indiscriminate taxation would be applied, that that indiscriminate taxation would be one which would make the two countries contribute exactly in proportion to their taxable capacities?—I do not think there is any passage which goes so far as that.

9322. Will you look at page 8 of Mr. Holland's paper? You will see there Lord Castlereagh says, talking of indiscriminate taxation, "By no system whatever could they "be made to contribute so exactly according to their "means, as by being subject to the same taxes equally "bearing upon the great objects of taxation in both "countries." Then on the next page he says, "Ireland "has by these means the utmost possible security, that "she cannot be taxed beyond the measure of her comparative ability, and that the ratio of her contribution "must ever correspond with her relative wealth and "prosperity." I ask you upon these two statements made by Lord Castlereagh is it not clear that when indiscriminate taxation was in his mind, he contemplated that that indiscriminate taxation should only make the two countries contribute in proportion to their relative wealth and prosperity?—I do not see how, if both countries were to be made subject to the same taxes, a differential system of taxation could have been possible, and if he contemplated indiscriminate taxation, I do not see how it was possible to provide that the mass of people should contribute relatively exactly according to their taxable capacities.

9323. Is it not clear from the first paragraph that according to his notion, which apparently is a wrong notion, but it was his idea, that under no system "could "they be made to contribute so exactly according to their "means, as by being subject to the same taxes equally "bearing upon the great objects of taxation in both "countries?" He starts with that proposition?—Yes, I presume he thought on the whole that Ireland's resources were relatively much the same as those of Great Britain.

9324. And it was upon that understanding that he looked forward to that indiscriminate taxation?—Yes, I presume so.

9325. And he says in the second paragraph I read to you that Ireland could never have to contribute anything more under the provisions of the Treaty of Union than in proportion to her relative wealth and prosperity?—Yes, so Lord Castlereagh said.

9326. Now, it turns out, does it not, by your statement the other day, and by the evidence given by other witnesses, that under the system of indiscriminate taxation Ireland does contribute more largely in proportion to her relative wealth and prosperity than Great Britain does?—That is my own personal opinion, as regards indirect taxation.

9327. (Mr. Sexton.) Is it not quite clear, if you apply that system of indiscriminate taxation to two countries, that you assume their resources are equal?—No doubt.

9328. And that there is no difference?—You cannot draw a distinction.

9329. (The O'Conor Don.) That was the assumption to which Lord Castlereagh apparently looked forward, namely, to indiscriminate taxation, as being a system under which Ireland would not pay more than in her proportion to her wealth and prosperity?—I think that is fair.

9330. (Mr. Currie.) Might not that assumption of Lord Castlereagh have been more justified at the time he lived than now, that is to say, was not the relative capacity of Ireland towards England greater than it is now?—I think there is no question about that. Great Britain then was a very poor country compared to what she is now.

9331. (Mr. Sexton.) Still, was there not a tremendous fallacy in the assumption that a system of indiscriminate taxation will find out the relative resources of two countries?—I think so.

9332. (Chairman.) I have some questions which Mr. Childers wished to put to you, and I will put them verbatim. This is Mr. Childers' language: I wish to ask some questions with regard to the comparative effects upon Great Britain and Ireland of the repeal of various taxes during the last 70 years. I think that the subject falls into two branches: (1) the repeal of taxes which extended to Great Britain only and not Ireland; (2) the repeal of taxes which affected both countries?—Yes.

9233. First with regard to the repeal of taxes which did not extend to Ireland. There are some striking figures given in one of the appendices prepared by Mr. Childers for the Select Committee of 1865, pages 144–146. But your attention has been called to these?—Yes, I know the figures to which Mr. Childers refers.

9234. Mr. Childers calculates that during the five years 1817 to 1821 the revenue derived from taxation which was not imposed upon Ireland amounted to rather over 20 millions a year on the average?—That is so.

9235. Then he shows that in the year 1845 this taxation, which affected Great Britain only, had sunk to about 14,000,000*l.* a year, including about 5,000,000*l.* produced by the income tax imposed upon Great Britain in 1842, but not extended to Ireland till 10 years later?—Yes, that is the case.

9236. Then again he shows that in 1853, 10 years later, the taxation which did not extend to Ireland was producing not quite 4,000,000*l.* a year?—Yes.

9237. It is now, I think, producing much about the same sum (about 500,000*l.*, more), so that there has been no general change since 1853?—That is almost the case. The taxes not imposed in Ireland at the present time are about 4,100,000*l.*, and in 1853–54 they only amounted to about 150,000*l.* less.

9238. The important thing to notice is that taxation from which Ireland was exempt was producing about 20,000,000*l.* a year in 1820; 14,000,000*l.* in 1845; and 4,000,000*l.* in 1853 and subsequently?—That is so, according to the figures quoted.

9239. Which there is every reason to suppose are substantially correct; you have no reason, have you, to find fault with them?—No, I believe the figures refer to actual receipts derived from Finance Accounts; therefore they may be presumed to be correct.

9240. This great change is chiefly due, is it not, to the abolition of various duties of minor importance, some duties which fell upon Great Britain, but did not extend to Ireland?—Yes, that is the largest part.

9241. I see on reference to the Report of the Inland Revenue Commissioners for 1870, Vol. II., p. [illegible], that in 1823 the excise duty on salt, which affected England only, was reduced at an estimated loss to revenue of 1,[illegible]*l.*, and that in 1825 the rest of the duty was repealed at an estimated loss of 381,000*l.*?—That is so, but it must be remembered that in Ireland there was an import duty upon salt, which may be presumed to have been the equivalent of the excise duty in England.

9242. (*The O'Conor Don.*) At what date was that?—I am referring now to about 1823.

9243. (*Chairman.*) The present supply of salt in Ireland is imported, is it not?—There are no salt mines in Ireland at all. Salt was imported from England, and there was an import duty on it.

9244. (*Mr. Sexton.*) It was an English product?—It was an English product.

9245. (*Chairman.*) Then there was an import duty in Ireland?—Yes.

9246. Was it of the same amount as the excise?—I could not say whether it was the same amount, but it was a corresponding duty.

9247. And probably it was intended to be a similar and corresponding duty?—I think so.

9248. In 1824 a small duty of cider was reduced and one on salt was was repealed?—Yes, that was the case.

9249. They affected Great Britain only?—Yes, these affected Great Britain only.

9250. In 1830 there was an abolition of a large duty which affected Great Britain but did not extend to Ireland that on beer, then estimated to bring in over 3,000,000*l.*?—Yes.

9251. In the same year the rest of the cider duty was repealed?—Yes; it is a trifling sum, about 25,000*l.*, I think.

9252. Then, in 1831, the duty on printed cottons, which brought in 625,000*l.*, and did not extend to Ireland, was repealed?—Yes, that is so.

9253. In 1832 the duty on candles, affecting Great Britain only, and producing 470,000*l.*, was abolished?—Yes.

9254. In 1833 the duty on soap, not affecting Ireland, was halved at a loss to revenue of 585,000*l.*?—Yes, that is so.

9255. I see that the rest of the soap duty was not abolished till 1853, when it produced 1,170,000*l.*?—That was one of the reductions effected by Mr. Gladstone in his first budget.

9256. In 1846 two small duties, affecting Great Britain only, viz., those on stone bottles and [illegible], were repealed?—Yes.

9257. In 1850 the duty on bricks, which did not extend to Ireland, and then produced 456,000*l.*, was repealed?—Yes, that is so.

9258. In 1861 the duty on hops, not extending to Ireland, was reduced at a loss of 103,000*l.*, and wholly repealed in 1862 at a further loss of 250,000*l.*?—Yes.

9259. I think that these are the chief excise duties, if not all, which fell upon Great Britain and not upon Ireland, and have now been removed. That has to be taken with the qualification you have stated with regard to the salt?—Yes, that is the case.

9260. I see that an observation is made on p. 17 of the yearly Return 313 of 1894 made by the Treasury to Parliament with reference to the duties on salt, beer, candles, bricks, soap, and hops. It is said "the incidence "of such duties may safely be assumed to have lain solely "on the part of the United Kingdom to which they were "confined, and no observation, therefore, is necessary in "respect of them. In support of such treatment it may be "mentioned that in all these cases a drawback was allowed "on articles sent from Great Britain to Ireland, except "hops, the trade in which enjoyed the equivalent advantage of being exempted from duty when sent from Great "Britain to Ireland." So that the removal of all these duties may be said to have benefited Great Britain but not Ireland. That again, I may observe myself, is true, subject again to the qualification you have mentioned with regard to the salt?—Yes.

9261. Because, if I understand you, the import duty upon salt in Ireland was abolished at the same time as the excise duty in England?—Yes.

9262. I return to Mr. Childers' questions. I do not wish to dwell now on the extension of the income tax to Ireland, or the elevation of stamp and spirit duties to the British level, but I should like to ask you one or two questions as to the relative effect on Great Britain and Ireland of the general changes in financial policy. May it be said, in your opinion, that the tendency of the policy inaugurated at the Reform Bill and carried out more by Sir Robert Peel, Mr. Gladstone, and others, was to abolish the duties on the raw materials of manufacturing industry and upon all except a very few articles of food?—Yes, that was the general tendency of the policy, no doubt.

9263. I think that the years 1842 and 1845 were marked by the abolition of a great number of small duties on raw materials of manufacturing industry?—Yes, I think that before the Budget of 1842 the customs tariff included about 1,200 articles, and about 750 of these were reduced or abolished between 1842 and 1845, which included the abolition of the duties on raw materials to a very great extent—there were very few duties on raw materials subsequently.

9264. One of the excise duties repealed in 1845 was, I see, that on glass, then estimated to produce 624,000*l.*?—Yes, and at the same time there was a large further clearance from the customs tariff.

9265. The budget of 1846 was distinguished, was it not, for a great onslaught on the taxes on food? The chief part of the duties on foreign corn, and the duties on the importation of live animals (cattle, sheep, and pigs) from abroad, and on salted dead meats, were abolished in that year?—Yes, that is so; in fact, the only remaining tax in respect of taxes on food was the sliding duty which remained on corn until 1849.

9266. The duties on butter and cheese from abroad were, I think, reduced in 1846, and abolished in 1860?—Yes, they yielded very small sums.

9267. In 1869, I believe, the remaining duty of 1*s.* a quarter on corn, then bringing in about 900,000*l.* a year, was repealed?—Yes, that is so.

9268. By Mr. Lowe?—Yes, by Mr. Lowe.

9269. Perhaps I had better now refer to the abolition during the same period of one or two other duties. The newspaper stamps, then bringing in 250,000*l.*, were, I believe, abolished in 1855?—Yes, that is so.

9370. The excise duty on paper was, I think, abolished in 1861, and was then producing about 1,300,000*l.* a year, was it not?—Yes, the paper duty was, as is well known, abolished by Mr. Gladstone in 1861.

9371. The customs duties on timber and pepper were repealed in 1866. They then, I think, were producing 300,000*l.* and 124,000*l.* respectively?—Yes.

9372. The duty on sugar was reduced in 1870 and 1873, and finally abolished in 1874, was it not?—That is so.

9373. In 1869 it was, I believe, producing about 5,300,000*l.* of revenue?—Yes, I think the exact sum was about 5,340,000*l.*

9374. These duties, unlike those to which I previously referred on soap, candles, hops, salt, bricks, &c., all extended, did they not, to Ireland as well as to Great Britain?—Yes.

9375. The general idea of taking off taxes on raw material was, I think, to lighten the springs of industry?—Yes, I think there is no doubt that that was the result.

9376. Was it not argued that if food were cheap, and raw material cheap, that would have a great effect in promoting manufactures and industry?—Yes, I think so.

9377. I suppose you would say that the policy has been very successful and justified by the results?—I think unquestionably that is the case.

9378. England has become a very successful manufacturing country. Would you say that this was because she had natural advantages for that purpose and was assisted by the financial policy?—I think it is unquestionable that the manufacturing interests of this country received a great spurt by that policy.

9379. Ireland does not seem to have great advantages for manufacturing industry. Do you think that the policy in question was equally advantageous to her?—No, I do not think it was. I think it stands to reason in fact, for Ireland is not a manufacturing country, and I suppose she was even less so 50 years ago than she is now.

9380. (*Mr. Sexton.*) Would you say she was less so 50 years ago?—I am speaking without book, but I should imagine so.

9381. She has two or three manufactures which have developed, but the bulk of her manufactures have disappeared?—But not the last 50 years? I should have thought if you go back further it would have been the case.

9382. (*Mr. Currie.*) Would you agree with the proposition that England has a larger relative share of the manufacturing industry of the world now than she had then?—I should have thought so.

9383. I should think certainly not, she had practically no rivals then, but she, and she has [illegible] rivals now?—Of course; but I was only thinking of her relation to Ireland.

9384. I do not think it can be said that the result has been to put England in a greater position as a manufacturing country than she was before, because undoubtedly there were no other manufacturing countries then, or practically none, and now there are?—No doubt, but at the same time no one, I think, will deny that the position which this country does occupy now as a manufacturing country, has to a great extent been assisted by the policy which has been pursued during the last 50 years.

9385. (*Mr. Sexton.*) And that that policy has not beneficially affected Ireland to a great degree?—Nothing so, but undoubtedly the vast increase of the wealth of Great Britain has to some extent been beneficial to Ireland, because Ireland has by that great increase been subjected to less taxation than she might otherwise have been.

9386. But the proportion drawn from Ireland has not been diminished, has it?—No; but additional taxes might have had to be imposed upon Ireland. The result of this vast increase of wealth in Great Britain has been that we have derived an enormous amount from direct taxation, and if it had not been for this vastly augmented wealth of Great Britain the Imperial Parliament could not have repealed all the indirect duties which have been repealed, and the repeal of which has affected Ireland very materially indeed.

9387. Do I understand you to say, if the income of Great Britain, instead of being as now 1,000,000,000*l.* a year, had been only, say, 1,000,000,000*l.* a year, that the increased levy upon Ireland owing to the increase of the spirit duty and the imposition of the income tax, would have been made still greater if the wealth of Great Britain had not been increased?—I do not see any other way of meeting the expenditure. The Imperial Parliament could not have made the large reduction in indirect taxation, if it had not been possible to throw a greatly increased weight of taxation upon the income-tax payers and other people who pay direct taxation.

9388. Do you suggest the Parliament of the United Kingdom would have been so inequitable as to ignore the fact that Great Britain has an income of 1,000,000,000*l.* a year, and make a still higher levy upon Ireland than at present?—I say nothing of the relative incomes of the two countries.

9389. I put the figures generally?—What I mean is that I do not see how the revenue could have been raised without subjecting Ireland to a higher levy. It is impossible—and I should think the present Chairman will admit with me that it would have been impossible—to reduce the sugar duties if it had not been for our ability to place the consequently increased burdens upon direct taxation, and if the sugar duties had not been reduced and finally repealed, Ireland would have been contributing and taxed under the head of sugar.

9390. Do you mean notwithstanding the general idea of the Act of Union and so on, that particular regard should be had to the circumstances of Ireland? Your view is that a system of indiscriminate taxation would necessarily have drawn a larger yield from Ireland than it has drawn if the difference of wealth among the people of England had not been such as to enable them to produce a larger share?—Yes; the greater is the amount derived from taxes on commodities, the more heavily would the poorer consuming country have to pay.

9391. Is not the way to put it that direct taxation falls more heavily on England than Ireland, whereas indirect taxation falls equally on both?—That is so.

9392. (*Chairman.*) Therefore the recent large increase of direct taxation as compared with indirect taxation has pro tanto been favourable to Ireland?—Yes, I think there is no doubt about that.

9393. In common with all other poorer parts of the United Kingdom?—Yes.

9394. (*Mr. Sexton.*) Of course you bear in mind that five-sixths of the Irish revenue does come now from indirect taxation?—I admit that, but I was thinking of the United Kingdom. I will not go beyond 1859-60, but the proportion of revenue derived from taxes in the United Kingdom then was 65 per cent. from indirect taxation and 35 per cent. from direct taxation. Now, in 1894-95, only 55 per cent. was derived from indirect taxation and 45 per cent. from direct taxation, and I presume it is manifest, therefore, that the poorer country to that extent has benefited by the tendency to shift the burden from indirect to direct taxation.

9395. I hardly see what the poorer country could have done in any case more than pay the tax on what was consumed?—Suppose it had not been possible to raise the enormous amount of revenue from income-tax, death duties, and inhabited house duties, and so forth, it is quite evident we could not have dispensed with such a duty as that on sugar, and if the duty on sugar had still been levied, Ireland, which is a large consumer of sugar, would unquestionably have been very much more distinctly burdened than she is now by taxation.

9396. (*Chairman.*) I return to Mr. Childers' questions. The duty on corn at the time of its abolition in 1846 was, I find, at the rate of 1*s.* each, on sheep 2*s.*, on pigs 5*s.*, on horses 1*l.*, and oxen 2*s.* 6*d.*, with a reduction to half these rates on animals coming from British possessions. Would not these duties, if continued, have brought in a considerable revenue at the present day?—I presume they would. I am afraid I have no figure to show what they might produce.

9397. And they are all animals which Ireland exports to Great Britain?—Yes, I believe that that is the case.

9398. So that the abolition of duties on foreign competitors in these animals was not an advantage to Ireland?—No, I do not think it could have been.

9399. Might Ireland have benefited, do you think, as a producer, by the retention of some duty on foreign corn?—I think that is rather a purely natural question to answer. I think it is almost impossible to say what the result might have been.

9400. (*Mr. Sexton.*) Have you any doubt that the repeal of the Corn Laws destroyed the market of the Irish farmer for cereals?—I think there is no doubt that it acted prejudicially to Ireland in many respects relatively to Great Britain; and indeed Sir Robert Peel at the time recognised that fact.

9401. (*Sir David Barbour.*) Do you mean that it would [illegible] on all classes in Ireland, or only on the agricultural class?—I was thinking mostly of the agricultural classes.

9402. (*Mr. Sexton.*) And collectively on those dependent on them?—Yes.

9403. (*Sir David Barbour.*) And I presume those persons who were not agriculturists got their food cheaper?—I have no doubt the masses got their food cheaper.

9404. (*Mr. Sexton.*) The masses in Ireland are agricultural, as they are?—I would speak of the lower classes generally.

9405. (*Chairman.*) I return to Mr. Childers' questions. Is it possible, do you think, to form any estimate as to the relative extent to which sugar is consumed in Great Britain and Ireland, to enable us to judge of the relative extent to which the two countries profited by the abolition of the duty? What are the figures as to the collection of the sugar duty in the two countries in 1869?—The amount, I think, collected, in Great Britain in respect of the sugar duty in 1869–70 was 5,300,000*l.*, and that in Ireland only 117,000*l.* But when we adjusted the figures according to the paper which has been laid before Parliament and before the Commission, a very different result was brought out, namely, that 4,700,000*l.* represented the amount contributed by Great Britain in respect of the sugar duty, and 700,000*l.* represented the amount derived from Ireland in respect of the sugar duty, that is to say, the percentages were about 87 per cent. in Great Britain and 13 per cent. in Ireland.

9406. (*Mr. Sexton.*) A little more than was put on by the income tax?—Yes.

9407. (*Chairman.*) Did most of the sugar come to Ireland, duty paid, from London?—Yes, I think there is no doubt about that, and these figures relating to collected revenue only show it.

9408. On page 11 of the Treasury return 313 of 1894, there are some figures as to the collection of duties on corn and timber in Great Britain and Ireland in 1839 and 1859 [illegible]. In 1839 as much as 98·71 per cent. of the corn duty seems to have been collected in Great Britain, and only 1·28 per cent. in Ireland. In 1859 81·06 per cent. was collected in Great Britain, and 18·94 per cent. in Ireland. To what do you attribute that change?—I speak under considerable reserve about that, but I think it may be inferred, possibly, that the habits of the Irish have changed, and that 10 years after the famine they were able and could afford to consume a larger amount of corn than 10 years before the famine. I think, possibly, also, that the proportion of pasture to tillage land had increased, and consequently the supply of home-grown corn had diminished.

9409. (*Mr. Sexton.*) Of course, obviously, as was said just now about the repeal of the Corn Laws, the corn seems to have been supplied from abroad, in part of it?—Yes.

9410. (*Chairman.*) In the case of timber the proportions do not seem to have changed in the two periods. In each year about 95 per cent. was collected in Great Britain and about 5 per cent. in Ireland?—Yes, that is so.

9411. Can you tell me how much of the newspaper duty, abolished in 1855, was collected in Great Britain and how much in Ireland?—I think about 480,000*l.* was collected in Great Britain and only about 30,000*l.* in Ireland.

9412. (*Mr. Sexton.*) The [illegible], of course, would be as collected?—Yes.

9413. (*Chairman.*) I suppose that would not need much adjustment, would it?—No, I do not think so.

9414. Is there any way of estimating the extent to which the abolition in 1845 of the duty on glass, and the abolition in 1861 of the tax on paper, relieved Great Britain and Ireland respectively?—The amount which the excise duty upon glass was producing in 1844 and 1845, was in Great Britain, about 663,000*l.*, and in Ireland only 7,000*l.*, and in 1861 the paper duty was yielding in Great Britain nearly 1,300,000*l.* and in Ireland about 60,000*l.*

9415. (*Sir David Barbour.*) Is that as collected?—That is as collected.

9416. (*Chairman.*) Because both glass and paper would be sent from Great Britain to Ireland, would they not?—Yes, I presume so.

9417. (*Mr. Sexton.*) Was the figure as to paper subject to adjustment?—I think it was merely as collected.

9418. Can you adjust them?—I am afraid we have no means of doing [illegible].

9419. But do they seem to you to require adjustment?—They seem to be out of proportion to the true figure.

9420. (*Mr. Currie.*) Does it not amount to this, that practically there were no glass or paper manufactures in Ireland?—No doubt, but it would appear to require adjustment for arriving at the true revenue.

9421. (*Chairman.*) Mr. Childers' next question is: Do you think that as much glass and paper was used per head of population in Ireland as in Great Britain?—I can give you the figures collected. In Great Britain the duty on glass, as collected, works out at 5½*d.* per head, and only a farthing in Ireland; and on paper it was 1*s.* 1*d.* per head in Great Britain, and 2¼*d.* in Ireland.

9422. (*Mr. Sexton.*) That is the consumption, is it?—I am afraid we have no means of adjusting that.

9423. But the Treasury professes to have adjusted all the accounts for all the years?—But there are one or two items we could not adjust separately.

9424. But we have the most imposing figures presented to us?—These are the best we can lay before the Commission, but I hope it has been understood throughout, that that paper is founded upon an enormous amount of hypothesis and conjecture and it cannot otherwise be the case.

9425. I am trying to get at your hypothesis about the paper?—We have made no estimate of the true revenue derived in both countries from that article.

9426. (*The O'Conor Don.*) You merely take the rate as collected?—Yes. I think it is obvious that Ireland must have consumed more glass and more paper than what appears to be the case by the collected figures.

9427. (*Chairman.*) I return to Mr. Childers' questions. These taxes upon paper and glass were sometimes referred to as taxes on light and knowledge, were they not?—Yes, that is the case.

9428. To what do you ascribe the fact that it was possible to carry through all these large reductions of taxes upon raw materials and food?—Should you say that it was chiefly due to the growth of the wealth and population of the United Kingdom, looked at as a whole, and consequent increased consumption of the remaining taxed articles? Or would you ascribe much part to the recovering the credit of the income tax, and to the enhancement of the taxation of spirits, beer and tobacco?—I think it must be looked upon as due to those causes collectively. There is no doubt that the income tax was a very valuable assistance in carrying out that financial policy.

9429. Should you say, generally, that the interests of the urban—industrial and the rural—agricultural classes and districts, have been equally considered in the financial legislation since the first Reform Bill?—I think that is a very difficult question to answer; I should not like to express any definite opinion upon that point. Local taxation plays so important a part in this matter.

9430. (*Mr. Sexton.*) And, of course, the repeal of the Corn Laws manifestly was beneficial to urban communities as distinguished from the rural communities?—I am not sure about that. Looking at the enormous prosperity of agriculture which followed the repeal, I think that in the first instance the agricultural classes may have even benefited as much as the urban communities. There was a great rise in wages in agricultural districts.

9431. The cheapening of food was an immense benefit?—No doubt.

9432. (*Mr. Currie.*) But then the man benefits who has the smallest income, does he not?—I think he benefits most, relatively, no doubt.

9433. (*Chairman.*) If you put that question to the landowner, the farmer, and the agricultural labourer, you would get very different answers, I suppose?—I do not think that would be the case for the first 20 years after the repeal of the Corn Laws. That agricultural industry flourished considerably.

9434. I am speaking of the present time?—It would be different at the present time.

9435. I return to Mr. Childers' questions. Should you say, from your experience at the Treasury, that it is easier for urban populations, when they have voting power, to put pressure upon Government, than it is for agricultural populations?—I think that is hardly a question for me to answer. Of course, under the Reform Bill of 1884, the county electors have become a very powerful body now.

9436. I may ask you in my own person whether the representatives of the agricultural interests have been backward or weak in Parliament, have they?—No, I do

Sir E. W. Hamilton, K.C.B.

11 June 189[illegible].

Relative [illegible]

not touch us at all. I think they have managed to press their case powerfully enough.

9437. (*Sir David Barbour.*) Do you think that both the urban and agricultural populations can put quite as much pressure on the Government as regards Treasury matters as it is desirable that they should be able to put upon it?—It is very difficult for me to express an opinion upon that.

9438. (*Mr. Sexton.*) Would you prefer there was no pressure at all?—The pressure is put on ministers of the day, not upon the Treasury.

9439. (*Chairman.*) I return to Mr. Childers' questions. I do not wish to criticise the fiscal policy of the period in question looked at from the point of view of the interest of the United Kingdom as a whole, but is it not possible that it has been disadvantageous to Ireland looked at separately?—I think that is rather a hypothetical question, but at the same time I do not think it is an unfair assumption to make. Of course, the manufacturing industries have benefited more than the agricultural industries, reviewing the whole period since the repeal of the Corn Laws, and one must remember that it is the agricultural industry which is the staple industry of Ireland; therefore, in that way Great Britain has relatively, I think, had a great pull over Ireland during the last 50 years from a fiscal point of view.

9440. Supposing that to some extent the old customs duties on live stock, dairy produce, corn, timber and so forth had been retained for revenue purposes, and that the taxation of tobacco, British spirits, and tea had been made less high, would not the incidence of taxation have been more favourable to Ireland?—That is possible, but it is difficult to imagine how the country could as a whole get on unless the imports of necessary food were practically free.

9441. (*Mr. Sexton.*) That answer shows the importance of the repeal of the Corn Laws?—No doubt, it does.

9442. (*Chairman.*) I return to Mr. Childers' questions. It has been represented to us that if you place taxation on tea for instance, upon two countries one of which chiefly consumes tea and the other coffee, you tax unequally. In the same circumstances, if you abolish a tax on tea, you benefit the two nations unequally, do you not?—Yes, that would be the case.

9443. I have hitherto been asking questions as to the relative effects upon Great Britain and Ireland of the abolition of various taxes. I should now like to refer to your existing taxes. According to the table on page 38 of your memorandum, the Irish population consumes more tobacco per head than that of Great Britain?—Yes, that was the result arrived at before the tobacco duties were adjusted afresh on the strength of further information elicited from Irish manufacturers.

9444. I think that subsequent investigations by the Board of Customs have shown that earlier more consumption of tobacco has to be confined to Great Britain and less to Ireland, but I suppose one may safely say that Ireland consumes at the least as much tobacco per head as Great Britain?—Yes, I think that may be said to be the case. I have had Table 24 in my memorandum which professes to give the annual expenditure incurred on tobacco in Great Britain and Ireland adjusted now, according to the latest figures the Customs have laid before the Commission, and I find that instead of coming out respectively at 11s. 7d. per head in Great Britain and 11s. 7d. per head in Ireland, the expenditure per head works out at 12s. 11d. in Great Britain and 10s. 5d. in Ireland, so that the fresh adjustment makes a material difference.

9445. Can you put in the adjusted table?—Yes, certainly.

9446. (*Mr. Sexton.*) You add 1s. per head to Great Britain and take 2s. off Ireland?—Yes, it works out in that way.

9447. We are entirely in the dark about the mode in which these repeated adjustments are made—that is the third adjustment made, is it not?—It is explained, I think, in the memorandum which is appended to the evidence which has been laid before Parliament. Mr. Fitter, I think, gave the explanation.

9448. You have now adjusted it on replies given by the manufacturers. I can understand that the value of the replies of the manufacturers on the amount of tobacco exported by them would very much depend on the form and extent of the inquiry and of the reply, and I would ask whether you can get the Inland Revenue to furnish information to the Commission?—The Customs, I believe, made the inquiry, or rather it was a joint inquiry made by the Customs and the Inland Revenue.

9449. The effect has been to subtract a quarter of a million a year from what you call the true revenue of Ireland, has it not?—Yes, I admit that.

9450. As compared with the results which you obtained from the information received from the Railway and Shipping Companies four or five years ago?—Yes.

9451. That is a very serious difference, is it not?—No doubt it is.

9452. And all we know is you tell us a certain question was put to manufacturers, and they returned a reply. I believe their reply was that they only gave us one [illegible] the total amounts of export a year?—The revenue officers who made the inquiries would be able to throw light upon this question. I thought Mr. Fitter had already explained to the Commission exactly what the line of inquiry had been. Perhaps in the [illegible] memorandum is given, that in the Financial Relations paper of last year, there is an explanatory note about the tobacco duty amended calculations.

9453. It is not printed to the question I think essential. What I should like to see would be a copy of the form of inquiry sent out to the manufacturers, and a copy of their reply sent in?—I am afraid I am not acquainted with the form.

9454. Could you not undertake to ask the Inland Revenue to furnish that?—I can and will ask the customs authorities to furnish the Commission with further particulars. No doubt Mr. Fitter would be able to furnish them even now.

9455. I noticed that the accumulative effect of all these repeated adjustments is always to lower the true revenue of Ireland?—The Commission must understand that the figures are necessarily hypothetical in the absence of a customs barrier.

9456. But they always go in one direction, that of lowering the true revenue of Ireland?—We cannot help that.

9457. But it excites a natural curiosity in the minds of some of us to ascertain how the thing is done?—I will get the forms of inquiry; but I think it may be more satisfactory for the Commission to hear the customs officers themselves who made the calculations in consultation with the Inland Revenue authorities.

9458. (*Chairman.*) If Mr. Sexton wishes it, Mr. Fitter could come before us again?—Certainly.

9459. I return to Mr. Childers' questions. The greater part of the cost of a pound of tobacco is due to taxation, is it not?—Yes, I think about 75 per cent. may be said to be what the duty represents.

9460. The total revenue derived from tobacco in 1894 was, I think, about 10,000,000*l.*; more than half the whole present customs duties?—Yes, that is so.

9461. I see by the Statistical abstract that in 1861 about 4½ millions were derived from tobacco, the whole revenue derived from customs being then more than 23,000,000*l.*?—Yes.

9462. The table on page 32 of your memorandum shows that the tax on spirits has never been reduced in England since 1865, and has risen from 7s. in 1823 to 11s. in 1894, and that in Scotland and Ireland the tax has risen from 2s. 10d. in 1823 to 11s. in 1894?—That is so; it is now 10s. 6d., or rather it is going to be 10s. 6d. as from the 1st July next.

9463. According to the table on page 39 of your memorandum, the Irish people drink more tea per head than the people in Great Britain?—Yes, according to the calculation I made with the help of the Customs authorities. I made out that the annual expenditure incurred on tea by Great Britain and Ireland was 10s. 1d. in Great Britain and 11s. 2½d. in Ireland, which is a marked difference.

9464. The tea tax has been very greatly reduced in 1890, was it not?—Yes, it was reduced by 2d. from 6d. to 4d.

9465. Was that, do you think, the reason why the revenue collected in Ireland was checked for a year in 1890 in its upward tendency, and was less by 300,000*l.* in 1892 than in 1891?—I am afraid I could not say so positively. It is very likely due to some holding back in the anticipation of reduction of duty or something of that sort.

9466. (*Mr. Sexton.*) I should like to ask whether you think the greater consumption of tea per head in Ireland is to be accounted for by the far more general use of beer as food in Great Britain?—I think that is quite possible. I have always understood—and I have often heard people who are acquainted with Ireland say they are not surprised to learn—that Ireland consumes rather more tea per head than England.

9467. Of course you know, do you not, that the consumption of beer in Great Britain is relatively double in proportion to the population?—Yes.

9468. And the custom, habit is to use beer at meals, which it is not in Ireland?—That is so, I believe.

9469. (*Chairman.*) I return to Mr. Childers' questions. On page 116 of the Report of the Select Committee on Irish Taxation, in 1865, there are some tables prepared by Mr. Chisholm giving the totals of taxes remitted and taxes imposed upon Great Britain and Ireland respectively, between 1816 and 1864. Do you attach much weight to statements of this kind?—I do not know that I do attach much importance to that table, because I think it is supposed to represent what the relief to the taxpayer is, and it is obvious that the actual amount which you lose by revenue does not represent the relief to the taxpayer, and *vice versa*. I think all these figures are very hypothetical unless they are held to mean the loss to revenue caused by taking off the taxes, but that does not, of course, in the least represent what the relief to taxation is.

9470. (*Mr. Sexton.*) These figures generally go on the wild assumption that when a tax is remitted a proportionate amount is taken off, and when a tax is imposed a proportionate amount ought to be added, but, of course, that is not so?—No, that it does not follow. The amount which is lost to the revenue by the reduction of a duty does not, of course, represent the relief to the taxpayer necessarily, and in the same way the imposition, of course, or the raising of a duty, does not necessarily represent the increased burden, because it is quite conceivable you may double the duty and get nothing out of it.

9471. And on the other hand, the reduction of one tax may increase the yield under another, may it not?—Certainly.

9472. (*Chairman.*) Or you may increase the yield by increasing the consumption?—I think these figures that we put here in the table are misleading.

9473. Then Mr. Childers has some questions with regard to Sir Joseph Prim's Return which I will now put. You have that Return, I daresay?—Yes, I have it here.

9474. According to that return, page 30, the true revenue of Great Britain was in 1819–20, 51,443,764*l*.?—Yes, that is so.

9475. The true revenue of Ireland was then 5,256,564*l*.?—Yes.

9476. In 1889–90 the true revenue of Great Britain was 84,[illegible]*l*., and that of Ireland 7,[illegible]*l*.?—Yes, that is so.

9477. Therefore, between 1820 and 1890, the true revenue of Great Britain had increased by 33,[illegible]*l*., or 39·3[illegible] per cent., and that of Ireland by [illegible]*l*., or 33·15 per cent.?—Those calculations are correct; I have checked them.

9478. The difference in the rates of increase is, therefore, not very great; but that of Great Britain is somewhat greater?—That is the case.

9479. I suppose that, generally speaking, increase in the proceeds of taxation may be due to either of two causes, viz., increase of taxable wealth in a community, or to increase of the number or weight of taxes?—I think that is a correct way of putting the case.

9480. Or it may be due partly to one of those causes and partly to the other in various proportions?—Yes, I think so.

9481. According to page 32 of your memorandum, the pressure of Imperial taxation per head of population in Great Britain was in 1819–20 2*l*. 14*s*. 10*d*., and in 1892–3 2*l*. 10*s*. 10*d*., was it?—Yes, that is taking the total revenue, but I think in talking of the pressure of Imperial taxation, the more correct way is to take the revenue derived from taxation. In that case the figures for Great Britain would be in 1819–20 2*l*. 12*s*., and in 1892–3 2*l*. 4*s*. 6*d*.; and in regard to Ireland, if I take the corresponding figures, namely, the amount derived from taxation at those two periods, the figures for Ireland would be in 1819–20 1*l*. 5*s*. 3*d*.; and the figure for 1893 works out practically the same as Mr. Childers', 1*l*. 12*s*. 11*d*. or 1*l*. 13*s*. Mr. Childers' figure takes the whole revenue, whether derived from taxes or other receipts, but I think as he talks of the pressure of Imperial taxation, the more correct way is to take only the amount derived from taxes, and not from the total revenue.

9482. Is this partly due to the fact that the population of Great Britain has increased, but that of Ireland has declined since 1820? In 1821 the population of Great Britain was 14,091,757, and in 1891 33,028,172. In 1821 that of Ireland was 6,801,827; and in 1891 only 4,704,750?—I think that must be the case, in calculations *per capita* such as these are.

9483. (*Mr. Sexton.*) Where revenue is mainly derived as in Great Britain from taxes on consumption, and almost exclusively derived from taxes on consumption as in Ireland, *per capita* calculations become of great importance?—No doubt they do.

9484. (*Chairman.*) Do you think that it can be safely said that in the case of Great Britain the increase of revenue since 1820 is due rather to the increase of the wealth and numbers of the community than to increase of the number of taxes or rates of taxation?—I think there can be no question about that. We know that the number of taxes has been greatly diminished, and that the rates of taxes are also known. Moreover, there is no better criterion of increased wealth than the large yield of the income-tax now as compared with what it was thirty years ago.

9485. Should you adopt the same view in the case of Ireland?—No, not to the same extent, certainly.

9486. According to the Primrose Return (page 14) the true Irish revenue in 1819 was 5,256,564*l*. It was about the same in 1829 and 1839, and rather less in 1849, then being 4,[illegible]*l*. In 1859 it had become 7,7[illegible]*l*., and has remained more or less at that level to present time. It may be said, then, may it not, that the whole rise of Irish revenue since 1819 practically took place in the decade 1850–1860?—Yes; I think that would be the case, owing to the fact that during that period the spirit duties had been assimilated to those in Great Britain and the income-tax had been imposed on Ireland.

9487. On a closer analysis, would it not appear that the bulk of the rise took place within the last six or seven years of this decade?—That would follow, certainly, dating from 1853, the time when the income-tax was put on.

9488. Ireland was paying rather under 5,000,000*l*. in 1850, and Great Britain rather over 51,000,000*l*., so that Ireland was paying at the rate of about one pound to ten. Do you think that, three years after the famine, this was too small a contribution on the part of Ireland?—No, I do not know that I can say it was too small a contribution.

9489. In 1860, Ireland was paying 7,[illegible]*l*., and Great Britain 61,[illegible]*l*., so that Ireland was then paying in the proportion of about one to eight, instead of one to ten. Would you attribute this change to increased taxation rather than to the increased consumption of taxed goods in Ireland?—It must be due to both causes, I think.

9490. Subsequently to the great enhancement of Irish taxation in the six or seven years previously to 1860 the Irish true revenue has not increased much. In 1860 it was, according to the Primrose Return, 7,[illegible]*l*. In 1893–94 it was according to the last Financial Return, 7,[illegible]*l*., or actually less than it was in 1860?—That is so, and I think the difference is still more marked if you take only the revenue derived from taxes. I think Mr. Childers has taken the total revenue—in fact I know he has, because he has taken it from that return. If you take only the taxed revenue in 1859–60 it amounted to 7,[illegible]*l*. and in 1893–4 to 6,[illegible]*l*., so that there is a decrease of about 700,000*l*.

9491. Meanwhile the true revenue derived from Great Britain has increased from 61,[illegible]*l*. in 1860 to [illegible]*l*. in 1893–94, an increase of more than 60 per cent. I suppose you would correct these figures again?—I should correct these figures in the same way; for instance, in 1859–60 the revenue derived from taxation in Great Britain was 57,[illegible]*l*., and in 1893–94 it was 7[illegible]*l*., an increase of about 1[illegible]*l*.

9492. Of how much per cent.?—I am afraid I have not got the percentage.

9493. Mr Childers puts it at 30 per cent. I see from a paper prepared by the Inland Revenue Department that during about the same period, 1861 to 1893, the gross assessments to income-tax had increased in Great Britain by 100 per cent., and in Ireland by 37 per cent., is that so?—Yes, I think that is correct.

9494. If that assessment can be taken as a more or less good test of increase of wealth would not the inference be that during the last 30 years wealth had increased in Great Britain about three times as fast as Imperial revenue derived from Great Britain?—Yes, certainly so.

Sir Edward W. Hamilton's evidence is continued at Question 9[illegible] (Twenty-fifth Day.)

Sir E. W. Hamilton, K.C.B.

13 June 1895.

Causes of increase of [illegible] of taxation.

Rise of Irish revenue between 1850 and 1860.

Rise of British revenue since 1860.

At Committee Room B, House of Lords.

PRESENT :

LORD FARRER, Chairman.

The Right Hon. THE O'CONOR DON.	THOMAS SEXTON, Esq., M.P.
Sir THOMAS SUTHERLAND, K.C.M.G., M.P.	J. E. REDMOND, Esq., M.P.
Sir DAVID BARBOUR, K.C.S.I.	HENRY F. SLATTERY, Esq.
The Hon. EDWARD BLAKE, M.P.	

Mr. B. H. HOLLAND, Secretary.

Mr. THOMAS LOUGH, M.P., re-called and further examined.

Mr. T. Lough, M.P. — 14 May 1895. — Emigration from Ireland.

9495. (Chairman.) I think we had got to page 8 of your brief, had we not?—Yes; but before I return to the brief, I want to answer a question that you put to me. When I was dealing with the subject of emigration you kindly accepted, and other members of the Commission kindly accepted, my view of Irish emigration, and you requested me to go to the Board of Trade and read their reports on emigration with a view of seeing whether the Board of Trade account of emigration as being due chiefly to the prosperity of trade was not a truer account of emigration than the account which I had given, namely, that the people were simply driven out of Ireland by oppression.

9496. I think the point Dr. Giffen thought he had discovered with reference to the general law of emigration was that the emigration was greater when the wages in America were greater, and less when the allowances in America were less?—Quite so. I thought that of such importance that I went to the Board of Trade, and I got all the reports, and prepared a brief memorandum on that particular point which I would like to put in before we return to the brief, because I think this will be the best time to put it in.

9497. Do you wish to state the upshot of it—the result of it?—Yes, I do; it will not take many minutes, and I would like to explain to the Commission that that is what kept me this morning. I only heard yesterday at 5 o'clock that I should be wanted to-day, and it is the preparation of that document which has kept me a little late this morning. It is a very brief memorandum, and one which I can read in about two or three minutes, and if you approve of it I would like it to go in as part of my evidence:—

"Memorandum prepared by Mr. Thomas Lough, M.P., on the Emigration from Ireland, at the request of the Royal Commission on the Financial Relations between Great Britain and Ireland.—As suggested by the Commission upon my answer to questions Nos. 8437–9, 8462–4, I have consulted the papers relating to emigration published by the Board of Trade, with a view to seeing whether their explanation of the causes of the increase or decrease of emigration in Great Britain could apply equally well to Ireland. In the report for the year 1891, the Board of Trade say that 'the low figures for emigration correspond with depression of trade, especially in the country of destination.' It is assumed throughout that large emigration always accompanies good trade, and that good trade in America and the Colonies is generally coincident with a prosperous condition of trade in Great Britain. My suggestion was that this explanation does not account for the emigration from Ireland which is caused by the condition of things in Ireland. Careful examination of the subject has confirmed this view. In Great Britain the movement is not one of emigration merely, but of immigration as well. The returns of the Board of Trade deal with one subject as fully as the other, the theory rests on the figures of one as completely as it does upon the other. Sometimes the number of immigrants into Great Britain exceeds the number of the emigrants; this occurred in 1877. In 1894 the figures practically balanced. In Ireland there is no immigration. The movement is one-sided. Since 1851 the population has been pouring in a steady stream out of the country, without any compensation in the shape of new arrivals for the loss the nation was sustaining. So much is this the case that Dr. Grimshaw, the Registrar-General for Ireland, publishes no statistics whatever of immigration."

That is my first point. My second point is:—

"The form of the returns of the two countries is arranged under different heads, which tend to make comparison difficult. In Great Britain the emigrant is described as one who goes to 'places out of Europe'; in the Irish returns he is described as one who 'leaves Ireland for the purpose of settling elsewhere.' These conflicting definitions make the Board of Trade returns worthless as far as recording the movement from Ireland is concerned. The vast numbers of settlers in Great Britain who are driven out of Ireland are not recognised in them. In 1876 the Irish emigrants, according to the Board of Trade, were 25,976, the actual number was 37,587; in 1877, 22,831 versus 38,503; in 1878, 29,492 versus 41,124."

9498. Did you ask at the Board of Trade what the amount of that difference was?—I did not; I had not time. I have had their latest papers, and I can give the reasons; in fact, I have given the reason already; the reason is that the emigration to Great Britain is not recorded by the British Board of Trade at all. It is assumed to be a healthy national movement that they do not recognise.

9499. (Mr. Sexton.) An internal movement perhaps?—Yes. An internal movement, which does not affect the political economy of Ireland. There are also mistakes apparently in the other direction. In 1894 the Board of Trade gives the Irish emigration as 43,000 instead of 35,809. I think it will be conceded that the Irish figures as prepared by Dr. Grimshaw are the true figures, and that an emigrant to Scotland is as much lost to Ireland as an emigrant to Canada.

9500. In his emigration to Scotland perhaps it is just as possible that he could not find a living in Ireland as if he went to Nova Scotia?—That is my point.

9501. (The O'Conor Don.) Was the temporary emigration to Scotland at that period recorded in the same way as permanent emigration?—No, that is carefully avoided by Dr. Grimshaw's returns; he says that he has specially excluded from the Irish returns all these temporary labourers who come over, for instance, and all who get a living in Ireland. Now, my third point is this: that there is no parallel between the numbers that leave the two islands relatively to the respective populations. From the 1st of January 1853 to the 1st of January 1894 the number that left Ireland was 3,037,363, or 65 per cent. out of an average population which was rapidly decreasing, while only 4,677,330 left Great Britain out of a population five times as large, which was increasing with phenomenal rapidity all the time.

9502. (Mr. Sexton.) Have you the percentage in the English case corresponding to the 65 per cent. in the Irish case?—I am sorry to say I have not, but it would be a very small percentage, something like 10 per cent., but I think that that figure of the total number in itself shows that no explanation given of one movement must be accepted as an explanation of the other movement. Another difference between the movement in the [illegible] countries is the larger number of females from Ireland. In the 43 years, 1851 to 1894, the figures nearly balance; in 1864 and 1865, and in 1893 and 1894, there are more females than males—this applies to the [illegible] as well as the [illegible]. From Great Britain the [illegible] males in every year are about [illegible] as [illegible] as the single females. The excess in the movement of females from Ireland establishes the "necessity" and upsets the theory that the emigration [illegible] is influenced by trade attractions. My fifth point is this: "The [illegible] of cabin passengers and the different classes [illegible] emigrate from Great Britain as compared with Ireland also indicate that in the former the movement may be associated with trade, but that in the latter the people are driven out by necessity. From London the cabin passengers were three-fourths of the total emigrants who left the port in 1894; from Southampton they were [illegible] of the whole. From Londonderry the cabin passengers were one-tenth of the whole; from Galway there was no cabin passenger; from Queenstown there were only 73 in [illegible] emigrants. From Liverpool [illegible] are cabin passengers; from Glasgow one-fifth, but no obvious deductions can be drawn from these ports, because as many Irish as well as British go from each of them." I think that shows that practically from Ireland you have had no cabin passengers.

9503. You mean so many Scotchmen as well as Irish?—Yes, the departures from Liverpool and Glasgow are mixed.

9504. The presence of the British would account for the large number of cabin passengers, would it not?—Yes, that is my point. I say I leave out Liverpool and Glasgow, because they are ports where both go from, but I take such ports as London and Southampton for British emigration, and Queenstown and Londonderry for Irish emigration, because they are all Irish from one and all British from the other. Now I think that that shows that the British emigrant is a man who looks round to see whether there are trade opportunities, but that the Irish emigrant is a man who is driven out by necessity, and who has not a pound to spare. Now with regard to the difference in the occupations of the emigrants. In 1894 nearly 10,000 who left Great Britain are described as "Gentlemen, professional men, and merchants," but of this class only 271 left Ireland. That is my sixth point. Now my seventh point on the contrast between the two is that "The destination of the emigrants from each country also illustrates the difference between the two movements. From Great Britain large proportions go to various countries as attractions may be offered by each. During the 43 years since 1853 almost half of the total number went to Canada, Australia, or other places than the United States, in 1894 only about [illegible] per cent. of the total number sailing from London went there. Particular years show great differences in the numbers that go to any given part of the world. In the Irish figures there is no such evidence of selection. During the 43 years over five-sixths of the total emigration went to the United States. In 1891 out of 33,[illegible] people sailing from Irish ports, 31,[illegible] went to the United States, and the proportion of the whole number of Irish emigrants going there in 1894 was 93·[illegible] per cent., in 1884, 91 per cent., in 1882, 91·[illegible] per cent., and in 1871, [illegible]·7 per cent. This shows that the Irish emigrants do not study the advantages of various countries; they know nothing about them, they simply go where they are [illegible], [illegible] about nothing except to escape from the misery and starvation in Ireland, with a [illegible] confidence that any place will be better than home." Then my eighth point is treating England and Scotland for the [illegible] as two separate countries:—"The movements of emigrants from England and Scotland always seem to 'march' together in every respect mentioned, showing that it may be safe to generalise about these two countries, but the figures of particular years in Ireland as well as the tendency of the whole period are different and often contradictory from both of the others. Out of many examples I quote the following:—In 1877 emigration decreased by one-fifth both in England and in Scotland, but it increased in Ireland on the figures of the previous year." That shows that a common explanation will not do. "In 1880 there was an increase all round in the figures. In England the increase was 7 per cent., in Scotland 14 per cent., but in Ireland it was 101 per cent., emigration having doubled in that year because of the famine of 1879."

Those are my points, which I think go to the bottom of everything the Board of Trade has said. I arrive at the following three broad conclusions, and each of these supports my former statement:—My first conclusion is that there is no common theory which will account for the emigration from the two islands. My second is that as regards Great Britain the generalisations of the Board of Trade may be true, but that the figures brought forward in support of them are misleading owing to the fact that they are mixed up with the Irish figures, and that to make the record valuable it should be reconstructed from the beginning, omitting Ireland. That is as regards Great Britain. And my third conclusion is that as regards Ireland, the efforts of the Board of Trade have only been effectual in obscuring one of the most important movements which have taken place in these islands during the last 40 years, and one of the saddest and most undeserved tragedies in the history of any country. That is my paper, and I should like it to be printed if the Commission do not object, and I put it forward as an explanation of my evidence.

9505. (Chairman.) That is then all upon that subject that you wish to say?—That is all. There was one other point, arising out of my evidence that I would like to mention in order to get it right. I was asked amongst a variety of other questions, which I was not prepared for the last day, about the wages for shipbuilding in Belfast, and I find I replied to one question, which I think was put by Mr. Sexton, that I thought the wages were less in Belfast than elsewhere. Well, I did not refer entirely to shipbuilders or particularly to shipbuilding, and I only spoke from memory, because if you look at my statement you will see nothing about wages. I did not see what it had to say to the subject, but since then I have got some particulars which support the statement that wages are lower in some respects, but in others, the wages paid in Belfast are quite up to the average paid by British shipbuilders. I will quote from a letter from the Amalgamated Society of Engineers, "Harland and Wolff in Belfast pay quite up to the average of British shipbuilders for men in our trade, and in some instances above, such as those on the north-east coast of England. With reference to Workman and Clark, they (although not such good employers as the other Belfast firm) are yet fairly up to the British average." Then with regard to ordinary labourers, I have got a longer letter, and I would like to be guided as to what you wish with reference to that.

9506. (Mr. Sexton.) What labourers—agricultural labourers?—The ordinary labourers in the shipbuilding yards in Belfast. The effect of the letter is that since the strike last year the wages are improved in Belfast, and that they are as good in Belfast now as on the Clyde, but not nearly so good as on the north-eastern coast of England.

9507. (Sir David Barbour.) Do you mean the wages for unskilled labour in shipbuilding yards?—Yes.

9508. Are you aware that some of the shipbuilding firms in Belfast—so I have been informed—have to send men to the south and west of Ireland to recruit unskilled labour?—I am not aware of it. I do not know anything about it.

9509. But they have, as I am informed by a gentleman who ought to know, to send their foremen to the south-west of Ireland, and pay them a bonus for every man they can recruit?—I never heard of it before.

9510. (Mr. Sexton.) The fact that there is only one shipbuilding firm in Ireland renders the comparison of very slight importance?—Yes. I only want to put it right for the sake of accuracy.

9511. (Chairman.) Is there any other point in connection with this matter that you wish to mention?—Yes, there is one other point. You may remember that there was a slight conflict about my statement that pauperism had greatly increased in Ireland. I said I had got figures from the Irish Local Government Board, and I criticised the way they prepared their figures, showing the daily average instead of the total number of paupers. In order to elucidate the matter I have prepared a table putting in the figures of the daily average of paupers in one set of columns with the total number of paupers in another set of columns.

9512. Do you wish to put that statement in?—Yes.

9513. (Mr. Sexton.) Your general argument is that the sum of pauperism cannot be inferred from the average number in daily receipt of relief as given by the Local Government Board?—That is one argument, and I have now got another valuable conclusion out of which I think will at all events the conflict between us. I have taken out the proportion of the daily average per 1,000 of the population in each year from 1864 to 1894 in one column, and alongside of it I have taken out the proportion of the total number of paupers.

Mr. G. Joseph, M.P.

14 June 1895

Emigration from Ireland.

Wages in shipbuilding yards at Belfast.

Increase of pauperism in Ireland.

9514. (Chairman.) Of the total number of individual paupers?—Yes, of the total number who obtain relief. The important point is that when you take out the figures for the 30 years both show exactly the same result. When you take the proportion per 1,000 of the average population both show the progress of the same movement that pauperism has doubled. I will just state to the Commission two figures. The daily average as given by the Local Government Board in Ireland in 1864, was 11·[illegible] to each 1,000 of the inhabitants in Ireland. In 1894 it was 21·79; the figures had doubled of the daily average, including outdoor and indoor paupers.

9515. (Mr. Sexton.) Proportionately to the population? —Yes, the figures have doubled proportionately to the population. Now the total number of paupers who obtained relief in 1864 were 23·[illegible] per 1,000, but in 1894 they were 95·8 per 1,000. That was the figure I stated the last day, which some members of the Commission questioned. I have now prepared this table to show that there is exactly the same movement apparent in the daily average number as there is in the total number of paupers, that is to say, both have doubled within the last 30 years.

9516. The element you add to the case as presented by the Local Government Board is that you take direct note of the increase in the volume of pauperism, having regard to the decrease in population?—That is it. I take in each year—the number of paupers in proportion to each 1,000 of the population.

9517. (Chairman.) Is not that what Mr. Robinson's return gives us?—I have not seen it.

9518. He says that, for 1862-3, for instance, the percentage of the total daily average of the population is 5·13. Then it varies and goes down, and in 1893-4 it is 8·17. I do not quite understand how the two results agree?—I have put in a table showing the total number of paupers and the increase of pauperism in Ireland between 1864 and 1894. The total number of emigrants in each year and the approximation between the figures of emigration and pauperism.

9519. (Mr. Sexton.) The introduction of the element of emigration does not affect your calculations?—No, it does not. In 1864 the number of paupers receiving outdoor relief in Ireland was 7,842, and in 1894 the number had increased to 57,000. That is progress. Now turn to indoor paupers. In the case of indoor paupers the daily average numbers in 1864 were 56,257, and that was on a population of nearly 6,000,000, whereas now we get 42,000 on a population of about 4,600,000. I should like to hand that paper in.

9520. I think it is obvious, assuming both the calculations to be accurate, the Local Government Board calculations and your calculations, that although you calculate the percentage per 1,000 of the population and they calculate it upon the population as a whole, yet if both calculations are accurate the percentages ought to agree? —Yes, and when I have had time to examine them I might probably be able to see why they conflict.

9521. (Chairman.) Perhaps you will take it and look at it before you put it in, and put in any explanation you can?—I will.

9522. (Sir David Barbour.) Is not the great increase in the total number of paupers mainly, if not entirely, due to the increase of outdoor relief?—It is not entirely due to it.

9523. But mainly?—It is due to a large extent to outdoor relief, but the number of indoor paupers has increased also in proportion to the population, but not very much.

9524. It is a correct percentage if you take column 5?—Yes.

9525. (Mr. Sexton.) You have attacked the whole theory that the true state and movement of pauperism are represented not by the total number relieved in the year, but by the daily average. What do you say upon that?—I have now worked out the daily average including indoor and outdoor, and it shows exactly the same result—namely that pauperism has doubled in 30 years.

9526. (Chairman.) That is where you are at variance with that return, but I think it is almost impossible for us to go into it, therefore will you take it and look into it?—Yes, I will.

9527. (Sir David Barbour.) From what year to what year do you count?—From 1864 to 1894.

9528. (Chairman.) Possibly that is because these figures show that the total has very largely increased from 1872 to 1873, if you look at the upper part of column 10?—Yes. May I point out that in 1862-3 this return gives 5·13 whereas 1893-4 gives 8·17. That is nearly double.

9529. (Sir David Barbour.) But you have got to add to that that the increase from 1862-3 is entirely in outdoor relief?—Very well. Outdoor relief has increased as much in Great Britain as in Ireland.

9530. I do not say it is not a legitimate increase—I am not attacking it?—I think there is a sort of assumption that it is new—that it is a special boon to Ireland—that outrelief. That is far from the truth.

9531. (Mr. Sexton.) Does not it rather appear that by the institution practically of the system of outdoor relief in 1862-3 what had previously been the sole method of relief within the house became supplemented by the system of outdoor relief afterwards?—Yes, and the increase in outdoor relief is continued and has been resorted to quite as much in Great Britain as in Ireland. Dr. [illegible] has made a calculation comparing the unions in London, which give outdoor relief largely, with the unions in Lancashire which give outdoor relief largely, and he finds that in those unions in Great Britain where outdoor relief is resorted to, there is a saving of 2s. 6d. per head of the population in the annual cost of the poor relief.

9532. (Chairman.) That is a subject of great controversy, is it not?—It is, but I only mentioned it to show that outdoor relief has been resorted to in Great Britain quite as much as in Ireland.

9533. (Sir David Barbour.) It is a remarkable fact, that in earlier years the persons who went into the workhouse stopped there for a longer time than they do now? —Yes, and a greater number of people constantly going into the workhouse even for a shorter period, surely shows a much worse state of the country, because then our workhouse was for the practically permanently incapable person who had to get the shelter somewhere, but now a large section of the population are so near the workhouse that they have got to go in for a period in every year.

9534. (Mr. Sexton.) It would appear that the system of outdoor relief had really no existence before 1862, but then it became part of the system, and after 1862 persons obtained benefit from outdoor relief who would [illegible] before the introduction of that system have gone into the workhouse?—That is it I think.

9535. So that, therefore, no conclusion can be drawn simply from the fact that the extension of outdoor relief is the main feature?—I do not think so; I think it rather tends the other way. But I have no doubt I will be able to reconcile my figures with the Irish Local Government Board's figures.

9536. (Chairman.) Now will you go on with your memorandum; it is at the foot of page 8, is it not?—Yes.

9537. Does Great Britain gain any benefit from the over taxation of Ireland?—Yes; as I understand it the only benefit obtained is 2,000,000l. per annum, the Imperial contribution which Great Britain receives from Ireland.

9538. That is to say, 2,000,000l. contribution to what the Treasury call Imperial purposes?—Yes, that is it; it is about 2,000,000l. per annum.

9539. It is the balance left after what they call the local expenditure?—Yes; I think we must accept that that is the total of the net advantage that this country, Great Britain, derives in a money contribution from Ireland. Well, I think in considering that we must remember what the total revenue of Great Britain is. I stated that it would be 1,300,000,000l., but it is now much bigger. In 1894 I believe it had increased to 1,[illegible],000,000l.

9540. That is the whole revenue of the country?—Yes, the total income.

9541. Not, of course, the revenue from taxation?—No, the total income. So that the 2,000,000l. is a small benefit anyhow; and it is in all probability not enough to weigh too closely against other advantages which might arise from relieving Ireland of even that contribution of 2,000,000l.

9542. Then you say that even the loss of that sum is unnecessary?—Yes. I suggest that even the loss of that sum is unnecessary, and I base that argument, notwithstanding some hostility with which I believe the idea is received, on the simple point first that it could all be saved in the cost of the [illegible]. It must cost 3,000,000l. I think at least per annum. There are nearly 31,000 soldiers kept there, and I have looked all over the country, and I believe the number kept in Ireland for 30 years past has never been under 25,000, so that it is practically kept up to that number.

2543. (*Mr. Sexton.*) The War Office have handed in a memorandum in which they say that the total military expenditure in Ireland is about 2,000,000*l.* in the year?—I thought it was higher; I put it roughly at 100*l.* a year per man, but I am prepared to accept that, because it is very hard to get at the expense of the army. The number of soldiers kept in Scotland through the same period has never been more than 3,000—about a tenth of what are kept in Ireland. I suggest then that this military expenditure might be abolished altogether, and the Army Vote could be reduced by that amount—in fact, I think the Army Vote could be reduced by a great deal more, and there is a very strong feeling arising in this country that we might get 5,000,000*l.* off the cost of the army, and reduce it from the total of 18,000,000*l.*, at which it stands now, to about 13,000,000*l.*, and if so you will save something for Great Britain as well as the 2,000,000*l.*, which I want to be saved for Ireland, and I cannot but say that the position of this camp in the Bog of Allen in Ireland, so far away from any centres of activity, is a most unsuitable place for a camp, and that the living of the soldiers is not practically cheaper than it would be somewhere in England. Therefore I think that on that item alone—on the army—this amount could be saved. I have got a [illegible] somewhere else that until a [illegible] of the [illegible] system I would not suggest that the army should be taken away, because there has been a great way of [illegible] one half of these expenditures in Ireland, and taking away the expenditure without reducing the taxes. I do not think the expenditure helps, but I still do not recommend a single soldier to be taken out of Ireland, nor a single policeman, until first double the cost of the soldier or policeman is taken off the backs of the unfortunate people.

2544. (*Chairman.*) You assume these 30,000 men are kept there because of the English connexion with Ireland, and that you might do away with them altogether if it were not for that?—To a large extent I do assume that. I believe that other ideas are now obtaining.

2545. (*Sir David Barbour.*) Are you aware of the fact that owing to the large number of troops abroad it is found necessary to keep a certain number of troops in this country in order to provide the necessary reliefs?—I do not quite accept that it is necessary; I do not accept the full statement on that point, but I say that if it is necessary it is not necessary for Irish purposes, and that the people of London who derive the benefit from keeping these troops abroad and who make the profit on these foreign possessions ought to pay for the army instead of [illegible] it on the Irish.

2546. Well, if that is the case, we cannot do away with these troops, even though you think it is not for Irish purposes that they are kept?—There is a feeling in the House of Commons, which I largely share, that we are wasting about 4,000,000*l.* a year upon the army, and that we could get an army quite suitable for all our purposes for about two-thirds of what we are spending now.

2547. I will ask you if you are aware that there are people who hold a different opinion from that which you express?—Yes.

2548. Are you aware that the Government of India has, as a matter of fact, had to pay extra sums of money to induce the British soldiers to prolong their service in India, because the establishment at home was not sufficient to send out the necessary reliefs?—I was not aware of that precise fact, but I would not think of denying it if you say it, only I do not think it implies any argument that the Irish peasantry ought not to pay it.

2549. (*Mr. Sexton.*) It is just a question whether the soldiers in Ireland are raised and maintained out of Ireland or whether they are raised and maintained in Ireland?—Yes.

2550. (*Chairman.*) Do not you think that the Irish people would object to the expenditure of this money being withdrawn from Ireland?—Well, possibly there might be a little objection at first, and that is why I think that previously to the expenditure being withdrawn there should be the large compensatory reduction of taxation, and then I think they would be reconciled to it.

2551. Can you suggest any other economies which Great Britain might effect?—Great Britain has lost consequently by doles and sops to Ireland, as they are called, and I need not repeat the evidence upon that point, as the Commission has had it at considerable length. For my own part, I think that although some of the figures submitted on this head are of a rather doubtful character, it would seem that at any rate 40 millions have been written off loans during the last 50 years, and any further loss of this kind would also be saved, amongst other benefits to Great Britain, if it were possible to make Ireland permanently prosperous, as I think ought to be done by relieving her of these burdens.

2552. Are any economies possible in Ireland?—I think there is room in Ireland apart from the Army, for great economies. The charges for the Irish establishments seem to me to be based upon a most extravagant scale. They could be reduced in my opinion, by another two millions; the charges in Ireland have not decreased as the population has diminished, the tendency is the other way. The extent has doubled as the population has halved, and there has been a most extravagant administration of everything, even new legislation like the Land Acts. We have only to go back less than 50 years to 1846 or 1847 to find that the figures in Ireland then justify all the statements and all my calculations through the remainder of the paper. The total Imperial and local charges in 1846 were only about six millions altogether, or six millions and a quarter, and although now the population has gone down nearly to half, the charges have gone up to 11½ millions, so we need only go back 50 years to find a justification for the statement that the growth has been extraordinary. During the Peel administration in Ireland the charges were as much as I have stated, so that if the charges could be reduced in proportion to the reduction of population there would be at least another two millions saved on the local charges.

2553. (*Mr. Sexton.*) In order to make up the 11½ millions out of the Imperial and local revenues?—Yes.

2554. (*Chairman.*) I understand you are of opinion that this question of the Imperial contribution is of slight importance compared with other financial considerations which are at issue between the two islands, and that if any trifling loss did occur it might be more than counterbalanced in some other way?—Yes. I am engaged in business in Great Britain, a business which I carry on partly with Ireland—I mean the wholesale tea trade—ever since I have been working at it, now for some 25 years, it has appeared to me, perhaps in an exaggerated way, still an example of the utter folly that Great Britain has been guilty of from a financial point of view, in not opening Ireland and allowing her to become a good customer instead of keeping her a poor and impoverished country as she is at present. Great Britain is a means of cheap-labour supplying everything; and Ireland, I think, in proportion to her wealth and population is, after all, the best customer that Great Britain has got. It cannot be good policy to ruin the nation which is your best customer; and I want to take the detailed example of my own business, which is the tea business, between the two countries. The Irish drink the finest quality and the largest quantity of tea of any part of the population of the United Kingdom. In the sixties and in the seventies, when Indian tea was introduced, it was not at all appreciated in England; but the Irish at once saw that it was a tremendous improvement on the wretched tea imported from China, and the result was that the moment the Indian tea was presented to them, the whole consumption turned to it. Now the English people have seen that that was a great historic example of Irish good taste, and they have slowly and reluctantly, in spite of the diatribes of Dr. Andrew Clark and others, commenced to drink entirely Indian and Ceylon tea.

2555. Do you endorse what we have been told, as mentioned by the Inland Revenue people, that the taste of the Irish for tea is better than that of the English?—Yes; it is far better, as in many other things.

2556. (*Sir David Barbour.*) You say that England has lost so much by Ireland not being prosperous, because if Ireland had been prosperous the people would have drunk more tea and there would have been a larger revenue. Certain witnesses have said that the Irish drink more tea because they are not prosperous, because they cannot afford good food; that view does not appear to be consistent with yours. If they were prosperous, according to that theory they would drink less tea and not more?—No, that is one of those exceptional things where really two ideas do not conflict at all. You take tea if you are very poor and cannot afford champagne, but if you are in easy circumstances tea is also a necessary article of consumption; that would be so in Ireland. Tea is no cardinal substitute for other kinds of food, but you take tea also as the best stimulating and the least harmful drink that you can use. The best proof of that is in the case of the Australians, who are a prosperous people; they drink 8 lbs. of tea per head of the population; they drink as much and half again as we do in this country.

* Sheer. [illegible]

[illegible]

9558. (*Mr. Sexton.*) Even if one drinks tea because of the poverty of food, that is no reason why he should prefer bad tea to good?—None. One pound of good tea will be worth 2 or 3 lbs. of the cheap China tea.

9559. Is not tea cheaper in Ireland than milk and other different articles of consumption?—Certainly as a stimulant, when you take into account the stimulating properties of the tea, it is a good variety of food.

9560. A pound of tea will last an economical family almost for a week, will it not?—Yes, it will. My argument is that if instead of the progressive ruin by emigration, a fair system had been applied to Ireland, say before 1871, so that her population, instead of continuing to fall would have continued to rise in proportion to the rise in Great Britain, Ireland would now be paying to us London 563,241*l.* each year more for tea, than what she is paying. This calculation goes upon the theory, that at some point England ought to take steps to stop the decay in Ireland, and if the reduction of the population had been checked and the population had continued to rise in 1871 in proportion to the rate of population in Great Britain, Ireland would now be paying us in London 562,241*l.* each year more for tea alone than she is paying.

9561. And if that population had been able to buy the tea?—Yes; I do not think we need question that, because their poverty could not be greater than it is now, and they are able to buy it now. It is based upon existing figures, and this is the calculation. In 1871 the population was 5,412,377; if that had increased as the population has increased in England, it would now be 26 per cent. more, or 6,896,873, whereas the actual population of Ireland is only about 4,500,000, or 2,390,000 less than it should be, judged by the English standard. That represents a loss exactly of 100,000 persons a year, so that we have lost in tea alone during the last 23 years nearly 12,000,000*l.* I submit a table showing what would have been consumed in the 23 years. I show at the first year when 100,000 people eat tea would have taken at 2*s.* a lb., consuming 3·97 per head, which was the consumption in 1871, and I reduce the price of tea gradually to 1*s.* 5*d.*, because tea has greatly fallen in price, and I make the calculation upon that basis, and it brings out the result I have stated.

9562. You would not accept Sir Edward Hamilton's general estimate that tea costs 1*s.* 11*d.* a lb.?—No, I do not think it costs 1*s.* 11*d.* a lb. now.

9563. But his calculation is based upon that assumption?—The average price of Indian tea sold on the London market now is only about 10*d.* a lb.—that is the average price of all Indian tea sold. The average price of China tea is only about 7½*d.*, and the average price of Ceylon tea is about 10½*d.* That is the average price of the whole crop.

9564. (*Sir David Barbour.*) That is the wholesale price?—Yes, in the Mincing Lane sale rooms.

9565. But in Ireland they drink a higher-priced tea, do they not?—I am allowing for that; I do not want to take an extreme price. I only want to take what Great Britain would get for the tea, and I have worked it down for the last three years to 1*s.* 5*d.*

9566. (*Chairman.*) That is not the sum that the Irish would give, but what the Irish wholesale merchant would give?—Yes.

9567. (*Mr. Sexton.*) And would the retail price be 1*s.* 11*d.*?—It might be; tea is a profitable article.

9568. (*Chairman.*) That is an assumption, of course, that the increased population would have purchased the same quantity that the present population purchase per head?—Yes, that is the assumption—just the same.

9569. I see that in the figures of "tea consumption" which you furnish you show that the amount consumed per head of the population has increased considerably within the last 23 years?—Yes; it has increased from 3·97 per head in 1871 to 5·83 in 1894.

9570. Do you, or do you not, think that this increased consumption may have had a deleterious effect upon the population?—I do not, because it is still 2½ lbs. less than people of the same blood consume in Australia, and it is not a large quantity spread over the whole year.

9571. You do not agree with those who think that it is any sign of the decadence of the population, or that it is a substitute for more nutritious food?—I do not think so, I think it is the most beneficial food that anybody can take, but perhaps I am a little prejudiced.

9572. (*Mr. Sexton.*) Your 5½ lbs. per head would give an average of about half a pound of tea per week for a family of five?—Yes.

9573. Which represents a very moderate figure?—Yes.

9574. (*Sir David Barbour.*) Of course they would not live on tea alone?—No, but it is a very moderate average.

9575. (*Chairman.*) Do the men drink it as much as the women?—I think so; it is an absolute necessity in all the cottages, I think.

9576. I notice that the price you give of the tea has rapidly diminished during the last 25 years. What reductions have taken place in the duty during that period?—The duty has only been reduced once; it has been reduced from 6*d.* a pound, which it was in the [illegible] and eighties, to 4*d.* a pound, which it is at the present time.

9577. (*Mr. Sexton.*) So that only 2*d.* in the fall of [illegible] is attributable to the duty?—That is all.

9578. (*Chairman.*) You wish to suggest that if the effect of reducing the taxation and other means was to cause an increase of population and prosperity England would make a great deal more by her commerce than she would lose by the reduction of direct contributions? —Yes; I suggested tea as only one example in a small trade that I have worked out. I have troubled the Commission with these details of tea because it is a small trade compared to many of the trades with Ireland, and I think it would be of enormous advantage to Great Britain in regard to very many of her staple industries if by any means the decay in Ireland could be checked. With regard to coal, for example, all the coal in Ireland comes from Great Britain; it is a tremendous traffic across the Channel, and all the iron, tin, slates, all cotton goods, boots, leather goods, furniture, clothes, sugar, spices, coffees, and everything else that is used in Ireland comes from Great Britain, and they must come from Great Britain, because Great Britain is the only market for the agricultural produce of Ireland; and this here is the case of the people who are most dependent upon us, and who are pouring their money into our hands, being so reduced and lowered by taxation that they are dragged from a good customer into a bad one. I think we should gain by stopping that movement far more than any loss of a couple of millions.

9579. In fact you think it is enormously to the advantage of England to make Ireland into a good customer?—Yes; far outweighing any trifling loss in taxation.

9580. (*Mr. Sexton.*) It has been held that some criterion of the capacity of Ireland to bear taxation is afforded by adding together her imports and exports, and if the exports of Ireland be the export of food too good for the people to consume, and if the import be chiefly an import of food of an inferior quality, they not being able to consume what they produce, do you see any reason in adding the exports and imports together, or in comparing the sum of the imports and exports of Ireland with the sum of the exports and imports of a country like England which imports [illegible] food and raw material and exports in large manufactures? —No, I have given a good deal of thought to that subject and I think it is one of the most cruel things in the argument between the two countries. The Irish exports and imports are really of a most pathetic character, they are the dead necessaries of the poorest quality, as Mr. Sexton has said, constantly passed, because the country has been reduced to such a state that it cannot produce that as it ought to produce them, whereas our exports and imports in Great Britain are the most highly developed products of the world. All the manufactures of our [illegible] people are such that we could almost support ourselves, but we do not do it, because it is not worth our while to do it in any operation in such a dull affair that we can afford to leave it alone.

9581. Will you tell me whether you think there is any true comparison between the exports and imports of a country which exports good food without being able to consume it, and the imports and exports of a country like England which consumes all the best food it produces itself. Is there any reasonable comparison between the two countries? —No. I think that the idea of forming an opinion from the total of exports and imports of one country in comparison with another, is perfect folly. It depends upon what the exports and imports are, they may reveal the poverty of the country, and in the case of Ireland I think they do reveal the poverty of the country, and in the case of Great Britain they reveal the richness of the country.

9582. (*Chairman.*) Does not it depend largely upon the profit which the country makes by its import and export trade?—Certainly.

9583. A country may be conducting a very large export trade in order to pay off a debt, but that does not increase the wealth of the country?—No.

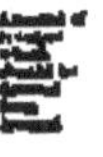

Mr. T. Lough, M.P. [illegible]

the British people. It is curious, but I believe the parallel is exact, but the Commission will remember the figures I gave at the commencement. We saw that the amount of taxation per head has not increased through the century in Great Britain, and I am now going upon the supposition that if the same phenomenon had taken place in Ireland we would be paying 2 millions at least and [illegible] taxes, and have a prosperous country, instead of nearly 12 millions and a ruined country.

9605. How do you think such a payment as you are describing would correspond with the payment that people have to make who live in Great Britain?—I believe they would be about the same.

9606. ([illegible]) I understand you are of opinion that it is not possible to go back to the figures of 1794?—I am afraid it is not possible; we must at any rate go step by step and it will be some time before we can get there. We must be content with a [illegible] [illegible] progression. Public wants have arisen since 1794 in connection with the improvement in the standard of existence. Foremost amongst them is education which costs a million and some odd pounds of money in Ireland, and this payment cannot be reduced and must, at first, be provided by the central Government. Public order must be maintained, and there will be charges for the poor, for lunatics, and some other things on a scale quite different from what they were 100 years ago. I think, probably, ultimately a good many of these charges which are discharged by the central authority now in Ireland will fall upon the local authorities, but we must get to that gradually too, and taking all these things into account, I think we could hardly expect to get the Imperial amount under 3,000,000*l.*, and then the local taxation might be reduced to something like 2,500,000*l.* or 2,000,000*l.*, making a total of 5,000,000*l.* altogether. I think that is all that Ireland should pay, and that an effective government could be very well provided out of that amount.

9607. (*Mr. Sexton.*) You mean the amount provided out of Imperial taxation?—Yes.

9608. (*Chairman.*) If the amount for the central administration were reduced to such a sum as you have mentioned, how about the Imperial contribution?—Of course that would serve as Imperial contribution, or in order to avoid raising any question of principle, let us say 10,000*l.* a year.

Question of contribution by Ireland to Imperial expenditure.

9609. But practically no contribution?—No, practically, no contribution. However, it is important to avoid any question of principle. I think Great Britain will have to admit that the Imperial demands would be quite as well secured theoretically by a payment of 10,000*l.* as 2,000,000*l.*, and, therefore, all that the question of the amount of [illegible] amounts to is, the question of what it is fair to ask out of Ireland, and I hold most strongly, and I have got very good authority for it, that 10,000*l.* a year would at present be an ample amount to withdraw for Imperial contribution.

9610. I think the Treasury calculation is that the Imperial contribution now is about 2,000,000*l.*?—Yes.

9611. And that 2,000,000*l.* would have to be found somewhere?—I dealt with that a few moments since, and I hold that it would not have to be found if the economies which I have mentioned were effected.

9612. You mean if economies in Imperial expenditure were effected?—Yes.

9613. Do you wish to give the Commission any further reasons in support of your view that there should be no substantial Imperial contribution?—Yes. The first point is necessity. I think after the statement of the century Ireland cannot afford it, and that is the bottom argument that you cannot make a country, any more than an individual, pay what she has not got, and Ireland has not got it, and therefore she ought not to be made to pay it. I think when 50 years of a better system had been experienced probably the 10,000*l.* might be increased to 100,000*l.*, an amount which ought to be regarded as a very considerable amount, and that no settlement should be made that would require any more permanently than that. Then in the second place the tendency of recent times is to withdraw the defences of the country from Ireland. Scarcely any money is spent upon the defences of the Empire in Ireland, nor would they be likely to be required there. We have had a very good example of that in the recent Naval Works Loans Bill. There is a project here for spending something like 8,000,000*l.*, and nothing is to be spent in Ireland. I do not complain of that, but it is a recognition of the fact that it does not tend to the safety of the Empire to spend anything in Ireland. 2,000,000*l.* was to be spent at Dover; that is right, that is a place where we might be hit; 2,000,000*l.* at Devonport; that is an important place, 2,000,000*l.* at Gibraltar, and 1,000,000*l.* [illegible], which I tried to prevent being spent, at Portland Harbour; but these are all places along the south coast of England of importance where the enemy might strike a vital blow. Well, she can strike no vital blow in Ireland. If the French were foolish enough to go and land in Galway I think they ought to be allowed to go until it was quite convenient for the English to clear them out. There is therefore no necessity for expenditure in Ireland.

9614. (*Mr. Sexton.*) The development of steam has altogether changed the circumstances with regard to the military importance of Ireland, has it not?—Absolutely. I think every general says that the thing has completely changed, and that no general would be so unskilled or so foolish as to make any attack upon Ireland now with any prospect of damaging the British Empire. That is my second reason why the Imperial contribution is not required. My third reason is that the naval and military expenses of this country after all are mainly incurred for a very practical purpose, to preserve the Colonial Empire, which is profitable, and protects the food supply of this country, and is very essential to us in Great Britain. The food supply from the Colonies is one main source of the impoverishment of Ireland, and the profit of the colonial trade accumulates in the great cities of Great Britain, so it would be quite fair on both grounds for Ireland to be exempted from any considerable payment.

9615. (*Sir David Barbour.*) It is enjoyed partly by the Irish who reside in those places?—I do not think they enjoy it, and such enjoyment as they do get we make them pay for in the form of tax, and it would be convenient for the Government to get the money to spend here and leave it to the merchants to recognise the thing and get a price that would repay them in the sale of the goods. I think as these naval and military expenses are incurred for the benefit of the mercantile communities of Great Britain it is very unfair to levy any part of them on the peasantry of Ireland who are really impoverished by the commerce.

9616. (*Chairman.*) Are those the three grounds you wish to put before the Commission?—Yes.

9617. Have you gone at all into the question of proportion or considered whether the amount of property assessed to the Income Tax and death duties in the two countries does not suggest a ratio between the contributions of Ireland and of Great Britain?—I have studied those figures carefully that were presented in connection with the two Home Rule Bills, and the evidence that was put before the Commission on the point. It seems to me impossible to fix any proportion between the two countries based upon the Income Tax and the death duties if we take what we ask for as that proportion simply the gross amount of these two taxes.

9618. (*Mr. Sexton.*) The gross produce, do you mean?—Yes, if we take the gross produce of the two taxes of the Income Tax and the death duties without going into the question of what each nation has got to do with its gross produce. I think it is essential to do this before we arrive at any conclusion with respect to the relative wealth. Therefore, I have come to the conclusion that it is impossible to fix a proportion between the two countries. That is the great point the Commission is enquiring into, and I think it is impossible to fix any proportion between the two countries, because the resources of the two countries differ so much in their amount and their nature. The resources of the one country are constantly increasing and the resources of the other country are constantly diminishing. Therefore any proportion fixed will become wrong immediately; and I would point out that after all the great mistake of the Union was fixing the proportion between the two, that broke down in 17 years, and its existence for even that short period has been a curse to Ireland ever since. Therefore the only available precedent supports my view that you cannot fix the proportion between the two countries, because they are so different from one another.

9619. The proportion might be just at the moment, but do you suppose that the proportion fixed at the time of the Union was just when it was fixed?—I do not. I think it was most unjust, and I am very doubtful about the capacity of fixing the correct proportion at the moment, because the two things are so unlike one another. There is no relation between the two as I think.

9620. What you mean is that as the two countries are constantly moving in opposite directions the measure fixed at any moment ceases immediately to be in any degree even just when it is fixed?—Yes; and I go further than that because I say that where one country has an annual income of 1,500,000,000*l.*, it is a very dangerous thing for

Mr. T. Lough, M.P.

14 June 1895.

legislature to fix any relation between it and a poor country that has only got 80,000,000l. per annum of income.

9621. (*Sir David Barbour.*) But you propose a relation yourself—a payment of 10,000l.?—It was not based upon a relation.

9622. (*Mr. Sexton.*) A proportion?—It was not based upon any proportion, but it was a sort of amount that a [illegible] country like Ireland might afford to contribute for those purposes.

9623. (*Chairman.*) You say the income of Great Britain may be taken at how much?—1,500,000,000l., as [illegible] Dr. Giffen's figure.

9624. And the income of Ireland how much?—80,000,000l.

9625. What is your reason for saying that the payment was not based upon any proportion?—I argued that out very fully in my answers go on, but I will answer it now if you like.

9626. I will go on with your Memorandum. I think you are of opinion that some of the calculations which have been based on these comparisons are fallacious?—Yes, one extreme fallacy may be indicated. These comparisons are based upon the gross instead of the net figures, and they must give a totally wrong result for all purposes of estimating the relative tax-bearing capacities of the two countries. The average gross income per head in Great Britain is 33l. It is more than that now—it is 42l. or 44l. now, but it was 33l. in 1891.

9627. What do you mean by gross as distinguished from net?—I mean the average population divided into the total income of the country.

9628. What do you mean by "net"?—By "net" I mean the income that remains after a certain moderate amount which is the lowest one can live on fairly for subsistence is deducted.

9629. The living wage?—No, I do not adopt the word wage; it is the minimum cost of meagre subsistence.

9630. (*Sir David Barbour.*) With which it is possible to live with a certain degree of comfort?—I would rather put it with meagre subsistence. I do not want comfort brought in nor starvation.

9631. Is it the minimum sum on which it is possible to maintain an existence?—Yes, on which it is possible to maintain a [illegible] decent existence, at [illegible] by a little [illegible].

9632. (*Chairman.*) Do you take any particular standard, for instance, to the standard of an English workman, or the standard of an Irish peasant, or the standard of a Hindoo?—I will take them all.

9633. Because in each of those cases the sum that would be required would be very different, would it not?—I will take them all, for although the sum that is required is very different yet the circumstances are different. The Hindoo lives in a sunny climate where he can live cheap. The Irishman may perhaps have favourable circumstances, but I think we can fix a common sum between Great Britain and Ireland.

9634. Therefore you assume for your purposes some sum which is necessary for existence?—Yes.

9635. And you take what is above that as the income of the country which is properly the subject of taxation?—Yes, that is my argument.

9636. (*Mr. Sexton.*) You adopt the figure as suggested by Dr. Giffen of 12l. a year?—Yes.

9637. I suppose you are aware that the average cost of supplying the inmate of an Irish workhouse only with food and clothing is 8l. a year?—Yes; I have not compared that figure yet, but I am coming to it; and when I come to it I will give a comparison for showing that it is not an unfair figure in Ireland. Now, to resume, the average gross income per head in Great Britain is 33l.; in Ireland it is 15l. From that it is assumed that the tax-bearing capacity per head is as 33 to 15. But this is obviously a wrong deduction. From both the gross amounts must be deducted a sum sufficient to live on. This is fixed at 12l. and the balance is the tax-bearing capacity. When this sum is deducted in each case, we find that the tax-bearing income in Great Britain is 21l. per head; in Ireland 3l. per head; so that the relation becomes as 21 is to 3 instead of as 33 is to 15. Therefore, to establish equality, only one-seventh of the tax paid in Great Britain should be demanded in Ireland per head of the population. And then it is a remarkable thing that that again brings us at once to the relation that existed before the Union. The moment we begin to take a reasonable view of the thing we get back to the figures of 1791.

9638. Your argument in principle is the same as Dr. Giffen's?—Yes, in principle.

9639. (*Chairman.*) Do not you think that 12l. is a large amount to take as necessary for subsistence in Ireland?—I think when you remember that 10,000,000l. of the produce of Ireland is monopolised by a few individuals, that is the rent of the landlords, and that the landlords are only allowed in our calculations to stand as taking 12l. per head per annum, when taken over the whole of Ireland, 12l. really means about 9l. or 10l. for the whole population of the country when the absentee landlords are left out. If you include them all I think 12l. for that reason is the lowest average which you can get to.

9640. (*Mr. Sexton.*) Even though the conditions of life in Ireland may be in some respects inferior, do you consider it would be tolerable to fix a lower minimum of subsistence for Ireland than for England in this calculation, thereby indicating that a larger proportion of the small income of the Irishman should be deducted than of the large income of the Englishman?—I do not think it would be safe at all, and I have had a large experience of working men, both in Ireland and in England, and of the lives of both people in both countries in connection with my business over there as well as here, and I do not think it would be safe for the Commission to adopt any lower standard in one than in the other.

9641. Would it be just, as a matter of fiscal law, to set up a barrier, and to say so much more of your income shall be taxed than of the other's?—No, I do not think it would; besides I do not think that food is generally cheaper in Ireland than it is in Great Britain. The rent of the same land is higher in Ireland than it is in Great Britain. The rent of houses is higher I think in Ireland—indeed much higher—than it is in Great Britain, even in London we can get houses of a much superior class built.

9642. They are not houses of the same class, are they?—Yes; the rent of houses of the same class I believe is cheaper in Great Britain than it is in Ireland, or as cheap; tea is as cheap as it is in England, and, therefore, all the means of subsistence are just as much available in Great Britain as in Ireland.

9643. Obviously all those various articles of food and other necessaries of life imported from Great Britain into Ireland are somewhat dearer than they are here, are they not?—Yes; and coal is dearer, which is a large item, and that has all to be carried from Great Britain.

9644. (*Sir David Barbour.*) The items that you export are cheaper?—Yes.

9645. (*Chairman.*) Supposing the whole standard of life in either of the two countries were to be raised, would you say that that amount of 12l. ought to be increased, and that the only taxable income was that which remained after paying for the higher standard of life?—I do not think I would.

9646. There is no doubt whatever that the standard of life amongst workmen in England has risen greatly within the last 50 years, has it not?—Yes.

9647. Would you say that income put the amount of income which was to be subject to taxation at a different point? Supposing, for instance, that the standard was equivalent to 10l. a year 20 years ago, and that it is equivalent to 12l. a year now, would you say that the surplus that could be made subject to taxation was that which was above 10l. then and that which is above 12l. now?—I think the growth would not be so rapid as what you suggest, but yet there might be a small growth. The living of people at a particular moment is relative to the wants that have been generated by the progress of the world up to that time, and relative to the degree of prosperity that is being enjoyed by other countries, therefore, the amount might rise a trifle, but it would depend upon circumstances. I do not think the tendency has been for the amount of 12l. to rise in either of these countries for the last 40 or 50 years, because 12l. purchases more now than it did before, therefore I think that checks it.

Taxable capacity.

9648. (*Mr. Sexton.*) The real point is that if you want to of equal capacity to bear taxation one man or two countries which have different incomes, you do not impose an equality of sacrifice, because the man of the larger income finds the taxation almost immeasurably less than the man with the smaller income, does he not?—That is so.

9649. (*Sir David Barbour.*) Will not that depend also upon the classes which there may happen to be among the men of the larger income?—I think it is modified very slightly. If these claims that you refer to are of a par-

[illegible] character they are a deduction from his income, and he is not a man of a larger income, but if they are of a character that he can use his judgment about, and income or dividends, then he can arrange for his taxation before he supplies them.

9650. (Chairman.) The point I want rather to get at is whether you can assume any absolute standard of living above which the income becomes taxable and below which it is not taxable, or whether that standard is not rather a thing varying with the different conditions of life with different people in different ranks of life, as well as in different countries?—I think the question may be answered by saying it is absolutely necessary for people who have got to tax a country to form a standard in their own mind—there must be a standard—there must be a standard in India, but it is relative to what will do for those there.

9651. Supposing the standard rises, does the man's capacity to bear taxation therefore diminish?—It does, slightly. I say the standard rises very little, but, undoubtedly, when the standard rises then his capacity to bear taxation becomes diminished.

9652. By the adoption of that principle of a standard and a taxable surplus you may get to some very curious conclusions, may you not?—Yes, you may. It takes a long time to alter these standards, but they do get altered. You will not get men to live in England now in the way in which they lived in Anglo-Saxon times; they will demand clothes, you will not get them to go about with skins over their shoulders.

9653. I think you suggest that a similar result to that which you have just given may be brought out in another way?—Yes, I have been talking hitherto of the result per head of the population. If we now take the figures of both countries you will see that they lead us to exactly the same conclusion. I have prepared a short table which is printed in my brief of evidence which shows that the total income in 1891 in Great Britain was 1,300,000,000*l*.

9654. The evidence is that it was 1,400,000,000*l*.?—Yes, it had been corrected. It was then 1,[illegible],000,000*l*., and in Ireland it was 65,000,000*l*. When we deduct the subsistence of 12*l*. per head per annum in the two countries we get the result out of [illegible],000,000*l*. as the taxable capacity of Great Britain, and 7,341,000*l*. as the taxable capacity of Ireland. Now that amount would be made [illegible] still if we corrected the figures, so we had better let them stand. The total of local and Imperial taxation in Great Britain is 118,000,000*l*., roundly—that was in 1890-91, and in Ireland it was 10½ millions, so that the whole of the Irish income according to this is paid in taxation—the whole of the taxable surplus is paid in taxation, and I believe myself we do not put the thing at all too strongly when we say that in Great Britain we only take 13·60 per cent. of it.

9655. (*The O'Conor Don.*) Where do you get the 10,000,000*l*. for rent if the whole is paid in taxation?—That is provided for before.

9656. You have to take that out of the 65,000,000*l*., have you not?—That is part of the cost of subsistence. That is what makes the 12*l*. a perfectly moderate amount for Ireland. The meaning of that is that the landlord levies about ten times as much or twenty times as much as he is entitled to.

9657. (*Sir David Barbour.*) If you took 13*l*. per head you would find the taxable quantity would become a minus quantity—what meaning would you attach to that?—The meaning would be that you would have put your calculation a little too high; but it is going back upon our [illegible].

9658. (*Mr. Sexton.*) Might not the meaning of it be that the people were living in such a miserable condition that they would be living upon what was below a reasonable minimum?—We could get a Government without much taxation; it is an entire mistake to suppose that it is the chief part of the duty of a Government to put on taxes. In Ireland years ago a great deal of the local authorities got their income from property apart from taxation, and the destruction of that local property and the substitution of taxes, as I tried to make out before, has led unhappily to that agricultural country being ruined.

9659. (*Sir David Barbour.*) But if the Government received the income from certain property that would be a deduction from the income of the people, would it not?—Yes, there would be to a certain extent.

9660. (*Mr. Sexton.*) You said it was a percentage of income which is now not got from property which has been alienated?—Yes.

9661. (*Sir David Barbour.*) But if you adopt a sum of 13*l*. per head, you get a minus quantity as the taxable quantity, how would you tax that minus quantity?—It would show that you had put the amount too high in making 13*l*.

9662. You must, in fact, adopt some figure that will leave you a reasonable amount of taxation to tax, must you not?—No, you must not, but you must put a figure which will enable people to live, but it must not be too high a figure.

9663. (*Mr. Sexton.*) In order to show that you have put a figure which was above the actual cost of subsistence, and that therefore the standard of living in that country was lower than it could be reasonably put at if the country was in a reasonably prosperous condition?—That is about it.

9664. You are of opinion that this plan of basing the contribution upon the gross revenue explains why the proportion of Ireland was fixed so high as it was in the discussions on the Home Rule Bill in 1886 and 1893?—Yes, I think so. We see that where the necessities of the population are taken out of the total Irish income the residue is very small indeed, whereas when the necessities of the population in Great Britain are taken out of the total income, there is a very large surplus, and that shows in my mind that you must not found the proportion simply upon the gross results of Income Tax and death duties collected in the two countries, and that is how people got at such a high figure as 4 or 5 per cent.

9665. Do you think Ireland would have been able to pay such a high contribution as was suggested in the Home Rule Bill of 1893?—I do not think so, and I stated so at the time of the discussion.

9666. (*Mr. Sexton.*) And not only thinks Dr. Giffen but Sir Edward Hamilton has said that "perhaps a better test "of the amount which the taxpayer can afford to pay for "being governed, protected, and educated is the residue "of income remaining after the bare necessaries of life "have been met?"—Yes, I read all through Sir Edward Hamilton's Memorandum, and I do not think I differ in principle at all from him. I think, therefore, that safe conclusions can only be drawn with regard to the relative tax-paying power of two countries from such figures when the population and other conditions of the two countries were somewhat assimilated to one another, instead of being, as in the case of Ireland and Great Britain, so extremely divergent.

9667. (*Chairman.*) Then, I understand, you think it is very difficult to get at any proportion at all?—That is my argument all through my paper that the figures are too far apart to afford a just basis for proportion.

9668. Can you state briefly how these Income Tax figures may be used safely so far as they can be used at all in calculating the respective contributions of the two countries?—In my opinion, the figures do afford valuable evidence, but it must be worked out. The steps are to take the gross amount assessed to Income Tax. To it add an estimate of the value of all other property. From this deduct what each nation has to provide for the support of its people respectively, and the proportion between the totals which remain is the true approximation to the taxable capacity of the two countries. That is practically summing up what I have said.

9669. And that does not really differ very much from what Dr. Giffen has stated?—I do not think so.

9670. Then I believe you wish to call attention to the evidence given by Dr. Giffen with regard to the tax-bearing capacity of the working classes in Ireland?—Yes, there is one point there in respect of which I differ from him a little in detail that I would like to mention. In the evidence given on the 20th March Dr. Giffen worked out the tax-bearing capacity of the working classes in Ireland at one-eighteenth of that of the same class in Great Britain, the average income of one being about 20*l*. and that of the other about [illegible] per annum, and the numbers in Ireland being one-ninth of those in Great Britain. In that evidence Dr. Giffen appeared to lend some support to the calculations that have been previously made by Sir Edward Hamilton and over the Home Rule Bill. True, Dr. Giffen recognises the necessity of making an allowance of 13*l*. per head for subsistence, but he did not carry that deduction to its logical conclusion, for his argument is summed up in these words: "If you are going upon "actual income, and considering Ireland's portion to be "one-twenty-fifth, you might reduce it still further, say "to a thirtieth, or something like that, to make some "allowance for the fact that its taxable resources upon the

Mr. T. Lough, M.P. [illegible]

"... some incomes are less in proportion than those of Great Britain. Some rough mode of calculation of that kind is all you can do." Now my feeling is that you cannot get upon actual incomes" [illegible] the income I have already stated, are justly "[illegible] Ireland's proportion to be only one-twenty-fifth." Surely we must consider what each country has got to do with its resources. The wages referred to are the earnings of the bread-winner. Let us suppose that in each country he supports five of the population. Before there is any taxable income the living of four persons must be deducted from his earnings. When this is done it will be seen that the English working man has [illegible] a year of taxable income, but the working man in Ireland has no taxable income whatever. He cannot provide a living of 12*l.*, or 10*l.*, or even 8*l.* per annum for four persons. He has got no surplus. Therefore, I cannot agree that "some rough calculation of that kind is all you can do." We can recognise that the working man in Ireland has no taxable income. Therefore, no proportion can be established between him and the inhabitant of Great Britain.

9671. Do you not think that 16*l.* per head is too large an amount for the subsistence of the working classes in Ireland?—I suggested that a moment since, but I put it here, that even if you take 10*l.* or 8*l.* it will come to the same thing.

9672. Do you not think it desirable that the working classes should contribute something to the support of the country?—No, certainly not, if you can avoid taxing them. We ought to let everybody off if we can, and tax certainly those who can pay most first. I would be very willing to let every person off.

9673-4. I would like to ask you then whether even a direct tax upon income or upon property must not always in the end fall more or less upon the working population?—They reach them in that way.

9675. You cannot avoid taxing the working classes, notwithstanding you make your taxation direct, and put it only on the comparatively rich?—I am prepared to admit in the way in which you now put it, but that does not directly tax them.

9676. I mean that you do not avoid taxing the working classes by making your taxation direct?—That I readily agree to, and seeing that they have got to pay that tax indirectly through the rich, we ought to be very glad if we possibly can to let them off.

9677. (*Sir David Barbour.*) Do not you think it desirable that a man who has a vote should feel that he is liable to pay taxation?—I do not think it is of any importance.

9678. Do you think it is desirable that there should be one class which controls the expenditure, and another which bears it?—I think so long as you have got a country in which one class monopolises most of the wealth, it is a very desirable thing if you can, to make them bear the chief burdens of taxation.

9679. That is not quite an answer to my question. My question is this: is it a desirable thing in any country to have one class which controls the expenditure, and an entirely different class which bears it directly?—That question was answered by what Lord Farrer said a moment since. He showed that this class which you say controls the expenditure——

9680. I did not say that any class controlled expenditure. I ask, as a matter of argument, is it a desirable thing to have in any country, one class controlling the expenditure, and another class which apparently bears the whole of the taxation?—It depends. I do not think it is. It depends upon whether these people lay undue burdens upon the other people who have most of the wealth.

9681. (*Mr. Sexton.*) I suppose you would say that any free country must control the public affairs of that country, and that if there be in that country a wealthy class, they should bear a share of the burdens in proportion to their wealth?—Yes, exactly.

9682. (*Chairman.*) I think the object of Sir David Barbour's question was to ascertain whether it is not desirable that the working classes, if they are to have a vote, should both bear the taxation, and should know that they bear it, not only that they should pay it indirectly by the loss of employment, and so on, but that they should know that they pay taxes of some kind, and feel that they pay them?—I think it would not make them a bit happier to know that they pay taxes.

9683. (*Sir David Barbour.*) But is it not desirable in the interests of the public good and the general welfare, that the men who have a voice, or perhaps a controlling voice, as regards expenditure, should also in the case of increased expenditure have to bear a portion of that increased expenditure?—If the circumstances were at all equal in the country, then it would certainly be desirable.

Mr. T. Lough, M.P.

[illegible]

Taxable capacity of [illegible]

9684. (*Mr. Sexton.*) Does it appear to you that in order to impress the ordinary citizen with a sense of responsibility it is desirable to place taxes upon him if those taxes place a burden upon him, which is out of due proportion between him and the rich citizens?—I do not think it desirable, certainly not.

9685. (*Chairman.*) But you would say at the same time that as the taxation must fall upon him, it is desirable that he should know that it falls upon him, would you not?—I do not see anything in that point. The ideal state would seem to me to be that each person should have a fair share of the wealth, and that each person should also pay a fair share of the taxes, and have a fair share of the responsibility.

9686. (*Mr. Sexton.*) A man should bear a fair proportion of the tax whether he is a voter or not, the circumstance that he is a voter is no reason why the tax should be laid upon him?—No; Sir David Barbour asked me whether he ought not to pay a fair share of the taxes without going into the question of having a fair share of the wealth. That is where I differ from him.

9687. (*Sir David Barbour.*) My question is, is it not desirable that the people who control the expenditure in a country should bear equally some proportion of the taxation which necessarily follows from an increase of expenditure?—Yes, but is that you are not saying quite enough. You say, is it not fair that he should pay something, but you say nothing about what he should receive or what he can afford.

9688. I do not say the considerations to which you refer are not matters to be taken into account. I merely ask you, do you or do you not accept the general principle that the people who control the expenditure of a country should immediately and openly bear some proportion of the taxation which necessarily follows from the increase of expenditure?—I think the relation of these tax-paying capacity must be dependent not upon their control of public affairs, but upon the share of the wealth they possess.

9689. Do you think that what I have stated is a thing that should be taken into consideration at all?—I think you have carefully excluded the one element which fits the person to pay taxes.

9690. You think the matter that I brought forward is not a matter that ought really to be taken into consideration?—I think there is a tendency to take it too much into consideration.

9691. Do you think it ought to be taken into consideration or not?—Not unless you can prove he has wealth sufficient to pay the taxes.

9692-3. (*Mr. Sexton.*) Taxation depends upon resources, does it not?—Yes, upon the purse.

9694. (*Chairman.*) But if direct taxation must ultimately fall in some form or another upon him, he must pay the taxes, and Sir David Barbour's question is whether he should do that in some way or other openly, so that he should know it?—I am in favour of direct taxation if that will answer the question, I think all indirect taxation should be done away with.

9695. (*Sir David Barbour.*) You are altogether against indirect taxation?—Yes, taking it all round I am against indirect taxation, and I am in favour of direct taxation.

9696. (*Mr. Sexton.*) But you do agree that, when a citizen is taxed, it is just as well that he should know it?—Yes, I do.

9697. (*Chairman.*) From your standpoint then, what is the true proportion in the case of Ireland if we assume that any proportion can be fixed?—I think no good results can be arrived at if we shrink from conclusions, and there seems to be no escape, if there is any truth in figures, from the fact that the taxable income of Great Britain is 300,000,000*l.*, and the taxable income of Ireland is something between 10,000,000*l.* and 15,000,000*l.* If it is the former sum Ireland should pay one-thirtieth, of whatever Great Britain pays, if it is the latter Ireland should pay one-twentieth; and this proportion will diminish rapidly as Great Britain continues to advance. It is a most serious thing on that point to remember that the advance in Great Britain is 10,000,000*l.* a year more or less. That is Mr. Giffen's calculation, that for the last 10 years we have advanced 10,000,000*l.* a year; so that we really advance

Taxable capacity of Great Britain and Ireland compared.

Mr. T. Lough, M.P. — 11 June 1895.

in respect of each year's income almost as much as what the total annual income of Ireland is. This proportion will diminish rapidly as Great Britain continues to advance, therefore the statement of it does not qualify my opinion, that it is impossible to fix any fair proportion. These figures again bring us back to something like the relative amount of taxes paid by each of the two countries before the Union.

5698. I understand that you do not wish the figures to conflict with what you have already said about the impossibility of fixing a proportion between the two countries?—No, I desire to stick to that opinion all through my evidence.

Amount of taxation which should be imposed upon Ireland.

5699. If the proportion suggested by you were adopted it would afford no Imperial contribution, nor even meet the Irish charges?—No, it would not meet the general Irish charges. Such a contribution would provide no assistance to Imperial outlay nor even defray the necessary charges in Ireland. It is only introduced to show how small Ireland's taxes would be if they bore the same proportion to the country's wealth as the taxes do in Great Britain.

5700. Do you think that a poor country can afford to pay a larger proportion of its wealth in taxes than a rich country can?—I do not think that a poor country can, strictly speaking, afford to pay a larger proportion of taxation than a rich country, but it is the same with a country as with poor individuals. It must depend upon the wealth of the one with which the comparison is made, and for many years to come I think Ireland will have to pay for the expenses of her government a sum in excess of what the inhabitants of Great Britain would have to pay for her expenses of Government.

5701. Supposing that Ireland were at this moment entirely independent she would no doubt have to pay for whatever Government she might choose to have of her own a larger sum in proportion to her wealth than the inhabitant of Great Britain would have to pay?—Yes, supposing that Ireland were at this moment entirely independent, and supposing she had the most economical statesmen in the world, I think, taking all the conditions into account she would have to pay more than we pay.

5702. (Mr. Sexton.) That means, I suppose, that a small country really has to pay more than a large country?—Yes, it has to pay more than a large one.

After an interval.

The Right Hon. The O'Conor Don, Chairman.

Public expenditure in Ireland.

5703. (Chairman.) We come now to the question of expenditure. You have seen it suggested that if large expenditure out of the taxes takes place in Ireland the people will be able to bear a greater amount of taxation. Do you think that is the case?—No, I do not think the amount of the expenditure at all tends to enable the people to bear taxation, and I think that if the situation could have been saved by such means as this, the distress in Ireland would not have arisen. As I have already said there have been nearly 30,000 soldiers in Ireland throughout most of the century; there has also been a most expensive Imperial Constabulary maintained which increased in numbers as the population diminished, but the presence of these men, well clothed, well fed, and treated has not prevented the village from sinking into want. The police barrack is now often the only building remaining on the spot where, in my recollection, a village stood.

5704. Do you think any harm arises from this large expenditure?—I was just going to add that the large judicial establishment in Dublin does not seem to me to confer any benefit upon the general community; I think there is harm in this large expenditure. It seems to me the opposite of beneficial. It creates a privileged class whose existence is no benefit to the people upon whom they are quartered, and attempts should be made to do justice to the wealth-producing and hard-working part of the population, rather than to increase the number of half idle officials.

5705. Are we to understand that you recommend a decrease of expenditure as the first step to be taken?—No; I always wish to guard myself against recommending any decrease of expenditure until after the taxes are swept away.

Public loans and grants in Ireland.

5706. You are aware that it has been suggested that the system of granting loans to Ireland may have to some extent compensated for the burdens of taxation; what do you think upon that point?—Well, I do not agree with that conclusion. I fear it only increases the evil. The system of granting loans establishes undesirable relations between the Government and the individual. I am inclined to think that such facilities should only be of a temporary character to tide over some great national crisis; for instance, I could imagine a system of granting loans at any period to enable the people to buy out their land and alter the system of landlordism in the country, but granting these small sums at all times for a great variety of purposes seems to me to be questionably beneficial to the country. The loans have got to be repaid, and the interest on them; and I do not think it is wise to bring a system like that into a part of the administration of a country. It seems to me to be open to all the objections that buying on credit rather than for cash in private affairs is open to. And then to suggest that the system of loans is a compensation for misgovernment of Ireland seems to me just like suggesting that if you take away the estate of a man whose affairs may be in your hands, you can compensate him by keeping him going on a system of loans at an exorbitant interest.

5707. Do you approve of the system of making grants to local authorities out of the Imperial taxation?—You mean that the Commission should recommend instead of reducing the taxation, the granting of loans.

5708. Going back to the previous question, do you think the grants to local authorities out of Imperial taxation is a satisfactory system?—I do not think so at all, because it does not seem to me to afford any assurance that the money would find its way back to reimburse the poorest people who are oppressed by the original taxation, and that is what you have got to provide for. I think the present system of local administration is quite sufficiently burdensome without increasing its weight, and then the grants that are made from the Treasury in Great Britain, it appears to me, go generally to relieve the rich ratepayer, while the great bulk of the taxes to provide these grants are paid by the poor.

5709. And what suggestion do you wish to make with regard to the best means of bringing the taxation of Ireland within the limits of the capacity of that country?—My suggestion is simply that we must go in the shortest way about what we have got to do. We think the taxes too high, then take off the taxes and reduce them to a proper amount. I believe no outlet will be found except that of reversing the policy of 1853, and altogether reconsidering the fiscal system. The policy of obtaining so large a proportion of the revenue from taxes on a few articles of diet operates unfairly in Ireland. That country pays five-sevenths of its present revenue by these indirect taxes, while Great Britain pays only two-fifths.

5710. (Mr. Sexton.) I think you will find it is somewhat more in Great Britain than two-fifths. I see in last year the total revenue from taxes in England was 60,000,000*l*., and the Customs and Excise amounted to 34,000,000*l*., which would be more near to three-fifths?—Does that include Scotland?

5711. The revenue from Scotland is 8,300,000*l*., and the Excise and Customs yield 5,600,000*l*. I think you will find if you enquire that the indirect taxes in Great Britain are three-fifths and the direct taxes two-fifths?—Perhaps so. However, the amount contributed in Ireland is larger than in Great Britain.

5712. (Chairman.) That is your point with regard to taxation?—Yes, that is my point. I do not think the precise proportion is quite so important. Then it seems to me that these few articles in one country, taking those in Great Britain first, form but portions of an ample dietary largely composed of bread, meat, cheese, fruit, and other such commodities, while in Ireland they are staples in a very limited dietary.

5713. Do you not think that it would cause great inconvenience to have different rates of duties on articles of consumption in different parts of the United Kingdom?—I do not think that the inconvenience that would arise from different rates of duty would be at all so serious as we are inclined to think. The main argument in favour of equalising the duties was that it would establish fiscal unity throughout the United Kingdom, but there is not fiscal unity at present; there is a railway duty, taxes on servants, carriages and land which it has been found impossible to enforce in Ireland. This may well lead us to enquire whether a further variation in the incidence of taxation is not demanded. The duties are levied for purposes of revenue solely. The revenue is required in Great Britain; it is not required in Ireland, therefore why levy it?

5714. Do you think that any real harm can be done to Ireland, even by the over-taxation of whiskey, if we grant that such takes place?—I think so. I do not think you can find a more direct way of oppressing the Irish people than overtaxing whiskey. It is to be borne in mind that whiskey, on which the heaviest impost has always been laid, is one of the leading articles of Irish manufacture, and is little made in England or Wales.

9715. What do you think with regard to tobacco as that a luxury?—I think tobacco is of far more importance, again, in Ireland than it is in Great Britain. As I said a moment ago, in the case of the duty, tobacco is one of the very few stimulants or comforts that the Irish have got, and it is far more essential to them than it is to the people of Great Britain, just in the same way as we find that tobacco is regarded as a far greater necessity in Germany and in many continental countries than here. I think the continental view of tobacco applies much more closely to Ireland than it does to Great Britain, and Ireland pays a million and a quarter, which is a terrible impost for a poor country to have to pay out of its pipe. Tobacco is a great Irish manufacture, and I think it would be grown in Ireland if it were allowed to be grown. There was evidence laid before the Royal Commission in 1861 about tobacco planting in Ireland in 1830, and it appears to me there is no doubt that the growth of tobacco would be developed in Ireland if the Revenue Department allowed it.

9716. I understand that you wish to call attention to a portion of the Channel Islands as an example of taxation?—Yes, I think the Channel Islands are an excellent illustration of some of the mistakes that is made with regard to Ireland, and of the best means of curing the mistake. In the Channel Islands no duties are levied on these articles, and the extraordinary prosperity of these little agricultural communities depends in no small degree on such immunity from taxes. In the description of these islands we read that, "Taxation is trifling. Customs duties very light. "Living cheap, pauperism unknown."

9717. (*Mr. Sexton.*) Do they make any contribution to the Imperial revenue?—Yes, they do; they make about such a contribution to the Imperial revenue as I suggested Ireland should make. If Ireland made the same contribution in proportion to her population that the Channel Islands make, she would pay about 10,000*l*. a year.

9718. We have been told that they make no contribution?—That is a mistake—there is a little balance. "The "bulk of the holdings contain only five to eight acres; "20 acres is a large farm. The exports to England "amount to 10*l*. for every acre of land, the Imperial contributions to [illegible] per annum for the five years ending in "[illegible]."

9719. Is that a direct payment as it is the produce of taxation?—Yes, it is a direct payment; it is a cheque and [illegible] as far as I can make out. I draw my [illegible] little arrangement about it, but that is the Imperial contribution. The population keeps on increasing; in 1881 it was [illegible]; in 1891, [illegible]. I think that one can make no difference upon this question, and I see no reason why equally good results should not arise in Ireland from a fresh adoption of a similar policy. I would like also to say that I believe in the Isle of Man we have a somewhat similar system. I have written to the [illegible] for some particulars which I have not received yet; but I believe that in the Isle of Man there are different duties, and although the duties are collected by the British Customs authorities the difference in the amount of duty makes no difference. The British authorities collect them although the amounts vary.

9720. (*Chairman.*) The rate differs?—Yes, the rate differs in the amount of some of the articles that are collected by the British authorities, and the system is found to work very easily.

9721. And what reform of taxation would you actually suggest?—I think that all indirect taxation ought to be done away with except a small tax upon spirits and beer. It appears to me to be necessary to get something, so I suppose I am influenced in favour of the English idea and in getting it out of spirits and beer. A duty of 5*s*. per gallon on spirits would produce [illegible], and a duty of 1*s*. 6*d*. per barrel on beer would yield [illegible]. All the direct taxation might be preserved as at present, and this amounts to [illegible].

9722. (*Mr. Sexton.*) That is including the miscellaneous revenue, is it not?—Yes, including the miscellaneous revenue certainly. I also include these, I think it is very important in Ireland. In this simple way we would obtain a revenue of [illegible], which I think would be amply sufficient under a re-organised system for the maintenance of an efficient central government in Ireland. After a few years, when the results of the present bad system had been got rid of, it would, no doubt, be possible to reduce this to three millions, or even a smaller amount. The tax of 2*s*. 6*d*. per gallon levied on whiskey in 1853 would now produce [illegible], and 1*s*. on beer would yield 103,000*l*.; making with the present direct taxation 3,013,000*l*. Now, in support of these figures I would like to point out that in the former, under Sir Robert Peel we were not far from these figures. I see that in 1850 the Imperial taxes were only 4,861,[illegible]. You will see that on page 4 of my evidence. So that if that amount in 1850 (and I think it was a little less, about 1846) were reduced in proportion to the reduction in population, you would get just such an amount as I have suggested, so that it really only amounts to the suggestion that we go back to the period before 1853.

9723. (*Chairman.*) Have you considered the objections that have been raised to this change?—I have considered them.

9724. Do you not think that a great reduction, for instance, in the tax on whiskey would lead to an increase of drunkenness?—I do not think it would. I stated my opinion fully upon that matter. It seems to me that the reduction of the tax on whiskey would increase the well-being of the people. They would have to pay less for a necessary stimulant so far as it is a necessary stimulant, and they would have more money available for clothes and other things.

9725. You do not think that they would drink any more than they do now?—No, I do not think so. I think hard drinking arises from a miserable condition of life, and we are keeping them in that miserable condition of life now.

9726. Would not any attempt to levy differential duties be regarded as a retrograde step after the legislation of the last 40 years?—I think it would, and that is the reason I gave it very full consideration. It would be regarded as a retrograde step, but when we come close up to the question we find very little objection to it. Whiskey is not a British manufacture, there is no trade done from England to Ireland in whiskey, the trade comes the other way. It is between Ireland and Great Britain. Therefore, England is not interested in this question; and on the other hand, I do not think the Irish would object to it; they would not be likely to either make or sell any less whiskey in Ireland because the duty was for a gallon instead of 10*s*. 6*d*. Equally as regards tobacco manufacture; I think tobacco would be a great deal more made and consumed in Ireland, especially if the population increased, if there was only a duty of 6*d*. or 1*s*. a pound upon it, and the fact of a heavy duty being imposed in England would not put them in a worse position than they are at present; and with regard to tea, we would find a larger market in Ireland for tea if the people had no duty to pay upon it. These things are not manufactured in this country to any considerable extent, therefore, none of the objections that might apply to protective duties could be urged against a reduction of the duties such as I suggest.

9727. Then, coming to the next point, do you consider that there might be a great saving and economy in various public departments?—Yes, but before I come to that question, the one inconvenience that I do admit would be the Customs relations between the two countries as being inconvenient to travellers. That is doubtless a point that would have to be well considered, I believe that the Isle of Man system would throw a great deal of light upon it. I think there is no search in the Isle of Man; it is arranged somehow by the Customs; but at any rate, even that point would not prevent my recommending a difference in the duty. I think it would be better that the few who travel should suffer inconvenience than that the whole population should be oppressed as they are at present.

9728. Then with regard to the last question, do you think that much might be done in the way of economy in the expenditure of the country?—Yes, I think a great deal of economy might be practised with regard to the Irish charges. I was going to furnish a budget, but I thought it was going into too much detail, and that it would require a great deal more consideration than one can give it in the hasty way in which it is necessary to prepare this evidence, but it is easy to lay one's finger on the charge for police and courts of justice, and other items, and say that they could be largely reduced. I think everybody agrees that there might be perhaps a million and a half of money saved in those items, but I think a great deal more than this will require to be done before the Irish establishment is placed on a moderate or proper scale appropriate to a poor agricultural country. I think that the expenses of the Local Government Board,

[Margin notes: [illegible], Esq. — 14 June 1895 — Proposed re-adjustment of taxation in Ireland. — Proposed economies in Irish administration.]

Board of Works, prisons, county courts, Chief Secretary's office, are a great deal more than a poor country like Ireland can afford to pay, and the enormous sum spent on public works and buildings throughout Ireland also calls loudly for economy, and it would be necessary to look at the matter as if we had a clean slate before us, and provide simple institutions which would be necessary to the country at the least possible expense.

9729. (Mr. Sexton.) You would not look to Great Britain as an example?—I think in the nature of the case it will appear to you that Great Britain is the worst country in the world we could look to for any precedents, merely because Great Britain is the richest country in the world, and she can afford most elaborate institutions, while Ireland is one of the poorest countries in the world, therefore it must have very economical institutions. I think Switzerland would be a country from which ideas might be obtained, Norway and Sweden and other continental countries, and also from our own Colonies, as to how arrangements might be made suitable to the wants of a poor nation.

9730. And small countries of moderate wealth and without an extensive commerce, as mainly farming communities?—Yes, exactly, and with a population somewhat near the population of Ireland, and the same class of occupations for the people.

9731. (Sir David Barbour.) But is it not the case that in point of fact we in Ireland rather go beyond the British standard with regard to the cost of these institutions?—Yes. We have gone ourselves beyond Irish institutions.

9732. (Mr. Sexton.) We have imitated England until we have utterly surpassed her?—Yes, we have.

9733. Of course, it is England that has done it?—Yes, England has one flooded Ireland with regard to Irish expenditure, but I meant also to include Scotland as a country from which ideals might be obtained. I believe all the charges in Scotland are really moderate charges—the local charges—and although it suffers a little, I think, from Imperial arrangements, yet it is in a great deal better position than Ireland.

9734. (Chairman.) Would not a large expense arise in connection with pensions in doing away with these offices in the transition from the present system to one such as you have sketched?—Yes, I quite admit that that is a difficulty. For the first few years there would be the expense of pensioning for the officers that might be displaced. This would no doubt involve a considerable extra charge, but it would grow less every year and would gradually disappear altogether. I do not think it would present any serious obstacle, because the charges for dealing with the officers would not be more than they will be at present in any one year under the existing system, and there would be an improvement in the system in every year as we went along.

9735. Do you think that economy is as necessary in the local expenditure as it is in the central administration?—I do; I think it necessary to introduce just as much economy in local expenses throughout Ireland if any change is to be made in the bad system which we now find in the rural districts.

Economy in local taxation, proposed abolition of workhouses.

9736. I believe that you wish particularly to call attention to the number of workhouses and to suggest that a considerable reduction in the number of those establishments is practicable?—Yes. I think the introduction of the English Poor Law in the crude way in which it was introduced into the Irish localities was a serious blow to Ireland. I think the workhouse system would have to be abolished altogether or reduced to the most humble proportions. There are now 163 workhouses. Within a very few years the number might be reduced to 32, one for each county, and the extra four for the four large cities. The present number was fixed when the population was nearly twice as large as it is now, and such institutions were built on such an extensive scale because the famine had previously commenced and every effort was put forward to meet the emergency. Since 1861 the workhouses have been half empty, and, as shown by figures already quoted, outdoor relief has grown up steadily in the place of the workhouse system of indoor maintenance. I do not think you will find in any agricultural country like Ireland such a system as the Irish workhouse system, it is only suited to a country where there are great cities and where there is very little agriculture.

9737. Are you in favour of outdoor relief?—Yes, certainly, especially in Ireland. I think outdoor relief would be much more economical; it would avoid the home being broken up and avoid the great charges for the maintenance of the staff and other expenses.

9738. Do not you think it would be much more difficult to check it?—I think it would require to be carefully checked; but may I point out that in the report of 1834, the great historic document on which the present Poor Law system was founded, the examples of extravagant expenditure are all in England. If I remember rightly that was the experience in English country districts, and there was never in those early years at any rate, any proof from Ireland that the system of outdoor relief would be objectionable.

9739. (Sir David Barbour.) That was the Report of 1834?—Yes.

9740. Was there any system of outdoor relief in Ireland at that date?—None at all; there was evidence furnished of the abuses that had grown up during the 30 years previous to 1834 from the somewhat indiscriminate relief in English country districts, but there was no such evidence furnished of abuses existing in Ireland at all.

9741. Because there was no such system of relief?—Yes.

9742. (Chairman.) You have never heard of any abuse of the system of outdoor relief in Ireland?—Except occasionally in the case of some of the unions, I do not mean to say that I have not heard of abuses.

9743. But you have not heard of boards of guardians being abolished, have you?—Yes, I have heard of that; but I think the whole expenditure in Ireland was not so abnormal that you need not bother about an odd instance of that kind; and on the whole I do not think it has been much abused, but such abuses as there are would be immediately checked if there was some proper local authority in Ireland to keep them in order.

9744. (Mr. Sexton.) What sum is allowed to give per week by way of outdoor relief now?—Half-a-crown and as low as 1s.

9745. And all these sums are liable to be surcharged by the officers?—Yes.

9746. (Chairman.) Is there not now a very great check upon out-door relief in consequence of the clause existing, that is to say, if the applicant is in the possession of a quarter of an acre of land he can get no out-door relief?—I am afraid that it is not an effectual check?—I think the country would be far better off if that check were removed.

9747. Do you think that if this were done there would be any limit to the extension of out-door relief amongst the small occupiers?—I think your question is probably based upon the existing condition of things. If you made one reform like that without reforming the whole of the system, you would find awkward results, but I think in a healthy condition of affairs you would not find any evil; and may I say that we removed that check in the House the other day. In all the distress Acts, what is done is to remove that check so as to abolish that law for the time being.

9748. You are not aware that it has led to very great abuses?—I do not pay much attention to those things under existing circumstances.

9749. (Mr. Sexton.) The total expenditure upon outdoor relief per annum in Ireland as compared with the number of the population and the number of those who are known to be very often in distress, does not seem to be a very extravagant amount, does it?—I do not think so. I think it is very reasonable. I believe the chief extravagance is in the workhouse establishments and that they are on too large a scale for the country.

9750. (Chairman.) And is that the definite suggestion you desire to make about the Poor Law system?—Yes. But I would like to say that in my opinion a change should be made in the direction I have stated, but I think it ought to be done continuously, and there ought to be some proper well-qualified Irish authority appointed to make these changes.

9751. Do you think that economies are practicable in any of the other local charges besides those connected with the relief of the poor?—I think there are; but there is one further point that I want to mention. It may be said that my statement about the increase of pauperism conflicts with the suggestion to abolish the workhouses. That is not necessarily so. I think the extravagant rating powers exercised by these organisations now do much in one season of the year to cause the poverty which they relieve in another portion of the year. The poverty in Ireland fluctuates very much, and is very temporary in its character. If the country were largely relieved of the present intolerable burden of taxation and the rates were reduced, I think pauperism would disappear. If this should be found to be too hopeful a view, a far more economical system of relief could be established.

9731. Then with regard to economies in any of the other local charges, have you any suggestion to make?—I was not going to make any definite suggestion about that, but I think it is probable that half a million of money could be saved in the county rate and the other local charges. I would rather not go into them in any detail. I think half a million would be a reasonable amount, and my calculation is based altogether upon a saving of half a million, in local charges and I think it would not be [illegible] to do that, but I am quite aware that in these suggestions of economy, we have to imagine a good deal in the way of change in the feeling of the people towards these things, before it can be carried out. But I do not think we will have a healthy state of things in Ireland until it is done.

9732. Might any beneficial results be reasonably expected when the over-taxation is redressed?—I think the first result would be that a great feeling of relief would be carried to every family and individual throughout the country. Everybody is struggling very hard in Ireland now, and even a very slight relief would be very acceptable indeed, I think, in the cottages all over the country. The large amount of the total taxation which is obtained by indirect taxes presses very heavily upon the poor families. I think the Commissioners have had before them certain budgets of poor families, which were printed in the first report of the Congested Districts Board, and which have been referred to by other witnesses; and they show that a large sum is paid annually in even the poorest households in Ireland through the medium of these indirect Imperial taxes. Therefore the very poorest would immediately share in the relief and every family throughout the country would also benefit by it. The total amount levied by means of the tobacco and breakfast table duties is 1,729,728l., so that a great deal of assistance would be given if they could be diminished. If the spirit duties were reduced to [illegible], and the duty on beer to [illegible], 2,058,919l., less would be collected from these two articles. Therefore the total amount of relief from Imperial taxation alone would be nearly 1,000,000l., or actually 3,598,641l.

9734. And you think that something like a million of money could be saved in local taxation?—Yes, I think, probably, [illegible] could be saved if we reclassify the [illegible] in local taxation. If we assume that there are 400,000 families in Ireland this would be equal to a contribution of [illegible] per annum towards the [illegible] of each family. If we may assume that rents will be reduced by three millions this would give another [illegible] of relief per family on the average, making altogether [illegible] per family per annum to be applied towards improved subsistence. Now I think this is beyond dispute that if any such thing as that could be done it would be very practical relief amongst a poor agricultural community.

9735. You also think that to grants to the local taxation or subsidies to railways would diminish those advantages so equally over the population?—No, I think nothing will stand but doing it in a perfectly simple way, especially as such as give an subsidies to railways would be liable to great abuse, and create a more expensive and costly system than we have got at present, and the effect of doing it in the way I have suggested by relief of taxation would be that people would begin to take a different view about life in Ireland, and would think it was possible to make progress there. I find almost everybody, even the most hard-working people in Ireland, have a hopeless feeling with regard to enterprise in Ireland. They say, if we are to do anything, the best thing is to clear out of this country; in order to improve things in Ireland a feeling of hopefulness must be created. Then the system of farming would rapidly begin to improve. New machinery would be introduced into districts, and greater variety would be seen in crops and produce. I think one great source of loss now is that so few crops are grown, and that there is no variety of produce such as you find in Great Britain or other countries.

9736. Then you think prosperity would spread from the country into the towns and villages?—Yes. I think the first evidence of contentment would be afforded by a decrease of emigration, and within five or ten years the population would probably begin to increase. On that point I think the decrease of emigration of 1894 was largely due to the hopefulness excited in the minds of the people by the discussions [illegible] of the Home Rule Bill. They did not exactly understand what was going on, but they thought that they were going to have a better state of affairs in Ireland, and the Commission asked me when I stated those figures whether I thought the reduction of emigration would be permanent, and I said I did not think it would. We have had since then the returns of emigration, and they show that the returns in the first three months of 1895 was 10,000, and if this goes on during the rest of the year the figures of emigration for the year 1895 will probably be 41,000 or 32,000, as compared with 38,000 in 1894. I think the first effect of some [illegible] Act of this kind would be that emigration would diminish, and then the people would begin to stay in the country.

9737. (*Mr. Sexton.*) There was a bad potato crop in the country last year, was there not?—Yes.

9738. But more tends to [illegible], is it not?—Yes, I [illegible] of that.

9739. (*Sir David Barbour.*) It was bad in 1894?—Yes, only I trace the decline in 1894 to the feeling of hopefulness created by the Home Rule Bill of 1893. You ought always to look to the Irish conditions in the year before the emigration took place. I think as soon as the farmers began to acquire some little surplus, however small, and the feelings of uncertainty and dread pass away from their minds, prosperity would spread to the towns and small local industries would arise. I do not think anything can be done in Ireland except something that commands the sympathy of the farmers and the agricultural population generally. I think the first change would be seen in the direction of utilising those mills I have mentioned; many of them are on good streams in good positions with plenty of water power. New machinery, too, is now very much cheaper than it was, and the slightest encouragement would set the mills going again, I think. Freed from the oppression of [illegible] rates, and with the means of living greatly cheapened, men would be found in good times, [illegible], spin and weave, even in competition with other countries, and we might hope for a gradual revival of manufactures.

9760. (*Chairman.*) And then to sum up your opinion, I think I may put it in this way, that it is difficult to gauge the relative capacity to bear taxation between Great Britain and Ireland, and that it is impossible to fix any proportion because the two islands are so different?—Yes.

9761. And each is moving rapidly in an opposite direction to the other?—Yes.

9762. And you think that Ireland can only contribute a [illegible] towards Imperial expenditure, and that if the country is to feed its people or cease to be a scandal to the system of government which is partly concerned, the taxation should immediately be reduced to [illegible] of what it is now?—Yes. That is putting it a little peremptorily, but it is exactly what I feel about it. I think the taxation ought to be reduced to half, and it is impossible to fix a proportion.

9763. Is there anything else that you wish to add to your evidence?—No, I do not think that there is. I think I have been a great deal of trouble to the Commission as it is.

9764. (*Sir David Barbour.*) I wish to ask you to refer to page 2, heading (b) of your Memorandum. You refer there to the fact that a great many articles which were formerly made in Ireland are now imported?—Yes.

9765. And you seem to think that there are not so many articles produced in Ireland as there used to be?—No.

9766. And those articles that have to be imported have to be paid for. I suppose they could only be paid for with Irish produce?—Yes.

9767. So that Ireland must produce something that is exported in payment for those articles?—Yes.

9768. And I suppose if she imports those articles instead of producing them at home it is because she finds it more profitable to import them?—Yes, perhaps so, to a certain extent. There is not the means of producing them at home that there used to be.

9769. How is that?—The local manufactures have been extinguished. Such machinery as there was has been allowed to go out of existence.

9770. Why?—Well, because of the depression of the people all the mills have practically ceased working.

9771. I suppose they would only go out of existence because they were not producing at a profit?—Perhaps so, to a great extent.

9772. And that the imported articles could be purchased more cheaply elsewhere?—Yes.

9773. And to pay for the imported articles, other articles are produced and exported?—Yes, but the reason they cannot produce them profitably is because the charges have been made so high.

9774. But does not that equally apply to the articles which they now produce and export in payment for the articles [illegible] M.P. — 14 June 1895. — [illegible]

that they [illegible]? These charges must affect all articles produced in the country?—No; the only thing they produce now is the present kind of agricultural produce; there is no manufacture.

9775. The people who produce that agricultural produce have to bear these charges, just the same as the people who make the other articles; that is to say, the charges they bear are no higher than if they were manufacturing cutlery or hardware?—Yes, there would be a much heavier tax upon the local manufacture of mills, or anything of that kind.

9776. In what way?—In the case of any manufacture.

9777. How would that be more heavily taxed than agriculture?—Because of the incidence of the rates. There is no manufacture in agriculture at all.

9778. Are there no rates upon agricultural land?—There are rates, but there is no manufacture. The cattle grow. There is no human employment.

9779. Then I would ask you to look at page 5 of your Memorandum. You give rather a dismal picture of the state of Ireland generally in your evidence; does that picture apply to all classes or are some classes better off than others?—Broadly it applies to all classes, but of course there is a difference in suffering.

9780. What are the classes that you think are not suffering, if you can draw any distinction?—The officials who get salaries from the Government.

9781. Anybody else. All the agriculturists are suffering?—Yes.

9782. The manufacturers are very few?—Yes.

9783. The trades-people, I suppose, depend upon the agriculture?—Yes, they do.

9784. And the exporters?—Yes.

9785. Now will you look at page 4 where you say that the prices of agricultural produce have fallen so much. The price of wheat was 26s. 4d. per quarter last year, and therefore it would now require three quarters of wheat to pay the same amount of taxation. The prices of agricultural prices generally have fallen very much?—Yes.

9786. And in about the same place you say that the wages of labour have doubled?—Yes.

9787. The man who gets wages twice as high as he used to get, and finds the price of produce very much lower, must have gained, must he not?—Yes, he has gained a little.

9788. A great deal I should think; double wages, and the price of produce is half what it used to be before?—These agricultural prices are half what they were.

9789. The articles of food?—Yes, but the taxes have been doubled.

9790. Increase of taxation would only balance a small proportion of the gain from double wages and half prices for food?—But the wages were very low at the beginning of the century. For instance, I quoted that in the beginning of the century the wages were sevenpence, and by the doubling of those wages they are now about 1s. 2d., I think.

9791. That may be, but is there not all round a great improvement?—Taking that fact apart from all others, no doubt the doubling of wages is a benefit to the working man, and reduction in the prices of the articles of food are a great benefit to him. But you must remember that three-fourths of the population of Ireland are farmers.

9792. You say that Ireland does not gain any advantage by what you call the foreign empire of Great Britain?—I do not think I quite said that, but I think it is a great [illegible].

9793. There is considerable advantage in some respects, is there not?—No, I do not think so.

9794. Take tea; it is a great gain to Ireland, is it not, that she gets her tea cheaper?—Yes.

9795. And that cheapness is undoubtedly due to the introduction of Indian and Ceylon tea, is it not?—Yes.

9796. And that tea in India and Ceylon would not have been produced, but for the existence of the British Empire?—I do not think that that follows. We got our tea from the Chinese before.

9797. But there was not an ounce of tea produced either in India or Ceylon until very recent times, was there?—No.

9798. And the growth of tea in India was practically started by the Government of India?—Yes, partly.

9799. And is now carried on by Englishmen, Irishmen, and Scotchmen, who are settled in those places?—Yes.

9800. And it is difficult to me to suppose that that would have happened, but for the existence of the British Empire in India?—They are producing a very good tea in Java now, and you cannot put it so strongly I think, as you do, that there would have been no tea grown there, except for the existing state of affairs; but I do not want to differ from you on the whole. We have developed tea cultivation in India, and I think that is the most splendid chapter in the annals of British commerce, but my argument is that the Irish pay the merchants who supply the tea a fair profit, which covers all costs of production. We are glad to sell Indian or Ceylon tea in France or in Turkey, as cheaply as in Ireland, though those nations pay no part of the cost of our Empire.

9801. On the other hand the Irish have the same opportunities of benefiting by the colonial empire of Great Britain that the English have, if they choose to avail themselves of them?—No, they have not the same opportunities.

9802. In what way have they not the same opportunities?—Because they have got to live in Connemara, and to benefit by those opportunities, they must come and live in England. If they come up here they can benefit by it, but the poor peasant living near Galway has no [illegible] more advantage from the large expense which keeps the fleet afloat.

9803. Take a poor crofter in Sutherlandshire, has he any direct gain?—Not much; it is a very hard case for the crofters too.

9804. With regard to that question of taxable capacity, you deduct from the total income of the country 12l. a head; of course you know that the calculation of the total income of any country cannot be made with perfect accuracy?—No, surely; but I do not think the figures are the less true on that account. It can be calculated nearly enough for every practical purpose.

9805. Nearly enough to show that the average Englishman is very much wealthier than the average Irishman?—Yes.

9806. Can you take the figures of the total income of a country as absolutely accurate?—I think you can get to a very great degree of accuracy about it.

9807. You deduct 12l. a head, but you are aware that there are a great many people in Ireland who have not got 12l. a head; take those typical budgets of families which were given to the Commission; they have not got 12l. a head or anything like it. Do you think it is right to deduct 12l. a head on account of the people who have actually got much less than 12l. a head?—On an average you cannot fix a less amount than 12l., because there are some people whom 12l. does not support; there is a rich landlord—a landlord would not live very well on 12l. a year.

9808. But may I point out that 12l. is not an average figure; it is the minimum necessary for subsistence?—It is the average all over the population.

9809. No, it is the actual minimum in the case of each person?—I beg your pardon, it is the average minimum.

9810. It is the minimum sum necessary for subsistence?—No, it is the average sum which is taken as the minimum for the whole population.

9811. Then do you mean to say that a man can live comfortably on less than 12l. a year?—He can live on it; I would rather leave out "comfortably."

9812. In a reasonably decent manner, to use your own phrase?—I do not think they can live on much less than 12l.

9813. Do you think it is right in making that calculation to deduct 12l. a head in the case of persons who have a smaller income?—Certainly.

9814. I rather think Dr. Giffen draws back from that deduction in all cases?—Yes, but Dr. Giffen does not go so far as I do. Dr. Giffen has not studied so much in Ireland as I have. Although I would like to say that I have studied Dr. Giffen's memoir here, and he does not [illegible] one jot or tittle of his argument that it is not safe to take less than 12l. broadly for the whole population.

9815. But I think in making the calculation he rather draws back from the actual deduction of 12l. in case of men who receive less than 12l.?—You cannot deduct it from men who do not receive that.

9816. He says that in case of persons receiving less than 12l. they ought to have the actual amount they receive deducted from the total income?—But he said sufficient to show that it was not safe to take any smaller amount.

9917. I think you will find that he holds that in making the calculation for persons who have less than 12l., you should deduct their actual income and not the 12l. per head?—No, I do not. I say you must take it broadly.

9918. You say the 12l. per head should be exempt from all taxation. If there is indirect taxation how are you to make that exemption, how can you carry it out in practice. For instance, if you tax the tobacco of a man whose family has less than 12l. per head, and who smokes tobacco, how are you to exempt them?—I have recommended that we should get rid of the tax upon tobacco and I would like to [illegible] all indirect taxation except away as far as possible.

9919. But what I want to point out is this in point of fact you cannot exempt that minimum of 12l. until you have got rid of indirect taxation. As long as you tax tobacco and whiskey, and so forth, there is some taxation falling upon that minimum in the case of such persons, is there not?—You say you cannot exempt it, but you can do this. You can allow the 12l. in your calculation and you say so that the total amount exacted from the country is such as can be paid after the 12l. is allowed.

9920. I agree you can do that with regard to the whole country, but you cannot do it as regards an individual?—I never suggested that, at least I do not suggest it.

9921. You do not suggest the exemption of the individual, but you merely say that in making the calculation for the whole country you should deduct an average rate of 12l.?—Yes. The way I put it is this. You ought to take from the total income of the country 12l. a head all round per head of the population; and then you should make your total taxes such as would be a reasonable amount to exact from the balance.

9922. But you do not propose to apply that minimum of 12l. to the case of each individual in the country, do you?—Yes, you would apply it to each individual, surely, as do not go round the country fixing each individual separately. I would recommend that the best way to relieve these people would be to exempt tobacco from taxation.

9923. You would like to see all indirect taxation removed, and if that is not practicable you would like to go as near to it as possible?—That is it.

9924. Then you compare the Channel Islands with Ireland?—Yes.

9925. The Channel Islands pay nothing towards Imperial expenditure and are prosperous, but there is not very much difference in climate between the Channel Islands and Ireland?—That makes no difference. There is a very good climate in Ireland.

9926. But are not the Channel Islands especially suited for the growing of fruit and vegetables; practically a sort of market garden?—Yes, but there are plenty of things that can be grown in Ireland too. Ireland might become a market garden if we encouraged it. That is the very point. And surely you could not urge that if Ireland is poorer and less favorably situated than the Channel Islands, therefore it is safe to oppress Ireland with heavy taxation.

9927. No, I do not think it is desirable or equitable to do that, but your argument was that the Channel Islands paid no Imperial taxation, and therefore they are prosperous, and you drew from that (as the inference) that if Ireland paid no Imperial taxation she would be equally prosperous. I ask you, are there not other differences in the circumstances affecting the two Islands, for instance, the difference in climate and so forth?—I do not think there are any differences that at all qualify my argument.

9928. (Sir Thomas Sutherland.) Not having been present, I have not quite apprehended the evidence you have been giving lately, but I gather that it is some proposal or suggestion that you have been making with regard to overcoming the difficulty of this great taxation under which Ireland labours?—Yes.

9929. I understand that you have made some suggestions upon the point?—Yes, I have.

9930. And that you have made some suggestions with regard to an alteration in the incidence of taxation?—Yes, I suggest the most sweeping alterations.

9931. For instance, the 5,000,000l. of indirect taxation which we collect in Ireland now, you propose to modify in some way or other?—Yes, by 2,000,000l. at least.

9932. By what means—by differential duties?—Yes.

9933. That, in fact, that would be equal to giving what I might call a sort of protection to Ireland?—No, I do not think there would be any disadvantage of that kind. I went into each of the three articles with the Government, and I showed that a duty now is not levied on articles of English manufacture, and that therefore there would be no disadvantage in that way.

9934. Would you have a different duty on whiskey in Scotland and a different duty on whiskey in Ireland?—I would rather not be made the exponent of Scotland. I would look at it as sympathetically as I could, and therefore I cannot answer without looking into the Scotch aspect of the question. But certainly I would reduce the duty in Ireland on whiskey, and I may say, speaking roughly, I have got a good deal of sympathy with the Scotch claim for a lower tax on whiskey also.

9935. Would you be in favour of lowering the duty on whiskey in Ireland and putting a heavier duty on beer in England?—No, not necessarily. I would let the duty on beer stay as it is, and I would like to say that I do not suggest reducing the tax in England on Irish whiskey. Let the English pay what tax they please.

9936. For example, I suppose you do not see your way to a differential duty on tea in England as compared with Ireland?—I do not see any great objection. I said a few minutes ago that we would sell rather more and not lose tea in Ireland if the duty was lower. Probably it would injure me a little, because I distribute a great deal of duty paid tea, but I would probably find some way of blending it in Ireland.

9937. Harking back to poverty and whiskey, which is a matter that weighs very much upon my mind, I dare say you have followed the cognate question of sugar. My constituency, I believe, has been to a very large extent ruined by what we call sugar bounties in foreign countries? —Yes.

9938. Greenock is, I suppose, about the only unprosperous town in the whole of Scotland, at any rate, a melancholy fact, which arose from the sugar refineries having been practically destroyed. There used to be about 16 or 18 very large and prosperous sugar refineries in Greenock, but there are now at the outside only three or four, which are not by any means too prosperous. At the same time I fear that the consumption of whiskey has not decreased in Greenock to the extent that it ought to have decreased relatively to the poverty of the place. How is it possible for any Government to deal with such a duty as the duty upon spirits upon the basis of richness or poverty, or to distinguish between the conditions of one population and another with regard to a question of that kind?—My experience upon both the days I have been examined, is that poverty tends to increase the consumption of whiskey rather than otherwise, for when the people get poor they get desperate, and they say "We may as well be hung for a sheep as a lamb," and they then drink more than if they were in a better condition, and you really find a flourishing community has given to excess in the way of intoxicants.

9939. You know of course that Sir William Harcourt has reduced the duty upon whiskey, because he found that the consumption was arrested by the higher duty?—Yes, but his duty was much too high for me.

9940. Party of reasoning suggests that whenever the duty on an article of luxury like whiskey is diminished, the consumption tends to increase, is not that so?—It is, within certain limits.

9941. And when the duty is put up the consumption is arrested, is it not, and when the duty is taken off the consumption increases, does it not?—Within certain limits.

9942. You know that very well, I think, that although everybody is in favour of a proper kind of taxation and that every man should be taxed in accordance with his means, that is one of those political ideas which unfortunately exists more in theory than in practice; and so far as I know is likely to exist, a poor professional man, for instance, pays, as no doubt he always will do in all probability, more in proportion to his means, than your rich capitalist; is not that your general idea?—Yes, I think that will be so to a certain extent.

9943. That affects all classes, and in practical politics those who have to collect the revenue have to provide the readiest and least expensive means of finding the revenue? —Yes.

9944. Now I have read over very carefully your examination the other day, which I had not the pleasure of hearing, and there is a good deal in it with regard to the question of local taxation and local burdens which you consider are very onerous duties in Ireland?—Yes.

Mr. [illegible] 11 June 1895.

Local government in Ireland.

9945. And which you think would be [illegible] to a very important extent if we could have a different system of Government in Ireland?—Yes.

9946. Now I think you are aware that although there is a very considerable difference of opinion amongst political parties on the question of what is called Home Rule, yet that there is very little difference of opinion with regard to the desire of all parties to give Ireland as full and complete a measure of what is local administrative Government as Ireland could wish to have?—No, I could not say yes to that question. The Unionists, so called, always find some ingenious reason for objecting to any practical proposal; as, for instance, they all divided against the Municipal Franchise (Ireland) Bill on Wednesday, at least a good many did; probably you did not.

9947. You are now going into details. I would rather ask you whether as a matter of broad principle you do not admit that you are not right upon that point?—No, I do not.

9948. To give Ireland every possible form of Government as it exists either in England or Scotland?—I have never seen any evidence of it up to the present moment.

9949. I rather gather from the general trend of your evidence that you are in favour of protection in Ireland?—No, I have not said so.

9950. You are rather in favour of [illegible] for Ireland?—No.

Contribution of Ireland to Imperial expenditure.

9951. Then I rather gather from your evidence also that you do not consider that Ireland derives any benefit whatever from the Imperial Navy or the Army for instance?—I did not put it quite so far, but I went a long way in that direction; she does not derive so much pecuniary benefit as we do in London.

9952. In fact, you think that she should be exempt from contributing towards that description of expenditure, that her position is so secure that she does not require the Army or Navy to contribute towards it?—Yes, only that her security is that of the poor man everywhere, he is not worth robbing, that is all. I may say I answered some questions to-day about that point, and went into a little detail, and you will find it printed.

Equality of taxation [illegible].

9953. (Sir [illegible].) Sir Thomas Sutherland has just admitted that it is desirable that everybody should be taxed in accordance with his means, but, of course, you understand that the question we have to investigate is not any such ideal perfection as between individual and individual; it is with regard to the relative resources of the two countries?—Yes, that is so.

9954. What we have to report is what Ireland as a whole can fairly afford to pay in comparison with Great Britain as a whole?—Yes, that is it.

9955. And if we can do that any question of unequal taxation in either country as between classes or individuals would be a question of internal regulation in that country?—I quite agree.

9956. Even supposing we could arrive at the result, that the taxation of all Ireland was made equitable in relation to the taxation of Great Britain, there undoubtedly would be still questions, as between classes and individuals in Ireland and in Great Britain as to whether the incidence of taxation was equal, would it not?—Yes, that would be so.

9957. So that the question of whether a professional man is robbed of his income to a greater extent than a person on another level of the social scale is an entirely distinct and separate question from the question before us here and you recognise that the reference to the Commission refers entirely to the taking of a proportionate sum from Ireland in relation to the sum taken from Great Britain, and not to the incidence of taxation between the classes or individuals in either country?—Yes, I quite agree.

9958. Sir Thomas Sutherland referred to the case of Scotland, but here we are inquiring into the case as between Ireland and Great Britain. I do not understand you to convey anything prejudicial to any claim which Scotland may have as between herself and England for re-arrangement or re-adjustment of the burdens of taxation?—None whatever; I think that there is a case for the Highlands of Scotland particularly, almost as strong as Ireland.

Proposal to reduce ordinary expenses in Ireland.

9959. Your plea for differential duties does not include any proposal for protection, or for bounties, nor do you think it has any such effect?—None whatever. I do not think the Irishman ought to be at all helped in sending his whiskey into England any more than the Scotchman in sending his whiskey. I do not think the authorities of Ireland should give him any help, and I do not think that he should be let in any more easily by the authorities in England; I do not think it is necessary to do so.

9960. You admit the difficulty of systems of differential duties, but finding that the tax in Ireland is greatly excessive and is inflicting serious evils upon that country, that you would not allow the principle of fiscal unity to stand in the way of a remedy if no other remedy could be found?—That expresses my views; I think it might be better if indirect taxation could be done away with altogether, as I said before, but when I see a country like Great Britain, which draws about 50 millions of its annual income from indirect taxation, I do not like being bold enough to suggest abolition in all that system. I therefore confine my suggestions to the small case of Ireland which I understand to be the one we are dealing with, or that the Commission have to deal with.

9961. We are instructed to find out what is equitable for Ireland?—Yes.

9962. And the principle, as I daresay you would state it, is, that as between convenience and equity, convenience must give way?—Yes, that is so, I think so.

9963. I suppose that if equity could be satisfied without rupture of the fiscal law you would be content?—I would so much so that I would strain a little to keep the duties the same. I say that in a qualified way. It is only since 1853 that they have been the same, and the two countries are so different (and nothing that has taken place since 1853 has made them any more alike, rather the other way) that I think we ought to sit down in one country and say what is best for this place? and do it; and then sit down in the other country and say what is best for that place, and do it.

9964. The only Imperial Statute, so far as I know, in which the question of taxation has been dealt with directly and openly from the point of view of principle, is the Act of Union, which declares that, even after the establishment of indiscriminate taxation, regard was to be had to such exemptions and abatements as circumstances might render desirable from time to time, and without limit of time?—Yes, without any limit.

9965. Therefore, on the authority of that statute, which was in the nature of a treaty, the principle even of differential duty is maintained?—Yes, I think so, and it was maintained for 50 years afterwards, and my theory is that that law was only abolished by Mr. Gladstone, Sir Robert Peel was thoroughly persuaded with the idea that you would sacrifice the prosperity of Ireland if you insisted that she could pay equal duties on articles of consumption.

9966. A small, poor country like Ireland, has been kept by indiscriminate taxation on an equal footing with the greatest and richest empire in the world, the taxation of which may pass far beyond the boundary of any surplus that Ireland possesses at any moment; it appears therefore to follow, that the system of equality of taxation might have the effect of driving the life out of the poorer country, and be scarcely felt by the richer country, is not that so?—Exactly, and I think it has done so. That is the whole argument of my evidence. I take the case of 1894, only last year, and we calmly accepted, judging from our own convenience here, that we wanted to spend 4,000,000 more, say, for our Navy, which we were entitled to do if we liked, but I say that such burdens bear with crushing effect upon a poor country like Ireland.

9967. And it is admitted, I think, by experts, that if you double the gross assessable to income tax, you have something like a good approximation?—Yes; there is a sentence in my Heads that I did not read on that very point, which I would like to read:—"It will be seen that "the property assessed (gross) to income tax in Ireland, "[illegible] in Great Britain about 700,000,000, fairly "justifies these figures, and bears a somewhat similar proportion to the total personal income in both countries. "In Great Britain it is as 700 is to 1,400, in Ireland it "[illegible]."

9968. So far therefore from its being the case that the estimates of income are speculative they have a reasonable basis and a basis of fact?—Yes, especially now with the facts that the income tax has given us.

9969. And beyond the income tax we have the wages and the number of men employed, and we have excellent data upon which to arrive at a conclusion with regard to the total income?—I think this Commission has amassed a volume of evidence that it would be impossible for anybody to gainsay upon that point.

Mr. [illegible] Lough, M.P. [illegible] June [illegible]. Manufactures in Ireland.

9870. You have a balance of about 1,000,000,000*l.* a year of taxable surplus in Great Britain and a balance in Ireland which at the maximum is put at 9,000,000*l.*, and at the maximum 22,000,000*l.*?—Yes.

9871. Almost one fiftieth of the taxable surplus of Great Britain?—Yes.

9872. Supposing in the event of any Imperial emergency this great country with its territories and interests in all parts of the globe and its immense heritage to keep open for food and commerce were engaged in a great war, the expenditure of this country might be doubled, might it not?—Easily.

9873. That would mean that the 75,000,000*l.* raised in Great Britain would become 150,000,000*l.*?—Yes.

9874. And doubling the Irish 7,000,000*l.*, that would take 14,000,000*l.*, which would exhaust the whole taxable resources of that country?—Yes.

9875. That is a proof, is it not, that under the deceptive guise of equity by equal rates of taxation you may [illegible] one, whilst the [illegible] burden is scarcely felt by the other?—I quite agree; I would like to say with regard to the one figure that you mentioned that I do not [illegible] the 22,000,000*l.* except as Ireland. I consider that when you would work the calculation up from the 22,000,000*l.* as expenditure to 74,000,000*l.* of gross income of Ireland; but I think that the surplus of Ireland must be something between 9,000,000*l.* and 16,000,000*l.* at the outside, or 15,000,000*l.*

9876. In the case I have stated the expenditure of the Empire being doubled by some extraordinary cause, only a small fraction of the taxable surplus of Great Britain would still be taken, but the whole taxable surplus of Ireland [illegible] by a thousand?—Yes. I have often said myself in conversation that this country could pay for 20 years to [illegible] the war indemnity that France had to pay to Germany and emerge at the end of the time, if her wealth kept up during the period, practically unimpaired; and any burden of that kind would ruin Ireland completely.

9877. Moreover a country like Great Britain might find a great expensive war a good investment, whilst it might not in any material way alter the condition of Ireland?—Yes, and that was so. The wealth of Great Britain increased steadily through the war ending in 1815.

9878. I believe that during that war, in which the nations of Europe were engaged in the field whilst England was enabled to pursue her industries at home, her financial position steadily improved and the community gained by the war?—Yes.

9879. What did Ireland gain?—National debt.

9880. So therefore it does not appear that it is so difficult, as Sir Thomas Sutherland suggested, to distinguish between the wealth and poverty of one community and another?—I do not think it is.

9881. With reference to what Sir David Barbour said with respect to the Channel Islands and Ireland, there is undoubtedly a difference in the climates, and that question has an effect upon those different communities that was not brought out, but it is not necessary to inquire into all the causes, we are engaged in inquiring into the causes at present?—Yes.

9882. Now Sir David Barbour suggested that Ireland imports almost all the requisites of life from Great Britain because she has found it profitable to do so; there was a time when she made many of them for herself, was there not?—Yes, certainly.

9883. There was a time when I think the manufactures in Ireland were discouraged and suppressed by Imperial Legislation?—Yes.

9884. (*Sir David Barbour.*) What time was that?—During the 18th century.

9885. Not in the present century?—There was the case I gave you of the tobacco industry being suppressed in [illegible].

9886. But that is common to England?—But it does not harm in England—that is just the point—it makes all the difference in the world because while it was essential to Ireland, England did not want to grow it.

9887. (*Mr. Sexton.*) At any rate it was at the time when the manufactures of England were being developed and encouraged by the same Legislature that discouraged them in Ireland?—Yes.

9888. And eventually manufactures in England reached a stage of organisation and development against which it became impossible for Ireland to compete?—Certainly.

9889. So that the Irish manufactures ceased?—Yes, and I think the sudden sweeping away of the Corn Laws was a thing which, looked at purely from the agricultural point of view, would not have been done in such a sweeping manner, had we ever had the time or the opportunity. The only thing that was thought of was the necessity of the English manufacturer, and a great blow was given to the great Irish industries, particularly to the tillage of flax.

9890. In a fairly prosperous community there would be an industrial class for the purpose of supplying the agricultural classes with its requisites, whilst the agricultural class supplies them with food?—Yes.

9891. That balance does not exist in Ireland, because Ireland finds its manufactured articles in another country?—Yes, she has to buy them in another country, and I do not think the fact of a country doing that is a proof that she finds it profitable to do so always. She may be driven by necessity to do it from certain economic reasons, although it would be very profitable for her to manufacture them at home if she could. Take flour, for example, how can it be right for Ireland, a great agricultural country, not to produce wheat and grind it at home, or not to make her own splendid oaten meal and grind it in Ireland, rather than send out cattle, and import Indian meal and flour from Chicago? It cannot be a paying thing for her to do that.

9892. (*Sir David Barbour.*) Why does she do it?—From necessity—from her terrible position.

9893. (*Mr. Sexton.*) I suppose it is manifest that the people of Ireland would prefer to eat the beef, and mutton, and butter, and eggs, and poultry, that they send out, if they could?—I think there is no doubt about that.

9894. They are compelled to send them out, because they cannot afford to eat them?—Yes.

9895. They have rent to pay, and other charges to meet, and they feel that if they were to consume the good food they produce, the situation would become intolerable?—Yes.

9896. Can there be a situation more indicative of poverty than that of a country producing good food, and exporting that good food, and importing cheaper food for consumption, and almost all the other requisites of life?—It seems to me to be the most terrible evidence of poverty that can exist, and that is what troubled me when Sir David Barbour was asking me why they do it?

9897. (*Sir David Barbour.*) I was not asking you with reference to the export of good food and the import of inferior food, which may be an indication of poverty, but of the export of certain goods in order to pay for the manufactures which are imported?—But that is really what it is. She exports cattle on which no labour has been spent, and eggs and other things on which hardly any labour has been spent, in order to enable her to import Indian meal.

9898. But I was referring more to the question of importing hardware or cutlery instead of producing these articles herself. If she exports certain articles of produce in order to import such an article, for instance, as cutlery, I ask you is not that a sign that she finds it more profitable to export these articles and import cutlery than to make the cutlery at home?—I think the explanation that was given in reference to meal and flour will also apply to furniture and hardware. I can remember myself when in every peasant's house in Ireland you would find much better furniture than the shoddy you see now; clocks and watches made at home were of excellent quality, but you cannot find anything like it now, and the explanation might be found just in the same train of reasoning as you admit in the case of grain and flour.

9899. But, I suppose, if necessary, they could have manufactured inferior clocks and watches in Ireland as well as good ones?—I suppose we could have manufactured inferior ones, but I do not think that that would have been much to her advantage.

9900. (*Mr. Sexton.*) It is obvious that at the time when the foundations of organised industry were being laid in both countries the Irish industries were placed at a disadvantage by legislation whilst the English industries were advanced and encouraged?—Yes.

9901. And the English industries reached a point at which the smaller and less encouraged industries became impossible?—Yes, I quite agree, and I think that principle is developing still. The railways in Ireland are not made to help the poor localities, but to attract the rich centres of population.

[illegible]

9902. If urban industries had been allowed to develop in the ordinary course in Ireland as they have in all civilized countries, you would have now some industries at least upon a moderate scale in Ireland sufficient to supply the wants of a local community and of taxable capacity, would you not?—I think so.

9903. Qualifying what Sir David Barbour called "the general progress of all classes," attention was pointed to the fact that the wages of the labourer had doubled in recent times, and that the prices of some of the commodities which the labourer has to buy were cheaper, but is there not a great change in the mode of living of the labourer, namely, that instead of subsisting upon native produce, which is mostly of a healthier and more suitable kind, he subsists upon imported goods, and buys them?—Yes, I think he does.

9904. Cheap American wheat and flour and tea instead of potatoes and milk, and other articles of home produce, which were the sustenance of the labourer 40 years ago?—Probably Sir David Barbour would says that he only takes them because he likes them.

9905. But it is not in itself even an indication of any material improvement in the condition of the class, is it?—No, it is not.

9906. It is an indication of change?—Yes, and I think some of the charges pressing upon the labourer in some of the conditions of his life have greatly increased while his wages have doubled. He used to get his fuel for nothing for the mere trouble of cutting it, but now bogs are the most highly rented parts of Ireland, and with respect to those small cabins of which you have heard, I do not think it was so hard to get hold of one of these years ago as it may be to get hold of one of these fourth-class houses, so that in many respects he was better off, he had a village green then, and now he has not a scrap of land upon which his children can play.

9907. The question is not whether the condition of the Irish labourer has improved, or whether his mode of life has changed, but what is the relation of it now to the corresponding class of labourer in England. We have it in evidence from Mr. Giffen that the average wages of labour in Ireland were about one half of what they are in Great Britain. Assuming that to be so, no argument with regard to an improvement in the condition of the Irish labourer, especially when it is disconnected from the improvement of the labourer in Great Britain, can affect the conclusions to which we ought to come?—I do not think so, not materially.

[illegible]

9908. Now we have heard a good deal of the commercial benefits that Ireland derived from the removal of commercial restrictions at the time of the union; what benefit has she derived—has she derived any foreign or colonial trade?—I do not think so; I think the development of modern trade has been extremely hard on places a little out of the way like Ireland. I am told that the Belfast Cork got short from Dublin until the famine, and there was a considerable trade done years ago between Ireland and European places which has gone out of existence now altogether. The development of modern trade has helped the great cities like London, Manchester, and Glasgow, and Belfast to a small extent, in respect of its own particular manufactures, but rural Ireland has suffered terribly.

9909. Therefore what benefit has she derived from the removal of the commercial restrictions?—I do not think she has benefited. An immense quantity of articles, including tea, used to come by ship to Dublin, to Liverpool, to Glasgow, and to Leith, and now not a pound of tea arrives in a year, except [illegible] a tremendous [illegible] has taken place, and therefore we have got this huge metropolitan community and the suffering of the rural population in Connemara is proportionately great.

9910. The trade of Ireland is the trade of Great Britain simply, is it not?—Yes.

9911. And whilst Ireland has no foreign or colonial trade, Great Britain has the greatest foreign and colonial trade in the world?—Yes.

9912. And it is mainly to protect and maintain that foreign and colonial trade, that the army and navy are maintained upon their present scale?—Yes, I think so. The navy has doubled since the Suez Canal has been opened.

9913. Ireland is not now politically independent; in all her affairs she is subject to correction, and is virtually under the orders of Great Britain, is she not?—Certainly.

9914. And she is very poor?—I think so, and I think her poverty is increasing.

9915. And very miserable?—I think so.

9916. Left all realized by discontent and poverty?—Yes.

9917. How does it appear then that she has any interest in the maintenance of army and navy of Great Britain, for the purpose of maintaining the extraordinary prosperity of Great Britain, or any interest commensurate with the scale of her taxation to Great Britain?—I do not think she has any interest in it. Nobody who wanted to hurt Great Britain would think of attacking her through Ireland.

9918. Now the trade of Ireland being solely, as you might say, with Great Britain, does that trade depend upon, or arise, from her political relations, or do you think it is a question of mutual convenience and advantage?—I think it is purely a question of mutual convenience and advantage. There is no sympathy shown in any way towards Ireland. If cattle come in from Canada for a little cheaper, I am sure that they would be bought in Glasgow or Greenock as freely as Irish cattle.

9919. Does the cross-channel trade depend upon the legislative union?—Not a bit.

9920. Which country, in your opinion, derives the greatest advantage, Ireland sending out her food which is too good for her to consume, and taking in cheaper food, or Great Britain taking in every description of food and other articles, and exporting in return her imports and manufactures?—I think Great Britain must have the advantage, because of the superior quality of her exports. Of course, it is an advantage to Ireland to have a market too.

9921. Now supposing Ireland were separated from England, and it was a separate kingdom, or even a country dependent upon another Power, is there any reason why the mutual convenience of the two countries should not maintain the cross-channel trade as it is at present?—No, I think Great Britain would probably find it to her advantage to do so.

9922. Then there is one other point I should like to ask you about with regard to the question of taxable capacity; it is suggested that a tax of 12l. a head cannot be laid, because many have less in Ireland, but many have less in Great Britain, have they not?—I quite agree.

9923. So that that reason cannot operate?—No, it cannot operate in one country more than in another. Many in the Highlands of Scotland have less than 12l.

9924. (Sir David Barbour.) I quite think it ought to apply to both countries?—Then we ought to leave it out.

9925. (Mr. Sexton.) Now let me make it clear what is suggested by the tax of 12l. a head; it is suggested that in either country many people have less than 12l.?—Yes.

9926. And it was suggested by Sir David Barbour as a reason why a general tax of 12l. should not be made that it was to be levied as a [illegible]; it is not an average [illegible]?—I think so. I have tried to put that as strongly as I could to Sir David Barbour; it is the average taken over the whole nation.

9927. What it means is this, is it not, that if you deduct for each person in a country 12l. a year you arrive upon the whole for that country at a sum which will probably represent the annual cost of supplying the whole community with the necessaries of life upon a reasonable standard?—That is it. I think that is a fair definition.

9928. And when you have laid that tax although it might appear to press heavily in the cases of certain individuals because they did not earn so much, while in other cases it would be ridiculously small, yet upon the average you do make such a deduction from the total income as leaves a balance which may be fairly described as the taxable surplus after the cost of living is defrayed?—Yes.

9929. And then the equity of taxation appears to suggest in the case of the two countries that that balance being ascertained for each, it should be drawn upon for taxation in the same proportion?—Yes, in the same proportion, or at any rate that there should be no larger deduction for purposes of taxation than that balance which remains will appear to justify.

9930. And the proportion that would be just would be such a proportion of the balance in each case as would discharge in the same percentage the total of the expenditure required. Let us say that the rich country had 1,000,000,000l. and the poor country had 100,000,000l. of surplus, and the total expenditure required was one-tenth of the 1,000,000,000l. the taxation should be taken in the proportion of one-tenth from each, should it not?—Yes, with one great qualification provided that the objects for which the taxation was taken were equally beneficial to both countries.

[illegible]. In your judgment the equity of the case requires that the sum to be taken from each of the two countries by way of taxation should be in the like proportion of the [illegible] that the like proportion of the taxable surplus after the cost of subsistence at an equal rate has been deducted? —That is exactly my point.

[illegible]. (*Sir David Barbour.*) You have stated that the Irish manufactures were repressed in the 18th century. I think you said that the English manufacturers got a great start then, so that the Irish manufacturers have never been able to compete with them?—I did not put that in my evidence but I am prepared to adopt it to some extent.

[illegible]. I ask you this question, because in your memorandum at page 7 you say that "in 1791 all things used "by people made in Ireland, all hardware, plate, cutlery, "clothes, boots, hats, agricultural instruments, furniture, "made at home, were all [illegible]"; and then I wish to point out to you that the worst came ten years afterwards, and that if these manufactures existed in 1791 it is difficult to suppose that they could have been destroyed in the ten years between 1791 and 1800?—But I did not say so. May I explain that the chief repression of the Irish manufactures by England was before 1782. In 1782 the Irish Parliament got perfectly free trade and equality between the two.

[illegible]. If in 1791 they existed as you say, how is it that the repression that took place before 1782 destroyed them? —Some of them were developed by the Irish Parliament. You are arguing [illegible] there, I think. You only asked me could I mention any case where Irish trade had been repressed by English Legislation.

[illegible]. I think you went in your answer to Mr. Sexton so far as to say that Irish manufactures generally had been repressed by the action of England in the 18th century, that English manufacturers had got a great start, and that was the reason why the Irish manufacturers had never caught them up?—It is undoubtedly historically true that everything that could be done in the 18th century was done by Great Britain to repress Irish manufactures. I remember one particular case of the fishermen of Margate and Ramsgate getting an Act through Parliament to prevent fishing in the Irish Sea, lest the Kent fishermen should suffer.

[illegible]. I merely point out that you have stated that in 1791 there were many manufactures in Ireland, which no longer exist, and that it cannot have been the repression that took place before 1782 that destroyed them?—No, I did not say it was. These particular manufactures undoubtedly existed then.

The witness withdrew.

Note.—In consequence of the dissolution of Parliament and the General Elections it was found to be necessary to adjourn the continuance of the evidence until the autumn.

TWENTY-FIFTH DAY.

At A. Committee Room, House of Lords, Thursday, 31st October 1895.

Present:

The Right Honourable Hugh C. E. CHILDERS, *Chairman*.

Lord Farrer.	J. E. Redmond, Esq., M.P.
Lord Welby, G.C.B.	Thomas Sexton, Esq., M.P.
The Right Hon. The O'Conor Don.	Henry F. Slattery, Esq.
B. W. Currie, Esq.	Gerald W. Wolff, Esq., M.P.

Mr. B. H. Holland, *Secretary*.

(*Chairman.*) I desire, gentlemen, before the public are admitted, to thank you very sincerely for the kind resolution you were good enough to pass, which I have not been able formally to acknowledge before. I am also very much obliged to you for excusing my attendance during the last three or four meetings of the Commission. I have, however, read carefully all that has passed, but I am very sorry I could not be present.

Sir Edward W. Hamilton, K.C.B., further examined.

[illegible]. (*Chairman.*) You have presumably read the evidence and the various statements laid before the Commissioners, and before your examination is concluded, I dare say you may wish to make some remarks that may occur to you at this stage?—There are one or two points of a general character which, with the leave of the Commission, I should like to touch upon, if I may; not really that I have any new points to raise, but since I submitted my memorandum, I have had the advantage of reading the valuable evidence that has been tendered to the Commission, and it is by the light of that evidence that I should like to make a few supplementary remarks. The Commissioners will, of course, understand that they are only remarks of a general character, and if I express any opinion it will be understood that it is only the personal opinion of one who has given a great deal of consideration to the question, and that it commits no one at the Treasury in any sort of way.

I take it that the practical question which has been referred to the arbitration of the Royal Commissioners is, whether, as compared with Great Britain, Ireland is, or is not, being overcharged by the Imperial Government relatively to her taxable capacity. But the past treatment of Ireland, financially, has been largely dwelt upon; and I venture first to summarise the principal aspects in which the historical part of the question strikes me.

In addition to the two periods of Grattan's Parliament and the first 16 years of the Union, before the two Exchequers were consolidated, there are, I submit, three subsequent periods which may be with propriety and indeed ought to be, separately considered.

With the leave of the Commission, I will make a few remarks on each of these five periods:—

I.—The Grattan Parliament, 1782–1800.

During that period I gather that nothing in the shape of unfair treatment has been seriously alleged against the Imperial Government. Ireland had to pay her own way, to provide means with which to meet the expenditure incurred within her own shores. With the exception of maintaining a limited number of soldiers abroad on foreign service, involving small cost, she was practically exempted from contributing to Imperial charges. What did affect Ireland's finances in a very serious manner towards the end of this period was the war with France, combined with her own disturbed state. But the expenditure on account

Sir E. W. Hamilton, K.C.B.

31 Oct. 1894.

Financial history. Second period.

of the war was expenditure incurred in the defence of Ireland herself, and the cost of repressing the rebellion was a charge which naturally and properly fell upon her.

II.—The Union with separate Exchequers, 1801–17.

The second period covers the first 16 years after the Union. During that time, notwithstanding that Ireland was incorporated with Great Britain for legislative purposes, there was a separate Irish Exchequer, a separate Chancellor of that Exchequer, a separate Irish Budget, and a separate system of Irish taxation with a necessary Customs cordon; all, of course, controlled by the Imperial Parliament. With the exception of the charges in respect of the British and Irish debts previously incurred, which were to continue to be borne severally by Great Britain and Ireland, the whole of the expenditure of the United Kingdom, local as well as Imperial, was aggregated, and Ireland's share was fixed at two-seventeenths, or 11·76 per cent. of that expenditure.

I believe the financial provisions of the Treaty of Union were carried out as nearly as could be, in conformity with its intentions. The Treaty was, I admit, and very explicitly worded in some respects, more especially as regards meeting the contingency of Ireland's having to borrow on her own account; and the consequence of that ambiguity has been, not unnaturally, that much has been said as to her having been made to bear the entire charge for the debt which she incurred during those 16 years. But I venture to think that it is clear that, had she not been debited with that charge, she might have largely evaded the provisions of the Treaty. As it was, considerably less in the way of war taxes was imposed on Ireland than on Great Britain, and, had Ireland been only required to pay two-seventeenths of the charge in respect of debt created on her account, she need scarcely have imposed any additional taxation with which to meet the great war expenditure. The Treaty did not contemplate—and it is not surprising that it did not contemplate—such a long double struggle with France; but neither could it surely have been intended that, if Ireland did not provide her quota out of the proceeds of taxes, she was only to bear less than 12 per cent. of the charge for borrowing the money with which to pay her quota.

A further important consideration to be borne in mind in connection with this period is that, out of the total amount with which Ireland was debited on account of her quota between 1801 and 1817, viz.: 99,000,000*l*., all but about 16,000,000*l*. was, according to the best records to which access can be had, incurred on and for Ireland. Accordingly, with that exception, I admit no inconsiderable one, Ireland, it may be said, would have fared no better financially, had there been no Union; for, anterior to the Union, as we know, she always bore, and not unnaturally, the whole of the public charges incurred within her own shores; and perhaps it is not unfair to assume that, had Ireland retained her own legislative independence, she would have been induced to contribute, even if she had not volunteered of her own accord to contribute, something more substantial towards the expenses to which the Imperial Government were exposed in carrying on the great war with France. I am, however, ready to admit that, though two-seventeenths of the public expenditure of the United Kingdom in times of peace might have been within the means of Ireland to cope with, yet two-seventeenths of the vast expenditure which was incurred in that international struggle was probably beyond her means, except at the cost of involving herself in an overwhelming, if not ruinous, debt. As the lengthened protraction of the war and the dimensions which it assumed could not have been foreseen when the Treaty was made, it follows that, if Ireland was made subject to an undue share of the public expenditure of the United Kingdom, it was due more than anything else, to the conflict of extraordinary circumstances, which upset, and could not fail to upset, all calculations.

III.—The Period following the Consolidation of the Exchequers, 1817–52.

Third period.

I come now to the third period. I take that period to be the first 35 years after the consolidation of the British and Irish Exchequers, 1817–1852. The reason why I take those years as a separate period will, I think, be immediately apparent, if already it is not so.

Apart from the remission of taxes effected on the conclusion of the war with France, from which no doubt, Great Britain derived relatively greater relief than Ireland, and with reason, because Great Britain had submitted, as she could afford to submit, to be more heavily taxed, a tolerably consistent policy was pursued. The essential feature of that policy was the great clearance of the tariff, accompanied during the last 10 years with the re-imposition of the Income Tax in Great Britain; in other words, the repeal of all duties on raw materials and the reduction or repeal of duties on a vast number of articles of consumption.

Now, Ireland not being, or perhaps rather having ceased to be, a manufacturing country, she unquestionably derived less direct advantage than Great Britain from the repeal of the duties on raw materials. On the other hand, Ireland, with one possible qualification, benefited equally with Great Britain from the repeal or reduction of duties on articles of consumption, and she was exempted from subjection to the Income Tax. The possible qualification to which I allude has reference to the repeal of the Corn Laws towards the close of this period. The starving condition of Ireland was, no doubt, a contributory cause of the repeal of those laws, but I will not venture to say whether that measure was less of an advantage to Ireland than to Great Britain. All I would point out is that it was the opinion of Sir Robert Peel that the change might bear hardly on Ireland, which was then, as now, essentially an agricultural country, and that he gave practical effect to that opinion by relieving her of her existing liability to bear on her own shoulders half the cost of the constabulary.

The net result, however, of the financial policy adopted by the Imperial Parliament during this period, was that Ireland emerged from the period rather less heavily taxed than she was at the commencement of it.

In 1819–20 (I am obliged to take the years for which we have the corrected figures), her total tax revenue amounted to 14*s*. 1*d*. per head of the population, and in 1849–50 to 13*s*. 11*d*., or, if we take separately the indirect and direct taxes, the comparison stands as follows:—

Year.	Indirect Taxes.	Direct Taxes.
	s. *d.*	*s.* *d.*
1819–20	11 0	3 1
1849–50	12 2	1 9
	+ 1 2	− 1 4

Therefore, there is apparently nothing serious to be laid to the charge of the Imperial Parliament as regards its treatment of Ireland during this period.

IV.—The Ten Years preceding the last Inquiry into the Taxation of Ireland, 1853–1863.

Here again I am obliged to take the nearest decennial periods, because these are the only years in which the figures have been corrected.

During that period, as compared with the past, Ireland was undoubtedly hit very hard. Not only were the spirit duties in Ireland levelled up to the English rates, from 2*s*. 8*d*. per gallon to 10*s*.; but the Income tax was extended to that part of the United Kingdom for the first time. The effect of this equalisation of one duty, and this imposition of another, was severely felt by Ireland. Her total tax revenue, which worked out at 13*s*. 11*d*. per head of population in 1849–50, had risen in 1859–60 to 1*l*. 4*s*. 1*d*. or, if we take the indirect taxes and direct taxes separately, the increases come out as follows:—

Year.	Indirect Taxes.	Direct Taxes.
	£ *s.* *d.*	*s.* *d.*
1849–50	0 12 2	1 9
1859–60	0 19 4	4 9
	+ 7 2	+ 3 0

It may be that, owing to the exodus during that period of large numbers of the poorest classes in Ireland, the taxable capacity of the average Irishman in 1859-60 was higher than that of the average Irishman 10 years previously. But, however that may be, it appears to me that the Commission might in 1864-5 have made out a stronger case than they did for Ireland. At the same time, one need not be surprised that their finding was not more conclusive. In the first place, they do not seem to have had the materials with which to draw the comparison properly; and, in the second place, they may well have been deterred from drawing any very definite conclusions by the obvious difficulties necessarily attending any proposals which involved the reversal of a policy only adopted so recently.

V.—The last Thirty Years, 1864-1894.

The main point to bear in mind in connexion with this period as compared with the preceding one, is, that Ireland has fared very differently. Though the expenditure for which the State has to provide has grown so vastly, from 70,000,000*l.* to 100,000,000*l.*, or by more than 40 per cent., yet Ireland is contributing to the common purse very little more now than she was 20 or 30 years ago. For, while her contribution to taxation in 1860 (I am obliged to adhere to the decennial periods prior to 1889-90) was 1*l.* [illegible] per head of her population, it is now about 1*l.* [illegible], or, if we confine the comparison to indirect taxes, and it is only indirect taxes which affect the consuming masses, we find that the increase is about 1*s.* [illegible] per head. I will not hazard a personal opinion whether the average Irish consumer is better able to afford to pay 1*l.* [illegible] in taxes now than 1*l.* [illegible] 20 or 30 years ago; though, according to Sir R. Giffen, the average wages or earnings of small farmers and labourers in Ireland have improved by at least 100 per cent. during the last half century. (Second Series of Essays on Finance, p. [illegible].) At any rate, however, the addition to taxation has been slight, and the comparative lightness of the contribution has, in view of the vastly augmented services which have been thrown on the State, only been made possible by the tendency which there has been throughout the period to shift the burden of taxation from indirect to direct taxation, whereby the poorer country of the two, which must relatively contribute less to direct taxation than the richer country, has necessarily benefited. The extent of this tendency is shown by the fact that, whereas in 1860 no less than 65 per cent. of the total tax-revenue was raised by indirect taxation and 35 per cent. by direct taxation, the respective proportions per cent. now are 53 and 47, and, in consequence of the increasingly large yield from the new "Estate Duty," such proportions are becoming more and more in favour of the consumer. By the changes of the last 30 or 35 years, resulting in great reductions of the duties on tea, coffee, and currants, and the total disappearance of the duties on sugar, timber, and pepper, Ireland must have been materially relieved. At any rate, it may be said that, had it not been for these changes, the consuming classes in Ireland would be at the present time much more heavily taxed. Moreover, in addition to the relief of indirect taxation at the expense of direct taxation, the great source of direct taxes—the income tax—has been made easier for those who have but small incomes. The total exemption has been raised, and the abatements have been extended. Accordingly, any part of the United Kingdom which has relatively a greater number of people of small incomes would benefit the most by this change.

It may, however, be said that, notwithstanding this shifting of burdens from the poor to the rich, there is the fact that, while the taxes extracted from British pockets show in the period of the last 30 or 35 years a decrease of about 5*s.* per head of the population, the amount similarly extracted from Irish pockets is not less, but more by about half-a-crown, and that, though every inhabitant in Ireland pays on an average about [illegible] per annum in taxes less than the inhabitant of Great Britain, yet that, regard being had to the estimated resources of the poorer country, a contribution of about 1*l.* [illegible] per head of its population is relatively a heavier amount to exact from Ireland than about 2*l.* [illegible] per head from Great Britain. This argument, which brings me to the consideration of the principal point of reference to the Commission, appears to raise a very difficult question, not only applicable to one particular period, but to all periods. It is this—are per capita calculations the correct test of the equalities or inequalities of taxation in one country as compared with another? In other words, can any correct conclusions be drawn as to the true incidence of taxation relatively on two countries from the fact that one pays *x* per head and the other pays *y* per head? I venture to think that such a test by itself is not an adequate or a fair test, and indeed may be a distinctly misleading one. It seems to me to be essentially necessary to follow up the comparison more closely by examining how much of the taxes taken out of the pockets of each country is spent on itself for which it may be considered that there is (as it were) "value received." For it is obvious that without such examination it might happen that the State which has the disposition of the proceeds of taxation might, while apparently taking more out of the poorer country relatively to its resources, be really undertaking for that country charges which the richer country has to provide for itself out of some other pocket. In fact, expenditure undertaken by the State may be a form of relieving burdens and adjusting inequalities of taxation. Indeed, it is the only relief which the State can administer to one part of a United Kingdom, short of imposing a differential system of taxation, and a most striking instance of what I may call relief by expenditure is furnished by the present local taxation grants, whereby the pockets of the ratepayers are saved at the expense of the pockets of the taxpayers. In the case of Ireland there is no doubt that resort has been had, ever since the time of Sir Robert Peel, to such form of relief; and it is often forgotten that, when the spirit duty was raised by Mr. Goschen in 1890 by 6*d.* a gallon, to which at the time strong exception, not unnaturally, was taken by the representatives of Ireland (and I may add, of Scotland), it was raised not for the purpose of replenishing the Imperial Exchequer, but for the purpose of assisting local authorities. In fact, nearly the entire proceeds of these increases in Ireland (i.e., [illegible] per cent. of the whole of the yield) were given back to Ireland. It may, of course, be said that this argument of relief by expenditure only holds good if, and so far as, the person who pays the taxes is the same as the person who benefits by the expenditure, that it is no consolation to the inhabitant of Dublin, who thinks himself overcharged by the State, to be told that the State is assisting the inhabitants of Galway by building light railways in that county. But to such a contention as this, I submit that there is the reply that for general purposes, especially where regard is had to the terms of reference to the Commission, we are bound to take the country as a whole, to treat Ireland as one unit and Great Britain as another unit.

Regard being had to these considerations, is not the conclusion to be drawn this?—That the best, and indeed the only true, standard whereby to determine whether Ireland is overtaxed as compared with Great Britain is to take the respective amounts which the State extracts from the taxpayers of the two countries for Imperial, as distinguished from local purposes, and to compare the amounts so extracted with the respective resources of each so far as they are ascertainable?

Let us see how this comparison stands with respect to Great Britain and Ireland. I take the decennial periods for which the accounts have been adjusted and the consecutive years from 1889-90 to 1893-94, and what do we find?

Year.	Balance of true Irish Revenue available for Imperial Services.	Amount of Imperial Charges.	Proportion of Ireland's Contribution to Imperial Charges.
	£	£	
1819-20	[illegible]	[illegible]	1/10th
1829-30	[illegible]	[illegible]	[illegible]
1839-40	[illegible]	[illegible]	[illegible]
1849-50	[illegible]	47,1[illegible]	[illegible]
1859-60	[illegible]	[illegible]	[illegible]
1869-70	[illegible]	[illegible]	[illegible]
1879-80	[illegible]	[illegible]	[illegible]
1889-90	[illegible]	[illegible]	[illegible]
1890-91	[illegible]	[illegible]	[illegible]
1891-92	[illegible]	[illegible]	[illegible]
1892-93	[illegible]	[illegible]	[illegible]
1893-94	[illegible]	53,34[illegible]	[illegible]

In order, however, to be absolutely fair towards Ireland, I will consider that half the charge for the Irish Constabulary and Dublin Police is an Imperial charge, just as much as if it were a military charge; and by so doing I, pro tanto, of course, increase Ireland's contribution to Imperial services.

When adjusted in this way the contribution works out as follows:—

Year.	Balance of Irish Revenue available for Imperial Services after deducting Irish Local Charges of Half the Police Charge.	Imperial Charges, including Half the Irish Police Charge.	Proportion of Ireland's Contribution to Imperial Charges.
	£	£	
1819–20 -	[illegible]	[illegible]	1/10th
1829–30 -	[illegible]	[illegible]	[illegible]
1839–40 -	[illegible]	[illegible]	[illegible]
1849–50 -	[illegible]	[illegible]	[illegible]
1859–60 -	[illegible]	[illegible]	1/10th
1869–70 -	[illegible]	[illegible]	1/11th
1879–80 -	[illegible]	[illegible]	1/17th
1889–90 -	[illegible]	[illegible]	1/19th
1890–91 -	[illegible]	[illegible]	[illegible]
1891–92 -	[illegible]	[illegible]	[illegible]
1892–93 -	[illegible]	[illegible]	[illegible]
1893–94 -	[illegible]	[illegible]	[illegible]

Now, I venture to think these are striking figures.

In the first place, it appears that the amount of Ireland's contribution to Imperial expenditure, which I take to be the true test of the justice of the present financial relations between Great Britain and Ireland is not in excess of Ireland's estimated relative resources. For, if the respective resources of the two countries are best comparable by the aggregate of the individual incomes of each (and this seems to be the view of a high economic authority), I gather that Irish resources may be said to be about one twenty-second of British resources. This would mean that, for every 22s. required to be disbursed in the shape of pay to the military and sailors of the United Kingdom, 21s. should be provided by Great Britain and 1s. by Ireland. As a matter of fact, Ireland only contributes to such pay 1s. for every [illegible] expended, or, if the allowance which I have made for police be taken into account, 1s. for every [illegible] so expended.

In the second place, the figures which I have adduced show how different is the position relatively to Great Britain which Ireland occupies now from that which she was occupying at the time when her case was last referred to arbitration. I am not able to say what the relative resources of the two countries were at that time. I take it that, owing to the continuous "leaps and bounds" made by Great Britain in wealth, and the comparatively stationary condition of Ireland, the relative resources were formerly not so divergent as they are now. But mark the enormous change that has taken place! Thirty-five years ago, the Imperial Government was receiving from Ireland, on the calculation which (as it were) gives her the benefit of the doubt as regards certain expenditure, one-tenth of the amount which was expended on Imperial services, and now such contribution is only one twenty-third. At any rate there has been a great reform, brought about not only by the shifting of the incidence of taxation from the poor to the rich, but also by the scrupulously just manner in which Ireland has been financially treated of recent years, as proved by the amounts of local taxation grants assigned to her. Whether or not that reform has been adequate, it is for the Commission, not for me to say.

At the risk of wearying the Commission, I should like to make one or two more remarks of a general character. A good deal has been said—and probably with reason—about costly administration and extravagant expenditure in Ireland. The "policing" of Ireland is an instance of costly administration. But this may or may not be due to the peculiar conditions of the country and to reasons of high policy which are beyond my province, and in these remarks of mine I have treated a part of the cost as an Imperial charge. It is otherwise with extravagant and useless expenditure. Without more information than I possess, I do not pretend to be able to lay my fingers on any weak spots specifically, but that there is room for economy there is probably little doubt. For instance, under the head of legal charges, the expenditure in Ireland is, relatively to the population, three times as great as it is in England. It may be asked what is the practical use of making an attempt to effect economies. There are the [illegible] difficulties connected with reducing expenditure in the shape of vested interests. A saving could only be effected gradually, and the net result would be small, while, even supposing that it were appreciable, it would mainly be the Imperial purse and not Ireland itself that would reap the benefit. I submit, however, that these arguments should have little force. If there be wasteful or unnecessary expenditure in the administration of justice or in any other branch of administration in Ireland it surely ought to be stopped. The existence of such expenditure is demoralising in itself, since it begets waste. But what is more important is that any money that can be saved might, without further encroachments on the common purse, be devoted to some really useful purpose in Ireland.

I feel sure that the Commission will wish to draw practical, not theoretical, conclusions, and that they will also wish that any suggestions which they may have to make may be of a practical or feasible kind. Therefore, whatever may be their finding, collectively or individually, I think I need not allude to the difficulties of setting up a system of differential taxes and to the grave inconveniences (to say the least) which would result therefrom, and might in the end militate against the real interests of Ireland.

I pass on, therefore, to another point which, though it may not be much more practical than a differential system of taxation, is one that is very likely to be urged by the representatives of England, though, perhaps, not of Scotland.

It may be argued that a country like Ireland, which, with the solitary exception of tea, has no necessary of life subject to taxation, can hardly be said to be overweighted by Imperial imposts, and that even if every allowance be made for the history, habits, and circumstances of the country, the remedy for being [illegible] taxed is in the Irishman's own hands by consuming less spirits and less tobacco. For if the Irishmen of to-day were content to drink spirits and smoke tobacco to the same extent as their fathers did about 35 years ago, I calculate that they would reduce the [illegible] [illegible] of taxation chargeable to (about) [illegible], which sum would be larger by about [illegible]. It has been taken into account in his calculation.

I confess that I do myself see a distinction between taxation on articles which are essential to existence and taxation on articles with which at any rate a large portion of the population finds itself able to dispense. The first kind of taxation is clearly more obligatory and unavoidable than the second. On the other hand, it may be contended, with considerable force, that it is the amount which you take out of the taxpayer's purse which is material, and not the manner in which you take it. Therefore, I do not wish to labour the point. All I will say is, that the increase in the consumption of spirits and tobacco per head of population since 1860, whether it is or is not necessary for the well-being of the people, would seem, at any rate, to be a satisfactory indication that the spending power of the present generation in Ireland is greater than the spending power of the last generation; and I would further point out that, granted that the taxes on such articles bear heavily on Ireland, it may be held that it would be unfair to relieve the smoker and the alcohol drinker at the expense of others who abstain from, or indulge more moderately in (what, at any rate, may be called) expensive tastes.

However that may be, I fear that the attainment of absolute equality of taxation between two parts of an United Kingdom is beyond the wit of man to devise. It is as difficult to attain an absolute "equality of sacrifice" between individuals.

This is a consideration which will doubtless weigh with the Commission, and therefore it is unnecessary for me to enlarge upon it.

In saying what I have said—and perhaps I have said too much—I feel I have made some grave admissions—admissions which may even reflect on past financial policies. But at the risk of being charged with presumption, what I have endeavoured to do is to take a broad view of all the questions involved in this difficult inquiry, and I hope it may be considered that I have partially, at any rate, attained my primary object, which has been to hold an even hand (as far as it is possible) between the British and Irish taxpayers. My sympathy extends to both equally.

It is often alleged that the Treasury will never admit that there are flaws in its administration of finance. I deny that the allegation is well founded. If there be flaws, let them be pointed out, and let every effort be made to try and remedy those flaws and the inequalities which may result from them. The difficulty of doing perfect justice, as J. S. Mill says, should not deter the State from doing as much justice as it can. But what is most important is that, in endeavouring to remedy one inequality, we should not redress it by creating another inequality—in other words, by shifting a burden from one set of shoulders which feels the pressure of it to another set of shoulders which is equally unable to bear it.

I must apologise to the Commission for the length of these remarks, but I thought, given in a consecutive form, in this way they might really be more helpful than if I gave them in evidence, which, of course, leads to cross-examination, and, therefore, I venture to give these remarks before the Commission, though, I admit, they do not really raise any new points; they are more a sort of review than anything else of the inquiry up to date.

9938. (*Lord Welby.*) Sir Robert Giffen, in discussing the relative capacity of Great Britain and Ireland to bear taxation, held, as I understood him, that no consideration ought to be given to the manner in which taxes levied from Ireland are spent. That is to say, we need not inquire how much of the taxation levied in Ireland is given back to Ireland. Do you think that this exclusion of the expenditure side of the question stated in what appears to me an absolute and unqualified manner is sound?—No, I confess I do not. With all due deference to the high authority by whom such an argument is held, I think it can be shown that, if pressed to its logical conclusion, such an argument may lead to most misleading results, and verge on a reductio ad absurdum. I think I can show that later on to the Commission, if they wish it, by some hypothetical illustrations.

9939. I propose to test the doctrine by an example or two, and I should like, in the first place, to take the police. I think the Imperial Exchequer pays, does it not, the whole charge of the Irish Police, but only a moiety of the police charge in Great Britain, the other being provided by local rates in England?—Yes, it is about a moiety, that is to say, the contribution to local taxation in Great Britain includes half the previous year's cost of pay and clothing of the police.

9940. In order to eliminate debateable points from the discussion, let us assume the fair charge for the Irish police to be the same in proportion to population as the police costs in Great Britain, charging the balance, for the purpose of our argument, as an Imperial service. On that assumption, I am not sure, but I think the cost of the Irish police would be about 600,000*l*.?—According to my calculation, I make it about 670,000*l*.; but for all practical purposes the cost may be taken at 600,000*l*.

9941. It will not cut upon the extensive side?—No, not on the excessive side.

9942. And the whole of that 600,000*l*. is now defrayed by the Imperial Exchequer, is it not?—That is so.

9943. No charge is made upon Irish rates?—None, except that there is a small contribution of about 40,000*l*. a year towards the cost of the Dublin police, which, I think, is practically a charge upon the rates in Ireland.

9944. Whereas if the Imperial Exchequer treated Ireland as unfavourably or in the same way as it treats Great Britain, it would only give her 300,000*l*., and Ireland would have to raise the moiety of her police charge, as Great Britain has now to do, by further rates?—Yes; if Ireland was treated exactly on all-fours with Great Britain as to regards the police, that would be so.

9945. And, in that case, Ireland would have to raise 300,000*l*. out of local rates?—Yes, assuming so large a police charge in Ireland was necessary.

9946. We are acting upon the assumption that a police force is necessary in Ireland, and that it bears the same proportion as it does in Great Britain?—Yes.

9947. Now is not this a special boon to Ireland, a special relief of her local taxation which Great Britain does not enjoy? In other words, if Ireland were not exceptionally favoured, or treated in this respect exceptionally, would not this contribution of 300,000*l*. cease, and would she not have to provide that amount out of local taxation?—That would be the case.

9948. And so far the two countries are treated differently in regard to the expenditure upon that particular head?—No doubt on that particular head of expenditure that is so.

9949. We may put it, may we not, in this way, that it is a special gift to Ireland in relief of local taxation?—Yes.

9950. Or, again, if a tax in Ireland producing 300,000*l*. a year were repealed, and if Ireland were left, like Great Britain and Scotland, to raise the moiety of her proper police charge by local taxation, would not the practical effect to Ireland be the same as the gift of that 300,000*l*. by the Imperial Exchequer to Ireland—a gift in which England and Scotland do not participate?—The arrangement connected with the pay of the police in Ireland is equivalent to remitting taxation in Ireland to the extent of over 300,000*l*. a year, assuming that her requirements could be met by a police force proportional to that of Great Britain.

9951. Therefore, in the instance of the police, is not this special gift to Ireland, in relief of local taxation, the equivalent of a reduction of Imperial taxation to that amount?—I think so; Ireland, like the rest of the United Kingdom, may be said to have two pockets—a tax pocket and a rate pocket, and it is practically the same thing to take one out of one pocket or out of the other, if you treat Ireland as an unit, as I think you must, for present purposes.

9952. Is there not in the next place another service to which we may apply the same argument, does not the same argument apply, in a great degree, to education?—Yes.

9953. The charge on rates is diminished in Great Britain; but, still, there is a very heavy charge on rates, is there not?—There is a very heavy charge, no doubt, in connexion with that. I am afraid I am not acquainted with the education system in Ireland, but I am under the impression that there is no charge in respect of education. I have always understood, but I shall be corrected by the honourable members who represent Ireland, that practically education is free in Ireland.

9954. (*Lord Farrer.*) And free at the cost of the Imperial Exchequer?—Yes, free at the cost of the Imperial Exchequer.

9955. (*Lord Welby.*) That, of course, is the point. We know that the rates in Great Britain have to provide for a very large proportion of the education?—Yes; and there is a point I may mention to the Commission now, and it is this: that when free education was granted to Great Britain in 1891, there was assigned to Ireland an equivalent grant, as it was called at the time by Mr. Goschen, though in fact she had already got the boon of free education. That is one of the things which I had in my mind when I said what I did about the just manner in which Ireland had been treated financially in recent years. The assignment of that equivalent grant of 185,000*l*. (I think it was) a year was erring on the side of generosity.

9956. Almost out of sympathy with Ireland?—Yes, perhaps that might be said.

9957. At all events, in the case of education also we find that the Imperial Exchequer contributes to Ireland a proportion of the education expenditure which it has contributed to education in Great Britain?—I presume that may be said to be the case.

9958. Let us press that question a little further, and test Sir Robert Giffen's conclusions by a somewhat enquiry other. Our Commission directs us to report upon what principle of comparison and by the application of what specific standards the relative capacity of Great Britain and Ireland to bear taxation may be most equitably determined. Sir R. Giffen, as an acknowledged authority, comes to aid us in answering that question, and he gives us a calculation, based, to a certain extent, upon conjecture,—I think we may say skilful and expert conjecture of the highest authority that we have, but still a conjecture,—which leads to the conclusion that the relative taxable capacity of Great Britain is to that of Ireland about as 20 to 1?—Yes, or thereabouts. I think it rather leans to one twenty-second, but I suppose for present purposes one-twentieth is sufficiently near.

9959. This is, in fact, advice proceeding from the highest and most respected authority that we have, that we should test the taxation actually raised from Ireland by that standard, and as a Commission is not appointed to express pious or abstract opinions, we must, if we accept Sir R. Giffen's opinion on relative taxable capacity, be expected to recommend remedial measures, and if Ireland pays more than one-twentieth of Imperial taxation, what must it be since we may not consider on the other side of the account any question connected with expenditure?—I think that seems to be the logical conclusion deducible from Sir Robert Giffen's reasoning.

9960. Now, supposing the Imperial legislature for some reason or other to have made an arrangement by which the whole of the local expenditure of Ireland were paid from the Exchequer, leaving the local expenditure of England and Scotland charged on the rates, the Commission would not, according to Sir Robert Giffen's canons, be allowed to take that important fact into consideration, and could only report that the taxes levied from Ireland largely exceeded the conjectural figure by which the relative capacity of the two countries to bear taxation is to be measured?—That would be so, unless I have misunderstood Sir R. Giffen.

9961. There is no other conclusion at which the Commission could arrive?—No; that appears to me to be the conclusion to be drawn from Sir Robert Giffen's argument, and perhaps I may be allowed to show by an illustration what seems to me to be the result of Sir Robert Giffen's canon, if pushed to its logical consequence. Supposing that in 1864-5 the Committee had come to the conclusion that Ireland was overtaxed, and recognising that it was impossible or impracticable at any rate to recommend the system of differential taxation, the Committee had recommended, that the whole of the expenditure charged upon rates in Ireland was to be undertaken by the Imperial Exchequer, and that the Government of the day had accepted that recommendation. If I understand Sir Robert Giffen rightly, then the Commission would be precluded from taking that consideration into account; though the inequality which the Committee of 1864-5 had found would have been practically adjusted by what I call relief by expenditure. In fact, I think that relief by expenditure out of the common purse is the only practical way of relieving an inequality in one part of the kingdom as compared with another, if it is found to be impracticable to have a differential system of taxation. According, however, to Sir Robert Giffen, unless I misunderstand him, no account could now be taken of such a remedy by the present Commission, because we must not see how the taxes taken from Ireland are spent.

9962. The impression left upon my mind by Sir Robert Giffen's evidence is precisely the same as the impression left upon yours. I could not trace any qualification of the assumption of his doctrine, and that is why I wanted to obtain your views upon the subject, because I feel that it is impossible in dealing with this as a practical question to accept in the unqualified manner in which it has been put forward, and by such a high authority, such a conclusion. In fact, the only conclusion to which one can come in considering that the taxation falls too heavily upon Ireland is redress by expenditure, is it not?—I think so.

9963. Of course within a reasonable limit?—Yes; within reasonable limits.

9964. Again, is it not the case that large sums have been granted for the construction of light railways in Ireland, no similar grants having been made to England?—There have been considerable sums granted for the construction of light railways in Ireland. I am afraid I have not got the exact figure with me, but I think the amount has been about 1,200,000*l.* in the last four or five years.

9965. And taking now these special grants to Ireland, can one avoid the conclusion that these grants that are given to one country and not to the other must be taken into consideration when we are endeavouring to judge of the burdens of taxation so levied, and also obliged to form that judgment upon what I think Sir Robert Giffen would admit is, to a certain extent, a conjectural estimate of the relative taxable capacity of the two countries?—I confess it appears to me to be absolutely essential to take the expenditure side into account for the reasons I have already given; otherwise we are doing an injustice to Great Britain, out of whose pockets the bulk of such expenditure in Ireland comes.

9966. The Commission is to advise how the relative capacity of Great Britain to bear taxation can be most equitably determined. Would it be equitable to Great Britain to assume an ever-more or less conjectural estimate of the incomes of the two countries, and measure by that standard the taxation levied in the two countries, and if the taxation levied in Ireland exaggerates that proportion to advise remedial measures without inquiring or examining whether the income received into the Exchequer from Great Britain and Ireland is expended upon like principles in the two countries?—I think the equity of such an assumption is open to very grave question, more especially where it is founded, to a great extent, upon conjecture.

9967. Sir Robert Giffen lays some stress, I think, upon the point that he found no precedent for taking into consideration the nature of the expenditure of the countries when comparing their finances, in order to ascertain whether the public burdens are equitably divided between them. May not the absence of such consideration be due to the fact that it would be difficult to find a precedent for the problem now before us?—I think that certainly is so. I do not suppose there is an exact precedent for it, but I think Sir Robert Giffen went even further than that and said that he was not aware there was any economic authority for drawing the distinction which we have drawn between Imperial and local expenditure. Now, I can adduce a very high economic authority for that distinction. It was Mr. Goschen himself who personally (as I think Lord Welby will himself remember) drew the lines of those Returns which have since been called the Financial Relations Papers, and therefore we have his authority, which is a very high one, for taking into account what is spent in one country as well as what is taken out of it in the shape of taxes. The distinction between Local and Imperial Expenditure may, I admit, be open to some question on certain details, but I do not think that there is room for any serious error in the returns to which I am referring.

9968. I think it is in both our memories that Mr. Goschen was specially responsible from his own experience of the Returns?—Yes, he took an enormous amount of trouble about them.

9969. But I think we must bear in mind that so far as this country is concerned a very special problem has to be considered, and that it is not sufficient to say that no precedent is to be found in Political Economists' writings?—No, more especially as you are not comparing two countries, but two parts of one country really.

9970. And endeavouring to make a distinction between them?—Yes.

9971. (*Lord Farrer.*) Are there not precedents to be found in the German or American Empires relating to that point?—I am afraid I am not sufficiently well acquainted with the financial systems of those countries to be able to describe them, or to say how far they may be said to have a bearing on the present inquiry.

9972. (*Lord Welby.*) How would you, with your long experience at the Treasury, during which you have constantly been called upon to draw papers as bases for the discussion of financial questions, regard the rule of Sir Robert Giffen's, would you feel justified in omitting all consideration of the nature and character of the expenditure in two countries if you were weighing their financial systems with a view to ascertain which of the two is the more heavily taxed?—No, I should not, for the reasons which I have already given.

9973. And I may go further, and ask, is not the exclusion of such an important consideration as the character of the expenditure likely to lead to a grave error on the part of financial authorities if they are practically told in such a problem as that before us that, in comparing the financial conditions of two countries, thriftiness in the one country and excessive expenditure in the other, are not essential parts of the problem?—I think so.

9974. I think in your remarks to-day you have already alluded to that matter?—Yes.

9975. And your view is very much in accordance with that?—Yes.

9976. And I think you have also, in the remarks which you have made to us, dwelt upon a point which is very strongly in my mind, namely, that if the expenditure on local services in Ireland is in any degree extravagant, that is a point which ought to be most carefully considered, inasmuch as it has a most important bearing upon the recommendations which it may be the duty of the Commission to submit?—I think so, certainly; indeed I do not see how, without taking into account the expenditure in Ireland, it is possible for the Commission to determine what she is now really contributing, and what she ought to contribute to Imperial expenditure, which is one of the main points, as I understand, of the reference to the Commission, and the principal point on which all recent discussions with respect to Irish finance have turned.

9977. I think your memorandum, which you laid before the Commission at an earlier stage, shows that statesmen of all parties have made it their object to establish identity of taxation in Great Britain and Ireland, at all events to the extent that customs and inland revenue officers shall not interfere with intercourse and trade between the two countries?—I think that has undoubtedly been so (ever since the consolidation of the two exchequers), and I am not aware that any responsible politician or financial authority has ever seriously advocated any departure from that policy.

9978. And this identity of taxation has been effected, the considerable exemption in favour of Ireland not being of a nature to hinder free intercourse?—Yes, that is so.

9979. If I heard your remarks rightly, you share the general impression that Ireland is a poorer country than Great Britain?—I do; I think that, viewed as a whole, there can be no question about that. If you take Sir Robert Giffen's estimate of the aggregate of the individual incomes of the two countries, he makes out, as I understand, that the aggregate income in Great Britain amounts to 1,[illegible],000,000*l*., as against 76,000,000*l*. in Ireland. That works out in Great Britain at 41*l*. 10*s*. per head of the population, and 16*l*. 4*s*. only in Ireland. I think that clearly shows that, man for man, Ireland is a poorer country. It may be that relatively to the total population there is in Ireland a larger percentage of those who have a struggle for existence than there is in Great Britain, but the difference in the aggregate result is more probably due to the presence in Great Britain, and to the absence in Ireland, of large incomes, rather than to there being more persons in Ireland relatively to Great Britain who have a struggle for existence. I do not think that can be satisfactorily proved unless Sir Robert Giffen could classify the number of persons as well as the aggregate incomes under the different heads of income tax payers, the intermediate classes, and the working classes. Therefore, I think it is very difficult to say whether the wage earners are relatively poorer in Ireland than those in Great Britain, but certainly as a whole, taken as a unit, there is no doubt that Ireland is a vastly poorer country than Great Britain.

9980. May I put it to you in this way, which I rather think represents Sir Robert Giffen's view, as to which I think some qualification ought to be made. He reckons what I may call the actual money-earning classes—that is to say, persons in employment—and if you take the income class, which you have just mentioned, I think he brings forward very considerable reasons for showing that what you may call unskilled labour in Ireland receives a much less monetary consideration than in England?—Yes, I should draw that inference from his figures.

9981. The qualification I suggested to you, and that I had struck upon in my question, was with reference to the word "employed." The weakness I think to a great extent in his deduction is, that he treats the whole of the people of England, and the whole of the people of Ireland as employed; he leaves out of consideration the vast amount of absolute poverty of unemployed labour that there is in Great Britain in the towns?—That is no doubt a material consideration.

9982. Have you read Sir Robert Giffen's evidence, and looked at the tables which he has handed in, showing the rates of wages which different classes of employment earn in the two countries?—Yes, I have studied those tables.

9983. And Sir Robert Giffen enjoys a most deserved reputation, [illegible] with acquaintance with the facts upon which an estimate of the rates of remuneration of labour must be based?—There can be no question about that.

9984. His expert evidence tends to support the general impression that Ireland is a poorer country than Great Britain in this respect, that the same kinds of labour in the two countries do not earn in the main the same rates of remuneration, that wages are lower in Ireland than they are in Great Britain?—That is the general conclusion to be drawn from Sir Robert Giffen's figures.

9985. I think a qualification must be put to that, because I think there is a considerable amount of reason for thinking that skilled labour is not paid very much less in Ireland?—No, I believe it is more in the unskilled labour where the difference is most marked.

9986. Do you think that Sir Robert Giffen makes sufficient allowance for the money which a considerable class of Irish labourers earn by coming over to England and for other extra sources of income?—I hardly feel competent to express an opinion upon that point.

9987. It did not strike you in reading Sir Robert Giffen's evidence that perhaps he did not lay sufficient stress upon that?—No, it did not so strike me, but I think it is a fair point to take, although I am afraid my opinion would be worth nothing.

9988. Have you any reason for questioning Sir Robert Giffen's data, or should you be prepared to accept his general conclusions that money payment for services is less in Ireland than it is in Great Britain?—I think that is a point upon which I should be inclined to defer entirely to Sir Robert Giffen's conclusions. He is a much greater authority upon these subjects than I can pretend to be, and therefore I should accept his conclusions upon that point, unless any information to the contrary were forthcoming which would lead one to form another conclusion.

9989. I say money payment because this conclusion rests, I think, upon the assumption that the labourer receives money payment for his services, and that he pays actual money for the articles which he consumes?—Yes, that appears to be the basis of the comparison.

9990. That is to say, [illegible] in the case of the agricultural occupier or owner that he produces so much corn, milk, and cattle, which he sells at certain prices, and with the money thus obtained he buys his food?—Yes, I think so.

9991. But must we not look a little closer into this matter in order to arrive at a true opinion?—I will put a somewhat extreme case. Take two families, one living in Cork, and one in Northumberland; if they live on the produce of their own land, consume their own oatmeal, milk, potatoes, and bacon, should we not fall into error if we measured their means of livelihood by the prices of their produce as current in their respective localities? A quart of milk is equally nourishing in Cork and Northumberland, and we should, in the case assumed, be in error in reckoning its value at 1*d*. in Cork and at 2*d*. in Northumberland. I am not asserting that that is so. I give it as an instance of a qualification that may affect the generalisation of Sir Robert Giffen?—I think there is a great deal of force in that contention, but here, again, I should not like to express a decided opinion; it is one of those points on which [illegible] extremely difficult to estimate the true resources of one country relatively to those of another.

9992. Then again, we will take into consideration that the inhabitants of one country may very often dress themselves as warmly but more cheaply as compared with those of another, take such an instance as this:—The French peasants, for instance, a well-to-do race, are quite content to wear sabots, which are much cheaper than leather boots; and again, the house which the Irish occupier or owner has built for himself may be cheaper than that for which the English labourer pays a rent?—That may be so.

9993. And the habits of the country will have to be taken into consideration, will they not, before you can accept the exact comparison which is given by rates of wages?—I admit that these are possible qualifications that may have to be taken into account.

9994. I am not suggesting for a moment that it is a desirable thing in the least that the French should wear sabots?—I quite understand.

[illegible]

9995. And must not possible qualifications on these heads be taken into account before we pronounce authoritatively that the relative means of livelihood in the two countries can be measured by the simple test of money payments for labour, as shown by rates of wages?—I think so, as far as it is possible to do so.

9996. Of course, at my age then, I do not wish to press you for the suggested qualification of the general conclusions which we should draw from Sir Robert Giffen's evidence. In dealing with the question of capacity to bear taxation, a body such as this Commission would not be justified in expressing an opinion without careful consideration of all the circumstances which may qualify the general conclusion to which expert evidence would lead us?—I think that is a fair way of stating the case.

9997. But after allowing for such qualifications, and with a reserve as to making such a conclusion as Sir Robert Giffen draws a sufficient reason for legislative action in the present state of our knowledge, would you incline to the opinion that labour on the whole is worse remunerated in Ireland than it is in Great Britain, that it has in Ireland a smaller command over the necessaries of life, and that therefore in all probability the ordinary labouring family in Ireland, whether occupiers of small farms or simple labourers, have a smaller margin out of which to pay taxes than a similar family in Great Britain?—I am inclined to think that that is so; all evidence apparently tends to show that at any rate.

9998. (Mr. Sexton.) That they have a smaller margin? —Yes.

9999. (Lord Welby.) If so, may not identity of taxation in the two countries subject wage earners in Ireland to heavier burdens proportionately to their resources than wage earners in Great Britain?—I think so, but I suppose it may be taken that the inquiry is more an inquiry into the relative resources of the two countries as a whole, and not the wage-earners of one as compared with the wage-earners of another. I introduce that qualification; because I understand that the Commission is regarding the two countries as a whole and not comparing a particular class in one country with the same class in the other country.

10,000. I am dealing with Sir Robert Giffen's evidence, because it struck me that his evidence led so completely up to the idea that almost without qualification there was such a uniformity of burthen in the two countries?—Quite so.

10,001. And that, of course, the question becomes one very much of the wage earner, because I think scarcely any one would come forward to argue seriously that a man with 1,000*l.* or 2,000*l.* a year in Ireland should pay less taxation than a man with a similar income in Great Britain; it is a question really of the poorer classes, is it not?—I admit that, and I feel that very strongly myself.

10,002. Then rather following out what you say with regard to that point, is it sufficient to speak of the classes actually earning wages as if taken together with the wealthy and professional classes they constituted the whole community. Are there not in Great Britain an enormous number of persons who do not earn the wages set down in Sir Robert Giffen's tables, and if once the question of identity of taxation is raised, have you not then a population with stronger claims to relief than the Irish wage-earners?—I am afraid there is no question that there are unfortunately a large number of the community in Great Britain who are on the verge of pauperism, and who have a great struggle for existence. And they, no doubt, have an equally good claim to be considered as their fellow strugglers in Ireland have.

10,003. And with respect to whom you might advance just as good an argument with reference to the incidence of taxation?—No doubt. That is one of the inherent difficulties connected with an inquiry like this, and it reminds one how careful one must be not to attempt to remedy one grievance by creating another.

10,004. Can you draw a distinction between the two classes?—I doubt whether that is practicable.

10,005. Is not this a sample of the enormous difficulties which would attend an attempt to differentiate taxes according to assumed capacity to bear taxation? —Certainly.

[illegible] 10,006. I take it from what you have told, that you are distinctly of opinion that if the Commission is to consider what Ireland contributes to the common purse, it should also consider what it gets from the common purse?—Yes, and that is the reason why I think that the fairest test of whether Ireland is or is not overcharged is to take the relative contributions of the two countries to Imperial expenditure, and compare them, so far as possible, with their estimated relative resources. [illegible]

10,007. In fact, if, as some argue, Ireland is to be considered a separate country for the purpose of contribution, she must also be considered a separate country for purposes of expenditure?—I think so.

10,008. As I understand Sir Robert Giffen, expenditure sanctioned by the Imperial Parliament is Imperial expenditure, even although it is granted for purely local purposes in Ireland; that is not a theory that the Treasury would accept, is it?—Certainly not. It is difficult to draw a line between Imperial and local expenditure, I admit; and I do not pretend to be able to supply a definition in which there are no flaws, but, perhaps, what best supplies such a definition is to take each head of expenditure and consider whether it would be incurred, were there no such identity in question.

10,009. And that is really the ground upon which Mr. Childers made those distinctions in the returns of which you have been speaking, is it not?—Yes, I think so.

10,010. I think that in your remarks which you have made to us to-day, you distinctly stated that, in your view, expenditure on public services in Ireland bears a greater proportion to population, business and resources than similar expenditure in Great Britain?—I think there is no question about that. The expenditure on local services in Ireland, met out of Exchequer revenue, amounts (according to the figures already placed before the Commission) to 16*s.* 1*d.* per head, as against 7*s.* 4*d.* in Great Britain, or, if I take the revenue paid into the Exchequer and to the Local Taxation Account, it works out to 19*s.* 7*d.* in Ireland and to 11*s.* 5*d.* in Great Britain, and no doubt the disparity is still greater when account is taken of the business and resources as well as of population. [illegible]

10,011. That is what you may call local services in the two countries?—Yes, 19*s.* 7*d.* in Ireland, and 11*s.* 5*d.* in Great Britain.

10,012. And is it not a likely result that expenditure on local administration will be extravagant in a case where a poorer country has a common purse with a richer country, and a representation out of proportion to its wealth and population?—I think that would be the result. I think Mr. M. O'Brien illustrated that tendency in rather a forcible manner by comparing Ireland's position to that of a person with a small income who had to keep up an establishment in forced partnership with a man of large means, and to contribute to every outlay which the richer partner incurred. I think that was the way in which Mr. O'Brien put it in his evidence.

10,013. Was he not thinking that the contribution of Ireland to your army and navy, and debt, and so on, was in that proportion?—I think that was so.

10,014. But I say where a rich country and a poor country are joined together, the tendency will be that the scale of salaries will be fixed upon a higher scale in the poorer country?—I think that is quite possible.

10,015. In fact, will there not be a tendency on the part of the Imperial Parliament, in the composition of which the richer country predominates, to measure the expenditure of the poorer country by that of its richer sister, for instance, to fix the salaries and pensions of judicial and other officers rather by the standard of the richer country than by the amounts which professional services earn in the poorer country?—I think there may be a tendency in that direction.

10,016. I think, as a matter of fact, we have only to turn to the Finance Accounts, and look down the judicial establishment charges, to see that there is, as you say, a tendency in that direction?—I think that may be said to be the case. I am under the impression that in Ireland the pay of the Government employés compares more favourably than in Great Britain with the scale of pay in commercial service.

10,017. And therefore, so far as that is the case, the revenue of Ireland is not laid out as efficiently as it would be if due regard were paid to the different circumstances of the two countries?—That may very well be the case.

10,018. And I would suggest to you that if it were conceded that Ireland is a poorer country than Great Britain, and that Ireland is paying the same taxes as Great Britain, is she heavily taxed, it must be conceded also that the expenditure ought not to be on the same scale as that of Great Britain?—I think so. I suppose every country ought, like individuals, to cut its coat according to its cloth, but the argument might not hold good, or entirely so, if the circumstances were very different; for instance, if the poorer country was a much more expensive country to govern than the richer country.

10,019. You must remember that in this case we are dealing with what might happen if Ireland were, financially, looking after her own affairs?—Just so.

10,020. Because otherwise we should be driven to the conclusion, that the taxpayer of Great Britain must make a contribution in order to maintain the cost of local services in Ireland at the level, or nearly the level, of the cost of similar services in Great Britain?—Yes, I suppose that would be so.

10,021. You cannot get out of that?—No.

10,022. I think you have already expressed the opinion in your remarks to-day that as a Treasury officer you are naturally interested in the orderly and thrifty expenditure of public money, and from that point of view do you think that extravagance in expenditure on local services in Ireland is at once demoralising to Ireland and injurious to the Kingdom as a whole?—Yes, I feel that very strongly; I think it has a very demoralising effect, and that a good deal of money is not turned to the best account in consequence.

10,023. In your memorandum you compare 1819–20 with 1893–94, and you show at page 31 the amount of taxation borne by Ireland at the two periods. In 1819–20, 4,790,000*l.* was levied in taxes, and in 1893–94 6,731,000*l.*, the increase being 1,941,000*l.*?—That is so.

10,024. If Ireland had been financially independent of Great Britain, she would have had to defray out of her own taxation the charge of her own Civil Government, and therefore would have had to provide for the increased demands which modern civilisation entails, would she not?—I suppose so, unless, of course, Ireland had chosen to go without more clearly in civilisation.

10,025. But still it is not unreasonable to suppose that she would not have lagged behind the rest of Europe? —No, I think that is quite a fair conjecture to make.

10,026. Every country, I think, spends money on education and police far in excess of what it spent in 1819–20, does it not?—I think there can be no question about that.

10,027. In your memorandum, table 8, page 35, you give the expenditure of Ireland on education at 1,250,000*l.*, and in the Estimates of the current year the expenditure on education, science and art in Ireland is at least 1,328,000*l.*, is it not?—Yes, I think that is about the figure.

10,028. You are doubtless aware that in 1819–20 the expenditure in Ireland on education was very small—not quite 160,000*l.*?—Yes, it was comparatively very small.

10,029. Therefore, if Ireland had been responsible for her own finances, she would have had to provide, upon your data, for 1893–4 about 750,000*l.* more than in 1819–20 for education alone, would she not?—That is so.

10,030. Do you know whether there has been any expression of dissatisfaction in Ireland against the expenditure on Irish education as being extravagant?—Not so far as I am aware; on the contrary, I think only the last session the question was raised in the House of Commons of some larger contribution to education.

10,031. So that we may probably take it that this item would not be condemned by the Irish themselves as excessive?—I think that may be assumed to be so.

10,032. Now, passing on to the police, in 1819–20 there was practically no police force in the three countries, we may say?—No, in those days I think it hardly existed.

10,033. And in the interval a considerable force has been created in each, has it not?—That is so.

10,034. Following, then, the ground of dividing the cost of the Irish Constabulary and putting a large portion of it as an Imperial charge, we may come to the conclusion, we will say, that that 650,000*l.* of which we have spoken represents what the charge of the police might be if Ireland had organised a police force the same as Great Britain has done, may we not?—I think that is a fair figure to take. The reason I took half was, that half was the original share that Ireland had to take on her own shoulders previous to the change made by Sir Robert Peel.

10,035. But am I not right, that a figure very much like 650,000*l.* was one at which we arrived upon the supposition that the police in Ireland was in number and in proportion about the same as it is in Great Britain?—Yes, that is about the figure we came to, I think.

10,036. Therefore, perhaps, for the purpose of our argument, we may say, may we not, that if Ireland had been financially independent, she would have maintained a police force such as exists in England and Scotland, the cost of which I put at 650,000*l.*?—Yes, I think that is a fair assumption to make.

10,037. Therefore Ireland for police alone would have had to provide in 1893–94 very nearly 650,000*l.* more than she had to provide in 1819–20, and if we add the Education, Science and Art Estimates for the present year she would have had to find some 1,750,000*l.* or 1,600,000*l.* more than in 1819–20?—That would be so.

10,038. If we add to these charges the charge for Public Works, that alone shows an increase on Parks and Public Works which more than accounts for the remainder of that increased burden of taxation which I mentioned, of 1,941,000*l.* levied since 1819–20, does it not?—Yes.

10,039. And these we may say are services which concern Ireland alone?—Yes, certainly.

10,040. May we not fairly then argue that Ireland would have had to find the money for these services, if she had had the charge of her own finance?—I think that may be fairly assumed.

10,041. And it follows that the extra taxation levied since 1819–20 is only that which was required for her own internal and local services?—Yes, that is so.

10,042. Passing now to the general account of Irish Revenue and Expenditure, does not your memorandum show that in 1819–20, after deducting local expenditure in Ireland from the total Irish revenue, the sum which Ireland contributed towards the charge of the National Debt and towards the Army and Navy was 1,[illegible]*l.*, whereas in 1893–94 her contribution to these services amounted only to 2,104,000*l.*?—That, speaking broadly, is correct, but there has been a slight adjustment in the figures since the figures you have mentioned were compiled, but it amounts to a slight change only. I think according to the latest adjustments in the calculations, the contribution of Ireland to Imperial expenditure was in 1819–20 2,[illegible]*l.*, and in 1893–94 1,[illegible]*l.* That, as you remember, was owing to the tobacco adjustment that was made, subsequently to the figures I used in my memorandum, but the adjustments are all to be found in the proof of the second volume of the Minutes of Evidence.

10,043. But the cost of Military and Naval Services has largely increased in the interval, and Great Britain has not only taken the whole of the increased charge of these services on herself, but has largely reduced the contribution which Ireland made towards these services in 1819–20, has she not?—That is so, no doubt.

10,044. I am not arguing that the contribution in 1819–20 was a proper one. I am only submitting for your opinion that Great Britain has been reducing since 1819–20 the contribution which she takes from Ireland, and that the whole of the sum derived from increased taxation in Ireland has been spent on services which Ireland, if she had been financially independent, must have undertaken?—That is no doubt, if you confine the comparison to the commencement of the period and the end of the period; but, of course, the contribution has not been at all uniform throughout the period, and for a certain number of years, about half way in the interval, it was largely increased, and therefore it is rather misleading.

10,045. You have already brought that out very clearly in your remarks and I think, in a very striking manner, but for all practical purposes we have to deal with the present?—Yes, no doubt.

* [illegible]

Q

10,046. Now the whole revenue of Ireland, including the non tax and receipts which are not taxes, amounted in 1819-20 to 5,[illegible]l., and in 1893-4 to 7,[illegible]l.; would not those figures have been modified since?—They would be modified slightly, no doubt; but for all practical purposes it does not make much difference.

10,047. For the purpose of argument I am putting it to you that the effect of the modifications would be rather to reduce Ireland's contributions, and so forth, than to increase it, would it not?—Yes.

10,048. Therefore the total increase of revenue of all kinds has been 2,[illegible]l.?—That is so.

10,049. And the sum which Ireland contributes to Debt, Army, and Navy is 1,[illegible]l. less than in 1819-20, making a total increase of expenditure in Ireland of 4,[illegible]l.?—Yes, that, I think, is correct.

10,050. I have brought to your attention expenditure on new services, namely, Education, Police, and Public Works, which is perhaps defensible, but which amounts to no less than 2,[illegible]l.?—Yes.

10,051. Therefore there is an increase in ordinary local expenditure in Ireland, independently of these new services, of more than 2,[illegible]l.?—Yes.

10,052. Do you think, looking at the circumstances of Ireland, which are always pleaded in favour of a poor country, that enormous increase is probably defensible?—Well, perhaps, not in itself, but of course part of that expenditure represents the means whereby the Imperial Government has endeavoured to rectify inequalities of taxation and to help Ireland.

10,053. So far as many of the services are concerned, that is the case; but would you consider what I may call extravagant judicial salaries, extravagant salaries in other directions, as a legitimate means of rectifying that?—No. I should exclude that. But extravagant expenditure of that kind would represent only a very, very small part of the large aggregate increase in the cost of Irish services.

10,054. Are you quite sure of that?—I imagine so, speaking generally. I was saying that there ought to taken into account the fact that large expenditure has been one of the modes in which inequalities of taxation in Ireland have been redressed; that was the point I wished to bring out this morning, or one of the points in the remarks I made. I admit that that would not apply to extravagant salaries like those of judges, and so forth; but I imagine that extravagant expenditure of that kind can represent only a small portion of the very large figure that you gave of the vast increase of expenditure on local services in Ireland, amounting to something like 4,000,000l.

10,055. It is not of course clear that, even in 1819-20, expenditure in Ireland was strictly economical, but when the question is raised of Ireland's capacity to pay taxes, must we not ask the necessity and justification of this enormous increase in local expenditure?—Yes, I think so. The Commission have from figures which I have already laid before them, that the local expenditure in Ireland has enormously increased; but it ought also to be borne in mind that the local expenditure in Great Britain has increased at a still more formidable rate, that is to say, it is six times as large now as it was in 1819-20.

10,056. But would it not be necessary to reduce the local expenditure to reasonable limits before considering relief?—I think that is no doubt a question which ought to be taken into consideration. The reasonable limits are not very easy to define, but I have no doubt that some reductions could be made with advantage.

10,057. Otherwise, if Ireland prefers to spend what is spent now on her local services, she must be content to bear the taxation required to meet it, must she not?—I do not know that that necessarily follows, because the relief afforded to Ireland during the last 20 or 25 years has been rightly or wrongly effected by means of larger assistance from the Imperial purse. I think that is an important point to bear in mind—I mean that it is by this large expenditure that the inequalities to a great extent have been redressed.

10,058. Just so, and what I say is this, that if Ireland as a country, or if its representatives and authorities, maintain that the present amount of taxation for local services is necessary, amounting, as it does, to this very high figure, then that they should be content to pay the taxation necessary for it. If they wish to reduce the taxation, they must begin by examining the expenditure, and seeing how far that expenditure is absolutely necessary, must they not?—No doubt, but, of course, you must remember that simply effecting a saving in Ireland would not necessarily relieve the Irish taxpayer, because the bulk of it would go in relief of the pockets of the British taxpayer.

[illegible]

10,059. Of course, but I am now dealing with the question which, I think, arises out of Sir Robert Giffen's evidence, namely, first of all, that Ireland is a poor country, and next, that she ought only to bear a certain amount of taxation, leading the Commission to the conclusion that relief in taxation ought to be given to Ireland, and then you very rightly point out that practically, that relief has been given in very large expenditure?—That is my view.

10,060. And I have brought that out by showing how very large that relief has been, and how, of late years, the whole tendency of the Imperial Parliament has been towards redressing that inequality by the grant of a larger sum to Ireland?—Yes, but I think it is only fair to say that the expenditure in Great Britain for local services has increased at a still greater rate.

10,061. But at present the English taxpayer is showing a patience of taxation; she is not complaining?—Yes.

10,062. (The O'Conor Don.) Has that large and costly and useless expenditure, to which Lord Welby has alluded, greatly increased since 1853?—An answer to that would involve the examination of many details, and without such examination I am not prepared to express a definite opinion offhand on that point.

10,063. Lord Welby has alluded to the fact that there has been an enormous increase in expenditure for local services in Ireland since 1853, and he has drawn the conclusion that a large proportion of that increase is due to what he terms costly and useless expenditure. Is that proportion, in your opinion, large or small?—I think the proportion is small.

10,064. And, as a matter of fact, taking what has been so often incidentally alluded to, namely, judicial expenditure in Ireland, is it not the fact that since 1853 the judicial establishments have been reduced instead of increased?—I think they have been reduced in some respects during the last 30 years, but of course the less that is spent on these costly and useless features, the stronger is my argument about what I call relief by expenditure.

10,065. Is not the whole of that expenditure under the control of the Imperial Parliament?—Yes.

10,066. And Ireland is not specially responsible for it?—No, she is not specially responsible for it. The Imperial Government is responsible for it.

10,067. And has not the tendency been to diminish useless expenditure?—I suppose within the last 20 years there have been some economical arrangements effected in Ireland, as there have been in England; but I believe there is much room for further economy still in Irish administration.

10,068. Just one other question upon your general examination by Lord Welby. Do you not think that a very great proportion of that examination has been what I may term cross-examination of Sir Robert Giffen through you?—I should hardly have thought so. I do not think Lord Welby has really seriously traversed Sir Robert Giffen's broad conclusions.

10,069. You do not think it had that tendency?—It did not occur to me that it had, when he put the questions he did to me.

10,070. Do you think that you are justified in assuming that Sir Robert Giffen has gone to the very great extent that is involved in Lord Welby's questions? For instance, are we to suppose that Sir Robert Giffen holds the doctrine that if the whole of the local taxation of Ireland for roads and bridges, and everything else, were transferred to the Imperial Exchequer, and a similar course were not adopted in England, then no account should be taken of that in regarding or in adjusting the relative taxation of the two countries?—I have read Sir Robert Giffen's evidence, and I may have misinterpreted it; but I certainly did not find any such qualification in it.

10,071. But if that is the case, would it not have been more satisfactory to have put these questions to Sir Robert Giffen himself?—I assumed they had been put to him, but I should like to be able to turn to the par-says where Sir Robert Giffen laid down that doctrine. He did not seem to me to lay it down with any qualification whatever, but I may be doing him an injustice, and therefore I should like to refer to the passages in his evidence.

10,072 I understand the tendency of Sir Robert Giffen's evidence to be that with regard to what might be called general expenditure it was a matter of indifference where it was made—that it regarded the whole Empire generally. For instance, if more soldiers were employed in one country than in another, that that should be regarded as general expenditure. But I do not think he ever laid down the doctrine that if the whole of the local taxation were done away with in one country and made Imperial, and if the whole of this local taxation were a separate charge on another country, that should not be considered, but that is the view taken by Lord Welby to-day. If you can show any statement of Sir Robert Giffen's that goes to that extent, I think it would be as well to recall Sir Robert Giffen again, to see if that was his meaning, because it raises a very important question?—I see Sir Robert Giffen says:—"The opinion which I have formed "is that on the whole it is not possible to make the "distinction between the different objects of Imperial "expenditure which is made in some of these returns "and documents; that, in fact, all the expenditure by "the Imperial Government is to be considered expen-"diture for Imperial purposes, and, although part of "it may be spent locally, you cannot consider it in any "way expenditure for the special benefit of that "locality." And then he says at the end:—"For these "reasons, practically, I cannot see any difference "in the objects of the Imperial expenditure by "the Imperial Government; they are all Imperial "from beginning to end, and you cannot consider "that any part of them is for the local benefit of a "particular part of the country." I can only draw one conclusion from that, namely, that Sir Robert Giffen says that you must not take into account anything like, for instance, local taxation grants in Ireland, because all you have got to look to is what you take out of the taxpayer's pocket, and not what you spend in the country. I think he states the case several times over; for instance, he goes on again (at No. 7811) to say:—"I may say that I know of no "economic authority of any sort or kind for the "proposition that in considering the question of "the equality of taxation throughout a community, a "distinction may be made between so-called Imperial "objects and objects special to some geographical "division of the community, or some special group of "taxpayers, so that in considering the question of "equality of taxation so far as that geographical divi-"sion or special group is concerned, the amount which "they receive back for expenditure for special objects "is to be deducted from the total contributions, so as "leave their contribution for so-called Imperial "objects."

10,073 (*Lord Farrer.*) Will you turn the Evidence to look at Question 7790, and read it?—Certainly; the question there put is:—"I do not want to [illegible] "to argue it at these [illegible] you now, but I want "to get at your view. Do you think, now, we ought "to consider the question of the taxation of Ireland, "independently and apart from the expenditure on "Ireland," and Sir R. Giffen's reply is, "I think "so, absolutely."

10,074 Will you be kind enough to read on?—The next question is, "And that we have nothing to do with "the expenditure of Ireland?—(A.) Nothing to do "with it." I certainly should not infer from those answers that he draws any distinction between Imperial and local expenditure.

10,075 (*The O'Conor Don.*) Then I may take it you do infer from Sir Robert Giffen's evidence the proposition I laid down a moment ago, that if all the local taxation of Ireland were charged upon the Imperial funds, and Ireland was completely free from all local taxation, England remaining as she is, Sir Robert Giffen would hold that that should not be considered in any way in discussing the question of the relative taxation of the two countries?—I think that the logical conclusion to be drawn from his evidence is that no such expenditure as that met out of (for instance) local taxation grants, which are in relief of rates, nor analogously any expenditure now charged on rates, if undertaken by the Imperial Government, could be taken into account in the question of the relative taxation of the two countries.

10,076 I should like to know whether that is what he means, because it is very important to ascertain what he really meant to convey?—He says distinctly that he cannot draw a distinction between Imperial and local expenditure, and when he is asked whether "we ought "to consider the question of the taxation of Ireland "independently and apart from the expenditure on "Ireland?" he says, "I think so, absolutely."

10,077. (*Mr. Sexton.*) Sir Robert Giffen regarded himself as an expert who came here to give evidence upon one question simply, namely, the relative taxable capacities of Great Britain and Ireland, and he disclaimed the right to limit himself to the reference to the Commission, namely, upon what principle and upon what standards their relative taxable capacity with reference to their resources should be determined?—I think if Sir Robert Giffen's dictum is followed out it may lead to very misleading results. Whether he meant to attach the signification to it which I do, I do not know. I have only read what appears in his evidence, and he certainly more than once lays down in decided language that expenditure in Ireland is to be considered apart from the question of Irish taxation.

10,078 His position is that the relative taxable capacity of the two countries is to be determined by their resources, and not by any other circumstance, and that is the instruction to the Commission?—Quite so.

10,079 (*Lord Farrer.*) I rather gathered from you that the local expenditure has increased very largely and, to a great extent, necessarily, in the same way as the local expenditure of other countries has increased? —Yes.

10,080 I gathered also from you that a great part of that increase would probably not have taken place if Ireland had had to manage her own resources, and had not been a partner with a rich country like England?—I think that is a fair conclusion to draw from my evidence.

10,081 And I suppose it is not possible for you to say to what extent that would have been the case, or to what extent any local expenditure which is now being made in Ireland is unnecessary?—No, I am afraid I could not do so.

10,082 Or to what extent, supposing Ireland to manage her own resources, she would be able to economise that expenditure?—No. There is the question of police, and I suppose if Ireland managed her own affairs she might make a large reduction under the head of police.

10,083 Is it possible to put any definite answer to that question so long as the present state of things exists under which there is a common purse from which a poorer country is able to draw to a large extent upon a rich country?—I think it would be extremely difficult to do so. I should not like to commit myself to any precise figures.

10,084 And you would not like to say to what extent, supposing Ireland had the entire management of her own resources, she would be able to economise her expenditure?—No; but I doubt if, with the exception of the police charge, she would be able to economise very materially.

10,085. (*Mr Sexton.*) You have said that if Ireland disappeared by some catastrophe of Nature, the expenditure which would then remain to Great Britain might be fairly considered Imperial expenditure?—Yes; but I think that is putting a very extreme case.

10,086. Now, supposing Great Britain disappeared by some catastrophe of Nature, what proportion do you really think of the five millions and a half Ireland would require to carry on her administration, would you have any doubt that she would carry it on for half the money?—No. If left to herself, I do not think she would be able to effect any great economy in civil administration, and she would certainly have to keep up a certain number of soldiers and a certain amount of sailors, and I presume she would not be content to be unrepresented abroad.

10,087 If you allow half-a-million for police and even a million for education, Ireland administered herself for much less than a million in Grattan's day, and I consider that two millions and a half would be

TWENTY-SIXTH DAY.

At A Committee Room, House of Lords, Thursday, 14th November 1895.

PRESENT

THE RIGHT HONOURABLE HUGH C. E. CHILDERS, *Chairman.*

LORD FARRER.	CHARLES E. MARTIN, Esq.
LORD WELBY.	J. E. REDMOND, Esq., M.P.
The Right Hon. THE O'CONOR DON.	THOMAS SEXTON, Esq., M.P.
Sir DAVID BARBOUR, K.C.S.I.	HENRY F. SLATTERY, Esq.
BERTRAM W. CURRIE, Esq.	

B. H. HOLLAND, Esq., *Secretary.*

Sir EDWARD WALTER HAMILTON, K.C.B., further examined.

10,088. (*Mr. Redmond.*) I am not quite sure, Sir Edward Hamilton, that I understand what you wish to convey when you say that your calculations or opinions do not commit anyone at the Treasury?—I meant to say that they were my personal opinions, the opinions of one who had given considerable attention to the subject referred to the Commission.

10,089. Your memorandum shows that you have studied very closely the questions referred to the Commission, but I should have thought that in an enquiry of this gravity, affecting the financial relations between Great Britain and Ireland, the Treasury would consider it to be a duty to present, what I may call, the Treasury view to the Commission?—I do not think that would be quite possible. The financial business of the Treasury is under my special charge, and, therefore, I appear before the Commission in that capacity, but I think it is extremely difficult for one individual to commit a body like the Treasury, which is a constantly changing body.

10,090. The Treasury is a dual body, one element constantly changes, and the other is permanent; do you refer to Ministers when you say your opinion commits no one, or to the permanent heads?—I mean the Ministers of the day, or the Board of Treasury; the Board, of course, changes according to the Government of the day.

10,091. You speak of the Lords Commissioners?—Yes.

10,092. Regarding the Treasury as a permanent Department, has the Treasury formed any opinion on the questions referred to this Commission?—I believe the opinion which I have formed myself, so far as I have been able to form one, is the opinion which the Treasury has formed. I have discussed the matter with some of my colleagues and talked over a good many points with them, but I do not like to commit other individuals besides myself.

10,093. Of course an inquiry of this kind could not be satisfactorily completed without ascertaining what might be regarded as the view of the permanent administration, and I suppose we may regard you as the exponent of the views of the permanent administration of the Treasury?—I think, perhaps, I might go so far as to say that. Lord Welby will correct me if I am wrong, but I think it might be said that my views represent those of my colleagues.

10,094. (*Lord Welby.*) I should say you appear before the Commission to give them such assistance from your experience and knowledge as you can, but at the same time, I think it is quite impossible for the permanent element of the Treasury to separate itself from its chief?—That I admit of course, but I do not want the honourable member to think that such conclusions as I have formed and placed before the Commission are the result solely of my own consideration. My colleagues have assisted me in the matter.

10,095. (*Mr. Sexton.*) I did not intend and did not wish to go into any discussion as to the elements of the Treasury. I want to ascertain your position as between the Treasury and the Commission, and I think you have said we may regard you as the exponent of such views as the Treasury has formed, or is disposed to express on the questions referred to the Commission?—I do not think that is an unfair way of stating the case.

10,096. Some two or three of what you call your general remarks on the last occasion appear to invite attention. At page 5 of what I may call your second memorandum you ask "are *per capita* calculations the "correct test of the equalities or inequalities of taxation "in one country as compared with another"?—Yes.

10,097. *Per capita* calculations have been very freely used by the Treasury, and by yourself in connection with the Inquiry, have they not?—No doubt they have, but all I meant to say was that I do not think they tell the whole truth of the story, because if you take merely the *per capita* calculations by themselves, they relate to only one side of the account; and what I hold is that you are obliged to take into account both sides of the account.

10,098. I am considering now merely the question of taxation?—And the question, as I understand, of what is the proper and fair contribution that Ireland should make to Imperial expenditure.

10,099. At present I direct myself simply to the question of taxation. Upon the question of taxation, are not *per capita* calculations of revenue actually raised at least as good as *per capita* calculations founded upon a long series of conjectures as to the consumption of certain articles?—Do you mean dutiable articles?

10,100. Yes?—I do not think I quite follow your point.

10,101. Are not *per capita* calculations founded upon actual money raised as valuable?—Yes.

10,102. As, for instance, your gauge of taxable [illegible] founded upon a long series of conjectures as to the amount of taxable articles consumed per head of the population?—Not conjectural. We hope that we have got fairly definite figures now. I do not know that the figures that have been put before the Commission now, have been seriously questioned.

10,103. Not conjectural?—But as regards the amounts contributed to revenue by the spirit duty and other duties, if I understood the honourable member rightly.

10,104. The consumption of tea is taken according to population, is it not?—Yes, partially so.

10,105. The consumption of tobacco has been altered three times, has it not?—Yes, but we hope now we have something definite to go upon.

10,106. But your hope may not be fulfilled?—It may not, but I think it is more than conjectural.

10,107. You began as to tobacco, with the carrying companies, then you passed on to another test, and finally you made application to some leading traders, and all, surely that is a conjectural test?—There is a certain amount of conjecture, but I think the result brought out looks as if it conformed to facts.

10,108. It looks so, but does it?—Of course, all we have been able to do is to put the best figures we can before the Commission.

10,109. Then with regard to beer, you also depend upon correspondence with some leading traders, and as regard to spirits, we know that grave errors have been discovered there. In the year 18[?], it was found that a whole branch was omitted, and in the year 1892–3, there was an error of £20,000?—I would rather the honourable member put those questions to those who are concerned with the question. I am not.

10,110. You are an expert in all these questions as compared with the members of the Commission, are you not?—I am sorry I am not acquainted with all the details of the calculations.

10,111. I am pointing out to you that your per capita calculations of consumption are founded upon a long series of intricate and arbitrary conjectures?—I do not admit that they are arbitrary.

10,112. Even as to price, you consider an average price for tea over the three Kingdoms of 1s. 11d.?—That I admit is an arbitrary calculation for what it is worth, but I think the actual figures relating to what we call the true revenue of the two kingdoms are something more than purely arbitrary figures.

10,113. I think you are rather wandering from my point, which was that per capita calculations of revenue actually raised are more valuable than your gauges of revenue founded upon a series of conjectures as to consumption?—I am not taking any other figures of consumption than those which were in my original memorandum.

10,114. If you think such conjectures as you state to be good enough for the foundation of per capita rates, how much better are the per capita rates which you expressed in your second memorandum, which are founded upon revenue actually raised?—I am not undervaluing those calculations at all. I only doubt whether, taken by themselves, they are the best gauge of whether Ireland is overcharged or not. That was my intention, but I may have conveyed it wrongly.

10,115. So far as the incidence of taxation is concerned, are they a good gauge?—If you look at one side of the account, yes.

10,116. You will allow me to confine myself at present to taxation?—Certainly.

10,117. Before I pass from that question of yours, may I also point out to you that your figures of relative consumption, as to drinkable articles in Great Britain and Ireland, are founded upon such other assumptions as these, that for every gallon of beer consumed inside a public-house four gallons are consumed outside, and that for every gallon of spirits sold outside a public house three gallons are consumed inside. These are large assumptions, not verifiable, are they?—I did not found any of my last remarks upon them. I was simply dealing with the amount of true revenue raised in Ireland and in Great Britain, respectively. None of those calculations have any reference to those to which the honourable member is referring in my original memorandum.

10,118. What you said was, "The correct test of the equalities or inequalities of taxation"?—Quite so, and what I meant was whether the amount raised per head in taxation in one country is a fair gauge of whether that country is overcharged or not overcharged.

10,119. Then you are mixing up another question with the question of taxable capacity, are you not?—No; I do not think so. — Sir E. W. Hamilton, K.C.B. / 16 May 1895.

10,120. What is taxable capacity?—I am not mixing up the two things. I think the honourable member refers to this: "Are per capita calculations the correct test," and I had just before been referring to what the amount of true revenue raised in Ireland was per head, as compared with the amount of true revenue raised in Great Britain per head. — Value of per capita calculations.

10,121. So far as per capita calculations may be taken as a measure, I understand you do not approach them as tests?—Not in the least.

10,122. So far as direct taxes are concerned per capita calculations present, in another and convenient form, the fact as to the proportion of taxed property in one country and the other; for example, the yield of direct taxes is about 1 to 24, the population about 1 to 5, and it follows from that that the rate per head of direct taxes in Ireland is as 1 to 5 in Great Britain, and that is putting in another form the proportion of 1 to 24, that is the use of the per capita rate as to direct taxation, is it not?—I think so. You said "three"; I counted it one-fourth.

10,123. It is three in round figures?—I make it nearer five. I think according to the latest year it is nearer forty.

10,124. What is the latest year in your return?—I have the figures for 1893–4 before me, and I see here that direct taxes in Great Britain, the true revenue was about £[illegible],000,000, and roughly speaking in Ireland it was about 1,300,000l., and the equal per-centage worked out as 95.5 to 4.5.

10,125. My point was that the yield being 1 to 24 and the population 1 to 5, it follows of necessity the rate per head is 1 to 5; and I find it verified in the years 1893–94, when the rate per head for Ireland was 5s. 10d., and the rate per head for Great Britain 1l. 6s. 9d., or 1 to 5?—Yes.

10,126. That is the function of per capita rates in relation to direct taxation?—I think so.

10,127. To show in a simpler form the proportion in which the property exists?—Yes.

10,128. In regard to indirect taxes to which the whole community and not any special class is liable, the per capita rate does discharge a most valuable function?—Certainly.

10,129. Because the average man would find it difficult to realise the relation between millions of population and revenue, but it is not difficult to realise that each individual on the average pays so much, and it is a just test, no doubt, of the pressure of taxation?—I admit that.

10,130. At page 7, paragraph 3, you say that it may be argued that a country like Ireland which, with the solitary exception of tea, has no necessity of life subject to taxation, can hardly be said to be overweighted by Imperial imposts?—Yes, I am using that as an argument which is constantly put forward. — [illegible] on test of taxable capacity.

10,131. Your own position as to tea, I think, has somewhat altered. You called it first a luxury and then an expensive taste?—Not tea, I think.

10,132. I thought you suggested it?—No, only spirits.

10,133. Did not you call it an expensive taste?—Yes; I think spirits are an expensive taste.

10,134. You doubted whether tea was a food, did you not?—I should doubt whether it is a food. I should call it a drink.

10,135. When the O'Conor Don pointed out to you that in Ireland, at any rate taking the great mass of the population, the choice is between tea and water, when they eat bread, I think you began to recognise, did you not, that if tea is not a food it is at least a necessary accompaniment to very poor food?—I think it may be said to be so. In this case I suppose there is a third alternative—milk. — (Tea.)

10,136. You know very little of Ireland if you think milk may be had in abundance by the labouring class?—I will not say in abundance.

10,137. Or at all, in some places. The farmers keep the milk to make butter. It is far easier to get tea than milk, and tea is cheaper. But even though Ireland be not taxed on necessaries of life, may she not be over-weighted? Is she not over-weighted?—As to being

Sir R. Giffen, K.C.B.

actually over-weighted, I am not prepared to say. I am only putting the arguments on one side and the arguments on the other side, and I leave that point to the Commission to decide. I thought that was the whole point the Commission had to decide—whether Ireland was or was not over-weighted with taxation. All I can put forward are the pros and cons that ought, I think, to be taken into account before a conclusion is arrived at.

10,138. You have put forward a good many cons; I want a pro. If possible the Commission depends upon evidence, and you are giving evidence?—Yes.

10,139. You have said already that, in your opinion, Ireland, relatively to her resources, is over-taxed?—If you take one side of the account only, Ireland, relatively to her resources, is over-taxed.

10,140. I am on taxation simply. She is over-taxed? —Yes, relatively to Great Britain.

10,141. Of course, that is the only question we are inquiring into. We are not inquiring so much into any absolute standard as into the relative capacity?—But you are quoting my words, and it was not a comparison with Great Britain at all. I was only taking the broad point as to whether a country could be said to be heavily over-weighted with taxation where there was no necessity of life taxed, with the solitary exception of tea.

10,142. That is an interesting question, no doubt, in social philosophy, but it is not the question referred to us?—Perhaps that paragraph to which you are referring is worth nothing, but I put it in because it was an argument which might, very likely, be brought forward, and I used the argument in the first paragraph by saying, "It may be contended that it is the amount "you take out of the taxpayer's pocket which is "material, and not the manner in which you take it;" I am only putting the pros and cons. I did not wish to commit myself on this particular point at all.

10,143. When the possible arguments of another, not shared by the witness, are put forward in this way, they are apt to be misleading. One might mistake them for the arguments of a witness, but I can hardly suppose you would imagine Ireland is not over-taxed when we all know now that the taxation is as 1 to 11, and the income, if measured by an equitable test, may be about 1 to 20?—Yes, relatively to Great Britain.

10,144. That is the question into which we are inquiring, is it not?—Yes.

10,145. That alone, even assuming income to be a test, contrary to the view of Stuart Mill and many other eminent men, Ireland is taxed double her relative share at present?—Yes, double her share in relation to income according to her relative aggregate resources.

10,146. As to taxes, other than those upon the necessaries of life, not weighing upon a community, does any civilised community confine itself to necessities of life?—No, but I do think there is a great difference between a country which has some of its necessaries of life taxed, and another country which has none of its necessaries of life taxed, because, after all, one class of taxation is more avoidable than the other class of taxation.

10,147. Neither is that question before us, because the two countries are alike in that respect?—Quite so.

10,148. Do you think it is admissible for the legislator to avail himself of the habits, perhaps ingrained and hereditary habits, of a community or the community in order to raise revenue, and then turn round and say, "If you give up these habits the revenue will "not be raised"?—No, I think that is a difficult point to give a direct answer to, and I have put it in the best way I can in those two paragraphs. I have guarded myself about it, and that is a point upon which I think I ought not to be asked to give a positive opinion. I have put the arguments for and the arguments against.

10,149. What I wish to ascertain is the argument you as a witness adopt?—Would you mind putting the question which you wish me to answer again?

10,150. When I press you upon what appears to be an argument in your memorandum, you tell me you put the arguments pro and con, as if you were rather acting as a judicial than in a testifying capacity, but I wish to ascertain what you as a witness put forward as defensible or justifiable?—I do not quite see how I am to give a direct answer to that question.

10,151. I do not think I need press you further than your admission that, relatively to income, Ireland pays double her share?—I admit that, relatively to income, Ireland does pay a larger share of indirect taxation than Great Britain.

10,152. You say:—"If the Irishmen of to-day were "content to drink spirits and smoke tobacco to the "same extent as their fathers did about 30 years ago, "I calculate that they could relieve themselves in the "matter of taxation amounting to about 1,000,000l., "which sum would be larger by about 300,000l. if "beer were taken into account." I do not know on what figures you found that computation?—I can hand them in if you like; I am not certain I have them here.

10,153. Does the Irishman to-day drink or smoke more than the inhabitant of Great Britain?—No, I think it is about the same as Great Britain.

10,154. But smoking is less; the last corrected return shows that he smokes less?—It is not materially less, I think, if I recollect rightly.

10,155. It is substantially less. He drinks a little more tea, smokes less; he drinks about the same quantity of spirits, and about half as much beer as an inhabitant of Great Britain; that is the result of your tables, is it not?—Yes.

10,156. Then the Irishman being a more moderate smoker and a far more moderate drinker than either the Englishman or Scotchman, where are we to look for the argument?—I am not suggesting it at all. If I worked out a similar calculation for Great Britain, I have no doubt I should bring out a still more striking calculation, and I should be able to point to Great Britain and say, "You must be much better off than "you were 30 years ago;" and that I should be able to show that Britishers might be able to save a great deal more than a million to-morrow if they drank and smoked at the same rate as their fathers did. But I think that would be a great proof of the increased prosperity of Great Britain.

10,157. Then that is a reflection, addressed in form to one country but applicable to both?—Certainly, and in a much more accentuated form in the case of Great Britain.

10,158. I suppose you are aware that since the last generation the habits of life in Ireland have changed very much; there is less home-grown produce consumed, and the people have to use a greater proportion of their money in purchasing food and other necessaries?—I dare say that may be so, but that is one of the disadvantages I labour under, because I am not sufficiently acquainted with the economical conditions of Ireland to be able to be of any real service to the Commission on such a point.

10,159. When you give these calculations, as to the abandonment of these indulgences, I may point out to you that if Irishmen were to give up tea, tobacco, spirits, and beer to-morrow, they would exist, no doubt, and the revenue would come down to about a million instead of being nearly seven millions; but do you suppose means would not be taken to make them contribute?—I think certainly in some form or other.

10,160. Suppose they became total abstainers to-morrow from all excisable articles, what would you say?—If in Ireland, and likewise in Great Britain, a serious change took place in the consumption of spirits, no doubt some fresh taxation would have to be found.

10,161. Or even in Ireland only?—Or even in Ireland only; but I am quite certain no tax would be applicable to Ireland alone. It would have to be made good throughout the United Kingdom.

10,162. When you exhort the Irishman who drinks the same quantity of tea, smokes less, and drinks less, what inducement do you hold out to virtue, if the result of total abstinence would be that he should pay the taxation in some other way?—There is no doubt that Great Britain would have to make up a good deal of it.

10,163. Do you not think that Great Britain would make Ireland make it up even if she had to tax potatoes?—No, I do not think so, to the full extent; some part of it. I think the natural tendency of all recent legislation has been to extract more from direct taxation than anything else; and direct taxation would not affect Ireland to the same extent as it would Great Britain, relatively.

10,164. If you will look into the figures you will see that the shifting of the burden from indirect to direct taxation has benefited the consumer in Great Britain materially, but the consumer in Ireland scarcely at all?—I am quite certain it has benefited the consumer in Great Britain and I do not see why it should not have benefited the consumer equally in Ireland; but I am open to be corrected upon that point.

10,165. The proportion of taxes paid by indirect taxation in Great Britain has fallen from 65 to 53 per cent.?—That is in the United Kingdom.

10,166. Are you aware that if you look into the figures the fall in Great Britain is almost identical with the fall in the United Kingdom, showing that no material reduction has been effected in Ireland?—Perhaps you will refer me to the figures.

10,167. Yes. I refer you to pages 188 and 189 of the second volume of evidence. If you will look at page 189, opposite the years 1859–60 and 1893–4, you will see that the total taxes in the United Kingdom on consumption fell from 68 to 53 of the tax revenue?—Yes.

10,168. Do you observe that in Great Britain, in the same time, they fell from 65 to 50?—Yes.

10,169. Is not that practically the same reduction in Great Britain as in the United Kingdom?—Yes.

10,170. On the other hand, observe, that in Ireland the taxes on consumption in the earlier year were 83 per cent. of the tax revenue, and they have fallen only to 75 per cent.?—It is not so great, I admit.

10,171. Hardly appreciable?—I do not know that it is hardly appreciable.

10,172. But in Great Britain it fell from 63 to 50, one-fifth of the whole, in Ireland from 83 to 75, one-eleventh of the whole?—I admit the difference is material between Great Britain and Ireland.

10,173. In Great Britain the consumer pays only about half the taxes, and in Ireland still three-fourths—where is the relief?—My argument was that if it had not been possible to make this transfer from indirect to direct taxation, Ireland would now be much more heavily [illegible] than she actually is.

10,174. Ireland, now paying double her due relative to income, would be paying more than double her share if a part of the burden of Imperial taxation had not been shifted to property?—I think that is so.

10,175. But that does not make paying double the share more tolerable, does it?—No, I did not say it did.

10,176. As to this question of smoking and drinking, the only real question for us is, not how Irishmen spend their money, which is their own affair in a free country, I suppose, but whether they can as well afford to pay the tax as the inhabitants of Great Britain, and whether the taxation is equally levied in both countries?—Certainly.

10,177. At a later stage of your evidence, in reply to Lord Welby, I think you rather attacked Sir Robert Giffen's evidence?—I had no idea of attacking Sir Robert Giffen, I only differed from what I understood to be his meaning, or the conclusions which he drew.

10,178. You at any rate suggested that his comparisons of gross aggregate income between Great Britain and Ireland and his comparisons of average individual income were to be received with caution, or with a qualification, because of the presence of large incomes in Great Britain, and because of the mass of unemployed labour in Great Britain. That is, I think, the effect of the answers to Questions 9979 to 82?—Yes, I think it was.

10,179. As to large incomes, your suggestion is that they may exist in Great Britain in such numbers as to throw up the average income of the population?—What I meant was that I thought the real test—or rather the best way of applying Sir Robert Giffen's figures—would have been this. He classified Great Britain and Ireland into income-tax payers, intermediate classes, and working classes. Now, I thought that, were it possible, it would be better if, instead of merely giving what he estimates to be the aggregate income of individuals under these classes in Great Britain and Ireland, he could have stated the numbers in the intermediate classes and the working classes against which he set the aggregates of these classes, in order that we might see to what extent the number of large incomes in Great Britain exceeded the large incomes in Ireland. That was what I had in my mind.

10,180. I doubt whether you have quite grasped the true tendency of Sir Robert Giffen's process. Sir Robert Giffen explained that the validity of his conclusions did not depend upon any comparison of aggregate incomes merely, but that it was established by the direct comparison of the proportions of income tax and of the rates of wages actually paid, qualified by the preponderance of the lowest rates of wages in Ireland?—Yes.

10,181. So you see his demonstration does not depend on the accuracy of the aggregate incomes?—I thought he rather set store on averages.

10,182. When you assented to Lord Welby's suggestion that Sir Robert Giffen's computations were conjectural, did you realise that Sir Robert Giffen really founded himself upon the assessments to income tax, which is not a conjecture, and that the remainder of his demonstration was a check of the conclusions yielded by income, and confirmed by various other tests?—I did not wish to question Sir Robert Giffen's figures in any way, but I suppose he would be the first person to admit that there must be an element of hypothesis about them.

10,183. Will you fix your attention on the fact that Sir Robert Giffen derived his ultimate proportion of 1 to 22 from the net assessment to the income-tax?—Yes, that is the main basis of his calculations.

10,184. And he then proceeded to inquire whether anything else disturbed that proportion?—Yes.

10,185. He tried wages, he tried intermediate incomes, he checked the sum of these three by a comparison of the gross assessments to income tax, and found it to tally; he checked it by the probate duty and by the probate and succession duty together, and he finally checked it by an independent estimate of the actual value of the yield of agricultural produce in Ireland. It was a demonstration founded upon fact, and confirmed by a variety of checks, and not a conjecture?—I never disputed Sir Robert's figures.

10,186. They are not really disputable from the point of view of calling them conjecture. Your suggestion as to the aggregate incomes is that these large incomes may be so numerous in Great Britain that being thrown into the mass of incomes and divided amongst the population they throw up the average substantially?—That was what was in my mind; I do not profess to be a statistician, but that was what occurred to me would very likely be the result if those further figures could be forthcoming.

10,187. You suggest in fact that there was some doubt whether the wage earners are relatively so much poorer in Ireland as his comparison would show?—No. I think there is no doubt the average wage in Ireland is lower than the average wage in Great Britain.

10,188. I think you said it was very difficult to say whether the wage earners were relatively poorer in Ireland than those in Great Britain?—What I believed was that while the average wage of the lowest class in Ireland was lower than the average wage of the corresponding classes in Great Britain, yet the difference was not great among skilled artisans.

10,189. Have you noted Sir Robert Giffen's figures, that putting the average income in Ireland at 35l., he finds 50 per cent. of the wage earners are at an average of only 19l., and 30 per cent. more at an average of about 25l.; whilst in England, the average being 48l., only [illegible] per cent. of the population are under that average of 48l.? That shows a great difference indeed between the wage-earners in Ireland and those in Great Britain?—Yes, I think that is a strong point to take.

10,190. The materials for comparison of large incomes are in your hands. Have you compared them?—I do not think they give what I suggest. I was taking the income tax payers and the non-income tax payers, and the Inland Revenue have no figures about the non-income tax payers.

10,191. But you can refer to the income tax mainly, because the income tax would contain all the large fortunes, and if you took them out, you would have a clearer average?—That might be done.

10,192. Have you examined it?—My recollection is, that I did ask for a calculation from the Inland Revenue, and they could not give it me.

10,193. I have here a return put in by Mr. Murrough O'Brien, as to Schedule D, which is, by far the most important schedule, is it not?—Yes.

10,194. As to Schedule A, I should think there are quite as many large landlords in proportion in Ireland as in Great Britain. Does it occur to you that, looking at what I have just said, that 80 per cent. of the people

Sir E. W. Hamilton, K.C.B. [illegible]

in Ireland are at rent under 10s., and 80 per cent. were under 15s., that if you took out the incomes of the large landlords, and a few brewers, distillers, linen manufacturers, and shipbuilders, the average income in Ireland would come out in a lower proportion to Great Britain?—I think it would probably come out in a lower proportion.

10,195. This return as to Schedule D. is very interesting. You will find it on page 160 of the second volume of evidence. The relative yield of income tax is as 1 to 20?—Yes, that is about it.

10,196. Look at the return at the bottom of the page?—I am afraid I have not studied that particular table.

10,197. You will see the proportion of Ireland to the United Kingdom, "persons and amounts"; do you see that the proportion of persons does not differ materially from the proportion of amounts?—I see it is so.

10,198. Does not that tend to negative your assumption that large incomes exist in a smaller proportion in Ireland?—That may be so.

10,199. When you look a little higher up, you will find that the proportions of the number of persons appear to be very much the same as the proportion of the total yield of the tax in Ireland and Great Britain, but when you pass beyond 4,000*l.* a year, the incomes are more numerous relatively in Great Britain than in Ireland?—Yes, in fact, commencing at 1,000*l.*

10,200. Somewhat, but not greatly. The gross yield is 1 to 21?—Yes.

10,201. So I think you have to go up to 4,000*l.* before you find a very material difference. I admit that when you pass 4,000*l.* the large incomes are more numerous relatively in Great Britain than the proportion of the yield of income tax between Ireland and Great Britain; but you see the income of Great Britain is so vast, both relatively and absolutely,—1,400,000,000*l.* or 1,500,000,000*l.* a year—that even if you deduct 100,000,000*l.* or 200,000,000*l.*, that is, take out all the large incomes, the proportion of income between Great Britain and Ireland, and the average between the two countries would not be materially altered?—I think not. You are referring now to income tax paying incomes.

10,202. Yes, and that is enough for the purpose of the argument. Now, if you will take the trouble to calculate the amount of these incomes over 4,000*l.*, you will find that they do not amount to 100,000,000*l.* altogether, and if you took them all out of the British incomes the proportion would not be materially altered?—No, I suppose not, materially.

10,203. Then, finally, as to the [illegible] you refer to the unemployed. You suggested that it was a weakness in Sir Robert Giffen's demonstration (or rather Lord Welby suggested it to you) that Sir Robert Giffen treated the whole of the people of England and the whole of the people of Ireland as employed, and that he leaves out of consideration the vast mass of absolute poverty there is in Great Britain in the towns. Do the unemployed earn wages?—I suppose not.

10,204. Do they pay taxes?—Not unless they consume dutiable articles.

10,205. If they did consume dutiable articles they would not pay the duty out of income?—Not unless they had something in their pockets in the shape of savings.

10,206. Have you any evidence that the unemployed in Great Britain are relatively more numerous than they are in Ireland, that is, that for every eight persons unemployed in Great Britain there is not one in Ireland?—No, I have no special information on that point.

10,207. When an effort is made in this way to qualify the force of a very closely reasoned demonstration it should be remembered that account has been taken, not only of the actual rates of wages but of the numbers of persons employed, according to the information of the Board of Trade, and I think it should also be borne in mind that Sir Robert Giffen in estimating the income and average rate of wages in Ireland and in Great Britain made no allowance—none whatever—for what he admitted to be the general inferiority of the earning power of the population of Ireland?—I believe that to be so.

10,208. Do you call to mind, for instance, that he pointed out that there are 5 per cent. more of the population in Ireland over 60 years of age than in Great Britain?—I read that in his evidence.

10,209. And between 20 and 40 there are 3 per cent. less in Ireland?—Yes.

10,210. And more children?—Yes, I believe that is so.

10,211. Do you call to mind that he made no allowance for the well-known fact, that agricultural labour, which is the mass of labour in Ireland, is precarious, and that whilst the rule in England is regular labour, in Ireland the agricultural labourer can only look for regular employment in the spring and harvest?—There must be a mass of very precarious employment in Great Britain as well.

10,212. No doubt there is an element of that kind in Great Britain, but the rule for the rural town is regular employment, while the rule in Ireland, I suggest to you, for agricultural labour, which is the great mass, is precarious and insufficient employment, except at spring and harvest?—That may be so.

10,213. If that were exhaustively estimated, do you not think it would tend to bring down the Irish average of wages actually received?—That is a statistical point on which I would rather not express an opinion. I am prepared to adopt the figures of Sir Robert Giffen, who is a much greater authority than I am.

10,214. I must say personally that I have never known a question so complicated dealt with in such a masterly manner as this has been dealt with by Sir Robert Giffen. I do not know whether that is your opinion?—I agree, but there are one or two points on which I do not agree with him.

10,215. You are familiar by this time—more familiar, perhaps, than is agreeable to you—with the text of the questions referred to this Commission?—Yes.

10,216. I think it might be convenient, if we could ascertain whether we have a common understanding of them. The Commission are instructed to report, "upon "what principles of comparison, and by the application "of what specific standards, the relative capacity of "Great Britain and Ireland to bear taxation may be "most equitably determined," and what is the true proportion. Do you understand that question to instruct the Commissioners to ascertain the means possessed by the people of Great Britain and Ireland to pay taxation?—I think so.

10,217. And to report that proportion?—I think so, but I admit the instructions have always been rather a puzzle to me. I do not think they are very explicit, but I think that is a fair inference to draw from them.

10,218. I think that part of it, so far as I have read, is hardly open to misunderstanding on the score of vagueness. It is plain enough. You ascertain taxable capacity, and you report the proportion, that is, whether you take the test to be income or resources you find the proportion which they bear to each other, and report the mathematical result?—Yes.

10,219. You report what is the true proportion. Now, glancing for a moment at your view of the connection between taxation and expenditure, whatever may be the expenditure in Ireland, can the expenditure in Ireland alter the reply to that question. Could the Commissioners, by reason of any expenditure, report the true proportion to be anything else than what they find to be the true proportion of the resources?—I should have thought they would have had to qualify the proportion very materially by looking at the other side of the account as well.

10,220. Are they instructed to do so?—I do not see how they can possibly approach the consideration of Question No. 2 without it.

10,221. At present I am not on No. 3?—But the third and the first two hang together.

10,222. I think, whatever answers may be given to No. 3 the answers to Nos. 1 and 2 will be unaffected by any answers that may be given to 3?—That may be so.

10,223. Then we are instructed to report "the history "of the Financial Relations between Great Britain and "Ireland at and after the Legislative Union." As that history is pretty well known already I take it the question means that we are to report our judgment or opinion upon any part of those transactions?—I presume so.

10,224. The next question is: "The charge for Irish "purposes on the Imperial Exchequer during that "period." That instruction does not oblige the Commissioners to accept any classification of "Irish purposes" so-called by the Treasury. The question is an open question so far as the Commissioners are concussed ?—I presume so. If they do not see fit to accept the classification of the Treasury.

10,225. They are at liberty to ask what are Irish purposes ?—I think so.

10,226. And whether there is any expenditure which can be classified as other than common expenditure of the United Kingdom ?—I think so.

10,227. Then we are to inquire what is "the amount "of Irish taxation legitimately available for contribution "to Imperial expenditure." That would again raise the question whether a part of the common expenditure of the kingdom can be classified as Imperial ?—Yes.

10,228. And it conducts us into the labyrinth of the Treasury adjustment of Irish revenue ?—Yes.

10,229. And raises the question whether your adjustment is accurate. Finally we are asked to report "what "is the Imperial expenditure to which it is considered "equitable that Ireland should contribute." That raises, as a matter of equity, the question whether, if you can classify a part of the expenditure of the United Kingdom as Imperial, the interest of Ireland in that expenditure is such that she should contribute according to her resources or at all, to all or some of that expenditure ?—I should have thought "at all" was rather more than was contemplated.

10,230. I think not. It is "the Imperial expenditure "to which it is considered equitable that Ireland should "contribute," which suggests there is some to which she ought not ?—Perhaps so.

10,231. I think there are two things; the first is that there is some to which it is not equitable she should contribute, and then there is the proportion of the remainder ?—I think that is arguable from the reference.

10,232. Your memorandum shows that you have given a very close study to the period of the Legislative Union and the period antecedent to it. What do you estimate to have been the income of Great Britain at the time of the Legislative Union ?—Do you mean the aggregate income ?

10,233. The gross income of Great Britain ?—The wealth, you mean ?

10,234. The annual income ?—Do you mean the aggregate of individual incomes, or the public income ?

10,235. I mean the aggregate of individual incomes ?—I am afraid I have no figures relating to the time of the Union.

10,236. You have not considered that question ?—No; I have no data to go upon. I do not know whether Sir Robert Giffen could furnish some. I have not seen any figures estimating the relative incomes of Great Britain and Ireland—I mean by that the aggregate individual incomes of the two countries—at the time of the Union.

10,237. You are not quite without data. For example, the income of Great Britain now, according to what Sir Robert Giffen calls the usual estimate of experts, which I suppose is a figure of great authority, is between 1,400,000,000*l.* and 1,500,000,000*l.* The population is 34,000,000 or 35,000,000; the population at the time of the Union we know to have been about 10,000,000, two-sevenths of the present population, two-sevenths of 1,400,000,000*l.* would be 400,000,000*l.*, so that if the individual income at the time of the Union were proportionate to what it is now, the gross income at the Union would have been 400,000,000*l.*; but we know, do we not, that whilst the increase of population in Great Britain during this century has been remarkable—more than treble—the increase in wealth has been much greater ?—I think so, certainly.

10,238. For example, in this generation, since 1850, the population has increased one-third, and the wealth has about doubled ?—Yes, I believe that to be the case.

10,239. The income has increased there more or less in the people, has it ?—Yes.

10,240. That seems to lead, does it not, straight to the conclusion that the income of Great Britain at the time of the Union, with two-sevenths of its present population, cannot have been so much as two-sevenths of its present income ?—I think that is quite possible.

10,241. Is it not quite certain, if the wealth during the century has advanced so much more quickly than the population, that the proportion of income per head must have been lower at the time of the Union ?—I think there is no doubt it was lower.

10,242. Mr. Holland has given us a very valuable return of income-tax assessments of lands and houses, which shows that in 1814, not so long after the Union, the assessment of lands and messuages in Great Britain was 52,000,000*l.*; the current return shows that the assessment of lands and messuages now is 189,000,000*l.*; the gross assessment now is 672,000,000*l.*—that is to say, the assessment of lands and houses is a little more than one-fourth of the total assessment. Looking to the increase of wealth other than lands and houses in Great Britain, I presume the assessment of lands and houses bore a higher proportion then than it does now to the total ?—I presume so.

10,243. The certainty is that lands and houses bore a higher proportion to the total property at the time of the Union than at present ?—I should think unquestionably so.

10,244. We have also the fact that there was an income tax in Great Britain at the time of the Union ?—Yes.

10,245. And in the year 1804-5 that income tax at 1*s.* in the pound on incomes of 150*l.* and upwards, that is to say, levied pretty much as it is levied now, yielded 3,600,000*l.* ?—Yes.

10,246. That approximately indicates an assessment of 72,000,000*l.* ?—Yes.

10,247. Then you have these suggestions, that the assessment to income tax about the time of the Union, in Great Britain, was an assessment upon about 72,000,000*l.*, and the lands and houses at the same time were assessed at 52,000,000*l.*, but if the population had the same proportionate income as now the income would be 400,000,000*l.* altogether. Should you be disposed to say that the income of Great Britain at the time of the Union was more than about two-thirds of the figure at which it would have stood if the proportion of income to population were the same as now ?—I do not like to give an opinion upon that straight off. I should like to consider the figures before I committed myself to them.

10,248. I may not have another opportunity of joining with you in the consideration of the matter, and I should like to advance it now. You have the estimate that the income is about 1,400,000,000*l.*, and you have the fact that wealth has advanced much more rapidly than population, and you have the fact that if the income had been the same in proportion at the time of the Union as now, it would have been 400,000,000*l.* Can you abstain from the conclusion that the income then would have been probably about 250,000,000*l.* at the outside ?—I think that may be a fair conjecture. But I am not certain that I am on the same lines as yourself. I find that in 1801-2 income tax in Great Britain yielded nearly 6,000,000*l.*

10,249. It was at a different rate from in that year; it was as far as that year ?—I am not certain that in 1801 it was; what year did you speak of ?

10,250. 1804-5 ?—That was 3,600,000*l.*, and in 1802-3 it was 5,000,000*l.*

10,251. In the year 1802 it was 2*s.* in the pound; I took 1804-5, at 1*s.* in the pound, indicating an approximate assessment of 72,000,000*l.* ?—Yes; and if I am right in my recollection I think Mr. Pitt estimated the yield of income tax in Ireland at 1,000,000*l.*, which would rather confirm, I think, what you had in your own mind.

10,252. The papers you know in their present estimated the rental of Ireland at only 6,300,000*l.* altogether. One would suggest a higher figure than 250,000,000*l.* for the income of that time in Great Britain ?—That may be so.

10,253. Have you considered what was the income of Ireland then ?—No.

10,254. Was it greater or less than now ?—I should think it was probably less.

10,255. Why was it probably less ?—I think that Ireland was a less wealthy country at the end of last century than it is now.

10,256. We are speaking of income, not of property ?—Yes, income; but I am afraid I have no data upon which to go, and any answer of mine would be worth nothing.

10,257. But you can reason and come to conclusions upon data as handed to you ?—I always like to see figures before coming to any conclusions, but I will do my best to facilitate the drawing of any conclusions at which you wish to arrive.

Sir E. W. Hamilton, K.C.B.

16 Nov. 1894.

Population of Ireland at time of the Union and at present.

10,258. The population of Ireland, at any rate, was greater by half a million at the time of the Union than at the present time?—Yes, that is so, according to the best calculations.

10,259. They had the same agricultural resources, had they not?—I do not know; that is a point I should not like to commit myself upon.

10,260. They had the same land, I mean?—Yes, the same land, no doubt, but I do not suppose there was so much in cultivation then as there is now; but that is a point upon which I really cannot express an opinion; I have not sufficient information to do so.

10,261. Those who are familiar with Ireland know that a good deal of land which was in cultivation in earlier times has now gone back to waste. Moreover, at that time, in Ireland, they had widely diffused manufactures up the cities and towns?—I believe so.

10,262. And they had a substantial foreign and colonial trade, had they not?—Yes.

10,263. Now, with a lower population, only the same agricultural resources, no manufactures, except in a couple of towns, and no foreign or colonial trade, can you commend to yourself the conclusion that the income of Ireland at that time could have been less than it is at present?—I am afraid any answer of mine would be worth little or nothing.

10,264. Do you see any reason for thinking that it was less?—I should have thought it would have been less; at least that is my idea. I should have thought Belfast and Dublin were then about a quarter the size they are now, and there would be nothing like the same amount of income derived from them as there is now.

10,265. If you look at Sir Robert Giffen's table of exports you will see the exports of whiskey, beer, and linen do not very materially pull up the aggregate, and that the essential thing is the agricultural income; and what I wish to ask you is, whether you are driven by these data, upon which we are agreed, that the income of Ireland was materially less at the period of the Union than it is at the present time?—I daresay not, but I think my opinion is worth nothing upon that point. I have never considered whether there are any data on which to base conclusions.

10,266. Those we have just discussed are unquestionable?—I admit that.

Proportions of contribution how fixed by the Act of Union.

10,267. If we take it that the Irish income, at that time, was as estimated now, say about 75,000,000*l.*, and the British income 220,000,000*l.*, it follows, does it not, that the proportion of 2 to 15 cannot have been founded upon income?—I do not think that the proportion ever professed to have been founded upon income. I should have thought that the main case to be drawn was that there were no data for estimating the relative incomes at the time of the Union, for I presume that, had there been such data, they would have been the first data which Lord Castlereagh and Mr. Pitt would have adopted. That is what has been always present to my mind on looking into the historical part of the question.

10,268. Whatever may have been the faults of the persons who passed the Act of Union, they were not persons who suffered from any lack of intelligence—they knew the movement to income tax in Great Britain?—Yes; but having no income tax in Ireland, I suppose they thought the income tax test was an impossibility.

10,269. No doubt, upon the materials at their hands they could form an intelligent view—from wages and other sources—they could form an estimate of the income of the people?—But as I have already said, I should have thought that, if it had been possible to ascertain what the relative incomes of the two countries were at that time, they would have been naturally taken as the test or standard of the relative capacities of the two countries.

10,270. At any rate, it is apparent on the most cursory examination of the subject, is it not, that the proportions of 2 to 15 were not founded on the relative incomes?—Not on the relative incomes; that is clear, I think.

10,271. What, then, were they founded upon?—They were founded upon a combination of commerce and consumption.

10,272. They were founded, ostensibly, upon current calculations, were they not?—Yes.

10,273. But upon what principle in regard to relative taxable capacity—the means of the people—were they founded?—On the value of the imports and exports, and the average amount consumed of dutiable articles.

10,274. Those were the pseudo arguments for debate; but if, as we have said, the income of Ireland may have been 75,000,000*l.*, and the income of Great Britain 220,000,000*l.*, if we apply to those figures—and we must remember the destitution of Scotland was then hanging—the doctrine as to the test is not the income, but the residue left after allowance for cost of subsistence, if we apply the figure of John Stuart Mill, of 10*l.* per head, or the figure of Sir Robert Giffen, of 12*l.* per head, to the population, which was then 5,000,000 of people in Ireland and 10,000,000 in England, it will leave a residue of 15,000,000*l.* in Ireland, and 120,000,000*l.* in Great Britain, or 1 to 8, corresponding very nearly to the proportion in the Act of Union?—That seems to be so; but I do not know whether I caught the argument, because, as I understand, your estimate is that the relative incomes of the two countries at the time of the Union were about 220,000,000*l.* to 75,000,000*l.*

10,275. I am suggesting it might have been so?—According to that argument, then, Ireland was undercharged in giving her a proportion of only 2 to 15.

10,276. My argument is that the promoters of the Act of Union recognised the unquestionableness of the test of income, and fixed it upon taxation?—I cannot say what they had in their minds more than what is recorded in their speeches.

10,277. In any proportion between two countries like Great Britain and Ireland—a great wealthy Power, a Power involved in every European complication, liable to great wars, and a small, poor country like Ireland, with purely domestic concerns—to tax two such countries in a fixed proportion, whatever it might be, without fixing a maximum sum beyond which the contribution of Ireland should not extend, must have proved extremely inequitable if the levy of taxation became high?—Yes, that may have been so; but what the framers of the Treaty of Union apparently had in view was, that, but for the amount of the debt in Ireland being less, proportionately, than the debt in Great Britain, Ireland would have been subjected indiscriminately to the full weight of taxation which was on Great Britain.

10,278. Does not that shed a very lurid light upon the entire scheme?—That may be so; but, unless I misread the speeches, I think it was simply the accident of the inequality of the debt burdens that prevented Ireland from being united financially as well as legislatively in 1800.

10,279. If there had been no debts, they would have made no inquiry at all into capacity, would they?—I take it that, if there had been no debt in either country, or if the debts had been what they considered to be proportionately fair, then Ireland would have been incorporated financially as well as legislatively.

10,280. If there had been no debts, there would have been no proportions, would there?—No doubt.

10,281. Would that have been equitable?—I do not say whether it would have been equitable or not. I say that that is apparently what the framers of the treaty had in their minds.

10,282. Would it have been equitable?—I do not think it would.

10,283. If there had been no debts, then there would have been no proportions; there would have been indiscriminate taxation; how could Lord Castlereagh have known whether the debts were in proportion to ability or not unless he inquired first what was the ability?—I cannot say.

10,284. Can you discover a glimmer of reason or equity in that sort of argument. If there were no debt there would have been no inquiry; the capacity would have been assumed to be equal; but as there were debts, they set about finding the relative capacity, and they fixed it at 2 to 15, yet the capacity being 2 to 15, if there were no debt they would have treated the capacity as 1 to 1. How did the minds of men operate to come to such conclusions?—I am afraid I cannot undertake to say what was in their minds at the time; as far as I can make out, their object was to make it a fair arrangement, and they took the best materials they had at hand.

10,285. That is just what I question. I say that tolerance on the part of Lord Castlereagh and others vitiates their whole position, because, if the capacity of Ireland to Great Britain stood in a certain proportion,

Sir E. W. Hamilton, K.C.B. 14 Nov. 1895.

the question of the presence or absence, or amount of debt should not subject her to indiscriminate taxation, her capacity being in a certain proportion?—That may be so.

10,286. Now as to the year 1816 and the extraordinary circumstances under which the transactions of that year were held to be justified, the capacity of Ireland to Great Britain being 2 to 15, can you discover in the circumstance that the debts came into the proportion of 2 to 15, that is, into the same proportion as the proportion of the capacity of the two countries relatively to each other, any reason why the proportion should be abolished—was it not one reason the more why the proportion should have been retained?—I do not think I follow that argument.

10,287. Ireland owed a debt, and Great Britain owed a debt; the debts were not in the relation of 2 to 15?—No; they had got out of that proportion, and the Irish debt was relatively higher than 2 to 15.

10,288. I am speaking now of the time of the Union. The debts were not in the relation of 2 to 15, and the capacity to bear taxation generally was held to be in that proportion?—Yes.

10,289. At a later date the debts were said to have come into the proportion of 2 to 15, but the capacity to bear general taxation being 2 to 15, why should the fact that the particular charge for debt came into the same proportion of 2 to 15 be held to alter the whole capacity to bear taxation?—But did it?

10,290. It was held to do so, because the proportionate system of 2 to 15 was abolished, and Ireland made subject to indiscriminate taxation?—But she did not come subject immediately to indiscriminate taxation, as we know, not for a good many years.

10,291. But it was held that she became subject to it?—No doubt, but as a matter of fact she did not become so.

10,292. She lost her right to proportionate taxation and periodical revision, and she became liable to indiscriminate taxation?—That may be so.

10,293. This is a matter of some importance, and really probes the core of the Union settlement. I ask you again: if the relative capacity of Ireland to Great Britain to bear taxation was 2 to 15, and if the particular charges for the debt came to bear the same relation of 2 to 15, that is the relation of the general capacity of the two countries, was not that one reason the more for maintaining the proportion of 2 to 15, and no conceivable reason for abolishing it?—I think that is a fair way of putting it, but Ireland did not continue to pay as 2 to 15 after the consolidation of the Exchequers.

10,294. (*Sir David Barbour.*) Was it not the case at that time that Ireland was no longer able to bear the proportion of 2 to 15, was she not practically bankrupt, when the Exchequers were amalgamated?—Yes, and therefore Great Britain took over the whole of the Irish debt.

10,295. (*Mr. Sexton.*) That touches the question I put a little while ago, whether any proportion whatever, no matter how low, could have been equitable as between a poor country and a rich one if the aim to be levied greatly rose, because it would encroach upon the small margin of the small country to a greater extent than upon the large margin of the large country?—No doubt; and that was the extreme misfortune of Ireland coming into the Union when she did, and having to face the frightfully high expenditure incurred by the Government of Great Britain.

10,296. The proportion of 2 to 15 was undoubtedly held out as a protection, was it not?—I think so.

10,297. And that protection, if it was worth, was taken away for a reason in which no trace of reason can be found, namely, that the charges for debt came into the same relation as the capacity, which would have been one more reason, if one were required, for maintaining the proportion. Now, I have been dealing with the question of whether the proportion was founded on reason, and I invite your attention to a remarkable declaration of Mr. Pitt in 1785, when he said: "The smallest burthen "on a poor country was to be considered when com"pared with those of a rich one, by no means in a "proportion with their several abilities, for if one "country exceeded another in wealth, population, and "established commerce, in a proportion of two to one, "he was nearly convinced that that country would be "able to bear near ten times the burthens that the "other would be equal to." Is it not evident from this passage that Mr. Pitt was of opinion that the relative capacities of countries to bear taxation do not correspond with their incomes?—I think that is a perfectly fair inference to draw from the passage.

10,298. Twice the means, he said; 10 times the burden. So far as Mr. Pitt was concerned, therefore, with the Act of Union, it might seem to be fair to infer that he did not apply the test of income, but the test of surplus?—Yes, apparently so, at least, that is not an unfair assumption to make.

Proportion of taxation was fixed by the Act of Union.

10,299. If we could consult Mr. Pitt at the present time with regard to two countries which stand to each other in population and wealth, not in the relation of 2 to 1, a relation which he said would justify 10 times the burden, but stand to each other in the relation as to capital of 1 to 24, as to population of 1 to 8, and as to income of 1 to 22, what proportion do you think Mr. Pitt would have said might properly exist between the taxation of the poorer of those countries and the richer?—I am afraid I cannot put words into Mr. Pitt's mouth, but I suppose it would be something comparatively small according to that view of his. I do not suppose, however, he would have considered that any hard-and-fast rule could be laid down, from which there would be no deviation. He would presumably have taken all the circumstances into account.

10,300. I have calculated the mean proportion as well as I can, and I make it 1 to 76. In your memorandum I think you adopt the principle stated by Sir Robert Giffen as the equitable principle of relative taxable capacity?—The aggregate individual incomes?

10,301. No, the principle, following Bentham and Mill, that the taxable revenue of a country is the income left after deducting the allowance necessary to maintain the population on a given standard of life?—I think there is a great deal to be said for that way of stating the case.

Taxable capacity and minimum individual subsistence.

10,302. In fact, I think you stated the same principle yourself?—I think I only quoted Sir Robert Giffen. I do not think I adopted it except in the way of a quotation.

10,303. You quoted Sir Robert Giffen and then you stated later on that the amount of a man's income is not necessarily a test of his capacity to bear taxation, and then you added, "Perhaps a better test of the amount which "the taxpayer can afford to pay for being governed, "protected, and educated is the residue of his income "remaining after the bare necessaries of life have been "met?"—Yes.

10,304. Have you considered Sir Robert Giffen's reasons for holding that there should not be a different minimum allowance applied to two countries standing in the relation of Great Britain and Ireland?—I think it is fair that a different minimum should be allowed to Ireland, which is a poor country, than to a country which is rich.

10,305. He said there should be no difference?—Not as regards the allowance necessary to maintain life.

10,306. Do you agree, looking to the fact that the same necessaries of life cost about the same in both countries, that the minimum allowance ought to be the same?—I think there is considerable force in that principle.

10,307. John Stuart Mill mentioned 10*l.* a head, but he added that he thought it insufficient; Sir Robert Giffen suggested 12*l.*?—Yes.

10,308. Do you think it could be fixed any lower?—I am afraid my opinion is worth little, but 12*l.* seems to me to be quite too large.

10,309. The 12*l.*, being an average, applies to all classes?—I believe so.

10,310. And is it, like all averages, flexible, and it really means allowing a higher sum to a higher class and a smaller sum to a lower class?—No; as I understand it, you make the same deduction from every individual's income. But that seems to me to be inapplicable to anything but the smallest incomes.

10,311. I do not quite see that, if you take 4,500,000 people, and deduct 12*l.* a head, that gives you for the 4,500,000 a subsistence fund of 54,000,000*l.*, and it allows of variation of expenditure according to the classes?—But it is inapplicable to make a deduction of 12*l.* a head from an individual who has a larger income than, say, 100*l.* a year. I think the deduction or allowance for the minimum of existence ought only to be taken from the very small incomes.

[illegible] 21 Nov. 1895. Taxable capacity [illegible]

10,312 No, the principle is to take it from all incomes?—I know it is; but I venture to question that principle.

10,313 It is an average, and being an average, is inapplicable to each individual income; we know, as a matter of fact, that with regard to the mass of incomes—for instance, 60 per cent. of the Irish wage-earners only get 10s. a week—no such deduction can be made, because their income is not so much; therefore it is obvious that the expenditure upon the necessaries of life in such a case as that, being much less, admits of the multiplication of the allowance where the income is so much larger?—That is probably so.

10,314 I do not know whether you have observed that Mr Robinson, of the Irish Local Government Board, told the Commission that the cost of supplying clothes and food alone to an inmate of an Irish workhouse is about 9l. a year?—No, I did not see that observation.

10,315 So that the minimum could scarcely be less than 12l., could it?—I have already said that I do not think that 12l. is a high minimum to fix.

10,316 You therefore, have adopted the principle that the residue is the most equitable test, and that in order to arrive at the residue, a minimum allowance of 12l. may be deducted all round from the income of the country?—Yes. I should doubt, as I have already said, whether it would be applicable to large incomes, but I defer to a higher authority, like Sir Robert Giffen.

10,317 Taking the income of Great Britain at 1,500,000,000l., and the income of Ireland at 76,000,000l., and making this identical allowance for the cost of subsistence, the conclusion is reached that the income left in Ireland after necessaries are provided, would be about 15,000,000l., and the residue in Great Britain would be about 1,180,000,000l., the residue bearing the proportion of about 1 to 70?—That was not what I made out. 12l. per head on a population of 4,600,000 would be 54,000,000l., and you have to deduct that from 76,000,000l.

10,318 76,000,000l. was the maximum figure stated?—I have put it at 76,000,000l., and I have always thought that not an excessive figure, for a reason which I will give, if you like.

10,319 Will you kindly pause for a moment on that point. 76,000,000l. is double the gross assessment?—Of course, the Commission understand that I do not profess to be a statistical authority, nor do I wish in the least to dispute Sir Robert Giffen's figures, but I determined to see if I could in any way corroborate it, and the way I went to work was to try and find out what Ireland was spending a year, and I have made up for what it is worth, a calculation which, curiously enough, comes to pretty much the same figure as Sir Robert Giffen gives—74,000,000l. My idea is that the gross expenditure of a country is almost a better test than the gross income; because, although it would not be safe to say so of individuals, I suppose what a nation spends is, at any rate, within its income. That is the reason why I say 76,000,000l. does not strike me as being too high a figure, although I think it did strike some members of the Commission in that light.

10,320 76,000,000l. is double the gross assessment to income tax in Ireland?—Yes, but I think I can make out that Ireland spends 74,000,000l.

10,321 That remains to be seen; it has not been proved yet. It is double the gross assessment, and we have it in evidence from Mr Murrough O'Brien and others, first, that Ireland is more strictly valued than England; secondly, that the valuation has remained unaltered during the recent fall in prices; and that on these grounds 4,000,000l. ought to be deducted. Then we have the absentee rents, mortgage interest, annuities, and various other payments amounting to 8,000,000l. more, so that if those deductions are made from the 76,000,000l., and I fail to see why they should not be made, you bring the figure down to 64,000,000l., which is also the figure reached if you apply to the non-agricultural population what Sir Robert Giffen has estimated to be the agricultural figure, namely, 40,000,000l. However, between the two figures 64,000,000l., which is the income of Ireland on the assumption that the whole income is the same as the agricultural, and 76,000,000l. which is the maximum figure named in evidence, you may take what figure pleases you best?—I only wished to mention the calculation I had made.

10,322 That leaves a margin of 22,000,000l.?—Yes. Then in Great Britain for a similar allowance you would have to deduct 408,000,000l. from the 1,475,000,000l.?

10,323 That is assuming the income of the United Kingdom to be 1,550,000,000l.?—Yes, and that would leave about 1,050,000,000l. as taxable income, and according to those figures they work out as 1 to 45.

10,324 Then your conclusion appears to be that the residuum is 1 to 11, the income is 1 to 22, taking the highest Irish income estimated, and the relative taxable capacity judged by the income remaining after the necessaries of life have been provided is 1 to 45?—That is what I made out, or rather, 1 to 44.

10,325 Now I wish to ask you a few questions about the hypothesis in your first memorandum, and the specific standard or gauge which you suggested there. I understand the hypothesis was a mere hypothesis?—Yes it was.

10,326 When you suggested that a man with 15s. a week in Ireland might get necessaries so much more cheaply than a man with 15s. a week in Great Britain, that his residue would be proportionately larger out of the 10s. than the other man would have out of 15s., you indulged, did you not, in a somewhat violent hypothesis?—Certainly, and I think when you are dealing with a point of that kind, the best illustration to take is a somewhat extreme case.

10,327 What you might call the obvious hypothesis, as the case is this, is it not: you have two countries lying beside each other in an atmosphere of free trade; in the one a man with 15s. a week will have a residue left after the necessaries of life have been provided, exceeding the residue which the man with 10s. a week would have, in a proportion much greater than the proportion of 15 to 10?—Presumably so.

10,328 If the man with 10s. a week can live on 8s. a week for necessaries, so can the man with 15s. a week, in which case the man with 15s. a week will have 7s. residue, while the man with 10s. a week would only have 2s. residue; in other words, the one would have five times as much as the other?—Yes.

10,329 I think you adopt the hypothesis in the other way now?—I only used the hypothesis to meet an argument which I thought was almost certain to be used.

10,330 As to the gauge, you took the expenditure upon certain taxed commodities?—Yes.

10,331 That was the same as one of Lord Castlereagh's tests at the time of the Union, was it not?—It was.

10,332 I think in your evidence you have attached but little importance to that test of his?—No, I have always said that I thought it was one of the few available tests he had to go upon.

10,333 But you never looked upon it as a test to be relied upon?—Not to be absolutely relied upon, and I do not pretend that my test can be relied upon.

10,334 What is your test in substance except this. What is it except taking the fact that the tax is paid as a proof that the tax is right?—No, I should have thought rather it was what the inhabitants of Great Britain and the inhabitants of Ireland respectively find themselves in a position to spend upon certain commodities.

10,335 Why upon certain commodities?—Because those are the only commodities I was able to test.

10,336 But they are not the only luxuries?—Certainly not, but I cannot test any others.

10,337 But then see how fallacious a test it is?—It may be. I only put it forward for what it is worth. When you have a very difficult question of this kind to deal with, you can only get at one or two contributory tests. It is not possible to set up one specific standard.

10,338 But if a test affords no guidance it can hardly be called a contributory test, it may contribute to confusion, may it not?—Personally, I should not say that, but other people may take a different view to me.

10,339 You know the opinion of Sir Robert Giffen with regard to offering as a test the yield of customs and excise?—I have read it, but I have forgotten what the exact words are.

10,340 He says, "It is only evidence that in matters "of taxation Ireland is virtually discriminated against "by the character of the direct taxes which happen to "be on articles of Irish consumption." Instead of being a proof of capacity. he considers it to be a proof of [illegible] against Ireland in fixing the taxes, and the rates of the taxes?—I should not take the same view on that point as Sir Robert Giffen. I do not see how it can help being a test of what a person finds himself able to spend.

10,241. How can it be a test of what a person finds himself able to spend unless it is an exhaustive test of what he spends?—I should like very much indeed to be able to apply an exhaustive test, but I believe such a thing is not [illegible].

10,242. Then this test is not exhaustive?—Certainly not; I do not say it is.

10,243. I think you agree, do you not, that the test of [illegible] is the same as the test of duty; you do not alter the [illegible] substantially by putting on the [illegible]. It would be pretty much the same if you took the duty simply?—It comes out not very different, I think.

10,244. The fact that a duty is paid is no proof that [illegible] or [illegible] is not unequally trenched upon in the two countries?—No.

10,245. In fact I think it is quite obvious, looking at the average income in Ireland of about 14l., and at the allowance of 12l., that the sum of 2l. just [illegible], if your calculation be at all correct, does represent, practically, what the mass of the people have to spare from the absolute necessaries of life?—That may be so, but unfortunately I have not the means of being able to follow that up.

10,246. You have the calculations of gross and average incomes, and you have the [illegible] allowance, and you know that this 2l. makes up about the difference, do you not?—Yes but one knows as a matter of fact that there is a great deal more spent.

10,247. Because there is a [illegible] of the average?—I mean, besides the expenditure which I have been able to calculate (for what it is worth), one knows there is a vast amount of other expenditure which I did not take into account in my memorandum. Since then I have tried to build up a table [illegible] the other side of the account, namely, what Ireland, as a whole, spends.

10,248. But the failure in your comparison is that there are not residues at all. In order to find the residue, you must take the income and make the allowance and the deduction?—No doubt.

10,249. It may be a residue in Ireland, but is it the residue in Great Britain?—Apparently not.

10,250. The average income in Great Britain is about 43l.; so that when you had come to it there, that out of an income of 14l. in Ireland you would allow 12l. for subsistence; and out of an income of 43l. in Great Britain, you would allow 27l. for subsistence, or twice [illegible] as much?—Yes, according to that way of putting it.

10,251. Then is it not obvious that what you call residue is not residue at all. You take certain articles of consumption and treat them as luxuries, and the expenditure upon them as the whole residue, these being substantially the only articles in Ireland, and you ignore entirely a vast mass of untaxed luxuries in Great Britain which Ireland cannot afford to use, and also a great mass of savings in Great Britain?—No doubt, and that is the reason why I tried to build up a total account of Ireland's aggregate expenditure, which I will give the Commission, if they like.

10,252. Then it seems to follow, does it not, that if you are to discover the taxable residue, that is, the whole income left after necessaries have been provided, you cannot proceed in this way, by taking [illegible] [illegible] and calling them residues, but you must take the whole income of either country and make an allowance for the cost of subsistence in that country, the residue left after subsistence being the taxable residue?—Yes, but I should have thought that that allowance ought only to have been deducted upon small incomes, and the exclusion of larger incomes might vitiate the comparison.

10,253. What I was upon at the moment was that your gauge is no gauge of residue, because what it calls residue in Great Britain is not the residue of Great Britain, but only a small fraction of it?—But I did not say it was a gauge of residue.

10,254. I think you have admitted that the taxable capacity of a country is the residue left from income after the necessaries of life have been provided, have you not?—Yes.

10,255. And your gauge was not that?—I do not see that the two things are quite connected.

10,256. You are measuring the relative taxable capacity?—Yes.

10,257. Your gauge was offered as evidence of it?—Yes.

10,258. I am pointing out that your gauge cannot be evidence of taxable capacity, because it does not show the real residue left after the necessaries of life have been provided?—Yes, I follow you.

Adjourned for a short time.

10,259. I think you have agreed that Sir Robert Giffen's method does not depend upon consumption, but that it is founded upon the proportions of the income tax assessment?—That is so; but of course the income tax assessment represents the whole of the national income, a considerable part of which is not subject to the tax at all.

10,260. But he tested the proportions derived from the net income tax assessment confirmed by various other tests?—That is so.

10,261. Namely, his estimate of wages of intermediate incomes, the assessment to the death duties, and the best estimate that could be formed of the value of agricultural produce in Ireland?—Yes.

10,262. It is important to observe that Sir Robert Giffen's estimate of 40,000,000l. is about midway between the Irish Registrar-General's estimate of 46,000,000l. and Mr. Murrough O'Brien's estimate of 37,000,000l., and that it relates to the year 1893, when there were comparatively high prices?—Yes.

10,263. Have you noted Sir Robert Giffen's observation, that if he were to go more deeply into the question and consider the tests given in his general tables as to the consumption of coal and various other items, he has no doubt the proportion of the average income of Ireland would be still further diminished?—I think I remember that that was a statement which he made.

10,264. Have you observed the remarkable figure in his table, that whereas [illegible] per cent. of the males employed in agriculture in the United Kingdom are in Ireland, the value of the agricultural produce of Ireland is only [illegible] per cent. of the whole?—No, I do not remember that statement.

10,265. So that the value of the produce is only about half, in proportion to the number of people employed in the two countries. Taking into account the question of rent, that test would appear to suggest, would it not, that the rate of wages in Ireland, so far as agriculture is concerned, cannot be more than half?—Yes, that would apparently be so.

10,266. Do you accept Sir Robert Giffen's view that, having regard to the extent to which the Irish revenue is raised by taxes upon consumption, the steady diminution of the Irish population, and the growth of wealth and population in Great Britain, in any proportion fixed between the two countries, allowance should be made for the constant divergence?—Yes, I think that is not unreasonable.

10,267. I notice a very strange discrepancy between the test which you proposed in your first memorandum and the test proposed in your second memorandum; in your first memorandum you accept the view that the best test of average taxable capacity is the amount of income remaining after the bare necessaries of life have been met, that is on page 439 of the minutes?—I think there I am quoting Sir Robert Giffen.

10,268. No, you first quote Sir Robert Giffen, and then you proceed yourself, to observe that the amount of a man's income is not necessarily a test of his capacity, and you proceed to say that a better test is the residue, and so on?—Yes, that is what occurred to me.

10,269. "A test better than income is the residue of "the income remaining after the bare necessaries of life "have been met." That was the principle adopted in your first memorandum, was it not?—Yes.

10,270. But now, in your second memorandum, which you call a review of the inquiry, you say that the best, and indeed the only true, standard whereby to determine

Sir R. W. [illegible] 11 Mar. 1896.

Taxable capacity, [illegible] residue [illegible] [illegible].

Sir R. Giffen's [illegible] of [illegible] [illegible] taxable capacity.

Question whether [illegible] [illegible] test of taxable capacity.

Mr. R. W. [illegible]

14 May 1895.

[illegible]

whether Ireland is overtaxed, as compared with Great Britain, is to take the respective amounts which the State extracts from the taxpayers of the two countries for Imperial as distinguished from local purposes, and to compare the amount so extracted with the respective incomes of each so far as they are ascertainable. Then a little later on you say, "If the respective conditions of "the two countries are best comparable by the "aggregate of the individual incomes of each (and this "seems to be the view of a high economic authority)" —who is he?—Sir Robert Giffen.

10,371. No?—I understood he said that was the best test.

10,372. No, on the contrary, Sir Robert Giffen holds that after finding the incomes, you must make allowance for the necessaries of life?—That he put forward afterwards, but I gather from his original evidence that he put forward as the best test of the resources of the two countries the aggregate income of individuals.

10,373. No, he says in his memorandum here that the proper mode of arriving at the surplus would be to deduct the whole of the incomes under the minimum, and then deduct the allowance from incomes above it. His view is that as a rough calculation a deduction of 12l. a head is good enough for the comparative purposes upon which we are engaged, and that the residue should be taken as the test?—I have no doubt that may be how he puts the case.

10,374. That also was your view in your first memorandum, was it not?—Rather I quoted Sir R. Giffen for that view.

10,375. How is it that in your second memorandum you shift your ground from the residue of income to income itself?—I do not know that I have shifted my ground. What I thought I had failed to do in my original memorandum was to bring out clearly the necessity, in my opinion, for taking into consideration the other side of the account.

10,376. Upon another question?—No. I ventured to put forward what occurred to me as the fairest standard, whereby it might be ascertained whether Ireland was or was not overcharged.

10,377. But there are two distinct questions which cannot be confounded with each other, the one is whether expenditure should be considered at all in estimating relative taxable capacity, and the other is whether in estimating relative taxable capacity, the income should or should not be the standard?—I hold it is impossible to take the amount derived from taxation by itself; you must take both sides of the account.

10,378. But that is not the question to which I am inviting your attention. The question I am asking you at present is not, whether expenditure should be linked with taxation in considering the taxable capacity, but whether, in considering the taxable capacity by itself, in the first instance, you should take income or residue as your test. You appear to suggest taking residue in your first memorandum, and in your second memorandum income?—I do not think so. I still adhere to the residue with this qualification—I think we ought to apply the residue to actual incomes of the two countries only.

10,379. Sir Robert Giffen says that it would be impossible to make an exact calculation of this kind, while a rough comparison seems good enough for comparative purposes—do you agree with that?—Yes; I think it very likely may be an impossibility.

10,380. Giving up the test of income, therefore, and adhering to the test of residue, you cannot still hold that even if your contention as to expenditure were admitted, the capacity of Ireland to bear expenditure should be 1 to 21, because that is the test by income. Your columns of figures depend upon the assumption that the capacity of Ireland is 1 to 21, but if residue be taken as the test, that proportion no longer applies, does it?—No, it would not.

Relation between expenditure and taxation in Ireland.

10,381. Now comes the question as to expenditure; I believe I am right in saying that the Treaty of Union, and the Acts confirming the Treaty, form the charter upon which the existing system of both taxation and expenditure in the United Kingdom rests?—I do not think that the terms of the Treaty of Union are applicable, since the consolidation of the two Exchequers, and since there has been practical assimilation of taxation throughout the two kingdoms.

10,382. I take the two Acts together—the Treaty of Union—the two Acts of Union confirming that Treaty and the Act of 1816—one is a development of the other?—It meant a very material change.

Mr. R. W. [illegible]

[illegible]

10,383. No doubt, but there are principles of the original Act of Union still in force, are there not?—I presume that the principles of the Act of Union, so far as they have not been repealed, are still in force, but they are hardly applicable to present circumstances.

10,384. Was there not a principle, for instance, that indiscriminate taxation in the case of Ireland was to be subject to such exemptions or abatements as her circumstances require—is not that in force still?—That may be so.

10,385. Has it been repealed by the Act of 1816 or any other Act?—No; it has not been repealed, but the whole position of affairs has become changed.

10,386. So much of the Act of Union as has not been repealed remains in force, does it not?—Yes; and the exemptions to which you refer have been to a certain extent carried out.

10,387. Which tends to confirm what I say, that the provision remains in force?—Yes.

10,388. Ireland, speaking in a parliamentary sense, though she came into this Union unwillingly, was a party to the Treaty and the Acts of Union?—No doubt.

10,389. And she has continuing rights under it?—I presume it may be said to be so.

10,390. And as by the Act of Union Ireland ceased to have the means of individual action by her own Legislature, would not you say there was an obligation of duty and honour upon the Imperial Parliament to respect those rights and to secure their observance?—I will not deny that.

10,391. In one respect the Act of Union and the Act of 1816 are alike, that they both deal with the common expenditure of the United Kingdom, is not that so?—Yes.

10,392. The Act of Union allowed of one separate charge and only one. The pre-Union debt of Ireland was a separate charge on Ireland?—Yes.

10,393. The pre-Union debt of Great Britain was a separate charge on Great Britain?—Yes.

10,394. Everything else was joint expenditure—common expenditure of the United Kingdom?—No doubt. I should like to point out that at that time what we call local expenditure—whether rightly or wrongly, was comparatively an insignificant affair. Practically the whole of the expenditure was what we now call Imperial expenditure, and I think that passage which you quoted several times from Lord Castlereagh clearly had reference to Imperial expenditure. The local expenditure was comparatively small in Ireland, about 900,000l.—not so much I think.

10,395. The expenditure of Ireland from the foundation of Grattan's Parliament up to the outbreak of the French war was to the extent of about one-half Civil Government charges, which you now call local expenditure. Internal government existed then as now, and though some charge it still had to be paid for?—No doubt, but what I meant was this, that the Civil Government charges in Ireland after the Union barely amounted to 1,000,000l. on an average, therefore it was a small amount compared to what we now call local expenditure.

10,396. Those primary charges of Government were then of smaller amount?—You are, I think, referring to the separate debt charges. I am referring to what we call now local charges, and to the fact that they comprised relatively a very small portion of the aggregate expenditure of the United Kingdom compared to what they do now.

10,397. The Act of 1816 went further in the direction of consolidation. It abolished the separate charges, and enacted that everything in future should be common expenditure?—Yes, that is so.

10,398. Let me call your attention to the language of the Act of Union. For 20 years after the Union Great Britain and Ireland were to pay certain contributions towards what? Towards the expenditure of the United Kingdom?—Yes.

[illegible]

10,399. And in the paragraph, Article 7, dealing with the consolidation, it says: "If it shall appear to the "Parliament of the United Kingdom that the respective "contributions of the two countries will thenceforth "consist of their contributing indiscriminately by equal "taxes imposed on the same articles in each to the "future expenditure of the United Kingdom"; and again it says when that declaration was once made, that "all future expense" thenceforth to be incurred should be defrayed indiscriminately. Do you see that?—Yes.

10,400. And further, "That from the period of such "declaration it shall be no longer necessary to regulate "the contribution of the two countries towards the "future expenditure of the United Kingdom"?—Yes.

10,401. And, moreover, that such taxes for such common expenditure should be imposed "subject only "to such particular exemptions or abatements in "Ireland, and particular exemptions or abatements in "Ireland and in that part of Great Britain called "Scotland, as circumstances may appear from time to "time to demand." That proviso is without any limit of time, is it not?—Yes.

10,402. It lasts for ever. It continues in full force now as on the day of the Union, does it not?—Yes, I presume so.

10,403. It provides that Ireland should have both exemptions and abatements, according to her circumstances; that is, according to her resources—according to her capacity relatively to Great Britain; is not that so?—The words are, "as circumstances may appear "from time to time to demand"; and "according to her condition."

10,404. Exemption means, and can only mean, that a tax imposed in Great Britain was not to be, in certain circumstances, imposed on Ireland?—Yes, that is the case, and has been the case.

10,405. And abatement means that a tax levied in Great Britain might be levied at a lower rate in Ireland, because of the circumstances of that country. Now what I submit to you is, that there are two fundamental principles of the Act of Union taken in connection with the Act of 1816 which remain in unchallenged force, and which Ireland, as a party under the Treaty, has a right to claim to be observed. The first of these is that the whole contribution of Ireland—not a part of it, but the whole of it—shall be in proportion to her resources, because she is entitled to claim exemptions or abatements as circumstances demand—is that so?—That, no doubt, may be held to be so.

10,406. The second is that the whole contribution of Ireland is a contribution to the common expenditure of the United Kingdom, and not to any part of it?—Yes.

10,407. Such being the constitutional rights of Ireland under the Treaty, do you think you are entitled to suggest that the common expenditure of the United Kingdom should be broken up into three categories, and that the resources of Ireland should be measured by her contribution to only one of those, and not to the whole expenditure?—I think so.

10,408. You think you are?—Yes.

10,409. Why?—Because I can see no other way of solving the difficulty connected with this inquiry. I can see no other way of ascertaining whether inequalities have been redressed in Ireland, or have not been redressed.

10,410. I say that the Act of Union denies you the right to make any such inquiry. In the speech of Lord Castlereagh, in which he moved the Articles, and at the close of which he confidently appealed to those gentlemen around him "who have a real stake in the interest "and happiness of this country, to pause and deliberate "before they allow arguments like those I have stated "to be rejected without discussion," a few minutes before he had said—"If the proportion of expense shall "be reliably fixed and ascertained upon just principles "for every part of the empire, it is immaterial to "Great Britain where the expenditure takes place"?—Quite so; but what does he go on to say? He is referring to military expenditure.

10,411. No, he illustrates it by military expenditure?—I think that must be read in that sense, for two reasons. One is, that he refers immediately afterwards to military expenditure, which is Imperial expenditure, and the other is that Imperial expenditure did practically represent the bulk of the expenditure of the United Kingdom.

10,412. It represented a larger proportion, but the principle is the same. The language of the Act is absolute—"the common expenditure of the United Kingdom"?—I should say distinctly he had in his mind Imperial expenditure.

Sir R. W. Hamilton, K.C.B.

14 Nov. 1895.

Relation between expenditure and taxation in Ireland.

Act of Union—resources of Ireland

10,413. I take his language. He had said a few sentences before, "It may be asked, sir, how Great "Britain can consent to an arrangement which "seems calculated to charge her with nearly half a "million in time of peace and a million in time of "war." He was arguing, whether peace or war prevailed, that Ireland would save, and why? Because, if Ireland paid her just proportion, Great Britain would save it and when the money was spent?—With all due deference to Lord Castlereagh, I consider it would be a reductio ad absurdum to apply that to present circumstances, because if that was the case you might perfectly well have applied the system of doing everything for Ireland in the way of undertaking the whole of her expenditure, rates and everything else, and have done nothing in the same way for Great Britain.

10,414. That is interesting, but it only shows the power of the human imagination. Does anyone suppose the Imperial Parliament is going to take the local rates of Ireland and Ireland only on the Imperial purse?—I was taking an extreme case. Let me take a less extreme case. Supposing the present Commission found that the contribution to Imperial expenditure now made by Ireland is excessive to the extent of half a million, how can that be remedied? I do not believe for one moment that a differential system of taxation would be listened to in Parliament.

10,415. I do not think that question is within the sphere of the Commission?—I venture to differ there, because it seems to me that is the only practical way of looking at it. How can an inequality be remedied unless the Imperial Government undertakes to do something for Ireland, the charge for which now comes out of some other pocket?

10,416. I asked you to fix your attention on the fact that the Minister in charge of the Act of Union gave an undertaking to the Irish House of Commons as one of the advantages of the Act, as one of the reasons why a poor country should be glad to come into union with a rich one, that if she was only content to pay her fair proportion to the common expenditure of the whole United Kingdom, the United Kingdom would gladly expend as much as might be required on Ireland, and not make it a reason for any larger taxation?—It is difficult to apply it to present circumstances.

10,417. But will you admit, if the Act of Union was passed upon such an understanding by the Minister in charge of the Bill, that same obligation remains?—Yes.

10,418. I have said, first that there is that fundamental principle that Ireland has only to contribute to the common expenditure according to her resources. If we find that the resources of Ireland are to a certain proportion, can you ask more under the Treaty of Union than that she should contribute in that proportion to the whole of the expenditure of the United Kingdom? Is that the provision of the Act or not?—I do not feel competent to say how a provision in an Act passed nearly 100 years ago should be interpreted under a totally different state of things.

10,419. But take the Act. "If it shall appear to "Parliament that the respective circumstances admit of "contributing by equal taxes to the future expenditure "of the United Kingdom, that all future expense "thenceforth to be incurred shall be so defrayed indiscriminately by equal taxes." Do not those terms of the Act, "all future expenses" to be "defrayed indiscriminately," directly forbid your theory and render it an infraction of the Act of Union?—A strict interpretation of the provision now might inflict an injustice on Great Britain.

10,420. Was it not one of the circumstances of advantage promised to the Irish?—That probably was so, but it seems to me conclusive that, if the Imperial Parliament undertakes expenditure in Ireland which Ireland would otherwise have to forego or have to find out of some other pocket, and if the Imperial Parliament does not do the same for Great Britain, Parliament has, I will not say adequately, but to some extent, redressed the inequality which might have arisen in consequence of due respect not being paid to the article which the honourable member quotes.

10,421. The validity of your argument depends upon many circumstances. This is a United Kingdom, is it not?—Yes.

Sir E. W. Hamilton, K.C.B.

[illegible] Nov. 1895.

Relation between expenditure and taxation in Ireland.

(Act of Union, question of [illegible] [illegible].)

10,422. Is it not the duty of the Imperial Government out of the common fund to make such expenditure in each part of the kingdom as the circumstances of that part require?—I think so.

10,423. Is not that a duty?—No doubt, and I think it is a very material consideration.

10,424. And if Ireland raises and pays her fair proportion according to resources to the common fund of the United Kingdom, what more can you ask of that country as a partner in the United Kingdom?—I am afraid I cannot admit that argument, because it is taking only one side of the account.

10,425. You are treating the United Kingdom in your suggestion as if it was a federation of States?—No.

10,426. I think so?—But surely this inquiry involves the treatment of Ireland and Great Britain as separate countries or not?

10,427. They are in a fiscal sense separate countries?—I do not hold that they are in a fiscal sense separate countries under our present financial system, but at the same time I think it is necessary to treat them as separate countries for the purposes of this inquiry.

10,428. We have no option in the matter. Ireland always has been, and is now, a separate entity in taxation?—I do not think I can admit that.

10,429. You admitted a moment ago that the proviso of the Act of Union remains in full force, that there were to be common taxes, subject to certain exemptions or abatements in Ireland, as circumstances require, from time to time?—Quite so, but I do not think that makes them separate entities. What is the meaning of indiscriminate taxation then?

10,430. It means as a general rule?—Then I say, as a general rule, they are not entities.

10,431. Subject to exemptions or abatements. How can you at any time investigate the claims of Ireland under that proviso unless by examining her special circumstances; and how can you do that unless you allow her to be a separate entity?—I admit that, I say, for the purposes of this inquiry, you are obliged to consider them as separate entities, but I do not admit that they are so in reality.

10,432. Is not Ireland a separate entity under the Act of Union?—I do not think so. I consider when Parliament provides that there is to be an indiscriminate system of taxation, Great Britain and Ireland are no longer entities, but become one United Kingdom.

10,433. But when you proceed to act under this proviso, which remains in force, and consider the circumstances of Ireland with a view to determine whether she is entitled to exemption or abatement, how can you consider her circumstances except separately?—I admit, for the purposes of this inquiry, you have to do so.

10,434. At any time?—No; I venture to think that a proviso is one thing, and an enactment another. The enactment is that there shall be indiscriminate taxation, though the proviso says that, as circumstances may appear from time to time to demand, there should be some abatements or exemptions.

10,435. From time to time, and at any time, till the end of time?—Yes.

10,436. A claim may be made on the part of Ireland, under this proviso, that her circumstances are such as to entitle her to exemption or abatement?—Yes.

10,437. And in the examination of that claim what is there, except to examine separately the condition of Ireland?—I quite admit we have to examine them separately for the purposes of this inquiry.

10,438. Then Ireland has been, since the Act of Union, is now, and will be as long as the Act of Union remains in force, a separate entity to the extent that her circumstances have to be considered when a claim or question arises under this proviso?—Yes; qualified in that way.

10,439. The Act of 1816 abolished the separate exchequers and constituted one exchequer, did it not?—That is so.

10,440. You propose now to set up those exchequers, do you not?—No; I am not proposing to set up those exchequers at all.

10,441. I admit you propose to keep them all under the same control, you do not propose to give one to Ireland?—The only possible way of approaching the consideration of this subject is, as I say, to treat Ireland and Great Britain as separate entities, and for that purpose and to that extent you have to regard the Irish Exchequer as distinct from the British Exchequer.

10,442. The only way of any form of considering legislation under the Act of Union, under which we, as the representatives of Ireland, can assert certain rights, is to take Ireland as a country as separate as if she were Canada or France, and to consider her circumstances by themselves alone, and by those circumstances alone, determine whether she is entitled to the exemption or abatement contemplated by the Act. You do in effect set up these exchequers; because, whilst the Act of Union declares that the contribution of Ireland—her whole contribution—shall be a contribution to the common expenditure of the United Kingdom—to one common fund—you propose to divide the common expenditure of the United Kingdom, as defined by the Act of Union, into three categories—charges for Irish purposes, charges for Imperial purposes, and charges for British purposes?—That is so.

10,443. Is not that striking at the whole theory and principle of the United Kingdom? Is it not treating the two countries as if they were two federated States, each raising a distinct revenue, devoting a portion of it to internal government, and handing over the remainder to a third exchequer as Imperial exchequer, for the discharge of a further category of charges classified as "Imperial"?—No doubt, but we should never have made the separation had we not been forced to do so; but to try and see what the relative financial position of these two countries was. It was begun when the inquiry was started in 1865, and it was due to that that we had to make the separation, otherwise it would not have been done at all.

10,444. Nothing has changed in principle since the Act of Union was passed; the provisions we have quoted remain in force; nothing has happened constitutionally or legally to change them?—No, the Act has never been repealed; but there have been great changes since.

10,445. If the Act is observed, and if the whole contribution of Ireland is measured by her resources, Ireland is protected by that Act, provided it be observed?—That would be so.

10,446. But what protection would remain to Ireland if your suggestion were adopted? Does it seem to you a matter of any concern whether the expenditure in Ireland by the Imperial Government is incurred with the assent or by the wish of the people of Ireland or her representatives?—I think that is a circumstance to be taken into account.

10,447. If it be found that the expenditure is wasteful, or if it is dictated by Imperial policy, and not for the good of the country alone, or if it be found that the scale of expenditure is caused by the fact of Imperial administration—all these would be reasons for diminishing the force of your argument, would they not?—That would be so certainly, and I have allowed for them to some extent.

10,448. Has this test which you suggest any real bearing upon Questions 1 and 2 referred to the Commission, as to the relative capacity of Great Britain and Ireland to bear taxation generally?—It is strictly pertinent to No. 3, and it would be difficult to separate 1 and 2 from 3.

10,449. The Legislature may consider it to be right to consider a question of this kind in relation to Questions 1 and 2, but we, as Commissioners here, being asked to determine the proportion of relative capacity, must found that proportion upon resources, without reference to expenditure?—That may be so; I do not express an opinion one way or the other, that is for the Commission.

10,450. I mean, if we found the proportion of resources upon taxation to be 1 to 22, or upon income to be 1 to 19, or 1 to 40, could we say in reply to the warrant that the proportion was something less than what we knew it to be, because there was certain expenditure in Ireland?—I confess, I think, that is the right thing to do.

10,451. To say the proportion was something else?—Yes.

10,452. The capacity?—The capacity must be qualified by the manner in which the money raised by taxation is spent.

10,453. That does not alter the capacity?—I think it does—that is to say, it alters the charge.

Sir R. W. Hamilton, K.C.B.

[illegible]

Relation between expenditure and taxation in Ireland.

(Act of Union purposes of Parliament.)

10,170. Unquestionably, under the Act of Union, Ireland contributes according to her resources, subject to such exemptions or abatements as circumstances may require, to the common expenditure of the United Kingdom?—Yes.

10,171. Your suggestion is that her revenue should be broken up into two parts; that as to the greater part of it the expenditure in Ireland should not be considered at all, but treated as if she had never paid it, and that the measure of her contribution should be the smaller sum, the balance contributed towards what are called Imperial purposes. Is that a reasonable policy, or one that can attach itself to the idea of a United Kingdom?—I say it is, and I do not see anything unreasonable in it.

10,172. You raise a revenue of nearly 7,000,000l. in Ireland. Ireland is entitled to have the whole of that revenue measured by her resources, and contributes the whole to a common fund. You say no?—No, I do not say "no."

10,173. You say "no" in this sense. You say "No, "we will not measure it by the 7,000,000l. contributed "to a common fund, we will ignore the 4,000,000l. "expended in Ireland and measure your resources by "a sum of 2,000,000l., the balance of your revenue, "which you contribute to purposes which we, the "Treasury, are pleased to call Imperial"?—Yes; that is my view.

10,174. I will refer you to the language of the Act. The English language, copious as it is, can afford no terms more exact and precise than those of the Act of Union, "all future expenses" and "the common expenditure of the United Kingdom." I stand on that Act and claim under that Act protection for Ireland and I ask you whether your suggestion is not directly contrary to it?—No. I do not think it is directly contrary to it, because the circumstances have so completely changed.

10,175. They have not changed in any essential respect or in any matter of principle?—I venture to think they have so completely changed.

10,176. The kingdom is still a United Kingdom, is it not?—Yes, but see what the expenditure was in Ireland a hundred years ago, and what it is now. There was no education, no police; the Civil Government charges were very small, and all that, as I understand you, is not to be taken into account at all.

10,177. I say that expenditure has been made by the Imperial Government in discharge of its duty, which is without regard to the revenue accruing from any part of the kingdom to spend in any part of the kingdom what that part requires. That was the view urged by Lord Castlereagh in asking the Irish Parliament to accept the Act of Union?—That, of course, is one view to take. I venture to take a different one; it is not for me to determine whether your view or mine is the correct view.

10,178. The law of the realm is, that Ireland should contribute according to her resources to the common expenditure. The common expenditure in the Act of Union is the whole of the expenditure of the United Kingdom?—Yes; but then there was practically no local expenditure.

10,179. There was a good deal indeed?—In Great Britain as well as in Ireland it was very small compared to what it is now.

10,180. But if the growth of expenditure, in your opinion, establishes any new relation, your theory can only be enforced by a repeal of those provisions of the Act of Union?—That may be so. I have only considered what appears to me to be the best test whereby you can measure whether Ireland is or is not being over-charged by the Imperial Parliament.

10,181. I say that it is no measure at all, because with regard to the greater portion of the revenue you decline to apply any test?—There we must agree to differ, I am afraid.

10,182. You have to admit that your theory only regards 2,000,000l. of revenue, have you not?—That seems to me to be fair, in considering whether Ireland is overcharged.

10,183. But surely the whole of Ireland's taxable surplus might disappear under your system. She has 10,000,000l. a year taxable surplus, we will say, the Imperial Parliament might take away the whole of it and expend it in Ireland for purposes useless, or purposes worse than useless?—That might be so.

Sir E. W. Hamilton, K.C.B.

10,484. And she would have no protection whatever if your principle were accepted?—She has the protection of the Imperial Parliament.

10,485. But she has no security?—No, nor has Scotland, nor has England.

10,486. We are taking Great Britain and Ireland as units?—Nor has Great Britain then.

10,487. Ireland has security in this Act?—She has.

10,488. Do you think we ought to abandon it?—I do not suggest the abandonment of it.

10,489. Perhaps we had better look for a moment or two at the expenditure; the phrase you have used, "relief by expenditure," is a somewhat questionable phrase?—I am afraid it is, but I really did not know what else to use.

10,490. It is relieving people with their own money, is it not?—No doubt.

10,491. It appears to admit, however, that the taxation is excessive?—Yes. I do not deny that.

10,492. But I hardly follow you when you say as a reason for examining the expenditure, that the expenditure in Ireland may be held to be "value received." Is it not the view that there is value received for all taxation?—Yes, I presume that may be said to be so, but not so directly as in the case of expenditure incurred upon the particular locality.

10,493. Would not that depend somewhat on whether the expenditure was incurred with the approval of the country?—Yes, I admit that; but I am not aware, with the exception of one item, which I admit is a very material item, that any expenditure in Ireland is objected to.

10,494. At any rate you are aware that Ireland has no means of making the test of her approval effectual with regard to any expenditure?—I do not think she is less able to do so than any other parts of the United Kingdom.

10,495. The other parts—there are only two parts under consideration—has an ascendancy of the House of Commons, and Ireland has one-seventh. In the expenditure part classification is a Treasury classification simply?—Yes. Mr. Goschen was the original authority for it, and it has been carefully considered since. I do not mean to say that exception may not be taken to the classification in certain respects; the line between Imperial and local expenditure is difficult to draw.

Local taxation grants.

10,496. I shall not dwell upon it very long, because my view is, that under the Act of Union we are entitled to regard the whole expenditure as common expenditure of the United Kingdom. You have put down "Irish charges" at 5,600,000l. The miscellaneous local charges paid out of local taxation represent a portion of the Imperial Revenue redistributed in about the proportion in which it has been raised?—So far as Ireland is concerned, it has been redistributed rather more favourably than a strict regard to proportion would justify.

10,497. Would not that be an expenditure of a strictly Imperial character?—It is classified as local expenditure.

10,498. But it is a uniform Imperial grant all over the kingdom, is it not?—It was intended to relieve the charges on rates in Ireland.

10,499. But being returned to Ireland in about the same proportion as she yielded it, there is no particular difference, is there?—No, it is taking it from one pocket and putting it in another.

10,500. I have often heard, so often that I cannot forget it, that Ireland in the matter of local taxation revenue has been treated justly and generously and sympathetically, and so forth. No doubt, according to the Treasury calculation, she contributes a quarter of a million and gets 320,000l., so that there would appear to be an advantage of 70,000l.?—I think those are the figures.

10,501. But is it not the fact that whilst the Exchequer grants were given to Great Britain, they were not given to Ireland?—No, but what happened in Great Britain was this—that a certain amount of expenditure was withdrawn from the Votes, and in place of it the licenses were handed over to local authorities. Great Britain by that change got an advantage, that is to say that the proceeds from the licenses were somewhat larger than the grants formerly on the Votes of Parliament.

10,502. Very much larger?—Considerably larger; and as a similar process could not take place in Ireland, a sum of 40,000l. was handed over, which was calculated to be the amount by which Great Britain has gained by the change.

10,503. The want of local government in Ireland, of course, is one of the disadvantages of the Imperial system, but the existence of that disadvantage is no reason why Ireland should not have received a corresponding benefit?—The sum of 40,000l. was supposed to, and I believe it did, represent the proportion to which Ireland would have been entitled had she received the same benefit as Scotland and England did.

10,504. I have often asked in the House for the foundation of that assumption, and I have never got it?—I think I can show you how the calculation was arrived at.

10,505. The licenses in Ireland are 200,000l. a year?—Yes.

10,506. The benefit she receives is only 40,000l.?—But there was nothing taken off the votes in Ireland, while large grants in aid were taken off the votes in Great Britain.

10,507. That introduces another element; it does not treat the local taxation grants alone?—No, I do not think so; for, while in Great Britain large votes were withdrawn from Parliament and revenue was handed over to local authorities instead, in Ireland, though there was a certain amount of revenue handed over to local authorities there in the shape of 40,000l., there was no withdrawal of grants.

10,508. You come back again to the old argument, you see, that Ireland receives more than her share of Imperial expenditure; but you are not able to show, are you, that the local taxation grants are administered in a generous manner to Ireland?—I certainly think that Ireland was treated generously with regard to local taxation arrangements.

10,509. She is said to have got 40,000l. a year as an Exchequer contribution, has she not?—Yes.

10,510. But you have locked it up as a guarantee?—For the moment, but it will come out again soon.

10,511. If you call five years a moment, yes. Really upon this local taxation question I may be pardoned for saying I see no generosity. Now you call the collection of taxes a local charge, do you not?—Yes. I think it is a moot question whether it ought to be an Imperial charge or a local charge.

10,512. Nearly a hundred years ago, when the collection of taxes was a much higher charge in Ireland than Great Britain relatively, it was admitted to be an Imperial charge and was so treated?—And it was so treated if I remember rightly in the Home Rule Bill of 1893.

10,513. Take the Post Office; is that an Imperial service?—I think, as I have already said, that it is a moot point whether that ought to be an Imperial charge. I should be quite prepared to regard the whole as an Imperial charge.

10,514. (*Lord Farrer.*) These charges, I think, are not high in Ireland, are they, as compared with the United Kingdom?—I do not think they are higher.

10,515. With regard to the Post Office?—The Post Office is, I think, rather high, but not the Customs and Inland Revenue.

10,516. (*Mr. Sexton.*) It is in the same relation as the revenue, 1 to 11?—Yes.

10,517. You charge Ireland for the Lord Lieutenant, do you not?—Yes. It was not so charged in the Home Rule Bill.

Lord Lieutenant.

10,518. As well as for a contribution to the Crown. Is any other part of the British Empire charged both for the representative of the Crown and for the Crown itself?—No, I think that is one of (what I may call) the moot items; and it is only a small item in five and a half millions; indeed it was treated as an Imperial charge in the Home Rule Bill.

10,519. Then take 81,000l. for the Queen's Colleges, and 1,038,000l. for primary education?—I am afraid I am not well acquainted with that class of expenditure.

10,520. Is it not the fact that that expenditure has been incurred in Ireland for purposes directly of Imperial policy—that those two systems were strongly disapproved of by the great bulk of the people of the country?—That may be so, and I dare say it is so; but

[illegible margin note]

I am not sufficiently acquainted with the subject of Irish education to be able to express an opinion which would be worth anything.

10,521. If the Queen's Colleges are not acceptable to the people of Ireland, as being secular in their constitution, and if the primary system is not acceptable, because of hindrance to religious teaching, because of excluding the language, literature, and history of the country, and because of the exclusion of such practical instruction as would be most useful in the future lives of the children, do not such facts indicate that expenditure on education has been incurred to satisfy Imperial ideas without regard to Irish opinion?—Possibly that may be so, but I have never heard any suggestion made that the charge for primary education in Ireland, despite of certain defects there may be in the system, should be reduced.

10,522. But that the Imperial system is imposed upon the people of Ireland without regard to their opinion?—I am, as I have already said, imperfectly acquainted with the educational systems in Ireland, as also with the views entertained by Irishmen on the question.

10,523. If that were so, would it not be an expenditure of an Imperial character?—I think that is open to argument.

10,524. I suggest to you that the two main characteristics of the expenditure in Ireland, incurred by the Imperial Government to satisfy its own ideas are these: firstly, that it is far more expensive than it need be because of the tendency in the scale of expenses in the local government, when Imperially administered, to approximate to the scale of Imperial expenses?—That may well be so.

10,525. That is to say, you pay in Ireland as much as if you were in Great Britain?—I think that is quite true.

10,526. And, secondly, that the administration is rendered far more costly by reason of being an administration from the outside, which, for that reason, is less acceptable, than it would be if it were domestic?—I think there is a great deal in that, too.

10,527. And, so far as these characteristics operate to raise the cost, they would appear to entail expenditure of an Imperial character, as distinguished from what they would be if the Government of Ireland were what the Government of England is, that is to say, dependent on domestic opinion?—To some extent there may, I admit, be an Imperial character about these expenses.

[illegible margin note]

10,528. Also with regard to the Chief Secretary and the police, the Chief Secretary is an Imperial officer whose function it is to effectuate Imperial control over local law in Ireland; that is hardly a local charge, is it; that is a charge of a strictly Imperial character, is it not?—So far as the expenses are incurred in this country, I think that is so; but I do not think one could say so, so far as the administrative expenses in Ireland are concerned.

10,529. The police you have admitted, have you not?—Yes.

10,530. And that you can only charge as much as would be incurred if the establishments were on the same relative scale as in Great Britain?—Yes.

10,531. It would seem, then, that a very great proportion of the Irish expenditure cannot be considered local?—I have excepted the very important item of the police; the other charges, to which a partially Imperial character may attach, would not amount, I think, to any very appreciable sum, even if one made up the account on the most liberal scale, and gave Ireland the benefit of all the doubts.

[illegible margin note]

10,532. I think under one or other of the two heads which you have admitted to be material almost every item of Irish expenditure would come in for review and considerable reduction. Take, for instance, the cost of the Local Government Board in Ireland, which is [illegible], and in Great Britain [illegible], the population being 1 to 8, the cost is as 1 to 5; Board of Public Works in Ireland, [illegible], in England [illegible], population 1 to 6, cost 2 to 3; law charges in Ireland, [illegible], in England, [illegible], more than half, the population being 1 to 6; the Supreme Court in Ireland, [illegible], in England, [illegible], one-third, the population being 1 to 6; prisons in Ireland, 110,000 l., England, [illegible], 1 to 5, the population being 1 to 6, does it not appear quite plain that the whole scale of expenditure in Ireland is vastly increased by the tendency of Imperial administration to be expensive?—I think there is a great deal in that, as I have already said.

10,533. Further, the classification of these items seems to me to rest upon the obvious fallacy that there is any parity of benefit between Ireland and Great Britain in regard to what you call Imperial expenditure?—Are you now speaking of the local charges?

10,534. No, Imperial. Is there any parity of benefit, in your opinion, between Ireland and Great Britain in regard to what you call Imperial expenses?—I will not say parity of benefit—and no one to contend a proportionate benefit. I do not like to determine the proportions.

[illegible margin note]

10,535. In proportion to their resources?—Well, perhaps in proportion to their resources.

10,536. What benefit has Ireland ever derived from the accumulation of the National Debt?—Ireland incurred an enormous debt on her own account, and that debt now forms part of the Imperial Debt.

10,537. For what reason did she incur it. It was charged to her during the sixteen years following the Union?—Yes.

10,538. For what reason?—Under the Treaty of Union.

10,539. But for what purpose was it expended?—The larger proportion of it going to the war between the United Kingdom and France, no doubt.

10,540. Was that an Irish war?—No, not an Irish war; but Ireland was very deeply concerned in it.

10,541. It was a British war with France, was it not?—No doubt, but I should say that Ireland's safety was quite as much at stake as that of Great Britain.

10,542. Her safety?—Yes.

10,543. Was it of more interest to Great Britain to hold Ireland as a territory of Great Britain than of Ireland to be held as a territory of Great Britain?—I should have thought it was quite as much to the interest of Ireland to have been defended at that time as it was to the interest of Great Britain. Ireland was the spot upon which France had fixed her eye for invasion.

10,544. But judging it by results, Ireland is now taxed to double the proportion of her income, and several times the proportion of her revenue. She has to take all her laws from an assembly where her members are one-seventh of the whole. If a desirable measure passes there unanimously, there is another assembly to reject it; she has no British capital, and her resources have gone on diminishing—all which appears to be the result of the Union. Now is it so self-evident that if Ireland had become independent, or had become connected with another power (we are engaged here in looking at practical interests), she would have been any worse off than she is at the present time. I mean where does the practical benefit appear?—I venture to think that so hypothetical a point is rather going beyond the scope of this inquiry. I do not think I should be asked to to give any direct answer to that question.

10,545. The debt was incurred, so far as the charge against Ireland was concerned for the purpose of defending Ireland, first as a territory attached to the Crown of Great Britain, afterwards as a part of the United Kingdom, against France?—Yes.

10,546. Was not that at least as much a British as an Irish object?—Certainly, I admit it was.

10,547. Suppose France had invaded Ireland in force, would Ireland have been expected to undertake the charge of resistance?—Not wholly so. Great Britain would undoubtedly, I presume, have come to her rescue.

10,548. Ireland in such a case, could only have contributed in a very moderate proportion?—These, I venture to think, are rather hypothetical questions.

10,549. To test the principle, if Ireland had been taken by France because her poverty rendered her unable to make resistance, would not Great Britain have spent her last shilling in winning Ireland back?—I presume so; certainly.

10,550. It appears then that the dominant interest was that of Great Britain?—Yes, I admit that.

10,551. It does not appear then that a debt incurred in defending Ireland, as an exposed part of the British territory could be in any measure reckoned as an Irish matter merely?—No.

10,552. Then I should think that as the only benefit Ireland has derived from a National Debt is the benefit of being held as a territory of Great Britain, with the results which we have stated, the advantages are of any

Sir E. W. Hamilton, K.C.B.

14 Nov. 1895.

Imperial expenditure, how much benefit to Ireland.

into open to argument?—Yes; but the amount which Ireland does contribute towards the debt is not a very large one now.

10,553. You know my position is that you cannot separate it in that way?—Yes, I am aware of that.

10,554. I pass now from the debt. You have said if Ireland ceased to exist to-morrow you would not spend a shilling less upon the army or upon the navy; is not that so?—I think that is very possible, but of course that is very hypothetical again. I doubt if we should reduce our army or navy.

10,555. These charges, then, are incurred without reference to Ireland, and would not diminish if Ireland ceased to exist, or to be a member of the kingdom?—Possibly so.

10,556. You class certain charges as Irish, because they would not be incurred if Ireland were not in question?—Yes.

10,557. In all these questions of revenue and expenditure the term "Imperial" is composed of two factors only, British and Irish, because the whole revenue is raised in those two countries?—No doubt.

10,558. If you take away the Irish, only British remains. Your position is, that certain charges are Irish, because they would not be incurred if Ireland were not in question; certain other charges would be incurred if it were not in question. What I submit to you is, all those other charges which you classify as Imperial, are substantially and in reality British?—They may be more British than Irish, but surely Ireland has a common interest in them.

10,559. It is very difficult to measure, is it not?—That may be so.

10,560. We know that Great Britain is a power which has territory in every part of the globe, capital invested abroad, great industrial enterprises everywhere, and that the freedom of the seas is essential to her existence?—No doubt.

10,561. She requires every man of her army and navy for the protection of British interests in every part of the globe?—Yes.

10,562. Ireland, on the other hand, is a country with purely domestic interests?—But if Ireland were an independent country, I take it she would certainly have to keep up as large an army or navy as, say, a country like Norway or Sweden.

10,563. I think Norway and Sweden are tolerably fair parallels, although Norway has one of the largest mercantile marines in Europe, and therefore has need for a navy which Ireland would not have?—If independence were to bring prosperity to Ireland, I should have thought that improved mercantile marine business might be one of the ways in which Ireland's prosperity would show itself.

10,564. That is speculation, is it not?—The whole of this is speculation.

10,565. I am taking the present situation. Are you aware that the army and navy of Sweden taken together cost about the same amount as the Irish police?—I am afraid I have not the details of Swedish expenditure, but I have the total, and I see it is about 6,000,000*l*. in all.

10,566. What is?—The expenditure of Sweden.

10,567. The whole expenditure?—Yes.

10,568. The army and navy cost about a million and a half?—That may be so.

10,569. A million and a half is enough for the army and navy in Sweden, with a mercantile marine only second to that of Great Britain; is not that so?—I daresay it is.

10,570. Do you not think that much less expenditure might suffice for Ireland?—Yes, but I reckon that Ireland barely pays as much as a million and a half now.

10,571. But if she were independent, a very moderate sum would be sufficient?—Very possibly.

10,572. Then Norway, a country of large territory and with powerful neighbours and a very extensive marine, expends on her army and navy together two-thirds of a million?—Yes.

10,573. So that you see the two examples set by yourself are examples in favour of the view that the expenditure of Ireland upon these charges, now called Imperial, might be very moderate indeed?—I think they would be very small, no doubt, but I do not know that they would be smaller than what she contributes now. I should doubt it.

10,574. I have not been able to discover in what respect Ireland as an agricultural and pastoral community, having no external relations, raising her crops and cattle, selling them and importing cheap food to be consumed, can be held to be concerned in the great benefit which a world-embracing community like Great Britain derives from a powerful army and navy?—No doubt. But my point is she contributes a very small proportion of the vast expenditure on the army and navy. I am not saying whether it is the right proportion or not.

10,575. According to your own test she contributes to the full extent of her resources, does she not?—That may be so; but it is a very small amount, and I cannot conceive of her being able to get on with less if she were an independent State.

10,576. But is it fair, as between a country whose income is not affected by the existence and operation of an army and navy and a country whose income is very largely affected by it, that they should contribute to the cost of these great institutions in proportion to their resources, the one being so slightly affected and the other so much?—I think that is a plea which may fairly be urged.

10,577. Upon the whole, I should be disposed to say with regard to these returns that under the Act of Union you cannot make such a classification at all, and that, if you do make a classification, the Irish expenditure, after deducting the collection of taxes and the Post Office, and making due allowance for the thousand men owing to Imperial administration, would fall to about half the present charge; and instead of classifying the other expenditure as Imperial and British, it is in substance British as a whole. Do you understand that view?—Yes.

10,578. You have divided the time which has elapsed since the Union into five periods, have you not, and you have considered each separately?—Yes.

Grattan's Parliament.

10,579. You say with regard to the period of the Grattan Parliament that nothing unfair is seriously alleged against the Imperial Government?—Yes.

10,580. And you have said already that there was an understanding that Ireland should pay all the expenditure incurred in Ireland?—I understand that that was the arrangement in force during Grattan's Parliament.

10,581. What is the evidence of that understanding?—Merely the facts, I think.

10,582. When you say that there was an understanding, of course one takes you to mean that there was something beyond and behind the fact of payment?—No; nothing beyond the fact that one knows that at different times an endeavour was made to get some more specific contribution towards Imperial expenditure from Ireland. During the period of Grattan's Parliament there were one or two efforts made to get a more specific contribution towards Imperial expenditure; and I should infer from that, that as regards expenditure incurred in Ireland, it was admitted to be chargeable upon Ireland.

10,583. In the Constitution of 1782 as established in Ireland there was no attempt to alter the arrangement as to contribution founded on the Irish Act of 1769?—No.

10,584. The system then was, that Ireland should contribute 3,000 men to the foreign service of Great Britain?—Yes.

10,585. About 100,000*l*. a year?—Yes.

10,586. That was a moderate sum compared with the actual expenditure in subsequent years?—No doubt it was.

10,587. And the Constitution of 1782, by not taking note of the matter appeared to recognise that sum as sufficient?—I imagine so.

10,588. There was also a moderate grant for the navy before the close of the American war, I think about 20,000*l*.?—Yes, I think so.

10,589. Then Mr. Pitt, in connection with commercial propositions, did suggest a contribution for military purposes?—That is so.

10,590. And it was ultimately agreed between the Irish Parliament and Mr. Pitt, that whenever the hereditary revenue of the Crown, that is, the customs, the hearth tax, and the inland excise, exceeded 656,000*l*. a year, and when there was no deficit on the year, that the surplus should go to the military uses of Great Britain?—Yes.

10,591. (*Sir David Barbour.*) Was that actually carried out or merely proposed?—It was agreed to by Ireland, but the proposals as a whole met with so much opposition in Great Britain, and were so altered by the British Parliament, that the arrangement fell through.

10,592. The commercial propositions were not rejected, were they?—It was those propositions which raised so much opposition in Great Britain.

10,593. (*Chairman.*) The commercial propositions broke down the whole thing, did they not?—No doubt.

10,594. (*Mr. Sexton.*) So far as we can learn, everybody agreed that the surplus of the hereditary revenue, over 650,000*l*., providing there was no deficit on the year, would be a reasonable contribution?—Yes.

10,595. That was very moderate, too, was it not, as compared with subsequent burdens?—No doubt.

10,596. I venture to submit to you that the Act of 1769, providing 3,000 men, and the Act of 1793, 5,000 men, and the propositions made by Pitt, and accepted by Grattan, all show the view which then prevailed, and what we might call the understanding as to what Ireland might fairly bear?—Yes, I think that may be said to be the case.

10,597. You, however, remark, in your memorandum, that the expenditure put upon Ireland was expenditure on account of the war. It was expenditure, you say, incurred in defence of Ireland herself, and the cost of suppressing the rebellion was a charge which naturally and properly fell upon her. By whom was all the cost incurred?—So far as the war was concerned, the expenditure may be said to have been incurred by Great Britain, so far as the rebellion was concerned, I suppose it was incurred by Ireland herself.

10,598. You are aware of the peculiar defect in the Constitution of 1782 that the Irish Ministers were not responsible to the Irish House?—I am.

10,599. Lord Castlereagh, and others, though called Irish Ministers, were really agents of the British Government, appointed by them and acting in concert with them, they were not responsible to the Irish House of Commons?—No doubt.

10,600. They held their offices without regard to adverse votes, and lived [illegible] through general elections?—Yes.

10,601. Holding their offices all the time?—Yes.

10,602. Therefore all this expenditure that was incurred in Ireland in the pre-Union period was expenditure dictated by the British Government who had control of the army and sent the troops to Ireland, and the accounts were made up by the Irish Ministers, who were not responsible to the Irish House. The expenditure, as you have said, was for the defence of Ireland as territory of the British Crown, as being an exposed and vulnerable part of such territory, and therefore requiring special defence?—Yes.

10,603. Do you think it was equitable to charge the whole of that expenditure, simply because it was incurred in Ireland, upon the Irish purse?—I think it was incurred in Ireland, in order to defend Ireland. Ireland might have been a separated country if it had not been for that large expenditure incurred in Ireland to protect her. It is very difficult at this distance of time to come to any definite conclusion, but I am not aware that there was any strong feeling expressed in or outside the House of Commons in Ireland that this was an undue expenditure to have charged upon her; at least, I have never come across any remonstrances on the part of the Irish Government.

10,604. Were there not continual remonstrances against the increase of taxation and debt?—That may be so.

10,605. And the Viceroy and Ministers acknowledged that effective answers were made?—Yes.

10,606. Was not the heavy expenditure in Ireland incurred, not merely to protect Ireland, but because it would have been extremely inconvenient and hazardous for Great Britain herself to have allowed France to have a footing in Ireland?—Probably so.

10,607. Then, was it equitable to charge the whole of the expenditure upon guarding that exposed and vulnerable territory, upon the Irish purse?—But, it must be remembered that Ireland contributed practically nothing at that time to the expenditure incurred outside her own shores. That was a material consideration.

Supposing that she had been contributing to the common purse at that time, and had been made to bear this vast expenditure in defence of herself, I should have said that it was unfair; but I do not know that it was unfair, seeing that she was exempted from making anything but a nominal contribution to the warlike expenditure outside her own shores.

10,608. Is there anything in principle to show, that, a special expenditure for the interest of Great Britain was incurred in Ireland, because of its being exposed territory, where therefore the heavy part of the expenditure was necessary, Ireland should pay the whole of it?—Great Britain, no doubt, had a very great interest in protecting Ireland, but, when I made the remark alluded to, I think I made it from an impression that Ireland did accept the expenditure. I do not know that she greatly remonstrated; on the contrary, she was most generous I should have said in the money contribution she made at that time. Some passages that I quoted in my original memorandum testified that she showed a very liberal spirit as [illegible] in the aid of the British Government.

10,609. The Irish Parliament was in the difficult position that the British Government dictated the expenditure of the Irish Ministers, who were not responsible to the Irish Parliament, but who made up the bills and called for payment. What would have been the position in Ireland, especially when martial law prevailed, if they had refused supplies to the army?—I admit the position would have been a very difficult one.

10,610. The fact that they were paid proves nothing?—That may be so.

10,611. As to the Rebellion, Sir David Barbour asked some questions suggesting that your estimate is not to be relied upon?—Please understand that it was only intended to represent the best I could make. I had so little to go upon as regards separating the expenditure.

10,612. I think you devised an excellent system?—I took the best I could.

10,613. First, you took the average ordinary annual military expenditure up to the year in which the French War broke out?—Yes.

10,614. Then you found how much was expended in addition after the outbreak of the war, and attributed that to the war?—Yes.

10,615. And then you attributed the further increase from 1796 to the rebellion?—Yes; it may have been a wrong principle, but it was the best I could adopt.

10,616. The whole cost of suppressing the Rebellion was also cast upon Ireland?—Yes.

10,617. Have you, in your study of the period, met with any evidence that the Rebellion was fomented by intrigue, or provoked by cruelties of the troops inflicted upon the people?—I have seen it stated so in history.

10,618. If that were so—if the Rebellion, from political reasons, was fomented to promote the scheme of Union, would it not have been a great additional injustice to charge the cost of suppressing it upon the people of Ireland?—Yes, if the assumption were correct.

10,619. After the Rebellion was suppressed (and that only took a few months), in 1798, have you observed that not only was the military force in the country maintained, but it was increased in the two years that elapsed between the closing of the Rebellion and the passing of the Act?—Yes, I am aware of that.

10,620. So that a larger force was kept for the purpose of suppressing manifestations of opinion against the Bill than was found necessary for suppressing the Rebellion?—I have always regarded that this increased military expenditure was incurred in order to avert a renewed outbreak of the Rebellion; and that is what I had in my mind.

10,621. Has your reading suggested to you that there was any indication of a possible renewal of the Rebellion?—I should have thought that the country was so disturbed that a recrudescence of an outbreak was more than possible, indeed very probable.

10,622. But are you aware whether, during the two years when the project of the Union was on foot, the principal use of the soldiery was to prevent meetings against the Bill?—I am aware that there was a great deal done in that way.

10,623. For instance, when the high sheriffs convened public meetings, they were dispersed by force?—I believe so.

10,624. It was a strong measure, was it not, to charge the whole cost of that establishment upon a country which had to submit unwillingly?—I think it was no [illegible] for the last year.

10,625. During the passage of the Bill, that is to say?—Yes.

10,626. As subject as to charge the 1,[illegible],000l. that was paid for the 85 votes that carried the Bill—paid to the patrons of borough seats contingent upon the passing of the Bill?—I am afraid that is a kind of expenditure that cannot be defended.

10,627. Taking the expenditure as a whole, what was the effect of it to Ireland; it raised the taxation from less than 1,000,000l. to 2,500,000l.; it raised the expenditure from 1,000,000l. to about 6,000,000l. or 7,000,000l., and it saddled Ireland, in seven years, with a debt of 26,000,000l. sterling; charging upon her the whole cost of the defence against France; charging upon her the whole cost of suppressing this fomented Rebellion; and charging upon her the whole cost of maintaining an army of occupation to suppress opinion during two years up to the passing of the Bill, a debt of 26,000,000l., in addition to an extraordinary increase of taxation, from 1,000,000l. to 2,500,000l. in the year. Was not that a severe experience to pass through, and one that entitles people to hold it in memory, and to have a strong opinion of it?—I can quite believe that.

10,628. Now this expenditure, so created, was useful, was it not, in promoting the project of Union?—That would be so to a certain extent, no doubt.

10,629. It created those apprehensions of bankruptcy and ruin to which Lord Clare, sincerely or not, gave expression in his speech. The Union being carried, or being secured, the next object was, I believe, to secure indiscriminate taxation?—I think that appears to have been the case.

10,630. And with a view to secure indiscriminate taxation, as it could not be granted at the moment owing to the debts, the next object was to establish such proportions as would be likely to facilitate indiscriminate taxation?—I do not think that you can find any real trace of that, I confess. I think that there was a wish among the framers of the Union that it should be the fairest arrangement that could be made. Whether they were mistaken or not is another thing, but I do not think that in the arrangement that they made at the time of the Union there is any evidence to show that they tried to lead up to an indiscriminate system of taxation, by pressing down Ireland with an extra load of weight, and thus to bring the respective debts into the proportion of 15 to 2.

10,631. Did they ever submit their data or proportions to any Committee of either House in Ireland or in England?—There were Executive Committees.

10,632. Yes, after the Union, but before the passing of the Act did they ever submit the proportions or data themselves to any Committee of either Parliament or to any Commission?—I think not, and I think exception was taken to that at the time.

10,633. Did they take any evidence of expert witnesses?—I have no proof of it.

10,634. They had no general election when the Bill was defeated?—No.

10,635. They proceeded, without consulting the electors, in the next year?—That was so.

10,636. Now we often hear of Lord Castlereagh's two tests of commerce and consumption—external trade and consumption of articles, but you have examined the speeches, and you may agree with me, that the real basis was what was called the ascertained proportion, what Mr. Pitt called the ascertained proportion, namely, that Ireland would be asked to contribute in the same proportion in which she had contributed?—I do not know quite what you mean by the ascertained proportion.

10,637. Mr. Pitt said that Ireland would be asked to contribute no more than the ascertained proportion; and Lord Castlereagh said the same—that the intention was to ask for no more than the ascertained proportion?—Do you mean the ascertained proportion of revenue?

10,638. Future revenue, of course?—I was thinking of expenditure.

10,639. I am on revenue. Will you turn to Lord Castlereagh's speech, which you will find at page [illegible], Volume I of the evidence. He professed there to found the proportion of 2 to 15 upon the proportions which had existed between the expenditure of Great Britain and Ireland; and referring to the peace establishment of Great Britain, in the year preceding the war, he said that it amounted to [illegible],000,000l., and that of Ireland to a million?—Yes, that is so.

10,640. But, in fixing that proportion, he excluded the debt charge from the British expenditure, and he also excluded the debt charge in taking the seven years preceding the Union, and also in taking the year 1799 alone. Did he not on all occasions exclude the debt charge from the British side of the account?—And from the Irish side of the account.

10,641. Well, I think not?—I am afraid I have not examined those particular figures for some time, and I have forgotten how they work out.

10,642. Was it just to exclude the debt charge from the British side?—I think he was justified in doing so if he excluded it from the Irish side as well.

10,643. Remember that Ireland, under the Union, became liable, not only in respect of the ordinary expenditure of the United Kingdom, but also in the proportion of 2 to 15 of all the debt that might be incurred after the Union?—Yes.

10,644. How, then, could her liability be properly estimated if you excluded the debt charge from previous expenditure? The different liability of Great Britain and Ireland to future debt was a necessary element to be considered in fixing the proportion of future expenditure, was it not?—Yes.

10,645. Was not that a fatal defect in his calculations?—I am afraid I have not worked out the particular calculations referred to.

10,646. I have worked it out, and I find that it did not include the debt charges, and I submit to you that any proportion founded upon the exclusion of the debt charges would not be a fair proportion for the future, as Ireland became liable for the full proportion of all future debt?—I think there is force in that.

10,647. Again, Lord Castlereagh, whilst he excluded the debt charge upon the British side, included upon the Irish side the whole cost of the Rebellion and the whole cost of the great military establishment in the two years after the Rebellion until the passing of the Act of Union. Was it just, do you think, in forming a basis for permanent charges to include transitory charges—charges for the Rebellion, which had been suppressed, and for the military establishment in connection with an Act which had been passed—to include those as forming a basis of the proportion for permanent expenditure in the future?—Very likely not; but his real basis was upon what I think the honourable member himself said, namely, upon the joint basis of commerce and consumption. What Lord Castlereagh said here in the way of expenditure was, I understand, intended to be a sort of confirmatory test to the [illegible] of the arrangement.

10,648. I know that the position of Pitt and Lord Castlereagh was this, that Ireland should be asked to pay no more than her ascertained proportion?—Yes.

10,649. And the ascertained proportion was calculated in the way I have stated, by leaving out the debt charge on the British side and by including heavy temporary charges upon the Irish side, and therefore it was doubly fallacious, and in both respects unjust to Ireland. I venture to suggest that these tests, foreign trade and consumption of certain articles (tests certified at the time and unverifiable since), are not the real basis, but merely ornaments to the main structure of the argument?—That may be so, but I certainly think that they must be considered to have formed the main basis of the respective proportions.

10,650. And it would appear, from the considerations that I have laid before you, that the proportions, so far as they were founded upon expenditure, were not just to Ireland?—That may be so.

10,651. (*Sir David Barbour.*) Was it not the case that Lord Castlereagh included upon the British side what you call the transitory expenditure on account of the great war with France?—I have not got the figures before me.

10,652. (*Mr. Sexton.*) What I submit is that inasmuch as Ireland under the Union became liable for all future debt, without exception, in the proportion of 2 to 15,

Sir E. W. Hamilton, K.C.B.

12 Nov. 1894.

the proportion in which the debts had been incurred respectively in Great Britain and Ireland before the Union should have been considered in measuring the future liability of Ireland?—I think there is something in that, but I have not examined for some time to the particular figures that Lord Castlereagh quotes with regard to expenditure.

10,653. (Chairman.) And that point, I think, was taken by Mr. Childers?—I do not remember whether it was or not.

10,654. (Mr. Sexton.) Again, I say that the extraordinary contention made at that time that if there had been no debts there would have been no proportion, but that indiscriminate taxation would have been at once applied, [illegible] doubt of the good faith of the promoters of the scheme; because if the ability was found to be in the proportion of 15 to 2, it would have been absurd to disregard that ability and to establish indiscriminate taxation merely because there was no debt. And it would have been still more absurd if the debt as well as the ability were in the proportion of 2 to 15; that would have been an additional reason, would it not, for the proportion?—Possibly so.

10,655. Can you really suggest any reasonableness in the declaration that if there were no debt, or if the debts had been in the relation of 2 to 15, the taxation would have been indiscriminate?—I think it was clearly the intention of the framers of the Treaty of Union to have applied indiscriminate taxation at once if they could have done so; but they found that they were precluded from doing so, because the charge for debt in Ireland was relatively smaller than the charge for debt in Great Britain.

10,656. They found the capacity to be in the proportion of 2 to 15?—That is so.

10,657. If so, why should they apply indiscriminate taxation?—They were precluded, as I understand, from applying indiscriminate taxation because the debt charge did not bear what they considered at the time to be an equitable proportion.

10,658. But even if there were no debt charge whatever, and if the capacity was so found to be in the proportion of 2 to 15, why should there even in that case be indiscriminate taxation?—That was their view at the time.

10,659. Is it your view?—My view is that, looking at Ireland as a part of the United Kingdom, indiscriminate taxation might have been the natural thing to apply; whether it would have been fair at the time I do not know.

10,660. But if the resources were in the proportion of 2 to 15, would indiscriminate taxation in that case have been fair?—It would not necessarily have been unfair.

10,661. (Sir David Barbour.) Did not Lord Castlereagh say, that by no means would Ireland have been made to contribute so justly in proportion to capacity as by indiscriminate taxation?—That is what he said.

10,662. Then he said they could not have indiscriminate taxation in that case, because it would be unfair to Ireland where debt was smaller?—That is the point that I wished to bring out.

10,663. And, therefore, he held it would be fair to find out what her capacity was, and to tax the two countries according to that capacity, leaving the debt charge to be met separately?—Exactly so.

10,664. (Mr Sexton.) I do not understand why, if the capacity was in the proportion of 2 to 15, either the absence of debt or the existence of debt, no matter in what proportion, should have deprived Ireland of her due proportion; and as to the quotation put to you by Sir David Barbour, I wish to show in what a fictitious and indefensible manner Lord Castlereagh applied himself to the question. He said, undoubtedly that, "by no system whatever could they be made to contribute so strictly according to their means as by being subject to the same taxes." Is that your opinion?—I think, on the whole, that indiscriminate taxation may be the fairest system.

10,665. Surely you can discriminate by indiscriminate taxation?—Not in the case of indirect taxation.

10,666. Surely, according to the consumption in each country. If you tax the articles consumed in one country and put high taxes upon them—although they are equal rates in both—and low taxes on the articles mainly consumed in the other country, you may take more revenue from one country than the other?—That I admit would not be a differential system.

10,667. No, an identical system. If you put identical rates upon the two countries upon articles consumed, so that you put low rates upon what is consumed in the one country and high rates upon what is consumed in the other, you take the burden of the revenue from one country?—Yes.

10,668. Moreover, in countries that stand as one to two in population, as Great Britain and Ireland did then, if you levy the taxation by identical taxes upon the main articles of consumption, if the consumption tends to be even in the two countries, they may contribute in the proportion of one to two?—That would be so, if the consumption were relatively the same.

10,669. Do you not see how that differs from a proportion of 2 to 15?—I admit that.

10,670. But they said that if there were no debt, they would make but do so, what reason was there in that?—I cannot interpret what Lord Castlereagh's views were at the time; I do not pretend to be able to do so; I do not know what was in the mind of the framers of the Treaty of Union more than what they said themselves and I do not see how I can go behind their own words.

10,671. I pass for a moment to the Act of 1816. In 1816 there was no reason, so far as I know, for assuming that the capacity of Ireland in relation to Great Britain, which was fixed at the Union as 2 to 15, had changed, but the debts which were in a different proportion in 1800 were held to have come into the proportion of 2 to 15. Can you say why the fact that the debts had come into the same proportion as the ability, should have entitled the Imperial Parliament to ignore the ability and to set aside the protection afforded by the ratio of 2 to 15, and to impose indiscriminate taxation, which in certain contingencies might possibly bring Ireland up to the proportion of 1 to 2. Why was that done?—Because, as I understand, what was found to be impracticable, because it was unfair to Ireland in 1800, was not found to be impracticable in 1816, for the assumed unfairness and injustice to Ireland had to some extent disappeared by reason of the fact that Ireland's debt had increased in the interval so materially that it was in the proportion of 2 to 15 as compared with Great Britain's debt.

10,672. But if the power of Ireland to bear the general burden was in relation to that of Great Britain as 2 to 15, why should the circumstance that the debt charge was in the same proportion as that general ability cause the abolition of that general ability scale and the assumption that the ability of Ireland was not as 2 to 15 but as much as that of Great Britain?—I am afraid I do not follow the argument.

10,673. I must say I think it is plain enough; the Act of Union ensured that Ireland should be taxed in the proportion of 2 to 15?—That is so.

10,674. That was said to be her capacity?—Her supposed capacity.

10,675. Her debt charge, which was lower in proportion, came into the same relation as her ability, 2 to 15?—Yes.

10,676. Why should the fact that that particular charge came into the relation of 2 to 15, dispose of and put aside the well-known fact that her capacity was only as 2 to 15 for general taxes, and render her liable to the same taxation as if she had the full capacity of Great Britain?—It was the view apparently held by successive Governments and by people of the time that it was fair.

10,677. Can you discover any justification for that view?—I admit that it is a point that may be argued.

10,678. (Sir David Barbour.) Was not the immediate effect of the amalgamation of the exchequers to make Ireland liable for less than 2 to 15; I do not say the ultimate effect, but the immediate effect?—For the moment that was so, no doubt.

10,679. (Mr. Sexton.) At the time of the Union, Ireland had 1,000,000l. a year of debt to pay, and Great Britain had 20,000,000l.?—Yes.

10,680. Because Great Britain had 20 times as much as Ireland to pay for debt it was held to be improper to include the debts in the joint charge?—That, I understand, was in the minds of the framers of the Treaty of Union.

Effect of consumption taxes on the two countries.

Change from proportionate contribution to indiscriminate taxation.

10,681. But then, in 1816, the amount of the debt charge upon Great Britain, and the amount of debt charge upon Ireland were held, at any rate, to have come very near the same proportion to each other as the general capacity?—Yes.

10,682. That is to say, 2 to 15?—Yes.

10,683. Therefore, if the debt charges in 1816 had been added to the joint expenditure, they would have made no change in the proportion of 2 to 15?—That is so.

10,684. Now we have come to the point; if the proportion had been continued and the debt charge added, then the actual proportion would still have been 2 to 15?—Yes.

10,685. Why was that proportion (presumably the proportion of capacity) abandoned?—I am afraid I can only refer to what was said in Parliament at the time. At any rate, Ireland, for the moment, got some benefit.

10,686. Can you suggest anything to justify that change?—I think the figures which I gave in my original memorandum will show that.

10,687. I am now on the principle. If the capacity was as 2 to 15, can you suggest anything to justify that change?—I think that what it came to was this; that, instead of having to pay in the proportion of 1 to 7½, she was to pay 1 to 15.

10,688. She never was able to pay 1 to 7½; that proved an excessive proportion?—That may be; she did not pay it, no doubt, and I have always admitted the probability that she was not able to pay it.

10,689. But you must admit one of two things: either that the proportions were a protection or that they were not. If they were a protection, that protection ought not to have been taken away in 1816; and if they were not a protection, the Union scheme was a mere pretence?—That may be so.

10,690. Just to suggest to you how Lord Castlereagh argued, he said "that by no system whatever could they "be made to contribute so directly according to their "means, as by being subject to the same taxes equally "bearing upon the great objects of taxation in both "countries;" and in the same speech, in the next column, arguing the question of proportionate taxation and revenue, he said, "Ireland has by these means the "utmost possible security that she cannot be taxed "beyond the measure of her comparative ability." In the same speech, therefore, he said that there was no system so good for equal taxation as indiscriminate taxation, and yet nothing so safe and secure for Ireland as the proportionate system; can you reconcile those two statements?—I presume he thought that the country would contribute to the revenue in proportion to its resources if there was one indiscriminate system of taxation all over the United Kingdom. I do not say that that was right, but that was apparently his position.

10,691. Of the two things both cannot be true; it cannot be true that a system of indiscriminate taxation was the best to discover the resources of the country, and also that a fixed proportion of 2 to 15 subject to periodical revision was the best. One or the other might have been the best, but he said that they both were?—I am afraid I cannot pretend to reconcile his conflicting statements.

10,692. (*Chairman.*) Is it not the theory that the virtue of the system of indiscriminate taxation (I do not say how high that is) depends upon the articles taxed?—To a very great extent.

10,693. Does it not almost entirely do so?—Yes; probably so.

10,694. (*Mr. Sexton.*) You have already agreed that under a system of nominally indiscriminate taxation there may be such discrimination in regard to particular articles, the subjects of consumption in either of two countries, as to take out of one country a tithe of the taxes and out of the other the whole burden, really?—Yes.

10,695. There is really, then, no security in indiscriminate taxation, except by equitable legislation in regard to the particular taxed subjects of consumption?—I take it so.

10,696. Now, Lord Castlereagh took as the basis, I think, of his assumption the anticipation that there would be two years of war and three years of peace, as in the eighteenth century, did he not?—I think so.

10,697. You have said that if peace had prevailed the proportions might have tested fairly?—Yes.

10,698. Do you mean by that that if Lord Castlereagh's anticipations in regard to the peace establishment had been realised, the burden upon Ireland would not have been excessive?—That is what I had in my mind.

10,699. He says here, in his speech upon the articles, "The produce of all the taxes in the last year amounted "merely to 1,950,000*l.*, and the present charges of the "debt alone are now 1,400,000*l.* Irish currency. I will, "however, admit that the revenues of this kingdom "have during the present year experienced an extra- "ordinary increase" (that was up to 3,460,000*l.*) "but "it is not possible to suppose that the whole of the "increase can be permanent when it can be accounted "for by the particular circumstances of the times." I suppose he refers there to the presence of so many men under arms in the country consuming dutiable commodities?—I presume so.

10,700. Lord Castlereagh was there of opinion that the taxation of Ireland could not have been brought above 2,500,000*l.*?—Apparently so.

10,701. And your view is, too, that if his peace establishment of 9,000,000*l.* a year had been the rule in the years succeeding the Union, Ireland would have been able to pay her debt charge of 1,250,000*l.* and a peace charge of 1,000,000*l.*, which would raise the taxation to 2,250,000*l.*, and in that case the proportion would not have been excessive?—I think that is possible. If Ireland had not had to incur any larger addition to her debt, such as she did, she ought to have been able to pay her way, I think.

10,702. Lord Castlereagh said, that on that assumption, Ireland would, in fact, save 500,000*l.*, and even if war prevailed her charge would be 1,000,000*l.* a year less than before the Union?—These have always seemed to me to be very hypothetical figures, which I have not been able to check.

10,703. The half a million saving in peace is founded on the assumption that the Civil establishment of Great Britain would be 9,000,000*l.*, and that Ireland's share would be 1,000,000*l.*, which, with the one million and a quarter of debt charge, would come to 2,250,000*l.* of taxation altogether?—Yes.

10,704. Whilst otherwise she would have had a peace establishment of 1,450,000*l.*, and have to spend half a million more?—Yes.

10,705. And as regard to war, he came to the conclusion that there would be a saving to Ireland of 1,000,000*l.*?—Yes.

10,706. But, however, it was very soon seen that there were not to be two years of war to three of peace, but that it was all war, and the Irish taxation, which had been 1,000,000*l.* in peace, before the Union, and 1,500,000*l.* upon the average, in war, before the Union, came up to an average of 5,000,000*l.* nearly for the 16 years; and the expenditure of Ireland, which had been, in peace, about 1,000,000*l.*, and in war about 3,000,000*l.*, before the Union, became 16,000,000*l.* a year during the 16 years; there was no maximum limit imposed as to the annual sum which Ireland was to pay; no matter how high the taxation ran, her proportion still applied to any amount of expenditure?—That was so.

10,707. The Imperial Parliament did nothing, as the effect of these proportions developed, to redress the grievance?—No, all they did was to appoint Committees year after year.

10,708. Committees, as you say, were appointed year after year. One Committee in 1803 asked for accounts, and none were provided till 1811?—That, I believe, was so.

10,709. And I believe it was only in 1815 that they struck the balance between the two countries?—I think it was before that. I think that in 1811 or 1812 they arranged to strike the balance.

10,710. That was a sort of approximation; but I think the precise balance was not struck till 1815, and the accounts themselves were not regularly balanced till 1825—the yearly accounts?—That is so.

10,711. Was that, do you consider, a proper way of dealing with such a matter?—No, I do not say that it was.

10,712. Do not you think that it would have been just and expedient if the Imperial Parliament, as the only legislative organ remaining (Ireland having been deprived of her power of action), had intervened when it became apparent, as it soon did, that Ireland was being overburdened, either by altering the proportions or by fixing a maximum sum per annum or in some mode relieving the country from the oppression under which she lay?—It would not have been an unnatural course to take.

10,713. The admission that the burden was oppressive was universal. I do not think there was anyone living at that time who denied it, so far as I know?—I think that was the general impression, no doubt, at the time.

10,714. Did the British taxes during that period yield what was anticipated from them?—I think in Great Britain the yield fairly came up to expectations.

10,715. The Irish taxes, on the other hand, did not, did they?—The Irish taxes certainly did not.

10,716. You have quoted McCulloch, a writer of such authority and of great research, as to the extent to which the taxation of Ireland in that period was oppressive?—I have.

10,717. He was of opinion, was he not, that the taxes in Ireland at that time were so heavy that they might be cited as an instance of the inutility and folly of making taxation so high as to render it unproductive?—Yes; that was his opinion.

10,718. And even the British Chancellor of the Exchequer, I believe, confessed that Irish taxes which had been estimated to yield 2,500,000*l*. had only yielded about 1,600,000*l*.?—Yes; but I have never been able to identify his figures.

10,719. (*Sir David Barbour.*) What was the date of McCulloch's writing?—I think it must have been in the forties when he wrote about that, but I am not quite certain.

10,720. (*Mr. Sexton.*) And I think the Chancellor of the Exchequer, or one of the chancellors of that day, was of opinion that taxes expected to yield 2,500,000*l*. had only yielded 1,600,000*l*. You quote that in your Memorandum?—I forget who it was said by—whether it was Mr. Goulburn.

10,721. I think it was Mr. Goulburn?—I am not certain.

10,722. Is it not the fact that one of the Select Committees, the Select Committee of 1811, upon considering the subject found a great falling off in the revenue of certain years?—Yes.

10,723. For instance, the revenue of 1802 was lower than the revenue of 1800 by 400,000*l*., and the revenue of 1804 was lower than the revenue of 1803 by 600,000*l*., and there were also considerable fallings off in the revenue in 1810 and 1811?—Yes.

10,724. Now considering these reductions of yield in connexion with the great increases in the rates of taxes between the Union and the consolidation of the Exchequers, is there not proof to demonstration that the burden of Ireland in that period trenched upon the subsistence of the people?—I think that is not an unfair inference to draw.

10,725. Would you look for a moment at your table of the changes in the rates of taxes in that period, showing what the increases were. You have them in the first part of the Memorandum?—I do not quite know to what you are referring. Do you mean the rates of duties?

10,726. Yes, the rates of duties?—I have not got the yields against them.

10,727. I think I have it here. I would ask you now whether there is a curious account of the fluctuations in revenue and the alterations of rates between the Union and the consolidation of the Exchequers. The Select Committee of 1811, upon an account showing that the revenues of Ireland had decreased in 1801 as compared with 1800 by about 400,000*l*.; in 1802 by a like amount, in 1804 by 600,000*l*., in 1810 by 800,000*l*., in 1811 by an additional fall of 600,000*l*., observed that in the last two years, and especially in the last, the Irish revenue had not only not increased in proportion to the augmented charge of the public debt, but had fallen considerably short of its former amount, and that the deficiency had occurred in the Department of Customs and Excise. They showed that the spirits customs had fallen from 718,000*l*. in 1810, to 225,000*l*. in 1811; the sugar duty from 408,000*l*. to 150,000*l*.; that all other customs had fallen—the excise on malt from 408,000*l*. to 248,000*l*., and the duties on spirits, which had yielded 1,325,000*l*. in 1807–8, had fallen to 908,000*l*. in 1808–9, to 730,000*l*. in 1809–10, and had only recovered to 895,000*l*. in 1810–11. As to the last-quoted they observed that the great reduction of duty in 1810 had not been attended with the expected effect of increasing the quantity brought into charge (a very significant remark). With the duty at 5s. 1d. the excise had fallen from 1,800,000*l*. to 300,000*l*.—that is, by about five-sixths, and the reduction of duty to 2s. 6d. had improved the yield to only about half the former amount. The heavy falls in gross and net produce in 1802, 1804, 1808, and 1811 occurred notwithstanding the increases in the spirit duty between 1800 and 1810 from 2s. 4d. to 5s. 1d., the duty on brandy from 4s. 7d. to 12s. 7d., on rum from 4s. 8d. to 10s. 8d., on malt from 1s. 2d. to 2s. 6d., on cheap teas from 20 to 34 per cent., on dearer teas from 35 to 84 per cent., and on tobacco from 1s. to 2s. 6d. It was found necessary to reduce the excise on spirits for two years, from 1810 to 1812, from 5s. 1d. to 2s. 6d., and in 1816 from 6s. 1d. to 5s. 7d., and the duty on malt in 1816 from 4s. 2d. to 2s. 4d. Putting these facts before you, these heavy falls in revenue in no fewer than 8 of the 16 years considered and connected with heavy increases, sometimes double, sometimes more than treble in the rates of the taxes from which the revenue on consumption was derived, is it not obvious that the taxes must have trenched so severely upon the subsistence of the people as to oblige them to abandon in a great degree these articles of common consumption?—I think that is a fair inference to draw.

10,728. Now the revenue of Ireland in those 16 years was 77,000,000*l*.; the tax revenue was 70,000,000*l*., apart from non-tax revenue; that is an average of four and three-eighth millions per annum. The tax revenue of Great Britain during the 16 years was 960,000,000*l*., and Great Britain yielded according to the Budget anticipations the full amount of 60,000,000*l*. a year. Ireland, however, in yielding four and three-eighth millions, suffered heavily. It was proved to be excessive taxation. It seems to follow, therefore, fairly, that all references to war taxes is irrelevant in this argument, because, if you take the whole of the taxes, Great Britain bore her share with comparative ease, whilst Ireland bore hers with great suffering. I presume, therefore, that the true relative capacity of Ireland at that time must have been less than the proportion of four and three-eighth millions a year to 60,000,000*l*.?—That may be so, but there is an important qualification with regard to income tax. I think the income tax must not be left out of account.

10,729. But would it have affected the situation?—The extent would be hypothetical.

10,730. Let us consider the point. The income tax in the 16 years produced in Great Britain 150,000,000*l*., and taking your own calculation it would have produced in Ireland 6,000,000*l*., or one twenty-fifth part of 150,000,000*l*. But the deficit of Ireland in the 16 years was 84,000,000*l*. Therefore even if the income tax had been imposed, it would only have affected the deficit of 84,000,000*l*. to the extent of 6,000,000*l*.?—No doubt.

10,731. That would not have altered the situation, would it?—It would to a limited extent, surely.

10,732. To the extent of 6,000,000*l*. out of 84,000,000*l*.?—I do not know how you arrive at 6,000,000*l*.

10,733. The income tax for Great Britain for the 16 years yielded 150,000,000*l*., and you suggested that it would have yielded 4 per cent. in Ireland?—That is, assuming that the contribution to income tax would have been the same as now relatively to Great Britain; which is very different to Mr. Pitt's estimate.

10,734. At that proportion it would have yielded about 6,000,000*l*. in the 16 years, or one twenty-fifth part of the 150,000,000*l*.?—Yes.

10,735. That 6,000,000*l*. would only have affected the deficit of Ireland to the extent of 6,000,000*l*. out of 84,000,000*l*.?—That would be so.

10,736. We may take it, therefore, I think (and I would invite you, if you think so, to concur), that the capacity of Ireland at that time was less than the proportion of 4½ to 60, because Great Britain bore the 60,000,000*l*. without apparent hardship, but Ireland did not so bear the 4½ millions, but on the contrary, the taxation obliged her to abandon her ordinary habits of consumption?—That is possible.

10,737. Therefore, the true proportion was less than 1 in 13, instead of being 2 in 15. You have not only suggested that there was some understanding that Ireland would pay all that was spent in Ireland before the Union, but also, I think, you have speculated in your sketch of the second period that Ireland would have fared no better than as we have just seen she did fare?—Not much better.

Sir E. W. Hamilton, K.C.B.

14 Nov. 1895.

[illegible]

10,738. If there had been no Union?—I qualified it to the extent of 16,000,000*l.*

10,739. She paid away 16,000,000*l.* to Great Britain, in addition to the expenditure in Ireland during those 16 years?—Yes.

10,740. And I think you went even so far as to say that if there had been no Union she might not only have yielded all that was required in Ireland, but that she might have paid the 16,000,000*l.* as well?—Yes.

10,741. I invite you to another line of [illegible]. If there had been no Union, the extended franchise of 1793, would have made [illegible] to Ireland, and no doubt Ireland would have demanded and would have secured responsible government—it could not have been long postponed if the Union measure had failed. Do you consider that with the extended franchise, and with Ministers responsible to the Irish House and not to British Ministers, Ireland would have gone on bearing a burden which imposed such hardship; that she would not have pointed out to Great Britain the interest of Great Britain, as well as of herself, in the defence of Ireland as a territory of the Crown; and that she would not have claimed from Great Britain a contribution?—It is quite possible.

10,742. Do not you think it very probable, at any rate that the Irish Parliament in the last resort would have used its constitutional power to limit the supplies to what the resources of the country allowed?—Yes; but, on the other hand, I have understood it to be held by the hon. member and his friends that, had Ireland been allowed to retain her separate Parliament, she would have been in a [illegible] condition than she was under the Union subsequently to 1800.

10,743. That may or may not be so, but all I submit to you is that whatever her resources might have been the Irish Parliament would have had the power, and probably would have used it, to say, we will contribute to this [illegible] (for it is a joint interest) as much as our resources allow, but no more?—That is perhaps probable.

10,744. And they would have had that power?—Presumably so.

10,745. I think I might add that, as in 1782, a great part of the expense in Ireland, under a domestic Government, might have been saved by a system of volunteers?—That may be so.

10,746. That is to say, that Ireland might have been garrisoned by volunteers, provided that the Government and people of the country were in accord, as they would have been if the Union had not been carried?—That is [illegible].

10,747. I suggest that to you as a reason for thinking that the burden imposed upon Ireland during all those 16 years could not have been imposed if there had not been a Union?—Perhaps so.

Sir Edward Hamilton's evidence is continued at Question 10,918 (Twenty-seventh Day).

TWENTY-SEVENTH DAY.

At A. Committee Room, House of Lords, Friday, 15th November 1895.

Present :

THE RIGHT HONOURABLE HUGH C. E. CHILDERS, Chairman.

The Right Hon. The O'Conor Don.	J. E. Redmond, Esq., M.P.
Bertram W. Currie, Esq.	Thomas Sexton, Esq., M.P.
Charles E. Martin, Esq.	Henry F. Slattery, Esq.

B. H. Holland, Esq., *Secretary.*

Sir Edward Walter Hamilton, K.C.B., further examined.

Sir E. W. Hamilton, K.C.B.

15 Nov. 1895.

[illegible]

10,748. (*Mr. Sexton.*) Considering the great care you have devoted to this question, and the main object of the reference to the Commission, I find it difficult to understand why, in that sketch of the five periods, in which you make many observations (not devoid of interest) you scarcely ever refer to the question of capacity, and never to the question of relative taxable capacity, which is really the question before us?—However, rightly or wrongly, I understood the main reference to the Commission to be, whether Ireland was or was not being overcharged. That was the only reason I put it in that way. I did not pretend to exhaust the whole subject by the few remarks I made. What I said was merely directed to that point which I took to be the main point of reference to the Commission, which was whether, in the opinion of the Commission, Ireland was or was not at the present moment overcharged.

10,749. Or rather, whether, admitting the overcharge, certain expenditure in one part of the kingdom may be regarded as a measure of relief?—It included that, certainly, but it included also whether, looking at the position as a whole, Ireland was now being unfairly or fairly treated, financially.

10,750. But, obviously, the most ready way to determine that would be to take to accepted tests, namely, the rise and fall of population; the rise and fall of income, the rise and fall of revenue, and the relation of those facts to each other in so far as they affect the two countries?—I admit that that is a line that may be and is taken by many persons. I hold a different view—the one which, after consideration, appeared to me on the whole to be the fairest; but, of course, my view may be an erroneous one.

10,751. What I mean is that, whatever the observations may be, if they are [illegible] and discursive in their character, they may more rather to lead away from the track of the main inquiry than to follow it?—Then I am afraid that is my fault. I thought as I had given a great deal more consideration to the subject since I put in my memorandum, that perhaps the few additional remarks I asked the Commission to hear, to might be of some interest and use, and if I have misled the Commission in any way, I am sorry I made them; at any rate, I certainly did not intend to mislead the Commission.

10,752. No doubt they are of very great interest, but what I have felt in reading your remarks is that they appeared, notwithstanding their interest, to lead one away from what are obviously the true rules of comparison, namely what, at each of these periods, was the relation in population, in income, and in surplus income between the two countries taxed?—All I can say is that I did not intend to mislead the Commission at all from the main point of the inquiry—at least, as I understand it.

10,753. The grievance of Ireland from taxation appears to be in the nature of a cumulative grievance.

Ireland undoubtedly suffered in the period next following the Union as compared with Great Britain, because the taxes in Ireland became unproductive through excess, whereas the taxes in Great Britain easily yielded the full amount, and since the middle of the century Ireland has gone on decreasing in population, and decreasing also in resources, while Great Britain all through the century has increased rapidly in population, and still more rapidly in wealth; is not that so?—Yes, that may be so.

10,754. And therefore from my point of view the grievance of Ireland is a cumulative grievance existing since the Union and more than ever increasing, but the effect of your mode of dealing with the question, separating the century into periods, and considering each by itself independently of the others, seems rather, instead of recognising the growing character of the grievance, to split it up into portions, and to treat each portion as if it were the whole?—It seems to me that the century divides itself in a very marked manner into these three periods since the consolidation of the exchequers. Of course the other two periods were obvious ones.

10,755. You appear to minimise in each period any hardship inflicted upon Ireland?—I do not think I at all minimised the hardship inflicted upon Ireland between 1853 and 1860—at least I should not say so; on the contrary, I thought I expressed myself rather strongly in the direction of showing that the fiscal legislation of that time bore very heavily upon Ireland.

10,756. Let us take that period for a moment as an example of what I mean; you do admit that during that period Ireland was hit very hard; but then you proceed to suggest that owing to emigration the average capacity of the Irishman may have been higher than it had been 10 years previously?—Yes.

10,757. That is in the direction of minimising, is it not?—Yes, but it is only fair to assume that that was probably in the minds of those who were responsible for the fiscal legislation of that time; and of course I am anxious not to reflect, or rather to avoid as far as possible, reflecting, upon those who were responsible for the finances in the past, and who were much greater authorities than myself upon the subject.

10,758. That probably is a more suitable way of expressing what I intended; it was not a surprising attitude of a Treasury officer that he should desire to bear lightly on what he considered to have been even an objectionable course on the part of those who preceded him in office and in responsibility?—Quite so; considering that it came from the highest financial authority at the time.

10,759. But you not only dwell lightly upon grievances, but your plan of dividing the century into periods has the effect, that whatever suffering or injury Ireland may have endured in any particular period, when you pass away from that period, you rather treat it as if it had never been; you look upon the next period as the beginning of all things, and only regard any fresh burden in the new period as worthy of consideration, forgetting what may have been the burden brought from the old period?—That may be so; but I regard that the treatment of Ireland in the distant past is hardly within the range of practical politics to deal with. I wished to draw attention specially to comparatively recent times.

10,760. I think that, looking at the difficulty of changing persons' standards of capacity, in the earlier periods, it is important to have, if possible, a clear idea of what was the degree of injustice inflicted upon Ireland at the earliest period, and to consider, in the light of what has occurred, whether that injustice has continued, diminished, or increased?—I quite admit that is a fair line to take, and interesting historically, but it did not seem to me to be a practical line to take.

10,761. You see, assuming that Ireland was unjustly treated in the 16 years after the Union, and that that injustice, upon the whole, has gone on increasing since, for instance, supposing it has doubled since, if you divide the century into five periods, and attribute to each period only a portion of the injustice undergone within that period, the effect upon the whole is to make the injustice to the people of Ireland to appear only a fraction of what it really was?—I think that is a legitimate criticism to make upon the remarks which I submitted to the Commission.

10,762. To pass now to the period you have just referred to, you suggest that the extraordinary increase in the taxation of Ireland between 1853 and 1860—an increase of nearly two-thirds—may have been in its incidence somewhat lightened by an increase of the average capacity of the Irishman owing to emigration?—Yes.

10,763. We know that that is rather more a technical argument than otherwise, because the payment of taxes on consumption, from which the Irish revenue is almost wholly derived, depends upon population, and though when you reduce population, arithmetically the proportion of property and income in the country may be held to be distributed at a higher rate per head, I think you will admit that the tax-paying capacity of the average individual has scarcely improved?—Yes, that may be so.

10,764. Now, I should like to refer you to a very important table, which was put in by the Irish Registrar-General, upon this point; you will find it at page 420 of Volume I. It touches the question whether the taxable capacity of the average Irishman increased between 1853 and 1862. You see there, "Table E.—"Average annual value of crops, stock, &c. disposed of, "exclusive of the portion of the crops used by stock." That is the view of the Registrar-General of Ireland of the gross value of the annual income of the agriculturists of Ireland, and in that table you may observe that the "average annual value in the years 1851-1855," the beginning of the period with which we are now concerned, was 72,600,000*l.*?—Yes.

10,765. Do you observe that the average annual value at the end of the period was only the same amount?—Quite so, but then I should have thought that, as the population has much diminished, the 72,600,000*l.* represented a larger annual value in proportion to the population in 1869 and 1870 to what it did between 1851 and 1855.

10,766. Yes, but now we come to my second observation. You observe that the increase occurred in stock, which is held in fewer hands and gives less employment?—Yes.

10,767. While the crops fall off from 43,000,000*l.* to 32,000,000*l.* per annum?—Yes.

10,768. And the crops are what constitute the tax-paying capacity of the small farmers and labourers, and does it not follow, therefore, that whilst the capacity of the persons taxed on property might have somewhat increased in that period, the capacity of the man depending on a small holding or upon wages, must have diminished?—I think that is quite a fair argument to found upon those figures.

10,769. It is highly important, upon the general question, to remember that these estimates have been subjected to severe criticism upon the score of exactness, but as they are all upon the same basis, they afford a good test of comparison of different periods, do they not?—Yes.

10,770. You see, therefore, that there is some point in my observation, namely, that whilst you admit that Ireland was, as you express it graphically, "hit very hard" during that period, there is no reason for thinking that the average capacity of the consumer in Ireland was larger, but that, on the contrary, it was rather smaller at the end of the period than it was at the beginning?—I think these figures rather tend to show that, but, at the same time, I presume, speaking generally, that the condition of Ireland was not quite so bad in 1863 as it was in 1853-1855, which was so soon after the famine. The reason why I alluded to a possible increase of Irish taxable capacity in 1863, was to anticipate what seems an obvious rejoinder to my contention that Ireland had been hit hard by the fiscal legislation of the 10 previous years, for anybody might say "Yes; but you have not to account the "fact that Ireland was not in such an impoverished "condition 10 or 16 years after the famine as she was "two or three years after the famine."

10,771. There were probably more people in absolute distress in Ireland, unable to pay taxes or to buy food, at the earlier period, were there not?—Yes.

10,772. But one doubts whether at the later period the capacity of the wage-earning class to bear taxes was materially different?—That may be so.

10,773. You have spoken somewhere of the great increase in wages during the last half-century; you said it had doubled, I think?—That is taken from Sir Robert Giffen.

Sir R. [illegible], K.C.B.

14 Nov. 1895.

Possible [illegible] of Ireland as [illegible] [illegible].

10,774. Have you any table of figures that you can put in which would show what the wages were at the beginning of the period and what they were at the end of the period, in order to ascertain what the doubling, in the amount of wages would represent?—I forget whether the [illegible] Office illustrated it by actual figures or not, but I could give you the reference to her essay again. It is one of her essays on [illegible] published about the year 1886, I think, if I recollect rightly.

10,775. Have you any doubt that the increase has been greater in wages in Great Britain than in Ireland?—No; I should think it had probably been greater, or quite as great.

10,776. For instance, we all know that in the last 50 years the resources of Ireland have diminished as tested by those returns of agricultural value, and we know from Mr. Bowley and other authorities, that in the United Kingdom the income has doubled, and rates of wages increased by 30 per cent. If that be so in the United Kingdom, and you take out Ireland, which is stationary, it is obvious that the percentage of increase in the case of Great Britain will be greater still?—That will be so.

10,777. Now, with regard to the period from 1800 to 1817, I think it is important here to call to mind a contemporary parliamentary judgment upon the effect of the proportion operating in those 16 years. The Select Committee of 1815, the last Committee which considered these questions, before 1817 reported, on the consolidation of the proportion fixed at the Union [illegible], in these terms: "And your Committee cannot "but remark that for several years Ireland has advanced "in permanent taxation more rapidly than Great "Britain itself, notwithstanding the immense exertions "of the latter country, and including the extraordinary "and war taxes." You see, therefore, that where reference is made to the war taxes in England at the time of the war with France as having been heavy, that observation taken alone, has a decidedly misleading effect, because the committee found that the taxation in Ireland increased more than in Great Britain, even including the war taxes paid by Great Britain?—Yes, that would appear to be so.

10,778. Then they say "The permanent revenue of "Great Britain has increased since 1801 in the ratio "of 16½ to 10, the whole revenue, including the "war taxes, in the proportion of 21 to 10, while in the "same period the revenue of Ireland has increased to "that of 23 to 10, and in the 24 years referred to your "committee the increase of Irish revenue has been "in the proportion of 46 to 10"—that is to say, it had nearly quadrupled?—Yes.

10,779. That evidence, added to what you gave us yesterday, does, I think, put beyond the sphere of controversy the fact that the proportion operated in Ireland during those 16 years so as to drive from Ireland with much hardship a bankrupting revenue, whilst it drew from Great Britain a revenue, which, from all appearance, she was able to bear without hardship?—Yes, I admit that, with one qualification, and that is with regard to income tax. The income tax, if it had been imposed on Ireland, would not have affected the masses of the consuming classes, but the propertied classes, and to that extent Ireland might have borne the income tax with some advantage, moreover, to the consuming classes.

10,780. Has it ever occurred to you to ask yourself why income tax was not imposed during those 16 years upon Ireland?—I presume it was because it was thought that Ireland was already sufficiently taxed, and that therefore it would be unwise to increase the taxation. At the same time, it has always seemed to me that what was left out of account was this, that if you had levied that tax it would not have been levied upon the consuming classes, but upon the propertied classes, and therefore I have always wondered that it was not levied.

10,781. It was recognised, on all hands that the taxation of Ireland was already excessive, was it not?—Yes, that I admit—excessive upon the consuming classes.

10,782. The Irish representatives of that day consisted almost wholly of the land owning class, did they not?—Yes, and no doubt they carried great weight in Parliament.

10,783. Probably they apprehended that if they complained of the excessive charge of debt against Ireland, the retort would have been "but the debt has "been piled up upon Ireland because her contribution "by taxes is insufficient, and we will remedy that "insufficiency by imposing income tax"?—I think that is very probable.

10,784. Does not that seem to account for the attitude of the Irish representatives?—Yes, I think it does.

10,785. (*Chairman.*) Might I ask you whether the extreme difficulty of collection at that time had not something to do with the non-imposition of income tax?—It may have had, but the machinery had never been started in Ireland, therefore we have no direct proof that difficulty would have arisen.

10,786. (*Mr. Sexton.*) It is natural to suppose, is it not, that if the Irish members thought that the only effect of strong remonstrance upon their part, against the piling up of the debt, would have been the reply upon the part of the Imperial Government, that the tax revenue being found inadequate, income tax would be imposed, they would see no benefit in pursuing a course that would only have the effect of increasing the burden of taxation upon the class in which they were most particularly interested?—Yes.

10,787. Now let us be clear about the income tax. The income tax yielded in Great Britain in 16 years was 180,000,000 sterling, and if it had been imposed upon Ireland it would, of course, have produced a proportionate amount; would that in your opinion, have effected any substantial alteration in the state of the case?—Perhaps not a substantial alteration, but it would have made some alteration.

10,788. It would have made the average of four millions and three-eighths per annum which Ireland paid in each of the 16 years into four millions and three quarters?—Yes.

10,789. And it would not have substantially altered the proportions raised by taxation in the two countries?—No.

10,790. The fact noted in the Report of the Select Committee of 1815 as to a greater increase of Irish taxes than of British taxes within that period, is partly due no doubt, to the conduct of Lord Castlereagh in fixing the proportions upon a comparison of the past expenditure which left out upon the one side the British debt, but on the other side, charged Ireland not only with the whole of the cost of defending Ireland in the period before the Union, but also with such temporary charges as were incurred in connection with the suppression of the rebellion and the passing of the Act of Union?—That may be so.

10,791. During those 16 years, while the energies of the other nations of Europe were concentrated upon the field of battle, England, whilst dispatching considerable armies to the scene of war, was free at home to pursue a course of manufacturing industry, and is it not certain that during these 16 years England did so pursue that course, and that she became the workshop of Europe and the first commercial nation of Europe at that time?—Towards the end of that time I think that was the case.

10,792. The gross expenditure of England in the whole 16 years was 1,200,000,000l.?—Yes.

10,793. And her income now in one year is about 1,400,000,000l.?—Yes.

10,794. Her income now, in one year, is greater than the whole taxation and debt that she incurred during the whole of those 16 years?—Yes, that is a very striking point.

10,795. Do you think from the point of view of the advancement of trade and the aggrandisement of income arising therefrom, England has ever made so good an investment since as when she expended those 1,200,000,000l. in those 16 years, chiefly in the war with France?—I think that is rather a difficult question to answer.

10,796. Did she not lay the foundation of her commercial greatness by the advantage she procured at home during that period while the war kept Europe busy?—No doubt she benefited immensely.

10,797. And I think we have to consider that it was in the nature of an investment, with returns postponed, but great when it came?—Yes, I think that may be said to be so.

10,798. On the other hand, what benefit did Ireland derive from the war?—It might be said that the war [illegible] her advantage in it.

Sir E. W. Hamilton, K.C.B.

18 Nov. 1895.

10,799. Ireland would have existed in any case?—Yes; but she might have been conquered for the time being.

10,800. Ireland is a country with purely domestic concerns; so long as the grass has crops and cattle the people can live?—No doubt; but I should have thought that her connexion with Great Britain, by which she has, no doubt, very greatly benefited—although, perhaps, the honourable member will not agree with me—had been of immense advantage to her. Owing to it, for instance, she has got extraordinary credit. I should have thought that upon the prosperity of Great Britain, and the soundness of Great Britain's credit, the prosperity of Ireland depended a great deal. Supposing, that, instead of having benefited from this great war, of having emerged triumphantly eventually from it, and of having built up a great commercial fabric, as Great Britain did after the war, the reverse had happened, surely Ireland would have found very difficulty after the peace was declared. Of course, all these are very hypothetical questions, and I do not think my opinion worth anything, but I can quite conceive that if the reverse, as I have said, had taken place, Ireland might have been a much more impoverished country.

10,801. The commercial relations between Great Britain and Ireland do not depend upon political considerations, they depend upon natural convenience and political economy, do they not?—Yes, I think so, mainly.

10,802. If Great Britain finds Danish butter cheaper and better, she buys it rather than Irish butter, does she not?—Yes.

10,803. It seems to me that, so far as the prosperity of Ireland depends upon commercial advantage, it is not dependent upon any political system?—No.

10,804. Then, with regard to the effect upon Irish credit of the Union, I have a test here which I would like to submit to you. At the time of the Union, Great Britain paid 1l. of debt charge for every 22l. of debt; and Ireland at the same time paid only 1l. of debt charge for every 23l. of debt, her credit was, therefore, better at the time of the Union tested by the cost of her debt than the credit of Great Britain?—That, I think, was mainly due to the fact that there was an enormous demand upon the capital of Great Britain, and a comparatively small demand upon the capital of Ireland. Great Britain's credit was consequently extremely bad for many years.

10,805. There is no other way of testing credit than by borrowing too much?—No.

10,806. But at the consolidation of the exchequers 16 years after, when Ireland had had the advantage of 16 years of Union, Great Britain instead of paying 1l. for every 22l. of debt, was paying 1l. charge for every 17l. of debt, while Ireland was only paying 1l. of charge for every 17l. 10s. of debt, and, therefore, her credit even at the time of the consolidation was somewhat better than that of Great Britain, but the Union seems to have pulled down the position of advantage which she had enjoyed in 1800, and reduced that to a position almost of identity with Great Britain?—That may be so. But I do not know whether you have taken into account the fact that the greater part of the debt that was raised on Irish account between 1800 and 1816, was raised in Great Britain, and that therefore that pro tanto increased the amount which had to be subscribed in England.

10,807. Yes; and I also notice, that the debt raised in Ireland before, as well as after, the Union was raised for a nominal capital not much exceeding the amount of the cash borrowed. [illegible] of money being borrowed for [illegible], of capital debt?—Yes, that was because Ireland had the good sense, as I think, to raise money on stock of a higher denomination than what was done in Great Britain at the time.

10,808. She paid a higher rate of interest?—Yes, and I think that was probably a much more financial step to have taken, than what was taken in this country, when Great Britain's large borrowings were made in stocks of a denomination which necessarily made the stocks go to a great discount.

10,809. Whatever the cause may have been the [illegible] of money raised in Ireland created a debt of only [illegible]—that is an addition of one fourth of capital, whilst the [illegible] borrowed in England for account of Ireland, before and after the Union, created a nominal debt of no less than 110 millions, and that contributed greatly to inflate the Irish debt, and so to render possible the calculation that was afterwards made?—No doubt; but there the condition of the test of credit—you must put the two borrowings upon the same lines before you can test what the credit is. Merely to say that the nominal capital of the debt was much more largely increased in Great Britain than in Ireland does not show that British credit was less good.

10,810. No; but it shows that the mode of borrowing pursued in Great Britain as compared with that pursued in Ireland tended artificially to inflate the amount of the debt of Ireland and to bring it into a certain relation to the inflated amount of the British debt, so as to establish unfortunate taxation in lieu of the system of proportion and particular [illegible]?—Yes.

10,811. Now as to the third period, from 1817 to 1853, a period of peace, taxation fell, and the policy was reversed?—That is so.

10,812. You have made the observation that Great Britain properly derived comparatively greater relief than Ireland from remissions because she had continued to be more heavily taxed. I believe Great Britain was paying [illegible], in 1816, by taxes not imposed in Ireland, and that [illegible] has been brought down to [illegible]?—I think that is so.

10,813. Great Britain has, therefore, benefited greatly in that way since the consolidation of the exchequers?—Yes, that would be so.

10,814. Now, why was Great Britain better entitled than Ireland to remissions—you have admitted that the four millions and three-eighths on an average levied in Ireland during these 16 years, as everybody admits, inflicted a great hardship, and even caused impoverishment of Ireland, and as Great Britain realised the full expectations, which is the best practical test of capacity, does it not seem that Ireland was in more need of remissions?—I think it is hardly fair to put it in that way. It is only reasonable to suppose that, as the inhabitants of Great Britain were suffering under a very heavy income tax, that claim should be one of the very first claims to be considered. There was no corresponding claim to be considered in Ireland. The great remission in Great Britain was the total remission of the income tax in 1816, when the Government, contrary to their own proposals, were forced by Parliament to make it.

10,815. That involves the question of a particular claim in one country, but admittedly, the country bearing the heavier burthen had the more urgent claim for remission, had it not?—Yes, it is fair to put it in that way.

10,816. Considering the effect of these remissions, you say that Ireland did not benefit as a manufacturing country, but that she benefited as a consumer. The policy of remission appears to have been most wisely devised in both its parts to render the maximum of benefit upon Great Britain, as it undoubtedly did, in the first place by opening the way to the admission of raw materials, cheapening their price (Britain having by this time become in the main a manufacturing country), it cheapened materials, stimulated manufactures, extended the labour market, and increased the tax-paying power of the country?—Certainly.

10,817. On the other hand, the labour market being extended, and wages increased, the remission of duties upon consumption, and the admission of food free, gave the wages of the earning classes in Great Britain a larger purchasing power, did it not?—That would be so.

10,818. They got better and more regular wages, and their wages were worth more in goods?—Yes, I admit that.

10,819. It was a system eminently well devised for the benefit of Great Britain, was it not?—Yes, no doubt.

10,820. There was more work for the workers, and cheaper food for the people?—Yes.

10,821. On the other hand, look at Ireland; she had no manufactures, and, therefore, she had no benefit whatever as a producer from the cheapening of raw materials, had she?—I do not know if it can be said that there were no manufactures in Ireland at that time.

10,822. Substantially there were none, they had ceased in the period since the Union. Then, having no benefit as a producer from the cheapening of raw materials, as an agricultural producer was she not severely injured by the repeal of the Corn Laws?—It is my opinion that she was injured.

[illegible] K.C.B. [illegible]

10,623. In what year were the Corn Laws repealed?—In 1846.

10,624. Do you know that, before 1846, Ireland was a great grower of cereals?—I believe so.

10,625. And that the export of wheat was one of her mainstays?—Yes.

10,626. But the export of wheat ceased, and the repeal of the Corn Laws depriving Ireland of advantages in the markets of Great Britain, led her to discourage the growing of cereals, and caused an economic revolution; and that was the chief cause that led to the change from the growing of grain to the raising of cattle, was it not?—I presume so.

10,627. And in that way led to the clearance of the better land for grazing, and the confining of the people to those barren tracts, that congestion of the population, which has become the greatest of Irish economic difficulties?—I take that to be one of the consequences, no doubt.

10,628. Ireland may have derived some benefit as a consumer of manufactured articles, from cheapening the price of raw material; but surely any benefit which she may have derived as a consumer of manufactured articles must be many times less than the injury inflicted upon her by free trade, which deprived her of all advantage in the markets of Great Britain?—It is very difficult to appraise the various advantages and disadvantages resulting from the legislation of that time.

10,629. You said the starving condition of Ireland was a contributory cause of the repeal of the Corn Laws; was not the continued increase of the means of the population in Great Britain a sufficient cause for it?—From what one reads in history, I doubt very much whether the measure would have been carried as soon as it was, if it had not been for the starving condition of Ireland. I think it was a very powerful weapon in Sir Robert Peel's hands at the time. I question whether he would have been able to carry the repeal of the Corn Laws, had he not been able to point to the condition of Ireland as one of the main reasons for introducing the measure.

10,630. It may have been useful in debate, perhaps, but how did the repeal of the Corn Laws beneficially affect the starving condition of Ireland?—By being able to increase the food of the people, and by opening the ports to foreign grain of all kinds.

10,631. But surely you do not suppose that the starving condition of Ireland was due to any want of food in the country?—I have always understood that it was owing to the failure of the potato crop. From what I have read I have always supposed that a large amount of food was imported into Ireland.

10,632. But there never was a time when there was not a sufficiency of food in the country to save the population from a famine if the means had been at hand to enable the population to avail themselves of it?—I defer to your superior knowledge of Ireland. I dare say you are quite right, but I was certainly under the impression that it was otherwise.

10,633. Do you consider, looking at the effect of the repeal of the Corn Laws in Ireland in producing that economic revolution, that there was any adequate compensation in the grant of half the cost of the constabulary?—I presume it was thought at the time by those responsible for the legislation that that was a means of making (what was thought) a fair compensation to Ireland for any injury that was done.

10,634. A measure which attacked fundamentally the means of living of the people could not have been compensated for by a grant of so many millions a year as there were hundreds of thousands. The policy of taxation pursued during this third period conferred upon England the enormous benefit, both as a manufacturing and also as a consuming country, without regard to the injury done to Ireland, and any benefit done to Ireland was only to make so [illegible] fundamentally from the benefit to Great Britain?—That seems to be a fair way of putting the case, according to the view held by the honourable member.

10,635. In your plan of separating each period from what has happened before it, you say here, "The "net result, however, of the financial policy adopted "by the Imperial Parliament during this period was "that Ireland emerged from the period rather less "heavily taxed." You do not say whether she had been too heavily taxed at the beginning?—No.

10,636. You say her taxes had fallen from—in 1819–20—[illegible] per head of the population to [illegible] in 1849–50. That was an infinitesimal reduction?—I admit that.

10,637. Then, is it not the fact that although the taxes on property fell somewhat in that period, the taxes upon the consumer increased in the same period from [illegible] to [illegible] per head?—That is so, according to the figures I cited.

10,638. And that whilst this increase took place in Ireland in a period of great calamity and great distress and great disease, in England the rate per head fell from [illegible] to [illegible] 7s. 6d. per head?—I think that is correct.

10,639. And that both the property owner and the consumer in Great Britain were relieved, for the rate per head on the property owner fell from [illegible] to [illegible] per head, and upon the consumer from [illegible] to [illegible]?—That is so, I think.

10,640. It would appear, therefore, that within the period the British consumer was much relieved and the Irish consumer was more heavily burdened; the pressure of British taxation, as tested by the rate per head, was relieved by one-third; and Irish taxation became heavier per head, and also heavier in absolute amount and in proportion to the taxation of Great Britain than it had been at the period of the Great War?—Hardly heavier, I think, as the figures show.

10,641. Yes, I think so. The taxation in the period of the Great War upon the average was [illegible] millions a year in Ireland for 15 years after the Union?—Yes.

10,642. In this year it was [illegible]; it, therefore, must have increased in amount?—Yes; but the population was larger.

10,643. I have also taken the rates per head for the consumer, which were heavier for Ireland?—That may be so.

10,644. The gross average sum paid by Great Britain in taxes was [illegible] for 15 years after the Union, and here at the end of that period it is [illegible]?—Yes.

10,645. So we see that Ireland, with a population of about the same number, or slightly less, is paying a larger sum, a larger rate per head, and a larger relative proportion of taxation than in the period of the war with France?—That may be the case.

10,646. Now, I pass away from that and come to the fourth period, in which you say that Ireland was hit very hard; you suggest that the Committee of 1864 might have made out a stronger case. I think anyone who has examined the matter would see that that is an absolutely non-contentious proposition; but, if you remember, the Committee of 1864, on the British members on it, rejected the Report of Colonel Dunne, the chairman, an Irish member, and adopted the Report of Sir Stafford Northcote against the Irish votes. The Irish members, therefore, were not responsible for the weakness of the case, and the British members did not apparently feel concerned to make out a strong case for Ireland?—I am under the impression that Colonel Dunne's report did not make out a very strong case.

10,647. At the same time it made out a rather stronger case than the case made out by Sir Stafford Northcote?—No doubt that is so.

10,648. Now, in that period you state the rates of taxation per head for Ireland—you say that in Ireland in 1849–50 the rate of indirect taxation per head was [illegible], and it became in 1859–60 [illegible] 7d., so that it nearly doubled?—Yes.

10,649. The direct rate was 1s. [illegible] and became [illegible], so that is nearly trebled?—Yes.

10,650. The total taxation had been [illegible] per head of the population in 1849–50, and it had risen in 1859–60 to [illegible], so that it almost doubled?—Yes.

10,651. Therefore the incidence of taxation in those ten years almost doubled in Ireland?—Yes.

10,652. During a period of diminishing population and of resources not increasing?—Yes.

10,653. Now in Great Britain the indirect taxation per head only increased from [illegible] to [illegible] 7d. and the direct taxation in about the same proportion, from [illegible] to [illegible] per head, so that in Ireland the taxation doubled while in Great Britain it increased but very slightly. Again I would point out to you that the increase of taxation in this period was 11,[illegible] and out of those eleven millions Great Britain, with its ... [illegible] consumption of [illegible], paid only [illegible] of the increase, which, assuming her income to be [illegible] or so, would be one-sixtieth of the income; that Ireland, with an income ... [illegible] of about [illegible] millions, paid two and three quarter millions of the increase, so that she paid one-twenty-second of her income in the increased taxation. It would, therefore, appear to follow that four times as much was exacted in proportion from Ireland as from Great Britain by increased taxation?—Yes, that may be so.

10,654. Then the British taxation within the period increased from [illegible] to 57,[illegible], or by about one-sixth, while the Irish taxation increased from [illegible] millions to 7½ millions, or by about two-thirds, so that there again we see a relative increase four times as great in Ireland as in Great Britain?—Yes.

10,655. Again, I compare this with the period of the separate exchequers—during the 16 years after the Union (when Ireland was so heavily burdened) she paid [illegible] millions a year, and now in this period she has to pay two-thirds as much again, while on the other hand Great Britain in those 16 years paid [illegible] in round ... [illegible] on the annual average. Now, with a population between doubled and trebled, and her wealth still more increased, she pays only about the same sum—57,[illegible]?—Yes.

10,656. Now, regarding the question from the point of view from which we have to consider it, these considerations seem to be conclusive, with regard to the past—the almost immeasurably greater pressure upon Ireland than upon Great Britain?—I think there was much greater pressure relatively upon Ireland than upon Great Britain during that period—undoubtedly so.

10,657. Now I may pass, I think, to the last period, and here you say that Ireland fared very differently from the manner in which she had fared in the preceding period. Did you mean that she fared better?—I meant that instead of having her taxation largely increased relatively to Great Britain, practically it was about the same.

10,658. It was somewhat easier?—Yes.

10,659. Therefore, if the case had been so bad in the preceding period and only because still worse in this last period, how has Ireland fared better?—In this sense—that instead of being very heavily mulcted as she was during those 16 years she was practically no more heavily mulcted at the end of the latest period than she was at the commencement of it.

10,660. Seeing what we have seen with regard to the ... [illegible] into which she had been brought by disproportionate exactions in the preceding period?—No, I put it in this way: that since 1853 there has been no tax imposed upon Ireland and there has been a considerable number of taxes remitted in Ireland; but exactly the reverse happened in the preceding 16 years; very considerable taxation was imposed upon Ireland. Therefore it is fair to say that Ireland has been treated very differently during the last [illegible] years from what she was during the preceding 10 years.

10,661. The reductions have been in Great Britain as in Ireland?—No doubt.

10,662. And the effect of it all is that bad as the taxation of Ireland was in the years from 1853 to [illegible], as shown in the figures just analysed, the incidence of taxation became heavier still in the last period of all, as the rate per head has increased in Ireland and has become lighter in Great Britain, and therefore the tendency, serious as it was in 1853-63, has become severer in the last period?—Relatively.

10,663. I am simply now upon the question of relative incidence?—Just so.

10,664. You point out that the expenditure has greatly increased—from 70,[illegible] to [illegible]—in the last period—the figures are I think [illegible] to [illegible]—but the increase in expenditure was over [illegible], while the increase in taxation was only 17,[illegible], the difference being met by non-tax revenue?—Yes.

10,665. Do you observe that whilst the increase in taxation has been 17,[illegible] a year, the increased amount expended in Great Britain would have been 23,[illegible] a year?—Yes, I am aware of that.

10,666. So that the increase of the burden has been due to increased expenditure in Great Britain?—My point was that practically there had been no increase of taxation.

10,667. We have seen that the taxpayer in Ireland pays more and more as time goes on, and the taxpayer in Great Britain less and less?—Yes, I admit that, but in the last [illegible] years large remissions of taxation have been made which have benefited Ireland; whereas during the preceding 16 years Irish taxation had been largely increased. That is why I said I thought Ireland had been treated very differently in the last period from what she had been in the penultimate period.

10,668. Say what you will about remissions or impositions, if you, as time goes on, find in every successive period that the Irish tax-paying community is paying more per head than he paid in the preceding period and that the British tax paying community is paying less per head, and that the invariable course of taxation is to increase the rate per head put upon the Irish, and to diminish the rate per head in Great Britain, what is that but a continuous hardship upon the one country relatively to the other?—I did not know that it was a hardship to take off taxes. Great Britain may have benefited from the remissions more than Ireland, but my point was that, taking the two periods—the last period and the penultimate period—the last period came out favourably as compared with the penultimate period. The revenue returns show that Ireland contributes more than she did to indirect taxation. How can that be accounted for except by the fact that the consuming power of Ireland has increased?

10,669. By the change of habit?—But surely the change of habit must be synonymous with an increased power of consumption.

10,670. Not necessarily. In the last generation in Ireland people had healthier and better food, and had, therefore, perhaps, less need for stimulants. Now they eat Indian meal, very inferior bread, and when they get out meat it is American bacon of very inferior quality. I think the tendency of the change of habit and of the vastly inferior food may be to create a natural craving for stimulants?—It may be so, but there must undoubtedly be a greater power of consumption now than there was in 18[illegible].

10,671. A greater tendency to consumption?—Yes; a greater consuming power.

10,672. (*Chairman.*) And greater consumption?—Yes, I call it a greater consuming power.

10,673. (*Mr. Sexton.*) Now I submit to you, that if the income of a man is, as it usually is in Ireland, so small that he cannot provide himself with the ordinary comforts of life in less abundance as a man usually can in Great Britain, then the tendency is naturally greater, possibly, in Ireland, or in any poor country, than it would be in Great Britain, or in any wealthy country, to spend, perhaps, a larger proportion of the insufficient income upon indulgences, than it would be in the case where decent comforts, good food, housing, and clothing can be amply provided?—It may be so.

10,674. Have you any doubt that in poor communities, a larger proportion of the income which is inadequate to command a fair supply of the comforts of life is spent upon stimulants, than in wealthy communities?—That is an economic question, which I am afraid I cannot express an opinion upon.

10,675. Even amongst social classes do not you think in the humblest class, where the income is least, the amount spent upon stimulants is larger in proportion to the income than in the case of the wealthier classes?—I do not feel competent to say whether that is or is not so.

10,676. Now, will you look at Sir Grimshaw's table at page 4[illegible] of volume I; do you see there that the average annual value of the crops and stock in the years 1851-55, and also from 18[illegible]-70 was [illegible] a year?—Yes.

10,677. Do you see that the value in 18[illegible] had fallen to [illegible] a year?—Yes.

10,678. And do you bear in mind, that when a particular year was taken and the percentage applied to it, namely, the year 18[illegible], for the purpose of this Commission the valuation for that year was [illegible]?—Yes.

10,679. Which Sir Robert Giffen has brought down to [illegible]. We, therefore have a sum compared with the valuation of [illegible] a year for agricultural

Sir E. W. Hamilton, K.C.B.

[illegible] Nov. 189[illegible]

Fiscal ... [illegible]

Consumption of drugs and ... [illegible]

Sir R. F. [illegible] K.C.B.

8 Nov. 1895.

Consumption of dutiable articles.

produce at the beginning of that very period, of 40,000,000*l.* a year at the present time; there is a diminution of nearly one half, which corresponds with what we know of the variation in prices?—But what is the first test we look to for the prosperity of that country? It is whether dutiable articles are being consumed in greater or smaller quantities—like tobacco, tea, and spirits—and if we find that the consumption is larger, and the revenue derived therefrom is consequently increased, we rightly or wrongly (and I believe Sir Robert Giffen would support me in that) should regard that as the best test of the increased spending power of the population. Therefore, I cannot get over the fact that whereas 35 years ago Ireland was able to spend so much, or rather did spend so much on dutiable articles, she spends relatively a great deal more on them now. I should have thought that that was a complete test of improved spending power.

10,880. The population of Ireland in 1861 was 5,798,000, and by the last census it was 4,700,000, and the income-tax assessments in the same period a reduction approximating to one-half; it is obvious, therefore, upon those figures that the spending power (that is the income after the necessaries of life have been provided) must have been diminished?—But where does the diminution come in?

10,881. Well I have already submitted to you that, whilst you test the prosperity by increased consumption, which may be a actual test in a country in an ordinary economic condition, where the income of the average working man allows him the means to live in comfort, it is not a actual test in a country the ordinary economic condition of which is the receipt of income insufficient for the necessaries of life?—That may be so. I will not dispute that proposition.

10,882. For instance, suppose a man has 1*l.* a week and is able to live in a comfortable house, and provide his family with good clothing and food, is there not a greater likelihood that when a man is struggling for existence in a chronic state of discomfort he is much more likely to spend a larger proportion of his small income upon some indulgence which mitigates privation?—That is quite possible.

Taxation, relative pressure on Great Britain and Ireland.

10,883. Now observe the cumulative effect of this Irish grievance of taxation, and the light it sheds upon the fallacy of regarding periods separately, looking at each period as if no grievance had arisen before. The rate per head in Ireland has increased in this last period from 1*l.* 6*s.* 6*d.* to 1*l.* 8*s.* 10*d.*, and side by side with that fact we have the fact that the British taxation per head has gone down from 2*l.* 12*s.* to 2*l.* 4*s.* 10*d.*?—Yes.

10,884. You have pointed out that between the beginning and end of this period the incidence of indirect taxation had, in the United Kingdom, fallen from 65 to 52 per cent., and in Great Britain, from 62 to 53 per cent.—that is a very substantial fall—the consumer was relieved to the extent of one-sixth of his previous quota; but in Ireland the indirect taxation at the beginning of the period was no less than 81 per cent. of the whole taxation, and it only fell to 78 per cent. Do you perceive that the proportion of Irish revenue still borne by the consumer is no less than three-fourths of the whole; that is to say, it is very considerably more than 65 per cent. and 62 per cent., the proportions borne by the average consumer in the United Kingdom, and in Great Britain respectively, even at the beginning of the period?—That may be so. I was taking the whole of the United Kingdom.

10,885. I should point out, I think, that the decrease in the United Kingdom is almost identical with the decrease in Great Britain, showing that Great Britain has got it all and that Ireland remains substantially in the same condition. Therefore the relief which has been very great to Great Britain has had no effect upon the incidence of taxation as between classes, but it has left the incidence as between classes in Ireland very much the same?—What I meant to indicate was that had it not been for the transfer from indirect to direct taxation which has taken place, Ireland would, as also Great Britain, probably be now having to pay a duty upon sugar and perhaps upon other commodities of that kind, and a higher duty upon tea.

10,886. But if Ireland is so heavily weighted now, how do you affect the argument that she is overweighted already by pointing out that if something else had happened she would be over-weighted more? But surely she is less over-weighted now than she was 35 years ago, in consequence of the remission of such duties as I have mentioned—the reduction of the duty upon tea, and the remission of duty upon sugar.

10,887. I have shown you, and you have admitted, that the only obvious course has been an increase of the rate per head upon the Irish consumer and a decrease of the rate per head upon the British consumer?—Yes.

10,888. The Irish consumer, enjoying a smaller income, has paid more and more per head, and the British consumer, enjoying a larger income, has paid less and less per head—what greater test can there be of the increasingly lighter pressure of taxation upon the one country and the increasingly heavier pressure of taxation upon the other?—I think it is quite fair to say that Great Britain has got greater relief during the last 35 years than Ireland has got, relatively.

10,889. If it be true that the crops and stock have fallen in value in the way indicated by Dr. Grimshaw's table, it is also true, is it not, that the resources of Ireland are actually less now than they were in 1860?—I have no means of being able to say what the actual resources of Ireland were in 1860 and comparing them with what they are now.

10,890. I will give you a very conclusive test in a moment. Take the assessment of income tax; the gross assessment to income tax in 1861–62 was in Great Britain, 299,000,000*l.*, and in Ireland, 21,000,000*l.*—that is, about 1 to 14 of the gross at that time—at the end of the period the assessment in Great Britain had become 673,000,000*l.*, or more than double, and in Ireland it had become 38,000,000*l.* The valuation of land in Ireland has not been lowered with the fall in prices. Therefore you must not take that full increase as having occurred; but even taking it as having occurred, the proportion between the two assessments at the beginning of the period was 1 to 14, and at the end of the period 1 to 18?—Yes, but I understood your point was that the resources of Ireland were actually less now than they were in 1860; while, according to that figure they show that they are more. I will not say largely so, or that there has been any substantial progress, but there is certainly not a diminution.

10,891. There is some apparent increase in the Irish income tax assessment, qualified by the fact just stated as to the valuation of land, but we have seen that the general agricultural returns show a decrease much greater than the increase in the assessment?—Yes.

10,892. Both the tests show a reduction in value approximating towards one-half?—Yes.

10,893. Now, I should like before I pass from this to put to you that the bulk of the benefit to the consumer has fallen to Great Britain, where, as has been shown, scarcely more than half the revenue is now derived from consumption. These are the rates per head within the period. At the beginning of the period the rate per head of indirect taxes in Great Britain was 21*s.* 7*d.*, and it has fallen to 16*s.*, and the indirect rate, which was 15*s.* 5*d.*, has increased to 16*s.* 6*d.* Therefore, the whole effect is that the rate per head has fallen from 45*s.* to 44*s.* 10*d.*, whilst in the same period, following immediately upon another period, of much graver calamity to Ireland, the rate per head of indirect taxation upon Ireland has gone up still further, namely, from 20*s.* 7*d.* to 23*s.*, and the direct from 4*s.* 9*d.* to 6*s.* 10*d.*, and the whole taxation from 25*s.* 4*d.* to 29*s.* 10*d.*?—Yes. I believe those are the figures in my table.

10,894. Now, taking a general view of the period, do we not find this—that within the period the proportion of the income of Ireland to that of Great Britain appears to have fallen off from 1 to 14 to 1 to 18?—Yes, according to the figures you have quoted.

10,895. The taxation, however, notwithstanding that failure in resources, has only decreased by one-tenth in amount, and her population has fallen off one-fifth so that the rates per head are even heavier than in the previous period; whilst in Great Britain the rate per head for consumption is one-fourth lower. At the opening of the last period Great Britain paid about one-twelfth of her income in taxation, and Ireland one-tenth; but at the end of the period, which you consider to have been rather a period of benefit to Ireland, Great Britain was paying only one-twentieth in taxation, but Ireland was paying one-tenth, as before; it is obvious that in the period which you consider to have operated less injuriously to Ireland than those which had gone before the pressure had severely increased; do you not assent to that?—Yes, but my point was that, although Great Britain may have been relieved, and has been relieved, more materially in that period than Ireland, yet there has been a relief to Ireland in the shape of taxation.

10,896. How?—By the remission of the duties I have mentioned.

10,897. A remission made to Great Britain, and therefore not to be withheld from Ireland?—I do not put it in that way.—I should say it was a remission of duty to benefit all parts of the United Kingdom.

10,898. It was a benefit inevitably resulting in some degree to Ireland from the greater benefit to Great Britain?—No doubt.

10,899. But where you find in a country a decreasing population and an increasing burden, an increasing rate per head, can it be looked at otherwise than in the light of an increasing pressure upon the people?—I think you are bound to see what the taxes are.

10,900. The taxes upon consumption?—Yes; but what are the articles consumed?

10,901. Whatever the article is the rate is paid all the same?—But I think it makes a considerable difference what that article is.

10,902. Not to the person who pays the money?—I do not see that. If I have my bread taxed I am bound to pay the tax if I am to keep body and soul together; but I am not bound to go and spend a portion of my very limited means upon articles which are taxed, but which are not absolutely necessaries of life.

10,903. But have I any assurance that if I do not spend it the State will not take it in relation to some other article?—At any rate the State has not done so.

10,904. As I said yesterday, if every Irishman were to give up the consumption of tea, tobacco, spirits, and beer do not you think that an Imperial administration, like yourself, would be ingenious enough next year to procure the same revenue in some other way?—I do not know about that; it would be an extremely difficult matter.

10,905. The question is not whether an individual is bound to buy a particular article or not, but whether the system of taxation which you have devised and carried out takes from one country a larger share of her revenue than it takes from another?—I have admitted that already, and I admit it again.

10,906. Then that being so, questions as to remissions of taxes can in no way affect the question of what is the relative pressure upon the populations now?—Perhaps I and [illegible] not argue the question any more, but I do not think there is any [illegible] difference between us.

10,907. Really, I think there is no difference, because we both agree. I think that however certain taxes may have been lightened 20 or 30 or 40 years ago, at the time of particular remissions in Great Britain and Ireland, if the taxation in Great Britain has gone on decreasing and the taxation in Ireland has gone on increasing since, the force of that fact cannot be affected by that remission which was made 20 or 30 or 40 years ago?—Just so.

10,908. Now again, I submit to you that there is this very remarkable fact. Taking the average population of Great Britain during the 16 years after the Union as, say, 12,000,000, and the average taxation per annum at [illegible]. Great Britain at that time paid £1 13s. 4d. a head per annum taxation; and taking the same period, Ireland paid 13s. 6d. The rate per head in Ireland at that time, when Ireland suffered by comparison, in comparison with Great Britain, was 13s. 6d. for Ireland and £1 13s. 4d. per head for Great Britain; that is, taking the average of the 16 years, the rate was really less than one-[illegible] of what it was in Great Britain. What has been the effect of the course of taxation since? Leaving out of our minds individual questions of the remission of that taxation and looking straight from the opening to the closing of the century, we find that Great Britain, which at the opening of the century paid £1 13s. 4d. per head, now pays £2 to 16d per head. The British taxpayer has been relieved although there is an increased amount of taxation, firstly, by the growth of population, and secondly, by the still greater growth of wealth, to the extent of more than one-half of the levy per capita which was made at the beginning of the century?—Yes, that is so.

10,909. In Ireland, on the other hand, the reverse process has been carried on to double the extent, for Ireland at the opening of the century, when the [illegible] admittedly oppressed her, paid 13s. 6d. per head per annum. Now with a smaller population, and [illegible] no longer [illegible], for her resources have all

a [illegible]

diminished during the last 20 years, she pays £[illegible] 10d. a head, does she not?—Yes; the calculations are, I think, deduced from the statements I have furnished to the Commission.

10,910. The taxation upon the British citizen halved in the century, and the taxation upon the Irish citizen doubled. In your own returns in the second volume, not taking averages at all, but taking two individual years, the first immediately after the close of the period of the separate Exchequers and the second now, we find that, that in 1819-20 the consumer in Great Britain paid £[illegible] 7d. per head, and now he pays 11s. 1d., exactly half?—Yes.

10,911. The taxes upon property in Great Britain were [illegible], and now they are £1 [illegible]; so that a close summary of the taxation in the case of Great Britain shows that the citizen who pays on property in Great Britain pays less than he did in the beginning of the century, and the consumer pays one-half of what he did then?—Yes, that is so.

10,912. On the other hand, in Ireland not only has the tax upon consumption increased from 11s. to [illegible], but the tax upon property has increased from [illegible] to [illegible] 10d., also exactly double?—That is so.

10,913. Passing away from that, I now wish to put one or two questions to you upon the adjustment of revenue. The Commission may be expected to report what is the total revenue of Ireland, and, by means of this labyrinth of Treasury adjustment, you have taken [illegible] a year off the revenue of Ireland as collected?—Yes, it comes to about that.

10,914. This adjustment has had a very [illegible] and varying effect. In the years following the consolidation of the Exchequers and up to 1870 the effect of the adjustment was to increase the contribution, was it not?—Yes, it was.

10,915. You added 1,[illegible] at first, and that gradually dwindled down to nothing, in 1870 and since then you have been deducting sums, small at first, but which have increased now to [illegible]?—Yes.

10,916. As you have quoted a politician of much distinction, Mr. Goschen, in regard to the question of considering expenditure in connection with taxation and the common plan of classifying expenditure into Imperial and local, I should like to mention another distinguished name in connection with adjustment of revenue. Do you remember that in 1893 Mr. Gladstone, in one of his speeches on the Home Rule Bill, stated that having regard to all that had occurred, it would be just and equitable to regard the revenue collected in Ireland as being the revenue of Ireland?—Yes. I am aware that he then imposed upon Ireland a much heavier contribution to Imperial expenditure in consequence of being unable to distinguish between the amount collected in Ireland and the amount Ireland actually paid. In 1886 he proposed to place upon Ireland a much lighter charge than what he did in 1893, because he was able, according to the best figures we could put before him, to arrive at what we considered to be the true revenue of Ireland. The two plans really came out almost identical, so far as Ireland was concerned.

10,917. Although he adopted another mode of computation in 1893, he took care that the amount to be taken from Ireland in that year, although computed upon the adjusted revenue, was not to be more than the amount that would be taken under the Bill of 1886, when the credit was given to her, did he not?—Yes, when he introduced the first Bill he did not think he had figures upon which to compute the true revenue of Ireland; but in the second Bill, after having considered the question for about two years, we were able to place some figures before him which he accepted as a fair approximation of Ireland's true revenue.

10,918. In the first scheme he took the proportion of Imperial charges, or of certain Imperial charges, and in the second scheme he took, not the Imperial charges, but the Irish revenue?—That was the second scheme specified by the Bill of 1893.

10,919. But he took care in the second Bill that the amount to be taken from Ireland should not be more than the amount to be taken under the plan upon which the Irish revenue was to be regarded as the revenue collected in Ireland, did he not?—Yes.

10,920. Does it not appear to you as rather hard in dealing between a wealthy country, such as Great Britain, and a poor and [illegible] country, such as Ireland, that [illegible] amount should be taken of the

Sir E. W. Hamilton, K.C.B.

12 Nov. 1895.

Adjustment of "true" revenue.

consumption of every pound of tobacco and every glass of spirits?—I do not see how it is possible to arrive at the incidence of taxation without it.

10,921. I should have thought that, in considerations of revenue between two such countries, the revenue collected might be allowed to stand as the revenue of Ireland?—It would be very misleading, I think.

10,922. Whilst on these various memoranda you explain so carefully the processes—and they are very various—it would be hardly possible for any except a Committee of experts sitting for a long time and having direct access to records and correspondence to check the Treasury work?—I do not think there is any very great element of doubt in them. The real practical question that affects Ireland is the adjustment of the spirit duty, and though we are aware that there was a blunder made some years ago, yet I believe that at the present time it may reasonably be assumed that the figures arrived at by the "permit" system are accurate. If the permit system is worked properly, it ought to be possible to trace the spirit revenue very accurately, and the principal factor in the whole revenue is the spirit revenue.

10,923. Tobacco and tea are very important, are they not?—They are important, no doubt.

10,924. Beer is also very important; and with regard to the spirit duty we are told that there were great errors up to 1888, and also in 1892-93; and upon the whole I am disposed to think that all we can do is to report that the Treasury Estimates are "expert and skilful conjectures," as you have described Sir Robert Giffen's evidence. Of course, if the question should become urgent, I should think there would be no difficulty in devising means for making a reliable partition of the revenue?—I do not think anything short of a Customs cordon would answer the purpose; at least nothing short of that would secure accuracy. Even then I do not think you could follow the entire revenue. For instance, I believe there is a certain amount of tea that goes into Ireland by the Parcel Post. How can you check that? However that may be, as I have already said, I do not think anything short of a Customs barrier would enable you to get accurate figures, but my belief is that they would not be materially different from the ones we have laid before you.

10,925. The question remains whether the true revenue of Ireland should be, as Mr. Gladstone held it should be, taken as the revenue collected there, or whether it should be taken as revenue adjusted upon your present plan?—But may I just say that I have a distinct recollection that the reason why he credited Ireland with the collected revenue in 1886, was that he had no figures to go upon at that time relating to true revenue. He was always anxious to take the true revenue of Ireland if he could.

10,926. I beg pardon, but I also have a very distinct memory of it, and that Mr. Gladstone distinctly stated that the balance of revenue against Ireland by adjustment was 1,400,000*l.* at that time?—I have no doubt that, if in 1886 the figures of true revenue had been obtainable, Mr. Gladstone would have adopted them.

10,927. Mr. Gladstone distinctly stated that the part of the revenue attributable to Ireland by reason of being taken as collected instead of as adjusted upon your present plan was 1,400,000*l.* at that time, did he not?—Yes.

10,928. And it would have been perfectly open to him to have deducted that sum, would it not?—It was too conjectural a sum, he could not possibly divide it under heads. We had never gone into the question of true revenue at that time, so he had nothing to go upon.

10,929. He could have enacted, or proposed to enact, in the Bill, that the contribution, whatever it was, should be deducted out of a revenue taken as adjusted, but he did not propose to do that; on the contrary, knowing the balance against Ireland to be 1,400,000*l.* a year, he decided that it was just and expedient, having regard to what had occurred between the two countries in finance, that the revenue of the country should be taken as collected there?—He would have taken it the other way if he had been able to do so in 1886.

10,930. I can only judge from his public action, and when it came to 1893 he took care that the amount to be taken from Ireland should be only the same as that taken under the previous plan, allowing the revenue to be taken as collected?—Yes, the two plans were practically identical. In the first place, Ireland was credited with more revenue and paid a larger contribution to Imperial expenditure. In the second place, she was credited with less revenue and debited with a much smaller contribution to Imperial charges.

10,931. Then the final question with which I have to trouble you relates to the management of the debt at the time of the Union?—I am afraid I may not know much about that.

10,932. I first desire to put one or two figures to you which I have extracted from the National Debt Report, which show that the debt of Ireland at the Union, after deducting debt redeemed up to the Union, was 28,000,000*l.*, and that the debt of Great Britain at the same time, after deducting debt redeemed up to that time, was 446,000,000*l.* These figures are correct, are they not?—Yes, I have no doubt they are.

10,933. The debts redeemed up to that time were deducted in computing the amount of debt existing at the time. I mean the gross debt contracted up to that time was not taken, but the debt remaining after deduction of debt redeemed?—Yes.

10,934. Now, in 1817, the debt of Ireland, after deducting the debt redeemed, was 112,000,000*l.*, was it not?—Yes, that is so.

10,935. And the debt of Great Britain after deducting the debt redeemed, was 737,000,000*l.*, and it appears that in the period between the Union and 1817 there was redeemed of Irish debt 27,000,000*l.* Do you note that figure?—Yes.

10,936. And 234,000,000*l.* of British debt redeemed?—Yes.

10,937. Now, as I conceive, the keynote of the whole question of the treatment of the debt was struck by Lord Castlereagh in his speech in introducing the Articles, when he said, "Ireland is to have no concern whatever "with the past debt of Great Britain," and then he adds, "but as to the future it is expected that "the two countries should move forward together and "unite with regard to their expenses in the measure of "their relative abilities," and later on he proceeds to explain the paragraph in Article 7, which deals with the event in which the debts might be consolidated and common taxation enacted; and you refer in your memorandum at page 377 to that passage in his speech, but when you come to the point at which he deals with the matter by illustration, you say, "But the figures "which he cited in support of his argument are not "easy to follow." I would submit to you that the figures you have described as "not easy to follow," are the figures about which we can have no shadow of doubt that they prove the purpose of the Act of Union to have been that only the debts incurred in each country previous to the Union should be counted in determining whether there ought to be common taxation?—That may be so.

10,938. These are the words of Lord Castlereagh; he was arguing upon the provision to be made for common taxes in case the debts came in to a certain proportion to each other, and he said, "I shall endeavour to obviate "an suggestion which may be made, that common "taxes with Great Britain will impose upon this kingdom heavier burdens than she would otherwise be "called upon to support. Let the House then first "consider that the charges of the debt of Great Britain "amount to 20,000,000*l.* a year" (it was twenty-one millions a year), "and the charges of the debt of Ireland "to 1,300,000*l.* British, a year; that common taxes are "not to take place, till either the past and separate "debts of both countries shall be liquidated, or till they "shall become to each other in the proportion of their "contributions, that is, in the ratio of 15 to 2." You does not he there clearly explain it that until the debts incurred before the Union have come into the proportion of 15 to 2 the consolidation could not occur, and common taxes could not be enacted?—I admit that I think that may be inferred from the speech.

10,939. And he makes it clearer still because he goes on to say, "before this can take place" (that is before common taxes can be enacted) "the taxes of Great "Britain must be reduced by the amount of ten millions "a year," that is to say, that the charge of 21,000,000*l.* should come down to about one half?—Yes.

10,940. That does not that mean that the debt of Great Britain would be reduced from 450,000,000*l.* to 200,000,000*l.*, and so come into the proportion of 15 to 2 to the Irish debt of 28 millions existing before the Union?—Yes, I presume so.

10,941. And then he goes on, "in which case the scale of her remaining taxation would be lowered to the scale of taxation in Ireland, and the adoption of British taxation would become a benefit, a similar result would take place, and in a greater degree, were the past debts of the two countries to be entirely liquidated; for, in that case, Ireland would be exempted from taxes to the amount of 1,[illegible] a year, and Britain to the amount of 20 millions; and the system of common taxation would become still more beneficial to Ireland." Is it not absolutely clear that in that explanation of the Bill, Lord Castlereagh had it clear that the debts of the two countries could not be amalgamated, and common taxation could not take the place of the proportionate system until the debts of the two countries incurred before the Union were brought to bear to each other the proportion of 15 to 2, or else extinguished altogether?—I think that is a fair inference to draw from the speech.

10,942. Now let us turn to Article 7. The first paragraph of that Article provides that the charge for the previous debt of each country should be a separate charge?—Yes.

10,943. Then I pass to paragraph 8, "That all moneys to be raised after the Union, by loan, in peace or war, for the service of the United Kingdom by the Parliament thereof, shall be considered to be a joint debt." Is not that a clear declaration of principle?—Yes, but the article is referring to debt incurred for the service of the "United Kingdom."

10,944. "That all moneys to be raised after the Union by loan, in peace or war, for the service of the United Kingdom by the Parliament thereof, shall be considered to be a joint debt"?—Yes, "United Kingdom"—not Great Britain or Ireland.

10,945. No, but a contribution to the joint expenditure by way of loans would be for the service of the United Kingdom?—No doubt.

10,946. Therefore, any debt incurred for the purpose of enabling either country to make up its contribution to the joint expenditure was a debt for the service of the United Kingdom, was it not?—Yes.

10,947. Therefore the general principle is laid down in accord with Lord Castlereagh's unmistakeable declaration, that debt subsequent to the Union was not to be separate debt but joint debt, a joint and inseparable debt falling as a charge upon the common expenditure?—I think it would have been impossible to have carried out the terms of the treaty under such an arrangement.

10,948. But that is the general principle, is it not, laid down by Lord Castlereagh?—Yes, for the service of the United Kingdom, but not if raised upon British account or Irish account.

10,949. But you have admitted that all sums required for the joint expenditure and raised by borrowing, were for the service of the United Kingdom?—Yes.

10,950. Here there are two exceptions, "provided that if at any time, the respective contributions hereby fixed for each country the Parliament of the United Kingdom shall judge it fit to raise a greater proportion of such respective contributions in one country within the year than in the other, or to set apart a greater proportion of sinking fund for the liquidation of the whole or any part of the loan raised on account of the one country than of that raised on account of the other country, then such part of the said loan, for the liquidation of which different provisions shall have been made for the respective countries, shall be kept distinct, and shall be borne by each separately, and only that part of the said loan be deemed joint and common, for the reduction of which the respective countries shall have made provision in the proportion of their respective contributions." Now, where was the difficulty in carrying out that provision?—It would have been impossible, as far as I can see, to have extracted from Ireland her quota, unless Ireland had been subjected to taxation in the [illegible] proportion.

10,951. But neither country found it in any year out of taxation?—No, but Great Britain was able to raise a much larger proportion out of taxation. I quite admit that it is a difficult point. I put the case as clearly as I could in my original memorandum, and I re-stated the case as it presents itself to me in the remarks I made the other day. I said, "I venture to think that "it was clear that had she not been debited with that "charge, she would have largely evaded the provisions "of the Treaty. As it was, considerably less in the "way of war taxes was imposed on Ireland than on "Great Britain; and, had Ireland been only required "to pay two-seventeenths of the charge in respect of "debt created on her account, she need scarcely have "imposed any additional taxation with which to meet "the great war expenditure. The Treaty did not contemplate—and it is not surprising that it did not contemplate—such a long drawn-out struggle with France, "but neither could it surely have been intended that, "if Ireland did not provide her quota out of the "proceeds of taxes, she was only to bear less than 12 per "cent. of the charge for borrowing the money with "which to pay her quota." That is the only alternative as far as I can see.

10,952. It must have been quite as apparent when the Act of Union was drawn as it is now, that the contributions of Great Britain and Ireland from taxation to joint expenditure would never have been in any year exactly in the proportion of 15 to 2, because Great Britain had a debt charge of 21,000,000l., and Ireland had only a debt charge of 1,000,000l., and these charges had to be paid by each country out of its revenue first, and therefore the fact that Great Britain and Ireland had to withdraw such different sums from the revenue before contributing the balance of revenue to joint expenditure, made it evidently very easy to foresee that the contributions of each country from taxes to joint expenditure would never in any year be in the proportion of 15 to 2?—That may have been so. I think it is impossible to say exactly what was intended by the framers of the Treaty upon that point.

10,953. The debt charges being so dissimilar, and having to be deducted first from the revenue, it follows that the proportion of revenue in each country available for joint expenditure would never be 15 to 2?—That I admit.

10,954. If the contributions from revenue to joint expenditure were not made in the proportion of 15 to 2, the balance of joint expenditure to be met by loans would be also dissimilar, would they not?—Yes.

10,955. Suppose that in the year after the Union the joint expenditure required was 34,000,000l. Great Britain's share of that would be 30,000,000l., and Ireland's share of it would be 4,000,000l. Suppose Great Britain, after paying her separate debt charge, had 15 millions of revenue to spare for joint expenditure, and contributed 15 millions out of taxes of the 30 millions she had to pay, that would leave her bound to borrow 15 millions; and supposing Ireland, towards her share of four millions, contributed out of taxes only one million, that would leave her in the position of borrowing three millions, so that 18 millions would have to be borrowed. Was not it the obvious intention of this Act that 17 millions of that 18 millions should be charged to joint debt, being in the proportion of 15 to 2, that the 17 millions should be joint debt, and that the balance of one million should be treated as the separate debt of Ireland?—I cannot say that I read it in that way; but the article itself is by no means clear.

10,956. I think it is. You admit the general principle was that all moneys raised after the Union, in peace or war, for joint expenditure, were for the service of the United Kingdom?—Yes, if the words "joint expenditure" had been used, I think it would have been different.

10,957. The debt was contracted, was it not, in respect of joint expenditure?—No, the debt was contracted in respect of Irish account, and in respect of British account. What they could not manage to provide out of taxation, wherewith to meet their contributions, they had to borrow.

10,958. But it was to make provision for the joint expenditure?—Yes, but the words "joint expenditure" are not in the article.

10,959. But there was no other service of the United Kingdom except the joint expenditure?—I am afraid I place a different interpretation upon the provision.

10,960. The service of the United Kingdom was, and could have been, nothing else than the joint expenditure; there was no other service of the United Kingdom than the joint expenditure?—That was so.

10,961. Therefore, the contribution of Ireland to joint expenditure was service of the United Kingdom?—No, not necessarily so. I see a distinction.

10,962. Where is it?—There is the general expenditure, and the expenditure which Ireland had to meet,

Sir E. W. Hamilton, K.C.B. [illegible]

18 Nov. 1895.

Act of Union, Art. 7, par. [illegible]

Mr. A. W. Samuels, Q.C. [illegible]

and which Great Britain had to meet respectively, representing their quotas. Now if Ireland or Great Britain had, in order to enable them to meet their quotas, to borrow, it seems to me that it was not for the service of the United Kingdom, but for the service of Great Britain or Ireland respectively.

10,963. But the article says: "That all moneys to be "raised after the Union by loan, in peace or war, for "the service of the United Kingdom by the Parliament "thereof, shall be considered to be a joint debt"?—Yes, that may be. I have just said what construction I put upon the provision.

10,964. Can you show me that any difficulty would have arisen if, in the case of a loan of 18,000,000l., of which 16,000,000l. was the share of Great Britain and 2,000,000l. the share of Ireland, 17,000,000l. being in the proportion of 15 to 2, had been treated as a joint debt, and the balance of 1,000,000l. as a separate debt of Ireland?—I think I described in detail the effect of joint borrowing in my original memorandum.

10,965. (Mr. Currie.) If the debt were not to be a separate debt, you put it, I assume, as part of the argument, that the contribution of Ireland would be up the ratio of 2 to 15?—Yes.

10,966. That was part of the bargain. When Lord Castlereagh said that all future debt was to be not a separate but a joint debt, did he not mean on the condition that the Act of Union should be carried out—that is to say that Ireland should contribute in the ratio of 2 to 15?—I think so. I see I explained in my original memorandum what my idea was of the result of working the provision by joint borrowing, and I illustrated it with figures. Perhaps as Mr. Sexton has used very much the same figures as I did, I may be allowed to quote what I said: "Let it be "assumed that the joint expenditure to which Great "Britain and Ireland had to contribute in a particular "year amounted to 34,000,000l. Accordingly Great "Britain's share would have been 30,000,000l., and "Ireland's share 4,000,000l. Let it further be assumed "that after the payment of the separate charges of "Ireland, the balance of her revenue did not exceed "2,000,000l. Consequently, the other two millions "required to make up her contribution would have had "to be borrowed. Now if it be held that this loan "could only be a joint debt, and if the charge on "account of it was 5 per cent., Ireland's share of the "charge would have been two-seventeenths of 100,000l., "or 11,764l., and the rest of the charge would have "fallen on Great Britain. Accordingly, Great Britain "would have had to contribute in the year, not "30,000,000l., but 30,088,235l., and Ireland would only "have contributed 3,911,765l., instead of 4,000,000l.; "while the future liability of Great Britain would have "permanently increased, and that of Ireland permanently diminished." That was the interpretation I put upon it.

10,967. (Mr. Sexton.) In the first place, you imagine a case that never occurred, where 34,000,000l. being required for joint expenditure, Great Britain paid all her share out of revenue, and Ireland paid only half out of revenue, and borrowed 2,000,000l.; but what occurred every year was this, that both countries borrowed, Great Britain in a lesser proportion than Ireland, and that was foreseen by the article, because it was necessarily foreseen that the contributions of the two countries from revenue to joint expenditure could never be in the proportion of 15 to 2. Nevertheless, with this clearly manifest, the general principle was laid down that all moneys to be borrowed were to be joint debt, and that the excess of either country over her due proportion should be separate debt. The article says clearly, that so much of the debt as is incurred by either country over her due proportion, should be her separate debt. Now, in the case you have put, if Great Britain borrowed nothing, she would incur no debt, and if Ireland borrowed 2,000,000l., that was a separate debt, but this is an imaginary case; it never occurred. In the ordinary case that arose from year to year both Great Britain and Ireland had to borrow to make up the joint expenditure. What this article declares is that the whole of what Great Britain borrowed, and as much of that was borrowed to make up the Irish quota as amounted to two-fifteenths of the sum borrowed by Great Britain, should have been joint debt; what was the difficulty in doing that?—I do not wish to set my opinion against yours. I have only stated how I read the provision. You put one construction upon it, I put another. It is a difficult point I admit.

10,968. In my opinion, the dealing with the debts in 1816 discloses a tampering unparalleled in the annals of national finance?—That may be. I do not venture to say what was at the time in the minds of the authors of the treaty.

10,969. Your argument is that if what was done had not been done, Ireland would have been relieved of a charge?—Yes.

10,970. Suppose 18,000,000l. to be borrowed in any year, England having to borrow 10,000,000l. and Ireland 8,000,000l., and supposing 17,000,000l. of that had been treated as joint debt, would not Ireland have borne her proportion of 2 to 15?—Yes, but I do not see how Ireland would have fared better.

10,971. If there were 18,000,000l. to be borrowed in the year, and Great Britain's share of it was 15,000,000l. and Ireland's share 2,000,000l., it follows that Ireland's proportion would have been 2,000,000l.; and supposing that 17,000,000l. had been treated as joint debt, Ireland would have paid that 2,000,000l., would she not?—Certainly.

10,972. Where, then, would occur the injustice, the joint debt would be fixed in the due proportion, and therefore would be borne in due proportion by the joint charge?—Yes, but I do not see what the answer is to the argument about joint borrowing.

10,973. What argument?—The argument I put forward in my original memorandum.

10,974. But yours is a supposititious case that never arose at all in the 16 years?—If I had taken different figures I would have shown that the result would have been the same to Ireland.

10,975. But you are taking a case that never arose in the 16 years, and as to which, if it did arise, the 2,000,000l. borrowed there would be the separate debt of Ireland; but I am taking a case that arose in every year, where there was borrowing by both countries, in a lesser proportion by Great Britain, and in a greater proportion by Ireland, and my contention is that in the clear language of the article, the rule ought to have been, and if it be so construed, that so much as Great Britain borrowed, together with so much of what Ireland borrowed as bore to the British borrowing, the proportion of 2 to 15, should have been treated as joint debt, but that such part of the Irish borrowing as exceeded the proportion should have been borne as the separate debt of Ireland?—That may be so. I think it is extremely difficult to go back upon that now after so many years have elapsed.

10,976. Has your attention been turned at all to paragraph 8, where it says that after the common taxes were remitted, the interest of "charges which may accrue "on account of any part of the separate debt with which "either country shall be chargeable and which shall not "be consolidated in [illegible] proportionably as above, "shall, until extinguished, continue to be defrayed by "separate taxes in each country." What does that mean?—I think it may be open to the construction that you put upon it, but I do not think it could possibly have been so worked in a practical way.

10,977. I assure you it could?—I think there probably would have been difficulty in doing so.

10,978. Lord Castlereagh said in the first place, did he not, that only the debts before the Union were to be remitted with a view to consolidation?—Yes.

10,979. If the Act had been carried out as intended, and if the British borrowing, and so much of the Irish borrowing as bore to the British the proportion of 2 to 15, had been made joint debt, that debt being joint would have been inseparable, and could not have been added to the pre-Union debts of Ireland and of Great Britain?—That is so.

10,980. Therefore, that Act was so administered that, instead of doing what the Act directed, and instead of making the borrowing of each year in the proportion of 15 to 2 the joint debt of the United Kingdom, every penny of the money borrowed after the Union was placed to the separate account of Great Britain or Ireland, in direct violation of the general rule laid down in the Act?—That may be, but I would rather not argue the point.

10,981. If in a year in which say 18,000,000l. were borrowed, 10,000,000l., the share of Great Britain, and 8,000,000l., the share of Ireland, 17,000,000l. of it had been put to the joint account, and 1,000,000l. to the separate account of Ireland, would any injustice have been done?—No; but the borrowing was not worked in that way.

10,982. Why not?—Because Ireland was not able to produce so much increase as Great Britain relatively, and therefore she always had to borrow proportionately more.

10,983. In each year there was a deficit in each country, was there not?—Yes, but I am afraid I do not follow your argument.

10,984. Will you kindly address yourself to the question I am putting to you. Was not there a deficit in each country in each year at the [illegible]?—Yes.

10,985. Was not each country obliged to borrow in each year?—Yes, certainly.

10,986. If the borrowing to the extent of 15 to 2 had been treated as joint debt, would not Ireland have borne every penny of the full charge upon her, and would not Great Britain have been relieved of any charge, except what she ought to bear?—Apparently, no injustice would have been done.

10,987. I will put the borrowing in any year at whatever amount you please, but what the Act of Union contemplated was this: That the proportion of 15 to 2 should have been joint debt; one country must have exceeded that proportion, or the other, and whichever country exceeded it, such part of the said loan, in the language of the Act, should have been taken as separate borrowing, and the borrowing of the two countries in the proportion of 15 to 2 should have been treated as joint debt, and that joint debt could never have been counted in with the pre-Union debt in order to consolidate the [illegible] [illegible] a [illegible] of a separate debt arising in each year, because the Act provided that such debt, even after the amalgamation and the institution of common taxes, should continue to be separately charged?—Yes, that may be so.

10,988. I submit, therefore, to you, in the first place, that the intention declared by Lord Castlereagh was obviously not carried out, because he said that only the debts before the Union should be considered, and that consolidation could not occur except the pre-Union debt of Great Britain was brought down to such a proportion as to be 15 to 2 to the debt of Ireland before the Union?—Or the Irish debt was raised.

10,989. No, certainly, not at all. What Lord Castlereagh said was, that until the British debt-charge was reduced by 11,000,000*l.* a year, consolidation could not take place. In other words, that it was only by reduction of the British debt, and not by increase of the Irish debt, that the consolidation could occur. Now, I say that in violation of the purpose declared by Lord Castlereagh and in violation of the Act itself, the Imperial Government in 1816, instead of considering only the pre-Union debts of both countries, which were to be the measure of consolidation, and instead of deducting from those debts the amount redeemed in the meantime up to 1816, treated the whole debt incurred after the Union by both countries, declared by the Act to be joint debt, as separate debt, thereby adding 113,000,000*l.* to the debt of Ireland, and professed to have brought it into the proportion of 15 to 2 with the debt of Great Britain in a manner [illegible] [illegible] either with the declarations of Lord Castlereagh, or, what is more important, with the [illegible] enactment in the Act itself?—That may be so.

10,990. Your view is different?—It is different; but, I think, only slightly different.

10,991. May I understand that, before the Commission conclude their inquiry, you will be willing to enter more closely into this particular section of the debt?—I will gladly reconsider it again, and, if I can satisfy myself that I can come to a different conclusion, I shall be quite happy to do so.

10,992. There are two questions which I should like you to consider, firstly, whether it was necessary, for a due distribution of the charges under the proportions, to charge all debt incurred after the Union as separate debt or only the amount required by either country in any year in excess of her due proportion?—Yes; I understand.

10,993. Or, might not the prescribed proportions of the charges have been duly apportioned between the two countries, if the debt in the proportion of 15 to 2 had been joint, and only any excess of borrowing by either country had been treated as separate debt?—I will consider that point.

10,994. The other question is whether any other debt except the debt incurred before the Union in either country should have been dealt with in the calculations of 1816 with a view to the establishment of common taxes and the consolidation of the Exchequers?—I will also consider that point.[*]

10,995. (*The O'Conor Don.*) Returning to the subject upon which you were first examined, there are three or four questions that I should like to put to you. I understand your contention now is, that while you admit that the taxation of Ireland is excessive, you consider that that excessive taxation is met, by expenditure for what you call local objects?—I would rather say, mitigated.

10,996. And I think you further hold that it is by this system of expenditure upon local objects that the mitigation of the excessive taxation can best be met?—I think it is one of the most practical ways of meeting it, if not the only way.

10,997. I think you further admitted, in answer to some questions I asked you upon the last occasion, that to a certain extent, the expenditure in Ireland is useless and extravagant?—Yes.

10,998. But so far as it is useless and extravagant, you surely would not set that off against the excess of taxation?—Perhaps not; but it is extremely difficult to express an opinion as to how much of the expenditure in Ireland represents extravagant expenditure.

10,999. Another portion of that expenditure I am sure you will admit is expenditure that would have to be incurred whether the taxation of Ireland was excessive or not?—No doubt.

11,000. For instance, supposing the spirit duties were done away with, and the tax upon tea abolished, and that in place of these some direct taxes were imposed, the result probably would be that the contribution of Ireland to the Imperial revenue would not be excessive?—That would probably be so.

11,001. If such a thing as that happened, is it not a fact that a very large proportion of that expenditure, for what you term local purposes, would still have to be met?—That might be so.

11,002. And so far as that is concerned, will you not also admit that that should not be placed against the excess of taxation?—I think it is very difficult to say how far any general contention about relief by expenditure can be qualified.

11,003. Will you not admit that a very large proportion, at least ought to be deducted from that local expenditure upon the ground that it is local expenditure that would have to be incurred whether the contribution of Ireland to Imperial taxation was excessive or not?—I admit that when once incurred, a great part of the expenditure would practically not admit of being put an end to.

11,004. You see you set off this local expenditure as a justification or a mitigation of the excess of taxation, is it not clear that you should not include in that set-off anything which you would not be justified in using as a set-off against a special tax upon Ireland?—It may perhaps be put in that way.

11,005. And if the revenue in Ireland were raised in such a manner as not to produce from Ireland more than in proportion to her resources, a very large proportion of this so-called local expenditure is of a nature that would still have to be borne, is it not?—I presume so.

11,006. And consequently cannot be used as a set-off against the excess of taxation?—However that may be, my real point was to show what Ireland was contributing towards Imperial expenditure, and how far such contribution was proportionate to her resources.

11,007. But I am sure you will admit that that portion of it which must necessarily be incurred as part of the Imperial expenditure, whether the Irish contribution is excessive or not, cannot be regarded as any set-off for excess of taxation?—I have admitted that to the extent of half the Constabulary charge.

11,008. Now, with regard to loans, on a former occasion when you were before us, it appeared that the average interest which the Treasury now charges upon loans is 3*l.* 11*s.* per cent., and you stated upon that occasion

Sir R. Giffen, K.C.B. [illegible] Nov. 1895. [illegible] [illegible] Expenditure and taxation in Ireland.

[*] See [illegible] statement by Sir E. Hamilton, in Appendix II., page 185.

Sir E. W. Hamilton, K.C.B. — 16 Nov. 1894. — Expenditure and revenue in Ireland.

that that interest could not be credited without loss to the local loans fund account, it appeared also, from your observation, that a sum of 130,000*l*. a year is set apart out of the income of those loans for the purpose of recouping the Exchequer for bad debts in former times?—Yes, that is so.

11,009. Then what would be the effect of doing away with that 130,000*l*. a year as regards the rate at which loans might be made; have you considered that if that 130,000*l*. a year was not set apart, loans could be made at a lower rate of interest, and if so, what would be the reduction that might be made if that 130,000*l*. a year were given up?—I think it would admit of a general reduction of about one quarter per cent.

11,010. What is the gross capital of the Local Loans Fund?—£3,000,000*l*.

11,011. How was this 130,000*l*. arrived at; why was that sum taken?—I think it was taken in this way—when Mr. Goschen established the Local Loans Fund, which was a great administrative improvement, he looked at the income and expenditure side of the account, and finding that there was or ought to be a margin, he thought it was fair that such margin, amounting to about 130,000*l*. a year, should be appropriated as a fund whereby the Exchequer might be recouped for losses previously incurred.

11,012. He did not make an estimate founded on any particular amount of bad debts?—No; as it was only a rough estimate.

11,013. He had no table of those bad debts made out, I suppose?—Yes, there was a table made out, showing what losses there had been. This 130,000*l*. a year may be regarded as a sort of additional sinking fund, which is paid over to the National Debt Commissioners, who cancel stock with it, and after so many years they would have cancelled stock sufficient to represent the amount of the losses that had been lost.

11,014. But in order to ascertain that, you must ascertain what were the losses that were lost, must you not?—Yes, and we made a calculation, and struck out all the Irish losses connected with the Irish famine.

11,015. Could you give us a table of the losses against which that 130,000*l*. was set?—Yes, it did not go into any great detail, but I can give you the calculation, I think.

11,016. (*Chairman*.) You mentioned, in answer to Mr. Sexton, that you had made some estimate of the expenditure upon all commodities in Ireland; have you any paper upon the subject, that you can give the Commission?—I have a rough estimate, which is at the disposal of the Commission. Of course I am only a statistician, and I do not know whether it is worth your while to use what I have made out, but if there is no objection to my putting in this table I will do so, with the permission of the Commission. It is partly made up from revenue figures, and also partly from Sir Robert Giffen's figures.

11,017. Will you be good enough to put it in as a memorandum?—Yes, I am afraid it may cause some controversial points, but I think it is rather interesting, and for what it is worth it shall be handed in.

The witness withdrew.

Adjourned for a short time.

Sir Robert Giffen, K.C.B., further examined.

Sir Robert Giffen, K.C.B. — 16 Nov. 1894. — Expenditure and revenue in Ireland.

11,018. (*Chairman*.) You have, I believe, been informed of the reason for which you have been asked to attend the Commission again?—I understand it to be the wish of the Commission, owing to some statements which had been made (especially with regard to my evidence as to the distinction between Imperial and local services), that I should look up my evidence and make a further statement upon the subject.

11,019. Your attention has been called to the criticisms in the course of the evidence made by Sir Edward Hamilton upon your statements as to Government expenditure in Ireland—a question has arisen as to your exact meaning, and we should be glad if you would give us a further explanation?—I understood that the Commission wished me to make a statement upon that point, and the substance of what I wish to say amounts to this, that what I said before was this, in a question of relative contributions and relative taxable capacity, you ought not to take account of the expenditure, because all the expenditure out of the Imperial Exchequer ought to be for the general benefit of the whole community governed. You ought not to make arbitrary distinctions between objects of expenditure and call some Imperial and some local, and then deduct from the taxation what you call "local expenditure," so as to show the contributions by two parts of the community to what you call Imperial expenditure. I say that because, as a matter of fact, you cannot make a distinction between what is Imperial and what is local, and your distinction is purely arbitrary, and I gave as an illustration the distinction attempted in the Treasury returns between military and police expenditure, the former being called Imperial and the latter local. I pointed out that, so far as internal government is concerned, both military expenditure and police expenditure is for precisely the same objects, namely the maintenance of civil order and repression of crime, and there is no distinction between them in their nature. If the one is Imperial, the other is Imperial. If the one is local, so far as civil government is concerned, then the other is local also, but there is no distinction in their nature between them. I pointed out that the distinction attempted between them, based on the fact that the expenditure in the one case is local and in the other case is not local, is really not sound. A large part of military expenditure is local; it is local in Ireland, and so long as there is a United Kingdom, the Imperial Government must spend whatever is necessary, whether on military or police as a mere detail. And I think I might go further now, and point out that even as regards naval expenditure, which, at first sight, you would not think is local to any part of the country, as a matter of fact, a certain part of naval expenditure is local. You have the coastguard service, for instance; you have a certain amount of appropriation of the naval forces to the protection of local fisheries; and I think in time of war you would find that a considerable part of your naval expenditure would have to be local according to the exigencies of particular localities. So that, altogether, I was led to the conclusion that this so-called distinction between Imperial and local services in the expenditure out of the Imperial Exchequer is purely arbitrary, and does not amount to anything, and therefore you cannot proceed to deduct what you call the expenditure on local services from taxation so as to show what goes for the other services which you describe as Imperial; that that is an improper procedure altogether.

11,020. Is this argument of yours traversed by what Sir Edward Hamilton has stated?—I think not. I think Sir Edward Hamilton confined himself very much to showing that certain services connected with the internal civil administration were obviously (and, no doubt, that is true to some extent) for the benefit of the particular locality; at any rate, they were services rendered in that locality, but he did not look at the other side of the account, and attempt to show that the services which he classed as Imperial were really distinguishable in their nature from services which he classed as local. He did not go into that side of the question at all.

11,021. Will you repeat your view as to the distinction taken in the Treasury returns between Exchequer money spent for local purposes and that spent for Imperial purposes?—What they seem to have had in their minds was that you can make a difference between expenditure for what they call local purposes, but which would be more correctly described as purposes connected with the internal civil administration of a particular locality, and other purposes of expenditure, the latter only being called Imperial. But, as I have now pointed out, the distinction is quite arbitrary, that the civil government of a locality, the internal civil administration, is only a portion of the general purposes for which an Imperial Government exists, and so, the expenditure connected with that internal administration falls under the same category as the whole of the expenditure of the Government, it ought to be expended on pretty much the same principles and for the same objects, and you must not simply regard the special benefit of the particular locality. The expenditure in both cases ought to be for the general benefit of the whole community and not for the special benefit of a particular locality. The localities, in fact, would be remote according to the best view of the Imperial Government as to the good of the whole, not according to population or contribution or any other test. A part

which [illegible] put forward by the Treasury unless he had [illegible] his views [illegible], and given his reasons for them; and, in the absence of any such statement, I do not think we can regard Mr Goschen as an authority for the method of handling these figures in these returns. I think it is fair to point out that if Mr Goschen is held responsible for this distinction between Imperial and local expenditure, then he must also be held to be [illegible], because, in his Local Taxation Report of 1870, he draws the ordinary distinction between Imperial and local expenditure, and all this division of Imperial expenditure is absolutely ignored, so that I cannot think Mr. Goschen, in this [illegible], can be cited as an authority.

11,026. (Mr. Sexton.) Have you read certain memoranda handed in by Professor Bastable and Professor Sidgwick?—I have glanced at them—I cannot say that I have read them very carefully, but I think Professor Bastable rather agrees with me, and I cannot say that I retain in my mind the nature of Professor Sidgwick's objections.

11,027. He also admits that there is no economic authority for a division between Imperial and local expenditure, but he says that if you do not [illegible] the distinction in regard to expenditure you ought not to [illegible] it in regard to the [illegible] of taxation?—It seems to me that that is really a very absurd contention to make, because [illegible] of taxation have been [illegible] [illegible], and there is a universal agreement amongst economists as to the principle of the equality of taxation, but I have never heard any discussion or any general [illegible] [illegible] to the principle of equality of expenditure in different localities. But it is hardly a question of authority, because I could not possibly have [illegible] to these two gentlemen as authorities in the matter, as they have not published their views. I was dealing with the state of opinion which I had gathered from the studies which I had made upon the subject up to that time.

11,028. (Chairman.) Do you agree in thinking that the whole question before us is a novel one?—It is novel to some extent, but it is not novel in this way—that you have had to deal for centuries, I think, with the common expenditure by united Governments. The incorporating Union with Scotland is nearly two centuries old, and I have never heard that in the expenditure within Great Britain regard has been had to the locality. I do not know of any case where it is so. The question has arisen in every case of an incorporating Union between two countries, and the people who have written on finance have had all the facts before them. Grants in aid and the like expedients are novel, but then they are also bad unless they are [illegible] in in such a way that the general good of the community is promoted as was the case with grants to localities in aid of police originally, a certain standard of efficiency being the condition of the grant.

11,029. Have you anything further to say about the method adopted by the Treasury?—No. But might I just say, [illegible] on the question of authority, that I think it would be of interest to the Commission if I were to state that Sir Robert Hamilton, with whom I discussed this subject, was quite in agreement with me as to the impropriety of this mode of handling the figures which the Treasury have followed, and that there ought to be no distinction between Imperial and local objects, such as Sir Edward Hamilton used there was.

11,030. You had an opportunity, did you, of meeting him between the appointment of the Commission and his death?—I think it was in the autumn of last year, shortly after the Commission was [illegible], that I had an opportunity of conversing with him upon a great many points which have been before you, and this was one of them, and I am quite sure that he was in entire agreement with me.

11,031. Are we to understand that, broadly speaking, you hold that excess of expenditure in Ireland cannot justify excess of taxation?—I think that is quite clear, that the fact that you spend a certain amount of money in Ireland has nothing to do with the question of inequality of taxation. My view is that you are bound to give good government to Ireland, whatever the expenditure may be, so that the good government of the whole country may result, and whatever may be necessary for that purpose you must spend.

11,032. Do you also think that, supposing it were to appear that there is excess of taxation in Ireland, it would not be right to give compensation by way of a special expenditure of revenue with a view to advancing the material prosperity of Ireland?—I think that is rather an [illegible] mode of arriving at the object which you have in view. I do not think that it ought to be shut out of view altogether, because if all parties are agreed you may contract yourselves out of any rule that you please; but on the whole I do not think that it is a desirable course upon which to embark, because you get into dangers and difficulties if you depart from the general principle of spending money out of an Imperial exchequer for the common benefit of the whole community governed.

11,033. (The O'Conor Don.) What is the distinction which you draw between local and Imperial expenditure?—Local expenditure is what is spent by local bodies out of moneys raised locally.

11,034. The distinction really is the raising and spending by the one body?—That is so.

11,035. But I suppose you will admit under that definition that of course there is expenditure, both in England and in Ireland, of a local character?—No doubt, but I think the [illegible] for it is, not that the Imperial Government is not responsible for it, but in order to ensure the necessary economy in what must be spent locally, you connect the local expenditure with the local revenue, and you leave it to the locality in that way.

11,036. But would you hold the extreme doctrine attributed to you by some of the questions asked of Sir Edward Hamilton, that if there were grants made in aid of the local expenditure in one part of the country that were not made in another, that should not be taken into consideration at all in considering the taxation of that part of the country as compared with the other?—I am so much opposed to grants of that kind altogether that I am perhaps hardly fit to express an opinion upon that point, but I should not admit, as a general rule, that a grant in aid of that kind was a thing to be deducted and set-off against excessive taxation. And I can give as an illustration the grants for police purposes in this country, in which instance the principle upon which they were made originally (I cannot say exactly as to what the present state of the law is) was this—that provided a locality maintained a police force sufficient in the eyes of the Imperial Government, the Imperial Government would give them so much to assist in the maintenance of that force. I think you might say that where the central authority had so much regard for efficiency, the grant in aid in that case was made for the general purposes of the welfare of the whole community, and that it was not to be considered in any way as a set-off against the inequality of taxation—and that was a proper grant in aid within certain limits.

11,037. It is quite clear from what you say that you are opposed to the system of compensation for excessive taxation, but assuming that that system which you call bad finance were adopted, and assuming the extreme case that was put by Lord Welby, that all the local taxes and rates were paid for, out of Imperial funds in one country and not in the other, would you not then consider that that was an element to be taken into consideration in estimating the excess or the [illegible] of taxation in that country, that received that large grant?—I should say it is so academic a case that it is of very little use considering it until you have such a case before you.

11,038. That is the interpretation, however, which has been put upon your evidence?—Then I think it has been put by people that have not read it, because I said I could conceive that, theoretically, exceptions might exist.

11,039. Your view is that the system of making contributions to the local expenditure is such a bad system of finance that it should never be adopted?—It possibly is not a desirable mode of finance. I do not say it is impossible, but I do not like to see it, and it is a dangerous course of finance to embark upon.

11,040. (Mr. Sexton.) I understand you to hold that in a case where it is admitted that the taxation drawn from a particular locality or country is excessive in proportion to the taxation of the remainder to the other part of the country, relief might be given, or special expenditure might be admitted by exceptional terms, provided that the country affected were in agreement with that course?—That is one of the conditions, I think, of the exceptions, that there should be practically an agreement about it, so that all the parties should contract themselves out of the rule—but I do not like the exception.

11,041. But I think your evidence at any rate goes to this, that if such expenditure is to be pleaded at all in mitigation of excessive taxation, it can only be pleaded when the country affected, by its representatives, assents?—I do not like to say it can be only pointed to as one of that kind, but that seems to me to be the most favourable case that you can plead for exemption. I do not like, after the way that one has been interrupted, to say that absolutely, mathematically, there can be no other case.

11,042. I think it should be easily understood that a practical man, as you are, addressing himself to these, did not propose to meet all possible theories and eventualities that might be suggested?—I think it is a great mistake sometimes to fall into, to concern oneself with theories and exceptions that are not material for the purpose you have in hand at that moment.

11,043. You applied sound doctrines to the facts as you found them?—That was the general idea that I had.

11,044. Now you have done unquestionable service by bringing to bear upon the questions referred to the Commission the accepted doctrines of great financiers, but your attention may not have been so closely directed to the circumstance relevant, I think, to the case, that all the financial relations between Great Britain and Ireland are founded upon the Treaty of the Union between the countries?—I have never gone into that specially to be able to answer questions with regard to the history of the financial relations between Ireland and Great Britain. I have looked up at different times what happened with regard to the Treaty of Union, and in 1816, but I have never followed the business accurately that I could answer questions about it, I think.

11,045. Perhaps you can answer this. If you found that the Minister in charge of the Bill of Union in the Irish Parliament told the Imperial Parliament at the moment of urging the Bill that, provided they came into the Union, and made their fair contribution to the expenditure of the United Kingdom, it would be immaterial to Great Britain where the expenditure was made, you would say that that Minister, even 100 years ago, had grasped firmly an economic doctrine which appears now not to be wholly appreciated, even in some official circles?—I think there was a good deal of intelligence, not only in economics, but otherwise, at that time, and some of the people at that period were very well acquainted with most of those matters.

11,046. And if you found that the Act of Union declared that Ireland should contribute, not to special charges, but to all charges according to her resources, and that that contribution should be to the common expenditure of the United Kingdom, would you consider that that special Treaty between the parties adds further force to the general doctrine which you have stated?—I do not know that I will even say that, because the doctrine was so universally held that the Treaty merely followed the commonly received doctrine, if that is the true account of it that you give.

11,047. Any breach would be a breach of the general doctrine, and incidentally of the particular Treaty?—It would be so.

11,048. Then I think I have only one other question to put to you. You have managed to make extremely clear, as I think, the most difficult points for laymen, that under the system of nominally equal taxes applying to two countries you may discriminate, and that, in fact, the existing system, as shown by the yield of the Customs and Excise, does discriminate as against Ireland. The Treasury appears to hold—at least Sir Edward Hamilton appears to express the view—that, the rates of taxation being equal, you cannot reduce inequality of taxation between the two countries except by differential rates. But may I not ask you as a recognised expert upon this subject, whether it is not quite possible and practicable under a system of equal rates of taxes applying to both countries, by discrimination of the objects of taxation to relieve one country or the other?—I think a great deal could be done in that way.

11,049. Without differential taxation?—Yes; having regard to the local circumstances of both countries; but I think that this idea that you arrive at equality of taxation by means of equal rates of taxes is a very unequal one, and it is one which has governed the proceedings of our financial authorities for a great many years, and which found expression in that Committee of 1865, but it is not a correct one at all. There were certain matters which those great authorities had neglected; and, I may say that I was just reading, after I was told that the Commission would like to hear me again, Mr Gladstone's financial statement in 1853 when he applied income tax to Ireland, and I find that the idea he was full of was the promotion of equality of taxation. He thought that by applying equal rates and the same taxes to both countries you were arriving at equality of taxation, and there is no doubt that Mr Gladstone was firmly impressed with the truth of that idea, and it certainly, according to the statistical knowledge we have now, is not a true idea; it is unsound.

11,050. A very admirable illustration of that has become quite familiar. It has been suggested that if England and France were bound together in a fiscal bond, and that the system of levy was by equal rates of taxes in both countries, by putting a high tax, identical in both countries, upon coffee, and a very low tax, identical in both countries, upon tea, you could free the tea drinking from the burden of taxation and place it upon the country in which coffee was most consumed?—Yes, that is so obvious that I wonder at the point being disputed.

11,051. Take spirits and beer. If there are two countries bound together in one system of taxation, and the people in one country consume spirits, and in the other beer, if you tax the beer lightly and the spirits heavily, though the taxes are the same in both countries, you make taxation press unequally?—Or take the case of China and England. Supposing we had a common Customs Union, and you put a duty upon opium, the Chinaman would not be free, and the Englishman would escape.

11,052. It may be reasonably assumed that as great inequality of taxation would be incurred under a system of equal rates of taxes as under a system of unequal taxes?—Yes, but I think we must admit that those great authorities must always have had in view a country where all the people were in much the same conditions—that there was no great difference between localities with reference to their general conditions; and, therefore, if you apply the same rates to all, you are arriving at the object of equality; but that idea was not a true idea, and they did not consider sufficiently the differences between localities and groups of people.

11,053. And as a practical illustration drawn from the actual state of things in Great Britain and Ireland respectively, suppose the tax upon beer were greatly increased, and the tax upon whisky much diminished, it is obvious that the relative proportions of taxation derived from Great Britain and Ireland would be greatly changed, is it not?—That could be easily done.

The witness withdrew.

Adjourned sine die.

APPENDICES.

APPENDIX I.

A.

MEMORANDUM by Mr. ROBERT GIFFEN, C.B., LL.D., in connexion with the EVIDENCE given by him to the COMMISSION.

1. My official position is Controller General of the Commercial, Labour, and Statistical Departments at the Board of Trade.

2. In that capacity, besides giving attention to statistical questions generally, I have had to give special attention to trade statistics, and lately to wages and other labour statistics.

3. I have also given some attention privately to questions of the relative resources of different countries and their relative capacity to bear taxation, and have written upon these subjects.

4. I have, first of all, to submit two tables, which I propose to put in, comparing wages paid in Ireland in different employments with wages in the United Kingdom generally. (*See Tables I. and II., post.*)

5. The general effect is that employment for employment the remuneration of labour is usually a good deal less in Ireland than in Great Britain, ranging from 10 per cent. and 15 per cent. up to 50 per cent.

This is shown most clearly by the first table, which deals with a great variety of employments. In the second table, which gives standard rates of wages, mainly in the building trades, there is a closer approximation of Irish rates to English rates, but this is quite consistent with the first table, which deals with larger masses of labour. Standard artisan rates in Ireland approximate to those of Great Britain, especially if we omit the Metropolis and Manchester, but the proportionate numbers receiving those rates are so much fewer in Ireland. In unskilled rates the difference between Ireland and the United Kingdom is more than for skilled labour.

6. It will be observed that the comparison in the first table is not between Ireland and Great Britain, but between Ireland and the average of the United Kingdom, the latter average being, of course, not so high as the average of Great Britain alone would be. In agriculture, owing to the large numbers there engaged, the striking of an average for the United Kingdom makes too low a figure for comparison with Ireland, and I have in that case stated the average for Great Britain as well as for United Kingdom.

7. I propose to point out afterwards, that allowing for the different distribution of people employed at high and low rates—the preponderance in Ireland of wages at the low rates for Ireland compared with the numbers at the low rates for Great Britain—these differences in the wages rates between Ireland and Great Britain suggest that the average remuneration of the wage earner, man for man, is probably only half, or little better, than the average remuneration of the wage earner in Great Britain. That is a question of the application of the figures, and I am first of all putting in the figures themselves for what they may be worth.

8. I have next to put in an extended comparison between Ireland and the United Kingdom on a great many points. I observe you have had similar tables from other witnesses, but shorter, and not including some important matters, and I have thought a table like what I now put in might be convenient to the Commission. This I also put in *pro tanto* [illegible], and as contributing to throw light on what I consider the main matter for investigation as to the relative resources of Ireland and the United Kingdom as a whole. (Put in table: Table III., with supplements.)

9. Proceeding with this investigation, I would suggest that in measuring the resources of two countries relatively to each other the first point to take account of is population. According to the latest figures, Ireland is not quite an eighth part of the United Kingdom in numbers.

	Millions.
Total population of the United Kingdom (1894) - - -	38·8
Total population of Ireland only	4·6
Proportion of Ireland to total -	11·9 per cent.

10. The next step in my view is to take account in the most general way of the condition of the two populations to be compared as indicated by the population returns themselves and the connected returns of births, deaths, and marriages, and of emigration, all population figures really. And one of the most important points for such an account is to compare the rates of the excess of births over deaths. Birth rates and death rates are often compared on the assumption that a high birth rate signifies prosperous conditions and a high death rate unprosperous, but these comparisons are found to be faulty by themselves. A high birth rate and a high death rate frequently go together. What is found by experience to be a most significant sign of general economic conditions is the rate above stated, viz., that of the excess of births over deaths. A high excess, when combined, as it usually is, with a low death rate, and with a moderate if not a low birth rate, is a good sign of prosperity.

11. On this head then, Ireland and Great Britain, taking the latest year in the Statistical Abstract, compare as follows:—

—	Births.	Deaths.	Excess of Births over Deaths.	
			Amount.	Proportion per Thousand of Population.
Ireland -	105,[illegible]1	[illegible]	[illegible]	[illegible]
England -	9[illegible]4,1[illegible]	[illegible]	[illegible]	11·[illegible]
Scotland -	12[illegible]	[illegible]	[illegible]	11·5

12. Such a difference between Ireland and Great Britain is in my judgment too great to be accounted for in any other way than by inferiority of general conditions in Ireland.

13. The broad conclusion, then, is that if Ireland in numbers is about an eighth part of the population of the United Kingdom, the presumption from the evident inferiority of the general conditions of living, man for man, is that the resources of Ireland must be very much less than in the proportion of one-eighth.

14. The different composition of a population according to age may also indicate differences of economic condition. On this head, I propose to put in tables showing the numbers and proportions of people in Ireland and also in England and Scotland at different ages. (*See Tables IV. and V., post.*)

15. These show that Ireland has more people in proportion above 50 than Great Britain has, and fewer

people in prime of life, i.e., between 20 and 40. The difference is notable. In Ireland no less than 16·[illegible] per cent. of the male population are upwards of 60, but in Scotland and England the percentages are 13·5 and 13·7 respectively. The percentage in Ireland between 20 and 40 is [illegible] per cent., and in Scotland and England [illegible] and [illegible] respectively. The percentages of the female population are much the same. Ireland has thus fewer people in proportion in the prime of life and more above 60 than Great Britain has.

16. These figures also agree with the facts as to the comparison of emigration from Ireland and Great Britain respectively. In Ireland there is a steadier stream of people in the prime of life (see Reports on Emigration). I put in a table on this head extracted from the Annual Reports on Emigration issued under my superintendence. (See Table VI., post.)

17. In 1893, while there were 116,000 passengers outward of English adult persons to places out of Europe, and [illegible] children—the children being thus about [illegible] per cent. of the total—and 19,000 adult Scotch persons with 4,000 children—the children being thus about 18 per cent. of the total—the corresponding records for Ireland showed an emigration of [illegible] adults and 4,000 children, the latter being thus about 8 per cent. only of the total.

18. These are general figures from the population statistics themselves, and I think they are fully confirmed by a more direct examination.

19. The main point to look to, I think, is a comparison of the aggregate of individual incomes in the countries compared. There is hardly any direct measure comparable of the resources of the two countries except incomes or property estimated in money, and income is a good measure because most services between individuals can be, and are in fact, measured in money. At any rate in two communities where the proportion of services not measured in money—such as the services of wives and other persons who belong to a household, are about the same—the comparison of the incomes which are measured in money seems to be what is most necessary. My plan is to take this measure as the primary one, and then enquire if there is anything else to suggest a different conclusion.

20. I do not think property quite so good a measure by itself, as incomes are not quite proportioned to the amount of property in a country. The United States and other new countries appear to have a larger income in proportion to their property than a country like England with large capital investments abroad, and generally a great accumulation of property of every description. But property should be compared if possible.

21. Dealing, then, with incomes, we find a portion of the incomes of Ireland and Great Britain dealt with for purposes of taxation. I refer to the income tax returns. If there were reason to believe that such incomes bore the same proportion to the total in the two countries compared, and that the returns were accurate to a fraction, hardly any other enquiry would be necessary. I propose, then, to examine the income tax figures first of all.

22. The basis of the income tax is the gross assessment of the whole of income from various kinds of property (land and houses), and the assessment of the income from other sources above the limit of 150l., now 160l., the object being to tax the incomes above the limit with certain deductions. From the income tax statistics, therefore, we get first a gross assessment, which includes all incomes above 160l. per annum from all sources, and in addition the whole of the incomes from certain property (land, houses, &c.), whether they are above or below that limit; second, a net assessment, which includes only incomes above 160l., with a deduction from incomes between 160l. and 500l.; and, third, the yield of the tax, which for the present purpose is, of course, much the same thing as the net assessment in another form. For our purpose the last two assessments appear the best, because the thing compared in the two cases is the aggregate of individual incomes above a certain standard, whereas the gross assessments deal with property which may exist in a different proportion in the two countries from what property or income generally does. We may look at all the figures, however.

23. We have first the gross assessment. I take the latest year 1892-3.

—	Amount Millions.	Per cent. of Total.
	£	
Ireland	38·8	5·4
England	[illegible]	[illegible]
Scotland	[illegible]	9·[illegible]
Total	718·8	100·0

On this showing Ireland is rather more than a twentieth part (5 per cent.) of the United Kingdom.

24. Next we have the net assessment, year 1892-3.

—	Amount Millions.	Per cent. of Total.
	£	
Ireland	[illegible]	[illegible]
England	[illegible]	[illegible]
Scotland	[illegible]	[illegible]
Total	[illegible]	100·0

Ireland, while appearing as rather more than a twentieth of the United Kingdom when gross assessments are taken, that is, assessments which include, besides all incomes above 160l., the whole of certain kinds of income, now appears when net assessments are taken, that is, incomes above 160l. only with certain deductions, as only about [illegible] of the United Kingdom.

I think the net, for the reasons already given, is more useful than the gross.

[illegible] We have next the yield of the tax.

In the Return No. [illegible], session 1893, the total yield of the income tax for England, Scotland, and Ireland separately is stated. A complication is introduced by [illegible] of the yield, [illegible], [illegible] from Imperial sources, but for [illegible] the amount will be here credited to England only. It is a matter of no importance. The comparison of the yield is:—

YIELD OF INCOME TAX IN IRELAND AND GREAT BRITAIN COMPARED, YEAR 1892-3.

—	Amount.	Per cent. of Total.
	£	
Ireland	[illegible]	[illegible]
England	[illegible]	[illegible]
Scotland	[illegible]	[illegible]
Total	[illegible]	100·0

[illegible] Here the results are substantially the same as those shown by the net assessment above given. The slight differences arising are obviously due either to the minor corrections introduced in the special return from which the figures of yield of the income tax are taken or the difference in the year to which the returns relate. The corrections are no doubt expedient in official work, to ensure trustworthiness in the accuracy of the figures, but they are immaterial for the present purpose. The difference of the year is also immaterial.

27. The general effect is that taking income tax figures alone as a guide, as showing a certain part of the incomes of the different communities compared, taken on the same basis, then Ireland is only about [illegible] part of the United Kingdom.

28. I disregard the minute adjustments in the return intended to bring out the exact contributions of England, Scotland, and Ireland respectively, as not being material for any purpose with which we are now concerned.

[illegible] To disprove the inference stated it would be necessary to show either that assessed income is not a good test for comparison, or the real proportion of two countries may not be measured by it, a point I have already discussed, or that Ireland has so much a larger share of that income which is not charged to income tax, that is, of incomes below 160l., than it has of incomes which are charged to income tax, as to alter the proportion of the aggregate income of the United Kingdom as appearing from the income tax returns only, and that appears to be the next point for investigation.

30. On this head I have now to call attention to the returns of wages I put in at the beginning of my examination. These show that whenever large masses of labour are compared it is found that wages in Ireland per man run a good deal less than wages in the United Kingdom generally or in the rest of the United Kingdom.

In almost every trade included in these returns where Ireland is at all represented there is hardly an exception to the rule of the average Irish wages being lower than the average of the United Kingdom, and in the case of the larger trades as a rule considerably lower. Linen, for instance, appears an exception. It is, however, a trade not carried on in the whole of Great Britain, but in Scotland only, where wages run lower than in England. The trades likewise where Ireland is not represented are, as a rule, the better paid trades of the order to which they belong, e.g., the cotton trade among textiles and various of the mining trades. Details if necessary.

31. On this head reference may also be made to more detailed tables at pages x, xv, xix, and xxix of the Report on Principal Textiles, page ix of the Report on Mines; and pages x, xx, xxvii, and xxxii of the Report on Police, Gasworks, Waterworks, &c., where details will be found as to the rates for the principal employments in several of the above trades, as well as the average of the whole. The difference in average wages especially is striking.

32. Agricultural wages, which are very important, are included in the tables above referred to, an average for the United Kingdom as well as for Ireland being stated according to the plan of the tables. That does not show the full contrast between Ireland and Great Britain, as the numbers of labourers or peasant farmers in Ireland are so great as to bring down the average for the United Kingdom. Stating an average for Great Britain separately, we find that while the run of agricultural wages in England and Scotland is from 12s. to 20s. per week for men, the prevailing rates in Ireland are no better than 8s. to 10s. While Irish agricultural wages may be taken as 9s. 6d. per week on the average, in Great Britain, the average is about 13s. 6d. per head.

33. While wages in Ireland are thus lower, employment for employment, than in Great Britain, the average per wage earner compared with the wage earner in Great Britain is further brought down by the preponderance in Ireland of employments paid at an inferior rate to others.

34. The relative numbers at different rates of wages is an important point in all such comparisons, and to show how important it is theoretically I quote from a paper I read four years ago at the meeting of the Australasian Association for Advancement of Science:

"It is quite conceivable that in one of two countries the earnings, and still more the nominal wages, may be higher than in the other in every single employment which can be enumerated and compared, and yet the average earnings of the average wage-earning man may be higher in the latter country than the former, the reason being the different distribution of the people according to earnings. This can be shown very clearly in a theoretical comparison. Take, first, a community of 1,000 wage earners, with the people distributed according to earnings in the following classes, A, B, C, D, and E, as follows:—

"FIRST COMMUNITY.

Class	Per Annum	Numbers	Total
	£	£	£
A earnings -	30	400	12,000
B " -	60	300	18,000
C " -	70	100	7,000
D " -	80	100	8,000
E " -	90	100	9,000
Total -	—	1,000	54,000

"Average per head 54l.

"And compare this with another community of equal numbers, in which there are also five grades, each remunerated at a lower rate than the corresponding grade in the first community, but in which the average of the whole is higher because of the different distribution of the people among the grades.

"SECOND COMMUNITY.

Class	Per Annum	Numbers	Total
	£		£
A earnings -	20	100	2,000
B " -	50	100	5,000
C " -	60	100	6,000
D " -	70	300	21,000
E " -	80	400	32,000
Total -	—	1,000	66,000

"Average per head 66l.

"In a comparison of rates of wages merely according to the nature of the employment, the wages in the first community would obviously appear higher than in the second, and this would be strictly true in a sense, but the inference would be untrue that the average earnings of the wage-earning classes in the first community, striking a true average, would be higher."

35. Applying this principle to Ireland, we have a case where not only all rates, or almost all rates, are lower in Ireland than in Great Britain, but there is also a disproportionate number at the lowest rates for Ireland as compared with the number at the lowest rates in Great Britain.

While in the United Kingdom, omitting agriculture, according to the evidence I gave before the Labour Commission, the average wage per man is about 60l. per head, about 15 per cent. of the wage-earning classes being above the average, about 60 per cent. about the average, and about 25 per cent. under the average, in Ireland the average could not be put at more than about 33l. per head, made up of about

		£
60 per cent. at 25l. only	- -	1,500
30 per cent. at 40l. only	- -	1,200
10 per cent. above 40l., at say 60l.	-	600
		£3,300

36. In other words, the incomes of the wage-earning classes in Ireland, man for man, are little more than half those of Great Britain, and as the population is only between 1/4th and 1/5th, this would make the Irish share of such income about 1/10th only of similar income in the United Kingdom. Allowing that the proportion of people in the prime of life in the two countries are the same, whereas in fact the proportion is lower in Ireland, this would not bring up the proportion of the total income very much, as the working class income is only about half of the total income.

37. There remains the question of the middle class incomes under the income tax limit, as to which no similar details are easily ascertainable, but the amount of that middle-class income, according to the census and income tax returns, must be relatively very small in Ireland. My estimate would be under 10,000,000l.

38. To bring the matter to a focus it would be desirable to make an estimate of the aggregate income of Ireland in much the same form as Dudley Baxter's in 1868, but this I have not ventured to do in the absence of complete official statistics at present for a detailed account. The conclusion, however, is not dependent on any such estimate, but on the direct comparison of the income tax already made, and on the comparison of rates of wages in different employments as qualified by the preponderance of the lower paid employments in Ireland. According to former experience, it appears a tolerably safe rule to double the gross assessment to income tax, which would give 76,000,000l. for Ireland, of which 37,000,000l. would be above income tax limit, 10,000,000l. intermediate between income tax and wages, and the remainder working class income. These figures compare with the usual estimate of about 1,400,000,000l. for the United Kingdom, which I gave

to the Labour Commission, and which was probably an under estimate.*

39. The next step is to inquire whether there are any other data as to the relative resources of Ireland and Great Britain in conflict with these conclusions as to income; and as the death duty figures are often referred to, I propose to deal with them.

40. There is no doubt that if in two countries the proportion of property passing at death to the total property was the same, that is, the same in the one that it is in the other, then a comparison of the property so passing at death would show the proportion of the two countries in respect of property to each other. There are reasons why such an assumption cannot be made. Rates of mortality vary. Communities are also differently constituted as regards the proportion of people at different ages; nor is there any certainty that even if they were constituted in precisely the same manner, and had the same death rate generally, the proportion of property passing at death would be the same in the one as the other. The special death rates of the people who had property might vary, although the general death rates were the same. Other causes of variation may be suggested. For instance, where the property passing at death is taken in an artificial manner, only the life interest of the successor being reckoned, as is the case with the succession duty, then in a country where property sells for a smaller number of years' purchase than in another, the property assessed will form a larger proportion of the total than in a country where property sells for a larger number of years' purchase. A comparison, then, between the amounts of property passing at death in two communities might be somewhat [illegible], and would not prove anything by itself (except within wide limits), though the items may be usefully looked at in conjunction with others.

41. Subject to these remarks, we get the following figures for Ireland and Great Britain:—

TOTAL NET VALUE of PROPERTY PASSING AT DEATH IN IRELAND and GREAT BRITAIN COMPARED—YEAR 189[illegible].

† (From page [illegible] of [illegible] Report of Inland Revenue.)

—	Millions.	Per cent. of Total.
Ireland	[illegible]	[illegible]
England	[illegible]	[illegible]
Scotland	[illegible]	[illegible]
Total	[illegible]	100·0

42. Here the indications are nearly the same as those of the gross assessment to the income tax. They are not sufficient, however, to suggest that the reasons above given for preferring the net to the gross assessment to the income tax are [illegible]. The suggestion already made as to the assessment of real property indicates that probably in Ireland the assessments approach more nearly the total value of real property than they do in England where the number of years' purchase of real property is higher than in Ireland. In Ireland the population is older, and successions, I should judge, probably more frequent than in Great Britain, where property is held very largely in proportion by people who have saved it themselves. Corporation property, also excluded, and probably more in Great Britain in proportion than in Ireland.

43. It has also to be considered that property cannot be looked at by itself—that the income of one country may be larger in proportion to its property than the income of another, so that there is no [illegible] between these figures of income and property.

44. The general conclusion is that there is nothing in the death duty figures inconsistent with the suggestion of the figures of income above as to the relative resources of Ireland and Great Britain.

45. The next suggestion I have to make is to inquire whether there is anything in the circumstances of the main industry in Ireland—agriculture—to throw doubt on the comparison of income generally which has been made.

Ireland is mainly an agricultural country, the industry of agriculture being the main pursuit of the inhabitants. If an independent estimate can be arrived at of what the annual value of the agriculture is, we have a basis for estimating within narrow limits what the total income of the country must be, because the return to agriculture in comparison with the numbers dependent on it can be compared with that of other pursuits and the numbers dependent on them. Such an estimate I have caused to be made and put in as a separate paper. (*See* Table VII, post.)

I have compared this statement with that of Dr. Grimshaw. Allowing for differences in form, the differences in estimates are mainly as to dairy produce and the amount of hay consumed non-agriculturally, a difference of 4,000,000*l.* on these two heads.

46. This statement shows the net income of the agricultural population of Ireland from agriculture to be about 40,000,000*l.* The question then is, what proportion of the Irish population is engaged in agriculture, and next, whether the remaining population probably earn less or more per head than those engaged in agriculture do.

47. Answering the first question, I have to refer to the census figures. The most general divisions of the Irish Census which it is necessary to refer to for the present purpose are as follows:—

OCCUPATIONS of the IRISH PEOPLE according to the IRISH CENSUS of 1891.

—	Total.	Males only.	Males above 20.
All persons	[illegible]	[illegible]	[illegible]
Do. of specified occupations	[illegible]	[illegible]	[illegible]
1. Professional class	[illegible]	[illegible]	[illegible]
2. Domestic	[illegible]	[illegible]	[illegible]
3. Commercial	[illegible]	[illegible]	[illegible]
4. Agricultural	[illegible]	[illegible]	[illegible]
5. Industrial	[illegible]	[illegible]	[illegible]
Total of occupied classes, as above.	[illegible]	[illegible]	[illegible]

48. On these data it is submitted that the best comparison as to the relative employment given by the different occupations is furnished by the last column of all, showing the occupations of males above 20. If we take the figures of the first column we get many females in the domestic class, which is not really a distinct class in the proper sense of the word, and whose numbers ought to be distributed among the other classes. The figures of the second column, again, are thrown out by the inclusion among them in the class professional of students and others not earning an income by the occupation they follow. The last column, in showing the proportions of the adult male population following different occupations, really shows the proportion of these different occupations in the whole industry of the people.

49. The general effect, then, is that out of 1,[illegible] male persons above 20 in Ireland following occupations, no fewer than [illegible] follow agricultural occupations; they are farmers, farm labourers, gardeners, &c. In other words, [illegible] per cent. of the population of Ireland is engaged in agriculture.

50. A further correction has to be made. It is stated in the Census of Ireland (General Report, note, page 11[illegible]) that the Industrial Class V includes persons called "general labourers," the majority of whom may be assumed to be agricultural labourers, although not having returned themselves as such. The total number of these "general labourers" is [illegible], and of these the number of the age of 20 and upwards is [illegible]. If we transfer three-fourths of these to the agricultural class we should increase that class to [illegible], and the proportion of this number to the above total of 1,[illegible] is nearly 64 per cent.

51. In assuming, therefore, that the labour of Ireland is occupied agriculturally to the extent of

* Evidence taken before Labour Commission, C—[illegible] [illegible] of 189[illegible], page [illegible].

† This is probate, legacy and succession duty together. (For details see [illegible] Report of Inland Revenue, p. [illegible], Appendix.) The [illegible] [illegible] to [illegible] duty [illegible] in the year in which the [illegible] [illegible] [illegible] [illegible].

nearly 64 per cent., we appear to be in accordance approximately with the census figures.

52. The only qualification to be made would be on the supposition that the labour of males under 20 and of female labour generally is more largely employed in non-agricultural than in agricultural industries; but while that may be the case to some extent, I doubt, looking at the total numbers of males under 20 and of females engaged in occupations altogether, whether any qualification of this sort would be serious.

53. If, then, 64 per cent. of the Irish people only produce a value of, say, 40,000,000*l.* per annum, the remaining 36 per cent., if their labour were no more productive per head, would produce, in round figures, about 23,000,000*l.*—total, 63,000,000*l.*

54. Is the remaining industry of Ireland more or less productive per man of those engaged in it than that of agriculture? Wages are, no doubt, higher in other industries than in agriculture; but, per contra, the value produced in agriculture includes the large element of rent, not merely the rent which goes to the landlord, but the immediate rent retained by tenants. A great part of this rent is interest and ordinary profit, and economic rent. I should doubt if there is any justification for considering that Irish incomes at much more per head than what is shown per head as the result of its agriculture to those engaged in it.

55. There is nothing in this mode of viewing the subject, therefore, to suggest that the above conclusions as to the relative resources of Ireland and Great Britain based on statistics of income in an earlier one, in crediting Ireland with too small a relative income. Before passing from this point I should like to put in another table comparing the numbers in Ireland and in England and Scotland respectively engaged in agriculture compared with other pursuits, so as to give an idea of how much Ireland is a purely agricultural country compared with England and Scotland. (See *Table VIII.*, post.)

56. Thus, whichever way the matter is looked at, the proportion of Irish income and capital to that of the United Kingdom comes out at about [illegible] to [illegible] only. All the facts combine to show that the population of Ireland only produces, man for man, less than half the value which is produced by the people of Great Britain, so that, as the numbers of Ireland are rather less than 1/8th of the numbers of the United Kingdom, the resources must be less than half that proportion, *i.e.*, less than 1/16th. In putting the proportion at 1/15th to 1/20th we cannot be far from the truth.

57. I have to refer next to the general table I put in early in the proceedings, comparing Ireland and Great Britain on many points. Looking at this table, we may affirm broadly that in no direction can the balance be redressed by the relative productions of Ireland in other respects than those I have dealt with. On the contrary, its inferiority would probably be rather increased than diminished by taking a strict account of all Irish productions.

58. The only facts in the table to suggest a different proportion are the amounts contributed by Ireland in Customs and Excise Revenue, the produce of indirect taxation, which is frequently considered by itself a sign of relative resources. In the face of all the above facts, however, it is only evidence that in matters of taxation Ireland is unequally discriminated against by the character of the indirect taxes which happen to hit articles of specially Irish consumption. This remark, however, is only made in passing. I am not dealing with the relative taxation of Great Britain and Ireland, but only with the resources.

59. There is nothing singular in various taxes discriminating against one of two communities although nominally at the same rate. We are acquainted with similar difficulties in the application of the most-favoured-nation clause in commercial negotiations. A country might give us most-favoured-nation treatment nominally, and yet by adjusting its tariff to the articles which it imports from other countries, excluding the special articles it imports from us, it might subject our trade to higher duties than it subjects the trade of other countries. The matter is one which is frequently before us in dealing with tariffs.

60. Altogether the conclusion I would come to is that the income of Ireland cannot be put at more than [illegible] of that of the United Kingdom, and the real proportion is probably less.

61. I would next suggest as very important in this connection that the proportion of Irish resources to those of Great Britain is constantly diminishing, owing to the rapid growth of Great Britain in population and wealth. If the proportion according to the actual latest figures is not higher than [illegible], then means that, for practical purposes, it should be taken at not more, perhaps, than [illegible], because in the course of a very few years the latter proportion must hold. In any case, some smaller proportion than the latest shown in the figures must be taken as the probable proportion in the immediate future.

62. In any arrangement as to relative taxable capacity also the probability of future changes should be allowed for by means of periodical revisions.

63. The next question is that of the relative taxable resources to be established on the basis of relative aggregates of individual incomes.

64. There are two points of view from which the question may be looked at. 1. Assuming that the Chancellor of the Exchequer is obliged to take all the revenue he can get, the question would be what in fact would be paid by two countries. The poorer might be made to pay more relatively than the richer, or vice versa. 2. Assuming that less is levied than could be levied in both cases, what is equitable as between them? What should be the proportion? It is the latter question only that concerns us at present.

65. Dealing with the latter question, then, I have to notice that there is a strong body of economical opinion that taxable capacity may be taken as in strict proportion to income, that all the members of the community should pay alike in proportion to income. But from this view, following John Stuart Mill, I should dissent, for what seem obvious reasons. (See *Mill*, *Book V.*, *chapter* 11, s. 3.)

66. Broadly, a poor population has necessarily a smaller taxable surplus in proportion to its gross income than a rich population. It has hardly a margin after a sum sufficient for decent living, whereas the rich man has a large margin.

67. Applying Mill's principle of allowing a minimum for subsistence per head before taxation should begin, say 15*l.* per head, then the taxable surplus of Ireland, giving Ireland an aggregate income of 70,000,000*l.*, would be about 22,000,000*l.* By the same method of calculation the taxable surplus of Great Britain would now be 900,000,000*l.*, or thereabouts.

Practically the British taxable surplus is not so great. There would be a great outcry if an attempt were made to levy so much as even a third part, and even in a great emergency. But there is an enormous interval in any case between 22,000,000*l.* and 900,000,000*l.*

68. No doubt, also, under existing conditions more than 22,000,000*l.* might be extracted from Ireland. The minimum for what is considered decent living is no doubt lower in Ireland than in Great Britain, however desirable it may be that this minimum should be raised. The sums actually raised for Imperial and local purposes together are about half that amount.

69. I may say that there is a technical slip in the calculation as originally put forward. The proper mode of arriving at the surplus would be to deduct the whole of the incomes under the minimum, whatever they may be, and then a minimum from the incomes above that. This would leave a larger taxable surplus than by deducting a minimum from every income. But it would be impossible to make an exact calculation of this kind, while the rough calculation seems good enough for comparative purposes.

70. There is, of course, no means of saying exactly what allowance should be made for the greater poverty of one community compared with another in estimating what its taxable surplus is from the aggregate of individual incomes. But I submit as a matter of equity that adjustments should be made.

71. I have not referred in these notes to the calculations of the relative accumulated wealth in Great Britain and Ireland respectively, given in my book on "The Growth of Capital." These figures are largely a reflex of the income tax returns. They are the income tax returns in another shape. But it may be stated that the calculation in this book that the Irish people only own 1/15th or 1/16th part of the accumulated wealth of the United Kingdom is not inconsistent with the figures I have now given as to income, and private property passing at death, showing a slightly higher proportion, as the accumulated wealth dealt with in the book including an estimate for public as well as private wealth, and allowance has also to be made for wealth which is not happen producing.

B.

Tables put in by Mr. Robert Giffen, C.B., LL.D., of the Board of Trade, in connexion with the Evidence given by him before the Commission.

1

STATEMENT showing the AVERAGE AMOUNT of WAGES paid per head to PERSONS engaged in different EMPLOYMENTS in IRELAND, compared with the WAGES paid per head in the same EMPLOYMENTS in the UNITED KINGDOM generally.

Employments	Average for Ireland.	Average for United Kingdom.	Employments.	Average for Ireland.	Average for United Kingdom.
Cotton trade	Not represented	[illegible]	Iron and steel shipbuilding	Not represented.	[illegible]
Woollen trade	[illegible]	[illegible]	[illegible] trades [illegible]	[illegible]	[illegible]
Worsted trade	Not represented	[illegible]	[illegible] trades [illegible]	[illegible]	[illegible]
Linen trade	[illegible]	[illegible]	Tin plate trade	Not represented	[illegible]
[illegible]	[illegible]	[illegible]	[illegible]	[illegible]	[illegible]
Jute trade	Not represented.	[illegible]	[illegible]	Not represented.	[illegible]
[illegible]	" "	[illegible]	[illegible] works	" "	[illegible]
Silk	" "	[illegible]	Coach and [illegible] building (including [illegible])	[illegible]	[illegible]
Carpet	" "	[illegible]			
Hosiery	" "	[illegible]	Boot and shoe factories (factory [illegible] only)	[illegible]	[illegible]
Coal and ironstone mining	[illegible]	[illegible]	Breweries	[illegible]	[illegible]
[illegible]	[illegible] *	[illegible]	Distilleries	[illegible]	[illegible]
[illegible]	Not represented	[illegible]	Brick and tile works	Not represented.	[illegible]
[illegible]	" "	[illegible]	[illegible]	" "	[illegible]
[illegible]	[illegible]	[illegible]	Printing and [illegible]		
[illegible]	Not represented	[illegible]	Large works	[illegible]	[illegible]
[illegible]	" "	[illegible]	Small works	[illegible]	[illegible]
Police (ordinary [illegible])	[illegible] †	[illegible]	[illegible]	[illegible]	[illegible]
[illegible]	[illegible]	[illegible]			
[illegible]	[illegible] ‡	[illegible]			
Waterworks	[illegible]	[illegible]	[illegible]	[illegible]	[illegible]
Railways [illegible]	[illegible]	[illegible]	Agricultural labourers [illegible]	[illegible] per week.	[illegible] per week
Railways [illegible]	[illegible]	[illegible]	Agricultural labourers [illegible]	[illegible] " "	[illegible] per week. [illegible]
[illegible]	Not represented	[illegible]			
[illegible]	[illegible]	[illegible]			

* The Irish returns here are quite unrepresentative.
† Including the Dublin Metropolitan Police as well as the Royal Irish Constabulary.
‡ [illegible]
§ This rate is based on only a small number of persons and is probably a little below the real average for Ireland.
‖ Based on [illegible] England only.

II.

STATEMENT showing the STANDARD RATES of WAGES in the under-mentioned EMPLOYMENTS at various places in IRELAND, compared with the STANDARD RATES existing at various localities in ENGLAND and WALES and SCOTLAND, derived principally from information supplied to the BOARD of TRADE by the different TRADE UNIONS.

[N.B.—The rates quoted are invariably for a full week's work, exclusive of overtime.]

Employments.	Irish Localities.		Per Week.	Localities in Great Britain.		Per Week.
CABINET AND CHAIR MAKERS.	Belfast	([illegible] hrs.)	[illegible] to [illegible]	Newcastle	([illegible] hrs.)	[illegible]
	Dublin	([illegible] hrs.)	[illegible]	Hull	([illegible] hrs.)	[illegible] to [illegible]
	Londonderry	([illegible] hrs.)	[illegible] to [illegible]	Bristol	([illegible] hrs.)	[illegible] to [illegible]
				Edinburgh	([illegible] hrs.)	[illegible] to [illegible]
				Blackburn, Bolton, and Rochdale.	([illegible] hrs.)	[illegible]
				Liverpool and Manchester.	([illegible] hrs.)	[illegible]
				[English provincial rates for [illegible] hours mainly range from [illegible] to [illegible]. London ([illegible] to [illegible] hrs.), [illegible] to [illegible].]		
LITHOGRAPHIC PRINTERS.	Belfast	([illegible] hrs.)	[illegible]	Newcastle	([illegible] hrs.)	[illegible]
	Cork	([illegible] hrs.)	[illegible]	Hull	([illegible] and [illegible] hrs.)	[illegible]
	Dublin	([illegible] hrs.)	[illegible]	Bristol	([illegible] and [illegible] hrs.)	[illegible]
				Edinburgh	([illegible] and [illegible] hrs.)	[illegible] to [illegible]
				[English provincial rates for [illegible] hours mainly range from [illegible] to [illegible]. London ([illegible] hrs.), [illegible]]		
PATTERN MAKERS.	Belfast	([illegible] hrs.)	[illegible]	Newcastle	([illegible] hrs.)	[illegible]
				Manchester	([illegible] hrs.)	[illegible]
				Hull	([illegible] hrs.)	[illegible]
				Sheffield	([illegible] hrs.)	[illegible]
				Cardiff and Swansea	([illegible] hrs.)	[illegible]
				Birmingham	([illegible] hrs.)	[illegible]
				Edinburgh and Leith	([illegible] hrs.)	[illegible]
				Glasgow	([illegible] hrs.)	[illegible]
				[English provincial rates for [illegible] hours mainly range from [illegible] to [illegible]. London ([illegible] hrs.), [illegible]]		
IRONFOUNDERS.	Belfast	—	[illegible]	Newcastle	—	[illegible]
	Cork	—	[illegible]	Manchester and South Lancashire generally	—	[illegible]
	Dublin	—	[illegible]	Hull, Leeds	—	[illegible]
				Birmingham	—	[illegible]
				Bristol	—	[illegible]
				Derby, Nottingham, and Leicester.	—	[illegible]
				Cardiff	—	[illegible]
				Southampton	—	[illegible]
				[London	—	[illegible]]
BLACKSMITHS AND MACHINE RULERS.	Belfast	([illegible] hrs.)	[illegible]	Newcastle	([illegible] hrs.)	[illegible]
	Dublin	([illegible] hrs.)	[illegible]	Manchester	([illegible] hrs.)	[illegible]
	Londonderry	([illegible] hrs.)	[illegible]	Hull	([illegible] hrs.)	[illegible]
				Bristol	([illegible] hrs.)	[illegible]
				Edinburgh	([illegible] hrs.)	[illegible]
				Cardiff	([illegible] hrs.)	[illegible]
				[English provincial rates for [illegible] hours mainly range from [illegible] to [illegible]. London ([illegible] hrs.), [illegible]]		
MILL SAWYERS AND WOOD CUTTING MACHINISTS.	Belfast	([illegible] hrs.)	[illegible] to [illegible]	Newcastle	([illegible] to [illegible] hrs.)	[illegible]
	Cork	([illegible] hrs.)	[illegible]	Nottingham	([illegible] hrs.)	[illegible]
	Dublin	([illegible] hrs.)	[illegible]	Bristol, Cardiff, and Newport.	([illegible] hrs.)	[illegible]
				[London	([illegible] to [illegible] hrs.)	about [illegible]]
BRASSFOUNDERS.	Belfast	([illegible] hrs.)	[illegible]	Newcastle	([illegible] hrs.)	[illegible]
				Manchester	([illegible] hrs.)	[illegible]
				Hull	([illegible] hrs.)	[illegible] to [illegible]
				Bristol	([illegible] hrs.)	[illegible] to [illegible]
				[London	([illegible] hrs.)	[illegible]]
SHIPWRIGHTS.	Belfast	([illegible] hrs.)	[illegible]	Newcastle	([illegible] to [illegible] hrs.)	[illegible] to [illegible]
	Larne	([illegible] to [illegible] hrs.)	[illegible]	Hull	([illegible] to [illegible] hrs.)	[illegible] to [illegible]
	Wexford	([illegible] to [illegible] hrs.)	[illegible]	Birkenhead	([illegible] to [illegible] hrs.)	[illegible] to [illegible]
	Dublin	([illegible] to [illegible] hrs.)	[illegible]	Bristol	([illegible] to [illegible] hrs.)	[illegible]
	Dundalk	([illegible] to [illegible] hrs.)	[illegible]	Southampton	([illegible] to [illegible] hrs.)	[illegible]
				Cardiff	([illegible] to [illegible] hrs.)	[illegible]
				Greenock, Leith	([illegible] hrs.)	[illegible] to [illegible]
				Barrow	([illegible] to [illegible] hrs.)	[illegible] to [illegible]
				[London	([illegible] to [illegible] hrs.)	[illegible]]
BOILERMAKERS AND IRON AND STEEL SHIP-BUILDERS.						
Angle-Iron Smiths.	Belfast	([illegible] hrs.)	[illegible]	The Tyne and Wear	([illegible] to [illegible] hrs.)	[illegible] to [illegible]
				Manchester and District	([illegible] hrs.)	[illegible]
				Hull	([illegible] hrs.)	[illegible] to [illegible]
				South Wales	([illegible] to [illegible] hrs.)	[illegible] to [illegible]
				The Clyde	([illegible] hrs.)	[illegible]
				Southampton	([illegible] hrs.)	[illegible]
				[London	([illegible] to [illegible] hrs.)	[illegible] to [illegible]]

Employments.	Irish Localities.			Localities in Great Britain.		
BOILER MAKERS, &c.—contd.			Per Week.			Per Week.
Platers (Heavy)	Belfast	([illegible] hrs.)	[illegible] to [illegible]	The Tyne and Wear	([illegible] to [illegible] hrs.)	[illegible]
				Manchester and District	([illegible] hrs.)	[illegible]
				Hull	([illegible] hrs.)	[illegible]
				South Wales	([illegible] to [illegible] hrs.)	[illegible]
				Southampton	([illegible] hrs.)	[illegible]
				The Clyde	([illegible] hrs.)	[illegible]
				[London	([illegible] to [illegible] hrs.)	[illegible]]
Platers (Light)	Belfast	([illegible] hrs.)	[illegible] to [illegible]	The Tyne and Wear	([illegible] to [illegible] hrs.)	[illegible]
				Manchester and District	([illegible] hrs.)	[illegible]
				Hull	([illegible] hrs.)	[illegible]
				South Wales	([illegible] to [illegible] hrs.)	[illegible]
				Southampton	([illegible] hrs.)	[illegible]
				The Clyde	([illegible] hrs.)	[illegible]
				(No London rates quoted.)		
Riveters	Belfast	([illegible] hrs.)	[illegible] to [illegible]	The Tyne and Wear	([illegible] to [illegible] hrs.)	[illegible]
				Manchester and District	([illegible] hrs.)	[illegible]
				Hull	([illegible] hrs.)	[illegible]
				South Wales	([illegible] to [illegible] hrs.)	[illegible]
				Southampton	([illegible] hrs.)	[illegible]
				The Clyde	([illegible] hrs.)	[illegible]
				[London	([illegible] to [illegible] hrs.)	[illegible]]
Holders-up	Belfast	([illegible] hrs.)	[illegible]	The Tyne and Wear	([illegible] to [illegible] hrs.)	[illegible]
				Manchester and District	([illegible] hrs.)	[illegible]
				Hull	([illegible] hrs.)	[illegible]
				South Wales	([illegible] to [illegible] hrs.)	[illegible]
				Southampton	([illegible] hrs.)	[illegible]
				The Clyde	([illegible] hrs.)	[illegible]
				[London	([illegible] to [illegible] hrs.)	[illegible]]
Caulkers	Belfast	([illegible] hrs.)	[illegible] to [illegible]	The Tyne and Wear	([illegible] to [illegible] hrs.)	[illegible]
				Hull	([illegible] hrs.)	[illegible]
				South Wales	([illegible] to [illegible] hrs.)	[illegible]
				Southampton	([illegible] hrs.)	[illegible]
				The Clyde	([illegible] hrs.)	[illegible]
				[London	([illegible] to [illegible] hrs.)	[illegible]]
[illegible]	Belfast	([illegible] hrs.)	[illegible]	Hull	([illegible] hrs.)	[illegible]
				Southampton	([illegible] hrs.)	[illegible]
ENGINEERING:						
Turners	Drogheda	([illegible] hrs.)	[illegible]	Newcastle	([illegible] hrs.)	[illegible]
	Dundalk	([illegible] hrs.)	[illegible]	Hull	([illegible] hrs.)	[illegible]
	Limerick	([illegible] hrs.)	[illegible]	Manchester	([illegible] hrs.)	[illegible]
	Londonderry	([illegible] hrs.)	[illegible]	Edinburgh	([illegible] hrs.)	[illegible]
	Newry	([illegible] hrs.)	[illegible]	Cardiff	([illegible] hrs.)	[illegible]
	Waterford	([illegible] hrs.)	[illegible]	Glasgow and District	([illegible] hrs.)	[illegible]
	Belfast	([illegible] to [illegible] hrs.)	[illegible]	Birmingham	([illegible] hrs.)	[illegible]
	Cork	([illegible] hrs.)	[illegible]	Leeds	([illegible] hrs.)	[illegible]
	Dublin	([illegible] hrs.)	[illegible]	Middlesbro'	([illegible] hrs.)	[illegible]
				Crewe	([illegible] hrs.)	[illegible]
				Derby	([illegible] hrs.)	[illegible]
				Wolverhampton and District	([illegible] hrs.)	[illegible]
				[London	([illegible] hrs.)	[illegible]]
Fitters	Belfast	([illegible] to [illegible] hrs.)	[illegible]	Newcastle	([illegible] hrs.)	[illegible]
	Dublin	([illegible] hrs.)	[illegible]	Hull	([illegible] hrs.)	[illegible]
	Cork	([illegible] hrs.)	[illegible]	Manchester	([illegible] hrs.)	[illegible]
	Drogheda	([illegible] hrs.)	[illegible]	Cardiff	([illegible] hrs.)	[illegible]
	Dundalk	([illegible] hrs.)	[illegible]	Leeds	([illegible] hrs.)	[illegible]
	Limerick	([illegible] hrs.)	[illegible]	Birmingham	([illegible] hrs.)	[illegible]
	Londonderry	([illegible] hrs.)	[illegible]	Middlesbro'	([illegible] hrs.)	[illegible] and [illegible]
	Newry	([illegible] hrs.)	[illegible]	Crewe	([illegible] hrs.)	[illegible]
	Waterford	([illegible] hrs.)	[illegible]	Derby	([illegible] hrs.)	[illegible] to [illegible]
				Wolverhampton and District	([illegible] hrs.)	[illegible]
				Edinburgh	([illegible] hrs.)	[illegible]
				Glasgow and District	([illegible] hrs.)	[illegible]
				[London	([illegible] hrs.)	[illegible]]
Smiths	Belfast	([illegible] to [illegible] hrs.)	[illegible]	Newcastle	([illegible] hrs.)	[illegible]
	Cork	([illegible] hrs.)	[illegible]	Hull	([illegible] hrs.)	[illegible]
	Dublin	([illegible] hrs.)	[illegible]	Leeds	([illegible] hrs.)	[illegible]
	Drogheda	([illegible] hrs.)	[illegible]	Middlesbro'	([illegible] hrs.)	[illegible] and [illegible]
	Dundalk	([illegible] hrs.)	[illegible]	Crewe	([illegible] hrs.)	[illegible]
	Limerick	([illegible] hrs.)	[illegible]	Manchester	([illegible] hrs.)	[illegible]
	Londonderry	([illegible] hrs.)	[illegible]	Derby	([illegible] hrs.)	[illegible]
	Newry	([illegible] hrs.)	[illegible]	Birmingham	([illegible] hrs.)	[illegible]
	Waterford	([illegible] hrs.)	[illegible]	Wolverhampton and District	([illegible] hrs.)	[illegible]
				Cardiff	([illegible] hrs.)	[illegible]
				Glasgow and District	([illegible] hrs.)	[illegible]
				[London	([illegible] hrs.)	[illegible]]

Contd.

ENGINEERING—*contd.*

Trade	Irish Town	Hours	Per Week.	English and Scottish Town	Hours	Per Week.
MILLWRIGHTS	Belfast	([illegible] hrs.)	[illegible]	Newcastle	([illegible] hrs.)	[illegible]
	Cork	([illegible] hrs.)	[illegible]	Hull	([illegible] hrs.)	[illegible]
	Dublin	([illegible] hrs.)	[illegible]	Leeds	([illegible] hrs.)	[illegible]
	Drogheda	([illegible] hrs.)	[illegible]	Crewe	([illegible] hrs.)	[illegible]
	Dundalk	([illegible] hrs.)	[illegible]	Manchester	([illegible] hrs.)	[illegible]
	Limerick	([illegible] hrs.)	[illegible]	Derby	([illegible] hrs.)	[illegible]
	Londonderry	([illegible] hrs.)	[illegible]	Birmingham	([illegible] hrs.)	[illegible]
	Newry	([illegible] hrs.)	[illegible]	Wolverhampton and District	([illegible] hrs.)	[illegible]
	Waterford	([illegible] hrs.)	[illegible]	Cardiff	([illegible] hrs.)	[illegible]
				Edinburgh	([illegible] hrs.)	[illegible]
				Glasgow and District	([illegible] hrs.)	[illegible]
				[London	([illegible] hrs.)	[illegible]]
PATTERN MAKERS	Belfast	([illegible] hrs.)	[illegible]	Newcastle	([illegible] hrs.)	[illegible]
	Cork	([illegible] hrs.)	[illegible]	Hull	([illegible] hrs.)	[illegible]
	Dublin	([illegible] hrs.)	[illegible]	Leeds	([illegible] hrs.)	[illegible]
	Drogheda	([illegible] hrs.)	[illegible]	Middlesbro'	([illegible] hrs.)	[illegible]
	Dundalk	([illegible] hrs.)	[illegible]	Crewe	([illegible] hrs.)	[illegible]
	Limerick	([illegible] hrs.)	[illegible]	Manchester	([illegible] hrs.)	[illegible]
	Londonderry	([illegible] hrs.)	[illegible]	Derby	([illegible] hrs.)	[illegible]
	Newry	([illegible] hrs.)	[illegible]	Birmingham	([illegible] hrs.)	[illegible]
	Waterford	([illegible] hrs.)	[illegible]	Wolverhampton and District	([illegible] hrs.)	[illegible]
				Cardiff	([illegible] hrs.)	[illegible]
				Edinburgh	([illegible] hrs.)	[illegible]
				Glasgow and District	([illegible] hrs.)	[illegible]
				[London	([illegible] hrs.)	[illegible]]
MACHINE MEN	Belfast	([illegible] hrs.)	[illegible]	Newcastle	([illegible] hrs.)	[illegible]
				Leeds	([illegible] hrs.)	[illegible]
				[illegible]	([illegible] hrs.)	[illegible]
				Birmingham	([illegible] hrs.)	[illegible]
				Wolverhampton and District	([illegible] hrs.)	[illegible]
				[London	([illegible] hrs.)	[illegible]]
BRASS TURNERS	Belfast	([illegible] hrs.)	[illegible]	Newcastle	([illegible] hrs.)	[illegible]
				Leeds	([illegible] hrs.)	[illegible]
				Middlesbro'	([illegible] hrs.)	[illegible]
				Wolverhampton and District	([illegible] hrs.)	[illegible]
				[London	([illegible] hrs.)	[illegible]]
COPPERSMITHS	[illegible]	([illegible] hrs.)	[illegible]	Leeds	([illegible] hrs.)	[illegible]
				Manchester	([illegible] hrs.)	[illegible]
				Birmingham	([illegible] hrs.)	[illegible]
				Cardiff	([illegible] hrs.)	[illegible]
				Glasgow and District	([illegible] hrs.)	[illegible]
				[London	([illegible] hrs.)	[illegible]]
BRASS FINISHERS	Belfast	([illegible] hrs.)	[illegible]	Leeds	([illegible] hrs.)	[illegible]
	Dublin	([illegible] hrs.)	[illegible]	Manchester	([illegible] hrs.)	[illegible]
	Dundalk	([illegible] hrs.)	[illegible]	Birmingham	([illegible] hrs.)	[illegible]
				Cardiff	([illegible] hrs.)	[illegible]
				Glasgow and District	([illegible] hrs.)	[illegible]
				[London	([illegible] hrs.)	[illegible]]

BUILDING TRADES.—(According to statements supplied by the National Association of Master Builders.)

Trade	Irish Town	Hours	Per Week.	English and Scottish Town	Hours	Per Week.
BRICKLAYERS	Belfast	Summer Rate—([illegible] hrs.)	[illegible]	Newcastle	Summer Rate—([illegible] hrs.)	[illegible]
				Manchester	([illegible] hrs.)	[illegible]
				Hull	([illegible] hrs.)	[illegible]
				Cardiff	([illegible] hrs.)	[illegible]
				Southampton	([illegible] hrs.)	[illegible]
				Bristol	([illegible] hrs.)	[illegible]
				Leith	([illegible] hrs.)	[illegible]
				[London	([illegible] hrs.)	[illegible]]
	Belfast	Winter Rate—([illegible] hrs.)	[illegible]	Newcastle	Winter Rate—([illegible] hrs.)	[illegible]
				Manchester	([illegible] hrs.)	[illegible]
				Hull	([illegible] hrs.)	[illegible]
				Cardiff	([illegible] hrs.)	[illegible]
				Southampton	([illegible] hrs.)	[illegible]
				Bristol	([illegible] hrs.)	[illegible]
				Leith	([illegible] hrs.)	[illegible]
				[London	([illegible] to 47 hrs.)	[illegible]]
MASONS	Belfast	Summer Rate—([illegible] hrs.)	[illegible]	Newcastle	Summer Rate—([illegible] hrs.)	[illegible]
				Manchester	([illegible] hrs.)	[illegible]
				Hull	([illegible] hrs.)	[illegible]
				Bristol	([illegible] hrs.)	[illegible]
				Cardiff	([illegible] hrs.)	[illegible]
				Southampton	([illegible] hrs.)	[illegible]
				Leith	([illegible] hrs.)	[illegible]
				[London	([illegible] hrs.)	[illegible]]

Irish Localities.			Localities in Great Britain.		
	Winter Rates—	Per Week		Winter Rates—	Per Week.
Belfast	([illegible] hrs.)	[illegible]	Newcastle	([illegible] hrs.)	[illegible]
			Manchester	([illegible] hrs.)	[illegible]
			Hull	([illegible] hrs.)	[illegible]
			Bristol	([illegible] hrs.)	[illegible]
			Cardiff	([illegible] hrs.)	[illegible]
			Southampton	([illegible] hrs.)	[illegible]
			Leith	([illegible] hrs.)	[illegible]
			[London	([illegible] hrs.)	[illegible])
	Summer Rates—			Summer Rates—	
Belfast	([illegible] hrs.)	[illegible]	Newcastle	([illegible] hrs.)	[illegible]
*Londonderry	([illegible] hrs.)	[illegible]	Manchester District	([illegible] hrs.)	[illegible]
*Dublin	([illegible] hrs.)	[illegible]	Hull	([illegible] hrs.)	[illegible]
*Queenstown	([illegible] hrs.)	[illegible]	Bristol	([illegible] hrs.)	[illegible]
			Cardiff	([illegible] hrs.)	[illegible]
			Southampton	([illegible] hrs.)	[illegible]
			Leith	([illegible] hrs.)	[illegible]
			[London	([illegible] hrs.)	[illegible])
	Winter Rates—			Winter Rates—	
Belfast	([illegible] hrs.)	[illegible]	Newcastle	([illegible] hrs.)	[illegible]
*Londonderry	([illegible] hrs.)	[illegible]	Manchester	([illegible] hrs.)	[illegible]
*Dublin	([illegible] hrs.)	[illegible]	Hull	([illegible] hrs.)	[illegible]
*Queenstown	([illegible] hrs.)	[illegible]	Bristol	([illegible] hrs.)	[illegible]
			Cardiff	([illegible] hrs.)	[illegible]
			Southampton	([illegible] hrs.)	[illegible]
			Leith	([illegible] hrs.)	[illegible]
			[London	([illegible] hrs.)	[illegible]]
	Summer Rates—			Summer Rates—	
Belfast	([illegible] hrs.)	[illegible]	Newcastle	([illegible] hrs.)	[illegible]
*Dublin	([illegible] hrs.)	[illegible]	Manchester	([illegible] hrs.)	[illegible]
*Cork	([illegible] hrs.)	[illegible]	Hull	([illegible] hrs.)	[illegible]
*Londonderry	([illegible] hrs.)	[illegible]	Bristol	([illegible] hrs.)	[illegible]
			Cardiff	([illegible] hrs.)	[illegible]
			Southampton	([illegible] hrs.)	[illegible]
			Leith	([illegible] hrs.)	[illegible]
			[London	([illegible] hrs.)	[illegible]]
	Winter Rates—			Winter Rates—	
Belfast	([illegible] hrs.)	[illegible]	Newcastle	([illegible] hrs.)	[illegible]
*Cork	([illegible] hrs.)	[illegible]	Manchester	([illegible] hrs.)	[illegible]
*Londonderry	([illegible] hrs.)	[illegible]	Hull	([illegible] hrs.)	[illegible]
			Bristol	([illegible] hrs.)	[illegible]
			Cardiff	([illegible] hrs.)	[illegible]
			Southampton	([illegible] hrs.)	[illegible]
			Leith	([illegible] hrs.)	[illegible]
			[London	([illegible] hrs.)	[illegible]]
	Summer Rates—			Summer Rates—	
Belfast	([illegible] hrs.)	[illegible]	Newcastle	([illegible] hrs.)	[illegible]
			Manchester	([illegible] hrs.)	[illegible]
			Hull	([illegible] hrs.)	[illegible]
			Bristol	([illegible] hrs.)	[illegible]
			Cardiff	([illegible] hrs.)	[illegible]
			Southampton	([illegible] hrs.)	[illegible]
			Leith	([illegible] hrs.)	[illegible]
			[London	([illegible] hrs.)	[illegible])
	Winter Rates—			Winter Rates—	
Belfast	([illegible] hrs.)	[illegible]	Newcastle	([illegible] hrs.)	[illegible]
			Manchester	([illegible] hrs.)	[illegible]
			Hull	([illegible] hrs.)	[illegible]
			Bristol	([illegible] hrs.)	[illegible]
			Cardiff	([illegible] hrs.)	[illegible]
			Southampton	([illegible] hrs.)	[illegible]
			Leith	([illegible] hrs.)	[illegible]
			[London	([illegible] hrs.)	[illegible])
	Summer Rates—			Summer Rates—	
Belfast	([illegible] hrs.)	[illegible]	Newcastle	([illegible] hrs.)	[illegible]
*Dublin	([illegible] hrs.)	[illegible]	Manchester	([illegible] hrs.)	[illegible]
			Hull	([illegible] hrs.)	[illegible]
			Bristol	([illegible] hrs.)	[illegible]
			Cardiff	([illegible] hrs.)	[illegible]
			Southampton	([illegible] hrs.)	[illegible]
			Leith	([illegible] hrs.)	[illegible]
			[London	([illegible] hrs.)	[illegible]]

* Computed from Trade Union Returns.

Employments.	Irish Localities.			Localities in Great Britain.		
BUILDING TRADES—*cont.*			Per week			Per Week
		Winter Rates—			Winter Rates—	
PAINTERS AND DECORATORS—*cont.*	Belfast	(51 hrs.)	[illegible]	Newcastle	(41½ hrs.)	[illegible]
	*Dublin	(48 hrs.)	[illegible]	Manchester	(47 hrs.)	27s. 3d.
				Hull	(47 hrs.)	27s. 3d.
				Bristol	(48 hrs.)	[illegible]
				Cardiff	(47 hrs.)	[illegible]
				Southampton	(50½ hrs.)	27s. 6d.
				Leith	(39 hrs.)	[illegible]
				[London	(44½ to 47 hrs.)	[illegible]]
		Summer Rates—			Summer Rates—	
SLATERS	Belfast	(54 hrs.)	[illegible]	Newcastle	(50 hrs.)	[illegible]
				Manchester	(54½ hrs.)	[illegible]
				Hull	(53 hrs.)	[illegible]
				Bristol	(54 hrs.)	[illegible]
				Cardiff	(51 hrs.)	[illegible]
				Leith	(51 hrs.)	[illegible]
				(No London rates quoted.)		
		Winter Rates—			Winter Rates—	
	Belfast	(51 hrs.)	[illegible]	Newcastle	(41½ hrs.)	[illegible]
				Manchester	(46½ hrs.)	[illegible]
				Hull	(47 hrs.)	[illegible]
				Bristol	(48 hrs.)	[illegible]
				Cardiff	(47 hrs.)	[illegible]
				Leith	(44 hrs.)	[illegible]
				(No London rates quoted.)		
		Summer Rates—			Summer Rates—	
BRICKLAYERS' LABOURERS	Belfast	(54 hrs.)	18s.	Newcastle	(50 hrs.)	[illegible]
				Manchester	(54½ hrs.)	[illegible]
				Hull	(53 hrs.)	[illegible]
				Bristol	(54 hrs.)	[illegible]
				Cardiff	(54 hrs.)	[illegible]
				Southampton	(56½ hrs.)	[illegible]
				Leith	(51 hrs.)	[illegible]
				[London	(50 hrs.)	[illegible]]
		Winter Rates—			Winter Rates—	
	Belfast	(51 hrs.)	18s.	Newcastle	(41½ hrs.)	[illegible]
				Manchester	(46½ hrs.)	[illegible]
				Hull	(47 hrs.)	[illegible]
				Bristol	(48 hrs.)	[illegible]
				Cardiff	(47 hrs.)	[illegible]
				Southampton	(50½ hrs.)	[illegible]
				Leith	(44 hrs.)	[illegible]
				[London	(44½ to 47 hrs.)	[illegible]]
MASONS' LABOURERS	Same as Bricklayers' Labourers			Same as Bricklayers' Labourers, except for Leith and Manchester, for which towns the rates are:—		
				Leith—		
				In summer	(51 hrs.)	[illegible]
				In winter	(44 hrs.)	[illegible]
				Manchester:—		
				In summer	(49½ hrs.)	[illegible]
				In winter	(47 hrs.)	[illegible]
PLASTERERS' LABOURERS	Same as Bricklayers' Labourers			Same as Bricklayers' Labourers, except for Newcastle and Manchester, for which towns the rates are:—		
				Newcastle—		
				In summer	(50 hrs.)	[illegible]
				In winter	(41 hrs.)	[illegible]
				Manchester—		
				In summer	(53 hrs.)	[illegible]
				In winter	(47 hrs.)	[illegible]
SHIP CARPENTERS	Belfast	(54 hrs.)	[illegible]	Newcastle	(54 hrs.)	[illegible]
				Hull	(53 hrs.)	[illegible]
				Birkenhead	(54 hrs.)	[illegible]
				Cardiff	(54 hrs.)	[illegible]
				Leith	(54 hrs.)	[illegible]
				[London	(54 hrs.)	[illegible]]

* Computed from Trade Union Returns.

Comparison of Ireland with the United Kingdom in respect of the undermentioned Particulars.

		Ireland.	United Kingdom.	Proportion of Ireland to Total.
				Per Cent.
Consumption of coal ([illegible])	Million Tons	[illegible]	[illegible]	[illegible]
Imports and exports ([illegible])	Millions Sterling	[illegible]	[illegible]	[illegible]
Income tax:				
Assessable [illegible]	" "	[illegible]	144·[illegible]	[illegible]
Net assessment of trades and professions	" "	[illegible]	[illegible]	[illegible]
" " quarries, mines, ironworks, &c.	" "	[illegible]	[illegible]	[illegible]
" " concerns not described in Rule No. 3, Schedule A.	" "	[illegible]	[illegible]	[illegible]
" " railways in the United Kingdom	" "	[illegible]	[illegible]	[illegible]
" " interest paid out of rates	" "	[illegible]	[illegible]	[illegible]
" " "other public"	" "	[illegible]	[illegible]	[illegible]
Property upon which Probate and Succession Duties were assessed ([illegible]):				
Net value of property upon which Probate Duty was charged	" "	[illegible]	[illegible]	[illegible]
Net value of property assessed to succession duty	" "	[illegible]	[illegible]	[illegible]
Shipping owned at ports (gross tonnage) [illegible]	Million Tons	[illegible]	[illegible]	[illegible]
Shipping built—average of [illegible]	Thousand Tons	[illegible]	[illegible]	[illegible]
Total tonnage of shipping entered and cleared in the foreign trade ([illegible])	Million Tons	[illegible]	[illegible]	[illegible]
Tonnage of shipping entered and cleared with cargoes in the coasting trade ([illegible])†	" "	[illegible]	[illegible]	[illegible]
Number of textile factories	Number	[illegible]	[illegible]	[illegible]
" spinning spindles	Millions	[illegible]	[illegible]	[illegible]
" doubling spindles	"	[illegible]	[illegible]	[illegible]
" power looms	Thousands	[illegible]	[illegible]	[illegible]
" persons employed in textile factories	"	[illegible]	[illegible]	[illegible]
Liabilities of banking companies ([illegible])	Millions Sterling	[illegible]	[illegible]	[illegible]
Cash received for goods sold—				
Co-operative Societies ([illegible])	" "	[illegible]	[illegible]	[illegible]
Deposits in Savings Banks ([illegible]):				
Post Office	" "	[illegible]	[illegible]	[illegible]
Trustee Banks	" "	[illegible]	[illegible]	[illegible]
Total	" "	[illegible]	[illegible]	[illegible]
Joint Stock Companies registered during [illegible]	Number	[illegible]	[illegible]	[illegible]
Capital of new Joint Stock Companies paid up at end during [illegible]	Millions Sterling	[illegible]	[illegible]	[illegible]
Number of Joint Stock Companies doing business in [illegible]	Number	[illegible]	[illegible]	[illegible]
Capital of Joint Stock Companies doing business in [illegible]	Millions Sterling	[illegible]	[illegible]	[illegible]
Letters delivered [illegible]	Millions	[illegible]	[illegible]	[illegible]
Letters delivered per head of population	—	[illegible]	[illegible]	—
Newspapers, book packets, &c., delivered [illegible]	Millions	[illegible]	[illegible]	[illegible]
Postcards delivered, [illegible]	"	[illegible]	[illegible]	[illegible]
Telegraph messages forwarded	"	[illegible]	[illegible]	[illegible]
Amount of money orders issued [illegible]	Millions Sterling	[illegible]	[illegible]	[illegible]
" postal orders issued [illegible]	" "	[illegible]	[illegible]	[illegible]
Deposits in Joint Stock Banks	" "	[illegible]	[illegible] / [illegible]	[illegible] / [illegible]
Local expenditure [illegible]	" "	[illegible]	[illegible]	[illegible]
Net receipts from Customs and Excise (excluding receipts on Local Taxation Account)	" "	[illegible]	[illegible]	[illegible]
Railways:				
Paid-up capital of Companies ([illegible])	" "	[illegible]	[illegible]	[illegible]
Number of passengers carried (excluding season ticket holders) ([illegible])	Millions	[illegible]	[illegible]	[illegible]
Tonnage of goods conveyed ([illegible])	Million Tons	[illegible]	[illegible]	[illegible]
Tramways:				
Capital paid up for tramways ([illegible])	Millions Sterling	[illegible]	[illegible]	[illegible]
Number of passengers carried ([illegible])	Millions	[illegible]	[illegible]	[illegible]
Gross receipts ([illegible])	Millions Sterling	[illegible]	[illegible]	[illegible]
Mining industries—estimated value of mineral produce at the mines or open works ([illegible])	" "	[illegible]	[illegible]	[illegible]
Population	Millions	[illegible]	[illegible]	[illegible]
Agricultural population:				
Males above [illegible] in agricultural class at census ([illegible])	No.	[illegible]	[illegible]	[illegible]
Net agricultural production	Millions Sterling	[illegible]	[illegible]	[illegible]

* [illegible] [illegible] [illegible]

† [illegible] § [illegible] Table VIII.

‖ [illegible]

A.—Supplement to Table III.

Joint Stock Banks.

Statement showing the Total Amounts of Deposits and Current Accounts held by the Undermentioned Groups of Joint Stock Banks in the United Kingdom, Summarised from the Banking Supplement to the "Economist" for the Half Year to June 1894 ("Economist" of [illegible] October 1894.)

	£
England and Wales (excluding Bank of England)	[illegible]
Bank of England	[illegible]
Isle of Man and Channel Islands	[illegible]
Scotland	[illegible]
Ireland	[illegible]
Colonial Banks with London Offices	[illegible]
Foreign " "	[illegible]
	[illegible]

	£
In addition Private Banks of England and Wales held	[illegible]

		£
Total for United Kingdom as above		[illegible]
Add — Private Banks of England and Wales		[illegible]
Grand Total for United Kingdom		[illegible]
Deduct —		
Colonial Banks with London Offices	£[illegible]	
Foreign Banks with London Offices	[illegible]	
	[illegible]	[illegible]
Net Total for United Kingdom, including English private banks, but excluding Colonial and Foreign banks having offices in London		£[illegible]

B.—Supplement to Table III.

Estimated Value of Import and Export Trade of Ireland in [illegible].

Exports.

	£
Direct exports from Ireland in the foreign trade	[illegible]
Estimated value of exports of principal articles from Ireland to Great Britain	[illegible]
Add for unenumerated articles, say	[illegible]
Estimated total value of exports	£[illegible]

Imports.

	£
Direct imports in the foreign trade	[illegible]
Estimated value of imports of principal articles from Great Britain	[illegible]
Add for unenumerated articles, say	[illegible]
Estimated total value of imports	£[illegible]

	£
Estimated total value of import and export trade of Ireland	[illegible]

IV.

Statement showing the Population of England and Wales, Scotland, and Ireland at different Groups of Ages according to the Census of 1891, distinguishing Males and Females.

Males.

Age.	England and Wales.	Scotland.	Ireland.	Total.
Under [illegible]	[illegible]	[illegible]	[illegible]	[illegible]
[illegible] to [illegible]	[illegible]	[illegible]	[illegible]	[illegible]
[illegible] to [illegible]	[illegible]	[illegible]	[illegible]	[illegible]
[illegible] and over	[illegible]	[illegible]	[illegible]	[illegible]
Total	[illegible]	[illegible]	[illegible]	[illegible]

Females.

Age.	England and Wales.	Scotland.	Ireland.	Total.
Under [illegible]	[illegible]	[illegible]	[illegible]	[illegible]
[illegible] to [illegible]	[illegible]	[illegible]	[illegible]	[illegible]
[illegible] to [illegible]	[illegible]	[illegible]	[illegible]	[illegible]
[illegible] and over	[illegible]	[illegible]	[illegible]	[illegible]
Total	[illegible]	[illegible]	[illegible]	[illegible]

Both Sexes.

Age.	England and Wales.	Scotland.	Ireland.	Total.
Under [illegible]	[illegible]	[illegible]	[illegible]	[illegible]
[illegible] to [illegible]	[illegible]	[illegible]	[illegible]	[illegible]
[illegible] to [illegible]	[illegible]	[illegible]	[illegible]	[illegible]
[illegible] and over	[illegible]	[illegible]	[illegible]	[illegible]
Total	[illegible]	[illegible]	[illegible]	[illegible]

V.

Statement showing the Percentage Proportion of the Population in England and Wales, Scotland, and Ireland at different Groups of Ages according to the Census of 1891, distinguishing Males and Females separately.

Males.

Age.	England and Wales.	Scotland.	Ireland.	Total.
Under [illegible]	[illegible]	[illegible]	[illegible]	[illegible]
[illegible] to [illegible]	[illegible]	[illegible]	[illegible]	[illegible]
[illegible] to [illegible]	[illegible]	[illegible]	[illegible]	[illegible]
[illegible] and over	[illegible]	[illegible]	[illegible]	[illegible]
Total	[illegible]	[illegible]	[illegible]	[illegible]

Females.

Age.	England and Wales.	Scotland.	Ireland.	Total.
Under [illegible]	[illegible]	[illegible]	[illegible]	[illegible]
[illegible] to [illegible]	[illegible]	[illegible]	[illegible]	[illegible]
[illegible] to [illegible]	[illegible]	[illegible]	[illegible]	[illegible]
[illegible] and over	[illegible]	[illegible]	[illegible]	[illegible]
Total	[illegible]	[illegible]	[illegible]	[illegible]

Both Sexes.

Age.	England and Wales.	Scotland.	Ireland.	Total.
Under [illegible]	[illegible]	[illegible]	[illegible]	[illegible]
[illegible] to [illegible]	[illegible]	[illegible]	[illegible]	[illegible]
[illegible] to [illegible]	[illegible]	[illegible]	[illegible]	[illegible]
[illegible] and over	[illegible]	[illegible]	[illegible]	[illegible]
Total	[illegible]	[illegible]	[illegible]	[illegible]

VI.

RETURN from STATISTICAL TABLES relating to EMIGRATION and IMMIGRATION for 1894, being TABLE XVIII, entitled "STATEMENT showing the ENGLISH, SCOTCH, IRISH, and FOREIGN EMIGRANTS to PLACES out of EUROPE, and not within the MEDITERRANEAN SEA, the NUMBER and SEX of ADULT EMIGRANTS, the EXCESS of MALES over FEMALES, the NUMBER of CHILDREN, and the PROPORTION of CHILDREN to TOTAL EMIGRANTS in each of the Years 1880 to 1894."

Nationalities.	Years.	Total Number of Emigrants.	Adults: Males.	Adults: Females.	Adults: Excess of Males over Females.	Children and Infants: Total Number.	Children and Infants: Proportion of Children to Total Emigrants.
		No.	No.	No.	No.	No.	Per Cent.
English	1880	[illegible]	[illegible]	[illegible]	[illegible]	[illegible]	[illegible]
	1881	[illegible]	[illegible]	[illegible]	[illegible]	[illegible]	[illegible]
	1882	[illegible]	[illegible]	[illegible]	[illegible]	[illegible]	[illegible]
	1883	[illegible]	[illegible]	[illegible]	[illegible]	[illegible]	[illegible]
	1884	[illegible]	[illegible]	[illegible]	[illegible]	[illegible]	[illegible]
	1885	[illegible]	[illegible]	[illegible]	[illegible]	[illegible]	[illegible]
	1886	[illegible]	[illegible]	[illegible]	[illegible]	[illegible]	[illegible]
	1887	[illegible]	[illegible]	[illegible]	[illegible]	[illegible]	[illegible]
	1888	[illegible]	[illegible]	[illegible]	[illegible]	[illegible]	[illegible]
	1889	[illegible]	[illegible]	[illegible]	[illegible]	[illegible]	[illegible]
	1890	[illegible]	[illegible]	[illegible]	[illegible]	[illegible]	[illegible]
	1891	[illegible]	[illegible]	[illegible]	[illegible]	[illegible]	[illegible]
	1892	[illegible]	[illegible]	[illegible]	[illegible]	[illegible]	[illegible]
	1893	[illegible]	[illegible]	[illegible]	[illegible]	[illegible]	[illegible]
	1894	[illegible]	[illegible]	[illegible]	[illegible]	[illegible]	[illegible]
Scotch	1880	[illegible]	[illegible]	[illegible]	[illegible]	[illegible]	[illegible]
	1881	[illegible]	[illegible]	[illegible]	[illegible]	[illegible]	[illegible]
	1882	[illegible]	[illegible]	[illegible]	[illegible]	[illegible]	[illegible]
	1883	[illegible]	[illegible]	[illegible]	[illegible]	[illegible]	[illegible]
	1884	[illegible]	[illegible]	[illegible]	[illegible]	[illegible]	[illegible]
	1885	[illegible]	[illegible]	[illegible]	[illegible]	[illegible]	[illegible]
	1886	[illegible]	[illegible]	[illegible]	[illegible]	[illegible]	[illegible]
	1887	[illegible]	[illegible]	[illegible]	[illegible]	[illegible]	[illegible]
	1888	[illegible]	[illegible]	[illegible]	[illegible]	[illegible]	[illegible]
	1889	[illegible]	[illegible]	[illegible]	[illegible]	[illegible]	[illegible]
	1890	[illegible]	[illegible]	[illegible]	[illegible]	[illegible]	[illegible]
	1891	[illegible]	[illegible]	[illegible]	[illegible]	[illegible]	[illegible]
	1892	[illegible]	[illegible]	[illegible]	[illegible]	[illegible]	[illegible]
	1893	[illegible]	[illegible]	[illegible]	[illegible]	[illegible]	[illegible]
	1894	[illegible]	[illegible]	[illegible]	[illegible]	[illegible]	[illegible]
Irish	1880	[illegible]	[illegible]	[illegible]	[illegible]	[illegible]	[illegible]
	1881	[illegible]	[illegible]	[illegible]	[illegible]	[illegible]	[illegible]
	1882	[illegible]	[illegible]	[illegible]	[illegible]	[illegible]	[illegible]
	1883	[illegible]	[illegible]	[illegible]	[illegible]	[illegible]	[illegible]
	1884	[illegible]	[illegible]	[illegible]	[illegible]	[illegible]	[illegible]
	1885	[illegible]	[illegible]	[illegible]	[illegible]	[illegible]	[illegible]
	1886	[illegible]	[illegible]	[illegible]	[illegible]	[illegible]	[illegible]
	1887	[illegible]	[illegible]	[illegible]	[illegible]	[illegible]	[illegible]
	1888	[illegible]	[illegible]	[illegible]	[illegible]	[illegible]	[illegible]
	1889	[illegible]	[illegible]	[illegible]	[illegible]	[illegible]	[illegible]
	1890	[illegible]	[illegible]	[illegible]	[illegible]	[illegible]	[illegible]
	1891	[illegible]	[illegible]	[illegible]	[illegible]	[illegible]	[illegible]
	1892	[illegible]	[illegible]	[illegible]	[illegible]	[illegible]	[illegible]
	1893	[illegible]	[illegible]	[illegible]	[illegible]	[illegible]	[illegible]
	1894	[illegible]	[illegible]	[illegible]	[illegible]	[illegible]	[illegible]
Total of British and Irish origin	1880	[illegible]	[illegible]	[illegible]	[illegible]	[illegible]	[illegible]
	1881	[illegible]	[illegible]	[illegible]	[illegible]	[illegible]	[illegible]
	1882	[illegible]	[illegible]	[illegible]	[illegible]	[illegible]	[illegible]
	1883	[illegible]	[illegible]	[illegible]	[illegible]	[illegible]	[illegible]
	1884	[illegible]	[illegible]	[illegible]	[illegible]	[illegible]	[illegible]
	1885	[illegible]	[illegible]	[illegible]	[illegible]	[illegible]	[illegible]
	1886	[illegible]	[illegible]	[illegible]	[illegible]	[illegible]	[illegible]
	1887	[illegible]	[illegible]	[illegible]	[illegible]	[illegible]	[illegible]
	1888	[illegible]	[illegible]	[illegible]	[illegible]	[illegible]	[illegible]
	1889	[illegible]	[illegible]	[illegible]	[illegible]	[illegible]	[illegible]
	1890	[illegible]	[illegible]	[illegible]	[illegible]	[illegible]	[illegible]
	1891	[illegible]	[illegible]	[illegible]	[illegible]	[illegible]	[illegible]
	1892	[illegible]	[illegible]	[illegible]	[illegible]	[illegible]	[illegible]
	1893	[illegible]	[illegible]	[illegible]	[illegible]	[illegible]	[illegible]
	1894	[illegible]	[illegible]	[illegible]	[illegible]	[illegible]	[illegible]
Foreigners	1880	[illegible]	[illegible]	[illegible]	[illegible]	[illegible]	[illegible]
	1881	[illegible]	[illegible]	[illegible]	[illegible]	[illegible]	[illegible]
	1882	[illegible]	[illegible]	[illegible]	[illegible]	[illegible]	[illegible]
	1883	[illegible]	[illegible]	[illegible]	[illegible]	[illegible]	[illegible]
	1884	[illegible]	[illegible]	[illegible]	[illegible]	[illegible]	[illegible]
	1885	[illegible]	[illegible]	[illegible]	[illegible]	[illegible]	[illegible]
	1886	[illegible]	[illegible]	[illegible]	[illegible]	[illegible]	[illegible]
	1887	[illegible]	[illegible]	[illegible]	[illegible]	[illegible]	[illegible]
	1888	[illegible]	[illegible]	[illegible]	[illegible]	[illegible]	[illegible]
	1889	[illegible]	[illegible]	[illegible]	[illegible]	[illegible]	[illegible]
	1890	[illegible]	[illegible]	[illegible]	[illegible]	[illegible]	[illegible]
	1891	[illegible]	[illegible]	[illegible]	[illegible]	[illegible]	[illegible]
	1892	[illegible]	[illegible]	[illegible]	[illegible]	[illegible]	[illegible]
	1893	[illegible]	[illegible]	[illegible]	[illegible]	[illegible]	[illegible]
	1894	[illegible]	[illegible]	[illegible]	[illegible]	[illegible]	[illegible]

* Excess of Females over Males.

VII.

The Agricultural Production of Ireland.

The annual value of Irish agriculture is the subject of certain official statistics. The crops are valued; there are means of estimating the quantity of dairy produce; the exports of cattle, sheep, and pigs to Great Britain, where the principal market is found, are known. What it now proposed is to make up an account stating, first, the annual value of such crops as go directly into consumption as the food of the people and are not exported from Ireland; second, the annual value of the dairy produce, which is not included among the crops, but is the result of the consumption of the forage, hay, and other crops of which valuations are given; and third, the annual value of the cattle, sheep, pigs, wool, and other produce exported or sold off the farm. All these items with deductions for seed and manure, must show the annual value of agriculture in Ireland.

On the first head it may be convenient to state at the outset the annual value of the crops in the gross for a recent average year.

The following is such a statement:—

Quantity and Value of Irish Crops (see note)

Crops.	Average Annual Produce of the Crops at the period [illegible]	Average Price assumed for the purposes of Valuation.	Estimated Annual Value of the Crops produced.
	Thousand Cwts.	Per Cwt.	Thousand £.
Wheat	[illegible]	[illegible]	[illegible]
Oats	[illegible]	[illegible]	[illegible]
Barley	[illegible]	[illegible]	[illegible]
Bere and Rye	[illegible]	[illegible]	[illegible]
Beans and Peas	[illegible]	[illegible]	[illegible]
Flax	[illegible]	[illegible]	[illegible]
	Thousand Tons.	Per Ton.	
Potatoes	[illegible]	[illegible]	[illegible]
Turnips	[illegible]	[illegible]	[illegible]
Mangolds	[illegible]	[illegible]	[illegible]
Hay	[illegible]	[illegible]	[illegible]
Total estimated annual value of the Crops			[illegible]

Note.—[illegible]

A similar estimate which I prepared two or three years ago, based on Thom's valuations, gave an almost identical total ([illegible]l.), though the different items in the accounts have, of course, been more or less varied.

These are the crops of about five out of 15 million acres of cultivated land in Ireland. They do not, however, include the value of the pasturage of the remaining 10 million acres of cultivated land, or the five million acres beyond that of waste. If we could put a figure on the annual value of such acreage, we should have an idea of the annual value of Irish agriculture making allowance for the additional cost of converting the raw material of much of the above crops and pasturage into beef, mutton, wool, and dairy produce. In the absence of such a figure we must separate from the above list the items which go direct into consumption, and then add the estimated value of the beef, mutton, &c., into which the other crops are converted.

We have to deal then, first, with the items going direct into consumption.

They appear to be as follows:—

	Thousand £.
Wheat	[illegible]
Oats (one half)	[illegible]
Barley	[illegible]
Flax	[illegible]
Potatoes	[illegible]
Hay, consumed for non-agricultural purposes	[illegible]
Total	[illegible]

This 15,000,000l. is the first item we get in reckoning up the value of Irish agriculture.

The second item it is proposed to take is the dairy produce. Mr. Rew in his paper read at the Statistical Society in April 1892, after studying many estimates of the produce of cows, finally reckons the produce of each milch cow, deducting 10 per cent from the numbers in the statistical returns for non-effectives, at 400 gallons per annum. This is for the United Kingdom. The average for Ireland, I am led to understand, would probably be less, but this account cannot pretend to be very exact, and if we take the United Kingdom average we cannot be supposed to underestimate.

Applying this figure then to Irish cows, stated to be 1,441,000 according to the last agricultural returns, but subject to a deduction of 10 per cent by Mr. Rew's method, making the number to be dealt with 1,300,000, we arrive at [illegible] gallons as the milk produce of Ireland. At 5d. per gallon, which I take to be a fair estimate allowing for the distance of many parts of Ireland from a market, this produce would be equal to an annual value of about 11,000,000l., which becomes the second item in our account.

The third item comprises the value of the cattle, sheep, pigs, &c., consumed or exported. The exports of cattle, sheep, and pigs have of late years averaged as follows in numbers:—

Cattle	[illegible]
Sheep and lambs	[illegible]
Pigs	[illegible]

Many of the cattle are stores and not equal in value to the average of the stock at home. But we may value the live stock exported, so as not to err on the side of deficit, at the following values, viz.:—Cattle at 10l., sheep at 2l., pigs 2l. 10s., being values somewhat less than the average given by Thom for the live stock in Ireland. The result is as follows:—

	£
Cattle	[illegible]
Sheep and lambs	1,722,000
Pigs	[illegible]
Total	[illegible]

Adding 1,000,000l. for export of horses and another 1,000,000l. for wool, poultry, &c., exported or sold off the farm, we get a total of about [illegible] as the export of live stock from the Irish farm.

Some addition must also be made for the consumption of meat in Ireland, which may be put, I think, at something like 30s. per head for the whole population, or in round figures 7,000,000l. Our third item altogether is thus about 17,000,000l.

The gross annual return of Irish agriculture on the basis of these data may accordingly be put as follows:—

	£
Potatoes, oats, &c., going directly into human consumption	[illegible]
Dairy produce	11,000,000
Value of cattle, sheep, &c. consumed or exported	17,000,000
Total	[illegible]

* One-tenth of Mr. Rew's estimate for United Kingdom.

C.

Papers put in by Mr Robert Giffen, C.B., LL.D., in connexion with his evidence before the Commission on [illegible] *March* [illegible].

EXPORT AND IMPORT TRADE OF IRELAND.—ESTIMATE of the VALUE of the PRINCIPAL ARTICLES exported from and imported into IRELAND during the YEAR [illegible].

A.—EXPORTS.

NOTE.—This statement deals with the *Principal Articles of Export only*. A complete estimate of the total value of Irish Exports is contained in Supplement B. to Table No. [illegible], page 17[illegible].

	£	Thousand £
Direct exports in the foreign trade:—		
British and Irish produce		[illegible]
Foreign and Colonial produce		[illegible]
Add for Irish exports to Great Britain:—		
Horses.—[illegible],000 at say [illegible] each		[illegible]
Cattle.—[illegible],000 at say [illegible] each		[illegible]
Sheep.—1,10[illegible],000 at say [illegible] each		[illegible]
Pigs.—[illegible],000 at say [illegible] 10s. each		1,[illegible]
Bacon and Hams.—Number of pigs in Ireland, 1,1[illegible]. Dr. Grimshaw estimates all to be turned out and disposed of in the year, but say 1,[illegible],000. Deduct from these the [illegible] exported = [illegible]. Suppose each one to weigh on an average [illegible] lbs. = [illegible] cwts. of bacon, each ham, 1[illegible] lbs. = 1[illegible] cwts. of hams, or [illegible] cwts. together—this quantity at 50s. per cwt. would represent a value of		[illegible]
Butter.—Dr. Grimshaw estimates the value of milk produced to be about 14,17[illegible]. The estimate adopted by Mr Giffen to be some 11,[illegible]. If we take the mean between these two we get a figure of 12,[illegible], which is perhaps near enough for our purpose. Suppose one-fourth of the quantity which this value represents, to be used for ordinary purposes as milk, we have a value of 9,[illegible] as the value of the quantity used in butter making. If we assume (roughly) that the increase in value due to labour, &c., in butter making is nearly balanced by loss in manufacture, this figure may be taken as an estimate of the value of butter made. Say one-half (a moderate estimate) sent to Great Britain		[illegible]
Poultry:—		
Turkeys.—Number according to Irish Agricultural Statistics, 1,[illegible], say one-half exported to Great Britain or [illegible],000, which at [illegible] each would give	77,000	
Geese.—Number according to Irish Agricultural Statistics, [illegible],000, say one-half exported to Great Britain = 1,[illegible], which at 3s. each would give	163,000	
Ducks.—Number according to Irish Agricultural Statistics [illegible], say one-half exported to Great Britain = [illegible], which at 1s. each would give	73,000	
Fowls.—Number according to Irish Agricultural Statistics, 9,[illegible]. Deducting [illegible] as an estimate of the number of laying hens = 7,[illegible]. Suppose one-fourth of these (1,[illegible]) to be exported to Great Britain and allowing a value of 1s. each we get a total of	94,000	
		[illegible]
Eggs.—The number of ordinary fowl in Ireland in [illegible] was 9,[illegible]. Dr. Grimshaw estimates one to four (or [illegible]) to be laying hens. If we suppose each hen to lay 100 eggs per annum we arrive at a figure of [illegible] or [illegible] dozen, which at [illegible] per dozen (the average import price) would give a value of [illegible], say, one-half to be exported to Great Britain, we get		[illegible]
Linen Yarn and Linen Goods.—Estimate as to Irish proportion of United Kingdom exports in the foreign trade only:—		
Linen Yarn.—Total value of United Kingdom exports in the foreign trade 1,[illegible], say one-half of this Irish made		[illegible]
Linen Piece Goods, plain.—Total value of United Kingdom exports in the foreign trade [illegible], say one-half of this Irish manufacture		[illegible]
Linen Piece Goods, printed.—Total value of United Kingdom exports in the foreign trade [illegible], say one-half of this Irish manufacture		[illegible]
Linen Sailcloth.—Total value of United Kingdom exports in the foreign trade 144,000*l*., say one-half of this Irish manufacture		[illegible]
Linen Thread.—Total value of United Kingdom exports in the foreign trade [illegible], say one-half of this Irish manufacture		[illegible]
Linen Manufactures, unenumerated.—Total value of United Kingdom exports in the foreign trade [illegible], say one-half of these Irish made		[illegible]
Spirits.—Irish made.—Quantity sent to Great Britain during [illegible] (see "Monthly Accounts of Trade and Navigation" for January 18[illegible]), [illegible] gallons, this at an assumed average of [illegible] per gallon would represent		[illegible]
Beer.—Quantity made in Ireland in 18[illegible] according to the "Monthly Accounts of Trade and Navigation" for January 18[illegible]), [illegible] barrels, say [illegible] per cent. of this sent to Great Britain for consumption and export (this proportion being based on the figures as to revenue from beer duty as given by the Treasury in the House of Commons Paper, No. [illegible] of [illegible]) = [illegible] barrels, which at 40s. per barrel would give 1,[illegible]		1,[illegible]
[The average export price as computed for the "Statistical Abstract for the United Kingdom," was [illegible] per barrel, but this would include cost of bottling and packing.]		
Wool.—The number of sheep of one year old and upwards in Ireland in 18[illegible] was [illegible]. Suppose each sheep to yield [illegible] lbs. of wool on the average, we should arrive at a figure of [illegible] lbs., which at the average import price of [illegible] per lb., would give		[illegible]
Fish.—The value of Irish-caught fish sent to Great Britain in 18[illegible], as estimated by the Irish Fishery Board, was		[illegible]
		[illegible]

3.—Imports.

Note.—This supplement deals with the *Presumed Arrivals* of Import only. A complete estimate of the total value of Irish Imports is contained in Supplement B. to Table No. III., page 174.

	Thousand £
Direct imports in the foreign trade	6,[illegible]
Estimated value of imports of under-mentioned articles from Great Britain:	
Coal.—Quantity received at Irish ports from Great Britain during 1893, 3,[illegible] tons; this at 9s. per ton (the average export price) would give	1,[illegible]
Cocoa.—The consumption per head in the United Kingdom in 1893 was 0·[illegible] lbs., but say for Ireland, 0·5 lbs. per head. The population of Ireland being 4,[illegible], the Irish consumption on this basis would be 2,[illegible] lbs., which at 7·[illegible]d. per lb. (the average import price) would give	76
Coffee.—The consumption per head in the United Kingdom in 1893 was 0·[illegible] lbs., say for Ireland, 0·[illegible] lbs. per head. Thus the Irish consumption would be 1,[illegible] lbs., which at the average import price of [illegible]s. per cwt. would give	70
Currants and Raisins.—The consumption per head in the United Kingdom in 1893 was [illegible] lbs., say for Ireland, 5 lbs. per head. Thus the Irish consumption would be 2[illegible] lbs.; but from this figure should be deducted 1,[illegible] lbs. imported direct, which would leave 20,[illegible] lbs. as an estimate of the quantity imported through Great Britain; and this at [illegible]s. per cwt. (the average import price) would give	1[illegible]
Foreign Spirits.—The consumption per head in the United Kingdom in 1893 was 0·[illegible] gallons, but say for Ireland 0·1[illegible] gallons per head. The Irish consumption on this basis would be about [illegible] gallons. Deduct [illegible] gallons imported direct = [illegible] gallons imported through Great Britain, which at an assumed average price of [illegible]s. per gallon would give	[illegible]
Tea.—The consumption per head in the United Kingdom in 1893 was 5·[illegible] lbs., but say for Ireland 5 lbs. per head. Thus the Irish consumption would be [illegible] lbs. Deduct from this the [illegible] lbs. imported direct, and we should have a figure of [illegible] lbs., which at [illegible]d. per lb. (the average import price) would give	[illegible]
Tobacco.—The consumption per head in the United Kingdom in 1893 was 1·[illegible] lbs. Assuming that there would be no great difference between consumption in Ireland and consumption in the United Kingdom generally, this rate would give 7,[illegible] lbs. as the Irish share. Deduct [illegible] lbs. imported direct = 7,[illegible] lbs., and this at 7·[illegible]d. per lb. (the average import price) would give	[illegible]
Wine.—The consumption per head in the United Kingdom in 1893 was 0·[illegible] gallons, but say 0·[illegible] gallons for Ireland alone. This would make the Irish consumption to be about 1,[illegible] gallons. Deduct from this [illegible] gallons imported direct = [illegible] gallons, and this at 7·[illegible]s. per gallon (the average import price) would give	170
Sugar, Raw.—The consumption per head in the United Kingdom in 1893 was [illegible] lbs., but say that the Irish consumption of imported raw sugar (whether refined in Great Britain or not) would be about [illegible] lbs. per head. Thus the Irish share of the total imports would be 1,[illegible] cwts., which at 14·[illegible]s. per cwt. (the average import price) would give	[illegible]
Sugar, Refined.—The consumption per head in the United Kingdom in 1893 was [illegible] lbs., but say [illegible] lbs. per head for Ireland alone. The Irish consumption on this basis would be [illegible] cwts. Deduct from this the [illegible] cwts. imported direct = [illegible] cwts., which at [illegible]s. per cwt. (the average import price) would give	[illegible]
Flax, Dressed and Undressed.—The total quantity imported into the United Kingdom in 1893 was 72,[illegible] tons. Suppose one-half of this ([illegible] tons) to have been intended for use in Ireland. Deduct from this the [illegible] tons imported direct, and we get [illegible] tons as imported through Great Britain, and this at [illegible]s. per cwt. (the average import price) would give	[illegible]
Manures, Phosphates.—The total quantity imported into the United Kingdom in 1893 was [illegible] tons. Suppose [illegible] ([illegible] tons) intended for use in Ireland. Deduct [illegible] tons imported direct, and we get [illegible] tons as the Irish share. This at [illegible] per ton (the average import price) would give	[illegible]
Manures.—*Other kinds.*—The total value imported into the United Kingdom in 1893 was 1,[illegible]. Deduct [illegible] for the value of re-exports, and we get 1,[illegible] as representing the net value imported. Supposing about [illegible] of this to be intended for Ireland, and allowing a little for direct importations, we get a figure of	[illegible]
Matches.—The total value imported into the United Kingdom in 1893 was [illegible]. Deduct [illegible] for the value of re-exports, and we get [illegible]. The proportion that Ireland would take, according to population, would be about [illegible] per cent., and on this showing we get	[illegible]
Linen Yarn.—The total quantity imported into the United Kingdom in 1893 was [illegible] lbs. Suppose one-third of this ([illegible] lbs.) to have been intended for use in Ireland. Deduct 4,[illegible] lbs. as having been imported direct, and we get [illegible] lbs. as the Irish share of the imports into Great Britain. This at [illegible]d. per lb. (the average import price) would give	[illegible]
Oil Seed Cake.—The total quantity imported into the United Kingdom in 1893 was [illegible] tons. The Irish share according to the number of cattle in Ireland would be about [illegible] per cent., but, taking into consideration the large extent of pasturage, we may perhaps assume a proportion of [illegible] per cent. Then, [illegible] per cent. of [illegible] tons = [illegible] tons, and deducting 7,[illegible] tons imported direct, we have [illegible] tons as the calculated quantity imported through Great Britain. This, at [illegible] per ton (the average import price), would give	[illegible]

		Thousand £.
Corn, Wheat.—		
Quantity produced in United Kingdom ([illegible]) . . Bushels. 40,[illegible],000 = [illegible] Qrs. = Cwts. 27,377,000		
Importation into United Kingdom in 18[illegible]	[illegible]	
	[illegible]	
Deduct exports of British wheat . . . . . Cwts. [illegible]		
" foreign wheat . . . . . [illegible]		
" British wheat flour . . . . . [illegible]	[illegible]	
Leaves for consumption . . .	[illegible]	
Irish proportion, [illegible] per cent. by population, but say 10 per cent. . .	[illegible]	
Deduct imported direct . . . . . [illegible]		
" produced at home . . . . . [illegible]	[illegible]	
Net for Ireland, through Great Britain . . .	[illegible]	
which at [illegible] per cwt. (the average import price) would give		1,0[illegible]
Corn, Wheat Flour.—		
Quantity imported into the United Kingdom in 18[illegible] . .	[illegible]	
Deduct re-exports	[illegible]	
	20,1[illegible]	
Irish proportion, 1[illegible] per cent. by population, but say 10 per cent. . .	[illegible]	
Deduct imported direct	[illegible]	
Net for Ireland, through Great Britain	407,000	
which at [illegible] per cwt. (the average import price) would give		1[illegible]
Rice.—The consumption per head in the United Kingdom in 18[illegible] was [illegible] lbs., but say 3 lbs. per head for Ireland. Then the Irish consumption would be [illegible] cwts., which at [illegible] per cwt. (the average import price), would give		[illegible]
Petroleum.—The total quantity imported into the United Kingdom in 18[illegible] was [illegible] gallons. Deduct [illegible] gallons re-exported, and we get [illegible] gallons. The Irish share by population would be 1[illegible] per cent., but [illegible] per cent. would probably be as much as Ireland would take. This would give [illegible] gallons, and deducting [illegible] gallons imported direct, there would remain [illegible] gallons as an estimate of the quantity imported through Great Britain, which at [illegible] per gallon (the average import price) would give .		7[illegible]
Boots and Shoes.—The population of Ireland is 4,[illegible]. Suppose that on an average each person has one pair per annum = [illegible] pairs. Assume that one-fourth supplied by Great Britain = 1,1[illegible] pairs, or [illegible] dozen pairs. Then at [illegible] per dozen pairs (the average export price) would give		[illegible]
Oranges and Lemons.—The total quantity imported into the United Kingdom in 18[illegible] was [illegible] bushels. Deduct quantity re-exported, [illegible] bushels, and we get [illegible] bushels. Taking the Irish share as being about [illegible] per cent., we have a figure of [illegible] bushels, and at [illegible] per bushel this would represent		[illegible]
Cotton.—Messrs. Ellison's estimate of cotton remaining for home consumption and stock in 18[illegible]—after deducting from the total quantity consumed, the waste in spinning, and the estimated quantity converted to goods and yarn exported—was [illegible] lbs., the Irish proportion by population would be 12 per cent., but say [illegible] per cent. This would give [illegible] lbs. of yarn, which at [illegible] per lb. (the average export price) gives [illegible]. Add [illegible] per cent. as an estimate of increased value by weaving, &c.		1,1[illegible]
		17,[illegible]

that the former question occupies nine pages of the Memorandum, whereas the latter is treated in scarcely a less than a page. The latter question is one of considerable difficulty, as well as great importance, and the brevity with which Sir R. Giffen has treated it suggests to me that he has not given it an amount of attention corresponding to its difficulty. In any case it will be well in these comments to keep the two questions entirely distinct.

I.

3. Sir R. Giffen begins by submitting two tables, comparing wages paid in Ireland in different employments with wages in the United Kingdom generally. He states the general effect of these tables to be that "the "remuneration of labour is generally a good deal less "in Ireland than in Great Britain, ranging from 10 and "15 per cent. up to 40 per cent."

4. This statement seems to me somewhat misleading. In Table I. I find that—omitting the case of employment in waterworks, in which the rate given is stated to be "based on only a small number of returns," and is obviously exceptional and untrustworthy for purposes of statistical inference—the highest difference given is 41 per cent. (in the woollen trade). Further, this difference is found in only one employment—the woollen trade, and only in three others—coal and ironstone mines, granite quarries, and gasworks—is the difference as much as one-third, while in 16 other cases the difference is less than one-third, besides three cases in which the Irish rates are higher.

5. I submit, therefore, that the *primâ facie* effect of Table I. would be more accurately described by saying that "the difference ranges generally from 10 or 15 to "[illegible] and 34 per cent., in one case rising as high as "40 per cent."

6. A small addition is required to obtain the difference between Irish rates and those of Great Britain, because the comparisons in Table I. are—except in the case of agriculture—between Ireland and the United Kingdom generally. But I gather from Sir R. Giffen's evidence (Q. 7717) that this correction is, in his view, so slight outside agriculture that he has not thought it worth while to calculate it.

7. In the second table, which gives more fully a comparison of average rates, chiefly in engineering and building trades, the general approximation of Irish to English rates is much closer, indeed, as Sir R. Giffen himself says, "you cannot say there is so very much "difference in average rates in Ireland and in Great "Britain." He goes on, however, to say that the general impression produced by the tables is materially changed when we "take into account the different "masses of labour at the different rates", the result being that the "average remuneration of the wage-"earner in Ireland is probably only half, or a little "better, than the average remuneration of the wage-"earner in Great Britain." But the grounds for this conclusion are so incompletely given, either in the Memorandum (page 4) or the evidence (Q. 7713, Q. 7719), that I am quite unable to estimate their force, and I cannot but express my surprise at the extremely loose reasoning which Sir R. Giffen seems to have thought sufficient to support so important a conclusion. He says that "in the United Kingdom, omitting "agriculture, the average wage per man is about 60*l.* "per head," while "in Ireland the average could not "be put at more than 32*l.* per head." Reading the Memorandum, I assumed (as Mr. Sexton appears to have done) that agriculture was omitted in calculating the average in Ireland as well as in England—though this was not expressly stated—because it seemed so obvious, considering the wages of agricultural labour in England, that a comparison which omitted agriculture on the one side and not on the other was *primâ facie* valueless for any conclusion of importance, theoretical or practical. But in his evidence (Q. 7717) Sir R. Giffen explicitly states that it is by just this process that his conclusion has been reached, and when the magnitude of the one-sided omission of agriculture is pointed out to him (Q. 7718) he answers vaguely that it would make no serious difference, because he had left out "the building trades on the other side, and "various other trades where wages are comparatively "high."

8. It is, of course, possible that the numerical result thus arrived at may be a rough approximation to the truth, but I confess that I should have been more disposed to accept it if it had been given as a bare statement of Sir R. Giffen's opinion than I am after learning the process by which it has been obtained.

9. There is another point in which Sir R. Giffen's evidence reveals a remarkable vagueness in his method of reasoning. He says that "peasant farmers below a "certain valuation" (apparently meaning a 15*l.* valuation) are, in estimates of income, to be taken as wage-earners, for "you will find constantly in the references to the "wages rates in Ireland the labourer is spoken of as "being better off than the peasant farmer who is "living on his own holding." I do not doubt that this is true of some peasant farmers; but in reasoning of this kind—as Sir R. Giffen has emphatically pointed out—everything depends on the numbers of the persons in the different classes distinguished. It may be presumed that Irishmen will not, generally speaking—any more than Englishmen—pay money to obtain a position that diminishes their income; therefore, in any district in which (*a*) agricultural labourers are employed to any considerable extent while (*b*) a tenant's interest in his holding has ordinarily an appreciable money value, the presumption that the farmer is ordinarily better off than the mere labourer is surely too strong to be overborne by a vague reference to the irresponsible statements of certain persons unknown.

10. In estimating the relative incomes of income-tax payers in the two islands the data are of a more satisfactory kind, and I see no reason for not accepting Sir R. Giffen's conclusion that the income-tax-paying wealth of Ireland is only about [illegible] of that of the United Kingdom. But when Sir R. Giffen goes on to say that he is "entitled to make the *primâ facie* "assumption that the proportion is likely to hold good "as regards the total income," I am quite unable to follow him. On the contrary, the general presumption, from the data already known, is clearly the other way, since, as the incomes in Ireland start from a lower level—as the tables of wages show—there must obviously be a larger proportion of the aggregate income in Ireland below the income-tax level.

11. A simplified example may make this plainer. Suppose that the distribution of wealth in Ireland and Great Britain were precisely similar, except that the incomes of all classes in Ireland were only two-thirds of the corresponding incomes in Great Britain, it is evident that, to make the income-tax-paying incomes bear a similar proportion to the total income in the two islands, the income-tax level would have to be lowered in Ireland from 150*l.* to 100*l.*

12. We start, then, with the presumption that the income-tax-paying income will bear a smaller ratio to the whole income in Ireland than in Great Britain. This presumption may of course be overborne by special evidence, but the burden of proving the opposite rests on Sir R. Giffen, and not, as he seems to think, on those who dispute his conclusions. But, as regards the wage-earning income, even his own estimate leads clearly to a conclusion opposed to that which he draws, since he explains (Q. 7713) that the wage-earning income of Ireland is "about one-seventeenth of the wage-earning income "in the United Kingdom." The question as to the incomes intermediate between the wage-earners and the income-tax payers is more complicated, and inevitably more uncertain, than either of the other two. But here, too, the data presented by Sir R. Giffen seem to me to point decidedly to a result materially different from the comparison of income-tax incomes.

13. Here the most important point seems to be the difference between the gross assessment to income-tax and the net assessment. This, as stated by Sir R. Giffen (Q. 7654), is 115.1 millions for the United Kingdom, and 10.9 millions for Ireland; that is, the ratio of the Irish share to the whole is little more than one-tenth, and is not much less than the ratio of the population. Now the greater part of this difference of [illegible] millions consists of incomes below the 150*l.* limit; 7,000,000*l.*—as Sir R. Giffen states (Q. 7780)—drops out of the gross assessment under Schedule B on this ground, whereas the corresponding deduction for England and Scotland is stated (Q. 7731) to be not more than [illegible]. Sir R. Giffen reduces the force of this consideration by pointing out that part of this 7,000,000*l.* is "probably permissible income." But even if we deduct 3,000,000*l.* on this account, the remaining 4,000,000*l.* will amount at least to nearly

one-tenth of the corresponding amount for England and Scotland; and, again, whatever is omitted here ought, I conceive, to be taken account of in estimating the incomes of the (agricultural) wage earners—the incomes of peasant farmers included in the gross assessment under Schedule B must be taken to be higher than the incomes of agricultural labourers, and must, therefore, raise the average of wage earners' incomes above that previously estimated by Sir R. Giffen.

14. On the whole, then, the general presumption above explained—that the whole income of Ireland will bear to the whole income of Great Britain a proportion considerably higher than the ratio of the income-tax-paying incomes in the two islands respectively—appears to me to be strengthened rather than weakened by an examination of the facts presented by Sir R. Giffen.

There is one more point on which I should like to make a remark before leaving this part of the subject. Sir R. Giffen seems to assume throughout that the relation of nominal to real income is practically the same in Ireland and in England. I do not think that this should be taken for granted, because Ireland is preponderantly agricultural, and there is a general probability that the purchasing power of money, relative to the commodities consumed by the labourer, will be somewhat higher in rural districts than it is in industrial and commercial centres and their neighbourhoods.

II.

15. I pass to consider the second question, viz., the principles of taxation to be applied in the distribution of taxation between Ireland and Great Britain, assuming the aggregate incomes of the inhabitants of the two islands respectively to have been ascertained.

16. On this point, Sir R. Giffen—in opposition, as he is careful to state, to a strong body of economic opinion—argues that "taxable resources" should be estimated by subtracting from aggregate income a certain sum per head, supposed to be the minimum necessary for subsistence. In his general idea—taken from J. S. Mill—of the desirability of avoiding the taxation of necessaries of life there seems to me to be much that deserves consideration; but the particular proposal in which he embodies this general idea I cannot but regard as crude and impracticable.

17. In the first place, it will be obvious that if the principle advocated by Sir R. Giffen is applied in computing the taxable resources of Ireland and Great Britain, its application cannot stop there; it must be applied in distributing the burden of taxation within, as well as between, Great Britain and Ireland. Nor does it appear that Sir R. Giffen shrinks from this [illegible] inference; at the same time he shows no sign of having thought out the method of applying his principle generally.

18. To apply it with any degree of exactness would involve a substitution of direct taxation of the poorer classes for the present indirect taxation. Now we might no doubt free from taxation not only the "breakfast tables" of the community, but also all forms of alcoholic potation and tobacco-smoking, and make up the deficit by an increased and extended income tax, allowing only a deduction of [illegible] a head for bachelors and spinsters, and of [illegible] a head for each member of a family; but I need not waste time in stating the overwhelming objections—financial, political, and moral—against any such scheme. If, however, Sir R. Giffen does not intend any such wild suggestion, if he approves or acquiesces in the method, actually adopted in our system of Imperial taxation, of taxing the poorer classes only indirectly, by taxes on a small number of commodities largely consumed—then he seems to have overlooked the impossibility, with such a system, of making taxation fall on individuals in any even approximate proportion to the excess of their income over the minimum required to provide necessaries of life. For if any considerable sum be raised by taxing necessaries, it will be impossible to avoid trenching on the minimum required for subsistence, in the case of the poorest class; and, in fact, Mill, in the discussion to which Sir R. Giffen refers, expressly excludes such taxes. If, on the other hand, the commodities selected for taxation, though widely consumed, are not necessaries of life, then the consumption of such commodities must be expected to vary almost

indefinitely within the same income class, from individual to individual, and from family to family. This is notoriously the case under the English system; many women, and not a few men, escape altogether the taxation of spirits, beer, and tobacco.

19. In fact it may be said that the English system of Imperial taxation carries out Mill's principle of not trenching on the minimum of subsistence in the only manner and degree in which it is really practicable, i.e., by relieving the poorer classes of all directly inevitable taxation, and only taxing them indirectly by the taxation of commodities which, however extensively consumed, are still, speaking broadly, luxuries.

20. Here I may perhaps excuse myself from discussing Sir R. Giffen's suggestion that spirits are a necessary of life to Irishmen (see Q. 7857, sqq.); since, if the Commission take it seriously, they will, I presume, refer the matter to physiological and medical experts. But I may point out that Mill, whom he is following, gives no support to this view. For in the same passage (Vol. II., § 3) in which he urges that incomes not exceeding 50*l.* should not be taxed "directly or by taxes on necessaries," he immediately adds that "this "arrangement constitutes a reason for maintaining "taxes on articles of luxury consumed by the poor"; and any doubt as to the articles which he has in view is removed by a later passage (v., § 5), in which he mentions "tea, coffee, tobacco, and fermented drinks" as examples of "real luxuries" consumed by the poor.

21. It may, however, be said, granting that if the poor are taxed, mainly or entirely, by the taxation of consumption, it is impossible to distribute the burden of taxation with anything like equality among different consumers, it is still possible and desirable to avoid gross inequality in the distribution of the burden among different social classes, and, especially, to avoid laying an undue weight of taxation on commodities which constitute a larger proportion of the non-necessary consumption of the poor than they do of that of the rich. I quite admit this, and I agree with Mill in regarding the income tax in the United Kingdom as required in equity to balance the heavy taxation of the luxuries of the poor. But in thus attempting to establish a rough approximation to equity as between different economic classes, I do not think that practically the right ideal to keep before us is that of "taxation proportioned to non-necessary consumption,"—chiefly for the following reasons:—

(a.) In the first place, it would be a serious error to regard all the expenditure of the higher income classes, in excess of the proposed minimum, as expenditure on "luxuries" or "indulgences" in the sense in which Mill applies these terms to the spirits and tobacco consumed by the poor, since a large part of it is expenditure which could not be [illegible] without economic detriment to society. In the case of all skilled labour, from the lowest to the highest, provision has to be made for the more or less prolonged education of the future labourers, and for their prolonged support while being educated. So far as this provision is thrown on parents, the minimum of economically necessary consumption must be increased, in varying degrees, for the classes that provide the various kinds of skilled labour, including, of course, commercial and professional as well as mechanical labour. Further, after education has been finished, a material part of the expenditure of the higher classes of labourers, besides what is required for their physical support, e.g., on books, instruments, conveyances, &c., is also either economically necessary or highly conducive to economic efficiency.

(b.) Inevitable taxation—such as that imposed by a fairly adjusted income tax—must be regarded as a burden severer in kind than taxation which can be reduced or avoided by restraining the consumption of non-necessary commodities. The difference does not, indeed, admit of any exact quantitative estimate, but it is not therefore to be disregarded in an equitable distribution of the total burden of taxation.

(c.) Another, even more important, consideration arises from the fact that the luxuries of the poor which bear the chief burden of indirect taxation are dangerous luxuries, largely consumed in excess. This point is expressly noted by Mill, who lays down (Vol. v., § 5) that for the reason "among luxuries of general consumption, "taxation should by preference attach itself to "stimulants"; and there can be no doubt that (e.g.) our present very high duty on spirits was proposed and is maintained—in spite of the obvious inequality which it involves in the incidence of taxation on different classes of consumers—as tending to reduce (excess) consumption, injurious to health or efficiency. Accordingly, Mr. Dudley Baxter suggests (*Taxation of the United Kingdom*, ch. iv.) that the extra contribution, levied through customs and excise, from those who drink to excess, should be regarded as a *fine* rather than a tax. The term "fine" is perhaps inappropriate; but the principle of equity implied in the suggestion seems to me in the main sound. For, on the one hand, the moderate drinkers in any class have no claim to be treated as overtaxed merely because their income class includes a minority of drunkards who materially increase the aggregate consumption of the class; on the other hand, to recompense the drunkards so far as such a class would be obviously contrary to the policy of the tax. It might, no doubt, be attempted to obviate this objection by drawing a line between moderate and immoderate consumption; but I think that any such line would be largely unsatisfactory—owing to the differences in the physical conditions of individuals—and would give rise to endless disputes.

(d.) In considering the equitable distribution of taxation in England, it has to be borne in mind that the main additional burdens imposed by any future war or similar emergency will certainly be borne by the income tax payers.

22. Taking these considerations together, I come to the conclusion that the idea of proportioning Imperial taxation to the amount of income over a subsistence minimum should be abandoned, and that the very rough approximation to equity which is alone possible, in a mixed system of direct and indirect taxation, is more likely to be attained if we aim at proportioning the normal contributions of different income classes to the total incomes of the respective classes; while carrying out Mill's principle of not trenching on the subsistence minimum, by excluding taxes on the necessaries of life as well as direct taxation of the poor.

23. And, as before said, if this is accepted as the right principle of distribution as between different income classes, we cannot consistently apply a different principle in estimating the different taxable capacities of different portions of the United Kingdom.

24. I have now, I think, dealt as fully as seems desirable with the points specially put before me by the Secretary to the Commission; but I should like before concluding to add a final remark on the general bearing of the whole discussion. I observe that Sir R. Giffen repudiates very emphatically the notion—apparently implied in the terms of the reference to the Commission—of distinguishing any portion of Imperial expenditure as devoted to specially "Irish purposes." He maintains (Q. 7796) that "all the expenditure by an Imperial "Government is to be considered expenditure for "Imperial purposes; although part of it may be spent "locally, you cannot consider it in any way expenditure for the benefit of the locality." And, again (Q. 7811), he "presses most strongly the absence of "common authority for the distinction which is "attempted, and its inconsistency with any view of "the functions of an overspreading Union of the two "countries which implies the abolition of all such distinctions." Sir R. Giffen's reference to "common authority" here is, I think, somewhat too emphatic, considering the vagueness and generality of the summary treatment which the leading English economists have usually given to the problems of public finance; still I do not doubt that, speaking broadly, the principle he lays down would have the support of economists generally. But I am surprised that he has failed to note a similar "absence of common authority" for the distinction which it is the apparent aim of his Memorandum to enforce—the distinction, that is, between the portion of Imperial taxation of commodities borne by the inhabitants of one locality within the United Kingdom as compared with that borne by the inhabitants of another locality. If the "overspreading "Union of the two countries" is held to abolish the one distinction it must surely be held equally to abolish the other; the arguments for uniformity are to a great extent similar in the cases; and the inconsistency of rejecting the one distinction while enforcing the other seems to me so gross and palpable, that it could not possibly have escaped Sir R. Giffen's notice, had it not been for the curiously limited attention which he appears to have given to the question of finance, as distinct from the commercial question. There is much to be said for refusing to inquire either how much of Imperial taxation is received from Ireland, or how much is spent on Ireland; but there is, I conceive, nothing to be said in favour of elaborately investigating the former question, while refusing, on principle, to consider the latter.

HENRY SIDGWICK.

---

2. *Note by Mr. C. F. Bastable, M.A., LL.D., Professor of Political Economy, Dublin University.*

The question of the just or equitable distribution of taxation has usually been discussed with reference to the contributions of individuals or classes within a single country, but the same general principles can, with some modifications, be applied to the case of different countries or districts subject to a single tax system.

Perhaps the easiest way of approaching the subject is to notice briefly the more important theories that have been advanced as to the true measure of relative contribution to taxation.

The once widely accepted doctrine "that tax contribution should be proportioned to benefit received," though now discredited as a general principle, yet deserves notice owing to the fact that it is to some extent the ground for the division of local from general taxation, and therefore applicable to cases of special outlay by the general government in the interest of one part of its territory. It may further be said that there is a distinct revival of favour towards the mode of remunerating the division of the cost of services that are readily measured, as evidenced in recent proposals like those for a "betterment" tax or assessment. In any "equitable" estimate of the "relative capacity "of Great Britain and Ireland to bear taxation" it seems proper in principle to exclude the extent to which each country benefits by Imperial expenditure incurred for its special advantage or by grants made to its local finances.

Quite independent of, and sometimes strongly opposed to, the "benefits" theory of taxation is the doctrine that taxation should be proportioned to "ability," "faculty," or "capacity," or, to put the same view in a different way, that it should involve an equal amount of sacrifice on the part of each contributor. The main arguments in support of this position are—(a.) The difficulty or even impossibility of measuring the services rendered by the State to each of its citizens; and (b.) the common interests of the citizens, which require that each should contribute according to his power or ability. These reasons have been regarded as conclusive by most writers on finance, even though some of them recognise the existence of exceptions to the application of the criterion.

But though the general rule of taxation in proportion to ability may be regarded as the accepted one for the distribution of the expense of those parts of State service that are not limited to particular persons or groups, the more difficult task of determining the objective criteria, or in the words of the reference, the "specific standards" by which ability can be gauged, remains for consideration.

One measure of ability largely used in the ruder systems of taxation was the amount of property or wealth possessed. The property tax was regarded as the fairest mode of levy. A little reflection, however, shows that mere property is an altogether inadequate criterion of the "ability" of either an individual or a community. Not only is it true that (a) the same amounts of property yield very different returns according to circumstances, but (b) a great deal of so-called "property," "wealth," or "capital" is merely an abstraction, having no real existence apart from the income by means of which (in comparison with the current rate of interest) it is computed. Still more important is (c) the fact that property cannot include the personal earning power of the community. Whether it be or be not true, as an eminent economist has recently argued (Professor Nicholson, *Money*, 2nd edition, pp. 346 seq.), that the living capital of the United Kingdom is five times as valuable as the dead capital or property, it is unquestionable that an estimate of taxable capacity which omits the value of personal services can be other than defective. According to Mr. Goschen's Budget statement in 1872, lawyers earned a larger aggregate income than cotton manufacturers, and doctors than the owners of coal mines, yet in an estimate based on property the earnings of these two learned professions would be left altogether out of account. For these reasons I should insist far more strongly than Sir R. Giffen does on the defectiveness of employing property instead of income as a measure of the ability of an individual or country to bear taxation.

The only case in which it seems at all admissible to use property as a standard for taxation is that in which a special levy is made once for all, and in which, therefore, it would be unfair to place a heavy charge on precarious incomes.

A far better criterion of taxable capacity is presented by income, which may provisionally be described as consisting of "the sum of new consumable goods obtained during a given period." Most economists have selected income or revenue as the proper measure of taxation, chiefly on the ground that it is the best test of ability to contribute, but sometimes also because it is supposed to measure roughly the amount of benefit received from the services of the State.

Income in this sense is, it should be said, wider than the income that appears in the Schedules of the Income and Property Tax, and includes the mass of commodities gained and services utilised during the period under examination. Its statistical determination for a country is always a difficult matter, whether the "personal" method—that of adding up individual incomes, or the "real" method—proceeding by enumeration of the various parts of products—be preferred. A small error in calculation, or the adoption of a different multiplier for purposes of comparison, even on plausible grounds, may lead to very surprising results.

The plainest and most obvious reason for taking income in the economic sense as the standard of taxable capacity is its disposability. Property may or may not be available, but by the nature of the case income is a new product which can be made use of. Again, not only is income disposable, it is also renewable, or, more correctly, recurs in each succeeding period. So far as property yields income, its abstraction for the purpose of taxation destroys the source of revenue, while future income is not directly impaired by taxation of existing income. The relation is, in truth, like that of a tree and its fruit. Moreover, the material enjoyments of the individual or the community are obtained out of its flow of income, which consists of its available material resources as distinct from its permanent possessions. It is difficult to conceive a tax system permanently resting on any other basis than that of levying a proportion of the national income, and this being so, there is a presumption of some strength in favour of taking income as the measure by which to estimate the ability of individuals or countries to contribute.

Nevertheless, objections have been frequently urged against the adoption of such a simple and ready criterion. Equal incomes do not, it is said, always mean equal power of contribution. Double the income may mean far more than twice the power. To put the objection in its most convenient form, it may be said that all income is not equally disposable, some of it is absolutely necessary for the receiver's support, and a still larger portion is desirable to make his productive capacity more efficient. It is only the surplus remaining after the above have been abstracted that should be dealt with for purposes of taxation.

The position contained in the preceding paragraph has been expressed in different ways, and not always carried to its extreme result. The best known form—at least in this country—is that which proposes to exclude the minimum of subsistence from taxation. This proposal, often said to have been originated by J. S. Mill, but really far older, takes, or may take, two different forms resting on separate grounds. Strictly construed, the minimum of subsistence can only mean the amount necessary for the preservation of life, and then in any society with an adequate poor law system not only is it not, but cannot be, taxed. Charges apparently levied on this part of income are necessarily, in technical language, "shifted" to those who have more than a minimum. This is but one part of the more sweeping doctrine of a famous French school, which held that all taxation, however raised, ultimately fell on land rent. The second form is that which would assign a suitable minimum standard of subsistence, and exclude it from the estimate of income available for tax purposes. Here the standpoint is altered. Instead of dealing with facts we consider what ought to be, and omit for the purpose of calculating taxable capacity not what must actually be expended on mere support, but something—in a country with a low standard of living probably a good deal more. It is this form of the doctrine which appears to be accepted by Sir R. Giffen, but whatever be the authority in its favour, it has the defect of treating what is really capable of being taxed as if it were not available for that purpose. The question of taxable capacity simply (apart from equitable considerations) is a question of fact which requires to be dealt with independently. It is as little admissible in principle to assume the same minimum standard for Great Britain and Ireland as it would be to take the same standard for the United Kingdom and India.

There are still more important considerations to be taken into account. Regarded scientifically, these theories as to the exemption of subsistence are but one part of the wider doctrine that it is net and not gross income that forms the true measure of capacity to contribute. It is argued with much apparent force that the expense of carrying on industry is not at the disposal of the income receiver. The term "necessaries," so frequently used in these discussions, is decidedly ambiguous. Sometimes it denotes merely what is "necessary for life," but it may be, and has been, used to include what is "necessary for efficient production." From this latter point of view each class would have its own necessary standard, and we might even say with Professor Marshall, "That the income of any class in the ranks of industry is below its necessary level when any increase in their income would in the course of time produce a more than proportionate increase in their efficiency." (*Principles of Economics*, Bk II., ch. 4.)

If this interpretation be adopted it seems plain that Sir R. Giffen's estimate of the relative taxable capacities of Great Britain and Ireland as being 800 : 16 or even 820 : 20 stands in need of correction. A large part of the income of Great Britain—how large it would be difficult to conjecture—is not free or disposable. The goods and clothing of the skilled artisans, even the "luxuries" of the business and professional classes, are not really available for the tax collector. They are needed to maintain the high standard of production which in its turn creates them. No one has put this point more clearly than Sir R. Giffen. "It is probable, besides," he says, "that as the consumption of every worker approaches very nearly his production, the condition of the production itself is that the worker should have an equivalent to consume. Strictly speaking, he could not produce at all at less wages than he receives. An artist or an author requires a certain comfort; the 'production' of a clever engine-driver, or other superior artisan, would equally be impossible unless with a certain command of food and other commodities, their wants and tastes would be excited to the utmost." (*Essays in Finance*, 2nd Series, p. 353.)

It is curiously confirmatory of this result to find that the real wages of skilled artisans in Ireland are only slightly, in some cases not at all, below their level in Great Britain, and in such cases as that of railway servants the work in the former country is decidedly easier.

Thus, it appears that if the true basis of the doctrine of the exemption of the minimum of subsistence be taken as our guide, it would lead to a very serious diminution of the fund really free for the purposes of the State. Nor is there anything inconsistent with them in this conclusion. It is a commonplace with writers on finance that only a small part of the gross revenue can be taken through taxation. About 15 per cent., or one-sixth, has been regarded as the limit by the best authorities, though for a short time a larger amount might probably be taken. But this simply means that the remainder is not obtainable even by the most rigorous taxation. In fact, the most correct way of looking at the aggregate of income is that which regards it as composed of different parts, each of different productive value to the treasury. We cannot draw a sharp line between "non-taxable" and "really taxable" income; there are rather several sections of different degrees of taxability.

Another question, however, arises here, viz.: Is the doctrine of net income as the measure for levying taxation really sound? So-called necessary expenditure involves the support of that machinery of civilised [illegible], the State. While it is clear that the fund from which taxation can come is the amount of disposable income, it does not follow that the distribution of taxation should be regulated by the relative proportions of net rather than gross income. That part of income which consists of absolute necessaries is a source of enjoyment, and may be used as part of the measure of contribution. The political argument that each citizen should bear some part of the public expenses leads in the same direction. More particularly does this hold good in the case of British and Irish taxation. The necessaries of life, with the doubtful exception of tea, are untaxed, and it is consistent with even J. S. Mill's view, that the luxuries of the poor should be taxed, and this course is actually recommended by him (Principles, Bk. V., ch. 6, par. 5). "The necessity extended to the [illegible] required for necessaries should depend on its being [illegible] expended for that purpose, &c." The fact that part of an income, [illegible] of the [illegible], is used to purchase other things than necessaries is conclusive evidence of the holder's opinion that he has something to spare.

On the whole, and having regard to the difficulties involved in any attempt to determine "disposable," as distinct from total, income, I would say that the fairest rough test—and no test can be looked on as more than an approximation—of taxable capacity is to be found in a comparison of total income rather than in any refined and doubtful calculations as to what is left after necessary expenses have been defrayed. It is, no doubt, desirable, both on social and technical grounds, to [illegible] taxation of very small incomes or taxes on strictly necessary articles of consumption, but these advantages can be obtained without departing from the broad rule of adjusting taxation to income.

Some additional points require to be noticed. One is the peculiar position of rent as a contributory to taxation. Without accepting the very extreme views sometimes put forth on this subject, it seems correct to hold that rent may be, and under the operation of ordinary economic forces often is, specially taxed. Now, it is evident that rent forms a much larger part of Irish than of British income. It includes, as Sir R. Giffen says, "not merely the rent "received by the landlord, but the beneficial rent "received by tenants." It is a tenable hypothesis that a good deal of Irish taxation, in its ultimate incidence, really falls on this particular part of income and so far is a special imposition on a special source.

Another matter of much importance is the treatment of harmful luxuries. Modern fiscal systems recognise the immense difficulties of raising revenue by direct taxation alone, and generally supplement it by taxes on the consumption of commodities. They are equally agreed in placing the chief weight of this part of the tax system on articles the use of which may be evil. Such a system may be criticised as a survival of sumptuary legislation, but it is in general operation. In recent years this method has taken the shape of heavy taxation on the stronger alcoholic drinks, together with moderate duties on, or even total exemption for, liquids with a small percentage of spirit (the *boissons hygiéniques* of French legislation).

This system may be right or wrong, but it is clear that such taxation stands on a different ground from other taxes. It is intended to be a penalty on a private vice, and its widespread employment proves that it rests on some strong basis of popular feeling or expert opinion. As the heavy taxation of Irish spirits is the main cause of the [illegible] proportion of her contribution, this point deserves consideration. Taxation of alcohol, in the opinion of those who impose it, is in the interest of the consumer quite as much as in that of the Exchequer. It is, besides, a levy not on a country but on a class, viz., the consumers of what is thought to be a particularly injurious article; it cannot therefore be placed on the same footing as other contributions in making up an account between the joint contributors to a common fund.*

A final point is the relation of central and local finance, which has already been referred to. The true point of view is, I think, that which regards all taxation, Imperial and local, as levied for the public advantage, and as forming one solid mass of public burdens. In considering its equitable distribution, however, allowance has to be made of the special local taxes levied for the sole benefit of the locality to its account. In the same way, Imperial expenditure, even though administered by central authorities, if it is solely for the advantage of a locality, should be charged to that locality. It is, of course, true that very few services are of purely local advantage, but this holds good quite as well of expenditure from local rates, which should therefore be treated in the same way.

C. F. Bastable.

* It may be suggested that the Irish spirit duties press more heavily on [illegible] than on Ireland.

APPENDIX II.

A.

1.—STATEMENT put in by Sir Edward Hamilton, in connexion with his Evidence before the Commission on 13th June 1895, SHOWING THE AMOUNT RECEIVED IN CASH as compared with the AMOUNT OF DEBT CREATED ON ACCOUNT OF IRELAND.

(1.) *Before the Union.*

Year ending	Amount received in Cash (British Currency) in respect of Loans raised in		How raised		Amount of Stock and Bills created in respect of Loans raised in		Terminable Annuities created.
	Ireland.	Great Britain.			Ireland.	Great Britain.	
	£	£		£	£	£	£
25 March 1793	[illegible]	—	5 per cent. Debentures		[illegible]	—	—
" 1795	[illegible]	—	5 per cent. Debentures, and an annuity of 1 per cent. for 15 years		*[illegible]	—	9,[illegible]
" 1796	1,4[illegible]	—	5 per cent. Debentures. And an annuity of 1l. 5s. per cent. for 15 years.	[illegible]			
			5 per cent. Stock. And an annuity of 1l. 5s. 6½d. per cent. for 15 years	1,[illegible]	†[illegible]	—	16,[illegible]
" 1797	[illegible]	—	5 per cent. Debentures, and an annuity of 1l. 5s. per cent. for 15 years		[illegible]	—	7,[illegible]
	[illegible]	—	5 per cent. Stock, and an annuity of 4l. 11s. per cent. for 15½ years		[illegible]	—	14,[illegible] 18 9
" 1798	[illegible]	—	5 per cent. Debentures		[illegible]	—	—
	461,[illegible]	—	Loan from Bank of Ireland at 5l. per cent., and an annuity of 3l. 12s. 6d. per cent. for 19 years		§[illegible]	—	16,791 0 0
	—	1,[illegible]	In 3 per cent. Stock. In 4 per cent. Stock. And an annuity of 6s. per cent. expiring in 1860.	[illegible] [illegible] —	—	‡[illegible]	4,[illegible]
" 1799	1,150,[illegible]	—	5 per cent. Debentures		1,[illegible]	—	—
	—	[illegible]	In 3 per cent. Stock, and an annuity of 4s. 11d. per cent., expiring in 1860		—	[illegible]	6,916 11 [illegible]
" 1800	1,844,154	—	5 per cent. Debentures. Exchequer Bills at 5 per cent.	1,844,154 454,[illegible]	[illegible]	—	—
Period to 5 Jan. 1800	—	[illegible]	In 3 per cent. Stock		—	[illegible]	—
" " 1801	2,[illegible]	—	In 5 per cent. Debentures. In Exchequer Bills at 5 per cent.	2,[illegible] [illegible]	[illegible]	—	—
Year ending 5 Jan. 1801	—	[illegible]	In 3 per cent. Stock		—	[illegible]	—
Totals	[illegible]	[illegible]			[illegible]	16,[illegible]	

* Includes [illegible]l., the dividends, &c. of which were payable at the Bank of England.
† The dividends, &c. on 1,[illegible]l. were payable at the Bank of England.
‡ Dividends on stock and annuity payable at the Bank of England.
§ Previous debt to Bank of Ireland ([illegible]l.) also raised from 4 to 5 per cent.

(B.) *After the Union until the Exchequers were amalgamated.*

Year ending	Amount raised in Cash (British Currency) in respect of Loans raised in: Ireland.	Great Britain.	How raised	Amount of Stock and Bills created in respect of Loans raised in: Ireland.	Great Britain.	Terminable Annuities created.
[illegible]	[illegible]	[illegible]	[illegible]	[illegible]	[illegible]	[illegible]
Totals	[illegible]	[illegible]		[illegible]	[illegible]	

* The Bank of Ireland were, during the continuance of their Charter, to pay all interest, annuities, and dividends on public loans payable at the said Bank without making any charge.

† This loan was raised for Ireland, but was charged upon and made payable out of the Consolidated Fund of Great Britain.

II.—STATEMENT SHOWING THE EFFECTIVE RATE PER CENT. AT WHICH LOANS WERE RAISED ON ACCOUNT OF IRELAND (1) in IRELAND and (2) in GREAT BRITAIN.

(1.) Loans raised by Stock in Ireland.

(a.) Before the Union.

Year ending	Amount received in Cash	Annual Interest payable on Stock and Annuity created	Rate per Cent. at which such Loan was raised
	£	£	£ s. d.
25 March 1794	[illegible]	14,[illegible]	5 0 0
" 1795	[illegible]	[illegible]	5 11 1
" 1796	1,[illegible]	[illegible]	[illegible]
" 1797	[illegible]	[illegible]	[illegible]
" 1797	[illegible]	[illegible]	[illegible]
" 1798	[illegible]	[illegible]	7 18 [illegible]
" 1799	661,[illegible]	[illegible]	7 15 0
" 1799	1,[illegible]	[illegible]	[illegible]
" 1800	1,[illegible]	[illegible]	[illegible]
Period to 5 January 1801	[illegible]	[illegible]	[illegible]
Totals	[illegible]	[illegible]	

AVERAGE RATE - £[illegible]

(b.) After the Union until the Exchequers were consolidated.

Year ending	Amount received in Cash	Annual Interest payable on Stock created	Rate per Cent. at which such Loan was raised
	£	£	£ s. d.
5 January 1802	—	—	—
" 1803	1,[illegible]	[illegible]	[illegible]
" 1804	—	—	—
" 1805	1,[illegible]	[illegible]	[illegible]
" 1806	—	—	—
" 1807	1,[illegible]	[illegible]	[illegible]
" 1808	—	—	—
1809	[illegible]	[illegible]	[illegible]
	1,[illegible]	[illegible]	[illegible]
" 1810	1,[illegible]	[illegible]	[illegible]
" 1811	—	—	—
" 1812	[illegible]	[illegible]	[illegible]
" 1813	[illegible]	[illegible]	[illegible]
" 1814	1,[illegible]	[illegible]	[illegible]
" 1815	[illegible]	[illegible]	[illegible]
" 1816	—	—	—
Totals	[illegible]	[illegible]	

AVERAGE RATE - £[illegible] 15 0

(B.) *Loans raised by Stock in Great Britain for Ireland.*

(a.) *Before the Union.*

Year ending	Amount raised in Cash.	Annual Interest payable on Stock and Annuity created.	Rate per Cent. at which each Loan was raised.
	£	£	£ s. d.
25 March 1798	1,500,000	[illegible]	6 5 10
" 1799	[illegible]	154,760	6 4 9
Period to 5 January 1800	[illegible]	157,[illegible]	5 5 0
Year ending 5 January 1801	[illegible]	94,[illegible]	5 11 2
Totals	[illegible]	[illegible]71,975	

AVERAGE RATE - - £5 10 11

(b.) *After the Union until the Exchequers were consolidated.*

Year ending	Amount raised in Cash.	Annual Interest payable on Stock created and Annuity	Rate per Cent. at which each Loan was raised.
	£	£	£ s. d.
5 January 180[illegible]	2,[illegible]	151,818	5 5 5
" 1803	[illegible]	79,171	5 19 2
" 1804	[illegible]	10[illegible]	5 2 0
" 1805	[illegible]	[illegible]	5 9 8
" 1806	[illegible]	1[illegible]	5 5 9
" 180[illegible]	1,[illegible]	87,[illegible]	5 16 4
" 1807	[illegible]	[illegible]	4 19 7
" 1808	[illegible]	91,[illegible]	4 16 7
	[illegible]	72,[illegible]	5 10 5
" 1809	[illegible]	118,179	4 14 6
" 1810	[illegible]	1[illegible]	5 12 10
" 1811	[illegible]	1[illegible]	4 4 7
	1,[illegible]	[illegible]	4 4 3
" 1812	[illegible]	251,[illegible]	5 15 6
" 1813	[illegible]	[illegible]	5 5 7
" 1814	[illegible]	[illegible]	5 10 6
" 1815	[illegible]	[illegible]	4 10 1
" 1816	[illegible]	[illegible]	5 11 5
Totals	[illegible]	[illegible]	

AVERAGE RATE - - £5 8 1

Statements put in by Sir Edward Hamilton, K.C.B., in connexion with his evidence given before the Commission on 13th June 1895.

TABLE I.

TABLE showing the ESTIMATED ANNUAL EXPENDITURE incurred on TOBACCO by the INHABITANTS of GREAT BRITAIN and IRELAND respectively as deduced from the adjusted REVENUE RETURNS for the year ending the 31st March 1893.

Tobacco.	Great Britain.	Ireland.	United Kingdom.
	lbs.	lbs.	lbs.
Annual consumption	[illegible]	[illegible]	[illegible]
Estimated cost *	£21,[illegible]	£2,[illegible]	£24,[illegible]
Percentage of total	88·23	11·77	100
Per head of population	[illegible]	[illegible]	[illegible]

* [illegible]

	s.	d.
Cigars	[illegible]	[illegible] per lb.
Cut and roll tobacco	[illegible]	[illegible]
Cigarettes, snuff, and other tobacco	[illegible]	[illegible]

The figures of total consumption and estimated cost for the United Kingdom are the same in the above table as in Table XXIV. of Sir Edward Hamilton's Memorandum (page 2[illegible] of C.-7720.-1). But the distribution of that total between Great Britain and Ireland has been re-adjusted in accordance with the proportions deduced from the Returns of Manufacturers and Dealers for the year 1893–4 (see Appendix IV. to the Minutes of Evidence, page [illegible] of C.-7720.-1).

TABLE II.

AN ACCOUNT showing the AMOUNT of SPIRITS (Foreign as well as Home) and BEER respectively, consumed by IRELAND, as represented by the true REVENUE derived from IRELAND under these heads, worked out for 1879–80 from the adjusted figures in Parliamentary Paper [illegible] of Session 18[illegible], and for 1889–90 and 1893–4 from the FINANCIAL RELATIONS RETURNS.

Quantities of Articles Consumed.	1879–80.	1889–90.	1893–4.
	Gallons.	Gallons.	Gallons.
Spirits—Home	*[illegible]	*[illegible]	[illegible]
Do. Foreign	†[illegible]	[illegible]	‡[illegible]
Total	[illegible]	[illegible]	[illegible]
	Barrels.	Barrels.	Barrels.
Beer	§[illegible]	[illegible]	[illegible]

* [illegible]

† [illegible]

‡ [illegible]

§ [illegible]

According to the above figures (subject to correction as regards spirits) the consumption has varied as follows:—

—	Spirits.	Beer.
	Gallons.	Barrels.
1879–80	[illegible]	[illegible]
1893–4	[illegible]	[illegible]
Increase (+) or decrease (−)	−[illegible]	+[illegible]
Increase or decrease per cent.	−[illegible]	+[illegible]

The average price paid for spirits and beer by the consumer in Ireland is, according to the estimate formed by the Inland Revenue authorities (page [illegible] of C.-7720.-1)—

	s.	d.	
For spirits	[illegible]	[illegible]	per gallon
For beer	[illegible]	[illegible]	

Applying these prices to the quantities consumed in 1879–80 and 1893–4 we obtain the following amounts as the estimated expenditure of the inhabitants of Ireland in those years on spirits and beer respectively:—

—	Spirits.	Beer.
	£	£
1879–80	[illegible]	[illegible]
1893–4	[illegible]	[illegible]
Increase (+) or decrease (−)	−[illegible]	+[illegible]

C.

Tables put in by Sir Edward Hamilton, K.C.B., in connexion with the Evidence given by him before the Commission.

1.—**Statement showing how much of the Estimated True Revenue derived from Great Britain and Ireland, respectively, represents the proceeds of Taxes on Commodities or Indirect Taxes, and how much represents the proceeds of Other Taxes or Direct Taxes, together with per capita Calculations, since the amalgamation of the British and Irish Exchequers.**

(N.B.—The estimated true revenue from taxes is the collected revenue in each Kingdom, exclusive of Imperial receipts, after being adjusted in accordance with Parliamentary Paper 313 of 1894.)

—	Taxes on Commodities.		Other Taxes.		Total Tax Revenue.		
	Great Britain.	Ireland.	Great Britain.	Ireland.	Great Britain.	Ireland.	Total.
	£	£	£	£	£	£	£
1819-20	[illegible]	[illegible]	[illegible]	[illegible]	[illegible]	[illegible]	[illegible]
Per head of population according to Census figures of 1st April 1821	[illegible]	[illegible]	[illegible]	[illegible]	[illegible]	[illegible]	—
1829-30	[illegible]	[illegible]	[illegible]	[illegible]	[illegible]	[illegible]	[illegible]
Per head of population according to Census figures of 1st April 1831	[illegible]	[illegible]	[illegible]	[illegible]	[illegible]	[illegible]	—
1839-40	[illegible]	[illegible]	[illegible]	[illegible]	[illegible]	[illegible]	[illegible]
Per head of population according to Census figures of 1st April 1841	[illegible]	[illegible]	[illegible]	[illegible]	[illegible]	[illegible]	—
1849-50	[illegible]	[illegible]	[illegible]	[illegible]	[illegible]	[illegible]	[illegible]
Per head of population according to Census figures of 1st April 1851	[illegible]	[illegible]	[illegible]	[illegible]	[illegible]	[illegible]	—
1859-60	[illegible]	[illegible]	[illegible]	[illegible]	[illegible]	[illegible]	[illegible]
Per head of population according to Census figures of 1st April 1861	[illegible]	[illegible]	[illegible]	[illegible]	[illegible]	[illegible]	—
1869-70	[illegible]	[illegible]	[illegible]	[illegible]	[illegible]	[illegible]	[illegible]
Per head of population according to Census figures of 1st April 1871	[illegible]	[illegible]	[illegible]	[illegible]	[illegible]	[illegible]	—
1879-80	[illegible]	[illegible]	[illegible]	[illegible]	[illegible]	[illegible]	[illegible]
Per head of population according to Census figures of 1st April 1881	[illegible]	[illegible]	[illegible]	[illegible]	[illegible]	[illegible]	—
1889-90	[illegible]	[illegible]	[illegible]	[illegible]	[illegible]	[illegible]	[illegible]
Per head of population according to Census figures of 1st April 1891	[illegible]	[illegible]	[illegible]	[illegible]	[illegible]	[illegible]	—
1893-94	[illegible]	[illegible]	[illegible]	[illegible]	[illegible]	[illegible]	[illegible]
Per head of population according to Registrar-General's estimate for 1st July 1893	[illegible]	[illegible]	[illegible]	[illegible]	[illegible]	[illegible]	—

II.—Statement showing how much of the Estimated True Revenue in Great Britain and Ireland has been derived from Taxes on Commodities or Indirect Taxes, and how much from Other Taxes or Direct Taxes, and the Proportion per cent. which the respective proceeds have yielded.

[N.B.—The estimated true revenue from taxes is the collected revenue in each Kingdom, exclusive of Imperial receipts, after being adjusted in accordance with Parliamentary Paper 313 of 1894.]

—	Great Britain.			Ireland.			Total Tax Revenue.		
	Taxes on Commodities.	Other Taxes.	Total.	Taxes on Commodities.	Other Taxes.	Total.	Taxes on Commodities.	Other Taxes.	Total.
	£	£	£	£	£	£	£	£	£
1819-20	[illegible]	[illegible]	[illegible]	[illegible]	[illegible]	[illegible]	[illegible]	[illegible]	[illegible]
Per cent.	[illegible]	[illegible]	100	[illegible]	[illegible]	100	[illegible]	[illegible]	100
1829-30	[illegible]	[illegible]	[illegible]	[illegible]	[illegible]	[illegible]	[illegible]	[illegible]	[illegible]
Per cent.	[illegible]	[illegible]	100	[illegible]	[illegible]	100	[illegible]	[illegible]	100
1839-40	[illegible]	[illegible]	[illegible]	[illegible]	[illegible]	[illegible]	[illegible]	[illegible]	[illegible]
Per cent.	[illegible]	[illegible]	100	[illegible]	[illegible]	100	[illegible]	[illegible]	100
1849-50	[illegible]	[illegible]	[illegible]	[illegible]	[illegible]	[illegible]	[illegible]	[illegible]	[illegible]
Per cent.	[illegible]	[illegible]	100	[illegible]	[illegible]	100	[illegible]	[illegible]	100
1859-60	[illegible]	[illegible]	[illegible]	[illegible]	[illegible]	[illegible]	[illegible]	[illegible]	[illegible]
Per cent.	[illegible]	[illegible]	100	[illegible]	[illegible]	100	[illegible]	[illegible]	100
1869-70	[illegible]	[illegible]	[illegible]	[illegible]	[illegible]	[illegible]	[illegible]	[illegible]	[illegible]
Per cent.	[illegible]	[illegible]	100	[illegible]	[illegible]	100	[illegible]	[illegible]	100
1879-80	[illegible]	[illegible]	[illegible]	[illegible]	[illegible]	[illegible]	[illegible]	[illegible]	[illegible]
Per cent.	[illegible]	[illegible]	100	[illegible]	[illegible]	100	[illegible]	[illegible]	100
1889-90	[illegible]	[illegible]	[illegible]	[illegible]	[illegible]	[illegible]	[illegible]	[illegible]	[illegible]
Per cent.	[illegible]	[illegible]	100	[illegible]	[illegible]	100	[illegible]	[illegible]	100
1893-94	[illegible]	[illegible]	[illegible]	[illegible]	[illegible]	[illegible]	[illegible]	[illegible]	[illegible]
Per cent.	[illegible]	[illegible]	100	[illegible]	[illegible]	100	[illegible]	[illegible]	100
1894-95	—	—	—	—	—	—	[illegible]	[illegible]	[illegible]
Per cent.	—	—	—	—	—	—	[illegible]	[illegible]	100

D.

III.—Statement showing the Estimated Local Expenditure incurred in Ireland, and the Balance of True Revenue which is available for Imperial Services after such Expenditure has been met.

—	Revenue as collected.	Adjustments (+) or (−)	Estimated True Revenue.	Estimated Local Expenditure.	Balance available for Imperial Services.
	£	£	£	£	£
1819-20	[illegible]	[illegible]	[illegible]	[illegible]	[illegible]
1829-30	[illegible]	[illegible]	[illegible]	[illegible]	[illegible]
1839-40	[illegible]	[illegible]	[illegible]	[illegible]	[illegible]
1849-50	[illegible]	[illegible]	[illegible]	[illegible]	[illegible]
1859-60	[illegible]	[illegible]	[illegible]	[illegible]	[illegible]
1869-70	[illegible]	[illegible]	[illegible]	[illegible]	[illegible]
1879-80	[illegible]	[illegible]	[illegible]	[illegible]	[illegible]
*1889-90	[illegible]	[illegible]	[illegible]	[illegible]	[illegible]
*1890-91	[illegible]	[illegible]	[illegible]	[illegible]	[illegible]
*1891-92	[illegible]	[illegible]	[illegible]	[illegible]	[illegible]
*1892-93	[illegible]	[illegible]	[illegible]	[illegible]	[illegible]
*1893-94	[illegible]	[illegible]	[illegible]	[illegible]	[illegible]

* The figures for these years do not correspond with those shown in the various Financial Relations Papers owing to the revised estimates of the tobacco figures; see Parliamentary Paper C.—7720 of 1895—Appendix IV.

E.

An Attempt made to estimate the Aggregate of Expenditure incurred by Individuals in Ireland.

[This estimate is submitted by Sir Edward W. Hamilton with much diffidence.]

Items of Expenditure.	Amount of Annual Expenditure.		References.
I.—Taxed Commodities.	£	£	
Tea	[illegible]		Minutes of Evidence, Vol. I, p. [illegible].
Tobacco	[illegible]		Do. Vol. II, p. [illegible]
Spirits	[illegible]		
Beer	[illegible]		
Wine	[illegible]		Estimate of Customs authorities.
Cocoa, coffee, dried fruits, &c.	[illegible]		Quantities given in Minutes of Evidence, Vol. II, p. [illegible]. Average retail prices estimated at— Cocoa [illegible] per lb. Coffee [illegible] Currants and raisins [illegible]
		[illegible]	
II.—Untaxed Commodities.			
Bread	[illegible]		Quantities of Irish grown wheat and imported wheat and flour given in Minutes of Evidence, Vol. II, p. [illegible]. Average retail price of bread estimated at [illegible] per lb.
Meat	[illegible]		Minutes of Evidence, Vol. II, p. [illegible]
Milk	[illegible]		Do. p. [illegible]. Value increased for difference between wholesale and retail prices.
Butter	[illegible]		Do. do.
Potatoes	[illegible]		Quantities [illegible] Annual [illegible] p. [illegible], and Minutes of Evidence, Vol. II, p. [illegible]. Average retail [illegible] estimated at [illegible] per [illegible]
Coal and turf	[illegible]		Consumption computed [illegible] each inhabited house at [illegible] per [illegible]

Items of Expenditure.	Amount of Annual Expenditure.		References.
II.—Untaxed Commodities—cont.			
Oats and [illegible]	[illegible]		[illegible] Minutes of Evidence, Vol. II, p. [illegible] [illegible]
Eggs, poultry, and fish	[illegible]		Eggs and poultry, Minutes of Evidence, Vol. II, p. [illegible] [illegible]
Potatoes	[illegible]		Valuation of Irish crops, Minutes of Evidence, Vol. II, p. [illegible]
		[illegible]	
[illegible]	—	[illegible]	Vol. II, Appendix III (4).
Local rates	—	[illegible]	C.—[illegible] of [illegible], p. 11.
House rent	—	[illegible]	Annual value of houses [illegible] [illegible]
Servants	—	[illegible]	[illegible]
Railway and tramway fares	—	[illegible]	One-fourth of passenger receipts, [illegible] pp. [illegible]
Post Office services	—	[illegible]	One half of contribution to Revenue. Vol. I, Appendix III (a).
Total		[illegible]	

Among items of expenditure which are omitted from the foregoing list, the following may be enumerated:—Clothing, furniture (annual depreciation), vegetables (other than potatoes), fresh fruits, salt, and other minor articles of food, books and newspapers, jewellery and other luxuries, amusements, investments (annual [illegible]), charities, and payments for personal services, as for lawyers, clergy, higher education, and domestic service.

F.

Further Memorandum by Sir Edward W. Hamilton on Points connected with the Treatment of Ireland in the matter of Debt in 1801–16.

I undertook to consider further the manner in which Ireland had been treated, under the Treaty of Union, in the matter of debt during the 16 years following the Act of Union.

The two points which Mr. [illegible] invited me to consider specially were—

1. Whether it was necessary for a due distribution of the charges under the proportions to charge the debt as a separate debt, or whether the due proportion of the charges might not have been equally apportioned between the two countries, if the debt in the proportion of 15 to 2 had been joint, and any excess of expenditure had been treated separately; and

2. Whether any other debt except the debt incurred before the Union in either country should have been included in the calculations of 1816 with a view to the establishment of common taxes and the consolidation of the two Exchequers.

1. Now, it is clear that there could have been only three ways of construing the 6th provision of the 7th article about which there has been so much controversy. "All monies" required "to be raised after the Union" might have been raised, either

(1) as joint debt, or

(2) as separate debt, or

(3) as partly joint debt and partly separate debt.

Let me illustrate the effect of each of these ways of borrowing with the figures assumed by Mr. [illegible].

He assumed that in a given year after the Union the expenditure of the United Kingdom, or the joint expenditure, towards which Great Britain was to contribute [illegible]ths and Ireland [illegible]ths, amounted to 34,000,000*l*. Accordingly, Great Britain would have been bound to contribute 30,000,000*l*. and Ireland 4,000,000*l*.

He further assumed that Great Britain raised 15,000,000*l*., or one half, of her contribution out of taxes, and that Ireland raised 1,000,000*l*., or one quarter, of her contribution out of taxes.

Let us see how this would have worked out under each of the three ways of raising debt.

1. *Under a system of joint debt.*

—	Great Britain.	Ireland.	Total.
	£	£	£
Joint expenditure	[illegible]	[illegible]	[illegible]
Raised by taxes	[illegible]	[illegible]	[illegible]
Amount required to be borrowed	[illegible]	[illegible]	[illegible]
Charge at 5 per cent. on the assumption that the debt was jointly raised, i.e., that Great Britain undertook [illegible] and Ireland [illegible] of the charge on a loan of [illegible]	[illegible]	[illegible]	[illegible]
Remaining charge on Revenue	[illegible]	[illegible]	[illegible]

2. *Under a system of separate debt.*

—	Great Britain.	Ireland.	Total.
	£	£	£
Joint expenditure	[illegible]	[illegible]	[illegible]
Raised by taxes	[illegible]	[illegible]	[illegible]
Amount required to be borrowed	[illegible]	[illegible]	[illegible]
Charge at 5 per cent. on the assumption that the debt was separately raised, i.e., that Great Britain undertook the charge of [illegible], and Ireland that of [illegible]	[illegible]	[illegible]	[illegible]
Remaining charge on Revenue	[illegible]	[illegible]	[illegible]

3. *Under a system of partly joint and partly separate debt.*

—	Great Britain.	Ireland.	Total.
	£	£	£
Joint expenditure	[illegible]	[illegible]	[illegible]
Raised by taxes	[illegible]	[illegible]	[illegible]
Amount required to be borrowed	[illegible]	[illegible]	[illegible]
Charge at 5 per cent. on the assumption that [illegible] was borrowed jointly in the proportion of 15 to 2, and that Ireland borrowed the remaining [illegible], separately	[illegible]	[illegible] (joint debt) [illegible] (separate debt)	[illegible]
Remaining charge on Revenue	[illegible]	[illegible]	[illegible]

It is obvious, and I think it has been generally admitted, that under the first course Ireland would have thrown on Great Britain a heavier charge in respect of debt than could have been contemplated by the Act of Union. In fact, "all the sums" could not have been raised jointly with due regard to the observance of the provisions of the Treaty, unless the amount raised by taxes in Ireland had been in exact correspondence, in the Union proportion of 2 to 15, with the amount raised by taxes in Great Britain.

As regards the second and third courses, I admit that either course might have been followed without involving an apportionment of the charges in contravention of the terms of the Treaty. But it is clear, I submit, from the illustrations that the charge on Ireland under the third course would have been identical with the charge on Ireland under the second course, which was the one adopted. This fact was recognised by the Committee of 1811, and I quote their words again:

"It does not indeed appear," they say, "that any part of the loans raised since the Union have (*sic*) been considered as joint debt; nor would it have made any other than a nominal difference, if so much of the Irish loan of each year as bore to the British loan the proportion of the respective contributions of Ireland, viz., 2 to 15, had been so considered; because the charge to be borne by Ireland, in respect of the two portions of the loan, viz., the joint and the separate portion, would in that case have been exactly equal to that which has been incurred on account of the Irish debt undivided."

Had the third course been adopted in preference to the second course, the amount of the separate Irish debt would, no doubt, have been found to be materially less, when the accounts came to be struck for the consolidation of the Exchequers in 1816. It would perhaps not have been in the proportion of 2 to 15. But what would have been the probable result? The consolidation of the Exchequers might have been delayed on the ground that the contingency for which the 7th provision of the 7th article had provided, had not arisen. Such delay would only have prolonged the crushing burden of the debt charge on Ireland, and she would have continued to be liable to contribute two-seventeenths of the expenditure of the United Kingdom in addition to her separate debt charge.

I fail, therefore, to see how the adoption of the third course could have benefited Ireland. It could not have mitigated her debt burden under separate exchequers, while it might have been the means of keeping that burden imposed upon her longer than it was.

Accordingly, with all due deference to Mr. Sexton, I can form no other conclusion than what I originally formed, namely, that there was not imposed upon Ireland any charge in respect of debt during 1801–16 which could have been avoided, except in violation of the spirit, if not the letter, of the terms of the Treaty of Union.

I pass on to Mr. Sexton's second point.

2. He infers from the speech which Lord Castlereagh made on the 5th February 1800, that it was only the debts incurred in each country previously to the Union that were intended to be taken into account, in determining whether the Exchequers should be consolidated and whether all expenses defrayed indiscriminately by equal taxes imposed on the same articles in each country. The passage in Lord Castlereagh's speech on which Mr. Sexton mainly relies is this:— Q. [illegible]

"Let the House then first consider that the charges of the debts of Great Britain and Ireland amount to 20 millions a year, and the charges of the debt of Ireland to 2,300,000*l*. (British) a year, that common taxes are not to take place till either *the past and separate debts of both countries shall be liquidated, or till they shall become to each other in the proportion of their contributions, that is, in the ratio of 15 to 2.*" [illegible]

I admit, and I said so in evidence, that these words may be held to support Mr. Sexton's contention, though "past and separate debts of both countries" may be read in two senses. But what has weighed with me, and still weighs with me, and what I venture to think ought to be taken into account, more than any present interpretation of a speech made nearly 100 years ago, is the interpretation which was placed on the 7th provision of the 7th Article by men who were themselves parties to or witnesses of the Union, and who had heard or read the discussions on the measure at the time.

The Report of the Select Committee of 1811 clearly shows that they entertained no doubt as to the propriety of including debt created after the Union in the calculations which should decide the question of amalgamation.

"It is obvious," they say, "even upon a slight examination of the Official Accounts of Great Britain and Ireland, that *the increase of the debt of Ireland since the Union* has been so much more rapid than that of Great Britain, that the value of the one must now bear to that of the other a proportion much more nearly approaching to that of 2 to 15, determined by *the Act of Union* as authorising *the Parliament of the United Kingdom* to declare . . . than it did when the Union took place." [illegible]

The Committee then presented actuarial valuations showing the existing proportions of the total debts of the two countries to one another, according to different modes of valuation, and, after pointing out that, whichever valuation might be adopted, the required proportions were very nearly approached, they added:

"And it is the more important that the attention of Parliament should be drawn to that circumstance as the words of the Act of Union may be thought capable of an interpretation by which, if Parliament should not think fit to carry into effect the con-

[illegible] of the debts and expenditure of the two countries at the period when such debts shall have arrived at the proportion stated, it might be precluded from afterwards doing so, until such proportion shall be restored."

Evidently the Committee were afraid that, if the right opportunity were allowed to slip, Ireland might, by the rapid increase of her debt, lose her claim under the Treaty of Union to be relieved of the obligation to pay her Union quota.

Moreover, when reporting in 1812, the Committee pressed upon the notice of the House the observations on this subject in their previous report; and they were quoted also by the subsequent Committee in the Report of 1815, which recommended that the question of consolidation should be considered by Parliament.

Finally, it may fairly be presumed that, if any doubt had been entertained at the time as to the interpretation of the provisions of the Act of Union, it would have found expression in the debate of 1816 on the resolutions for consolidation. Several Irish members took part in the debate, and of these two at least, Sir John Newport and Mr. Ponsonby, could not be suspected of any indifference to the interests of Ireland. But there was no hint of any objection to the circumstances on which the proposal for consolidation was based; and, if Lord Castlereagh may be accepted as an authoritative exponent of the meaning of his own utterances, his remarks in this debate should set at rest any doubts as to what was intended by the Union speeches. Defending the Union arrangements, he said:

> "It was fit that Ireland should only pay her quota of the national expenditure while her public debt was so much below that of England. Now that her debt had risen so as to do away that distinction which had formerly been made, it was fitting that (such) an arrangement should cease to operate, and that the taxes should take their natural course in both countries on a footing of equality."

E. W. Hamilton.

28th November 1895.

APPENDIX III.

Paper put in by Mr. Murrough O'Brien in connexion with his evidence before the Commission on 6th March 1895. (*See Vol. I. of Evidence, page [illegible]*)

PRINCIPAL PAYMENTS from IRELAND to ENGLAND constituting a drain on the ECONOMIC RESOURCES of IRELAND, i.e., PAYMENTS and EXPENDITURE out of the ANNUAL GROSS INCOME of IRELAND for which there is little or no corresponding RETURN.

—	Amount known approximately.	Probable Amount.
	£	£
1. Value of property owned by absentees, confined to rural property in the Return* 167 of April [illegible], 1876	2,470,416	[illegible] (items 1–3)
2. Similar proportion of urban properties	[illegible]	
3. Residue of London Co.'s estates	[illegible]	
†4. Mortgages of English Insurance Cos. as estimated by Dr. Coffee in 1886, 14,000,000*l.* at [illegible] per cent.	[illegible]	[illegible] (all absentee mortgages and annuities)
5. Average annual paid by Church Fund as interest for [illegible] years to 31st March 1894	[illegible]	[illegible]
6. Average annual amount of capital repaid by Church Fund for 19 years	[illegible]	[illegible]
‡7. Interest on Board of Works and Public Works Loan Commissioners loans (average taking as payment in 1893) (Hamilton's Return [illegible], 17th August 1893)	[illegible]	[illegible]
8. Repayment of capital by same lodgers	[illegible]	[illegible]
9. Quitrents and Crown rents	[illegible]	[illegible]
10. Land loan annuities 4 per cent. on [illegible]	[illegible]	[illegible]
11. Remittances of capital for deposit in Post Office and Trustee Savings Banks. Average annual increase of deposits for past 21 half years	[illegible]	[illegible]
12. Interest at 3 per cent. on Post Office and Trustee Bank deposits on which [illegible] per cent. is paid to depositors, while they are lent back to Ireland at not less than [illegible] per cent.	[illegible]	[illegible]
13. Extra cost of Irish Private Bill legislation, estimated (see debate in 1871) to cost [illegible] times as much as if conducted in Ireland	Not ascertained	—
14. Expenses of 103 M.P.s in England per annum	[illegible]	[illegible]
	[illegible]	[illegible]

* This return was well known to be an under estimate, many small [illegible] and [illegible] were [illegible]. [illegible]

† [illegible]

‡ The benefit of most of this expenditure is represented in the [illegible] interest and capital.

The "absentee drain" payments in the foregoing table are chiefly those from rural estates.

In addition it should not be overlooked that a considerable proportion of all large Irish incomes, even of persons who are not absentees, is spent in England.

Where two countries like England and Ireland are connected, the natural tendency of wealthy persons in the poor and dependent country is to spend some of their time and a good deal of their income in the wealthier country, where the attractions of society, the means of gratifying their desires, and the facilities for pleasure are greater. It is well known that this is the case. For example, nearly all persons residing in Ireland who are in easy or wealthy circumstances send their children to England for education, and spend no small part of their income there.

The following table from the Inland Revenue Report of 1885 shows the number of incomes assessed under Schedule D in the United Kingdom and Ireland. In the higher classes, Ireland's proportion is very small, and the increase in her total assessment during the past 15 years is almost nothing.

Of the larger incomes no small part is spent in England, but the amount can only be a matter of conjecture, and not of even approximate estimation.

NUMBER of PERSONS charged to INCOME TAX, SCHEDULE D., TRADES and PROFESSIONS in UNITED KINGDOM and IRELAND, and PROPORTION of IRELAND to UNITED KINGDOM, 1883–84, in CLASSES.—Twenty-eighth Report of Inland Revenue, 1885 [C.—4474.]

Class.	United Kingdom.	Ireland.	Proportion.
	No.	No.	
Under 150*l.*	[illegible]	[illegible]	1 to [illegible]
150*l.* to 200*l.*	[illegible]	[illegible]	1 to [illegible]
200*l.* to 300*l.*	[illegible]	[illegible]	1 to [illegible]
300*l.* to 400*l.*	[illegible]	[illegible]	1 to [illegible]
400*l.* to 500*l.*	[illegible]	[illegible]	1 to [illegible]
500*l.* to 600*l.*	[illegible]	[illegible]	1 to [illegible]
600*l.* to 700*l.*	[illegible]	[illegible]	1 to [illegible]
700*l.* to 800*l.*	[illegible]	[illegible]	1 to [illegible]
800*l.* to 900*l.*	[illegible]	[illegible]	1 to [illegible]
900*l.* to 1,000*l.*	[illegible]	[illegible]	1 to [illegible]
1,000*l.* to 2,000*l.*	[illegible]	[illegible]	1 to [illegible]
2,000*l.* to 3,000*l.*	[illegible]	[illegible]	1 to [illegible]
3,000*l.* to 4,000*l.*	[illegible]	[illegible]	1 to [illegible]
4,000*l.* to 5,000*l.*	1,117	[illegible]	1 to [illegible]
5,000*l.* to 10,000*l.*	[illegible]	[illegible]	1 to [illegible]
10,000*l.* to 50,000*l.*	[illegible]	[illegible]	1 to [illegible]
50,000*l.* and upwards	[illegible]	[illegible]	1 to [illegible]

NUMBER of PERSONS and NET AMOUNT charged to INCOME TAX, SCHEDULE D., TRADES and PROFESSIONS in UNITED KINGDOM and IRELAND, 1868–69, and PROPORTION of IRELAND in NUMBER and AMOUNT to UNITED KINGDOM [C.—4474.]

—	Number of Persons.		Amount charged.		Proportion of Ireland to United Kingdom.	
	United Kingdom.	Ireland.	United Kingdom.	Ireland.	Persons.	Amount.
			£	£		
Number and amount 1883–4	[illegible]	19,761	[illegible]	[illegible]	1 to [illegible]	1 to [illegible]
Do. do. 1868–9	[illegible]	[illegible]	[illegible]	[illegible]	1 to [illegible]	1 to [illegible]

In 15 years to 1883, the assessment of the United Kingdom increased [illegible] per cent. under the head, Schedule D., Trades and Professions. In the same period, Ireland increased only [illegible] per cent., i.e., the United Kingdom's increase was [illegible] times as much as Ireland's.

The Parliamentary Return by the Inland Revenue Department (C—[illegible] of [illegible]) has enabled me to prepare tables for the year [illegible] for comparison with the tables for [illegible] given at the end of the foregoing paper by Mr. Murrough O'Brien.

[illegible],
Secretary.

I.—Table showing Number of Persons charged to Income-Tax, Schedule D., Trades and Professions in the United Kingdom and Ireland, and Proportion of Ireland to United Kingdom, [illegible], in Classes. (P.P. [illegible] of [illegible].)

Class.	United Kingdom.	Ireland.	Proportion.
	No.	No.	
Under 150l.*	[illegible]	[illegible]	1 to 17·[illegible]
150l. to 200l.	[illegible]	[illegible]	[illegible]
200l. to 300l.	[illegible]	4,778	[illegible]
300l. to 400l.	[illegible]	[illegible]	[illegible]
400l. to 500l.	[illegible]	764	[illegible]
500l. to 600l.	[illegible]	476	[illegible]
600l. to 700l.	[illegible]	[illegible]	[illegible]
700l. to 800l.	[illegible]	164	[illegible]
800l. to 900l.	[illegible]	[illegible]	[illegible]
900l. to 1,000l.	[illegible]	[illegible]	[illegible]
1,000l. to 2,000l.	[illegible]	[illegible]	[illegible]
2,000l. to 3,000l.	[illegible]	[illegible]	[illegible]
3,000l. to 4,000l.	[illegible]	[illegible]	[illegible]
4,000l. to 5,000l.	[illegible]	[illegible]	[illegible]
5,000l. to 10,000l.	[illegible]	[illegible]	[illegible]
10,000l. to 50,000l.	[illegible]	[illegible]	[illegible]
50,000l. and upwards	[illegible]	[illegible]	[illegible]

II.—Table showing Number of Persons and Net Amounts charged to Income-Tax, Schedule D., Trades and Professions in the United Kingdom and Ireland, and Proportion of Ireland to United Kingdom in Number and Amount for the periods [illegible].

	Number of Persons		Amounts charged.		Proportion of Ireland to United Kingdom.	
	United Kingdom.	Ireland.	United Kingdom.	Ireland.	Persons.	Amount.
Number and amounts, [illegible]	[illegible]	[illegible]	[illegible]	[illegible]	[illegible]	[illegible]
" " [illegible]	[illegible]	[illegible]	[illegible]	[illegible]	[illegible]	[illegible]
" " [illegible]	[illegible]	[illegible]	[illegible]	[illegible]	[illegible]	[illegible]

III.—Table showing Number of Persons and Net Amounts charged to Income-Tax, Schedule D., Trades and Professions in Great Britain and Ireland, and Proportion of Ireland to Number and Amount to Great Britain, [illegible], in Classes. (P.P. [illegible] of [illegible].)

Class.	Number of Persons		Amounts charged		Proportion of Ireland to Great Britain.	
	Great Britain.	Ireland.	Great Britain.	Ireland.	Persons.	Amounts.
Under [illegible] per annum	[illegible]	[illegible]	[illegible]	[illegible]	[illegible]	[illegible]
[illegible] and under 1,000l.	[illegible]	[illegible]	[illegible]	[illegible]	[illegible]	[illegible]
1,000l. and under [illegible]	[illegible]	[illegible]	[illegible]	[illegible]	[illegible]	[illegible]
[illegible] and upwards	[illegible]	[illegible]	[illegible]	[illegible]	[illegible]	[illegible]
Total	[illegible]	[illegible]	[illegible]	[illegible]	[illegible]	[illegible]

* Note.—[illegible]

A.

Table handed in by Mr. Henry A. Robinson, Local Government Board for Ireland, in connection with his evidence before the Commission on 6th December 1894. (See Vol. I. of Evidence.)

Showing for each Fifth Year, from 1852 to 1892, and for each Year from 1882 to 1893, the Number of Persons in Receipt of Indoor and Outdoor Relief, with the Total Number thereof, and the Daily Average Number of such Persons, with the Percentage of those Averages on the Population of the Country.

Year.	Numbers relieved in Workhouses and at Institutions for the Blind, &c.	Numbers in receipt of Outdoor Relief	Total numbers Relieved.	Average daily numbers in receipt of Relief, with Percentage of such average on Population.					
				In Workhouses and Institutions for the Blind, &c.	Percentage of Indoor on Population.	Numbers in receipt of Outdoor Relief (approximately)	Percentage of Outdoor on Population.	Total daily average number	Percentage of total daily average on Population
1.	2.	3.	4.	5.	6.	7.	8.	9.	10.
1852-53	[illegible]	[illegible]	[illegible]	[illegible]	[illegible]	[illegible]	·04	[illegible]	[illegible]
1857-58	177,863	6,031	[illegible]	[illegible]	·75	[illegible]	·03	[illegible]	·8
1862-63	[illegible]	[illegible]	[illegible]	[illegible]	[illegible]	[illegible]	·1	[illegible]	[illegible]
1867-68	[illegible]	[illegible]	[illegible]	[illegible]	[illegible]	[illegible]	·27	[illegible]	[illegible]
1872-73	[illegible]	[illegible]	[illegible]	[illegible]	[illegible]	[illegible]	·53	[illegible]	1·4
1877-78	[illegible]	[illegible]	[illegible]	[illegible]	·9	[illegible]	·63	[illegible]	[illegible]
1882-83	[illegible]	[illegible]	[illegible]	[illegible]	[illegible]	[illegible]	1·17	[illegible]	[illegible]
1887-88	[illegible]	[illegible]	[illegible]	[illegible]	[illegible]	[illegible]	[illegible]	[illegible]	2·31
1892-93	[illegible]	[illegible]	[illegible]	[illegible]	·9	[illegible]	[illegible]	[illegible]	[illegible]
			Similar particulars for each year from 1882 to 1893, inclusive.						
1882-83	[illegible]	[illegible]	[illegible]	[illegible]	[illegible]	[illegible]	1·17	[illegible]	[illegible]
1883-84	[illegible]	[illegible]	[illegible]	[illegible]	·97	[illegible]	[illegible]	[illegible]	[illegible]
1884-85	[illegible]	[illegible]	[illegible]	[illegible]	[illegible]	[illegible]	1·17	[illegible]	[illegible]
1885-86	[illegible]	[illegible]	[illegible]	[illegible]	·96	[illegible]	1·2	[illegible]	[illegible]
1886-87	[illegible]	[illegible]	[illegible]	[illegible]	·95	[illegible]	[illegible]	[illegible]	[illegible]
1887-88	[illegible]	[illegible]	[illegible]	[illegible]	·94	[illegible]	[illegible]	[illegible]	[illegible]
1888-89	[illegible]	[illegible]	[illegible]	[illegible]	·91	[illegible]	[illegible]	[illegible]	[illegible]
1889-90	[illegible]	[illegible]	[illegible]	[illegible]	[illegible]	[illegible]	1·21	[illegible]	[illegible]
1890-91	[illegible]	[illegible]	[illegible]	[illegible]	[illegible]	[illegible]	[illegible]	[illegible]	[illegible]
1891-92	[illegible]	[illegible]	[illegible]	[illegible]	[illegible]	[illegible]	[illegible]	[illegible]	[illegible]
1892-93	[illegible]	[illegible]	[illegible]	[illegible]	·9	[illegible]	[illegible]	[illegible]	[illegible]
1893-94	—	—	—	[illegible]	[illegible]	[illegible]	[illegible]	[illegible]	[illegible]

B.

Table put in by Mr. Thomas Lough, M.P., in connexion with his evidence before the Commission on the 16th June 1896.

TABLE showing the TOTAL NUMBER of PAUPERS and the INCREASE of PAUPERISM in IRELAND between 1864 and 1894, the TOTAL NUMBER of EMIGRANTS in each YEAR, and the APPROXIMATION between the FIGURES of EMIGRATION and PAUPERISM.

Year	Population	Daily Average of Paupers			Paupers			Emigrants.	Proportion per 1,000 of Population.		
		Indoor.	Outdoor.	Total.	Indoor.	Outdoor.	Total.		Daily Average Paupers.	Total Paupers.	Emigrants.
1864	[illegible]	[illegible]	[illegible]	[illegible]	[illegible]	[illegible]	[illegible]	[illegible]	[illegible]	[illegible]	[illegible]
1865	[illegible]	[illegible]	4,749	[illegible]	[illegible]	[illegible]	[illegible]	[illegible]	[illegible]	[illegible]	[illegible]
1866	[illegible]	[illegible]	[illegible]	[illegible]	[illegible]	[illegible]	[illegible]	[illegible]	[illegible]	[illegible]	[illegible]
1867	[illegible]	[illegible]	[illegible]	[illegible]	[illegible]	[illegible]	[illegible]	[illegible]	[illegible]	[illegible]	[illegible]
1868	[illegible]	[illegible]	[illegible]	[illegible]	[illegible]	[illegible]	[illegible]	[illegible]	[illegible]	[illegible]	[illegible]
1869	[illegible]	[illegible]	[illegible]	[illegible]	[illegible]	[illegible]	[illegible]	[illegible]	[illegible]	[illegible]	[illegible]
1870	[illegible]	[illegible]	[illegible]	[illegible]	[illegible]	[illegible]	[illegible]	[illegible]	[illegible]	[illegible]	[illegible]
1871	[illegible]	[illegible]	[illegible]	[illegible]	[illegible]	[illegible]	[illegible]	[illegible]	[illegible]	[illegible]	[illegible]
1872	[illegible]	[illegible]	[illegible]	[illegible]	[illegible]	[illegible]	[illegible]	[illegible]	[illegible]	[illegible]	[illegible]
1873	[illegible]	[illegible]	[illegible]	[illegible]	[illegible]	[illegible]	[illegible]	[illegible]	[illegible]	[illegible]	[illegible]
1874	[illegible]	[illegible]	[illegible]	[illegible]	[illegible]	[illegible]	[illegible]	[illegible]	[illegible]	[illegible]	[illegible]
1875	[illegible]	[illegible]	[illegible]	[illegible]	[illegible]	[illegible]	[illegible]	[illegible]	[illegible]	[illegible]	[illegible]
1876	[illegible]	[illegible]	[illegible]	[illegible]	[illegible]	[illegible]	[illegible]	[illegible]	[illegible]	[illegible]	[illegible]
1877	[illegible]	[illegible]	[illegible]	[illegible]	[illegible]	[illegible]	[illegible]	[illegible]	[illegible]	[illegible]	[illegible]
1878	[illegible]	[illegible]	[illegible]	[illegible]	[illegible]	[illegible]	[illegible]	[illegible]	[illegible]	[illegible]	[illegible]
1879	[illegible]	[illegible]	[illegible]	[illegible]	[illegible]	[illegible]	[illegible]	[illegible]	[illegible]	[illegible]	[illegible]
1880	[illegible]	[illegible]	[illegible]	[illegible]	[illegible]	[illegible]	[illegible]	[illegible]	[illegible]	[illegible]	[illegible]
1881	[illegible]	[illegible]	[illegible]	[illegible]	[illegible]	[illegible]	[illegible]	[illegible]	[illegible]	[illegible]	[illegible]
1882	[illegible]	[illegible]	[illegible]	[illegible]	[illegible]	[illegible]	[illegible]	[illegible]	[illegible]	[illegible]	[illegible]
1883	[illegible]	[illegible]	[illegible]	[illegible]	[illegible]	[illegible]	[illegible]	[illegible]	[illegible]	[illegible]	[illegible]
1884	[illegible]	[illegible]	[illegible]	[illegible]	[illegible]	[illegible]	[illegible]	[illegible]	[illegible]	[illegible]	[illegible]
1885	[illegible]	[illegible]	[illegible]	[illegible]	[illegible]	[illegible]	[illegible]	[illegible]	[illegible]	[illegible]	[illegible]
1886	[illegible]	[illegible]	[illegible]	[illegible]	[illegible]	[illegible]	[illegible]	[illegible]	[illegible]	[illegible]	[illegible]
1887	[illegible]	[illegible]	[illegible]	[illegible]	[illegible]	[illegible]	[illegible]	[illegible]	[illegible]	[illegible]	[illegible]
1888	[illegible]	[illegible]	[illegible]	[illegible]	[illegible]	[illegible]	[illegible]	[illegible]	[illegible]	[illegible]	[illegible]
1889	[illegible]	[illegible]	[illegible]	[illegible]	[illegible]	[illegible]	[illegible]	[illegible]	[illegible]	[illegible]	[illegible]
1890	[illegible]	[illegible]	[illegible]	[illegible]	[illegible]	[illegible]	[illegible]	[illegible]	[illegible]	[illegible]	[illegible]
1891	[illegible]	[illegible]	[illegible]	[illegible]	[illegible]	[illegible]	[illegible]	[illegible]	[illegible]	[illegible]	[illegible]
1892	[illegible]	[illegible]	[illegible]	[illegible]	[illegible]	[illegible]	[illegible]	[illegible]	[illegible]	[illegible]	[illegible]
1893	[illegible]	[illegible]	[illegible]	[illegible]	[illegible]	[illegible]	[illegible]	[illegible]	[illegible]	[illegible]	[illegible]
1894	[illegible]	[illegible]	[illegible]	[illegible]	[illegible]	[illegible]	[illegible]	[illegible]	[illegible]	[illegible]	[illegible]

APPENDIX V.

A.

(1.) Table showing Revenue as Collected in Great Britain and Ireland for every Tenth Year from 1819 to 1890, with the relative Percentages and Amounts per Head in each Country.

—	Great Britain. Revenue as Collected.	Ireland. Revenue as Collected.	Total Revenue.	Great Britain. Percentage.	Ireland. Percentage.	Great Britain. Per Head.	Ireland. Per Head.
	£	£	£			£ s. d.	£ s. d.
1819 to 5 January 1820	[illegible]	[illegible]	[illegible]	[illegible]	[illegible]	[illegible]	[illegible]
1829 to 5 January 1830	[illegible]	[illegible]	[illegible]	[illegible]	[illegible]	[illegible]	[illegible]
1839 to 5 January 1840	[illegible]	[illegible]	[illegible]	[illegible]	[illegible]	[illegible]	[illegible]
1849 to 5 January 1850	[illegible]	[illegible]	[illegible]	[illegible]	[illegible]	[illegible]	[illegible]
1859–60 to 31 March 1860	[illegible]	[illegible]	[illegible]	[illegible]	[illegible]	[illegible]	[illegible]
1869–70 to 31 March 1870	[illegible]	[illegible]	[illegible]	[illegible]	[illegible]	[illegible]	[illegible]
1879–80 to 31 March 1880	[illegible]	[illegible]	[illegible]	[illegible]	[illegible]	[illegible]	[illegible]
1889–90 to 31 March 1890	[illegible]	[illegible]	[illegible]	[illegible]	[illegible]	[illegible]	[illegible]
1893–94 to 31 March 1894	[illegible]	[illegible]	[illegible]	[illegible]	[illegible]		—

Note.—In Table 1 the revenue as collected in Great Britain includes that revenue which is attributable to Imperial sources and derived therefore neither from Great Britain nor from Ireland (see Return C. [illegible] of 1894, page [illegible]). This revenue has been deducted from Table 2. The annual amount of such revenue is the difference between the totals in Tables 1 and 2.

B.

(2.) Table showing True Revenue, as estimated by the Treasury, of Great Britain and Ireland for every Tenth Year from 1819 to 1890, with the relative Percentages and Amounts per Head for each Country.

—	Great Britain. Estimated True Revenue.	Ireland. Estimated True Revenue.	Total Revenue.	Great Britain. Percentage.	Ireland. Percentage.	Great Britain. Per Head.	Ireland. Per Head.
	£	£	£			£ s. d.	£ s. d.
1819 to 5 January 1820	[illegible]	[illegible]	[illegible]	[illegible]	[illegible]	[illegible]	[illegible]
1829 to 5 January 1830	[illegible]	[illegible]	[illegible]	[illegible]	[illegible]	[illegible]	[illegible]
1839 to 5 January 1840	[illegible]	[illegible]	[illegible]	[illegible]	[illegible]	[illegible]	[illegible]
1849 to 5 January 1850	[illegible]	[illegible]	[illegible]	[illegible]	[illegible]	[illegible]	[illegible]
1859–60 to 31 March 1860	[illegible]	[illegible]	[illegible]	[illegible]	[illegible]	[illegible]	[illegible]
1869–70 to 31 March 1870	[illegible]	[illegible]	[illegible]	[illegible]	[illegible]	[illegible]	[illegible]
1879–80 to 31 March 1880	[illegible]	[illegible]	[illegible]	[illegible]	[illegible]	[illegible]	[illegible]
1889–90 to 31 March 1890	[illegible]	[illegible]	[illegible]	[illegible]	[illegible]	[illegible]	[illegible]
1893–94 to 31 March 1894	[illegible]	[illegible]	[illegible]	[illegible]	[illegible]	—	—

Note.—The figures of estimated true revenue to 1890 are taken from the Return C. [illegible] of 1894 (Prime Return), and as to year 1893–94 from the Return C. [illegible] of 1894 (Financial Relations Return). A subsequent correction by the Treasury has assigned the estimated true revenue for 1893–94 [illegible].

The figures per head are based on the decennial census of 1821 and onwards.

The figures for 1889–90 and 1893–94 in each Table exclude the sums collected as Exchequer revenue but handed over under recent legislation to local authorities.

C.

Table showing for every fifth year from 1819-20 to 1889-90, and for every year from 1890-94 (1) the Total Exchequer Revenue collected in Ireland; (2) Total Civil Expenditure in Ireland; and (3) the Balance applicable to other Purposes.

Year	Total Exchequer Revenue collected in Ireland.	Total Civil Expenditure in Ireland.	Balance.
	£	£	£
1819-20	[illegible]	[illegible]	[illegible]
1824-25	[illegible]	[illegible]	[illegible]
1829-30	[illegible]	[illegible]	[illegible]
1834-35	[illegible]	[illegible]	[illegible]
1839-40	[illegible]	[illegible]	[illegible]
1844-45	[illegible]	[illegible]	[illegible]
1849-50	[illegible]	[illegible]	[illegible]
1854-55	[illegible]	[illegible]	[illegible]
1859-60	[illegible]	[illegible]	[illegible]
1864-65	[illegible]	[illegible]	[illegible]
1869-70	[illegible]	[illegible]	[illegible]
1874-75	[illegible]	[illegible]	[illegible]
1879-80	[illegible]	[illegible]	[illegible]
1884-85	[illegible]	[illegible]	[illegible]
1889-90	[illegible]	[illegible]	[illegible]
1890-91	[illegible]	[illegible]	[illegible]
1891-92	[illegible]	[illegible]	[illegible]
1892-93	[illegible]	[illegible]	[illegible]
1893-94	[illegible]	[illegible]	[illegible]

Note.—The figures of revenue collected in Ireland are taken from the table furnished by Sir Edward Hamilton and printed at page [illegible] of the first volume of evidence and appendices published by the Commission. The figures of civil expenditure in Ireland are taken from the tables on pages [illegible] and [illegible] of that volume. They include the expenditure upon postal service and collection of taxes in Ireland.

B. H. Holland,
Secretary.

D.

Table showing for every tenth year from 1819 to 1890, and for the years 1893-94, (1) the true Irish Revenue as estimated by the Treasury; (2) the Expenditure on Services classified as Irish by the Treasury, and (3) the Balance applicable in each year to other Purposes.

Year	Estimated True Irish Revenue.	Expenditure on Irish Services ‡	Balance.
1819-20	[illegible]*	[illegible]	[illegible]
1829-30	[illegible]*	[illegible]	[illegible]
1839-40	[illegible]*	[illegible]	[illegible]
1849-50	[illegible]*	[illegible]	[illegible]
1859-60	[illegible]*	[illegible]	[illegible]
1869-70	[illegible]*	[illegible]	[illegible]
1879-80	[illegible]*	[illegible]	[illegible]
1889-90	[illegible]*	[illegible]	[illegible]
1893-94	[illegible]†	[illegible]	[illegible]

* Taken from Return C [illegible] of [illegible]. A subsequent [illegible] by the Treasury has reduced the estimated true Revenue for [illegible] to [illegible].

† Taken from Return C [illegible] of [illegible].

‡ [illegible] by [illegible]'s Table [illegible], p. [illegible] of first volume of Evidence.

B. H. Holland,
Secretary.

RETURN APPLIED FOR BY FINANCIAL RELATIONS COMMISSION, APRIL 1894.

A Return showing the approximate Amount of Imperial Revenue paid into the Bank of Ireland in the Financial Years mentioned below, the Amounts paid in Ireland for Irish Expenditure, and the Balance transferred to England, so far as these particulars can be obtained from the entries in the Bank Books.

N.B.—The Index Numbers to the Columns refer to explanatory remarks attached to this statement.

Index No.	Year.	1. Total Amount paid into H.M. Exchequer.	2. Estimated Amount from Customs, Excise, Stamps and Post Office General.	3. From other Sources.	4. Total Amount paid out of H.M. Exchequer.	5. Amount transferred to England.	6. Amount expended on Irish Services.	7. Interest on Debt, Funds, Annuities, &c.	8. Other special Payments, if any.
		£	£	£	£	£	£	£	£
1	[illegible]	[illegible]	[illegible]	[illegible]	[illegible]	Nil	[illegible]	[illegible]	[illegible]
2	[illegible]	[illegible]	[illegible]	[illegible]	[illegible]	Nil	[illegible]	[illegible]	[illegible]
3	[illegible]	[illegible]	[illegible]	[illegible]	[illegible]	[illegible]	[illegible]	[illegible]	[illegible]
4	[illegible]	[illegible]	[illegible]	[illegible]	[illegible]	[illegible]	[illegible]	[illegible]	—
5	[illegible]	[illegible]	[illegible]	[illegible]	[illegible]	[illegible]	[illegible]	[illegible]	..
6	[illegible]	[illegible]	[illegible]	[illegible]	[illegible]	[illegible]	[illegible]	[illegible]	—
7	[illegible]	[illegible]	[illegible]	[illegible]	[illegible]	[illegible]	[illegible]	[illegible]	—
8	[illegible]	[illegible]	[illegible]	[illegible]	[illegible]	[illegible]	[illegible]	[illegible]	..
9	[illegible]	[illegible]	[illegible]	[illegible]	[illegible]	[illegible]	[illegible]	[illegible]	—
10	[illegible]	[illegible]	[illegible]	[illegible]	[illegible]	[illegible]	[illegible]	[illegible]	—
11	[illegible]	[illegible]	[illegible]	[illegible]	[illegible]	[illegible]	[illegible]	[illegible]	—
12	[illegible]	[illegible]	[illegible]	[illegible]	[illegible]	[illegible]	[illegible]	[illegible]	—
13	[illegible]	[illegible]	[illegible]	[illegible]	[illegible]	[illegible]	[illegible]	[illegible]	—
14	[illegible]	[illegible]	[illegible]	[illegible]	[illegible]	[illegible]	[illegible]	[illegible]	—
15	[illegible]	[illegible]	[illegible]	[illegible]	[illegible]	[illegible]	[illegible]	[illegible]	[illegible]
16	[illegible]	[illegible]	[illegible]	[illegible]	[illegible]	[illegible]	[illegible]	[illegible]	—
17	[illegible]	[illegible]	[illegible]	[illegible]	[illegible]	[illegible]	[illegible]	[illegible]	—
18	[illegible]	[illegible]	[illegible]	[illegible]	[illegible]	[illegible]	[illegible]	[illegible]	—
19	[illegible]	[illegible]	[illegible]	[illegible]	[illegible]	[illegible]	[illegible]	[illegible]	—
20	[illegible]	[illegible]	[illegible]	[illegible]	[illegible]	[illegible]	[illegible]	[illegible]	—

* Sinking Fund. † Bank of Ireland for repayment of Treasury Bonds. ‡ Silver Tokens shipped to England. § Sale of Gold and Crown Notes. ‖ [illegible] Redemption of Government Stock. ¶ Pensions paid to Lord Lieutenant, &c.

In the letter received from the Secretary to the Financial Relations Commission, dated 23rd March last, the following returns were asked for:—

1st. Annual receipts from Imperial taxation paid into the Bank of Ireland in the financial year 1819–20, and at intervals to 1894–5.
2nd. The amount of expenditure for Irish services paid out of these receipts.
3rd. The balance transferred to England.

In endeavouring to comply as far as possible with the above request considerable difficulties were experienced. At different periods changes appear to have been made in the method of working the Revenue and Exchequer accounts, and particularly in the earlier periods under review, the entries in the books (most probably kept in accordance with instructions from the Treasury authorities) afford scant information.

After consideration it was decided to furnish the returns in the present form, as being less liable to lead to erroneous conclusions than would be the case had we endeavoured to condense them.

Much care has been taken in preparing the figures for these returns, and taking into consideration the difficulties encountered and the limited time at our disposal, they are believed to be fairly correct.

With regard to the Postal Revenue, from the year 1820 to the year 1851 there appear to have been considerable sums credited to Her Majesty's Exchequer account by the Postmaster-General, but about the last-named year these credits ceased, and no arrangement of the working of the Postmaster-General's account in the books here does not afford the means of obtaining such information as could be made available for these returns.

Remarks

Nos. 1, 2, and 3.—It would appear that during these periods the Customs, Excise, and Stamp Revenues were paid direct into Her Majesty's Exchequer account, and not by daily transfers from separate cash accounts as at present. Included in total amount (column No. 1) paid into Exchequer, are sundry items for repayment of loans to ports and harbours.

In the year 1834–5 there are the following special credits:—

			£
5th January 1835		Paid into Bank of England by Wm. Uff	102,333
25th April	..	Per Vernon and Hume	170,000
30th June	..	Ditto ditto	131,[illegible]
31st October	..	[illegible]	[illegible]

The debits and credits for silver coin represent transactions connected with the withdrawal of silver tokens from Ireland by Act of Parliament and the substitution of standard silver coins.

No. 4.—In this and succeeding financial years sundry amounts were paid into the Bank of England and accounted here for account Excise and Customs Revenue. They are included in the amount in column No. 2.

No. 5.—In this year we first find amounts of Woods and Forests, transfers from which account go direct to London without passing through Her Majesty's Exchequer account. They are set out separately in columns 1 and 3.

No. 6.—The financial year was changed in [illegible] from 5th January in each year to 31st March. In this year Income Tax Revenue is first credited to Her Majesty's Exchequer account.

No. 15.—In this and the following financial years large sums were transferred from Stamp, Revenue, Excise, and Customs accounts to Local Taxation (Ireland) account, Consolidated Fund Local Purchase account, &c., and appear separately in columns Nos. 3 and 6. In this year there was a payment out of Her Majesty's Exchequer account of [illegible] for the redemption of Consols, which is noted in the returns.

J. E. [illegible],
Accountant-General, Bank of Ireland.

24th April 1896.

Note by Sir Edward Hamilton with regard to the above Return furnished to the Chairman.

I venture to think that this Return will confuse the issue before the Royal Commission, inasmuch as it cannot agree with any of the statements which have been laid before the Commission. I offer one or two explanations about the discrepancies, which cannot be avoided.

The statements already presented have related on the one hand to the expenditure incurred on Irish Local services, and on the other hand either to the revenue collected in the country, or to the revenue estimated to be contributed by Irish taxpayers.

This Return shows "the approximate amount of "Imperial revenue paid into the Bank of England" over a series of years, "the amounts paid in Ireland "for Irish expenditure, and the balance transferred to "England."

The amount of Revenue paid into the Bank of Ireland cannot agree with the amount collected in that country, because, among other reasons—(1) some of the Revenue collected in Ireland may be, and is, paid by cheques drawn on English banks, and (2) Post Office Revenue collected in Ireland (amounting to about 750,000*l.*) is not brought to account at the Bank of Ireland, but treated like Post Office Revenue collected in the provinces on this side of St. George's Channel. The amounts paid at the Bank of Ireland include certain payments in respect of Imperial services, such as interest on the debt inscribed in the books of that bank, while a part of the Irish local expenditure may be met by cheques drawn on Irish banks.

"The amount remitted to England," or "the balance transferred to England" is equally misleading, inasmuch as the remittances include the proceeds of taxation which were collected in Ireland, but contributed by British taxpayers.

It may be pointed out in conclusion that, whereas according to this Return, the amount paid into Her Majesty's Irish Exchequer (e.g.) in 1893–4 was, including Crown revenues, [illegible], the amount actually collected in Ireland was, apart from Local Taxation Revenue, [illegible] (see p. [illegible] of the Parliamentary Paper issued by the Royal Commission, C.—7720).

Her Majesty's Treasury, E. W. HAMILTON.
6th July 1896.

A.

At page 480 of the first volume of evidence and appendices published by the Commission there are tables relating to assessments to Income Tax in Great Britain and Ireland down to the year 1893. The figures for 1894 have now been received from the Inland Revenue Department, together with some slight corrections to the figures for 1893. The figures for these two years are therefore given below.

B. H. HOLLAND,
Secretary.

July 1895.

No. I.—ENGLAND AND WALES.

Account for the years 1893 and 1894 of the Annual Value (1) of Lands; and (2) of Houses in England and Wales, assessed to Income Tax under Schedule A.; (3) of Railways assessed under Schedule D., and (4) of "Other Property" (including Quarries, Mines, Ironworks, Gasworks, Waterworks, Canals, &c.), also assessed under Schedule D.

Year ending 5th April.	Lands, including Tithes.	Houses.	Railways.	"Other Property" as defined above.	Total.	Amount of "Other Property" transferred to Schedule D.	Remarks.
	£	£	£	£	£	£	
1893 -	[illegible]	[illegible]	[illegible]	[illegible]	[illegible]	[illegible]	—
1894 -	[illegible]	[illegible]	[illegible]	[illegible]	[illegible]	[illegible]	New assessment, except Metropolis.

No. II.—SCOTLAND.

Account for the years 1893 and 1894 of the Annual Value (1) of Lands, and (2) of Houses in Scotland assessed to Income Tax under Schedule A., (3) of Railways assessed under Schedule D., and (4) of "Other Property" (including Quarries, Mines, Ironworks, Gasworks, Waterworks, Canals, &c.), also assessed under Schedule D.

Year ending 5th April.	Lands, including Tithes.	Houses.	Railways.	"Other Property" as defined above.	Total.	Amount of "Other Property" transferred to Schedule D.	Remarks.
	£	£	£	£	£	£	
1893 -	[illegible]	[illegible]	[illegible]	[illegible]	[illegible]	[illegible]	—
1894 -	[illegible]	[illegible]	[illegible]	[illegible]	[illegible]	[illegible]	—

No. III.—IRELAND.

Account for the years 1893 and 1894 of the Annual Value (1) of Lands, and (2) of Houses in Ireland assessed to Income Tax under Schedule A., (3) of Railways assessed under Schedule D., and (4) of "Other Property" (including Quarries, Mines, Ironworks, Gasworks, Waterworks, Canals, &c.), also assessed under Schedule D.

Year ending 5th April.	Lands, including Tithes.	Houses.	Railways.	"Other Property" as defined above.	Total.	Amount of "Other Property" transferred to Schedule D.	Remarks.
	£	£	£	£	£	£	
1893 -	[illegible]	[illegible]	[illegible]	[illegible]	[illegible]	[illegible]	—
1894 -	[illegible]	[illegible]	[illegible]	[illegible]	[illegible]	[illegible]	—

No. IV.

Table showing, for the years 1893 and 1894, the Total Gross Assessment to Income Tax (1) in Great Britain, (2) in Ireland, in respect of Lands (including Tithes), Houses, Railways, and "Other Property" (including Quarries, Mines, Ironworks, Fisheries, Canals, Gasworks, &c.).

Year ending 5th April.	Great Britain.	Ireland.
	£	£
1893 - - - - - -	[illegible]	[illegible]
1894 - - - - - -	[illegible]	[illegible]

B.

The following Tables are taken from the Thirty-eighth Report of the Commissioners of Inland Revenue (C. 7854 of 1895):—

Net Amount of Property and Income charged under each Schedule of the Income Tax Acts for the Years ended 5th April 1894 and 1895, and the Amount of Duty charged thereon.

Schedule.	Year ended 5th April 1894. Amount of Property and Income charged in — England.	Scotland.	Ireland.	United Kingdom.	Amount of Duty charged.*	Year ended 5th April 1895. Amount of Property and Income charged in — England.	Scotland.	Ireland.	United Kingdom.	Amount of Duty charged.†	Schedule.
	£	£	£	£	£	£	£	£	£	£	
A.	[illegible]	[illegible]	[illegible]	[illegible]	[illegible]	[illegible]	[illegible]	[illegible]	[illegible]	[illegible]	A.
B.	[illegible]	[illegible]	[illegible]	[illegible]	[illegible]	[illegible]	[illegible]	[illegible]	[illegible]	[illegible]	B.
C.	[illegible]	—	[illegible]	[illegible]	[illegible]	[illegible]	—	[illegible]	[illegible]	[illegible]	C.
D.	[illegible]	[illegible]	[illegible]	[illegible]	[illegible]	[illegible]	[illegible]	[illegible]	[illegible]	[illegible]	D.
E.	[illegible]	[illegible]	[illegible]	[illegible]	[illegible]	[illegible]	[illegible]	[illegible]	[illegible]	[illegible]	E.
Totals	[illegible]	[illegible]	[illegible]	[illegible]	[illegible]	[illegible]	[illegible]	[illegible]	[illegible]	[illegible]	Totals.

* At [illegible] in the £. † At [illegible] in the £.

C.

DEATH DUTIES.

Gross Value of Estates and Net Capital paying Probate Duty,* or Estate Duty under the Finance Act, 1894, in the Year 1894–95. (In Thousands of Pounds.)

	(1)	(2)	(3)	(4)	(5)	(6)	(7)	(8)	(9)	(10)	(11)	(12)
	£	£	£	£	£	£	£	£	£	£	£	£
England — Probate Duty	[illegible]	[illegible]	[illegible]	—	—	—	—	—	[illegible]	[illegible]	[illegible]	[illegible]
England — Estate	[illegible]	[illegible]	—	[illegible]	[illegible]	[illegible]	[illegible]	[illegible]				
Scotland — Inventory Duty	[illegible]	[illegible]	[illegible]	—	—	—	—	—	[illegible]	[illegible]	[illegible]	[illegible]
Scotland — Estate	[illegible]	[illegible]	—	[illegible]	[illegible]	[illegible]	[illegible]	[illegible]				
Ireland — Probate Duty	[illegible]	[illegible]	[illegible]	—	—	—	—	—	[illegible]	[illegible]	[illegible]	[illegible]
Ireland — Estate	[illegible]	[illegible]	—	[illegible]	[illegible]	[illegible]	[illegible]	[illegible]				
United Kingdom — Probate Duty	[illegible]	[illegible]	[illegible]	—	—	—	—	—	[illegible]	[illegible]	[illegible]	[illegible]
United Kingdom — Estate	[illegible]	[illegible]	—	[illegible]	[illegible]	[illegible]	[illegible]	[illegible]				

* Including Account Duty.

APPENDIX VIII.

RELATIVE CHANGES during PERIOD [illegible] to [illegible] of the TOTAL and AVERAGE INCOMES and WAGES of the WHOLE POPULATION of the UNITED KINGDOM.

The following paper is extracted from a paper read by Mr. A. L. [illegible], M.A., before the Royal Statistical Society on the [illegible] March [illegible], and printed in the June number, [illegible], of the journal of that Society. The paper was referred to by Sir Robert Giffen in his evidence before the Commission (A. [illegible]). The table is a summary of what appears to be a very careful analysis of the information derived from various sources.

R. H. [illegible]
Secretary.

Year.	1	2	3	4	5	6	7	8	9	10	11	12	13	14	15	16
	[illegible]				Total Annually Paid in Wages. (From Cols. [illegible])		Total Income not Received as Wages.						Average Income of Nation (From Cols. [illegible])		Col. [illegible] and Col. [illegible] Corrected by [illegible]	
							Subject to Income Tax.		Not Subject to Income Tax.							
	Number of Persons [illegible] Independent Incomes	Number of Manual Labourers	[illegible]	[illegible]	Amount	Percentage of Col. 11	Amount	Percentage of Col. 11	Amount	Percentage of Col. 11	[illegible]	[illegible]	Amount	Percentage [illegible]	Real Average Wages	Real Average Income
[illegible]	[illegible]	[illegible]	[illegible]	[illegible]	[illegible]	[illegible]	[illegible]	[illegible]	[illegible]	[illegible]	[illegible]	[illegible]	[illegible]	[illegible]	[illegible]	[illegible]
[illegible]	[illegible]	[illegible]	[illegible]	[illegible]	[illegible]	[illegible]	[illegible]	[illegible]	[illegible]	[illegible]	[illegible]	[illegible]	[illegible]	[illegible]	[illegible]	[illegible]
[illegible]	[illegible]	[illegible]	[illegible]	[illegible]	[illegible]	[illegible]	[illegible]	[illegible]	[illegible]	[illegible]	[illegible]	[illegible]	[illegible]	[illegible]	[illegible]	[illegible]
[illegible]	[illegible]	[illegible]	[illegible]	[illegible]	[illegible]	[illegible]	[illegible]	[illegible]	[illegible]	[illegible]	[illegible]	[illegible]	[illegible]	[illegible]	[illegible]	[illegible]
[illegible]	[illegible]	[illegible]	[illegible]	[illegible]	[illegible]	[illegible]	[illegible]	[illegible]	[illegible]	[illegible]	[illegible]	[illegible]	[illegible]	[illegible]	[illegible]	[illegible]
[illegible]	[illegible]	[illegible]	[illegible]	[illegible]	[illegible]	[illegible]	[illegible]	[illegible]	[illegible]	[illegible]	[illegible]	[illegible]	[illegible]	[illegible]	[illegible]	[illegible]
[illegible]	[illegible]	[illegible]	[illegible]	[illegible]	[illegible]	[illegible]	[illegible]	[illegible]	[illegible]	[illegible]	[illegible]	[illegible]	[illegible]	[illegible]	[illegible]	[illegible]
[illegible]	[illegible]	[illegible]	[illegible]	[illegible]	[illegible]	[illegible]	[illegible]	[illegible]	[illegible]	[illegible]	[illegible]	[illegible]	[illegible]	[illegible]	[illegible]	[illegible]
[illegible]	[illegible]	[illegible]	[illegible]	[illegible]	[illegible]	[illegible]	[illegible]	[illegible]	[illegible]	[illegible]	[illegible]	[illegible]	[illegible]	[illegible]	[illegible]	[illegible]

NOTE.—To compare [illegible] progress of total [illegible] and total [illegible] wages, see Columns [illegible] and [illegible].
Do. compare [illegible] wages and average [illegible], see Columns [illegible] and [illegible].

Tables and Observations reprinted from Vol. IV. of the General Report of the Census of England and Wales in the year 1871.

I. Occupations.

Occupations of the Inhabitants of the United Kingdom and its several Divisions, and the Proportions of Persons engaged in such Occupations to the Total Population.

Classes, Orders and Subdivisions.	Numbers.				Rates per Million.			
	England and Wales.	Scotland.	Ireland.	United Kingdom.	England and Wales.	Scotland.	Ireland.	United Kingdom.
PROFESSIONAL CLASS.	[illegible]	[illegible]	[illegible]	[illegible]	[illegible]	[illegible]	[illegible]	[illegible]
1. Civil Service and Local Government	[illegible]	[illegible]	[illegible]	[illegible]	[illegible]	[illegible]	[illegible]	[illegible]
2. Defence of the country	[illegible]	[illegible]	[illegible]	[illegible]	[illegible]	[illegible]	[illegible]	[illegible]
3. Professional (with subordinate subdivisions) —								
a. Clerical —								
1. Clergymen, priests, ministers	[illegible]	[illegible]	[illegible]	[illegible]	[illegible]	[illegible]	[illegible]	[illegible]
2. Nuns, [illegible], church, cemetery officials, &c.	[illegible]	[illegible]	[illegible]	[illegible]	[illegible]	[illegible]	[illegible]	[illegible]
b. Legal —								
1. Barristers, solicitors	[illegible]	[illegible]	[illegible]	[illegible]	[illegible]	[illegible]	[illegible]	[illegible]
2. Law clerks, &c.	[illegible]	[illegible]	[illegible]	[illegible]	[illegible]	[illegible]	[illegible]	[illegible]
c. Medical —								
1. Physicians, surgeons, general practitioners	[illegible]	[illegible]	[illegible]	[illegible]	[illegible]	[illegible]	[illegible]	[illegible]
2. Sick nurses, midwives	[illegible]	[illegible]	[illegible]	[illegible]	[illegible]	[illegible]	[illegible]	[illegible]
3. Others	[illegible]	[illegible]	[illegible]	[illegible]	[illegible]	[illegible]	[illegible]	[illegible]
d. Educational —								
1. Teachers	[illegible]	[illegible]	[illegible]	[illegible]	[illegible]	[illegible]	[illegible]	[illegible]
2. Students over 15	[illegible]	[illegible]	[illegible]	[illegible]	[illegible]	[illegible]	[illegible]	[illegible]
e. Others	[illegible]	[illegible]	[illegible]	[illegible]	[illegible]	[illegible]	[illegible]	[illegible]
DOMESTIC CLASS								
a. Domestic offices or services	[illegible]	[illegible]	[illegible]	[illegible]	[illegible]	[illegible]	[illegible]	[illegible]
COMMERCIAL CLASS	[illegible]	[illegible]	[illegible]	[illegible]	[illegible]	[illegible]	[illegible]	[illegible]
1. Commercial occupations	[illegible]	[illegible]	[illegible]	[illegible]	[illegible]	[illegible]	[illegible]	[illegible]
2. Conveyance of men, goods, and messages —								
a. On railways	[illegible]	[illegible]	[illegible]	[illegible]	[illegible]	[illegible]	[illegible]	[illegible]
b. On roads	[illegible]	[illegible]	[illegible]	[illegible]	[illegible]	[illegible]	[illegible]	[illegible]
c. On canals, rivers, seas	[illegible]	[illegible]	[illegible]	[illegible]	[illegible]	[illegible]	[illegible]	[illegible]
d. Storage, porterage, messengers	[illegible]	[illegible]	[illegible]	[illegible]	[illegible]	[illegible]	[illegible]	[illegible]
AGRICULTURAL AND FISHING CLASS	[illegible]	[illegible]	[illegible]	[illegible]	[illegible]	[illegible]	[illegible]	[illegible]
1. Agriculture —								
a. Farmers	[illegible]	[illegible]	[illegible]	[illegible]	[illegible]	[illegible]	[illegible]	[illegible]
b. Farmers' sons, grandsons, &c., over 15	[illegible]	[illegible]	[illegible]	[illegible]	[illegible]	[illegible]	[illegible]	[illegible]
c. Farm bailiffs	[illegible]	[illegible]	[illegible]	[illegible]	[illegible]	[illegible]	[illegible]	[illegible]
d. Agricultural labourers, farm servants, cottagers	[illegible]	[illegible]	[illegible]	[illegible]	[illegible]	[illegible]	[illegible]	[illegible]
e. Shepherds	[illegible]	[illegible]	[illegible]	[illegible]	[illegible]	[illegible]	[illegible]	[illegible]
f. Gardeners, nurserymen, &c.	[illegible]	[illegible]	[illegible]	[illegible]	[illegible]	[illegible]	[illegible]	[illegible]
g. Engaged about animals	[illegible]	[illegible]	[illegible]	[illegible]	[illegible]	[illegible]	[illegible]	[illegible]
h. Others	[illegible]	[illegible]	[illegible]	[illegible]	[illegible]	[illegible]	[illegible]	[illegible]
2. Fishing	[illegible]	[illegible]	[illegible]	[illegible]	[illegible]	[illegible]	[illegible]	[illegible]
INDUSTRIAL CLASS	[illegible]	[illegible]	[illegible]	[illegible]	[illegible]	[illegible]	[illegible]	[illegible]
9. Books, instruments, prints, maps	[illegible]	[illegible]	[illegible]	[illegible]	[illegible]	[illegible]	[illegible]	[illegible]
10. Machines, tools, and implements	[illegible]	[illegible]	[illegible]	[illegible]	[illegible]	[illegible]	[illegible]	[illegible]

[1] [illegible]

Classes, Orders, and Sub-Orders.	Numbers.				Ratio per million.			
	England and Wales.	Scotland.	Ireland.	United Kingdom.	England and Wales.	Scotland.	Ireland.	United Kingdom.
INDUSTRIAL CLASS—continued.								
11. [illegible]:—								
a. Building trades	[illegible]	[illegible]	[illegible]	[illegible]	[illegible]	[illegible]	[illegible]	[illegible]
b. [illegible]	[illegible]	[illegible]	[illegible]	[illegible]	[illegible]	[illegible]	[illegible]	[illegible]
12. Carriages and harness	[illegible]	[illegible]	[illegible]	[illegible]	[illegible]	[illegible]	[illegible]	[illegible]
13. Ships and boats	[illegible]	[illegible]	[illegible]	[illegible]	[illegible]	[illegible]	[illegible]	[illegible]
14. Chemicals and compounds	[illegible]	[illegible]	[illegible]	[illegible]	[illegible]	[illegible]	[illegible]	[illegible]
15. Tobacco and pipes	[illegible]	[illegible]	[illegible]	[illegible]	[illegible]	[illegible]	[illegible]	[illegible]
16. Food and lodging:—								
a. [illegible]	[illegible]	[illegible]	[illegible]	[illegible]	[illegible]	[illegible]	[illegible]	[illegible]
b. [illegible]	[illegible]	[illegible]	[illegible]	[illegible]	[illegible]	[illegible]	[illegible]	[illegible]
c. [illegible]	[illegible]	[illegible]	[illegible]	[illegible]	[illegible]	[illegible]	[illegible]	[illegible]
17. Textile fabrics:—								
a. Wool, worsted	[illegible]	[illegible]	[illegible]	[illegible]	[illegible]	[illegible]	[illegible]	[illegible]
b. Silk	[illegible]	[illegible]	[illegible]	[illegible]	[illegible]	[illegible]	[illegible]	[illegible]
c. Cotton	[illegible]	[illegible]	[illegible]	[illegible]	[illegible]	[illegible]	[illegible]	[illegible]
d. Flax, linen	[illegible]	[illegible]	[illegible]	[illegible]	[illegible]	[illegible]	[illegible]	[illegible]
e. [illegible]	[illegible]	[illegible]	[illegible]	[illegible]	[illegible]	[illegible]	[illegible]	[illegible]
f. [illegible]	[illegible]	[illegible]	[illegible]	[illegible]	[illegible]	[illegible]	[illegible]	[illegible]
18. Dress	[illegible]	[illegible]	[illegible]	[illegible]	[illegible]	[illegible]	[illegible]	[illegible]
19. [illegible]	[illegible]	[illegible]	[illegible]	[illegible]	[illegible]	[illegible]	[illegible]	[illegible]
20. [illegible]	[illegible]	[illegible]	[illegible]	[illegible]	[illegible]	[illegible]	[illegible]	[illegible]
21. Mineral substances:—								
a. Mining	[illegible]	[illegible]	[illegible]	[illegible]	[illegible]	[illegible]	[illegible]	[illegible]
b. [illegible]	[illegible]	[illegible]	[illegible]	[illegible]	[illegible]	[illegible]	[illegible]	[illegible]
c. [illegible]	[illegible]	[illegible]	[illegible]	[illegible]	[illegible]	[illegible]	[illegible]	[illegible]
d. [illegible]	[illegible]	[illegible]	[illegible]	[illegible]	[illegible]	[illegible]	[illegible]	[illegible]
e. [illegible]	[illegible]	[illegible]	[illegible]	[illegible]	[illegible]	[illegible]	[illegible]	[illegible]
f. Others	[illegible]	[illegible]	[illegible]	[illegible]	[illegible]	[illegible]	[illegible]	[illegible]
22. [illegible]:—								
a. [illegible]	[illegible]	[illegible]	[illegible]	[illegible]	[illegible]	[illegible]	[illegible]	[illegible]
b. [illegible]	[illegible]	[illegible]	[illegible]	[illegible]	[illegible]	[illegible]	[illegible]	[illegible]
c. [illegible]	[illegible]	[illegible]	[illegible]	[illegible]	[illegible]	[illegible]	[illegible]	[illegible]
d. [illegible]	[illegible]	[illegible]	[illegible]	[illegible]	[illegible]	[illegible]	[illegible]	[illegible]
23. [illegible]	[illegible]	[illegible]	[illegible]	[illegible]	[illegible]	[illegible]	[illegible]	[illegible]
CHILDREN AND ADULTS WITH NO SPECIFIED OCCUPATION	[illegible]	[illegible]	[illegible]	[illegible]	[illegible]	[illegible]	[illegible]	[illegible]
TOTAL POPULATION	[illegible]	[illegible]	[illegible]	[illegible]	[illegible]	[illegible]	[illegible]	[illegible]

We do not propose to examine the figures in the foregoing table in great detail. Confining ourselves, however, to the six great classes, we may give the following summary view of the comparative conditions as regards occupations of the three main sub-divisions of the United Kingdom.

Class	Proportions per 1,000 of all Ages.			
	England and Wales	Scotland	Ireland	United Kingdom
Professional	[illegible]	[illegible]	[illegible]	[illegible]
Domestic	[illegible]	[illegible]	[illegible]	[illegible]
Commercial	[illegible]	[illegible]	[illegible]	[illegible]
Agricultural and Fishing	[illegible]	[illegible]	[illegible]	[illegible]
Industrial	[illegible]	[illegible]	[illegible]	[illegible]
Unoccupied	[illegible]	[illegible]	[illegible]	[illegible]
Total	1,000	1,000	1,000	1,000

It is curious to note that the proportion borne by the professional class to the total population is much higher in Ireland than in England and Wales, or than in Scotland. This is partly due to the large number of soldiers quartered in Ireland, but mainly to the exceedingly large number of persons over 15 years of age returned as "students" in that division of the Kingdom. These amounted to no less than [illegible], or from three to four times as many as in Scotland, and [illegible] as many as in England and Wales, notwithstanding that the population of this latter is more than six times that of Ireland. What may be the explanation of this enormous excess of students over 15 in Ireland we are quite unable to say. The numbers of what are ordinarily termed the learned professions, with the exception of the clergy, were not in excess in that country, as is shown in the following table, which gives the average number of persons to one clergyman or priest, one lawyer, one doctor, and one teacher.

Profession	Persons to each Professional			
	England and Wales	Scotland	Ireland	United Kingdom
Clergyman, priest, minister	[illegible]	[illegible]	[illegible]	[illegible]
Lawyer	[illegible]	[illegible]	[illegible]	[illegible]
Medical man	[illegible]	[illegible]	[illegible]	[illegible]
Teacher	[illegible]	[illegible]	[illegible]	[illegible]

In the domestic class, which consists almost entirely of servants and washerwomen, the English proportion, as might be anticipated, far exceeded those of Scotland and of Ireland, which latter two were in this respect practically on an equality.

The commercial class was also more fully represented in England and Wales than in Scotland, though not to a very great degree; but in both the proportions vastly exceeded that in Ireland. The Irish proportion was low in all the sub-divisions of this class, namely, those engaged in what are ordinarily known as commercial businesses, and those engaged in transport, whether by rail, road, or water.

Still greater is the contrast between the several countries in the agricultural and fishing class. In England and Wales only [illegible] per 1,000 of the population were grouped in this class. In Scotland the proportion was [illegible], and in Ireland no less than [illegible]. In Ireland, with a population only one-sixth of that of England, there were almost twice as many persons returned as farmers as in the larger country, while the farmers' sons or nephews, or other male relatives, over 15 years of age, living with the farmer, and without specified occupation, and who were presumably assisting in farm work, were more than four times as numerous. The large excess in Ireland of these farmers' relatives, who practically take the place of farm servants, and the imperfect way in which the agricultural labourers are returned throughout the kingdom, but especially in Ireland, prevents due comparison of the figures under this last heading. Even if we take the figures as they stand in the table, however, without correction, the proportion of agricultural labourers in Ireland vastly exceeded the proportions in England and Wales, and in Scotland. Scotland, on the other hand, exceeded both England and Ireland in the proportion of shepherds, while the only agricultural persons in which the English and Welsh proportion largely exceeded the Scotch and Irish was that of gardeners, including nurserymen and seedsmen. There were more than ten times as many persons thus engaged in England as in Scotland, and more than twenty times as many as in Ireland.

The returns of fishermen in England and Wales, as has been pointed out on an earlier page, considerably understate the number so employed. When, however, the fullest allowance has been made for this, the proportion of fishermen to population in England and Wales still remains far lower than in Ireland, while in Ireland it is only one-third as high as in Scotland.

The proportion of persons in the industrial class to the total population was [illegible] to 1,000 in England and Wales and [illegible] in Scotland, figures practically coincident, but only [illegible] in Ireland; the only industry in which the Irish proportion was higher than in the other divisions being the flax and linen manufacture, which is almost extinct in England, is carried on to a large extent in Scotland, but in Ireland alone assumes notable proportions.

8. Physical Infirmities.

The total number of persons returned as blind in the United Kingdom was [illegible], of whom 18,270 were of the male and [illegible] of the female sex. These figures give [illegible] blind persons per million living, [illegible] per million males and 790 per million females.

The proportions, however, varied much in the different divisions of the kingdom. In Scotland there were only [illegible] blind persons per million population; in England and Wales there were [illegible], and in Ireland as many as 1,[illegible]. Moreover, while the proportion of blind males considerably exceeded the proportion of blind females both in England and Wales and in Scotland, in Ireland the opposite was the case, and the female proportion was somewhat the higher, there being 1,168 blind females but only 1,[illegible] blind males per million of the corresponding sex.

The Blind, [illegible] and Aged.

The total number of persons returned as deaf-mutes in the United Kingdom was 1[illegible], or [illegible] per million persons living. Of the total, 10,7[illegible], or [illegible] per million living, were of the male, and [illegible], or [illegible] per million living, of the female sex. In England and Wales the proportion of deaf-mutes was [illegible] per million living, in Scotland it was [illegible], and in Ireland 71[illegible]. In each division of the kingdom the male proportion largely exceeded the female proportion; the male proportions per million living being [illegible], [illegible], and 77[illegible], respectively in England and Wales, in Scotland, and in Ireland, while the female proportions per million living, taking the divisions in the same order, were respectively [illegible], [illegible], and [illegible].

Deaf and Dumb; Sexes and Ages.

—		All Ages.	0–	15–	25–	35–	45–	55–	65–	75–	85 and upwards.
England and Wales	Males	[illegible]	[illegible]	[illegible]	1,17[illegible]	[illegible]	[illegible]	[illegible]	[illegible]	[illegible]	5
	Females	[illegible]	1,[illegible]	1,419	1,[illegible]	[illegible]	[illegible]	[illegible]	[illegible]	[illegible]	10
Scotland	Males	1,[illegible]	[illegible]	[illegible]	17[illegible]	16[illegible]	[illegible]	[illegible]	[illegible]	10	1
	Females	[illegible]	[illegible]	1[illegible]	[illegible]	11[illegible]	[illegible]	[illegible]	41	[illegible]	1
Ireland	Males	1,[illegible]	[illegible]	[illegible]	[illegible]	[illegible]	[illegible]	17[illegible]	[illegible]	[illegible]	3
	Females	1,[illegible]	[illegible]	[illegible]	[illegible]	27[illegible]	[illegible]	1[illegible]	[illegible]	[illegible]	[illegible]
United Kingdom	Males	10,7[illegible]	[illegible]	[illegible]	1,[illegible]	1,[illegible]	[illegible]	[illegible]	[illegible]	[illegible]	18
	Females	[illegible]	[illegible]	1,[illegible]	1,[illegible]	1,[illegible]	[illegible]	[illegible]	[illegible]	[illegible]	19
	Persons	19,[illegible]	[illegible]	4,1[illegible]	[illegible]	[illegible]	1,[illegible]	1,[illegible]	[illegible]	[illegible]	[illegible]

The total number of persons returned as suffering from some or other form of mental derangement was 1[illegible], or 3,[illegible] per million persons living. The proportion was lowest in England and Wales, 3,[illegible] per million, and lower in Scotland, [illegible] per million, and highest in Ireland, [illegible] per million, so that the last division of the kingdom suffered considerably more than either of the other two divisions from each form of physical infirmity dealt with in the Census. Again, while the female insane rate exceeded the male rate very considerably in England and Wales, and slightly in Scotland, the opposite was the case in Ireland, where there were 4,7[illegible] insane males and only [illegible] insane females per million living of corresponding sex.

Insane; Sexes and Ages.

—		All Ages.	0–	15–	25–	35–	45–	55–	65–	75–	85 and upwards.
England and Wales	Males	[illegible]	[illegible]	[illegible]	[illegible]	9,714	6,1[illegible]	5,7[illegible]	3,41[illegible]	[illegible]	11[illegible]
	Females	51,991	[illegible]	4,[illegible]	[illegible]	10,[illegible]	10,5[illegible]	[illegible]	3,1[illegible]	1,[illegible]	[illegible]
Scotland	Males	7,[illegible]	[illegible]	9[illegible]	1,31[illegible]	1,[illegible]	1,[illegible]	[illegible]	[illegible]	1[illegible]	[illegible]
	Females	[illegible]	[illegible]	[illegible]	1,[illegible]	1,[illegible]	1,[illegible]	1,[illegible]	7[illegible]	[illegible]	1[illegible]
Ireland	Males	[illegible]	[illegible]	1,[illegible]	2,[illegible]	2,[illegible]	2,1[illegible]	1,[illegible]	[illegible]	17[illegible]	[illegible]
	Females	[illegible]	[illegible]	1,[illegible]	1,91[illegible]	[illegible]	[illegible]	1,[illegible]	17[illegible]	[illegible]	[illegible]
United Kingdom	Males	[illegible]	[illegible]	[illegible]	12,47[illegible]	[illegible]	[illegible]	[illegible]	4,[illegible]	[illegible]	1[illegible]
	Females	[illegible]	[illegible]	[illegible]	[illegible]	[illegible]	[illegible]	[illegible]	[illegible]	[illegible]	[illegible]
	Persons	[illegible]	[illegible]	[illegible]	[illegible]	[illegible]	[illegible]	[illegible]	[illegible]	[illegible]	[illegible]

3. *Institutions.*

The total number of persons in receipt of indoor relief in the United Kingdom was [illegible], or [illegible] per million population. The proportion, however, was only [illegible] per million in Scotland, while in England and Wales it was [illegible], and in Ireland no less than [illegible].

The total number of patients in hospitals was [illegible], or [illegible] per million population. The proportion per million was highest in Scotland, where it reached 1,[illegible]; then in England and Wales, where it was [illegible]; and smallest in Ireland, where it was only [illegible].

The total number of persons afflicted with some or other form of mental derangement in the United Kingdom was, as shown in the last section, [illegible], and of these [illegible], or [illegible] per cent., were inmates of asylums. In England and Wales [illegible] per cent. of the lunatics were inmates of asylums, in Scotland [illegible] per cent., and in Ireland only [illegible] per cent.

There were at the date of the Census [illegible] prisoners in the United Kingdom and [illegible] inmates of certified reformatories or industrial schools, making together a total of [illegible] persons in some or other place of detention. The proportion of such persons to the total population was highest in Ireland, [illegible] per million living; next highest in Scotland, [illegible] per million, and lowest in England and Wales, where it was only [illegible] per million. The high proportion in Ireland was entirely due, and in Scotland was mainly due, to the excessive number of young persons in reformatories or industrial schools, the proportion of prisoners, or, speaking generally, of adult criminals, being lower in Ireland than in either of the other divisions of the kingdom, and though higher in Scotland than in England and Wales, not nearly so much higher as was the proportion of the inmates of the reformatories and industrial schools.

	Number of Special Inmates.				Proportion per Million of Total Population.			
	England and Wales	Scotland	Ireland	United Kingdom	England and Wales	Scotland	Ireland	United Kingdom
Workhouses (including Infirmaries and Schools)	[illegible]	[illegible]	[illegible]	[illegible]	[illegible]	[illegible]	[illegible]	[illegible]
Hospitals	[illegible]	[illegible]	[illegible]	[illegible]	[illegible]	[illegible]	[illegible]	[illegible]
Lunatic Asylums*	[illegible]	[illegible]	[illegible]	[illegible]	[illegible]	[illegible]	[illegible]	[illegible]
Prisons	[illegible]	[illegible]†	[illegible]	[illegible]	[illegible]	[illegible]	[illegible]	[illegible]
Certified Reformatories and Industrial Schools	[illegible]	[illegible]	[illegible]	[illegible]	[illegible]	[illegible]	[illegible]	[illegible]

* [illegible]

† [illegible]

4. *Marriage.*

Proportion per 1,000

Civil Condition	England and Wales		Scotland		Ireland	
	Males	Females	Males	Females	Males	Females
Single	[illegible]	[illegible]	[illegible]	[illegible]	[illegible]	[illegible]
Married	[illegible]	[illegible]	[illegible]	[illegible]	[illegible]	[illegible]
Widowed	[illegible]	[illegible]	[illegible]	[illegible]	[illegible]	[illegible]

APPENDIX X.

Note by the Secretary.

It is thought that the following extracts from the work of so careful an investigator of statistics as Mr. Charles Booth may be of service to the Commissioners in considering the historical aspects of the case.

The extracts are taken from a paper on the Occupations of the People of the United Kingdom, which Mr. Charles Booth read before the Statistical Society on May 18, 1886.

After analysing the census returns for England and Scotland at several periods with a view to show the changes in the proportions of population employed in the given groups of occupations, Mr. Booth makes the following observations:—

Observations by Mr. Booth.

The picture we have now completed of the industrial development of England since 1851, and her apparent position in 1881, is, on the whole, one which may be regarded with satisfaction. Nor could any changes since 1881 seriously affect this result. Every line of it shows vitality and an innate power of meeting changes of circumstance, which seems to give promise of continued prosperity.

The growth of the population of Scotland (10, 9½, and 11½ per cent. for the three decades, 1851–1881) has been slower than that of England (12, 13, and 14½ per cent.), and the proportions engaged in each main division of industry are somewhat different, but the points of similarity are much more noticeable than the points of difference. We see a similar falling off in the proportion connected with agriculture, a similar constancy in those connected with building and manufacture, and a similar increase under other heads.

The figures show that the two countries share each other's fortunes, and make the union of feeling between them easy to understand.

But it is far different with the sister island.

If the picture given of the condition of agriculture in England and Scotland is gloomy, that of the whole condition of Ireland is much more so, and needs a treatment far more exhaustive than can here be pretended to.

In adopting the method already employed for England and Scotland, it must be remembered that in place of increasing, the whole population has decreased. The amount of this decrease from 1841 to 1881 is three millions out of eight millions of persons, and is made up as follows:—

From 1841 to 1851	1,623,000	3,000,000*
" '51 " '61	753,000	
" '61 " '71	386,000	
" '71 " '81	238,000	

The general picture at each period stands as under. 1841 is taken as the starting point, because it is necessary to begin from before the famine of 1846–47, and the returns of 1841 for Ireland appear to be sufficiently correct:—

* The preceding increase of population had been:—

From 1821 to 1831	965,000
" '31 " '41	408,000

TABLE A.—Showing Occupations of the People of Ireland by Percentages.

Occupations.	1841.		1851.		1861.		1871.		1881.	
Agriculture, &c.	[illegible]	[illegible]	[illegible]	[illegible]	[illegible]	[illegible]	[illegible]	[illegible]	[illegible]	[illegible]
Fishing	[illegible]		[illegible]		[illegible]		[illegible]		[illegible]	
Mining	[illegible]		[illegible]		[illegible]		[illegible]		[illegible]	
Building	[illegible]	[illegible]	[illegible]	[illegible]	[illegible]	[illegible]	[illegible]	[illegible]	[illegible]	[illegible]
Manufacture	[illegible]		[illegible]		[illegible]		[illegible]		[illegible]	
Transport	[illegible]	[illegible]	[illegible]	[illegible]	[illegible]	[illegible]	[illegible]	[illegible]	[illegible]	[illegible]
Dealing	[illegible]		[illegible]		[illegible]		[illegible]		[illegible]	
Industrial Service	—	[illegible]	—	[illegible]	—	[illegible]	—	[illegible]	—	[illegible]
Industry	—	[illegible]	—	[illegible]	—	[illegible]	—	[illegible]	—	[illegible]
Public and Professional Service	[illegible]	[illegible]	[illegible]	[illegible]	[illegible]	[illegible]	[illegible]	[illegible]	[illegible]	[illegible]
Domestic Service	[illegible]		[illegible]		[illegible]		[illegible]		[illegible]	
Others	[illegible]		[illegible]		[illegible]		[illegible]		[illegible]	
	—	100·0	—	100·0	—	100·0	—	100·0	—	100·0

With approximate apportionment to each class, the following are the figures:—

TABLE B.—Showing Means of Support of the People of Ireland by Percentages (Estimate.)

Occupations.	1841.		1851.		1861.		1871.		1881.	
Agriculture, &c.	[illegible]	[illegible]	[illegible]	[illegible]	[illegible]	[illegible]	[illegible]	[illegible]	[illegible]	[illegible]
Fishing	[illegible]		[illegible]		[illegible]		[illegible]		[illegible]	
Mining	[illegible]		[illegible]		[illegible]		[illegible]		[illegible]	
Building	[illegible]	[illegible]	[illegible]	[illegible]	[illegible]	[illegible]	[illegible]	[illegible]	[illegible]	[illegible]
Manufacture	[illegible]		[illegible]		[illegible]		[illegible]		[illegible]	
Transport	[illegible]	[illegible]	[illegible]	[illegible]	[illegible]	[illegible]	[illegible]	[illegible]	[illegible]	[illegible]
Dealing	[illegible]		[illegible]		[illegible]		[illegible]		[illegible]	
Industrial Service	...	[illegible]	—	[illegible]	—	[illegible]	—	[illegible]	—	[illegible]
Industry	—	[illegible]		[illegible]	—	[illegible]	—	[illegible]	—	[illegible]
Public and Professional Service	[illegible]	[illegible]	[illegible]	[illegible]	[illegible]	[illegible]	[illegible]	[illegible]	[illegible]	[illegible]
Domestic Service	[illegible]		[illegible]		[illegible]		[illegible]		[illegible]	
Others	[illegible]		[illegible]		[illegible]		[illegible]		[illegible]	
	—	100·0	—	100·0	—	100·0	—	100·0	—	100·0

* Army and Navy were omitted from the census of Ireland in 1841 and 1851.

† It is probable that domestic service should be 1 per cent. more in this year, and farm service (agriculture) 1 per cent. less. The returns prove inconclusive in this respect.

The numbers employed in agriculture have decreased since 1841 by 859,000, out of a total of 1,844,000, and those who may perhaps be counted as supported by agriculture by [illegible] out of five millions. Nor is this all, for their reductions being proportionately greater than those for the whole population, the percentage employed in or supported by agriculture has decreased as well as the total numbers.

The land in England and Scotland employs as many, and probably supports nearly as many, as it did in 1841, and meanwhile other productive industries support the bulk of our great increase of population. In Ireland, on the other hand, not only does the land fail to support half of those it once in some fashion maintained, but other productive industries (e.g., building and manufacture) are even worse off, and, like agriculture, show it both in numbers and percentage, those engaged in building and manufacture (taken together) being 10·9 less in percentage, as well as [illegible] fewer in number, than in 1841.

It is when taken together that these facts appear so serious as evidence of decadence. It might be well that fewer people, or that a smaller proportion of the population, should attempt to obtain a living from the land; and, on the other hand, the abandonment of industries for which the country has no advantages might be no loss, whether accompanied by a general loss of population or not; and, although a painful process, a general reduction in numbers of population by death and emigration, may finally conduce to the benefit of those who remain; but if all these things happen at once—if a reduced population finds less work to do per man—it is hard to obtain any encouragement from the figures. The best that can be hoped is that some ultimate advantage may lie at the end of a road not yet all trodden.

Nevertheless, the view is commonly held that in general well-being Ireland has enormously improved since the famine. No evidence of this improvement is to be found in the occupation returns, which, on the contrary, point to a diminution of industry likely to be the cause, as well as consequence, of poverty and waning trade, and certain to be the source of political discontent. I know that figures may be, and are, drawn from bank deposits and other returns which seem to tell a different story. I shall not attempt to reconcile this conflict of evidence. To do so would be beyond the scope of this paper. I can only state the conclusions to which the census returns point.

There may be much that is delusive in the rather golden picture of the industrial condition of England and Scotland that has been given; the tale may have varied since 1881, or even before; and the number of the unemployed or partly employed in each trade, whose lack of employment is not considered in our comparative returns, may make the reality very different; but in the picture of desolation which the Irish figures afford there seems little room for delusion. While industries decay, those who have been supported by them cling to their employment as long as possible, and what in England may have happened, that the numbers given include many who no longer find a living in what they profess to do, has certainly occurred in Ireland. In such a case the facts are assuredly worse than the figures disclose.

The subject may be taken from another side. It will be seen that the percentage of the Irish population actually returned as engaged in productive industry (in agriculture, fishing, mining, building, and manufacture) has fallen from 80·6 per cent. in 1841 to 60·1 per cent. in 1881, or progressively thus:—

1841.	1851.	1861.	1871.	1881.
Per cent.	Per cent.	Per cent.	Per cent.	Per cent.
80·6	74·0	68·7	63·1	60·1

the percentage of those otherwise engaged having risen in proportion from about 20 per cent. to about 40 per cent. I shall try to show what proportion of the increase in non-producers offers any compensation. It is divided thus:—

	Per Cent.
Increase in Transport	1·7
,, Dealing	2·8
,, Industrial Service	5·3
,, Public and Professional Service	3·6
,, Domestic Service	6·6
,, Property Owning	0·6
	[illegible]·0
Decrease in Indefinite	1·8
	[illegible]

The increase under Transport is connected with improvements in commercial system, and is not to be objected to. Of that under Public and Professional Service, which is very considerable, it is impossible to say much without entering upon ground more political than economical. The items in detail are as follows:—

—	1841.	1881.
	Per cent.	Per cent.
Administration	6,000, or 0·1	11,000 or 0·3
Army and Navy	—* —	48,000 ,, 1·7
Police and Prisons	11,000 ,, 0·3	1[illegible],000 ,, 0·[illegible]
Law	5,000 ,, 0·1	5,000 ,, 0·2
Medicine	7,000 ,, 0·2	7,000 ,, 0·2
Art and Amusement	4,000 ,, 0·1	5,000 ,, 0·1
Literature and Science	— —	1,000 —
Education	17,000 ,, 0·5	27,000 ,, 1·0
Religion	7,000 ,, 0·2	14,000 ,, 0·3
	57,000 ,, 1·6	171,000 ,, 5·0

* The soldiers in Ireland were omitted from the census 1841.

We may compare these with the parallel figures for Scotland, which are as follows:—

—	1841.	1881.
	Per cent.	Per cent.
Administration	4,000, or 0·1	16,000, or 0·4
Army and Navy	3,000 ,, 0·1	5,000 ,, 0·1
Police and Prisons	2,000 ,, 0·1	5,000 ,, 0·2
Law	4,000 ,, 0·2	7,000 ,, 0·2
Medicine	3,000 ,, 0·1	10,000 ,, 0·3
Art and Amusement	1,000 ,, 0·1	5,000 ,, 0·1
Literature and Science	— —	1,000 —
Education	7,000 ,, 0·3	18,000 ,, 0·5
Religion	3,000 ,, 0·1	6,000 ,, 0·2
	35,000 ,, 1·3	73,000 ,, 1·9

The increase in Ireland, though large, does not (if the Army and Navy be omitted) bring the percentage for 1881 so high as that of Scotland, or by any means so high as in England, and, except for the items of Police and Prisons, there is not much to be objected to.

It is otherwise with the increases under all the other heads. It is impossible to account satisfactorily for the increase which is to be found in the numbers as well as percentage of the dealers—those who live by buying and selling. The increase cannot be traced to any improved system of distribution, nor can we account for it, as we may in England and Scotland, by the fact that increasing production or greater wealth increases the volume to be distributed, and that our foreign trade has made of Great Britain a shop to which all the world comes to buy. It seems evident that the multiplying of this class in Ireland can only be taken as a sign of want of more useful employment.

In *Industrial Service* the commercial portion of the class was 11,000 in 1841, and 16,000 in 1881, an increase which, like that in Transport, may be satisfactory, as pointing to improvements of system, but this is not so with the main increase in this class—that of general labourers, from 21,000 in 1841, to 144,000 in 1881.

These labourers (who no doubt to some extent belong to the agricultural class) can hardly be added to the ranks of productive industry. They take their origin from the doubtful class who appear in the return of 1851 (after the famine) as "unclassed," and who, dropping out of that unnatural position, appear in 1861, and continue in 1871 and 1881, as "general labourers." It is true that this class is, relatively, almost as num-

[illegible] in England and Scotland as in Ireland, but there is a great difference in the fact that in the former countries they have always been a [illegible] order connected with the manufacturing and building industries, whereas in Ireland they have no such basis of support, and sprang into existence, not from any need of their services, but as the outcome of agricultural and industrial distress and [illegible] on an [illegible] scale.

Domestic Service has risen with a steady progression from 9·4 per cent. in 1841, to 13·0 per cent. in 1881. It may perhaps be conceivable that the loss of a large poor population should increase the proportion, to the whole, of those classes who can afford to keep servants; but this would not account for the large positive increase in the total number of servants ([illegible]), nor for the extraordinary fact that the proportion of servants to population in so poor a country as Ireland is considerably higher than it is in England, and as much as 31 per cent. higher (comparing the percentages) than it is in Scotland. And it must be remembered that it was not so in 1841, when the percentage for Ireland was much less than for England and Scotland. The figures are as follows, taking the proportions first to the employed, and second to the whole population:—

	On the Employed		On the whole Population	
	1841	1881	1841	1881
	Per cent.	Per cent.	Per cent.	Per cent.
England -	[illegible]	[illegible]	[illegible]	[illegible]
Scotland -	[illegible]	[illegible]	[illegible]	[illegible]
Ireland -	9·4	13·0	[illegible]	[illegible]

What is the explanation of these remarkable figures? It would be simplest to show that they are inaccurate, but apart from some difference in the method of tabulation (alluded to in the Census Report for 1881, but not specified), I have found no loophole of escape, and the comparison of successive decades shows how gradually the position of Ireland was reversed from being the most economical to being the most extravagant in Domestic Service. The only explanation that suggests itself is that servants are more numerous where poverty makes service cheap.*

The slight increase in the percentage under Property Owning would also be unimportant, if any conclusion could be fairly drawn from the figures, but, as we have already seen in the case of England, the returns under this head are entirely defective.

Against these increases has to be set off a decrease in the Indefinite class, which is returned as [illegible] in 1841, against [illegible] in 1881.

To bring the figures roughly together, so as to show what portion of the increase of non-producers may be satisfactory or not unaccountable, and what portion must, as I think, be considered unsatisfactory, I submit the following table. The difference in condition and industrial utility between the small dealers and general labourers and the unskilled class is probably very slight, and for this purpose they may be counted together:—

TABLE C.—SHOWING TRANSFER OF EMPLOYED FROM PRODUCTIVE TO NON-PRODUCTIVE INDUSTRY BETWEEN 1841 AND 1881.

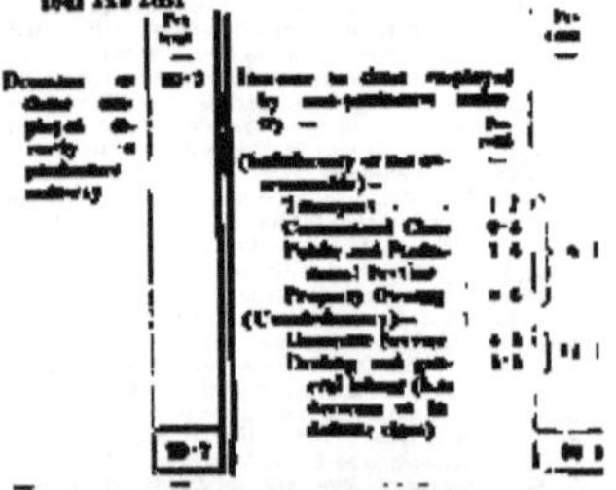

	Per cent.		Per cent.	
Decrease of those employed directly in productive industry	[illegible]	Increase in class employed by non-productive industry:—		
		(Satisfactory or not unaccountable):—		
		Transport	[illegible]	[illegible]
		Commercial Class	[illegible]	
		Public and Professional Service	[illegible]	
		Property Owning	[illegible]	
		(Unsatisfactory):—		
		Domestic Service	[illegible]	[illegible]
		Dealing and general labour (less decrease in indefinite class)	[illegible]	
	[illegible]			[illegible]

* The total number of persons engaged as domestic servants [illegible] [illegible] [illegible] [illegible] [illegible] (Irish Census Report 1881, Part II., p. [illegible]) [illegible]

Although this calculation must be accepted with very great reserve, it may yet give us a fair idea of the extent to which Ireland, besides its great decrease of numbers, has also deteriorated in the quality of work performed by those who remain. It shows us that since 1841 more than 14 per cent. of the employed population have been transferred from direct production to occupations which can at best add little to the wealth of the community.

In confirmation of this, if we turn to the details of those who figure under the head of Manufactures, we find only one occupation which has increased considerably in percentage, while on the whole there has been so great a decrease; this is under the heading [illegible]; and going into further detail we find that in [illegible] it is the [illegible] only who have increased in numbers, viz., from 47,[illegible] to 71,[illegible], so that once more it is only in the last refuge of destitute women that we find any increase.

A detailed review of productive industry in Ireland, to which we will now return, will show us more clearly where the falling off has occurred.

The decrease in those employed in Agriculture, though affecting each branch, shows itself, of course, mainly in the labourers and farm servants, which have fallen from [illegible] in 1841, to [illegible] in 1881, or [illegible] per cent. The decrease in farmers, from [illegible] to [illegible], is only [illegible]. The figures in regard to those engaged about animals, which show a large decrease, are fallacious, because a great number of persons who were in the earlier census classed as herds, have in 1881 been included with farm servants, which would tend to make the decline in the farm servants even worse than appears.

Fishing and Mining are small industries in Ireland. The former has increased from [illegible] to [illegible], or from 0·2 per cent. to 0·5 per cent. of the employed population; mining has fluctuated considerably at each decade, but ultimately shows a slight falling off in bulk. In percentage, however, it has risen from 0·2 per cent. to 0·4 per cent.

In 1841 there were [illegible] persons occupied in Building. In 1881 there were but [illegible], nevertheless the percentage to the total employed population has increased by 0·4 per cent.

The total employed in Manufactures has dropped from [illegible] to [illegible] (or [illegible] per cent.), and the percentage to the whole occupied population from [illegible] per cent. to 14 per cent. Machinery and tool makers employ a very much smaller proportion of workers than do these trades in England and Scotland, but the numbers have risen slightly, and now form [illegible] per cent. of the employed. The way in which Ireland has failed to share in the growing prosperity of the other portions of the kingdom is, however, strikingly exemplified in these trades, for while the great development of machinery during the last 40 years has enabled England and Scotland combined to add nearly [illegible] to their number of workers in this branch, Ireland during the same period has found a new opening in this direction for barely [illegible] persons. This will be found to throw a strong light on our next great (textile) industry, where more strongly than elsewhere we find the evidences of industrial decay.

It appears that in 1841, [illegible] persons were engaged in or employed in textile and dyeing industries. Since then the decline has been startling, to [illegible] in 1851, [illegible] in 1861, [illegible] in 1871, and finally to [illegible] in 1881. In the meantime England, starting with only [illegible] in 1841, has progressed to [illegible] in 1881. These figures include spinning, and it is to the loss of this hand industry, which passed to English machinery, that the reduction is largely to be traced. There is no body of women engaged in the Irish spinners to be found in the English returns of 1841, though there is a large number of women weavers who fall away later. It may be that domestic spinning existed in England and was not returned at all, or it may be that a larger share of this industry fell to Ireland. At any rate, we have the singular fact that in 1841 Ireland returns more workers in this section (textiles) than England, but in 1881 not one-[illegible] of the number. If the spinning industry was spread over the country, and an aid to every family whose men only were needed on the land, it would go some way to explain a wreck of prosperity.

The figures for textile manufacture show a very general decline, to which even flax and linen cannot be considered exceptions.

The detailed facts as to the textile industries of Ireland are as follows:—

(In thousands and decimals of a thousand.)

Occupations.	1841.	1851.	1861.	1871.	1881.
Woollen cloth manufacture	[illegible]	[illegible]	[illegible]	[illegible]	[illegible]
Worsted and stuff manufacture	[illegible]	[illegible]	[illegible]	[illegible]	[illegible]
Flannel manufacture	[illegible]	—	—	—	—
Carpet and rug manufacture	—	[illegible]	[illegible]	[illegible]	[illegible]
Woollen knitters	—	[illegible]	[illegible]	—	—
Others, in wool	—	—	—	—	[illegible]
Cotton and calico goods manufacture	[illegible]	[illegible]	[illegible]	[illegible]	[illegible]
Silk and silk goods manufacture	[illegible]	[illegible]	[illegible]	[illegible]	[illegible]
Ribbon manufacture	[illegible]	[illegible]	—	—	—
Crape, gauze, shawls, and fancy goods (textile) manufacture	[illegible]	[illegible]	[illegible]	[illegible]	[illegible]
Weavers, spinners, and factory hands (undefined)	[illegible]	[illegible]	[illegible]	[illegible]	[illegible]
Flax, linen, and damask manufacture *	[illegible]	[illegible]	[illegible]	[illegible]	[illegible]
Canvas and sailcloth manufacture	—	[illegible]	[illegible]	—	[illegible]
Sacking and bag manufacture	—	—	[illegible]	[illegible]	[illegible]
Hemp, jute, and cocoa-fibre manufacture	—	—	—	—	[illegible]
Rope, twine, and cord makers	[illegible]	[illegible]	[illegible]	[illegible]	[illegible]
Net makers	[illegible]	[illegible]	[illegible]	[illegible]	[illegible]
Mat makers	[illegible]	[illegible]	[illegible]	[illegible]	[illegible]
Lace manufacture	[illegible]	[illegible]	[illegible]	[illegible]	[illegible]
Embroiderers	—	[illegible]	[illegible]	[illegible]	[illegible]
Thread manufacture	[illegible]	[illegible]	[illegible]	[illegible]	[illegible]
Tape manufacture	—	—	—	—	[illegible]
Trimming manufacture	[illegible]	[illegible]	—	[illegible]	[illegible]
Artificial flower makers and others	—	—	—	—	[illegible]
Dyeing	[illegible]	[illegible]	[illegible]	[illegible]	[illegible]
Total of textiles and dyeing	[illegible]	[illegible]	[illegible]	[illegible]	[illegible]

* The apparent decrease, under the heading of "Flax and linen," between 1871 and 1881 is [illegible]

TABLE giving a COMPARISON of the INDUSTRIAL CONSTITUTION of ENGLAND with that of SCOTLAND, and that of IRELAND, at each Decade, 1851 to 1881.—(In Thousands.)

	1851.		1861.		1871.		1881.		Increase.		Decrease.	
	No.	Per-centage.	No.	Per-centage.	No.	Per-centage.	No.	Per-centage.	In Thousands.	Of Per-centage.	In Thousands.	Of Per-centage.
Agriculture—												
England and Wales	[illegible]	[illegible]	[illegible]	[illegible]	[illegible]	[illegible]	[illegible]	[illegible]	—	—	[illegible]	[illegible]
Scotland	[illegible]	[illegible]	[illegible]	[illegible]	[illegible]	[illegible]	[illegible]	[illegible]	—	—	[illegible]	[illegible]
Ireland	[illegible]	[illegible]	[illegible]	[illegible]	[illegible]	[illegible]	[illegible]	[illegible]	—	—	[illegible]	[illegible]
Fishing—												
England and Wales	[illegible]	[illegible]	[illegible]	[illegible]	[illegible]	[illegible]	[illegible]	[illegible]	[illegible]	[illegible]	[illegible]	—
Scotland	[illegible]	[illegible]	[illegible]	[illegible]	[illegible]	[illegible]	[illegible]	[illegible]	[illegible]	[illegible]	[illegible]	—
Ireland	[illegible]	[illegible]	[illegible]	[illegible]	[illegible]	[illegible]	[illegible]	[illegible]	—	[illegible]		—
Mines—												
England and Wales	[illegible]	[illegible]	[illegible]	[illegible]	[illegible]	[illegible]	[illegible]	[illegible]	[illegible]	[illegible]	—	—
Scotland	[illegible]	[illegible]	[illegible]	[illegible]	[illegible]	[illegible]	[illegible]	[illegible]	[illegible]	[illegible]	[illegible]	—
Ireland	[illegible]	[illegible]	[illegible]	[illegible]	[illegible]	[illegible]	[illegible]	[illegible]	—	—	[illegible]	[illegible]
Building—												
England and Wales	[illegible]	[illegible]	[illegible]	[illegible]	[illegible]	[illegible]	[illegible]	[illegible]	[illegible]	[illegible]	—	—
Scotland	[illegible]	[illegible]	[illegible]	[illegible]	[illegible]	[illegible]	111	[illegible]	[illegible]	[illegible]	—	—
Ireland	[illegible]	[illegible]	[illegible]	[illegible]	[illegible]	[illegible]	[illegible]	[illegible]	—	[illegible]	[illegible]	—
Manufacture—												
England and Wales	[illegible]	[illegible]	[illegible]	[illegible]	[illegible]	[illegible]	[illegible]	[illegible]	[illegible]	—	—	[illegible]
Scotland	[illegible]	[illegible]	[illegible]	[illegible]	[illegible]	[illegible]	[illegible]	[illegible]	[illegible]	—	[illegible]	[illegible]
Ireland	[illegible]	[illegible]	[illegible]	[illegible]	[illegible]	[illegible]	[illegible]	[illegible]	—	—	[illegible]	[illegible]
Transport—												
England and Wales	[illegible]	[illegible]	[illegible]	[illegible]	[illegible]	[illegible]	[illegible]	[illegible]	[illegible]	[illegible]	—	—
Scotland	[illegible]	[illegible]	[illegible]	[illegible]	[illegible]	[illegible]	[illegible]	[illegible]	[illegible]	[illegible]	[illegible]	—
Ireland	[illegible]	[illegible]	[illegible]	[illegible]	[illegible]	[illegible]	[illegible]	[illegible]	[illegible]	[illegible]	—	—
Dealing—												
England and Wales	[illegible]	[illegible]	[illegible]	[illegible]	[illegible]	[illegible]	[illegible]	[illegible]	[illegible]	[illegible]	—	—
Scotland	[illegible]	[illegible]	[illegible]	[illegible]	[illegible]	[illegible]	[illegible]	[illegible]	[illegible]	[illegible]	—	—
Ireland	[illegible]	[illegible]	[illegible]	[illegible]	[illegible]	[illegible]	[illegible]	[illegible]	[illegible]	[illegible]	—	—

TABLE—*continued*

[illegible]	[illegible] No.	Per cent.	[illegible] No.	Per cent.	1871 No.	Per cent.	[illegible] No.	Per cent.	Increase In Numbers.	Of Percentage.	Decrease In Numbers.	Of Percentage.
Industrial Servants—												
England and Wales	[illegible]	[illegible]	[illegible]	[illegible]	[illegible]	[illegible]	[illegible]	[illegible]	[illegible]	[illegible]	—	—
Scotland	[illegible]	[illegible]	[illegible]	[illegible]	[illegible]	[illegible]	[illegible]	[illegible]	[illegible]	[illegible]	[illegible]	—
Ireland	[illegible]	[illegible]	[illegible]	[illegible]	[illegible]	[illegible]	[illegible]	[illegible]	[illegible]	[illegible]	—	—
Total of Industrial—												
England and Wales	[illegible]	[illegible]	[illegible]	[illegible]	[illegible]	[illegible]	[illegible]	[illegible]	[illegible]	—	—	[illegible]
Scotland	[illegible]	[illegible]	[illegible]	[illegible]	[illegible]	[illegible]	[illegible]	[illegible]	[illegible]	—	—	[illegible]
Ireland	[illegible]	[illegible]	[illegible]	[illegible]	[illegible]	[illegible]	[illegible]	[illegible]	...	—	[illegible]	[illegible]
Public and Professional Services—												
England and Wales	[illegible]	[illegible]	[illegible]	[illegible]	[illegible]	[illegible]	[illegible]	[illegible]	[illegible]	[illegible]	—	—
Scotland	[illegible]	[illegible]	[illegible]	[illegible]	[illegible]	[illegible]	[illegible]	[illegible]	[illegible]	[illegible]	—	—
Ireland	[illegible]	[illegible]	[illegible]	[illegible]	[illegible]	[illegible]	[illegible]	[illegible]	[illegible]	[illegible]	—	—
Domestic Servants—												
England and Wales	[illegible]	[illegible]	[illegible]	[illegible]	[illegible]	[illegible]	[illegible]	[illegible]	[illegible]	[illegible]	—	—
Scotland	[illegible]	[illegible]	[illegible]	[illegible]	[illegible]	[illegible]	[illegible]	[illegible]	[illegible]	[illegible]	—	—
Ireland	[illegible]	[illegible]	[illegible]	[illegible]	[illegible]	[illegible]	[illegible]	[illegible]	[illegible]	[illegible]	—	—
Others—												
England and Wales	[illegible]	[illegible]	[illegible]	[illegible]	[illegible]	[illegible]	[illegible]	[illegible]	[illegible]	[illegible]	—	—
Scotland	[illegible]	[illegible]	[illegible]	[illegible]	[illegible]	[illegible]	[illegible]	[illegible]	[illegible]	[illegible]	—	—
Ireland	[illegible]	[illegible]	[illegible]	[illegible]	[illegible]	[illegible]	[illegible]	[illegible]	—	—	[illegible]	[illegible]
Total Non-Industrial—												
England and Wales	[illegible]	[illegible]	[illegible]	[illegible]	[illegible]	[illegible]	[illegible]	[illegible]	[illegible]	[illegible]	—	—
Scotland	[illegible]	[illegible]	[illegible]	[illegible]	[illegible]	[illegible]	[illegible]	[illegible]	[illegible]	[illegible]	—	[illegible]
Ireland	[illegible]	[illegible]	[illegible]	[illegible]	[illegible]	[illegible]	[illegible]	[illegible]	[illegible]	[illegible]	—	—
Whole Dependent on Self-Supporting Population—									[illegible]		[illegible]	
England and Wales	[illegible]	[illegible]	[illegible]	[illegible]	[illegible]	[illegible]	[illegible]	[illegible]	[illegible]	[illegible]	—	—
Scotland	[illegible]	[illegible]	[illegible]	[illegible]	[illegible]	[illegible]	[illegible]	[illegible]	[illegible]	[illegible]	—	—
Ireland	[illegible]	[illegible]	[illegible]	[illegible]	[illegible]	[illegible]	[illegible]	[illegible]	—	—	[illegible]	[illegible]

Summary of Whole Population

Employed—												
England and Wales	[illegible]	[illegible]	[illegible]	[illegible]	[illegible]	[illegible]	[illegible]	[illegible]	[illegible]	—	—	[illegible]
Scotland	[illegible]	[illegible]	[illegible]	[illegible]	[illegible]	[illegible]	[illegible]	[illegible]	[illegible]	—	..	[illegible]
Ireland	[illegible]	[illegible]	[illegible]	[illegible]	[illegible]	[illegible]	[illegible]	[illegible]	..	—	[illegible]	[illegible]
Dependent—												
England and Wales	[illegible]	[illegible]	[illegible]	[illegible]	[illegible]	[illegible]	[illegible]	[illegible]	[illegible]	[illegible]	—	—
Scotland	[illegible]	[illegible]	[illegible]	[illegible]	[illegible]	[illegible]	[illegible]	[illegible]	[illegible]	[illegible]	..	—
Ireland	[illegible]	[illegible]	[illegible]	[illegible]	[illegible]	[illegible]	[illegible]	[illegible]	..	[illegible]	[illegible]	—
Total Population—									[illegible]			
England and Wales	[illegible]	[illegible]	[illegible]	[illegible]	[illegible]	[illegible]	[illegible]	[illegible]	[illegible]	[illegible]	—	—
Scotland	[illegible]	[illegible]	[illegible]	[illegible]	[illegible]	[illegible]	[illegible]	[illegible]	[illegible]	[illegible]	—	—
Ireland	[illegible]	[illegible]	[illegible]	[illegible]	[illegible]	[illegible]	[illegible]	[illegible]	—	—	[illegible]	[illegible]
United Kingdom	[illegible]	—	[illegible]	..	[illegible]	..	[illegible]		[illegible]	[illegible]	—	—

Mr. [illegible] has kindly prepared, for the assistance of the Royal Commission, the following Notes with reference to the results of the Census of 1891.

IRELAND.—NOTES ON THE CENSUS OF 1891.

Since 1881 the population has further decreased to 4,704,[illegible], a reduction of 471,[illegible] in the 10 years, making a total decrease since 1841 of 3,471,[illegible], or 42½ per cent.

The proportion of the population engaged in each group of occupation is as follows:—

(Compare with Table A., page 114.)

Occupations, 1891.

	Per cent.	
Agriculture	39·7	44·1
Fishing	·5	
Mining	·2	
Building	2·6	20·4
Manufacture	17·8	
Transport	2·6	6·0
Dealing	3·4	
Industrial service		6·6
Industry total		79·4
Public and professional service	5·6	20·6
Domestic service	13·2	
Others	2·6	
		100·0

Of those engaged in productive industry (or agriculture, fishing, mining, building, and manufacture), although in actual numbers there has been a decline of 79,000 in the 10 years, the proportion to the total of those employed shows an apparent increase from 63·6 in 1881 to 64·6 in 1891. This increase is, however, in reality mainly due to the changed method (already noted) of enumerating those engaged in domestic work, which, by transferring a great body of women from the occupied to the unoccupied class, has reduced domestic service by 6 per cent., and has correspondingly increased the proportions of the other occupied classes.

The decline in the textile industries, though considerable, is not nearly so great as at previous decades, as will be seen by comparing the subjoined statement with that on page 6:—

Textile Industries, 1891.

(In thousands and decimals of a thousand.)

Occupations, 1891.	—
Woollen cloth manufacture	6·5
Worsted and stuff	·1
Flannel manufacture	—
Blanket	—
Carpet, rug, and felt manufacturers	·8
Woollen [illegible]	—
Cotton and cotton goods manufacturers	2·2
Silk and silk goods	·5
Ribbon manufacturers	—
Crape, gauze, shawls, fancy goods	4·0
Weavers, spinners, and factory hands	7·4
Flax, linen, and damask manufacturers	65·7
Canvas and sail cloth manufacturers	—
Sacking and bag	·3
Hemp, jute, and cocoanut fibre	·8
Rope, twine, and cord makers	1·0
Net makers	·1
Mat	·1
Lace manufacturers	·6
Embroiderers	4·3
Thread manufacturers	1·1
Tape	1
Trimming	1
Artificial flower maker and other	—
Dyeing	1·0
Total, textile industries	116·0

The following Table compares the Industrial Constitution of the three Countries in 1891, in continuation of the Table on pages 215 and 216:—

(In thousands.)

—	England and Wales.		Scotland.		Ireland.		Total.	
	No.	Per cent.	No.	Per cent.	No.	Per cent.	No.	Per cent.
Agriculture	1,[illegible]	9·6	21[illegible]	11·6	[illegible]	43·7	2,4[illegible]	14·0
Fishing	[illegible]	·2	[illegible]	1·8	11	·5	[illegible]	·4
Mining	674	4·9	10[illegible]	6·3	5	·2	[illegible]	4·5
Building	[illegible]	6·1	10[illegible]	5·8	[illegible]	2·6	[illegible]	5·8
Manufacture	4,[illegible]	32·2	[illegible]	35·4	[illegible]	17·8	5,[illegible]	29·9
Transport	[illegible]	7·0	1[illegible]	6·6	[illegible]	2·6	1,1[illegible]	6·6
Dealing	1,[illegible]	9·1	1[illegible]	7·7	110	3·5	1,[illegible]	7·7
Industrial service	[illegible]	6·6	1[illegible]	6·0	140	6·6	1,1[illegible]	6·6
Total of Industry	[illegible]	[illegible]	1,[illegible]	7[illegible]	1,[illegible]	79·4	1[illegible]	7[illegible]
Public and professional service	797	5·9	[illegible]	4·5	1[illegible]	5·6	1,0[illegible]	5·7
Domestic service	[illegible]	15·2	[illegible]	11·9	[illegible]	13·2	[illegible]	15·0
Others	947	6·9	11[illegible]	6·8	[illegible]	2·6	1,1[illegible]	6·5
Total Non-industrial	[illegible]	27·4	[illegible]	[illegible]	[illegible]	20·6	[illegible]	[illegible]
Total employed or self-supporting population	13,[illegible]	100·0	1,[illegible]	100·0	[illegible]	100·0	17,[illegible]	100·0
Employed	13,[illegible]	47·3	1,[illegible]	46·0	[illegible]	44·7	17,[illegible]	46·[illegible]
Dependants	15,[illegible]	52·[illegible]	2,1[illegible]	54·0	[illegible]	55·3	[illegible]	53·[illegible]
Total population	29,0[illegible]	100·0	4,0[illegible]	100·0	4,7[illegible]	100·0	37,7[illegible]	100·0

A.

Table furnished by Mr T. J. Pittar, Principal of the Statistical Office, Customs Department, showing the Average Value per lb avoirdupois, per cwt., or per gallon, as the case may be, of the several Principal Articles subject to Customs Duty, as declared upon Importation into the United Kingdom, the Rates of Duty, the Total Import Prices inclusive of the Duty, and the Proportions per cent which the Declared Value and the Duty respectively bear to the Total Cost of the Articles as shown in Column 4.

1.		2.	3.	4.	5.	6.	7.
Articles in Customs Tariff		Average declared Value on Importation.	Duty.	Total	Proportions per Cent which the Declared Value and the Duty respectively bear to the Total Cost of the Articles as shown in Column 4		
					Declared Value	Duty.	–
		£ s. d.	s. d.	£ s. d.			
Coffee, raw	cwt	4 14 4½	14 0	5 10 [illegible]	87 41	12 [illegible]	100
Cocoa	lb	0 0 7¾	0 1	0 0 8¾	88 37	11·63	100
Brandy	gall.	[illegible]	11 4	0 19 [illegible]	[illegible]	[illegible]	100
Rum	"	0 1 [illegible]	11 4	0 12 [illegible]	[illegible]	[illegible]	100
Geneva	"	0 [illegible] [illegible]	11 4	0 14 [illegible]	[illegible]	[illegible] 31	100
N.O.E. unenumerated	"	0 0 11½	15 4	0 [illegible] [illegible]	7·84	[illegible]	100
Tea	lb.	0 0 [illegible]	0 6	0 1 [illegible]	[illegible]	[illegible]	100
Tobacco, unmanufactured	"	0 0 [illegible]	[illegible]	0 [illegible] 9	[illegible]	[illegible]	100
Cigars	"	0 4 [illegible]	[illegible] 0	0 11 [illegible]	[illegible]	11·41	100
Manufactured, (3 sorts)	"	[illegible] 4 [illegible]	4 0	0 10 [illegible]	[illegible]	[illegible]	100
Wine, still, in cask and bottle	gall	0 4 10½	1 [illegible] (average)	0 6 [illegible]	[illegible]	[illegible]	100
Sparkling	"	[illegible] [illegible] 10	2 [illegible]	1 7 10	[illegible]	[illegible]	100

B.

Note furnished by the Inland Revenue Department as to Comparative Taxation of Beer and Spirits in relation to Alcoholic Strength (See Vol. I of Evidence Q. [illegible])

When the evidence was given the spirit duty was 11s the proof gallon, and the beer duty [illegible] a gallon.

The average quantity of spirits present in beer is about 11 per cent.—rather over than under. The duty on the spirit in 100 gallons of beer would therefore be 11s. × 11 = 121s.

Duty on 100 gallons of beer would be—

$$\frac{100 \times 6s.\ 9d}{36} = 18s.\ 9d$$

Then $\frac{121s}{18s\ 9d}$ = 6·45. The alcohol in beer was therefore charged 6·45 times less than spirits.

At the present rate of the spirit duty—10s 6d, the ratio would be 6·16.

$$\frac{11 \times 10s\ 6d = 115s\ 6d}{\text{Beer duty} = 18s\ 9d} = 6·16$$

3rd December 188[illegible]. J. [illegible]

Statement furnished by the Inland Revenue Department with regard to Changes in the various Inland Revenue Duties since the Year 1817.

A.—STATEMENT of DUTIES REPEALED, EXPIRED, or REDUCED, and of DUTIES IMPOSED in each Year from 1816.

General Note by Sir Alfred Milner, K.C.B.

The figures showing the actual fiscal results of remissions or impositions of duty are only approximate. As far as the years prior to 1875 are concerned the figures are taken from old Inland Revenue Reports. The principle on which the amount of gain or loss resulting from particular changes of taxation was stated in those Reports, it is not now possible accurately to determine. As a general rule, the Budget estimate of the effect of a proposed change seems to have been taken, though in some instances the figure given represents the actual result of the remission or imposition of duty in the first complete year after such remission or imposition. Notes are appended in all cases where the exact principle of calculation adopted for the years prior to 1875 is accurately known. The figures showing results of impositions or remissions of taxation since 1875 are now published for the first time. With regard to these, the principle of calculation adopted is fully explained in the notes. It is evident that neither of the two most feasible systems of calculation can be regarded as entirely satisfactory. The Budget estimate of the effect of a change of taxation may be falsified by events. On the other hand, the actual increase or decrease in the yield of a duty following a change in the amount of that duty may be due to causes quite independent of such change. It is impossible, as a matter of fact, to disentangle the effect of that change from other influences simultaneously affecting the yield of the tax. There is thus no absolute reliance to be placed on any of the figures, though in most instances they are probably fair approximations to fact.

EXCISE.

Year	Duties repealed, expired, or reduced.	Consequent Loss of Revenue	Duties imposed or augmented.	Consequent Increase of Revenue
		£		£
1816	Malt War Duties, 2s. per bushel. Repealed	[illegible]	Hard Soap. Increased from 2½d. to 3d. per lb.	[illegible]
	Licences to Retail Dealers of [illegible] only (Scotland), various rates. Repealed	17,000		
	Spirits (Ireland). Reduced from 6s. [illegible] to 5s. 7½d. per gallon	[illegible]		
1817	Sweets or Made Wines. Reduced from [illegible] per barrel	4,000	Stone Bottles. Increased from [illegible] per cwt.	[illegible]
1818	Vinegar. Reduced from [illegible] per barrel to 4d. per gallon	9,000	Paper (Ireland). Excise Duty increased to 3d. per cubic foot	1,900
1819	Plate Glass. Reduced from [illegible] per cwt.	14,000	Spirits (England). Increased from 10s. [illegible] to 11s. 8½d. per gallon	[illegible]
			Malt (Great Britain). Increased from [illegible] to 3s. 7¼d. per bushel	[illegible]
1820	Malt in Scotland made from Bere or Bigg. Reduced from 3s. 7¼d. to 3s. 1d. per bushel, and subsequently to 2s. 10d.	[illegible]	Malt (Ireland). Increased from [illegible] to 3s. 6¼d. per bushel	[illegible]
1822	Malt. Reduced from 3s. 7¼d. (Great Britain) and 3s. 6¼d. (Ireland) to 2s. 7d. per bushel	[illegible]	—	—
	Hides and Skins, various rates. Reduced to one-half the former rates	[illegible]		
	Irish Spirits imported into England. Reduced from 11s. 8½d. to 11s. 1¼d. per gallon	[illegible]		
1823	Salt (England). Reduced from 15s. to 2s. per bushel	[illegible]	Intermediate Beer. New duty of 5s. per barrel	[illegible]
	Spirits. Reduced from [illegible] (Scotland) and [illegible] (Ireland) to 2s. 4¾d. per gallon	[illegible]		
1825	Flint Glass. Duty on the [illegible] repealed, and a duty of 6d. per lb. imposed on the Fluxed Materials	97,000	Paper (Ireland). Duties imposed on the several classes of Paper manufactured, in lieu of Excise Duty repealed	12,000
	Salt (England). The remaining duty, of 2s. per bushel, repealed	[illegible]	Flint Glass. Duty of [illegible] per cwt. extended to Ireland	[illegible]
	Licences, various rates. Reduced	[illegible]	Hides and Skins (Ireland). Duty charged on Leather by weight	[illegible]
[illegible]	Cyder (Great Britain). Reduced from [illegible] per hogshead to [illegible] per gallon	[illegible]	Spirits (Scotland and Ireland). Increased from 2s. [illegible] to 2s. 10d. per gallon	[illegible]
	Vinegar. Reduced from 4d. to 2d. per gallon	[illegible]		
	English Spirits. Reduced from 11s. 8¼d. to 7s. per gallon	[illegible]		
	Sweets. Reduced from [illegible] per barrel to 6d. per gallon	[illegible]		
	Printed [illegible], [illegible] per yard. Repealed	[illegible]		
	Tawed Sheep and Lamb Skins, 1½d. per lb., and Kid Skins 1s. per dozen. Repealed	19,100		
	Gilt Wire (Great Britain), 1s. 6d. per oz. and Silver Wire, 1s. [illegible] per oz. Repealed	[illegible]		

Excise—continued.

Year.	Duties repealed, expired, or reduced.	[illegible] Loss of Revenue.	Duties imposed or augmented.
		£	
1830	Hides and skins, various rates. Repealed	350,000	Spirits (England). Increased from 7s. to 7s. 6d., and (Scotland and Ireland) from 2s. 10d. to 3s. 4d. per gallon.
	Licences to Tanners, Curriers, &c. Repealed	18,000	Licences to Retailers of Beer, Cyder, and Perry, 2l. 2s.
	Beer (Great Britain), various rates. Repealed	3,064,000	
	Cyder and Perry (Great Britain), [illegible] per gallon. Repealed	25,000	
	Malt in Ireland, made from Bere or Bigg. Reduced from 3s. 7d. to 2s. per bushel	5,000	
1831	Printed Cottons (Great Britain), 3½d. per square yard. Repealed	560,000	——
	Licences to Calico Printers, 20l. Repealed	1,000	
1832	Candles (Great Britain), viz., Tallow 1d. per lb., and Wax and Spermaceti 3½d. per lb. Repealed	470,000	——
	Licences to Candle Makers, 2l. and 1l. Repealed	4,000	
	Flint Glass. Duty on Fluxed Materials reduced from 6d. to [illegible] per lb., and 6d. per lb. imposed on the Manufactured Article	—	
1833	Tiles, various rates. Repealed	34,000	——
	Soap (Great Britain). Reduced to one-half the former rate, viz., Hard, to 1½d. per lb., and Soft to 1d. per lb.	[illegible]	
1834	Stone Bottles (Great Britain), 5s. per cwt. Repealed	3,000	Retail Spirit Licences. Increased 10 per cent.
	Starch (Great Britain), 1½d. per lb. Repealed	91,000	Retail Beer Licences. Altered.
	Sweets, 6d. per gallon. Repealed	5,700	
	Spirits for consumption in Ireland. Reduced from 3s. 4d. to 2s. 4d. per gallon	500,000	
1835	Country Spirit Licences. Reduced	30,000	——
	Flint Glass. Reduced from 6d. to 4d. per lb.	60,000	
1836	Stained Paper, 1½d. per square yard. Repealed	60,000	Countervailing Duties on [illegible] Spirits and [illegible] Various Rates
	Licences to Stained Paper Makers, 4l. Repealed	300	
	Paper. Reduced to one uniform rate of 1½d. per lb.	235,000	
	Additional Duty of 10 per cent. on Spirit Licences. Repealed	140,000	
1837	——	—	Sugar made from Beetroot. New duty of 1l. 4s. per cwt.
1839	Bricks (Great Britain), various rates. Reduced	2,000	——
1840	——	—	5 per cent. additional imposed on All Duties excepting Post Horses and Spirits.
			Spirits (England). Increased from 7s. 6d. to 7s. 10d.; (Scotland), 3s. 4d. to 3s. 8d.; and (Ireland) from 2s. 4d. to 2s. 8d. per gallon.
			Sugar. The duty of 1l. 4s. per cwt. extended to Sugar made from any material.
1842	——	—	Spirits (Ireland). Increased from 2s. 8d. to 3s. 8d. per gallon.
			Licences to Malt Roasters. New duty of [illegible] per annum.
			Licences to Dealers in Roasted Malt. New duty of 10l. per annum.
1843	Spirits (Ireland). Reduced from 3s. 8d. to 2s. 8d. per gallon	[illegible]	——
1844	Flint Glass. Reduced from [illegible] to [illegible] per lb.	[illegible]	——
	Vinegar, 2d. per gallon, and 5 per cent. additional. Repealed	25,000	
1845	Auctions, various rates. Repealed	300,000	Licences to Auctioneers. Increased from [illegible] to 15l.
	Glass, various rates. Duty and licences repealed	624,000	
	Sugar (British). Reduced from 1l. 4s. per cwt. and 5 per cent. additional to 14s. per cwt.	3,000	
1846	——	—	Licences to Chemists and others using Stills (England). New duty of 10s.

Excise—continued

Year.	Duties repealed, expired, or reduced.	Consequent Loss of Revenue.	Duties imposed or augmented.	Consequent Increase of Revenue.
		£		£
1849	—	—	Licences to Dealers in Spirits for retailing Foreign Liqueurs. New duty of [illegible]	[illegible]
1850	Bricks (Great Britain), various rates. Repealed	[illegible]	—	—
	Sugar (British). Reduced from 14s. to 13s. per cwt.	—		
1851	Sugar (British). Reduced from 13s. to 12s. per cwt.	—	Sugar used by Brewers. New duty of 1s. 4d. per cwt.	100
1853	Soap, soft 1d. and hard 1½d. per lb. Repealed	[illegible] 1,170,000	Post Horse Licences (Great Britain). Substituted for duty; various rates, according to the number of horses and carriages kept	-
	Hackney Carriages (London). Weekly duty reduced from 10s. to 7s. (and 6s. if not used on Sunday), and Licences altered from 5l. yearly to 1l. annual	[illegible]	Spirits (Scotland). Increased from 3s. 8d. to 4s. 8d. per gallon; and (Ireland), from 2s. 8d. to 3s. 4d. per gallon	[illegible]
	Post Horse Duty and Licences repealed, and new Licence Duties substituted	—		
Ended 1 May 18[illegible]	—	—	Malt from Barley. Increased from 2s. 8d. and 5 per cent. to 4s. per bushel; and from Bere or Bigg, increased from 2s. and 5 per cent. to 3s. 1d. per bushel	[illegible]
			Sugar (British). Increased from 12s. per cwt. to 13s., 14s., 15s., and 17s., according to quality	—
			Sugar used by Brewers. Increased from 1s. 4d. to 1s. 6d. per cwt.	—
			Licences to Brewers using Sugar. New duty of 1l.	430
			Spirits (Scotland). Increased from 4s. 8d. to 6s. per gallon; and (Ireland) from 3s. 4d. to 4s. per gallon	[illegible]
1855	Stage Carriage Mileage Duty. Reduced from 1½d. to 1d. per mile, and Supplementary Licence from 1s. to 1s. each	[illegible]	Spirits. Increased from 7s. 10d. (England), and 6s. (Scotland), to 8s. per gallon; and (Ireland) from 4s. to 6s. 2d. per gallon	[illegible]
	Sugar used by Brewers. Reduced from 1s. 6d. to 1s. 4d. per cwt.	—	Sugar (British). Increased from 13s., 14s., 15s., and 17s. per cwt. to 13s. 6d., 15s., and 18s. 4d. per cwt., according to quality	—
			Licences to Makers of Methylated Spirit, 10l. New imposed	140
1857	Malt War Tax (imposed in 1854). Repealed	[illegible]	—	—
	Sugar used by Brewers. Duty ceased	—		
1858	—	—	Race Horses. Transferred from Assessed Taxes	[illegible]
1859	—	—	Spirits (Ireland). Increased from 6s. 2d. to 8s. per gallon	[illegible]
1860	Hops (Great Britain). Reduced from 2d. and 5 per cent. to 1½d. per lb.	[illegible]	Spirits (United Kingdom). Increased from 8s. to 10s. per gallon	[illegible]
			Licences. Refreshment Houses, &c. New duty at various rates	[illegible]
			Licences, Game (Great Britain). Transferred from Assessed Taxes, and rates of duty altered	[illegible]
1861	Paper Duty. Repealed (About average receipt of three years to 1860–61.)	1,[illegible]	Licences, Beer and Spirits. Certain new rates imposed	[illegible]
1862	Hops, 1½d. per lb. Repealed	[illegible]	Licences to Brewers, various rates. Increased	(Annual) [illegible]
			Licences, Tobacconist's [illegible]. New duty of 5s.	[illegible]
1864	Stage Carriages, Mileage Duty and Licences. Reduced on carriages to convey not more than eight persons, and Daily Licences created	—	Licences, Beer, &c. Certain rates altered	[illegible]
1865	Licences to sell Tea, &c. Reduced	[illegible]	Licences to Hawkers, Dealers in Plate, Appraisers, House Agents, Pawnbrokers, Sellers of Playing Cards, and of Patent Medicines, transferred from Stamps	[illegible]
			Licences, Occasional, to sell Wine, Beer, and Tobacco. New duty	1,030
			Sugar used in Brewing. 1s. 4d. per cwt. imposed	[illegible]
			Chicory Duty imposed in 1860, and gradually increased	[illegible]

Year ended 31 Mar.	Duties repealed, expired, or reduced	Consequent Loss of Revenue	Duties imposed or augmented	Consequent Increase of Revenue
		£		£
1866	Malt Duty on Light Grain. Reduced	10,000	—	—
1867	Stage Carriage Mileage Duty. Reduced to ½d a mile	[illegible]	—	—
	Licences to let Horses for Hire, various rates. Reduced	[illegible]		
1869	Licences to Retailers of Methylated Spirits. Reduced from [illegible] to 10s.	—	Sugar (Home-made). Various rates	—
			Sugar used in Brewing. Increased from [illegible] to [illegible] per cwt.	[illegible]
			Licences to keep Dogs (Great Britain). Duty of [illegible] imposed in lieu of assessed tax	[illegible]
1870	Licences to Tea Dealers. Repealed	[illegible]	Armorial Bearings, [illegible] transferred from assessed taxes	[illegible]
	Post Horse Licences. Repealed	[illegible]	Carriages with four wheels, weighing 4 cwt., [illegible], with less than four wheels, or having four wheels but weighing less than 4 cwt., [illegible], transferred from assessed taxes	[illegible]
	Stage Carriages. Duty and licence repealed	[illegible]	Male Servants, [illegible] each person, transferred from assessed taxes	[illegible]
	Hackney Carriages. Duty and licence repealed	[illegible]	Horse Dealers (Great Britain), [illegible] each, transferred from assessed taxes	[illegible]
			Horses (Great Britain), at [illegible] each, transferred from assessed taxes	[illegible]
			Licences to carry Guns, 10s. each imposed	[illegible]
1871	Licences repealed:— Post Masters; Paper Makers; Soap Makers; Vendors of Playing Cards; Salt Makers; Makers of Watch Cases	[illegible]	Sugar used in Brewing. Duty increased to 7s. 6d. per cwt.	[illegible]
	Sugar, Home-made. Reduced to:— Refined [illegible]; Not equal to 1st class [illegible]; 2nd [illegible]; 3rd [illegible]; 4th [illegible]; Molasses [illegible]	[illegible]		
[illegible]	Chicory. Duty reduced	[illegible]	—	—
[illegible]	Licences, Male Servants employed by Hotel and Refreshment House Keepers. Repealed	[illegible]	Sugar used in Brewing. Duty increased to [illegible] per cwt.	[illegible]
	Sugar, Home-made. Duty reduced from May 1873:— Refined [illegible]; Not equal to 1st class [illegible]; 2nd [illegible]; 3rd [illegible]; 4th [illegible]; Molasses [illegible]	—		
[illegible]	Licences. Horses and Mules, Horse Dealers, and Race Horses. Repealed	[illegible]	Sugar used in Brewing. Duty increased to [illegible] per cwt.	[illegible]
	Sugar, Home-made. Repealed	[illegible]		
[illegible]	Brewers' Licences. Reduced. Brewers of Beer, other than Black or Spruce, for every 50 barrels or fractional part of 50 barrels, [illegible] (Other licences as before.)	[illegible]	—	—
1877	Licences, Male Servants. Repealed as regards boys or men casually employed	[illegible]	—	—
[illegible]	—	—	Licences to keep Dogs. Duty increased to 7s. 6d., but Farmers' and Shepherds' Dogs exempted from duty	[illegible]
[illegible]	Malt. Duty repealed (See note †)	[illegible]	Beer. Duty from 1st October, [illegible], [illegible] for every 36 gallons of worts of gravity of [illegible] degrees	[illegible]
	Sugar used in Brewing. Duty repealed	[illegible]	Licences. Brewers, for sale, [illegible]. Private Brewers, [illegible] imposed	[illegible]
	Licences. Repealed. Maltsters or Makers of Malt, Roaster of Malt, Dealer in Roasted Malt, and Brewer of Beer for Sale	[illegible]	Publicans' Spirit Licences. Duties increased and revised generally	[illegible]

† Note.—In addition to this the malt drawback allowed on [illegible] in hand was [illegible].
* Budget estimate figures. No more exact estimate available. [illegible] Mean produce three years to [illegible].
[illegible] Based on produce of [illegible]. [illegible] [illegible] [illegible]. [illegible] Estimated produced in [illegible].

EXCISE—continued.

Year ended 31 Mar	Duties repealed, expired, or reduced	Consequent Loss of Revenue	Duties imposed or augmented.	Consequent Increase of Revenue.
		£		£
188[illegible]	Beer. Duty repealed on Materials for Brewing used by farmers and others living in houses between value of 10*l* and 15*l*.	10,[illegible]	Licences to Private Brewers living in houses between value of 10*l* and 15*l*.	8,[illegible]
1883	Railway Duty. Modification of Cheap Trains Act, 46 & 46 Vict. c. 167 (Local)	11,[illegible]	Coffee Mixtures or Substitutes	[illegible]
1884	Railway Duty. Duty on Urban District Traffic reduced to 2*l*. per cent. and Fares under 1*d*. per mile exempted	c[illegible]	—	—
1885	Licences. Hackney Carriages, with four wheels, &c., reduced	*[illegible]	—	—
1886	Licences, Private Brewers, &c. Reduced to 4*s*.	[illegible]	—	—
1887	Licences, Private Brewers, on Rentals under [illegible] exempted	14,[illegible]	—	—
1889	Licences, Hawkers (United Kingdom) Reduced to 2*l*.	11,[illegible]	—	—
	Carriages. Amended:			
	Four or more wheels, fitted to be drawn by two or more horses or mules or by mechanical power, 2*l*. 2*s*.			
	Four or more wheels, fitted to be drawn by one horse or mule only, 1*l*. 1*s*.			
	Less than four wheels, 15*s*. per annum	[illegible]		
1890	Licences (England). Certain duties handed over to Local Authorities in lieu of grants from Exchequer	a[illegible]	Beer. Standard specific gravity reduced to 1,055°	a[illegible]
	Vinegar Makers. Licence duty reduced to 5*l*. per annum	[illegible]		
1891	Beer. 3*d*. a barrel handed over to local authorities	b[illegible]	—	—
	Licences (Scotland). Certain duties handed over to Local Authorities in lieu of grants from Exchequer	b[illegible]		
1895	—	—	Beer Duty increased 6*d*. per barrel	44[illegible]
			Spirit Duty increased 1*s*. per gallon	4[illegible]

c Loss of duty in first year of change. * Budget estimate figures. No more exact estimate available.
a Approximate amount. b Result in 1890–91.
d The amount of the Spirit Duty for one year only much exceeded the withdrawals from bonded warehouses for consumption, and the actual increased revenue was consequently very small.

STAMPS.

Year	Duties repealed, expired, or reduced	Consequent Loss of Revenue	Duties imposed or augmented.	Consequent Increase of Revenue
		£		£
1816	Marriage Licences, 10*s*. Repealed	—	Certain Legal Instruments, various rates (Ireland)	—
	Receipts for Stamp and Tax Duties (Ireland) Repealed	—	Certain Certificates, 5*l*. and 8*l*.; Conveyances, 5*l*.; Licences to Notaries, 5*l*. and [illegible] (Ireland)	[illegible]
	Certain Legal Instruments, various rates (Ireland). Reduced	—		
1819	Recognizances for Persons, &c. (Ireland) Repealed	23,[illegible]	—	—
1821	Certain Legal Instruments, various rates (Ireland). Repealed	—	Certain Duties on Law Proceedings termed "Law Fund Duties," various rates (Ireland)	42,[illegible]
	Handbills, ½*d*. (Ireland). Repealed	71		
1830	Certain "Ad Valorem" Duties, various rates Repealed or reduced	—	—	—
	Bankers' Notes under 5*l*. (Ireland). Reduced from 3*d*. to 1½*d*.	[illegible]		
	One horse Carriages Conveying Passengers for Hire (Great Britain). Reduced	—		
1832	—	—	Certain Duties on Law Proceedings termed "Equity Exchequer Fund and Chancery Fund Duties" (Ireland)	14,[illegible]

STAMPS—continued.

Year.	Duties repealed, expired, or reduced.	Consequent Loss of Revenue.	Duties imposed or augmented.	Consequent Increase of Revenue.
		£		£
1824	Duties on certain Proceedings at Law and Equity, various rates. Repealed	274,556	—	—
	Duties on certain Proceedings in the Court of Admiralty, the Ecclesiastical Courts, and the Court of Delegates (Ireland), various rates. Repealed	—		
	Civil Bill Proceedings (Ireland), various rates. Repealed	—		
1825	Revenue Bonds 20s. (Great Britain), and 10s. (Ireland). Reduced to 5s.	63,750	—	—
	Debentures on Certificates entitling to Drawbacks (Great Britain). Reduced	1,000		
	Do. (Ireland). Reduced from 2l. 10s. and 1l. [illegible] to 5s.	—		
	Lease Duties, 2l. 5s. and 5s. (Great Britain). Repealed	7,000		
	Conveyance on Sale or Mortgage of Property in Ships. Repealed	—		
	Duties on all Proceedings in Bankruptcy, various rates (Great Britain). Repealed	—		
	Appointments to [illegible] (Great Britain). Reduced from [illegible] to [illegible]	—		
1826	Bankers' Small Notes, 1l. and 10l. (England). Repealed	39,160	—	—
	Additional Duties on Plate Licenses, [illegible] and 1l. 10s. (Great Britain). Expired	7,000		
	Duties on all Proceedings relating to Insolvent Debtors, various rates (Great Britain). Repealed	—		
1827	Indentures of Seamen's Apprentices and Seamen's Articles (Great Britain). Reduced from 1l. and 1l. 10s. to 5s.	—	—	—
	Seamen's Articles (Ireland). Reduced from 1l. to 5s.	—		
	Lottery Stamps (Great Britain). Expired	5,000		
1828	Playing Cards, 2s. 6d. (Great Britain), and 2s. (Ireland). Reduced to 1s.	13,301	Dice (Ireland). Increased from 10s. to 1l. per pair	—
	Protests of Bills of Exchange or Promissory Notes (Ireland). Reduced from 5s., 6s., and 10s., to 2s., 3s., 5s., and 10s.	3,570	Licenses to Makers of Cards and Dice, &c.	—
1831	—	—	Hackney Carriages (London). Licenses increased from 5l. 10s. to 5l.	300
1832	Bonds given by persons letting horses for hire, 10s. (Great Britain). Repealed	1,134	Stage Carriage Licenses (Great Britain). Increased from 10s. to 5l.	20,100
	Certain "Law Fund Duties," various rates (Ireland). Expired	5,025	Post Horse Licenses (Great Britain). Increased from 5s. to 7s. 6d.	400
	Admission into Corporations (Ireland). Reduced from 2l. to 1l.	—		
1833	Receipts for sums under 5l., 2d. (Great Britain), and 1½d. (Ireland). Repealed	20,000	—	—
	Pamphlets, 3s. (Great Britain), and 2s. (Ireland). Repealed	1,000		
	Advertisements (Great Britain). Reduced from 3s. 6d. to 1s. 6d.	65,000		
	Do. (Ireland). Reduced from 2s. 6d. to 1s.	7,000		
	Insurances on Agricultural Produce, &c. (Great Britain), 3s. per cent. Repealed	20,000		
	Do. do. (Ireland), 2s. 6d. per cent. Repealed	—		
	Marine Insurances on Foreign Voyages, various rates, reduced	—		
	Applications and Affidavits for granting Pensions (Ireland), 2s., 3s., 4s., 5s., and 6s. Repealed	—		
1834	Almanacks (Great Britain), 1s. 3d. Repealed	27,200	Certain Affidavits and Certificates under the Act for the Abolition of Fees and Gratuities, 2s. and 4s. 6d. (Ireland). Imposed	—
	Almanacks (Ireland), 6d. and 1s. 6d.; Debentures (Ireland), 6d.; and Affidavits to qualify as Voters (Ireland), 2s. Repealed	1,654		
	Certain "Law Fund Duties," various rates (Ireland). Expired	3,000		
1835	Life Insurances for sums not exceeding 100l., 20s. (Great Britain), and 10s. (Ireland). Reduced to 2s. 6d. and 5s. according to amount of insurance	—	—	

STAMPS—continued

Year	Duties repealed, expired, or reduced	Consequent Loss of Revenue	Duties imposed or augmented	Consequent Increase of Revenue
		£		£
[illegible]	Transfers of the East India Company's Territorial Debt, when made in England. Reduced to [illegible]	—		
	Letters of Attorney for Voting at Election of East India Directors, 1l. Repealed	—		
	Certain Admissions to Inns of Court (Great Britain), 25l. Repealed	—		
	Seamen's Agreements for Wages, and Indentures of Apprenticeship (Ireland), 2s. Repealed	—		
	Appointment of Sub-Sheriff (Ireland), 1l. Repealed	—		
	Duties payable on certain Proceedings in Equity (Ireland). Reduced	—		
	[illegible] Deeds, Bonds, &c. (Ireland), 1l. Repealed	—		
1855	Race Horses (Great Britain), 3l. 5s. Repealed	1,179	—	—
	Newspapers and Supplements (Great Britain), 1d and 2d. Reduced to ½d, 1d, 1½d, and 2d, according to size	200,000		
	Certain Legal Instruments and Advertisements relating to Bankruptcy (Ireland). Repealed	—		
	Newspapers (Ireland). Reduced from 1½d to 1d	14,879		
	Bonds given by Printers of Newspapers (Ireland), 1l. Repealed	—		
1858	Procurator's Admissions, 1l. (Great Britain) Repealed	—	Licences to Drivers, Conductors, and Watermen of Metropolitan Carriages (London), 5s	1,725
1859	Mileage Duty on Stage Carriages (Great Britain), various rates. Reduced	34,[illegible]	—	—
1860	Procurator's Admissions, 5l. and 1l. (Ireland) Repealed	—	—	—
	Certain "Law Fund Duties" (Ireland), 5s. and 1s. Repealed	5,000		
1861	Affidavits in Courts of Law or Equity, &c., (Great Britain), 2s. 6d. Repealed	—	—	—
1862	Stage Carriage Licences (Great Britain), reduced from 5l. to 3l. 3s.	6,475	Supplementary Stage Carriage Licences (Great Britain). Increased from 1s. to 5s.	1,024
	Mileage Duty on Stage Carriages and Railway Passengers. Repealed, and one uniform duty of 1½d per mile granted in lieu on Stage Carriages, and a duty of 5l per cent. on Railway Fares (Great Britain)	71,[illegible]	Stamp Duties in Ireland assimilated to those payable in Great Britain. Increased	101,744
	Bills of Lading (Great Britain), reduced from 1s. to 6d	16,[illegible]	Pawnbroker's Licences (Ireland), 5l. 10s. to and 1l. Imposed	4,487
	Charterparties (Great Britain), reduced from 5s. to 6d	—	Licences to keep a Lunatic Asylum (Ireland), 15s. Imposed	—
	Duties on certain Ecclesiastical Preferments. Repealed and others granted (Great Britain)	—		
1863	Do. extended to some not before specified (Great Britain)	—	Certificates of Registration of Druggists (Ireland), 5l. Imposed	—
	Marriage Licence Bonds (Ireland), 1l. Repealed	—		
	Certain Legal Instruments relating to Leases (Ireland), 1l. 10s. Repealed	—		
1864	Customs and Excise Bonds for obtaining Drawbacks, &c. Repealed	—	—	—
	Marine Insurance (Great Britain), various rates. Reduced	101,[illegible]		
	Do. (Ireland), various rates. Reduced	—		
	Agreements under Hand, containing not more than 1,080 words (Great Britain). Reduced from 2s. 6d. to 6d	—		
	Certain Deeds relating to Joint Stock Companies. Reduced from 5s. to 2s. 6d	—		
	Duty on Railway Fares not exceeding 1d per mile, 5l per cent. (Great Britain). Repealed	—		
1865	Copies or Extracts from Memorials, &c. (Ireland). Reduced from 5s. to 1s.	—	Appraiser's Licences (Great Britain). Increased from 10s. to 2l.	4,780
	Certain "Law Fund Duties" (Ireland), various rates, reduced	—	Do. (Ireland). Increased from 10s. to 2l.	—
			Certain Legal Instruments issued from the Registry Office (Ireland), 1s. Imposed	—

Year	Duties repealed, expired, or reduced	Consequent Loss of Revenue	Duties imposed or augmented	Consequent Increase of Revenue
		£		£
1848	Admissions into Corporations (Scotland), reduced from [illegible] to [illegible] -	—	—	—
	Certain Bonds, [illegible], and certain Warrants, [illegible] (Ireland). Repealed	—		
	Certain Leases (Ireland). Reduced from [illegible] to [illegible]	—		
1850	Agreements, Bonds, Conveyances, and other Legal Instruments. Reduced	[illegible]	Certain Duties termed "Deputation Fund Duties" (Ireland) -	[illegible]
			Certain Duties termed "Law Fund Duties" (Ireland) -	—
1851	—	—	Certain Duties termed "Civil Bill Fund" (Ireland) -	[illegible]
1853	Supplements to Newspapers. Reduced -	[illegible]	Legacy Duty on Succession to Real Property imposed at various rates -	Ultimately [illegible]
	Attorney's Certificates, various rates. Reduced -	[illegible]		
	Policies of Life Insurance, various rates. Reduced -	[illegible]		
	Receipts, various rates. Reduced to one uniform rate of 1d. upon every sum amounting to 2l. or upwards, and extended to Drafts or Orders on Demand -	*[illegible]		
	Advertisements (Great Britain), 1s. 6d., and (Ireland), 1s. Repealed -	[illegible]		
Ended 31 Mar. 1855	Bills of Exchange, various rates. Reduced, and extended to Foreign Bills -	[illegible]	Admiralty Court Fee Stamps, various rates -	[illegible]
1855	Stamp Duties on Newspapers repealed except for transmission by post	[illegible]	—	—
1858	—	—	Drafts 1d. Extended to all cheques -	[illegible]
			Probate and Divorce Court Stamps, various rates -	[illegible]
1860	—	—	Probates and Letters of Administration. Graduated duty extended on amounts exceeding 1,000,000l. -	—
1861	—	—	Various alterations and impositions of new duties -	[illegible]
1862	—	—	Licences of Furnished Houses, to 5l. -	[illegible]
			Licences to let [illegible] -	[illegible]
			Registrars of District Probate Courts. Stamps in lieu of Fees, various rates -	[illegible]
1862	Cards. Duty reduced from 1s. to 3d. per pack -	[illegible]	Foreign Bonds and Securities, same duty imposed as on other Bonds -	[illegible]
	Hawkers Trading with One Horse. Reduced from [illegible] to [illegible] -	—	Land Registry Fee Stamps (England), various rates -	[illegible]
1864	Licences to Hawkers, Dealers in Plate, Appraisers, House Agents, Pawnbrokers, Sellers of Playing Cards, and of Patent Medicines, transferred to the Excise -	[illegible]	Registration of Deeds, Fee Stamps (Ireland), various rates -	[illegible]
	Fire Insurance Duty on Stock-in-Trade. Reduced from 3s. to 1s. 6d. per cent.	[illegible]		
	Probates and Letters of Administration, where the effects do not exceed 100l. exempted from duty -	[illegible]		
1865	Fire Policies. Reduced to 1d. -	[illegible]	Record of Title Fee Stamps (Ireland), various rates -	[illegible]
	Fire Insurance Duty. Reduced to uniform rate of 1s. 6d. per cent. (actual decrease in [illegible]) -	[illegible]		
	Conveyances, Appointments, Awards, and certain other Instruments. Duties altered and reduced -	—		
1866	—	—	Companies Registration Fee Stamps, various rates -	[illegible]
			Admiralty Court Fee Stamps. Extended to Ireland -	[illegible]
1867	Marine Insurance. Reduced to uniform rate of 3d. per cent. on Policies for Voyages, and to 3d. and 6d. on Time Policies (actual decrease in [illegible], compared with [illegible]) -	[illegible]	Common Law Court Fee Stamps. Produce included in General Stamp Revenue -	[illegible]
			Chancery Court Fee Stamps (Ireland), various rates -	[illegible]

* Budget Estimate. [illegible] The [illegible] produce after an interval of [illegible] years was only [illegible]

[illegible] The result was obtained after an interval of [illegible]

Stamps—*continued*.

Year ended 31 Mar	Duties repealed, reposed, or reduced	Consequent Loss of Revenue	Duties imposed or augmented	Consequent Increase of Revenue
[illegible]	—	£ —	Copyhold Inclosure and Tithe Commission Fee Stamps, various rates	£ 1,000
			Public Record Fee Stamps (England), various fees	3,000
1870	Fire Insurance Duty. Repealed (Produce of 1867–68)	1,[illegible]	—	—
1871	Impressed Stamps on Newspapers. Repealed	*[illegible]	—	—
	Duties reduced on [illegible], Carts, Boats, and Plate Glass Insurance Policies	1,300		
	Various alterations in duty per Stamp Consolidation Act, 33 & 34 Vict. c. 97	*[illegible]		
1876	Duty on Appointments and Dispensations repealed	[illegible]	—	—
1878	Duty on Appointments to Benefices	[illegible]	—	—
1879	Duty on Ecclesiastical Licences	[illegible]	—	—
[illegible]	—	—	Probate, &c. Duties. Revision of Scale	[illegible]
[illegible]	Legacy Duty of 1 per cent. on Lineals	c720,000	Do. Rates of duty consolidated into 3 per cent (approximately), deductions being allowed for debts and funeral expenses; Duty on estates under £300 fixed at 30s; Legacy duty imposed on sums under £20	b1,[illegible]
[illegible]	—	—	Corporation, &c. Property. Duty imposed 5 per cent. on net annual income	[illegible]
			Bonds to Bearer. Increased to 1s for 10l. or fraction of 10l.; Substituted Securities. Increased to 6d for 10l. or fraction of 10l.	314,173
[illegible]	Marine Insurance. Duty on Policies with premium [illegible] per cent. Reduced to 1d	7,200	Transfers of Debenture Stocks, &c. Duty increased	*[illegible]
[illegible]	Probate Duty. One-third handed over to Local Authorities in 1888–1889	1,[illegible]	Succession Duty. Increase of ½ per cent on Lineals, 1½ per cent. on Collaterals	*[illegible]
			Companies' Capital Duty 2s per cent. imposed	[illegible]
			Foreign Securities to Bearer	[illegible]
			Registered Bonds. Increase from 6d to 1s per cent.; Contract Notes. Increase from 1d to 6d	[illegible]
			Improved Regulations for Prevention of Evasion of Duty	*[illegible]
[illegible]	Probate Duty. Transfer to Local Authorities increased to one-half. Increase over 1888–89	[illegible]	Estate Duty, temporary, imposed on Real and Personal Estate of and over 10,000l	c1,[illegible]
[illegible]	Gold and Silver Plate Duty. Repealed	[illegible]	—	—
	Apprenticeship Indentures. Duty reduced to uniform rate of 2s 6d	—		
	Insurance. Policies against Sickness or Injury. Duty 1d. only	—		
[illegible]	Patent Fee Stamps. Reduced	*[illegible]	—	—
[illegible]	Foreign and Colonial Share Certificates. Repealed	[illegible]	Contract Notes above 1l. Duty increased from 6d. to 1s.	[illegible]
[illegible]	—	—	Estate Duty (in substitution of Probate, Account, Old Estate Duty, &c.)	d2,[illegible]

* Budget estimates. No exact actual figures being available. a Estimated result after an interval of several years.
b Actual result, after allowing for [illegible] receipts at old rates of duty at March [illegible]
c and d. Estimated result after an interval of years when [illegible] would be [illegible]

Year.	Duties repealed, expired, or reduced.	Consequent Loss of Revenue.	Duties imposed or augmented.	Consequent Increase of Revenue.
		£		£
1816	Horses used in Husbandry (Great Britain), various rates. Reduced	[illegible]	—	—
	Do. certain rates. Repealed	[illegible]		
	Servants (Great Britain), Labourers in Husbandry. Repealed	[illegible]		
	Horses (Ireland), various rates. Reduced	[illegible]		
	Hearths (Ireland). Reduced	[illegible]		
	Carriages, Servants, and Horses kept for Hire (Ireland), various rates. Reduced	[illegible]		
	Jaunting Cars (Ireland), various rates. Reduced	[illegible]		
1817	Houses and Windows (Great Britain). Tenements employed solely for the Purposes of Trade, or as Warehouses. Various rates reduced	[illegible]	—	—
1818	Carriages, Four-wheeled (Great Britain), various rates. Reduced	[illegible]	—	—
1819	Servants (Great Britain), Under Gamekeepers, &c. Reduced	[illegible]	—	—
	Do. certain Apprentices, &c. Repealed	[illegible]		
	Windows, Carriages, Servants, Horses, and Dogs (Ireland). Reduced	[illegible]		
	Horses (Great Britain). Hunters' Horses and Horses under 13 hands high, &c., various rates. Reduced	7,313		
	Do. Mares kept for the Sole Purpose of Breeding, various rates according to the number kept. Repealed	[illegible]		
1822	Horses used in Husbandry (Great Britain). Repealed	[illegible]	—	
	Hearth Money (Ireland). Repealed	[illegible]		
	Windows (Ireland). Repealed	[illegible]		
1823	Houses and Windows (Great Britain). Reduced to half former rates	[illegible]	—	—
	Do. Duties on Windows in Shops, &c. Repealed	27,731		
	Servants (Great Britain). Reduced to half the former rates	[illegible]		
	Do. (Ireland). Repealed	[illegible]		
	Carriages (Great Britain). Reduced to half the former rates	[illegible]		
	Do. (Ireland). Repealed	[illegible]		
	Horses (Great Britain). Reduced to half the former rates	[illegible]		
	Do. (Ireland). Repealed	[illegible]		
	Dogs (Ireland). Repealed	[illegible]		
	Composition (Ireland). Repealed	[illegible]		
	Coach Masters (Ireland). Repealed	[illegible]		
1824	Dogs (Great Britain) kept by Small Farmers for Care of Sheep. Repealed	[illegible]	—	—
	Houses and Windows (Great Britain). Offices and Counting-houses. Repealed	[illegible]		
	Servants (Great Britain). Occasional Porters, &c. Repealed	[illegible]		
1825	Horses (Great Britain). Certain Farmers' Horses, &c. Reduced	[illegible]	—	—
	Do. Mules carrying Ore, &c. Repealed	[illegible]		
	Houses and Windows (Great Britain). Dwelling-houses under 10l. per Annum Rent, and Windows in all Houses not containing more than Seven. Repealed	[illegible]		
	Servants (Great Britain). Occasional Waiters at Taverns, &c. Repealed	[illegible]		
	Carriages (Great Britain). Taxed Carts and Four-wheeled Carriages drawn by Ponies. Repealed	[illegible]		
1826	Do. Certain Four-wheeled Carriages. Reduced	[illegible]	—	
	Do. Certain Carriages with less than Four Wheels. Repealed	[illegible]		
	Horses used by Common Carriers (Great Britain). Reduced	218		
	Servants (Great Britain). Employers' Sons under Age of 21. Repealed	[illegible]		

ASSESSED TAXES—*continued.*

Year	Duties repealed, expired, or reduced	Consequent Loss of Revenue	Duties imposed or augmented	Consequent Increase of Revenue
		£		£
[illegible]	Horses (Great Britain) used by Licensed Persons for Hire in Carriages drawn by One Horse only. Repealed	3,[illegible]	Licences at [illegible] or [illegible] (Great Britain) [illegible] per annum. Imposed	[illegible]
1822	Carriages (Great Britain). Carts with less than Four Wheels, various rates. Reduced	[illegible]	—	—
	Servants (Great Britain). Male Persons employed as Shopmen under 18 years of age, &c. Repealed	[illegible]		
	Stage Coaches (Great Britain). [illegible] per annum. Repealed	[illegible]		
1823	Servants (Great Britain). Travellers, Clerks, Book Keepers, Shopmen, Bailiffs, &c. Repealed	1[illegible]	—	—
	Houses (Great Britain). Duties reduced on Inhabited Dwelling-houses rated at from [illegible] to [illegible] per annum	[illegible]		
	Carriages (Great Britain). Carts with less than Four Wheels. Repealed	[illegible]		
1834	Houses and Windows (Great Britain). Duties on Inhabited Houses under 3 & 4 Will. 4, c. 39, and on Windows in certain Farmhouses, various rates. Repealed	1,188,750	—	—
	Servants (Great Britain). Certain Male Servants under 18 years of age. Repealed	[illegible]		
	Horses ridden by Bailiffs, &c., and certain Husbandry Horses, &c. Repealed	1[illegible]		
	Dogs used in the Care of Sheep or Cattle. Repealed	[illegible]		
1840	—	—	Race Horses (Great Britain). Altered from [illegible] to [illegible] per annum	[illegible]
1840	Carriages kept to be Let for Hire with Horses. Reduced	[illegible]	10 per cent. additional on Assessed Taxes (Great Britain)	[illegible]
1851?	Windows. Various rates. Repealed	1,876,850	Inhabited Houses (Great Britain). 6d. and 9d. in £ per annum. Imposed	[illegible]*
Ended 31 Mar. 1853	Servants, Horses, and Carriages. Various rates. Reduced	[illegible]	—	—
1856	Race Horses. Transferred to Excise	[illegible]	—	—
1861	Game Certificates. Transferred to Excise	1[illegible]	—	—
1864?	Dogs. Reduced from 12s. to 5s.	[illegible]	—	—
1865?	Dogs. Transferred to Excise	[illegible]	—	—
1869?	Assessed Taxes. Repealed generally, and, except for Hair Powder, Excise Licences substituted, viz.:—		—	—
	Hair Powder, [illegible] per annum for each person	[illegible]		
	Armorial Bearings. Various rates	[illegible]		
	Carriages. Do.	[illegible]		
	Horses. Do.	[illegible]		
	Servants. Do.	[illegible]		
	Horse Dealers. Do.	[illegible]		

* As estimated, the gross produce of the first two complete years was [illegible].

INCOME TAX.

Year	Duties repealed, expired, or reduced	Consequent Loss of Revenue	Duties imposed or augmented	Consequent Increase of Revenue
		£		£
1816	(Great Britain). Tax ceased. 2s. in £, or 10 per cent. on Incomes derived from Real Property, and on Incomes of 150*l.* and upwards derived from Trades or Professions. Various rates on Incomes from 50*l.* to 150*l.* derived from the latter source	14,512,475	——	—
1842	——	—	(Great Britain). Re-imposed 7*d.* in £ on Incomes of 150*l.* and upwards	5,100,000
1853	——	—	Extension to Ireland at same rates as above, but with 5*d.* in £ from 100*l.* to 150*l.* throughout the United Kingdom	700,000
Ended 31 Mar. 1855	——	—	Increased to 1s. 2d. and 10d. respectively	[illegible]
1856	——	—	Increased to 1s. 4d. and 11½d. respectively	[illegible]
[illegible]	(United Kingdom). Reduced to 7d. in £ on Incomes of 150*l.* and upwards, and 5d. from 100*l.* to 150*l.*	[illegible]	——	—
[illegible]	Reduced to 5d. in £ on Incomes of 150*l.* and upwards	[illegible]	——	—
[illegible]	——	—	Increased to 9d. in £ for Incomes of 150*l.* and upwards, and 6½d., 100*l.* to 150*l.*	[illegible]
1860	——	—	Increased to 10d. and 7d. respectively	[illegible]
[illegible]	Reduced to 9d. in £ on Incomes of 150*l.* and upwards, and 6d. 100*l.* to 150*l.*	[illegible]	——	—
[illegible]	Rate 7d. in £ on Incomes of 100*l.* and upwards. Abatement of duty on 60*l.* allowed on Incomes under 200*l.*	[illegible]	——	—
[illegible]	Reduced to 6d. in the £. Abatement as before	[illegible]	——	—
[illegible]	Do. to 4d. Do.	[illegible]	——	—
[illegible]	——		Increased to 5d. in £. Abatement as before	[illegible]
[illegible]	——	—	Do. to 6d. in £ Do.	[illegible]
[illegible]	Reduced to 5d. in £. Abatement as before	[illegible]	——	—
[illegible]	Do. to 4d. in £ Do.	[illegible]	——	—
[illegible]	——	—	Increased to [illegible] in £. Abatement as before	[illegible]
[illegible]	Reduced to [illegible] in £ on Incomes of [illegible] and upwards	[illegible]	——	—
	Abatement of duty on [illegible] on Incomes under [illegible]	*[illegible]		
[illegible]	Reduced to [illegible] in £ on Incomes of [illegible] and upwards, with abatement as before	[illegible]	——	—

* Approximate amount.

INCOME TAX—*continued*.

Year ended [illegible]	Duties repealed, reduced, or relieved.	Consequent Loss of Revenue.	Duties imposed or augmented.	Consequent Increase of Revenue.
		£		£
[illegible]	Reduced to [illegible] in £ on Incomes of [illegible]l. and upwards, with abatement as before	[illegible]	—	—
[illegible]	Abatement of [illegible]l. on Incomes under [illegible]l. (Incomes under [illegible]l. exempted)	*[illegible]	Increased to [illegible] in £ on Incomes of [illegible]l. and upwards, with abatement as per contra	[illegible]
[illegible]	Allowance for Wear and Tear of Machinery	*[illegible]	Increased to [illegible] in £. Abatement as before	[illegible]
[illegible]	—	—	Do. to [illegible] in £ Do.	[illegible]
[illegible]	Reduced to [illegible] in £. Abatement as before	[illegible]	—	—
[illegible]	—	—	Increased to [illegible] in £. Abatement as before	[illegible]
[illegible]	Reduced to [illegible] in £. Abatement as before	[illegible]	—	—
[illegible]	—	—	Increased to [illegible] in £	[illegible]
[illegible]	—	—	Do. to [illegible] in £	[illegible]
[illegible]	Reduced to [illegible] in £	[illegible]	—	—
[illegible]	Do. [illegible] in £	[illegible]	—	—
	Relief to Tenant Farmers on Lands [illegible] Profits to made [illegible]	[illegible]	—	—
[illegible]	—	—	Increased to [illegible] in £	*[illegible]
[illegible]	Schedule A., Relief under Lands and Houses from Income, abatements to [illegible]	[illegible] [illegible]	Increased to [illegible] in £	*[illegible]

* Approximate estimates.

B.

Statement furnished by the Board of Customs with regard to Changes in the Rates of Customs Import Duties on certain Principal Articles from 1814 to 1885.

(*Note.*—In the earlier years of the period comprised in this Return the principal articles in the Customs tariff were also subject to duties of excise. The variations in the rates of Customs duty do not, therefore, necessarily indicate the variations in the taxation to which such articles were subject. *Nor does the repeal of the Customs duty on any particular article* (where the same is set forth in this table) necessarily mean that such article became free of duty altogether.)

CHANGES in the RATES of CUSTOMS IMPORT DUTIES on certain PRINCIPAL ARTICLES from the year 1814 to 1885.

Years.	Duties repealed, expired, or reduced.	Duties imposed or augmented.
1814	—	Tobacco (Great Britain and Ireland) increased from [illegible] to 1s. per lb. Sugar (Great Britain and Ireland) East India increased from [illegible] to 37s. per cwt.
1816	Sugar, unrefined (Great Britain and Ireland). East and West India and foreign sugar reduced 3s. per cwt. from 5th September	Sugar (Great Britain and Ireland) East India increased from 37s. to [illegible], and from 5th May increased to [illegible] per cwt.
1818	—	Sugar, unrefined (Great Britain and Ireland) increased 3s. per cwt. on various rates.
1819	Sugar, unrefined (Great Britain and Ireland), reduced from 5th May 3s. per cwt. on various rates, from 5th September further reduced 1s. per cwt. Sugar, refined (Great Britain and Ireland). Reduced from [illegible] to [illegible] per cwt. Tea (Great Britain). Customs duty repealed. Tobacco (Great Britain). Customs duty repealed.	Sugar Candy (Great Britain and Ireland). Brown increased from [illegible] to [illegible] per cwt. White increased from [illegible] to [illegible] per cwt. Tea (Ireland). Tea sold at the East India Company's sales in London above the price of 2s. per lb. increased from [illegible] to [illegible] per cent. Wine (Great Britain and Ireland). French wine increased from [illegible] to [illegible] per gallon.
1820	—	Spirits (Ireland). Acquavitae, Hungary water, and Lavender water increased from [illegible] to [illegible] per gallon. British content not above proof. Brandy and Geneva increased from [illegible] to [illegible] per gallon. British content not above proof. Rum from British Plantations increased from [illegible] to [illegible], and rum of other sorts from [illegible] to [illegible] per gallon. British content not above proof. Cinnamon water increased from [illegible] to [illegible] per gallon. British content not above proof. Usquebaugh increased from [illegible] to [illegible] per gallon. British content not above proof. Cordials, &c. increased from [illegible] to [illegible] per gallon. British content not above proof. —— (Ireland). The produce of any place within the limits of the East India Company's charter or imported from Cape of Good Hope and the Territories and Dependencies thereof. Brandy and Geneva increased from [illegible] to [illegible] per gallon. British content not above proof. Rum increased from [illegible] to [illegible] per gallon. British content not above proof. Arrack increased from [illegible] to [illegible] per gallon. British content not above proof. Tobacco, unmanufactured (Ireland). The produce of Spain or Portugal increased from [illegible] to [illegible] per lb. —— manufactured and segars (Ireland). Increased from [illegible] to [illegible] per lb. —— —— (Great Britain). Duty of [illegible] per lb. imposed.
1824	Rum (United Kingdom). The produce of any British Colony or plantation in America reduced [illegible] per gallon, above proof reduced [illegible] per gallon.	—
1825	—	Spirits (Great Britain). Rum not above proof increased [illegible]; above proof increased [illegible] per gallon. —— (Great Britain). The produce of British plantations in America not above proof increased [illegible]; above proof increased [illegible] per gallon. —— (Great Britain). The produce of any place within the limits of the East India Company's charter not above proof increased [illegible], above proof increased [illegible] per gallon.
	Tobacco (United Kingdom). From 5th July 1825. From British Possessions in America reduced from [illegible] to [illegible] per lb. From other parts reduced from [illegible] to [illegible] per lb.	Tobacco unmanufactured (Great Britain). The produce of Spain or Portugal, duty of [illegible] per lb. imposed. —— Of any other place [illegible] per lb. imposed.

Years.	Duties repealed, expired, or reduced.	Duties imposed or augmented.
[illegible]	Tea. Importation prohibited except into the port of London.	Snuff (United Kingdom). Duty of [illegible] per lb. imposed. Wine (United Kingdom. Cape wine increased from [illegible] to [illegible], French wine from [illegible] to [illegible], Madeira from [illegible], Portuguese from [illegible], Rhenish from [illegible], Spanish and other sorts of wine from [illegible] to [illegible] per gallon.
[illegible]	Spirits (United Kingdom). Duty at various rates repealed and others substituted, the effect of the change being a reduction, in the case of Rum from [illegible] to [illegible] per gallon, Brandy and Geneva from [illegible] to [illegible] per gallon; the new rates of duty were as follows, per proof gallon, viz. :— The produce of any British Possession in America, [illegible]. The produce of any British Possession within the limits of the East India Company's Charter, [illegible]. Of any other place, [illegible]. — Sweetened or mixed so that the strength cannot be exactly ascertained, viz. :— The produce of any British Possession in America, [illegible] per gallon. Of any other place, [illegible] per gallon.	—
		Sugar (United Kingdom). Increased from [illegible] to [illegible] per cwt. Wine (United Kingdom). French wine increased from [illegible] to [illegible] per imperial gallon; other sorts, except Cape wine, increased from [illegible] to [illegible] per imperial gallon.
[illegible]	—	Tea (Ireland). Not allowed to be removed to Ireland until the duty of excise had first been paid in Great Britain.
[illegible]	Sugar, unrefined (United Kingdom). From British West Indies reduced from [illegible] to [illegible] per cwt., from East India reduced from [illegible] to [illegible] per cwt.	Rum (United Kingdom). Increased from [illegible] to [illegible] per proof gallon.
[illegible]	Wine (United Kingdom). French wine reduced from [illegible] to [illegible] per gallon.	Wine (United Kingdom). Cape wine increased from [illegible] to [illegible] per gallon. — Other sorts (not French) from [illegible] to [illegible] per gallon.
[illegible]	—	Tea (United Kingdom). Duty imposed at the following rates, viz. :— Bohea, per lb. [illegible]. Congou, Twankay, Hyson Skin, Orange Pekoe, and Campoi, per lb. [illegible]. Other sorts, per lb. [illegible].
[illegible]	Sugar, unrefined (United Kingdom). Of any British Possession within the limits of the East India Company's Charter into which the importation of foreign sugar is prohibited and imported from thence, reduced from [illegible] to [illegible] per cwt.	—
	Tea (United Kingdom). All sorts except Bohea, reduced to [illegible] per lb.	Tea (United Kingdom). Bohea increased from [illegible] to [illegible] per lb.
[illegible]	—	Spirits (United Kingdom). All rates increased [illegible] per gallon. Sugar (United Kingdom). All rates increased [illegible] per cent. Tea (United Kingdom). All rates increased [illegible] per cent. Tobacco, cigars, and snuff (United Kingdom). All rates increased [illegible] per cent. Wine (United Kingdom). All rates increased [illegible] per cent.
[illegible]	—	Tobacco, unmanufactured (United Kingdom). From British Possessions in America, increased from [illegible] to [illegible] per lb.
[illegible]	Sugar, unrefined (United Kingdom). The growth of any foreign country, the sugar of which Her Majesty has declared to be admissible as not being the produce of slave labour, reduced from [illegible] to [illegible] per cwt.	—
[illegible]	Sugar (United Kingdom). Reduced various rates.	—
[illegible]	Spirits (United Kingdom). Rum reduced from [illegible] to [illegible] per gallon. Brandy and Geneva reduced from [illegible] to [illegible] per gallon. Sugar (United Kingdom). Reduced various rates.	—
[illegible]	Sugar (United Kingdom). Reduced various rates. Spirits, rum, reduced from [illegible], in England to [illegible], Scotland to [illegible], and Ireland to [illegible] per gallon.	—
[illegible]	Sugar (United Kingdom). All rates reduced. Spirits, rum, England, Scotland, and Ireland. Reduced [illegible] per gallon.	—

[illegible]

Years	Duties repealed, expired, or reduced	Duties imposed or augmented
1849	Wine (United Kingdom). From British Possessions, reduced from 2s. 6d. to 1s. 3d. per gallon. Sugar (United Kingdom). All rates reduced.	—
1850	Sugar (United Kingdom). All rates reduced.	—
1851	Sugar (United Kingdom). All rates reduced.	—
1852	Sugar (United Kingdom). Various rates reduced.	—
1853	Sugar (United Kingdom). Various rates reduced. Tea (United Kingdom). Reduced from 2s. 2¼d. to 1s. 10½d. per lb.	Spirits, rum (Ireland). Increased from 3s. to 3s. 4d.; (Scotland) from 4s. to 4s. 8d. per gallon. Wine. Of British Possessions other than the Cape of Good Hope, increased from 1s. 3d. to 2s. 10½d. per gallon (United Kingdom).
1854	Tea (United Kingdom) reduced from 1s. 10½d. to 1s. 6d. per lb.	Spirits, rum (Ireland), increased from 3s. 4d. to 4s. 1d.; (Scotland), increased from 4s. 8d. to 6s., and afterwards to 6s. 2d. per gallon. Sugar (United Kingdom), all rates increased.
1855	—	Spirits, rum (Ireland), increased from 4s. 1d. to 6s. 2d.; (Scotland), increased from 6s. 2d. to 8s. 1d. per gallon. Sugar, unrefined and refined (United Kingdom). Uniform rate imposed on sugar of whatsoever growth and whencesoever imported, as follows, viz.:— Equal to White Clayed, per cwt., 17s. 6d. Not equal to White Clayed, per cwt., 15s. Not equal to Brown Clayed, „ 13s. 9d. Refined, per cwt., 18s. being an increase of duty in the case of sugar of British Possessions. Tea (United Kingdom), increased from 1s. 6d. to 1s. 9d. per pound.
1857	Sugar (United Kingdom) duties reduced, viz.:— Equal to White Clayed from 17s. 6d. to 16s. per cwt. Not equal to White Clayed, from 15s. to 13s. 10d. per cwt. Not equal to Brown Clayed, from 13s. 9d. to 12s. 8d. per cwt. Refined, from 18s. to 18s. 4d. per cwt. Tea (United Kingdom) reduced from 1s. 9d. to 1s. 5d. per lb.	—
1858	—	Spirits, rum (Ireland), increased from 6s. 2d. to 8s. 1d. per gallon.
1860	Spirits (United Kingdom), Brandy and Geneva, reduced from 15s. to 8s. 2d. per gallon. Wine, Foreign (United Kingdom), reduced from 5s. 9¾d. to 3s. per gallon.	Spirits (United Kingdom), rum, Colonial and Foreign. Rum imported from the country of its production increased from 8s. 2d. to 8s. 4d. Other rum increased from 8s. 2d. to 8s. 5d. per gallon, and subsequently increased to 10s. 2d. and 10s. 5d. per gallon respectively. Brandy and Geneva, increased from 8s. 2d. to 10s. 5d. per gallon.
1861	Wine (United Kingdom), of whatever growth, and whencesoever imported, duties reduced according to degrees of strength to the following rates, viz.:— Imported in casks containing less proof spirit than— 18 degrees, 1s. per gallon. 26 „ 1s. 9d. per gallon. 40 „ 2s. 5d. „ 45 „ 2s. 11d. „ Imported in bottles, and containing less proof spirit than 40 degrees, 2s. 5d. per gallon.	—
1862	Wine (United Kingdom) rates altered as follows:— Imported in casks and containing less proof spirit than— 26 degrees, per gallon, 1s. 42 „ „ 2s. 6d. Imported in bottles, and containing less proof spirit than— 42 degrees, per gallon, 2s. 6d. Imported in casks or bottles, and containing more proof spirit than— 42 degrees per gallon, 2s. 6d., and 3d. additional for every degree beyond 42.	—
1863	Tea (United Kingdom), reduced from 1s. 5d. to 1s. per lb. Tobacco Manufactured (United Kingdom), reduced from 9s. 6½d. to Segars, 5s.; Foreign Cavendish, 4s. 6d., other sorts, 4s. per lb.; snuff from 6s. 3½d. to 3s. 9d., and 4s. 6d. per lb. according to more or not more than 13 lbs. of moisture in every 100 lbs. weight thereof.	Tobacco, unmanufactured (United Kingdom), containing less than 10 lbs. of moisture in every 100 lbs. weight thereof, increased from 3s. 1½d. to 3s. 6d. per lb.

Years.	Duties repealed, expired, or reduced.	Duties imposed or augmented.
1864	Sugar (United Kingdom), unrefined :— Equal to White Clayed reduced from 16s to 11s. 8d. per cwt. Not equal to White Clayed reduced from 15s. 10d. to 10s 6d per cwt. Not equal to Brown Clayed, the duty on which was 12s 8d per cwt., was divided into two classes, viz. :— Equal to Brown Muscovado, with a duty of 9s. 4d. per cwt., and not equal to Brown Muscovado, with a duty of 8s 2d per cwt. —— Refined, reduced from 18s 4d to 12s. 10d. per cwt.	——
1865	Tea (United Kingdom), reduced from 1s to 6d per lb.	——
1866	Wine (United Kingdom), imported in bottles, duty divided into two classes, viz. :— Containing less than 26 degrees of proof spirit, 1s per gallon. Containing less than 42 degrees of proof spirit, 2s 6d per gallon.	——
1867	Sugar (United Kingdom). Unrefined, which had been classified under the four headings of "Equal to White Clayed," "Not equal to White Clayed," "Equal to Brown Muscovado," and "Not equal to Brown Muscovado," with duties of 11s 8d, 10s 6d., 9s 4d, and 8s 2d per cwt. respectively, were reclassified and duties imposed according to standard samples deposited with the Lords of the Treasury and approved by them as follows, viz. :— First Class, 11s 8d, per cwt. Second " 10s 6d " Third " 9s 7d " Fourth " 8s " The effect of this was a slight reduction. —— Refined, reduced from 12s 10d to 12s per cwt.	——
1870	Sugar (United Kingdom). Unrefined reduced 1st Class from 11s. 8d to 6s 0d per cwt. 2nd " " 10s 6d " 5s 3d. " 3rd " " 9s 7d " 4s 9d " 4th " " 8s " 4s " —— Refined, reduced from 12s to 6s per cwt.	Perfumed spirits and Cologne water (United Kingdom) increased from 14s to 16s 4d per gallon.
1873	Sugar (United Kingdom). Unrefined reduced 1st Class from 6s 0d to 3s 0d, per cwt. 2nd " " 5s 3d " 2s 8d " 3rd " " 4s 9d. " 2s 5d " 4th " " 4s " 2s. " —— Refined, reduced from 6s to 3s per cwt.	——
1874	Sugar (United Kingdom). Unrefined and refined, duty repealed.	——
1876	——	Tobacco (United Kingdom). Unmanufactured increased 4d per lb. —— Manufactured increased 4d per lb.
1878	——	Tobacco (United Kingdom). Cigars increased 6d per lb.
1881	Spirits (United Kingdom). Brandy and Geneva, and rum unsweetened imported, reduced from 10s 5d to 10s 4d per gallon.	Spirits (United Kingdom). Rum sweetened imported, increased from 10s 2d to 10s 4d per gallon.
1886	Wine (United Kingdom). Strength admitted at 1s. rate of duty increased from "containing less than 26 degrees of proof spirit" to "not exceeding 30 degrees of proof spirit."	——
1887	Tobacco (United Kingdom). All kinds reduced 4d. per lb. Cigars reduced 6d per lb.	——
1888	——	Wine (United Kingdom). Sparkling wine, additional duty of 1s and 2s. 6d per gallon, according as the market value was less or more than 15s per gallon, imposed.
1890	Tea (United Kingdom). Reduced from 6d to 4d per lb.	Spirits (United Kingdom). Additional duty of 6d per gallon imposed for local taxation purposes.
1893	Wine (United Kingdom). Additional duty changed to 2s per gallon, irrespective of the market value.	——
1894	——	Spirits (United Kingdom). All kinds increased 6d per gallon.
1895	Spirits (United Kingdom). Reduced 6d per gallon.	——

APPENDIX XIII.

LOCAL LOANS FUND, IRELAND

Authority through whom Advance was made by National Debt Commissioners	Total Amount advanced to 31st March [illegible]	Total Amount of the Repayments made from [illegible] up to the 31st March [illegible] in respect of such Advances, including Repayments of Capital and Interest			Remitted up to 31st March [illegible]	Balance outstanding on 31st March [illegible]
		Capital	Interest	Total		
	£	£	£	£	£	£
Commissioners of Public Works, Ireland	[illegible]	[illegible]	[illegible]	[illegible]	[illegible]	[illegible]
Irish Land Commissioners under Land Purchase Acts	[illegible]	[illegible]	[illegible]	[illegible]	[illegible]	[illegible]
Total - -	[illegible]	[illegible]	[illegible]	[illegible]	[illegible]	[illegible]
Public Works Loan Commissioners	[illegible]	[illegible]	[illegible]	[illegible]	[illegible]	[illegible]
H.M.'s Treasury - -	[illegible]	—	—	—	[illegible]	—
Grand Total - -	[illegible]	[illegible]	[illegible]	[illegible]	[illegible]	[illegible]

NOTE.—This table is a summary of that printed on page [illegible] of the first volume of Evidence, which [illegible] to the 31st March [illegible].

APPENDIX XIV.

[illegible]

[illegible]

[illegible]

[illegible]

APPENDIX XV.

TABLES REPRINTED FROM THE STATISTICAL ABSTRACT. C.—7675 OF 1895.

TOTAL LENGTH, PAID-UP CAPITAL, TRAFFIC, RECEIPTS, and WORKING EXPENSES of RAILWAYS in ENGLAND and WALES, SCOTLAND, and IRELAND.

Years.	Length of Line open at the end of each Year.	Paid-up Capital at the end of each Year*: Ordinary.	Guaranteed, Preferential, and Loans and Debenture Stock.	Total.	Number of Passengers conveyed (exclusive of Season-Ticket Holders).	Weight of Goods and Minerals conveyed.	Gross Receipts: From Passenger Traffic.	From Goods Traffic.	Average Receipts from Passenger and Goods Traffic per Mile of Line open.	Miscellaneous.	Total.	Working Expenditure.	Net Receipts.	Proportion of Working Expenditure to Gross Receipts.
	Miles.	£	£	£	No.	Tons.	£	£	£	£	£	£	£	Per Cent.
ENGLAND AND WALES.														
[illegible]	[illegible]	[illegible]	[illegible]	[illegible]	[illegible]	[illegible]	[illegible]	[illegible]	[illegible]	[illegible]	[illegible]	[illegible]	[illegible]	[illegible]
SCOTLAND.														
[illegible]	[illegible]	[illegible]	[illegible]	[illegible]	[illegible]	[illegible]	[illegible]	[illegible]	[illegible]	[illegible]	[illegible]	[illegible]	[illegible]	[illegible]

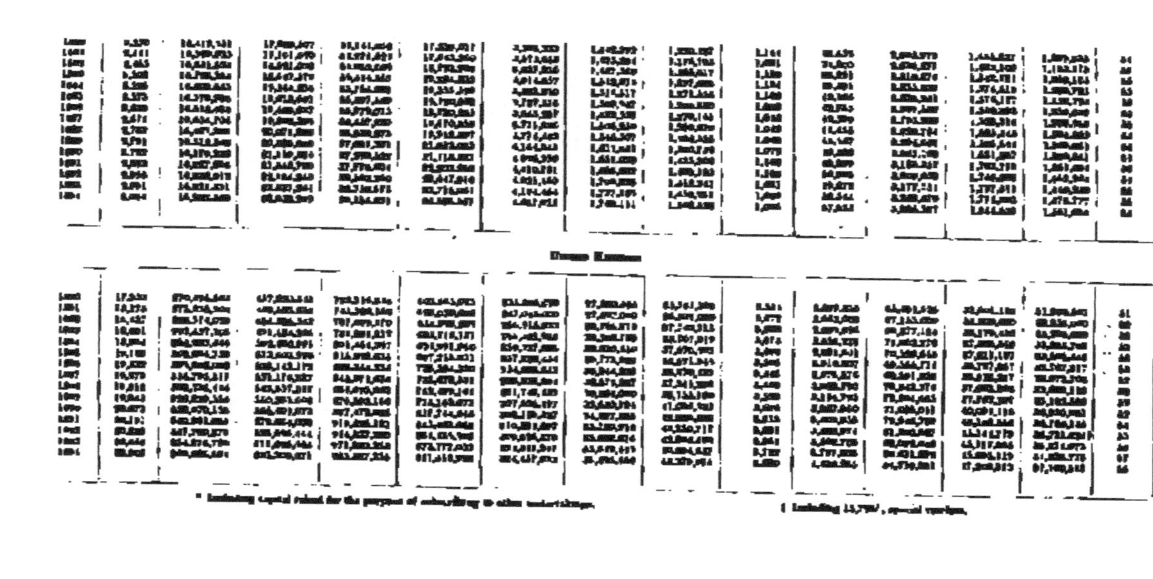

* Including capital raised for the purpose of subscribing to other undertakings.

† Including 13,750*l*. special receipts.

APPENDIX XVI.

It has been thought that a review of the financial arrangements existing in certain composite States might be of assistance to the Royal Commission. The following statement with regard to Austria-Hungary, the German Empire, Sweden and Norway, and Switzerland has been chiefly prepared from information specially obtained, through the courtesy of the Foreign Office, from Her Majesty's representatives in those countries.

B. H. Holland,
Secretary.

April 1895.

AUSTRIA-HUNGARY.

The Exchequers of Austria and Hungary are entirely distinct, but certain expenditure is common to the two countries, namely, that upon the army and navy, the foreign office and diplomatic service, and the finance ministry and department, by whom the common revenue and expenditure is superintended.

The Budget for common expenses is laid before delegations from the Parliaments of the two countries for their respective sanctions. The delegations consist of an equal number of representatives of each House of Parliament in the two kingdoms.

The system upon which the common expenditure is defrayed is as follows:—

Under the Pact (Ausgleich) of 1867 between the two divisions of the monarchy, which has been twice renewed since that date, "the net proceeds of the common "customs are deducted from the amount required, "then 2 per cent. of the remainder is debited to "Hungary, and lastly of this remainder 70 per cent. "is paid by Austria and 30 per cent. by Hungary. A "common loan may be taken, and the floating debt, "consisting of bills, is guaranteed jointly by both. "The other debts are not regarded as common, but "Hungary pays, on account of ordinary debt contracted "before 1868, a yearly sum of 30,112,980 florins." (Statesman's Year Book, 1895.)

The deduction of 2 per cent. debited to Hungary is made on account of the territory of the "military frontier" having been incorporated into Hungary subsequently to the Pact of 1867.

The basis upon which was settled the proportion in which Austria and Hungary respectively should contribute to so much of the joint expenditure as the receipts of the common customs were unable to meet is explained by Sir Edmund Monson in the following letter addressed by him to the Earl of Kimberley on 20th February 1895:—

(No. 11, Commercial.)

My Lord, Vienna, February 20, 1895.

In answer to the query contained in the enclosure to your Lordship's Despatch No. 6 of that series, of the 9th instant, I have the honour to state, for the information of the Royal Commission on the Financial Relations between Great Britain and Ireland, that the main principle observed in estimating the comparative wealth of Austria and Hungary when the "Ausgleich" or Pact of 1867 was concluded was that of taking the returns of direct taxation as a basis.

The matter gave rise to much discussion, not as to the character of the test to which recourse was had, but as to the results deducible therefrom. Taking the average contributions of both parties to the negotiation during the six years 1860–1865 as a starting point, the Hungarian deputies arrived at the conclusion that the share of their country was a little over 25 per cent. The Austrian rejoinder was that in dealing with the figures the Hungarian deputies had left sundry items out of the account: no notice of the State debt, for instance, having been taken, that, moreover, certain excise duties, such as those on spirits and sugar, which were levied in the same way in both countries, should be taken into consideration, and that the proper proportion, without reckoning the debt, was a little over 29 per cent. for Hungary, whilst the last items of charges that amongst brought the ratio up to something above 31 per cent., leaving not quite 69 per cent. to be borne by Austria.

"The deputies were unable to come to an agreement, and a compromise was finally adopted by the ministers on both sides, who decided on 30 per cent. and 70 per cent. being taken for the contributions towards joint expenses of Hungary and Austria respectively, and also for their shares of charges for debt, after first striking off from the whole an annual sum of 25,000,000 florins, Austrian currency (say 2,000,000*l.* sterling) to be borne by Austria alone.

This plan was ultimately accepted, and has remained in force ever since, subject to the modification mentioned in my Despatch on this subject, No. 65, of the 29th of November last, and caused by the incorporation into Hungary of the region formerly known as the military frontier. It is liable to revision only when the "Ausgleich" itself expires, that is to say, 10 years after each renewal. The Pact originally took effect on the 1st of January 1868, and has subsequently been since twice renewed.

I have, &c.
(Signed) Edmund Monson.

The Earl of Kimberley, K.G.,
&c. &c. &c.

The following observations are quoted from the Report for the years 1892–3 on the Finances and Taxation of Austria, published in the Foreign Office Annual Series (C. 6855–80):—

"It is to be observed that the receipts from customs in Austria are far larger than those realised in Hungary, amounting in that country alone to nearly 3,000,000*l.* sterling net. Obviously the greater portion of the import duties are levied by Austrian officials on goods coming from Germany, France, Italy, Russia, Great Britain, &c., while to a very large extent the imported goods consumed in Hungary have paid duty on the Austrian frontier, or at Vienna, whence they are forwarded to the Hungarian consumer or importer. This difference in the sums actually raised by customs duties in Austria and Hungary has, however, no effect upon the proportional contributions of the two countries to the common finances, because this revenue is brought as a total to the common exchequer irrespective of the amount levied in either country.

"I should add that the gross receipts from customs levied in Austria amounts to 37,400,000 florins, or 3,116,000*l.*, a sum which is decreased owing to certain refunding of duties, by 80,000*l.*, and by costs of administration by a further total of 1,400,000*l.*

"Little more than 1 per million of the whole amount is derived from duties on exports.

"It would extend beyond the limits of this report to explain here many of the complex arrangements between Austria and Hungary in financial matters, especially in regard to the apportionment of the proceeds of the indirect taxes. No barrier existing between the two halves of the monarchy, these taxes, such as those on sugar, beer, spirits, and mineral oils, go, as a rule, into the exchequer of that country in which the taxable establishments exist, although the consumer in the other country pay virtually the tax in the price of the article taxed. By this arrangement sugar and beer, which are more produced in Austria, give an advantage to that country, as a great deal of Austrian sugar and beer is consumed in Hungary. The reverse is the case in regard to spirits and mineral oil, of which a surplus over the Hungarian production goes to the Austrian consumer. The tax, however, thereon remains in the Hungarian exchequer.

"Hungary is just now endeavouring to secure her share of the profits of the excise on sugar, and grants every possible facility for the erection of new sugar manufactories within its territory, in order to obtain the tax on the sugar consumed by its inhabitants."

Austro-Hungarian Budget for [illegible]

Expenditure.	Ordinary. Florins.	Extraordinary. Florins.	Florins.	£	Revenue.	Florins.	£
Foreign Department—Central Office	[illegible]	—	—	—	Diplomatic service fees, &c.	[illegible]	
Secret service, &c.	[illegible]	—	—	—	Consular ... and fees	[illegible]	
[illegible]	[illegible]	[illegible]	—	—		[illegible]	[illegible]
Consular	[illegible]	[illegible]	—	—			
	[illegible]	[illegible]	[illegible]	[illegible]			
War Department—Army	[illegible]	[illegible]	[illegible]	[illegible]		[illegible]	
Navy	[illegible]	[illegible]	[illegible]	[illegible]		[illegible]	
	[illegible]	[illegible]	[illegible]			[illegible]	[illegible]
Finance Department	[illegible]	..	[illegible]	[illegible]			
[illegible]	[illegible]	—	[illegible]	[illegible]		[illegible]	[illegible]
Audit	[illegible]	—	[illegible]	[illegible]			
Total	[illegible]	[illegible]	[illegible]	[illegible]		[illegible]	[illegible]
					Customs revenue, estimated		
					On Austria [illegible]		
					Trans-Leithania [illegible]		
Deduct receipts	[illegible]	—	—	[illegible]	Bosnia and Herzegovina [illegible]		
					[illegible]		
					Less sums for above purposes of [illegible]		
					And deficiency for ... charges of [illegible] [illegible]		
Remainder	[illegible]	[illegible]	[illegible]	[illegible]		[illegible]	[illegible]
Of which Austrian States contribute			[illegible]	[illegible]		[illegible]	[illegible]
And Hungarian			[illegible]	[illegible]			

THE GERMAN EMPIRE.

The following Report with regard to the relations between Imperial and State Finance in Germany has, at the request of the Secretary of the Royal Commission, been obtained by the Foreign Office from Her Majesty's Ambassador at Berlin:—

Sir, Berlin, February 20, 1893.

I have the honour to lay before your Excellency a report upon the relations between Imperial and State Finance in Germany.

In order to make these relations as clear as possible, I have endeavoured to trace (1) the sources of Imperial revenue at the time of the creation of the German Empire in 1871; (2) the Customs Reform of 1879; (3) the working of the reformed system from 1879 to the present day; and, lastly, the recent measures proposed by the Imperial Government to remedy the present unsatisfactory financial system.

I have, &c.

(Signed) Reginald Tower.

His Excellency Sir E. B. Malet, G.C.B.

The Relations between Imperial and State Finance of Germany.

Contents.

[illegible]

The principal objects of Imperial expenditure are:— (margin: Imperial expenditure.)

Reichstag and Federal Council.
Imperial Chancellor and Chancery.
Foreign Office. (Allowances in favour of Bavaria, Saxony, and Wurtemberg on account of their separate diplomatic representation described below.)
Ministry of the Interior (including contributions for maintenance of museums at Nuremberg and Mayence, schools and international exhibitions; for encouragement of sea fisheries, subsidies to German Postal steamship lines running to Asia, Australia, and East Africa; precautions against cattle disease on Russian and Austrian frontiers, &c.)
Army (exception in favour of Bavaria, described below)
Navy
Post and Telegraphs (exceptions for Bavaria and Wurtemberg, see below)
Railways (Imperial, i.e., Alsace-Lorraine)
Imperial Administration of Justice.
Imperial Treasury
Pensions
Imperial Debt

Imperial finances are administered at the Imperial Treasury in Berlin, under the direction of a Secretary of State for the Treasury (Staatssekretär des Reichsschatzamts) and an Under Secretary of State. (margin: Administration of Imperial finance.)

To the Imperial Treasury belong the preparation of the Imperial Budget, the control and account of the moneys, matters affecting coinage, issue of notes, and the Imperial loans, the administration of Imperial revenue, (so far as it is not otherwise controlled), and the preparation of matters regarding Customs and taxation.

Prussian finances are administered by the Prussian Minister of Finance, who is a Minister of State. (margin: Of Prussian finance.)

Sources of State (Prussian) revenue*:—
- Direct taxes (including Income Tax, Buildings Tax, Industrial Tax, &c.).
- Indirect taxes (the principal items of which are Stamp and Succession Duties).
- Lotteries.
- Woods and Forests, Agriculture, &c.
- Mines and Saltworks.
- State railways.
- Customs and tobacco duties, excise on brandy and stamp duties paid back by the empire as Assignments (*Ueberweisungen*).
- Extraordinary revenue.

On the creation of the German Empire it was laid down by the Imperial Constitution of April 16, 1871 (Article 70), that the "accruing balance, as well as the "revenues derived from Customs, Excise duties, and the "Posts and Telegraphs Administration, serve towards "defraying common (i.e., Imperial) expenditure."

In the first years after 1871, expenditure increased in such a manner as to exceed revenue derived from the above sources, and it became necessary to put a severe strain upon the Confederated States by the exaction of matricular contributions (*Matrikular-beiträge*), according to the further provisions of Article 70, that "in case these sources (i.e., from Customs, "&c.) are not sufficient to cover common expenditure, "and so long as Imperial taxation is not introduced, "contributions shall be laid on the Confederated "States according to the rate of their population, and "these contributions shall be administered by the "Imperial Chancellor, their amount being fixed by the "Budget."

These contributions are assessed in the Budget at a uniform rate throughout all the States, and may be regarded as a kind of poll tax, which presses heavily on some of the smaller States, where the average population is poor.

In June 1877, a proposal was put forward by Prussia to impose Imperial Stamp and Succession Duties, and a Commission appointed in that year and composed of experts from the Confederated States reported in favour of the imposition of Imperial Stamp dues.

In 1879 the Franckenstein Clause, passed by the Reichstag (paragraph 8 of the Customs Tariff Law of July 15, 1879), provided that no amount, not exceeding [illegible] from the proceeds of Customs and Tobacco duties should be credited to the Empire, and that the remainder should be made over to the Confederated States. These payments are called Assignments (*Ueberweisungen*).

Imperial stamp duties were imposed by the law of July 1881, and increased by that of May [illegible], 1885.

By paragraph 44 of the Imperial Stamp Law of June [illegible], 1885, and paragraphs 39 and 43 of the Brandy Excise Law of June 24, 1887, the total net revenue from Imperial Stamp duties, as well as the surtax to the [illegible], is paid to the Confederated States.

Customs duties were further increased by the laws of May [illegible], 1885, and of December 21, 1887.

The present principal sources of Imperial revenue are:—

I. Customs and Excise, including:—
- (a.) Customs duties.
- (b.) Tobacco duties.
- (c.) Sugar Tax.
- (d.) Salt Tax.
- (e.) Brandy Excise.

(a.)–(e.): common to all "*Zollverein*" States.

- (f.) Beer Excise, from which Bavaria, Wurtemberg, Baden, and Alsace-Lorraine are exempted.

II. Stamp duties, exclusive of—
- Duties on playing cards, bills of exchange, shares, [illegible], and bonds.
- On lotteries, both State and private.
- On statistical fees.

III. Posts and Telegraphs Administration, surplus (Bavaria and Wurtemberg are exempt).

IV. Railways (Imperial, i.e., Alsace-Lorraine), surplus.

V. Imperial Bank.

VII. Imperial Invalid Fund.

VIII. Sundry receipts from administrative and other sources.

IX. Extraordinary Revenue.

X. Matricular contributions.

* [illegible]

† [illegible]

II. Beer Excise.

The law of May 31, 1872, imposing an excise on beer, applies to the whole Empire within the Customs Union, with the exception of the Kingdoms of Bavaria and Wurtemberg, the Grand Duchy of Baden, and Alsace-Lorraine. These States do not, in return, share the revenue derived therefrom.

For this exemption from Beer Excise, Bavaria, Wurtemberg, Baden, and Alsace-Lorraine are required to pay to the Imperial Treasury additional sums which are added to their matricular contributions.

In the estimates for 1894-95 these sums amount to:—

	£
Bavaria	[illegible]
Wurtemberg	[illegible]
Baden	[illegible]
Alsace-Lorraine	[illegible]

These amounts are assessed according to the rate of population.

The total receipts from Beer Excise are estimated (1894-95) at [illegible]. The population of all the States sharing in the above receipts, i.e., with the exception of Bavaria, Wurtemberg, Baden and Alsace-Lorraine, amounts to [illegible]. The corresponding equivalents, therefore, for the non-sharing States are, as have been above given, calculated at the rates of their respective populations, viz., Bavaria, [illegible]; Wurtemberg, [illegible]; Baden, [illegible]; and Alsace-Lorraine, [illegible].

III. Posts and Telegraphs.

Article 52 of the Constitution of April 16, 1871, states:—"The legislation respecting posts and telegraphs, "respecting the legal relations of both these Depart-"ments to the public, and respecting the postage, is in "the hands of the Empire. But the Regulations and "Tariff Rules for the internal postal and telegraphic "communication in Bavaria and Wurtemberg are laid "down by those countries themselves. The regulations "for the postal and telegraphic communication with "the exterior are also under the Empire, with the "exception of those affecting the immediate com-"munications of Bavaria and Wurtemberg with the "Non-German States bordering on them, which regu-"lations are determined by Article [illegible] of the Postal "Treaty of November [illegible], 1867."

"Bavaria and Wurtemberg have no share in the "revenues which the Empire derives from the Posts "and Telegraphs."

In the Estimates for 1894-5 the surplus from Posts and Telegraphs is put at [illegible]. In this amount Bavaria and Wurtemberg have no share, and, in view of these separate administrations, are required to pay the following sums to the Empire, the amounts being added to their matricular contributions.

These are fixed at:—

	£
Bavaria	[illegible]
Wurtemberg	[illegible]

The above are likewise computed according to population, the total population of all the States except Bavaria and Wurtemberg being [illegible], while that of Bavaria is [illegible], and Wurtemberg [illegible].

IV. Railways.

Article 41 of the Constitution states:—"Railways, "which are considered necessary for strategical "purposes or in the interests of general traffic, may "be constructed on account of the Empire, by virtue "of an Imperial law, even against the will of such "Confederated State as is traversed by the railway, or "a concession may be granted to private constructors "and with rights of expropriation."

With this exception, and the Imperial control over the rates of freights (Article [illegible]), each State administers its own railways.

Bavaria is, however, placed on a different footing by Article 46, which states that the provisions of the regulations respecting railways in the Empire do not apply to that Kingdom, except for strategical purposes.

Army.

By Article 63 of the Constitution it is stated:—"The whole of the land forces of the Empire shall form "a united army in war and peace, under the orders of "the Emperor."

Bavaria, Saxony, and Wurtemberg have War Ministers of their own, though their military Budgets are all on the same footing.

Bavaria.

By the Treaty with Bavaria of November 23, 1870 (Sections III., [illegible], and IV.), Bavaria reserved to contribute her quota, as in the case of other States, to the Imperial military chest, but this quota is kept entirely apart, and the mode in which it is expended is left to her. The details do not appear in the Imperial Budget. In peace time, her army is under the King of Bavaria, but, on mobilisation, in time of war the Emperor takes the command. The organisation, training, &c. of her army are, however, assimilated to the system of the Imperial military forces.

In return Bavaria has no share in the administration of the Imperial military forces.

Saxony and Wurtemberg.

The military budgets of Saxony and Wurtemberg are prepared in Berlin.

On the revenue side of the Budget for 1884-85, the sum of [illegible] is estimated from leases of buildings, sale of ground, material, &c.

In view of the independent condition of the Bavarian military funds, that Kingdom is required to pay a contribution of [illegible], to the Imperial Exchequer, the sum being added to her matricular contributions, and calculated, as in the case of exemptions from Beer Excise and Postal Administration, according to the proportion of her population.

On the expense incurred for Imperial diplomatic representation, 1884-85, the following abatements are credited to Bavaria, Saxony, and Wurtemberg, in view of their separate representation:— [illegible margin note]

	£
Bavaria	[illegible]
Saxony	[illegible]
Wurtemberg	[illegible]
Total	[illegible]

MATRICULAR CONTRIBUTIONS. ESTIMATE for 1884-5.

—	Amount.	Population (1880.)	—	Amount.	Population (1880).
	£			£	
1 Prussia	[illegible]	[illegible]	15 Anhalt	[illegible]	[illegible]
2 Bavaria	[illegible]	[illegible]	16 Schwarzburg-Sondershausen	[illegible]	[illegible]
3 Saxony	[illegible]	[illegible]	17 Schwarzburg-Rudolstadt	[illegible]	[illegible]
4 Wurtemberg	[illegible]	[illegible]	18 Waldeck	[illegible]	[illegible]
5 Baden	[illegible]	[illegible]	19 Reuss (elder branch)	[illegible]	[illegible]
6 Hesse	[illegible]	[illegible]	20 Reuss (younger branch)	[illegible]	[illegible]
7 Mecklenburg-Schwerin	[illegible]	[illegible]	21 Schaumburg-Lippe	[illegible]	[illegible]
8 Saxe-Weimar	[illegible]	[illegible]	22 Alsace-Lorraine	[illegible]	[illegible]
9 Mecklenburg-Strelitz	[illegible]	[illegible]	23 Lippe	[illegible]	[illegible]
10 Oldenburg	[illegible]	[illegible]	24 Lübeck	[illegible]	[illegible]
11 Brunswick	[illegible]	[illegible]	25 Bremen	[illegible]	[illegible]
12 Saxe-Meiningen	[illegible]	[illegible]	26 Hamburg	[illegible]	[illegible]
13 Saxe-Altenburg	[illegible]	[illegible]			
14 Saxe-Coburg and Gotha	[illegible]	[illegible]	Total	[illegible]	[illegible]

ORDINARY REVENUE and EXPENDITURE of the EMPIRE between 1872 and 1878-9, being the ACTUAL REVENUE and EXPENDITURE, exclusive of the FRENCH WAR INDEMNITY or EXTRAORDINARY EXPENDITURE.

—	1872.	1873.	1874.	1875.	1876-7 (15 months).	1877-8.	1878-9.
	£	£	£	£	£	£	£
Recurring expenditure	[illegible]	[illegible]	[illegible]	[illegible]	[illegible]	[illegible]	[illegible]
Non-recurring expenditure	[illegible]	[illegible]	[illegible]	[illegible]	[illegible]	[illegible]	[illegible]
Total	[illegible]	[illegible]	[illegible]	[illegible]	[illegible]	[illegible]	[illegible]
For covering the above expenditure, the sources of Imperial Revenue are:—							
1 Customs and Excise duties	[illegible]	[illegible]	[illegible]	[illegible]	[illegible]	[illegible]	[illegible]
2 Stamp duties on playing cards	—	—	—	—	—	—	[illegible]
3 On bills of exchange	[illegible]	[illegible]	[illegible]	[illegible]	[illegible]	[illegible]	[illegible]
4 Surplus from posts and telegraphs	[illegible]	[illegible]	[illegible]	[illegible]	[illegible]	[illegible]	[illegible]
5 Surplus from Imperial railways	[illegible]	[illegible]	[illegible]	[illegible]	[illegible]	[illegible]	[illegible]
6 Other sources of revenue	[illegible]	[illegible]	[illegible]	[illegible]	[illegible]	[illegible]	[illegible]
Total	[illegible]	[illegible]	[illegible]	[illegible]	[illegible]	[illegible]	[illegible]
[illegible] for account not common to all States:—							
[illegible]	[illegible]	[illegible]	[illegible]	[illegible]	[illegible]	[illegible]	[illegible]
[illegible]	[illegible]	[illegible]	[illegible]	[illegible]	[illegible]	[illegible]	[illegible]
Total	[illegible]	[illegible]	[illegible]	[illegible]	[illegible]	[illegible]	[illegible]
Amount of expenditure [illegible] by revenue	[illegible]	[illegible]	[illegible]	[illegible]	[illegible]	[illegible]	[illegible]
Percentage of above expenditure	[illegible]	[illegible]	[illegible]	[illegible]	[illegible]	[illegible]	[illegible]
Matricular contributions	[illegible]	[illegible]	[illegible]	[illegible]	[illegible]	[illegible]	[illegible]

Whilst Imperial expenditure from 1879 to 1893-4 rose from 14,[illegible] to 29,[illegible], or, in round numbers, 5,000,000l., the ordinary revenue had only increased from 13,[illegible] to 14,[illegible], or about 1,271,000l., and the percentage of expenditure covered by ordinary revenue rose from 12.5 per cent. in 1872 to 27.7 in 1878-9.

This state of affairs brought about the Customs Reform of 1879, and the Franckenstein Clause, which have been already described.

The increase of revenue (Imperial) effected by that law, and by subsequent legislation, has resulted in the fact that, in spite of the continuous increase of Imperial expenditure, the matricular contributions were not only balanced by the assignments (derived from Customs and Stamp Duties and Excise on brandy), but every year to 1892-93 a considerable excess was paid by the Empire to the Confederated States.

The comparison between matricular contributions and assignments from 1879-80 to 1892-3 is shown as follows:—

Year.	Matricular Contributions (exclusive of the Amounts determined by Supplementary Budget, but exclusive of the equivalent for Beer Excise)	Assignments derived from Customs, &c.	Assignments compared to Matricular Contributions.
1879-80	2,[illegible]	101,[illegible]	− 2,[illegible]
1880-81	3,[illegible]	1,818,[illegible]	− 1,[illegible]
1881-82	4,[illegible],104	2,[illegible],319	− [illegible]
1882-83	4,[illegible]	4,172,[illegible]	− [illegible]
1883-84	3,[illegible],764	4,97[illegible],105	+ 577,[illegible]
1884-85	[illegible]	[illegible]	+ 2,049,[illegible]
1885-86	[illegible]	[illegible]	+ [illegible]
1886-87	[illegible]	[illegible]	+ [illegible]
1887-88	[illegible]	[illegible]	+ [illegible]
1888-89	10,[illegible]	13,[illegible]	+ 3,[illegible]
1889-90	10,[illegible]	17,751,[illegible]	+ [illegible]
1890-91	[illegible]	18,[illegible]	+ [illegible]
1891-92	17,[illegible]	19,[illegible]	+ [illegible]
1892-93	16,[illegible]	17,[illegible]	+ 2,141,164

In a Memorandum attached to a new Bill for the improvement of the financial system, submitted to the Reichstag during the present session, it is stated:—

"Except for some fluctuations in 1879-80 to 1884, both the matricular contributions and the assignments have increased largely in amounts from 1884 to 1891-92.

"For the financial year 1893-94 the matricular contributions amount (inclusive of their increase by supplementary Budget of July 1893, of over one million sterling to cover the half-yearly army increase) to 18,[illegible], or, roughly, exclusive of the above-mentioned army increase, 1,500,000l. in excess of the previous year.

"The assignments, which also up to 1891-92 became constantly larger, showed in 1892-3 a diminution, compared to the preceding year, from 19,165,000l. to 17,912,000l., and, for the year 1893-4, they were estimated at about 17,450,000l. The excess of assignments over matricular contributions has been reduced from 5,[illegible] in 1889-90, to 2,138,000l. in 1892-3.

"For the year 1893-4 the excess would, according to the estimate, have amounted to only 130,000l., if the above-mentioned army increase expenses are not taken into account. In consequence of these expenses having been charged to the matricular contributions for six months only, the total assignments are reduced to 1,010,000l. less than the matricular contributions.

"In view of the fact that the available revenue does not increase in a corresponding amount with Imperial expenditure, the Empire, with its present sources of revenue, would have no choice but to call upon the Confederated States to increase their matricular contributions without making any increase in the assignments.

"Were this done, the object of the Franckenstein Clause, which gave to the Confederated States the surplus from Imperial revenues, would be frustrated.

"Further, should it prove in the future, as seems inevitable from the experience of the last years, that the matricular contributions continue to increase in excess of the assignments, then the Confederated States will no longer be in a position to satisfy the demands made upon them, and will be compelled to resort to borrowing.

"The finances of the States have been arranged for years past upon the certainty of assignments being in excess of matricular contributions. Not only does their expenditure rise side by side with the matricular contributions, but they have reduced their revenue, particularly by the abolition and diminution of direct taxes, duties, &c. for the relief of the poorer classes. The deficits which have resulted from these causes, and which appear likely in the future to assume larger proportions, cannot be met by the Confederated States, in view of the increasing claims of the Empire.

"Sources of indirect taxation are closed to them for the benefit of the Empire; direct taxation is in most cases carried as far as possible, and any increase to be hoped for on the score of increasing prosperity must necessarily be both slow and limited in degree.

"If, then, the Confederated States are to be saved from grave financial difficulties, the Imperial Budget must be placed in a position to meet the budgets of the States from its revenues, at least to a moderate extent. It is in the political and financial interest both of the Empire and of the Confederated States to adjust the financial conditions of the Empire in such a way as to render this possible. A state of affairs which prevents the Empire from assisting the Confederated States, and still more, one which throws difficulties in the way of any fixity of arrangement and adjustment of their finances on account of the rise and fluctuation of the demands, would be attended with grave danger.

"By the Clause Franckenstein and subsequent legislation, the bond of union between Imperial and State finances was not only maintained but strengthened and developed. The annual assignments and matricular contributions were made dependent, the former on customs receipts and special taxes, and the latter according to special requirements; and the whole risk of fluctuation both on the amounts of revenue and in relation of these amounts to the matricular contributions is thrown, not on the Empire, but on the Confederated States.

"It is above all in the interest of the Confederated States that these serious fluctuations between assignments and matricular contributions must be restricted.

"It has been already seen how large these fluctuations have been since 1879-80. If only the years are taken into account in which the assignments exceed the matricular contributions, the amounts are seen to vary from 5,[illegible] in 1889-90 to 283,000l. in 1883-4.

"The uncertainty to which the Budgets of the Confederated States are exposed is still heightened by the frequent augmentation of the matricular contributions, as originally estimated, by means of a supplementary Budget. These augmentations during the last five years have been as follows:—

	£
1889-90	449,[illegible]
1890-91	2,[illegible]
1891-92	[illegible]
1892-93	385,[illegible]
1893-94	1,[illegible]

"The manner in which the estimated amount of Assignments is altered before the final account is shown by the following table:—

Year	Estimate	Final Amount	Comparison of Estimate with Final Account
1879-80		401,[illegible]	+ 401,[illegible]
1880-81	2,[illegible]	1,818,[illegible]	− 113,[illegible]
1881-82	2,[illegible]	2,[illegible],319	+ [illegible]
1882-83	4,[illegible]	4,172,[illegible]	− [illegible]
1883-84	4,[illegible]	4,97[illegible]	+ [illegible]
1884-85	4,[illegible]	5,[illegible]	+ [illegible]
1885-86	5,[illegible]	5,[illegible]	+ [illegible]
1886-87	7,[illegible]	6,[illegible]	− [illegible]
1887-88	7,[illegible]	8,[illegible]	+ 1,[illegible]
1888-89	12,[illegible]	13,[illegible]	+ [illegible]
1889-90	14,[illegible]	17,751,[illegible]	+ 2,[illegible]
1890-91	17,[illegible]	18,[illegible]	+ 1,[illegible]
1891-92	16,[illegible]	19,[illegible]	+ 2,[illegible]
1892-93	11,[illegible]	17,[illegible]	+ [illegible]

"The object in view can only be attained if the matricular contributions are placed in a fixed relation to the assignments, in such a manner that, if the final account exceeds the estimate (in consequence of a surplus from customs duties, &c. over the estimated totals), the surplus should go to the Empire, and that, on the other hand, if the final amount is less than the estimate (in consequence of customs duties, &c. falling short of the estimate), a corresponding amount of the matricular contribution should not be levied."

The above extracts have been quoted at length in order to show the effect of the present financial system upon the Empire and upon the Confederated States.

In view of the unsatisfactory complications arrived at, fresh legislation on the subject is, in the opinion of the Imperial Government, urgently required.

In the second session of 1893–4, a Bill was submitted to the Reichstag for the improvement of the financial system of the Empire, but was dropped, after being read a first time and then referred to Committee.

In the present session, January [illegible], 1895, a new Bill, of which the following is a translation, has been submitted to the Reichstag:—

Bill respecting the further improvement of the finance system of the Empire.

We, William, by the grace of God German Emperor, King of Prussia, &c., ordain in the name of the Empire, with the consent of the Federal Council and the Reichstag, as follows:—

The provisions shall come into force from April 1, 1895, till March 31, 1901 (?).

Paragraph I. Matricular contributions, exclusive of the special supplementary contributions (*Ergänzungsbeiträge*), payable by the Confederated States to the Imperial Treasury, shall be included in the Imperial Budget for each financial year, at a sum not exceeding the estimated total assignments (*Ueberweisungen*), made over to the Confederated States according to law which are derived from customs, tobacco duties, Imperial stamp duties, and excise on brandy, as well as the [illegible] in the same.

Should the receipts from these sources exceed the estimated amount for a financial year, the surplus shall be credited to the Empire, and the amounts to be handed over to the Confederated States from customs, &c. are reduced in proportion to the total population, which formed the basis of the original apportionment.

If the assignments for the financial year do not, in the final account, reach an equivalent of the amount of the matricular contributions fixed in the Imperial Budget, a corresponding amount of the latter shall not be levied, and shall be deducted from the estimated matricular contributions of the Confederated States according to the proportion of their contributions, exclusive of the supplementary contributions mentioned in Paragraph I.

Paragraph II. Any surplus in the final account of the Imperial Budget shall be devoted to a special fund, which shall provide for any deficit that may subsequently arise.

Paragraph III. When this fund, described in Paragraph II (*Ausgleichungsfonds*), has reached the sum of 40 million marks (2,000,000*l.*), any additions to it beyond that sum shall be devoted to the redemption of Imperial loans.

Detailed provisions with regard to the disposal of the surplus will be contained in the Budget law.

Paragraph IV. The Imperial Chancellor shall administer the fund described in II. The capital of this fund shall be invested only in State obligations and Treasury Bills. Interest to be added to the fund.

The amount of the fund and any fluctuations which occur shall be communicated to the Federal Council and the Reichstag at their regular yearly sessions.

Paragraph V. To cover the deficit in the Imperial Budget resulting from the recurring and non-recurring expenditure of the ordinary Budget, so far as the provisions of II of this law do not come into operation, the stamp and excise duties accruing to the Empire may be increased.

The provisions as to what duties may be increased, to what amount and for what length of time, are contained in a special law.

The second part of the Reform is the Tobacco Duty Bill, which was submitted to the Reichstag on January [illegible], 1895. This introduces an ad valorem duty on manufactured tobacco, which is fixed at 25 per cent. for cigars and cigarettes, and 40 per cent. for smoking, chewing, and snuff tobacco. Statistics are published in the *exposé des motifs* appended to the new Bill, showing that, in all other European countries tobacco is taxed considerably higher than in the German Empire. By the Tobacco Duty Law of 1879, the yearly receipts from tobacco amounted to 2,000,000*l.* During 1893–4 they amounted to about 2,100,000*l.* In Great Britain and Ireland the receipts from tobacco duties are put down in 1892–3 at 10,[illegible]*l.*

The present Bill claims that an increase of 1,[illegible]*l.* will be thereby obtained.

The new Finance Bill was read a first time on Tuesday, February [illegible], and was then referred to the Committee on Tobacco Taxation.

Prussia.

TABLE I.—ESTIMATED REVENUE for the Year 1893–4.*

Description	Amount
	£
Ministry of Agriculture—	
Woods and forests	[illegible]
Agriculture	[illegible]
Stud farms	[illegible]
Ministry of Finance—	
Direct taxes	9,[illegible]
Indirect taxes	[illegible]
Lotteries	[illegible]
Seehandlung	[illegible]
Ministry of Commerce and Industry—	
Mines and salines	[illegible]
Ministry of Public Works—	
State railways	46,[illegible]
General Finance Administration—	
Customs duties and tobacco tax†	[illegible]
Tax on spirits	[illegible]
Stamp duties	[illegible]
Moneys on deposit	[illegible]
Sundries	[illegible]
Ministry of Justice	[illegible]
" the Interior	[illegible]
Various administrative departments	[illegible]
Extraordinary revenue	[illegible]
Total	[illegible]

* Published in No. [illegible], F.O. Annual Series, 1894.
† Handed over to Prussia by the Imperial Treasury.

Prussia.

TABLE II.—ESTIMATED ORDINARY EXPENDITURE for the Year 1893–4.

Description	Amount
	£
Department of Agriculture—	
Woods and forests	[illegible]
Department of Finance—	
Collection of direct taxes	[illegible]
" indirect "	[illegible]
Lotteries	[illegible]
Management of mints	[illegible]
Department of Commerce and Industry—	
Mines and salines	[illegible]
Department of Public Works—	
State railways	[illegible]
Endowments and General Finance Administration—	
Endowment to the annual income of the Crown	[illegible]
Interest on National Debt	[illegible]
Sinking Fund	[illegible]
Annuities	[illegible]
Expenses of management	[illegible]
House of Peers	[illegible]
Chamber of Deputies	[illegible]
Prussia's contribution to the Imperial Budget	[illegible]
Appanages, annuities, compensations, allowances, and subventions	[illegible]
Ministry of State	[illegible]
Ministry for Foreign Affairs—	
Foreign Office	[illegible]
Prussian Diplomatic Service	[illegible]

Description.	Amount.
Ministry of Finance—	£
Pensions	[illegible]
Salaries of officials, widows' and orphans' institutions, office expenses, reserved fund, &c.	[illegible]
Ministry of Public Works	[illegible]
Ministry of Commerce and Industry	[illegible]
Ministry of Justice—	
Upper district courts	[illegible]
Provincial courts of justice	[illegible]
Disbursements in civil and criminal cases	[illegible]
Office expenses and sundry disbursements	[illegible]
Ministry of the Interior—	
Buda police	[illegible]
Provincial police administration	[illegible]
Provincial police	[illegible]
Criminal administration	[illegible]
Officials and employés of provincial courts of justice	[illegible]
Other and sundry expenses	[illegible]
Ministry of Agriculture, Woods and Forests—	
General expenses of administration, agricultural schools, cattle breeding, fish breeding, veterinary schools, and other State concerns	[illegible]
Stud farm	[illegible]
Ministry of Education and of Sundry and Ecclesiastical Affairs—	
Elementary education	[illegible]
Universities	[illegible]
Higher educational establishments	[illegible]
Schools combining religious and other instruction	[illegible]
Art and science	[illegible]
Technical education	[illegible]
Evangelical church and clergy	[illegible]
Roman Catholic church, bishops, and clergy	[illegible]
Office and sundry other expenses	[illegible]
Ministry of War—	
Buda armoury	[illegible]
Total	[illegible]

TABLE III.—BOSNIAN EXTRAORDINARY EXPENDITURE for the Year 1893–4.

Description.	Amount.
	£
Ministry of Finance	[illegible]
Pensions	[illegible]
Ministry of Public Works—	
Railway administration	[illegible]
Management of roads and public buildings	[illegible]
Ministry of Commerce and Industry	[illegible]
Justice	[illegible]
the Interior	[illegible]
Ministry of Agriculture, Woods and Forests—	
Woods	[illegible]
Forests	[illegible]
Agriculture	[illegible]
Stud farm	[illegible]
Ministry of Education and of Ecclesiastical and Sundry Affairs	[illegible]
Ministry of War	[illegible]
Total	[illegible]

DETAILS of BUDGET of IMPERIAL REVENUE for 1894–95.*

Item.	Description.		Estimated Revenue, 1894–95.
			£
I.	Customs and excise—		
	(1) Revenue shared by all the Reichsrath States:—		
	Customs duties		[illegible]
	Tobacco duty		[illegible]
	Sugar tax		[illegible]
	Salt		[illegible]
	Brandy tax		[illegible]
	(2) Revenue not shared by Bavaria, Württemberg, Baden, and Alsace-Lorraine:—		
	Beer tax		[illegible]
	(3) Receipts from increase against the Reichsrath:—		
	(a) Revenue shared by all Reichsrath States (as above)		[illegible]
	(b) Beer tax, not shared by South Germany and Alsace-Lorraine		[illegible]
II.	Stamp duties—		
	On playing cards		[illegible]
	On bills of exchange		[illegible]
	On shares, coupons, and bonds		[illegible]
	On sales and other transactions		[illegible]
	On lottery tickets (State and private)		[illegible]
	On stamped bills		[illegible]
III.	Post and Telegraph Administration—	£	
	Gross receipts	[illegible]	
	Expenses	[illegible]	
			[illegible]
IV.	Printing department—		
	Gross receipts	[illegible]	
	Expenses	[illegible]	
			[illegible]
V.	Railways—		
	Gross receipts	[illegible]	
	Expenses	[illegible]	
			[illegible]
VI.	Imperial Bank		[illegible]
VII.	Sundry receipts from administration and other sources		[illegible]
VIII.	Imperial invalid fund		[illegible]
IX.	Interest on Reichstag Palace building fund		[illegible]
X.	Sundry receipts, sale of portions of ground		[illegible]
XI.	Balance from Budget of past financial years		[illegible]
XII.	Contributions from Constituent States		[illegible]
XIII.	Extraordinary revenue		[illegible]
	Total		[illegible]

* Published in No. 1838, F.O. Annual Series 1895.

TABLE showing IMPERIAL EXPENDITURE for 1894–5, as compared with FIGURES of previous Year.

Item	Description	1894–5 Per annum Ordinary	1894–5 Non-recurring Ordinary and Extra-ordinary	1893–4 Per annum Ordinary	1893–4 Non-recurring Ordinary and Extra-ordinary
		£	£	£	£
I	[illegible]				
II	[illegible]	[illegible]		[illegible]	—
III	[illegible]	[illegible]	[illegible]	[illegible]	
IV	[illegible]	[illegible]	[illegible]	[illegible]	[illegible]
V	Home Office	[illegible]	[illegible]	[illegible]	[illegible]
VI	Army and [illegible]	[illegible]	[illegible]	[illegible]	[illegible]
VII	Admiralty and Navy	[illegible]	[illegible]	[illegible]	[illegible]
VIII	Justice*	[illegible]	[illegible]	[illegible]	[illegible]
IX	Treasury	[illegible]	[illegible]	[illegible]	[illegible]
X	Imperial Bank [illegible]	[illegible]	—	[illegible]	
XI	Imperial Debt [illegible]	[illegible]		[illegible]	—
XII	Audit Office	[illegible]	—	[illegible]	—
XIII	General Pension Fund	[illegible]		[illegible]	—
XIV	Imperial Invalid Fund	[illegible]	—	[illegible]	—
XV	[illegible]	[illegible]		—	—
XVI	Post and Telegraphs	—	[illegible]	—	[illegible]
XVII	Printing Office	—	[illegible]	—	[illegible]
XVIII	Administration of Railways		[illegible]		[illegible]
	Total	[illegible]	[illegible]	[illegible]	[illegible]

* [illegible]

SWEDEN AND NORWAY.

Sweden and Norway present an instance of two countries united by the Crown and by nothing else. They have not, like the German Empire and that of Austria-Hungary, a common revenue derived from customs and other sources, and supplemented by contributions from the component States based upon a fixed principle of assessment.

It will be seen from the following statement, prepared by Her Majesty's Minister at Stockholm, that if for a time certain proportions have been observed in the payments made by Norway towards the Civil List and Diplomatic and Consular expenses, such observance has been voluntary, and of late has been interrupted.

MEMORANDUM.

"In the United Kingdoms of Sweden and Norway the objects of common expenditure are:—

(1.) The Civil List of the Royal Family.

The Swedish Riksdag and the Norwegian Storthing vote their contributions separately. The proportion between the contributions of each Kingdom is not fixed, and before 1893 the allowances have during a number of years been nearly corresponding to the proportions between the two countries' populations, viz., about [illegible] from Sweden and [illegible] from Norway.

"In Sweden the amount voted at the beginning of the reign of the present King was raised in [illegible] in consequence of the marriage of the Crown Prince.

"In Norway a corresponding amount was allowed in [illegible], but for the financial years July [illegible] to June 30, [illegible], the Norwegian Storthing reduced in [illegible] and [illegible] the allowance for the King from [illegible] crowns to [illegible], or by [illegible], and for the Crown Prince from [illegible] crowns to [illegible], or by [illegible].

(2.) Diplomatic Budget.

"The Minister of Foreign Affairs reports the budget each year in a council composed by members of the Cabinets of both countries. The amount asked is divided, according to existing custom, between both countries in proportion to the populations at the rate of [illegible] for Sweden and [illegible] for Norway.

"Thereafter the King decides in the council of each country to make propositions to Riksdag and Storthing.

"After July 1 of the present year ([illegible]) no contribution from Norway to diplomatic expenses has been received.

(3.) Consular Budget.

"The contributions are direct State allowances and consular tonnage dues and fees. The proportion between the State allowances of each country are determined in the Consular Ordinance, section [illegible], to four-sevenths for Sweden and three-sevenths for Norway, on the basis of a calculation made by the Consular Commission of [illegible].* There is no stipulation concerning the amount of the State allowances, but during a number of years these allowances have been [illegible] crowns from Sweden and [illegible] crowns from Norway.

"In the last Budget the contributions of consular tonnage dues and fees were estimated at [illegible] crowns from Sweden and [illegible] crowns from Norway. The reason why these contributions are greater from Norway than from Sweden is that the navigation of Norway is larger than that of Sweden. On the other side the direct State allowance is, as previously noticed, larger from Sweden than from Norway, in consequence of the larger population and commerce of Sweden.

"In the last Budget the contribution of each country to the Consular Budget, State allowances and consular dues and fees included, has been estimated at [illegible] crowns from Sweden and [illegible] crowns from Norway, showing a proportion between the contributions of about three-sevenths from Sweden and four-sevenths from Norway. When the State allowances and consular dues and fees together attain a larger amount than that required for the Consular Budget the exceeding part is paid back to each country in proportion to the whole contribution of each country to the consular fund of the Foreign Office, as well as of State allowances as to consular dues and fees.

"After July 1, [illegible], the ordinary Norwegian State allowance has not been received, but the Norwegian Government has declared that as far as expenses legally incumbent on the Norwegian State, and connected with the common consular service of the United Kingdoms, cannot be covered by consular dues and fees contributed to the common consular fund of the Foreign Office, the remaining part will be paid by the Norwegian Treasury.

"Stockholm,

"December, 1894."

* [illegible]

SWITZERLAND.

The Federal revenue of Switzerland is now derived from customs and non-tax revenue and the Confederation has no power to levy direct taxes on individuals.

In certain contingencies, which have not yet occurred, the several cantons are liable to be called upon for special contributions to Federal expenditure, and the principle upon which the cantons should be assessed has been a subject of inquiry.

It appears from the information furnished by Her Majesty's Minister at Berne that the Federal Constitution of [illegible], by its [illegible] Article, provided that the contributions of the cantons to Federal expenditure shall be paid upon a scale which should be revised every [illegible] years upon the basis of the population of the several cantons and their wealth and productive capacities. The difficulty of ascertaining relative wealth and productive capacity led to the appointment of a Parliamentary Committee to inquire into this question. In its Report ([illegible] April [illegible]) the Committee pointed out the difficulties of this task, and suggested certain amendments to the then existing scale. For this purpose, they said, it was necessary "to make oneself familiar with all the "different circumstances which have to be taken into "consideration in order to form a judgment upon the economic situation of a canton, thus, using a free judgment, and without taking too rigorous a basis, to tax each canton according to a certain test."

The suggestions of this Commission were carried into effect by the Federal Law of 9th July 1851, which divided the cantons into [illegible] classes, rated from [illegible] centimes to [illegible] francs per head of their total population. After an interval of [illegible] years this arrangement was continued by a resolution of the Federal Assembly on the 12th July 1861.

Under the revised Constitution of 1874, Article 42, after directing to meet the expenses of the Confederation the Customs, posts and telegraphs, and other indirect or non-tax revenues, it is provided that in the contingency (which has not happened) of these proving insufficient, these expenses shall be met by contributions from the cantons, which shall be regulated by Federal legislation, having regard especially to their wealth and taxable resources (their richesse et de leurs ressources imposables).

On the 7th October 1874 the Federal Council addressed a message to the Federal Assembly, in which, after pointing out the difficulty of finding any single exact test of the relative means of cantons, some of which raised their own revenue chiefly by direct and others by indirect taxation, and others again partly from public property, and whose modes of expenditure are as diverse as their sources of revenue, it was concluded that, in accordance with the opinion of the Committee of 1851, the scale of contributions could not be established upon a mathematical basis, but must be determined in accordance with a certain appreciation (d'après une certaine appréciation). The Council suggested certain alterations in the existing scale, based upon economic changes in the conditions of the several cantons, and their suggestions were carried into effect by the Federal Law of 9th March 1875, the contingents then being fixed for a period of 20 years. The [illegible] cantons are under this law divided into eight classes, which are variously assessed at from 10 to [illegible] centimes per head of population.

The period of 20 years, from the 9th March 1875, being about to expire, it became necessary either to revise the scale or to continue it for either a definite or an indefinite period. A message was addressed on the [illegible] February 1895 by the Federal Council to the Federal Assembly proposing not to proceed, at present, to a revision of the existing scale. The reasons given in the message are (1) the difficulty of estimating the relative taxable capacity (Täxbarkeit, responsabilité) of cantons possessing such different forms of taxation; (2) the quarrels and discussions to which such a revision might lead; (3) the fact that in ordinary cases there will, probably, never be any necessity to call for the cantonal contributions.

On consideration of that message, the Federal Assembly have resolved (subject to the result of a referendum if demanded) to maintain in force for an indefinite period the scale fixed by the Federal Law of 9th March 1875.

It is to be remembered that circumstances have not as yet rendered any cantonal contributions under this scale necessary, and that the provisions is not likely to come into force, except in case of a war.

APPENDIX XVII.

Note.—With a view to completeness it has seemed to be desirable to print the following extract from a speech by Lord Clare, in addition to the extracts from other speeches relating to the financial clauses in the Act of Union, and already published in the first volume of Evidence and Appendices.

B. H. HOLLAND, Secretary.

June 1895.

Extract from Speech by Earl of Clare, Lord High Chancellor of Ireland, in the House of Lords of Ireland, February 10th, 1800.

"Look to your finances, and I repeat you have not redemption for three years from public bankruptcy, or a burthen of taxation which will sink every gentleman of property in the country.

"Perhaps it will occasion some surprise to hear that the debt of Ireland is now 25,6[illegible], and that the annual interest and charges upon it amount to 1,[illegible]. In stating the debt of Ireland, I speak of the capital created, not the money paid into the Exchequer by the public creditor. If I am compelled to borrow money on onerous terms, my debt is the sum which I contract to pay, not the sum which I may happen to have received, and therefore it is a gross deception in stating the public debt to take it on any calculation but of the capital for which the nation must stand security. The increase of debt in the last seven years has been: principal, 23,[illegible]; interest and charges in the same period increase, 1,[illegible].

"Of these 23,[illegible] of increase in the capital of your debt during the last seven years, no less a sum than 18,[illegible] has accumulated in the years 1798, 1799, and 1800, the interest and charges in the same three years amount to [illegible], and on recurring to the fluctuations in your debt for the last 10 years, it will be seen to have kept exact pace with the distraction of the councils of Ireland in the cause of dignity and independence.

25th of March.	Principal.	Interest and Charges.
	£	£
1791, the debt was	2,44[illegible]	14[illegible]
1792 "	2,44[illegible]	1[illegible]
1793 "	2,44[illegible]	1[illegible]
1794 "	3,1[illegible]	17[illegible]
1795 "	4,[illegible]	[illegible]
1796 "	[illegible]	[illegible]
1797 "	7,[illegible]	[illegible]
1798 "	11,[illegible]	7[illegible]
1799 "	17,[illegible]	1,[illegible]
1800 "	25,[illegible]	1,[illegible]

"In 1793, at the beginning of the war, the debt of Ireland was 2,44[illegible], and so long as we had none but a foreign enemy to contend with, our war expenses were scarcely 1,000,000*l.* in the year. In 1795 the debt was 4,[illegible], so that during the first two years of the war, it did not increase quite 2,0[illegible]; but the old Irish custom of pressing forward political claims in times of common danger and calamity, was again maintained in 1795, a period peculiarly suited for it, for by that year the French had made themselves masters of Brabant, Flanders, and Holland, and the rebel government of United Irishmen was pretty well established. Mr. Oliver Bond and Mr. Neilson stated before the Secret Committee of this House, that the military organisation of the province of Ulster was completed on the 1st May 1795, and had got into a state of forwardness in the other provinces before the end of that year; it was, therefore, found necessary to increase the military force of the country for mere internal defence against a confederacy of foreign and domestic enemies, and accordingly, in the year ended at Lady Day 1796, our war expenses were double what they had been in either of the preceding years; and in every subsequent year they have progressively increased with the growth of faction and rebellion, until we were obliged, in defence of our own existence, to increase the public debt in the last year nearly 4,500,000l., and in this year above 5,000,000l. And this expense must necessarily continue, not to enable Ireland to contribute to offensive war, but to keep down the brutal fury of the mass of the Irish people who have been goaded to madness by every wicked artifice that disappointed faction can devise, and to protect the country from foreign invasion, equally solicited by a gang of Irish traitors who have connected themselves with the rulers of the French Republic; and if we are to continue this scale of expense for the next three years, a revenue of 2,[illegible]l. must be raised for payment of the interest of the public debt alone, or public bankruptcy will necessarily ensue.

"Let us now see what is the present state of our revenue. In the last year the net revenue of Ireland, including the loan fund, was 1,8[illegible]l. only; if it had continued at the same amount in this year the surplus, after defraying the interest and charges of the debt, would have been under [illegible]l. for the support of all your other establishments; but if the current quarter keeps up to the produce of the last three, your net revenue in this year will be somewhat about 2,700,000l. A considerable portion, however, of the great increase in the revenue of this year has been adventitious. During the rebellion importation was checked, the deficiency has of course come into this year's accounts, and there has been an unusual importation of Portugal wines in consequence of the apprehensions of increased duties entertained in this country; and therefore I consider it to be a sanguine calculation that the produce of our present revenue is to continue at 2,500,000l.

	£
The capital created by the loan of last year is	5,[illegible],100
Interest and charges	345,000
1801, capital	5,[illegible],100
Interest and charges	345,000
1802, capital	5,[illegible],100
Interest and charges	345,000
1803, capital	5,[illegible],100
Interest and charges	345,100
Capital, three years	[illegible]
Interest and charges	1,035,000
Present debt	[illegible]
Present interest and charges	1,395,733
Total capital 1803	[illegible]
Total interest 1803	2,430,733

"On this calculation the produce of your present revenue to continue at 2,500,000l., there will remain at the end of three years, on your present scale of expense, a surplus only of 70,000l. for the whole of the establishment—civil and military. Let me ask, if we remain as we are, how is this enormous deficit to be made up? Can you raise an additional revenue in Ireland of more than 1,000,000l. in the present state of our resources without recurring to a land-tax or an income-tax, or both? And, if recourse be had to land or income, the [illegible] in those taxes [illegible] considerably more than the actual deficit, I should say it would not be much less than 2,000,000l. For either tax would inevitably diminish in a great proportion your customs and excise. If we make up the deficit by annual loans, bankruptcy is inevitable. By misapplying the sinking fund you may postpone the period of insolvency for a year or two at the expense of a breach of faith with the public creditors, but bankruptcy is the ultimate issue. I know it is the fashion to say that England has our war expenses to answer for, and that our financial difficulties arise from a French war, and a Dutch war, and a Spanish war. No, our present difficulties arise from an Irish war, a war of faction, a Whig war, and an United Irishmen's war; the increase of your debt for the last 10 years proves the fact, and if England was at peace at this hour with all the Powers of Europe your establishments would be a melancholy proof of the fact: you would be compelled to maintain a war establishment for defence against your own people. It has been demanded triumphantly, how we are to be relieved by Union? I answer, first we are to be relieved from British and Irish faction, which is the prime source of all our calamities. Next, if we incorporate our people with England the army of the Empire will be employed where it is most wanted for general service, and so long as it is found necessary to garrison every district in Ireland for the internal safety of the country, the necessary force may be stationed here without incurring additional expense to either country. And, therefore, in time of war we may hope to be relieved from the separate expense entailed upon Ireland by domestic treason, and in peace it [illegible] to the general service of the Empire where the army may be quartered. Again, by Union, the resources of Ireland must necessarily increase; if we have but grace to remain in a state of tranquillity for a few years, I have no doubt our resources would augment most rapidly; if we have but grace to abjure faction, I feel sanguine hope on the restoration of peace that Ireland will participate in British capital and British industry; and until we can find employment for the poor, and teach them to feel and value the comforts of life, it is vain to expect that they will be reclaimed from barbarism."

APPENDIX XVIII.

Memorandum as to the Terms on which Government Loans are made for Public Works in Ireland and particularly for the Building, &c. of Lunatic Asylums, by John Ribton Garstin, J.P. and D.L., M.A., &c. (Braganstown, Castlebellingham.)

Submitted, by desire of the governors of the "Richmond" (or Metropolitan) district, to the Royal Commission on the Financial Relations between Great Britain and Ireland, May 1895.

"The maintenance (as well as the housing) of pauper lunatics in Ireland was (under the Acts 1 & 2 Geo. IV. c. 33 and 18 & 19 Vict. c. 109) for many years provided for [illegible] out of the local tax known as county cess, which is assessed on lands and houses. Consequently, incomes derived from other sources escaped contributing for these purposes. This anomaly was partially corrected in 1874, and since then a capitation grant of 4s. per head per week has been granted by Parliament out of Imperial taxation in respect of each patient. This amount was supposed to be about equivalent to the local contribution, and it is still so in some country districts where the cost of maintenance has not varied much, but in many districts it now falls far short of supplying one half of the cost of maintenance, and should be raised by about one-fifth if that proportion is to be restored. In 1893 the total Government grant was 112,221l., as against 1[illegible]l. raised locally

The money requisite for the building and equipment of the asylums throughout Ireland for the housing of the lunatics is advanced on loan, under the Acts already cited, from funds at the disposal of the Treasury, repayments being charged exclusively on the county cess. Previous to 1877, when the Public Works Loans Act (40 & 41 Vict. c. 27, s. 3) was passed, these loans were managed in Ireland by the Paymaster-General's Office, and were granted free of interest, the capital being repayable in 20 annual or 40 half-yearly instalments. This exemption from interest operated, like the capitation grant for maintenance, to relieve the burthen on real property, and was in aid from Imperial taxation. Under the Act of 1877, however, a new system was introduced and interest was charged. The loans were made extinguishable, by annuities of fixed amount payable during 14 years by 28 equal half-yearly instalments. The interest was calculated at 3½ per cent., and added to the allowance for extinguishing the principal. These together were equivalent to 8l. 5s. 2d. per cent. per annum. This was included in the county cess, and secured by compulsory presentments. The total amount of these loans advanced by Government up to the 31st of March 1877, free of interest, was 1,181,[illegible]. Of this sum there had been remitted [illegible], and there remained outstanding at that date, in course of repayment, [illegible], rather less than one-third. In the following 16 years, ending 31st March 1893, the advances increased at about the same rate, then reaching [illegible], and the amount at present outstanding, and being gradually paid off, with interest as above stated, is about one-sixth of that sum. The local distribution of these loans is shown up to date in a table appended, which was obligingly compiled for me by direction of the Commissioners of Public Works.

It recently became evident that, owing to the great and rapid increase in the number of lunatics, it would be necessary in the near future to provide largely increased accommodation. The board of the Richmond district found themselves confronted by the necessity for expending sums which are now estimated as likely to reach [illegible] plus [illegible], in fact, for their district alone, an amount far exceeding that of the debt still outstanding for all the asylums in Ireland. The Richmond district is only one of [illegible] into which Ireland is divided, but it is the most important, being formed of Dublin city and county, added to the counties of Wicklow and Louth, with Drogheda town. Its present asylum in Dublin (between the North Dublin Workhouse and the Royal Barracks) houses a lunatic population of over [illegible], rapidly increasing and likely to be augmented by the addition of the lunatics of the several workhouses. In view of this serious responsibility, the governors resolved on 17th January 1893 (on the motion of the writer), to endeavour to obtain from Government the necessary advances on better terms as to repayment, and at a more equitable rate of interest, having regard to the altered circumstances of the money market.

In the first place, they approached the Board of Control, which is a Government board—practically a branch of the Board of Works—specially entrusted with the issue and administration of these loans. They were received with much sympathy by that board, and Mr. Justice Holmes, the chairman, not only promised to represent the case favourably to the Treasury, but he addressed a letter to the Richmond Board, from which the following is an extract:—

"The Board of Control are deeply impressed with the importance of the subject. In their communications with the governors of provincial asylums they have found that the greatest obstacle in the way of providing adequately for the insane poor, is the necessity of repaying in a few years expenditure for permanent purposes, the benefit of which will extend over half a century. The increase of mental disease makes this a pressing question . . . . Having regard to the ample security which the county cess affords for such loans and the substantial nature of the buildings, the Board of Control are prepared, by the strongest expression of opinion, to support any steps taken to obtain by legislation terms equally favourable as those granted under Acts" for other public loans (specified).

Notwithstanding this powerful expression of opinion redress was not obtained, and it was found that without further legislation satisfactory terms could not be granted by the Treasury. It was, consequently, decided by the Richmond Board, in concert with representatives from the Belfast, Antrim, Londonderry, and Armagh Boards, to apply to the Irish Government, and on the [illegible] of June 1893 a deputation placed the case before the Under Secretary, Sir David Harrel, the press not being present.

The result was so far satisfactory, that a short Act, "The Public Works Loans (No. 2) Act, 1893," was introduced in Parliament by the Secretary of the Treasury, and received the Royal assent on the [illegible] of December following. It enacted that the term for repayment might be extended to 50 years, and that these loans should bear interest at 3¼ per cent, "or such other rate as may, in the judgment of the Treasury, be necessary to enable the loans to be made without loss to the Exchequer" (56 & 57 Vict. c. [illegible] s. 3).

In pursuance of that Act, the Treasury altered the rules regulating these loans to the following as notified by circular in June last (after the lapse of six months), by the Board of Works, which administers the Treasury loans in Ireland:—

"1. (a) Loans for permanent works and buildings, or for the acquisition of land, or for any outlay incurred in connection therewith, &c.:—

If repaid within [illegible] years, at [illegible] per cent. per annum.

If repaid within 50 years at 3½ per cent. per annum.

(b) Loans for furniture, fittings, &c.:—

Maximum period for repayment, [illegible] years at [illegible] per cent. per annum.

2. The principal to be repayable by equal half-yearly instalments on the balance from time to time outstanding."

The Irish Government issued a circular to boards of governors of asylums ([illegible] September, 1894), stating that these "favourable terms" had been granted by the Treasury (on their strong representations), "in view of considerations peculiar to the case of lunatic asylum loans," and "only for so long as in the judgment of the Treasury they continue to be such as will secure the Exchequer from loss." The ratepayers may bear a loss so long as the Exchequer is safe. The terms are doubtless "favourable," but not to them.

Disappointing as were the terms authorised by the Act as regards the rates of interest fixed, the Government appears to have been unwilling to give the ratepayers the full benefit conceded by Parliament, for, in notifying the Treasury sanction to a loan to buy land for a site for the Richmond Auxiliary Asylum, at Portrane, the Board of Control, writing on the [illegible] of March 1894, said, "the loan will be repayable in 50 years, with interest at the rate of 3½ per cent." (besides, of course, the instalment of principal) that is actually ¼ per cent. over the then existing rate, which the governors regard as exorbitant. And though this higher rate is charged (without any apparent reason), the loan was not extended to the full term sanctioned by the Treasury for loans charged at that rate until after remonstrance from the governors.

The inadequacy of the concession made by the Treasury led to several protests from public bodies affected, and the Lord Mayor of Dublin convened a meeting of representative governors of Irish asylums to arrange for further action, and to interview the Chief Secretary, as suggested in a circular issued by Colonel Cooper, H.M.L., Chairman of the Sligo Board, and by the Richmond Board, as proposed by the writer. Accordingly, an influential deputation, introduced by the Lord Mayor, waited on Mr. Morley, at Dublin Castle, on the [illegible] of January last. The interview was fully reported by the press.

The Louth Grand Jury, finding remonstrance unavailing, refused one of the presentments at last Spring Assizes, by way of protest against the exorbitance of the rate charged (as well as against being only allowed one representative on the Richmond Board of [illegible] governors, and against having to bear part of the cost of providing for Dublin lunatics, their own space being still sufficient), and though the Board of Works officials and counsel appeared to support the presentment they failed to supply the requisite proof, and the application was refused by Chief Baron Palles.

The upshot of the deputation to the Chief Secretary, was that Mr. Morley has induced the Treasury to agree to a further reduction of ¼ per cent., leaving the rate for repayment of 50 year loans 3¼ per cent., plus [illegible] per cent. for capital. Many of the ratepayers who pay for the housing of lunatics are labourers or artisans or tenants, who, as such, are given better terms.

It will be observed that the new system applies only to new loans, and affords no relief in respect of the unexpired portion of previous loans. Also, that while extending the period for repayment, it makes the amount, taking principal and interest together, heavier at the commencement of the terms, though granting relief as regards the extension of time for repayment. Rates of repayment which may have been generous in bygone years, have now, owing to the altered state of the money market, become exorbitant.

Assuming, as is unquestionably the fact, that, with Consols at or over [illegible] ex dividend, and becoming 2½ per cent. stock in 1903, eight years hence, the Government can borrow at 2½ per cent., it is manifest that (even allowing for cost of management), the loans must be a source of profit to the Government at the cost of the Irish ratepayers, and charged solely on landed property.

It is submitted that this is unreasonable, and contrary alike to sound policy and to the professions of the Government.

The preamble of the Irish Church Disestablishment Act declares the expediency of appropriating the pro-such thereof "mainly to the relief of unavoidable calamity and suffering," and Mr. Gladstone named the lunatic asylums as having the first claim on the funds released by disestablishment, so as to relieve the over-burdened payers of county cess. To quote his speech in Committee, 1st March 1869 (Hansard, 3rd Ser., vol cxciv):—

"The wants that I speak of in Ireland are at this moment partly unsupplied, and they are partly supplied through a medium which we think defective, and which might be greatly improved. The medium I speak of is the county cess, a heavy and increasing tax . . . a tax not founded, like the poor law, to some extent on value, but going down to the most miserable hut or cabin. The holders of these most wretched tenements are now required in Ireland, and required increasingly from year to year, to pay . . . for that class of want and suffering which ought undoubtedly to be met, and which, in every great community, ought to be liberally met, but which can only be met by the expenditure of large and considerable funds in comparison with those which avail for the support of the pauperised population. Now what are these? I take first the lunatic asylums. The care of lunatics is one of the great duties of the community, and in Ireland . . . the expenditure is defrayed by the county cess, collected from the class of occupiers I have described."

Commenting so recently as 1891, on these observations of the ex-Premier, the Inspectors of Lunatics in Ireland observe (40th Report, p. 20):—

"Many charitable, educational, and industrial objects have obtained assistance from the large sums of money set free by the disendowment of the Irish Church, but, as it seems to us, by the very irony of fate, not one shilling of this money has been appropriated to the objects, then specifically indicated as affording the most just and proper application of these funds . . .

"To us, at least, it seems clear that the time has come when it is most desirable that, if possible, some such assistance should be afforded from Imperial sources, whether by grants towards necessary buildings, or by reducing the interest on loans contracted for the purpose" . . . "The disproportionately large number of lunatics is to be explained (as it seems to us, to some extent at least, by the operation of those causes, economic or other, which have led to the impoverishment of such a large portion of the population of Ireland."

The obligation of the State to provide for the care of insane poor is recognised in every civilised country as paramount, and I am told that even in Japan, asylum buildings are an Imperial charge. It will scarcely be contended that our own Government is justified in carrying on a profitable money-lending business. I have been shown a calculation that, at 3½ per cent. for 50 years, each 100l. lent produces at 3 per cent. compound interest, 155l. 0s. 3d. In the case of tenant farmers, purchasers under the Land Act, it is expressly stated in the Land Commission "Explanations," p. 7, that the rate of interest to be allowed "shall be as nearly as may be equivalent to the average rate of interest earned on the investments of the National Debt Commissioners"—a variable rate, assumed at the time to be about 2¾ per cent.

As regards the incidence of taxation for asylum building loans, it falls wholly on landed property, whereas a fair share of such burthens should be borne by other descriptions of property, as laid down by the Chancellor of the Exchequer in introducing the Finance Bill last spring, and that principle is recognised in the Government capitation grant contributed towards the maintenance of the insane in Ireland, as above explained.

In order to enable comparisons with the terms for kindred loans in England, it may be stated that, under the Housing of the Working Classes Act (53 & 54 Vict. c. 70), commonly called "Dilke's Act," the following rates are charged:—

On loans for	20 years	3¾	per cent.
"	30 "	3½	"
"	40 "	3¾	"
"	50 "	3½	"

And the rates for loans for artisans' dwellings (in England largely used) are on a somewhat similar scale, and issued on security of the buildings, and sometimes to companies by whom they can be and are worked as commercial speculations, yielding a profit.

Under the Labourers Acts, Ireland (46 & 47 Vict. c. 60 and 48 & 49, c. 77), passed in 1883, where the funds were [illegible], the rates of interest are:—On loans for 35 years, 3½; 40 years, 3¾; and 50 years, 3½ per cent., secured on the rates of the electoral division only.

Irish tenants, however, have secured the most favourable terms from Government to induce them to become owners of their farms, for advances to them, issued through the Land Commission, are extinguished—capital and interest—by the payment of 4 per cent. during 49 years. The rate for interest appears to be 2¾ per cent.

Apart from the general considerations of State policy affecting this question, the following reasons are adduced in favour of the issue of loans for lunatic asylum building, &c., in Ireland, either free of charge for interest, or at a minimum rate, and with generous terms for repayment:—

1. The loans are not voluntarily undertaken, but forced by Government on the several local areas, access to the open market being precluded, except in the case of Belfast, which obtained special power by Act of Parliament in 1892 (55 & 56 Vict.). That city as well as Dublin, if the loans could be raised on their credit (which is, of course, out of the question), could give terms better than those of the Government.
2. The expenditure of these loans is at the sole discretion of a Government board styled the "Board of Control." To quote a letter from the Chief Secretary to the governors of Kilkenny Asylum, 23rd December 1891, the considerations constituting this board "consist at present of seven members appointed by the Lord Lieutenant, viz.:—(1) a judge of the High Court of Justice, (2) the Chairman of the Board of Works, ex officio, (3 and 4) the two inspectors of lunatics and (5, 6, and 7) three non-official members" . . . "As the law now stands, neither the ratepayers nor the rating authority (? and formerly), the Grand Jury, have any control over the sums spent in erecting or enlarging district asylums." Though the public pay the piper, the Board of Control "calls the tune." If their outlay is sanctioned it is only by the advisers responsible to Government, and not by those who have to bear the cost; and if they occasionally consult the board of governors of the several asylums concerned, it is only as a matter of favour.
3. The 22 boards of governors, who have the management of the asylums when built, are appointed from year to year by the Lord Lieutenant, and, though one-half of each board is usually appointed on the recommendation of the grand juries, such nominations are not always regarded. In fact the governors are all Crown nominees, enjoying (?) Government appointment of a rather trying nature, not only without salary, but with a considerable outlay, not of time only, but in some cases also of money necessarily expended in travelling.
4. Owing to the requirements of the Board of Control as regards cubic space per inmate and land, &c., the buildings are of a more expensive and solid character than what would suffice for ordinary requirements. Under the Government rules 60 square feet, or in rooms 10 feet high, 600 cubic feet per inmate are required.
5. The security cannot be surpassed, being by imperative proceedings under Government warrant charged on each entire county. There has been no default in repayment of these loans, and the remissions have not amounted to 1 per cent.
6. That taxation falls wholly on the occupiers and owners of land, a class in Ireland, much impoverished. In the Richmond district the contemplated expenditure would largely increase the taxation of Dublin and associated counties, where the local rates are already oppressive. The advantages for pauper lunatics would probably be doubtful. It is now for Ireland over 3d. of the county cess, but in Derry and Wexford nearly 6d. in the pound.
7. The preponderance of lunacy in Ireland as compared with Great Britain and the great increase in lunacy in Ireland is partly attributable to "severe agricultural depression and destitution," and the unsettled relations of landholders in

recent years. The total number in Irish asylums in 1880 was [illegible]. It rose regularly in 10 years to [illegible]. The rate of increase is now diminishing slightly.

I understand that in England these buildings are now provided for chiefly by county councils, who may borrow in the open market, if they prefer not to take advances from the Local Loans Fund formed under the Act of 1887, and represented by Government stock paying 3 per cent., now quoted at about 10[illegible].

As regards the recent extension of the period for repaying the capital sum, a concession in the case of compulsory loans, it is fair, only if the rate of interest charged meanwhile is moderate. If otherwise, such a prolongation of payment is only the aggravation of an exaction, and is especially objectionable if proceeding from any Government professing to be paternal.

The considerations embodied in this memorandum apply to a considerable extent to other loans advanced through the Commissioners of Public Works, such as those for county purposes, public buildings, fishery piers, land improvement, glebe houses, and dispensaries, schools, libraries, &c., as shown in statement passed by the Board in December 1892, the rates of interest being now excessive, since the value of Government stock has risen so considerably of late years.

The Richmond Board of Governors will not be satisfied with any terms inferior to those granted for other public purposes of a less urgent nature, or which will allow the State to make a profit as money-lenders, and they consider that the loans for building lunatic asylums should now be supplied at [illegible] per cent., having regard to the altered state of the money market.

In conclusion, I append a letter in reply to one on this subject, addressed to the Auditor-General, premising only that the rates above referred to, cover the "expenses of administration," and that there has been no loss on the loans which the memorandum mainly relates to:—

"Somerset House, (London,)

"SIR, "December [illegible], 1894.

"The Comptroller and Auditor General directs me to acknowledge your letter of the [illegible] ult., on the subject of loans to lunatic asylums.

"The administrators of the expenditure incurred on these buildings are the Commissioners of Public Works in Ireland, and details of the advances and repayments appear in their annual reports presented to Parliament.

"The accounts of the Commissioners, including the loans, are audited in this Department, and the statement in your letter with regard to the terms of the advances and the punctuality of repayment appear to be correct.

"With regard to the disposal of the 'profit' to which you refer, you are probably aware that the Local Loans Act of 1887 placed all the transactions of the Exchequer with regard to borrowers on a new footing. The fund from which the loans are made is a stock, called the 'Local Loans' stock, on which the Government pay dividends at 3 per cent.

"There is, therefore, as you will see, a smaller margin of profit than you supposed to meet the expenses of administration.

"The apparent intention of the Chancellor of the Exchequer in bringing in the Bill was to establish an equilibrium, so that the inevitable bad debts that would occur might be met from general profits.

"I am to add that the arrangements under which the loans are sanctioned rest with the Treasury, subject to the control of Parliament.

"As a matter of fact the results of the various years' workings since 1888 have eventuated sometimes in a slight loss, and sometimes a slight profit.

"I am, Sir, yours faithfully,

"RICHARD A. [illegible]

"J. M. [illegible], Esq., J.P., D.L."

From this letter it is obvious that, as there have been no bad debts on the asylum loans, a profit must be made on them, and from the last report of the Board of Works it appears that this profit has been applied in discharging losses incurred on other loans, notably those for the extension of railways in the West of Ireland. This seems a very questionable misappropriation of funds raised for the benefit of the lunatic poor. The benevolent intentions of Parliament, as indicated by the Act of [illegible], will be frustrated if it is not checked.

APPENDIX.

RETURN showing the INDEBTEDNESS of COUNTIES on 31st MARCH 1894 for LOANS for LUNATIC ASYLUM BUILDINGS.

County	Amount of Principal outstanding on 31st March 1894	County	Amount of Principal outstanding on 31st March 1894
	£ s. d.		£ s. d.
Antrim	[illegible]	Brought forward	[illegible]
Armagh	[illegible]	King's	[illegible]
City of Belfast	[illegible]	Leitrim	—
Carlow	[illegible]	Limerick	[illegible]
Town of Carrickfergus	[illegible]	City of Limerick	[illegible]
Cavan	[illegible]	Londonderry	[illegible]
Clare	[illegible]	Longford	[illegible]
Cork	[illegible]	Louth	[illegible]
City of Cork	[illegible]	Mayo	[illegible]
Donegal	[illegible]	Meath	[illegible]
Down	[illegible]	Monaghan	[illegible]
Dublin	[illegible]	Queen's	[illegible]
City of Dublin	[illegible]	Roscommon	[illegible]
Town of Drogheda	[illegible]	Tipperary	[illegible]
Fermanagh	[illegible]	Tyrone	[illegible]
Galway	[illegible]	Waterford	[illegible]
Town of Galway	[illegible]	City of Waterford	[illegible]
Kerry	[illegible]	Westmeath	[illegible]
Kildare	[illegible]	Wexford	[illegible]
Kilkenny	[illegible]	Wicklow	[illegible]
City of Kilkenny	[illegible]	Total	[illegible]
Brought forward	[illegible]		

Office of Public Works,
Custom House, Dublin.
[illegible] day of February 1895.

G. H. [illegible],
Accountant.

NOTE.—The remittances made in 1893 were:—[illegible], Kilkenny, [illegible], Mullingar, [illegible], Sligo, [illegible]. Total—[illegible]. This sum is not 1 per cent. on the loans, and would about equal the profit over [illegible] per cent. which would be made by Government in three years on the forthcoming advances to be forced upon the Richmond Board alone for expenditure now required.

APPENDIX XIX.

Note by the Secretary as to the History of the Extension of the Income Tax to Ireland in 1853.

The Budgets of 1842 and 1845.

In the year 1842 there was a deficit of nearly 2½ millions, and for some years previously there had been deficits. Sir Robert Peel, in his financial statement of that year, proposed to establish an income tax of 7d. in the pound for a period of three years, and declared that his object was by means of this tax, estimated to produce 3,771,000l., not only to meet the deficit, but to be able "to propose great commercial reforms which will "afford a hope of reviving commerce and such an improvement in the manufacturing interests of the "country as will re-act on every other interest in the "country." (*Hansard*, 61, p. 438.) These reforms chiefly consisted in taking a great number of small items off the raw materials of manufacture, with the view, as he said in the same speech, of removing the "burden that presses on the springs of manufacture "and commerce." He said that if any great war should arise, then, in his opinion, Ireland ought to contribute towards the income tax, but that apart from this contingency, it would not be expedient to extend the tax to Ireland. His reasons were—(1) that Ireland had not been subject to the income tax during the great war, and (2) that, as Ireland was not subject to assessed taxes, no machinery for the collection of the income tax existed in Ireland as it did in Great Britain, so that the revenue would hardly pay the cost of collection. He proposed, however, as an equivalent, to add 1s. a gallon to the duty on spirits in Ireland, which would produce 250,000l., and to equalise the Irish stamp duties with the British, which would produce 160,000l., altogether additional Irish taxation of 410,000l. This he considered would be almost as much as would be produced by the extension of the income tax to Ireland.

In the year 1845 the first period fixed for the income tax had expired, and Sir Robert Peel proposed the renewal of the tax for another three years. On this occasion there was no question, as in 1842, of meeting a deficit, since the revenue, independently of income tax, had become almost sufficient to meet expenditure. Sir Robert Peel stated that he proposed to renew the tax "distinctly for the purpose of enabling me to make "the great experiment of reducing other taxes." (*Hansard*, 77, p. [illegible].) It was proposed on this occasion (especially by Mr. Hume and Mr. Roebuck), that income tax should now be extended to Ireland. Sir Robert Peel in reply repeated his explanation, that his reason for not extending the tax to Ireland in 1842 was the absence of machinery for its collection. He said that neither Pitt nor Fox, nor Lord Sidmouth, nor Lord Grenville, nor any other minister, had attempted to impose the income tax in Ireland, because of the great local difficulties that existed. "We adopted the same course, and not from any desire "to favour Ireland at the expense of Great Britain, "but because of the great local difficulties in the way "of collecting such a tax in that country." Sir Robert Peel, however, gave on this occasion a new reason for not extending the income tax to Ireland. He said that if "we now" proposed again to continue the income tax for "a limited period, in order to effect a commutation of "taxation bearing upon the manufacturers of the "United Kingdom." He said that it was impossible to disregard the fact that although Ireland would benefit in some respects from the proposed remissions, yet that "from the peculiar circumstances of Great "Britain as compared to Ireland, the advantage of "this course will not be chiefly for Ireland, but for "this part of the United Kingdom." He went on to prove this in some detail, with regard to the remissions which it was then proposed to make, adding that he was led to the conclusion "that from the remission of "duties upon important manufactures, Great Britain "will derive by far the greater advantage." (*Hansard*, 77, p. 780, &c.)

The Consolidated Annuities.

Large loans of public money were made under the authority of Acts of Parliament to meet the distress in Ireland consequent with the famine of 1846–7, and to establish the workhouse and poor law system in Ireland. The repayment of these loans was secured on local rates. The balances of these remaining outstanding, after certain large remissions, were consolidated under the Consolidated Annuities Act, in 1850 (13 Vict. c. 14), and were known as the "Consolidated Annuities." A Select Committee of the House of Lords inquired, in 1852, into the claims which were made for the remission of these debts.

The Report of the Committee divided the sums then outstanding in respect of these charges into the following heads, viz.:—

	£
1. Debt for building workhouses -	1,192,707
2. Debt due for temporary relief advances under 10 Vict. c. 7. This money had been spent in direct distribution of food.	763,328
3. Debt for advances for works under 1 Vict. c. 21, and 9 Vict. c. 1.	170,928
4. Debt for advances for relief of distressed unions. 13 Vict. c. 14.	830,984
5. "Labour rate" advances, spent on relief works. 9 & 10 Vict. c. 107.	2,246,784*

The Report of the Committee recommended the total remission of the last of these debts, viz., the labour rate advances. In making this recommendation, the Report said, "The Committee are fully aware how important "it is to adhere to and enforce all engagements entered "into with the public. They are of opinion that no "persons should be released from contracts voluntarily "made, except on undeniable grounds of equity or "sound policy. In a case like the present, the creditor "should be satisfied that any claim which he abandons, "however small, is one which he would not be justified "in enforcing. A debtor should be convinced that a "claim enforced, though great and oppressive, is one "which, on principle, he is bound to discharge." Mr. Moore and Mr. French, two Irish members, brought this Report to the notice of the House of Commons, on the 7th April 1853, two or three weeks before the Budget statement of that year was made.

Mr. Moore, in calling the attention of the House of Commons to this Report, summed up certain of the findings of the Lords' Committee as follows. They found "that the mode of relief under which the greatest "part of the famine charges was incurred, was, in "itself, utterly unsuited to meet the exigency with "which it had to cope; that it was adopted and set on "foot after due and timely warning of its inadequacy "and inevitable failure; that it was persevered in "long after it had been proved and admitted to be not "only inadequate and unfit for the preservation of life, "but destructive to property and subversive of society "itself; that when it was found impossible to expend "these loans on works of public utility, it was stipulated "as the next best test of their fitness, that such works "should be at least useless to those who were "ultimately to pay for their execution; that not only "were works so executed no test of destitution and no "fit mode of relieving famine, but that they enticed "multitudes from their regular employment; and "while they generated disease and death among the "feeble and infirm, they deteriorated the value of "property, and shortened the future means of human "subsistence, by greatly diminishing the agricultural "labours that would otherwise have contributed to the "coming harvest."

The opinion of the Committee of the House of Lords is well condensed in this sentence from their Report, page xvii.:—

"The uselessness of a great proportion of the works executed, their incompleteness, and the enormous waste of labour and capital which they have produced are proved by the great majority of the witnesses."

* See Report of Select Committee, &c. of 1852, and Sir C. Trevelyan's Report of [illegible], on the Consolidated Annuities. It should be noted that half the labour rate advances had already been [illegible], in [illegible], together with other loans in connection with the famine. [illegible] [illegible] [illegible]

Mr. Gladstone, then Chancellor of the Exchequer, in reply to these speeches, after taking an objection to a financial suggestion originating in the House of Lords, said that Mr. Moore and Mr French had "not made good the case which they stated "their intention to prove, namely, a case of wrong "and oppression on the part of Government against "Ireland at the period of the famine, upon the ground "of which wrong and injustice they claimed a "remission of 2,000,000*l.* or 3,000,000*l.*, not as a matter "of mere equitable consideration, but as a matter of "strict restitution due on the ground of right," and he said "it was not the intention of Government to give "their ultimate judgment on the subject of the "Consolidated Annuities, except in connexion with "their financial arrangement."

Colonel Dunne, in the course of the same debate, said that "the grounds upon which the present appeal was "made upon behalf of every union in Ireland were "that the works which had been executed were useless "to that country; that they were executed against "the will of every class in Ireland, that the disposal "of the funds for those works was taken out of the "hands of the Irish people, and that the plans for their "construction were inefficiently carried out. . . . . He "regretted that the Chancellor of the Exchequer "could not see the justice of the arguments which "had been adduced . . . and he trusted that "upon a reconsideration of the subject he would deem "it advisable to come to a different conclusion with "respect to it from that at which he seemed to have "arrived."

Mr. Butt, in the same debate, said that "When the "Chancellor of the Exchequer asked them to make "this question dependent upon the convenience of the "Budget he asked them to do one of two things, "either to admit that the claim put forward was not "one of justice, but a question of the expediency of "taxation; or to vote that the concession of a claim of "justice was to depend upon the convenience of the "the Minister of Finance."

A division was taken, in which Mr. Moore's motion was defeated by the majority of 161 to 95. (*Hansard*, 125, p. 780.)

The Budget of 1853.

In 1853 the income tax was legally expiring, and the question was whether it should be renewed for a further term of years. *Mr. Gladstone* proposed that the tax should be renewed for seven years, so that by its means might be completed "the noble work of commercial "reform, which is so far advanced." This reform consisted in the abolition of a number of remaining Customs duties on manufactures and semi-manufactures, on fruit and dairy produce, and the reduction of the duty on tea and foreign sugar. It also included the final abolition, at a cost of over a million a year, of the excise duty on soap, and of that on newspaper advertisements. It was calculated that the gross loss of revenue would be nearly 5,400,000*l.* per annum. This loss, it was calculated, would be met partly by the extension of the income tax to Ireland, the reduction of the line of exemption from 150*l.* to 100*l.*, the imposition of a succession duty, and an increase of the duties on Irish and Scottish spirits. It was estimated that all this additional taxation would produce for the current year 1,344,000*l.*, and in future years, when the taxation had reached its maximum, as much as 3,1[illegible],000*l.* The rest of the loss of revenue, it was calculated, would be made up by the increase of consumption and increase which would follow the fiscal reforms.

It seems to be desirable to give in some detail Mr. *Gladstone's* statement on this occasion, so far as it relates to the point in question. *Mr. Gladstone* began his financial statement (*Hansard*, 125, p. 1350) by showing a current surplus of upwards of a million.

With regard to the proposed renewal of the income tax for seven years, he said—

"I think it also most desirable that effectual measures should be taken to mark this tax as a temporary tax . . . My own opinion is decidedly against the perpetuity of this tax as a permanent ordinary portion of our finances. . . . If you determine to renew the income tax, will you make its early extinction your first and sole object, or will you in order to bring to completion the noble work of commercial reform which is so far advanced, once more associate the income tax with a remission of duties, extensive in itself and beneficial to the community?"

After giving his reasons for reducing the line of exemption from 150*l.* to 100*l.* per annum, *Mr. Gladstone* said:—

"I now come to another great exemption, the exemption of Ireland. Ireland in like manner has received the benefit of the income tax through the changes in our fiscal system, but at the same time the equivalent which was intended to be taken has not been exacted. That equivalent was twofold. In the first place it consisted of a duty upon spirits of 1*s.* a gallon, which was abandoned almost as soon as it was enacted. In the second place it consisted of an augmentation of the stamp duties—which augmentation was indeed levied for some years, but in 1850 my right honourable friend the President of the Board of Control (Sir C. Wood) made a great reduction in the stamp duties, both of this country and of Ireland, and in that reduction disappeared the increase which was enacted in Ireland as an equivalent for the income tax. I am not able to speak with absolute precision, but as nearly as we can make out, it would appear that the rate at which Ireland now pays stamp duties on her transactions is as nearly as possible, on an average, the same as it was in 1842.

"It is indeed true that since the first enactment of the income tax, Ireland has been visited with an awful calamity, and although that scourge has been mercifully withdrawn, yet traces of it still remain in many social and economical forms, and especially in the form of a very heavy and burdensome debt. That debt is but a fraction indeed of the generous aid accorded by the Imperial Parliament to the necessities of Ireland; but at the same time it cannot be denied that it is a very heavy and enduring burden, not on Ireland generally, but on its most distressed parts. Those, however, who look at Ireland cannot avoid being struck by the fact that all Ireland is not alike, that there are certain districts which do not need to shrink from their full taxation, and which have no reasonable charge or plea to offer for exemption.

"Let me remind the Committee what exemption means. It does not mean that we have got a bottomless purse, and that we can dispense exemptions to one man without injuring another. No, sir, the exemption of one man means the extra taxation of another, and the exemption of one country means the extra taxation of another. And, as this applies to changes in the income tax generally, so it applies to Ireland relatively to England.

"What we think, therefore, is, that the case of Ireland demands very special consideration in connexion with the burdens that have been imposed on her, with respect to which I will say more bye-and-bye, as a sequel or corollary to the present branch of my subject; but in the meantime I have to say that we see no reason why the income tax should not be levied on Ireland, as she, through the income tax which Great Britain has borne, has received a good portion of the benefit attending the remission of taxes up to the present time, and is likely also to profit largely by the remissions which I have to propose to the House. The produce of the income tax in Ireland . . . I estimate at 460,000*l.* a year."

In a later part of his speech, Mr *Gladstone* proposed an additional duty of 8*d.* a gallon on Irish spirits. Then, returning (p. 1402) to the question of the extension of the income tax, he referred to it as "a measure "which if you adopt it, as I trust you will, will operate "as one great step towards establishing an equalisation "of taxation between the three countries. It is true "that the income tax is of temporary duration, but "you will show by levying it that there is a fixed "intention and a rational prospect of equalising the "taxation."

He then stated that the 4,500,000*l.* of Consolidated Annuities included 1,300,000*l.* of debt that strictly belonged to the establishment of the Poor Law in Ireland, which he described as "a great social and "national good, a great and permanent good to Ireland." The other 3,000,000*l.* he said consisted of debts connected with the famine. Mr Gladstone then said that the Government proposed to remit the whole of the Consolidated Annuities. He added "In "remitting these charges and in proposing an income "tax upon Ireland, you will grant away an enormous "sum of money, but you will make a great stride "towards that, the advantages of which I hardly know "how to appreciate, namely, bringing the two countries "towards the establishment of the principle of "equalised taxation. . . . Now we are asking you "to remit a capital sum which was nearly 4,500,000*l.*, "and is still above 4,000,000*l.*, and to remit an annual "charge of 245,000*l.* Three-fourths of that annuity "would continue for forty years, and one-fourth for "various periods of from ten to thirty years. The "taxation we propose for Ireland would in the first "two years be considerably higher than the taxation "we propose to [illegible]; but if we look to the time "when, as I have said, Parliament will be in a position "to part with the income tax, Ireland will enjoy, and "enjoy for a long term of years, a much larger remis- "sion of consolidated annuity than it will have to bear "of additional burdens in the shape of the spirit "duty."

The income tax question was next discussed on the 8th April 1853.

Mr. Fagan, in opposing the extension of the tax to Ireland, said that "it was held out as an inducement "to Irish members to vote for an income tax for their "country that the Consolidated Annuities should be "abandoned. Now, he solemnly and earnestly pro- "tested against bringing those annuities into the "discussion at all. He recollected some months ago "forming one of a very distinguished deputation to "the Chancellor of the Exchequer on the subject of those "annuities. At its head was Lord Monteagle. There "was no part of the remarkable and lucid statement "then made by that experienced nobleman in which he "more fully concurred than where he called upon the "Chancellor of the Exchequer to act, as regarded the "Consolidated Annuities, on the strict principles of "justice, without any reference to the Budget, with "which it had nothing whatever to do. The claim "made was founded on simple justice, and nothing "could be more unfair than to put forward the remis- "sion of the annuities as a compensation for the pro- "posed income tax. It was the will of Providence to "visit in 1846–47 the United Kingdom with an unpre- "cedented and widespread famine, and he was always "of opinion that the advances made by Government "to meet the exigency of the crisis should have been "provided as a grant from the Imperial resources." He referred to the report of the committee of the House of Lords and its result "the calm and sober conclusion "of recommending to Parliament that the demand for "the labour rate should be abandoned." He then re- ferred to the beneficial effects which the imposition of the income tax on Great Britain in 1842, and the conse- quent lightening of the burdens on materials of manu- facture and food have had in Great Britain. "One only "can over-estimate the vast mass employment to the in- "dustrious classes in England which this has produced. "No wonder for the Manchester school to be so in love "with the income tax. But in this respect what "service has it been to Ireland? They had scarcely "any manufactures, and the extent of their chief "fabric—linen—had rather diminished than increased, "at all events since 1835." *Mr. Fagan* went into the point in some detail, and then argued that "By the "solemn treaty of the Union Ireland was not bound "to contribute to the general expenditure beyond her "relative ability with the ability of England." He then contended that at the existing date "Ireland now "pays more than she ought under the terms of her "treaty with England."

The same line of argument was followed by many other Irish speakers in the course of these debates. Some English members also spoke against the exten- sion of the income tax to Ireland, and among these *Mr Disraeli*, who said that he saw no connexion between the income tax and the Consolidated Annuities. He also said, "Four months ago we had to consider the "extension of the income tax to Ireland, and, after "mature consideration, we unanimously came to the "conclusion that it would be unwise and inexpedient "to extend it to Ireland. We not only thought it un- "wise to extend it to Ireland at that time, but the "considerable period which we proposed to Parliament "to interest us with the tax proved we had no im- "mediate intention of changing our policy in this "respect. It was our opinion for reasons which I need "not give, but it was arrived at after ample and anxious "consideration by the late Government, that it was "quite out of the question to extend the income tax to "Ireland."

Mr. Disraeli also said that the late Government had been prepared to bring forward a proposal with regard to the Consolidated Annuities, which was "one founded "upon equity, and which would, I think, have given "satisfaction to all those who were interested in the "affair."

Among the speakers in favour of the extension of the income tax to Ireland was *Mr Cobden*, who supported it chiefly for the reason that "there must be a perfect "equality between the two countries, and every tax "paid by this country must be paid by Ireland."

www.ingramcontent.com/pod-product-compliance
Lightning Source LLC
Chambersburg PA
CBHW021520210326
41599CB00012B/1331

* 9 7 8 3 7 4 2 8 3 2 6 4 1 *